LISTENING

토익마법
2주의 기적
990

이교희 지음

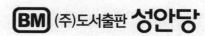
BM (주)도서출판 **성안당**

머리말

독자 여러분께

'토익 마법 – 2주의 기적'에 이어 **'토익 마법 – 2주의 기적 990'**을 내놓았습니다. 전작은 토익 LC 문제 중 시험에 자주 출제되는 유형들을 주로 소개했고, 청취력이 부족하여 잘 알아듣지 못한 문제도 맞힐 수 있는 기술을 알려주면서, 700점 이상을 달성하기에 알맞은 어휘력을 목표로 연습 문제를 제공했습니다. 이번에는 토익 시험에 출제되는 LC 문제의 모든 유형을 빠짐없이 다루면서, 고득점을 원하는 독자들을 위한 고난도 문제를 대거 포함시켰습니다. 이 책에 없는 유형은 시험에 나오지 않는다고 볼 수 있으며, 못 알아들은 문제를 맞히는 기술을 전수받으면서 동시에 청취력 완성을 위한 훈련도 할 수 있습니다.

공부를 시작하기 전에 '필독 서론'과 '이 책의 학습법'을 반드시 읽고 숙지하기 바랍니다. 유형에 대한 설명을 꼼꼼히 읽고, 예문은 항상 큰 소리로 여러 번 따라 읽어 보기 바랍니다. 연습 문제를 푼 후에는 워크북을 활용해 복습을 철저히 해야 합니다. Actual Test를 풀 때는 반드시 먼저 Today's Vocabulary를 따라 읽으면서 암기하고, 마찬가지로 워크북을 활용해서 복습해야 합니다. 정답을 맞힌 문제를 포함하여 모든 문제의 해설을 자세히 읽어 보고, 몰랐던 단어는 따로 정리해서 외우기 바랍니다.

토익 공부에 쓸 시간이 충분히 있다면 책 제목대로 2주, 주말 빼고 열흘 만에 공부를 끝내 보세요. 시간이 충분하지 않다면, 하루치로 제시되어 있는 양을 2, 3일에 나누어 공부해서 20일이나 한 달 만에 끝내는 것도 괜찮습니다. 열흘이든 한 달이든, 성실한 자세로 책에서 제시하는 문제 풀이와 훈련 방식을 그대로 따라 하면 확실히 목표를 달성할 수 있습니다.

엄마가 젖을 빠는 아기를 보며 기쁨에 산고(産苦)를 잊는 것처럼, 이 책을 통해 토익을 정복해 나아갈 독자 여러분을 생각하면 저도 참으로 행복합니다. 저에게 이런 행복을 주신 하나님께서 여러분의 앞날을 더 큰 행복으로 채워 주시기를 진심으로 기도합니다.

저자 이교희 올림

추신 이번에도 책이 출간될 수 있게 힘을 모아 주신 성안당과 이재명 부장님, 김은주 부장님, 과정에 참여하신 모든 직원 여러분, 안산이지어학원 김창로 원장님, 남편과 아빠를 학원과 책에 양보해 준 사랑하는 나의 가족, 늘 쉼 없는 기도로 함께해 주는 아름빛 교회 형제 여러분, 고맙습니다.

목차

이 책의 구성과 특징

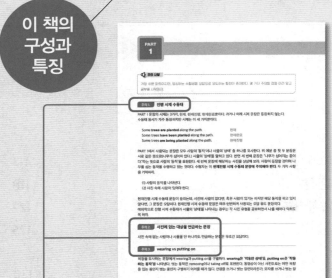

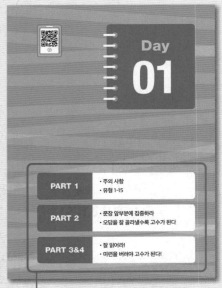

1 못 알아들은 문제도 정답을 알아내는 비법!

각 파트, 유형마다 문장 전체나 지문 전체를 알아듣지 못해도 정답을 맞힐 수 있는 비법을 알려줍니다.

2 전무후무, 매일 모든 파트 학습

다른 토익 교재에서는 볼 수 없는 방식.
매일 모든 파트를 공부함으로써 균형 잡힌 학습이 가능해집니다.

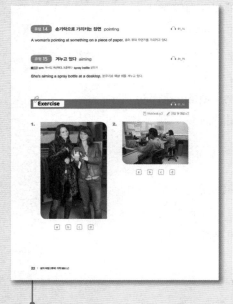

3 풍부한 실전 문제

문제 풀이 기술을 배웠다면 실전 문제에 적용하는 무한 반복 훈련이 필요합니다.
매일 충분한 연습 문제와 Actual Test를 풀며 실전 감각을 기를 수 있습니다.

5 고득점의 열쇠는 어휘력

점수 상승이 정체되는 가장 큰 원인은 어휘력
입니다. Exercise와 Actual Test마다 정리되어
있는 단어를 따라 읽으면서 암기하세요. 모르는
단어가 없게 해서 LC 만점에 도전해 보세요.

4 상세한 해설과 실전에 유용한 팁

모든 문제의 정답과 오답에 대해 자세하게
설명합니다. 저자 자신의 풍부한 응시 경험
(만점 10회)과 오랜 연구와 강의를 통해 얻은
실전에 유용한 팁도 함께 제공합니다.

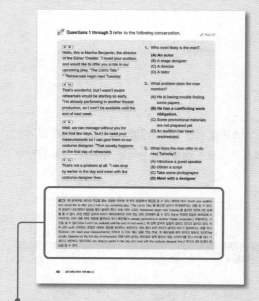

7 정기 토익과 같은 성우 구성

출연 성우들의 출신 국가와 성별을 정기 토익과
같게 구성해서 각 나라 특유의 발음과 억양을
익히게 해 줍니다.

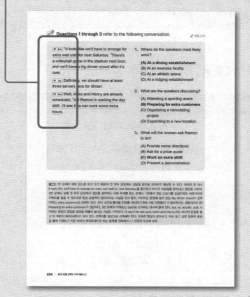

6 받아쓰기

받아쓰기를 연습할 수 있는 워크북을 제공합니다.
매일 꾸준히 연습해서 귀가 뚫리는 즐거움을
누려 보세요.

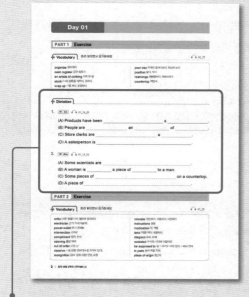

TOEIC이란?

▶ TOEIC

Test Of English for International Communication(국제적 의사소통을 위한 영어 시험)의 약자로, 영어가 모국어가 아닌 사람들이 비즈니스 현장 또는 일상생활에서 원활한 의사소통에 필요한 실용영어 능력을 갖추었는가를 평가하는 시험이다.

▶ TOEIC 시험 구성

구성	PART	유형		문항 수	지문	번호	시간	배점
L/C	1	사진 묘사		6		1~6	45분	495점
	2	질의 응답		25		7~31		
	3	짧은 대화		39	지문 13 x 3	32~70		
	4	짧은 담화		30	지문 10 x 3	71~100		
R/C	5	단문 빈칸 채우기 (문법/어휘)		30		101~130	75분	495점
	6	장문 빈칸 채우기 (문법/어휘/문장 고르기)		16	지문 4 x 4	131~146		
	7	지문 독해	단일 지문	29	지문 10	147~175		
			이중 지문	10	이중 지문 2 x 5	176~185		
			삼중 지문	15	삼중 지문 3 x 5	186~200		
Total	7 PARTS			200 문항			120분	990점

▶ TOEIC 평가 항목

Listening Comprehension	Reading Comprehension
단문을 듣고 이해하는 능력	읽은 글을 통해 추론해 생각할 수 있는 능력
짧은 대화문을 듣고 이해하는 능력	장문에서 특정한 정보를 찾을 수 있는 능력
비교적 긴 대화문에서 주고받은 내용을 파악할 수 있는 능력	글의 목적, 주제, 의도 등을 파악하는 능력
장문에서 핵심이 되는 정보를 파악할 수 있는 능력	뜻이 유사한 단어들의 정확한 용례를 파악하는 능력
구나 문장에서 화자의 목적이나 함축된 의미를 이해하는 능력	문장 구조를 제대로 파악하는지, 문장에서 필요한 품사, 어구 등을 찾는 능력

TOEIC
수험 정보

▶ TOEIC 접수 방법

1. 한국 토익 위원회 사이트(www.toeic.co.kr)에서 시험일 약 2개월 전부터 온라인으로 24시간 언제든지 접수할 수 있다.
2. 추가 시험은 2월과 8월에 있으며 이외에도 연중 상시로 시행된다.
3. JPG 형식의 본인의 사진 파일이 필요하다.

▶ 시험장 준비물

1. 신분증: 규정 신분증(주민등록증, 운전면허증, 기간 만료 전의 여권, 공무원증, 장애인 복지 카드 등)
2. 필기구: 연필과 지우개(볼펜이나 사인펜은 사용 금지)
3. 아날로그 손목시계(전자식 시계는 불가)

▶ TOEIC 시험 진행 시간

9:20	입실 (09:50 이후 입실 불가)
09:30 ~ 09:45	답안지 작성에 관한 오리엔테이션
09:45 ~ 09:50	휴식
09:50 ~ 10:05	신분증 확인
10:05 ~ 10:10	문제지 배부 및 파본 확인
10:10 ~ 10:55	듣기 평가 (LISTENING TEST)
10:55 ~ 12:10	읽기 평가 (READING TEST)

▶ TOEIC 성적 확인

시험일로부터 약 10~12일 후 인터넷 홈페이지 및 어플리케이션을 통한 성적 확인이 가능하다. 최초 성적표는 우편이나 온라인으로 발급받을 수 있다. 우편으로는 발급받기까지 성적 발표 후 약 7~10일이 소요되며, 온라인 발급을 선택하면 즉시 발급되며, 유효기간 내에 홈페이지에서 본인이 직접 1회에 한해 무료로 출력할 수 있다. TOEIC 성적은 시험일로부터 2년간 유효하다.

▶ TOEIC 점수

TOEIC 점수는 듣기 영역(LC)과 읽기 영역(RC)을 합계한 점수로 5점 단위로 구성되며 총점은 990점이다. TOEIC 성적은 각 문제 유형의 난이도에 따른 점수 환산표에 의해 결정된다. 성적표에는 전체 수험자의 평균과 해당 수험자가 받은 성적이 백분율로 표기되어 있다.

필독 서론

토익 LC 고득점을 목표로 정한 수험생이 필수적으로 읽어야 하는 서론이다.
고득점을 위해 수험생은 두 가지 목표를 세워야 한다.
첫째는 '못 알아들은 문제도 맞히는 **'기술'**을 익히는 것이며,
둘째는 못 알아듣는 문제가 없도록 **'청취력'**을 완성하는 것이다.

1. 못 알아들은 문제도 맞히는 기술

LC 각 파트의 출제 방식을 알면 문장을 완벽하게 이해하지 못해도 정답을 알아낼 수 있는 기술을 습득할 수 있다.

PART 1

출제되는 사진 속 장면이 무작위가 아니다. 지난 40여 년간 시험에 등장한 장면들을 모두 분류하면 100가지가 채 안 되는 유형으로 정리할 수 있다. 또한 거의 모든 장면의 정답 문장에서 정해진 키워드나 문장 특유의 구조나 패턴을 파악할 수 있다. 가장 효과적인 학습 방식은 각 유형의 사진이 나올 때마다 항상 **정답임을 알려주는 키워드나 문장 구조를 익히는 것**이다.

PART 2

(1) 우리말은 동사가 문장 끝에 있어서 끝까지 들어야 화자가 말하고자 하는 바를 올바르게 파악할 수 있다. 반면 영어는 문장 맨 앞에 주어와 동사가 있기 때문에 **대부분 앞부분이 핵심**이다. 원활한 문제 풀이를 위해 질문 맨 앞부분을 놓치지 않는 것이 중요하다.

(2) 출제위원들은 수험자가 영어를 모국어로 사용하지 않는 사람이라는 점을 이용한다. 혼동을 일으키기 위해 발음이 비슷한 두 단어를 들려 준다거나 무언가 관련이 있어 보이는 표현들을 사용하는 방식으로 문제를 구성한다. 수험자는 이런 것들이 오답을 유도하는 장치라는 사실을 알고 있어야 한다.

(3) **의문사 의문문은 의문사마다 정답 문장의 패턴이 존재**한다. 제안/부탁 의문문이나 선택 의문문도 자주 정답으로 사용되는 표현들이 있다. 이런 것들을 익혀두면 더 수월하게 정답을 파악할 수 있다.

PART 3, 4

이 파트에서는 질문과 선택지가 모두 문제지에 적혀 있다. 이것은 **듣는 능력과 동시에 읽는 능력도 필요하다**는 것을 의미한다. 대화나 담화를 못 알아들어도 정답을 알아내는 기술에서는 바로 '읽는 능력'이 핵심이다. 대화나 담화가 나오기 전에 문제를 잘 읽어 두면 못 알아듣는 부분이 있어도 웬만한 문제는 해결이 가능하다. 반대로 잘 읽어 두지 않으면 대화나 담화를 완벽히 알아들어도 정답을 고르는 일이 쉽지 않을 것이다.

2. 청취력

당연한 이야기이지만 청취력이 좋은 사람이 좋은 점수를 얻을 수밖에 없다. 청취력 향상을 위해 세 가지 학습법을 사용하자.

(1) 어휘력 배양

못 알아듣는 말은 대부분 모르는 말이다. 되도록 시험에서 모르는 단어가 나오지 않도록 어휘력을 향상시키는 데 최선을 다하자. LC 시험에서 듣는 단어는 RC 시험에서도 보게 되므로 철자를 정확히 암기해야 한다. 철자만 알고 발음을 모르면 알아들을 수가 없으므로 발음도 확실히 외워야 한다. 가장 좋은 어휘 암기 방식은 음원을 따라 읽으면서 여러 번 써보는 것이다.

(2) 받아쓰기

받아쓰기를 처음 시도해 보는 수험생이라면 그 효과가 나타나는 속도에 놀랄 것이다. 어휘력이 풍부할수록 받아쓰기의 효과가 더 빨리 나타나는데, 심지어 며칠만 훈련해도 청취력이 상당히 좋아지는 것을 경험하게 될 것이다. 받아쓰는 문장의 구조와 문장 곳곳에 나타나는 문법 관련 요소들을 생각하는 것이 훈련의 효과를 극대화한다는 사실도 기억하자.

(3) 따라 읽기

받아쓰기를 한 문장은 반드시 '큰 소리로' 따라 읽어보자. 중얼거리지 말고 반드시 '큰 소리로' 따라 읽어야 한다. 되도록 성우와 똑같이 읽도록 노력하자. 연음되는 부분, 강하게 읽는 부분과 약하게 읽는 부분, 미국 발음과 차이가 나는 영국과 호주 발음 등에 신경 써서 읽어야 한다. 속도까지 따라할 필요는 없지만, 받아쓰기 할 때와 마찬가지로 문장의 구조와 문법 요소들을 생각하며 따라 읽는 것이 훈련의 효과를 훨씬 높여준다.

이 책의 학습법

Day 01부터 Day 10까지 열흘 동안 LC 모든 파트를 매일 공부하자. 일일 학습 진행 순서는 다음과 같다.

1	Part 1 사진 유형 및 정답 문장 & Exercise
2	Part 2 유형별 공략법 & Exercise
3	Part 3, 4 유형별 공략법 & Exercise
4	Today's Vocabulary
5	실전 문제

각 파트의 유형별 공략법을 자세히 읽고 연습 문제를 풀어보자.

실전 문제를 풀기 전에는 반드시 Today's Vocabulary를 따라 읽으면서 암기하자.

이 책은 Workbook을 잘 활용하는 게 중요하다. 모든 문제는 풀어본 후에 반드시 Workbook을 이용해서 복습하자. 문장을 반복해서 들으면서 빈칸을 채우고, 빈칸 채우기를 완성한 후에는 큰 소리로 따라 읽으면서 청취력 완성을 도모하자.

토익 고득점을 노리는 수험생이라면 LC는 만점을 목표로 공부하자. RC 만점자는 드물지만 LC 만점자는 쉽게 만날 수 있다. 매 시험마다 전국 평균 점수를 보면 보통 LC 점수가 RC보다 50점 정도 높다. 게다가 RC와 달리 LC는 4–5 문제를 틀려도 만점이 나온다. RC는 오랫동안 상당히 많이 공부한 수험생도 만점을 받기 어렵지만, LC 만점은 저자가 제시하는 지침대로 성실하게 공부하기만 하면 반드시 달성할 수 있다고 확신한다.

학습 계획

1. **10-Day Plan** - 하루에 많은 시간을 투자할 수 있다면 열흘에 공부를 끝내자.
2. **20-Day Plan** - 시간이 부족하거나, 초보자라서 많은 양의 학습이 부담스럽다면, '파트별 학습 + Today's Vocabulary'와 ACTUAL TEST로 나누어서 이틀에 하루치를 공부하자.
3. **30-Day Plan** - 하루에 많은 시간을 내기 힘들면 '파트별 학습 → 복습, Today's Vocabulary → Actual Test로 나누어서 사흘에 하루치를 공부하자.

나만의 학습 플랜 및 체크리스트

● 10일 플랜

1 ☐ Day 1 / PART 1, 2, 3 & 4 ☐ ACTUAL TEST	**2** ☐ Day 2 / PART 1, 2, 3 & 4 ☐ ACTUAL TEST	**3** ☐ Day 3 / PART 1, 2, 3 & 4 ☐ ACTUAL TEST	**4** ☐ Day 4 / PART 1, 2, 3 & 4 ☐ ACTUAL TEST	**5** ☐ Day 5 / PART 1, 2, 3 & 4 ☐ ACTUAL TEST
6 ☐ Day 6 / PART 1, 2, 3 & 4 ☐ ACTUAL TEST	**7** ☐ Day 7 / PART 1, 2, 3 & 4 ☐ ACTUAL TEST	**8** ☐ Day 8 / PART 1, 2, 3 & 4 ☐ ACTUAL TEST	**9** ☐ Day 9 / PART 1, 2, 3 & 4 ☐ ACTUAL TEST	**10** ☐ Day 10 / PART 1, 2, 3 & 4 ☐ ACTUAL TEST

● 20일 플랜

1 ☐ Day 1 / PART 1, 2, 3 & 4 ☐ Today's Vocabulary	**2** ☐ ACTUAL TEST	**3** ☐ Day 2 / PART 1, 2, 3 & 4 ☐ Today's Vocabulary	**4** ☐ ACTUAL TEST	**5** ☐ Day 3 / PART 1, 2, 3 & 4 ☐ Today's Vocabulary
6 ☐ ACTUAL TEST	**7** ☐ Day 4 / PART 1, 2, 3 & 4 ☐ Today's Vocabulary	**8** ☐ ACTUAL TEST	**9** ☐ Day 5 / PART 1, 2, 3 & 4 ☐ Today's Vocabulary	**10** ☐ ACTUAL TEST
11 ☐ Day 6 / PART 1, 2, 3 & 4 ☐ Today's Vocabulary	**12** ☐ ACTUAL TEST	**13** ☐ Day 7 / PART 1, 2, 3 & 4 ☐ Today's Vocabulary	**14** ☐ ACTUAL TEST	**15** ☐ Day 8 / PART 1, 2, 3 & 4 ☐ Today's Vocabulary
16 ☐ ACTUAL TEST	**17** ☐ Day 9 / PART 1, 2, 3 & 4 ☐ Today's Vocabulary	**18** ☐ ACTUAL TEST	**19** ☐ Day 10 / PART 1, 2, 3 & 4 ☐ Today's Vocabulary	**20** ☐ ACTUAL TEST

● 30일 플랜

1 ☐ Day 1 / PART 1, 2, 3 & 4	**2** ☐ PART 1, 2, 3 & 4 복습 ☐ Today's Vocabulary	**3** ☐ ACTUAL TEST	**4** ☐ Day 2 / PART 1, 2, 3 & 4	**5** ☐ PART 1, 2, 3 & 4 복습 ☐ Today's Vocabulary
6 ☐ ACTUAL TEST	**7** ☐ Day 3 / PART 1, 2, 3 & 4	**8** ☐ PART 1, 2, 3 & 4 복습 ☐ Today's Vocabulary	**9** ☐ ACTUAL TEST	**10** ☐ Day 4 / PART 1, 2, 3 & 4
11 ☐ PART 1, 2, 3 & 4 복습 ☐ Today's Vocabulary	**12** ☐ ACTUAL TEST	**13** ☐ Day 5 / PART 1, 2, 3 & 4	**14** ☐ PART 1, 2, 3 & 4 복습 ☐ Today's Vocabulary	**15** ☐ ACTUAL TEST
16 ☐ Day 6 / PART 1, 2, 3 & 4	**17** ☐ PART 1, 2, 3 & 4 복습 ☐ Today's Vocabulary	**18** ☐ ACTUAL TEST	**19** ☐ Day 7 / PART 1, 2, 3 & 4	**20** ☐ PART 1, 2, 3 & 4 복습 ☐ Today's Vocabulary
21 ☐ ACTUAL TEST	**22** ☐ Day 8 / PART 1, 2, 3 & 4	**23** ☐ PART 1, 2, 3 & 4 복습 ☐ Today's Vocabulary	**24** ☐ ACTUAL TEST	**25** ☐ Day 9 / PART 1, 2, 3 & 4
26 ☐ PART 1, 2, 3 & 4 복습 ☐ Today's Vocabulary	**27** ☐ ACTUAL TEST	**28** ☐ Day 10 / PART 1, 2, 3 & 4	**29** ☐ PART 1, 2, 3 & 4 복습 ☐ Today's Vocabulary	**30** ☐ ACTUAL TEST

LISTENING

토익마법
2주의 기적
990

Day

01

PART 1	• 주의 사항 • 유형 1-15
PART 2	• 문장 앞부분에 집중하라 • 오답을 잘 골라낼수록 고수가 된다
PART 3&4	• 잘 읽어라! • 미련을 버려야 고수가 된다!

가장 쉬운 파트이지만, 방심하는 수험생을 오답으로 유도하는 함정이 존재한다. 몇 가지 주의할 점을 미리 알고
공부를 시작하자.

주의 1. **진행 시제 수동태**

PART 1 문장의 시제는 3가지, **현재, 현재진행, 현재완료**뿐이다. 과거나 미래 시제 문장은 등장하지 않는다.
수동태 동사가 자주 등장하지만 시제는 이 세 가지뿐이다.

Some **trees are planted** along the path.	현재
Some trees **have been planted** along the path.	현재완료
Some trees **are being planted** along the path.	현재진행

PART 1에서 사용되는 문장은 모두 사람의 '동작'이나 사물의 '상태' 중 하나를 묘사한다. 위 예문 중 첫 두 문장은
서로 같은 뜻으로(나무가 심어져 있다.) 사물의 '상태'를 말하고 있다. 반면 세 번째 문장은 "나무가 심어지는 중이
다."라는 뜻으로 사람의 '동작'을 표현한다. 세 번째 문장에 해당하는 사진을 상상해 보라. 사람이 등장할 것이며 나
무를 심는 동작을 수행하고 있는 것이다. 수험자는 이 **현재진행 시제 수동태 문장에 주의해야 한다.** 두 가지 사항
을 기억하자.

(1) 사람의 동작을 나타낸다.
(2) 사진 속에 사람이 있어야 한다.

현재진행 시제 수동태 문장이 들리는데, 사진에 사람이 없다면, 혹은 사람이 있기는 하지만 해당 동작을 하고 있지
않다면, 그 문장은 오답이다. 현재진행 시제 수동태 문장은 매우 빈번하게 사용되는 오답 유도 문장이다.
예외적으로 진행 시제 수동태가 사물의 '상태'를 나타내는 경우는 각 사진 유형을 공부하면서 나올 때마다 익히도
록 하자.

주의 2. **사진에 없는 대상을 언급하는 문장**

사진 속에 없는 사람이나 사물을 단 하나라도 언급하는 문장은 무조건 오답이다.

주의 3. **wearing vs putting on**

복장을 묘사하는 문장에서 wearing과 putting on을 구별하자. **wearing은 '착용한 상태'**를, **putting on은 '착용
하는 동작'**을 나타낸다. 벗는 동작은 removing이나 taking off로 표현한다. 동영상이 아닌 사진으로는 어떤 복장
을 입는 중인지 벗는 중인지 구별하기 어려울 때가 많다. 안경을 쓰거나 벗는 장면이라든가, 모자를 쓰거나 벗는 장

면을 상상해 보면 이해가 될 것이다. 따라서 입거나 벗는 '동작'을 나타내는 putting on, removing, taking off가 들리는 문장은 거의 항상 오답이다. 대신 wearing을 사용하여 착용하고 있는 복장을 설명하는 문장은 자주 정답으로 출제된다.

주의 4. **위치 표현을 알아들어야 한다**

PART 1 문장에는 위치 표현이 포함되는 경우가 많다. 많은 수험생들이 알아듣기 어려워하는 위치 표현들을 암기하자.

> on top of ~의 위에
> at the bottom[foot] of ~ 맨 아래에
> in front of ~ 앞에
> at the rear of ~ 뒤쪽에
> on both sides of / on either[each] side of ~ 양옆에
> in(to) the distance 저 멀리, 먼 곳에
> against the wall 벽에 붙어서[기대어]

이제 시험에 등장하는 모든 사진 유형들과 각 유형에서 정답으로 출제되는 문장들을 차근차근 익혀보자.

●● 장면을 상상하면서 큰 소리로 여러 번 따라 읽으세요.

유형 1　무언가를 보고 있다　거의 매회 출제!　🎧 01_01

사용되는 동사

look, stare, view, gaze, review, face, examine, study, inspect, read, admire, check, watch, focus, peer, consult

어휘 scenery 경치, 풍경　contents (문서의) 내용　face ~과 마주보다, 대면하다　article (물건) 한 점　attach A to B A를 B에 붙이다　produce 농산물　spoke (수레바퀴의) 바퀴살　inspect 점검하다, 검사하다　admire 감탄하며 바라보다　peer into ~을 자세히 들여다보다, 유심히 보다　browse 둘러보다, 훑어보다　consult (정보를 위해) 찾아보다, 참고하다　diner (식당의) 식사하는 사람[손님]

They're looking at a book that's open. 펼쳐져 있는 책을 보고 있다.

They're looking over the side of a boat. 배 옆면 너머로 내려다보고 있다.

They're staring into the distance. 먼 곳을 응시하고 있다.

People are viewing some artworks in a gallery. 미술관에서 미술 작품을 보고 있다.

He's gazing out at the scenery. 바깥 경치를 보고 있다.

Passengers are gazing at a city landscape. (유람선) 승객들이 도시 전경을 보고 있다.

They're reviewing the contents of a notebook. 공책의 내용을 검토하고 있다.

One man is facing a group of people. 한 집단의 사람들과 마주보고 있다.

A customer's examining an article of clothing. 옷 한 벌을 살펴보고 있다.

She's examining a tag attached to a suitcase. 여행 가방에 붙어 있는 가격표를 보고 있다.

They're examining some produce. 농산물을 살펴보고 있다.

A patient's teeth are being examined. 환자가 치아를 진찰받고 있다.

cf. The man is treating the boy's arm. 남자아이의 팔을 치료하고 있다.

A couple is studying a sign. 표지판을 (자세히) 살펴보고 있다.

The spokes on a wheel are being inspected.
바퀴살을 점검하고 있다.

Two students are reading from the same book. 같은 책을 읽고 있다.

He's admiring some paintings. 감탄하면서 그림을 보고 있다.

A woman is checking her appearance in a mirror. 거울 속의 자기 모습을 살펴보고 있다.

A woman is watching a man work on a motorbike. 남자가 오토바이 고치는 것을 지켜보고 있다.

The group is focusing on the computer monitor. 컴퓨터 모니터를 집중하여 보고 있다.

Some scientists are peering into the microscopes. 현미경을 자세히 들여다보고 있다.

The women are browsing in a bookstore. 서점 안을 둘러보고 있다.

They're searching for some books. 책을 찾고 있다.

A woman is searching a bookshelf. 책꽂이를 찾아보고 있다.

He's consulting a manual. 매뉴얼을 찾아보고 있다.

Some sculptures have drawn the woman's attention. 조각품들이 여자의 주목을 끌었다.

The menus have been provided for diners. 손님들에게 메뉴판이 제공되었다.

유형 2   마주보고 있다 🎧 01_02

Two women are facing[looking at] each other. 서로 마주보고 있다.

유형 3   탁자[카운터]를 사이에 두고 마주보는 장면에서는 🎧 01_03
across가 들리면 정답!

어휘 across from ~의 바로 맞은편에 diner 식사하는 사람[손님]

The women are across the desk from each other. 책상을 사이에 두고 마주보고 있다.

Some diners are seated across from one another. 손님들이 서로 맞은편에 앉아 있다.

유형 4   전화 통화하는 장면 🎧 01_04
대부분 talking on the (tele)phone이나
making a (phone) call이 들리는 문장이 정답!

어휘 conduct (특정한 활동을) 하다

One of the women is talking on the telephone. 전화 통화를 하고 있다.

He's making a phone call. 전화 통화를 하고 있다.

The man is conducting a phone conversation. 전화 대화를 하고 있다.

유형 5   프레젠테이션[연설/강연] 하는 장면 🎧 01_05

| give
make
deliver | a(n) | presentation
speech[address]
lecture |

어휘 address 연설(하다); ~에게 말을 걸다[하다]

A man is giving a presentation to the crowd. 사람들에게 프레젠테이션 하고 있다.

One man is delivering a speech. 연설하고 있다.

The speaker is addressing a group. 한 무리에게 연설하고 있다.

A presentation is being shown on a screen. 스크린에 프레젠테이션을 보여주고 있다.

An audience is listening to a presentation. 프레젠테이션을 듣고 있다.

Some people are watching a presenter. 발표자를 보고 있다.

Some people are attending a presentation. 프레젠테이션에 참석하고 있다.

She's speaking into a microphone. 마이크에 대고 말하고 있다.

유형 6 인터뷰하는 장면

🎧 01_06

어휘 take place 발생하다 crew (함께 일하는) 팀, 조, 반

A woman is being interviewed on the street. 길거리에서 인터뷰를 받고 있다.

An interview is taking place. 인터뷰가 벌어지고 있다.

A camera crew is recording something outdoors. 카메라 팀이 야외에서 무언가를 촬영하고 있다.

유형 7 회의하는 장면

🎧 01_07

어휘 be involved in ～에 몰두하다 engage (이야기 등에) ～를 끌어들이다

People are having a discussion at the table. 테이블에서 토론하고 있다.

They're involved in a discussion. 토론에 몰두하고 있다.

Some women are engaged in a friendly discussion. 사적인 논의에 참여하고 있다.

They're discussing the document. 서류를 보며 논의하고 있다.

A team is having a meeting. 회의를 하고 있다.

유형 8 대화하고 있다

🎧 01_08

어휘 doorway 출입구 receptionist 접수 담당자

A group is having a conversation over a meal. 식사하면서 대화하고 있다.

A conversation is taking place next to a window. 창문 옆에서 대화하고 있다.

The women are talking by a doorway. 출입문 옆에서 이야기 나누고 있다.

A guest is chatting with a receptionist. 손님이 접수 직원과 이야기 나누고 있다.

The receptionist is explaining something to the guest. 접수 직원이 손님에게 무언가를 설명하고 있다.

유형 9 손을 흔들고 있다 waving

🎧 01_09

어휘 wave (손, 팔을) 흔들다

The colleagues are waving good-bye. 서로 손을 흔들어 작별인사 하고 있다.

유형 10　고르고 있다 selecting, choosing

🎧 01_10

어휘 be involved in ~에 몰두하다　engage (이야기 등에) 끌어들이다

A man is selecting an item from a display. 진열품 중에서 물건을 하나 선택하고 있다.
A folder is being selected from a drawer. 서랍에서 폴더를 선택하고 있다.
The woman is choosing what to eat. 먹을 것을 고르고 있다.
She's choosing an item off a shelf. 선반에서 선택한 물건을 꺼내고 있다.

유형 11　손을 뻗고 있는 장면 reaching

🎧 01_11

어휘 reach (손, 팔을) 뻗다, 내밀다　extend (팔, 다리를) 뻗다, 내밀다　outstretch 펴다, 뻗다

She's reaching for something on the shelf. 선반 위의 무언가를 향해 손을 뻗고 있다.
A man's arms are extended over the table. 테이블 위로 팔을 뻗고 있다.
The man's arms are outstretched. 팔을 뻗고 있다.

유형 12　물건을 꺼내는 장면 taking, removing

🎧 01_12

어휘 volume 책　baked goods 구운 제품, 제과류　carton 판지 상자

He's taking a volume from the bookshelf. 책꽂이에서 책을 꺼내고 있다.
Merchandise is being taken off a shelf. 선반에서 상품을 꺼내고 있다.
He's removing loaves of bread from the oven. 오븐에서 빵 몇 덩이를 꺼내고 있다.
Baked goods are being removed from an oven. 오븐에서 제과류를 꺼내고 있다.
cf. The cover has been removed from a carton. 상자에서 뚜껑을 제거해 놓았다.
　　 A door has been taken off its frame. 문짝이 틀에서 떨어져 있다.

유형 13　팔짱을 끼고[다리를 꼬고] 있다

🎧 01_13

어휘 fold (양손, 양팔)을 끼다　cross (양다리)를 꼬다

The man is folding his arms. 팔짱을 끼고 있다.
He has his arms folded. 팔짱을 끼고 있다.
The woman is sitting with her legs crossed. 다리를 꼰 채로 앉아 있다.
cf. The clerk is folding some clothes. 점원이 옷을 개고 있다.

유형 14 손가락으로 가리키는 장면 pointing　　🎧 01_14

A woman's pointing at something on a piece of paper. 종이 위의 무언가를 가리키고 있다.

유형 15 겨누고 있다 aiming　　🎧 01_15

어휘 aim 겨누다, 겨냥하다, 조준하다 spray bottle 분무기

She's aiming a spray bottle at a desktop. 분무기로 책상 위를 겨누고 있다.

Exercise　　🎧 01_16

📖 Workbook p.2　　✏️ 정답 및 해설 p.2

1.

ⓐ ⓑ ⓒ ⓓ

2.

ⓐ ⓑ ⓒ ⓓ

●● 기본 공략법을 익히기 위해 예제를 풀어보자.

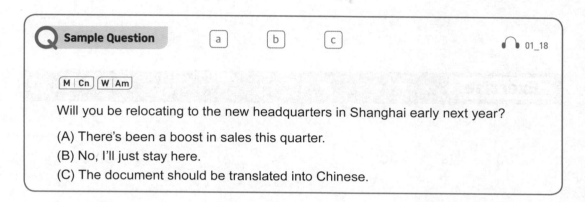

예제를 분석하면서 가장 중요한 풀이 원칙 두 가지를 기억하자.

1. 질문 앞부분에 집중하라!

질문 앞부분 Will you be relocating(옮겨 가실 건가요?)만 이해해도 (B)가 자연스러운 대답이라는 것을 알 수 있다. 영어 어순의 특징을 이용하자. 영어 문장은 언제나 '주어 + 동사'로 시작한다. 다른 문장 성분은 없을 수 있지만, 주어나 동사가 없는 문장은 존재할 수 없다. 즉, 주어와 동사는 구조와 의미면에서 모두 핵심 성분이므로 수험자는 질문의 앞부분에 집중하는 습관을 들여야 한다. 그러나 앞부분은 놓친 채 문장 뒷부분만 이해한 경우라면, 아무 문제도 풀 수 없을 것이다. 질문의 요점을 놓쳤기 때문이다. 고득점의 생명은 질문 앞부분에 있다.

2. 오답을 잘 골라낼수록 고수가 된다!

질문에 들어 있는 단어 headquarters의 quarter가 (A)에서 반복된다. 이처럼 질문에 들어 있는 어떤 단어가 대답에서 반복되거나 그것과 발음이 비슷한 단어가 들리면 거의 오답이다. 또한 질문에서는 지명 Shanghai가 들리는데, (C)에서는 Chinese가 들린다. 이와 같이 질문에 있는 어떤 단어에서 연상되는 단어나 표현이 들리면 십중팔구 오답이다. 출제위원들이 외국인을 대상으로 사용하는 이러한 오답 유도 장치들을 숙지하자. 오답 두 개를 잘 걸러내면 나머지 하나는 자동으로 정답이 되므로 문장을 완벽하게 알아듣지 못해도 정답을 맞힐 수 있다.

질문 앞부분에 집중하는 습관을 들이고, 오답을 걸러내는 훈련을 성실히 하면 거의 모든 문제를 맞힐 수 있다.

Exercise 🎧 01_19

📄 Workbook p.3   ✏ 정답 및 해설 p.2

1.   (A)   (B)   (C)   **6.**   (A)   (B)   (C)

2.   (A)   (B)   (C)   **7.**   (A)   (B)   (C)

3.   (A)   (B)   (C)   **8.**   (A)   (B)   (C)

4.   (A)   (B)   (C)   **9.**   (A)   (B)   (C)

5.   (A)   (B)   (C)   **10.**   (A)   (B)   (C)

PART 3, 4에서 고득점의 관건은 '잘 읽기'이다. 반드시 대화나 담화가 나오기 전에 질문과 선택지를 미리 잘 읽어 두어야 한다. 잘 읽어 두는 능력은 청취력만큼이나 점수에 큰 영향을 미치기 때문이다. '미리 잘 읽기'와 문제 풀이에 대한 요령을 숙지하고 연습 문제 풀이와 시험에 활용해 보자.

1. 파본 검사 시간

"수험자 여러분께서는 문제지를 밑에서부터 한 부씩 가지고 뒤로 전달하시기 바랍니다."라는 안내 방송이 나온 후 약 2분 20초가 파본 검사 시간으로 주어진다. 이 시간을 RC 문제를 푸는 데 사용할 수도 있지만, RC의 시간 부족 문제는 '토익 마법 - 2주의 기적 RC'와 '토익 마법 - 2주의 기적 990 RC'에서 제시하는 문제 풀이 기술을 잘 익혀서 해결하도록 하자. 이 시간에는 PART 3 문제 읽기를 권장한다. 보통 파트마다 후반부의 문제가 더 어려우므로 56-70번 문제를 읽어 두자.

2. LC Directions, PART 1 Directions, PART 2 Directions

표지(1쪽)를 넘겨 2쪽을 보면, LC 시험 전체에 대한 안내와 PART 1 Directions 및 Part 1 예제가 있다. 성우가 이 부분을 모두 읽고 예제까지 풀어주는 시간은 약 1분 35초다. 6번 문제의 네 문장을 모두 읽고 나면 정답을 고르는 데 5초, 페이지를 넘기는 데 5초가 주어지며, 곧이어 PART 2 Directions를 읽어주는 데 30초가 소요된다. 다 합치면 PART 2의 첫 문제가 나올 때까지 40초의 틈이 있다.
이 두 번의 자투리 시간을 활용하여 Part 4의 후반부 86-100번 문제를 읽어두자.

3. PART 3 Directions

PART 3을 읽어주는 30초 동안 바로 나올 대화의 32-34번 문제를 읽어야 한다.

4. 키워드 듣고 정답 선택하기

질문과 선택지를 미리 읽어두면 대화나 담화가 나올 때 정답을 알려주는 키워드가 다른 부분보다 더 또렷이 귀에 들어온다. 키워드가 들릴 때 낚시하듯이 정답을 낚아채자.

5. PART 3, 4의 정답 표시는 문제지에

두 문제의 키워드가 전혀 틈을 주지 않고 연달아 나오는 경우가 많기 때문에, 답안지에 마킹을 하면 다음 문제의 키워드를 놓치기 쉽다. 정답을 낚아채되 답안지 마킹은 하지 말고 문제지에 살짝 표시만 해 두고 넘어가자. 98-100번 문제의 담화가 끝난 후에 한꺼번에 얼른 마킹하고 RC로 넘어가자. 32번부터 100번까지 69문제의 정답을 모두 마킹해야 하므로 시간을 절약하기 위해 연필은 반드시 뭉툭하게 만들어서 가져가자. 심이 납작한 샤프를 사용하는 것도 좋은 방법이다. PART 3, 4와 달리 PART 1, 2는 문제가 나올 때 바로 정답을 마킹하자. 문제마다 5초의 간격이 있기 때문에 마킹할 시간은 충분하다.

6. 질문을 읽어 주는 시간

대화나 담화가 끝나고 성우가 세 문제의 질문을 읽어 준 후 정답을 선택하는 8초가 주어진다. 세 문제를 모두 읽어 주고 정답을 고르도록 주어지는 시간은 보통 총 40-45초다. 이 시간은 당연히 다음 세 문제를 읽는 데 활용해야 한다. 이 방식으로 문제를 풀면 앞서 미리 읽어두었던 56-70번과 86-100번 문제는 두 번씩 읽게 된다. 각 파트 후반부에 나오는 어려운 문제를 좀 더 수월하게 해결하려면 이렇게 반복해서 잘 읽어두는 게 필요하다.

★
7. 미련을 버려야 고수가 된다.

대화나 담화가 끝났는데 정답을 알아내지 못한 문제가 있다면, 바로 아무거나 '찍고' 다음 문제를 읽어야 한다. 이것은 지극히 상식적인 이야기이지만, 막상 수험자에게는 쉬운 일이 아니다. 누구나 풀지 못한 문제에 대해서는 미련이 남기 때문이다. 그러나 놓친 문제들을 계속 생각하면, 다음 문제들을 읽을 시간이 줄어들고 정답을 알아내기 어려워지는 악순환이 계속되어 그날의 LC 시험 전체를 망칠 수도 있다.
기억하자. 미련을 버려야 고수가 된다! 미련을 못 버리는 사람 미련한 사람!

●● 문제를 미리 잘 읽어두고 키워드를 통해 정답을 알아내는 기술을 예제를 통해 확인해 보자.

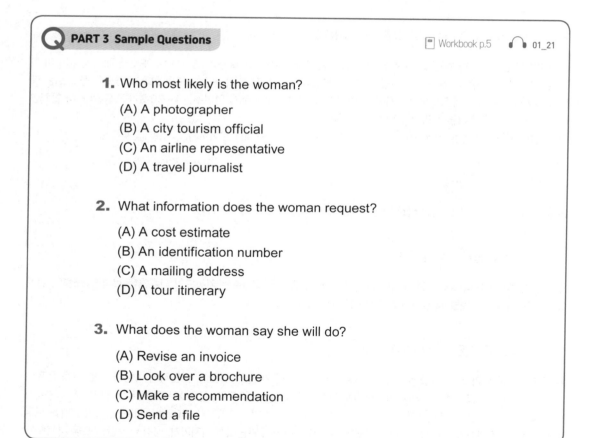

Q PART 3 **Sample Questions**   🖺 Workbook p.5   🎧 01_21

1. Who most likely is the woman?

(A) A photographer
(B) A city tourism official
(C) An airline representative
(D) A travel journalist

2. What information does the woman request?

(A) A cost estimate
(B) An identification number
(C) A mailing address
(D) A tour itinerary

3. What does the woman say she will do?

(A) Revise an invoice
(B) Look over a brochure
(C) Make a recommendation
(D) Send a file

M | Cn

Hi, this is Ezra Goldman from the city tourism office. Your photos were recommended to me by one of my colleagues. I've been looking over your Web site, and [1]I'd like to purchase your aerial photo of the city. We'd like to include it in a tourist brochure.

W | Am

Great! I have several different shots. [2]Could you tell me the ID number next to the photograph?

M | Cn

Sure, it's 78231.

W | Am

OK. Um... you can go ahead and make a payment on my Web site, and then [3]I'll e-mail you the file with the high-resolution version of the picture.

1. Who most likely is the woman?

(A) A photographer
(B) A city tourism official
(C) An airline representative
(D) A travel journalist

2. What information does the woman request?

(A) A cost estimate
(B) An identification number
(C) A mailing address
(D) A tour itinerary

3. What does the woman say she will do?

(A) Revise an invoice
(B) Look over a brochure
(C) Make a recommendation
(D) Send a file

● 문제를 미리 잘 읽어두기만 하면 대화 중에 키워드가 그대로 들리는 경우가 많기 때문에 매우 쉽게 정답을 알아낼 수 있다.

PART 3

1. Who most likely are Keith and Susan?

(A) Property managers
(B) Maintenance workers
(C) Building inspectors
(D) Potential home buyers

2. What are Keith and Susan concerned about?

(A) The placement of smoke detectors
(B) The measurement of a property
(C) The cost of major repairs
(D) The number of occupants

3. What is mentioned about the current owner?

(A) She has decided to take on a new job.
(B) She owns multiple properties.
(C) She can recommend skilled workers.
(D) She is available only in the afternoon.

PART 4

4. What is being advertised?

(A) A cleaning service
(B) A computer shop
(C) An Internet service provider
(D) An accounting firm

5. What does the speaker emphasize about the service?

(A) Its reliability
(B) Its reasonable prices
(C) Its speed
(D) Its user-friendliness

6. According to the speaker, what is available on the Web site?

(A) Discount codes
(B) Promotional videos
(C) Software applications
(D) Customer testimonials

Today's Vocabulary

●● Actual Test를 풀기 전에 이 단어들을 암기하자.

dining car (기차의) 식당차

part 부품

organize 정리하다

in alphabetical order 알파벳순으로

let *sb* in ~를 들어오게 하다

contractor 하청업자, 도급업자

initial 첫 글자[머리글자]를 표시하다

interoffice 사내의

revision 수정, 정정

browse 둘러보다

staff forum (온라인) 직원 토론 게시판

post 게시하다

alike (앞에 언급한 두 사람[사물]) 둘 다, 똑같이

view 보다

exhibit 전람회, 전시회

unveil 처음 공개하다

feature 특별히 포함하다; 기능, 특징

a wide selection of 다양하게 엄선한

architect 건축가

power 동력을 공급하다, 작동시키다

solar panel 태양 전지판

make use of ~을 이용하다, 활용하다

present 제출하다, 제시하다

employee ID badge 사원증

monitor 감시하다

upcoming 다가오는, 곧 있을

newsletter 소식지, 회보

make sure to–V 반드시 ~하도록 하다

identification 신분증

track 탐지하다, 추적하다

carry 휴대하다, 가지고 다니다

valuables 귀중품

with + N + 형용사[분사] ~가 ~인 채로

Actual Test

PART 1	1-3
PART 2	4-12
PART 3	13-21
PART 4	22-30

Part 3, 4 '미리 잘 읽기' 전략

LC Directions 시간:	16-18번 읽기
Part 1 Directions 시간:	19-21번 읽기
Part 2 Directions 시간:	28-30번 읽기
Part 3 Directions 시간:	13-15번 읽기
19-21번 문제 읽어주는 시간:	22-24번 읽기
Part 4 Directions 시간:	25-27번 읽기

Actual Test

📱 Workbook p.8   ✏️ 정답 및 해설 p.7

LISTENING TEST

지금 16-18번 읽기

In the Listening test, you will be asked to demonstrate how well you understand spoken English. The entire Listening test will last approximately 45 minutes. There are four parts, and directions are given for each part. You must mark your answers on the separate answer sheet. Do not write your answers in your test book.

PART 1

지금 19-21번 읽기

Directions: For each question in this part, you will hear four statements about a picture in your test book. When you hear the statements, you must select the one statement that best describes what you see in the picture. Then find the number of the question on your answer sheet and mark your answer. The statements will not be printed in your test book and will be spoken only one time.

1.

3.

2.

PART 2

Directions: You will hear a question or statement and three responses spoken in English. They will not be printed in your test book and will be spoken only one time. Select the best response to the question or statement and mark the letter (A), (B), or (C) on your answer sheet.

4. Mark your answer.   (A)   (B)   (C)

5. Mark your answer.   (A)   (B)   (C)

6. Mark your answer.   (A)   (B)   (C)

7. Mark your answer.   (A)   (B)   (C)

8. Mark your answer.   (A)   (B)   (C)

9. Mark your answer.   (A)   (B)   (C)

10. Mark your answer.   (A)   (B)   (C)

11. Mark your answer.   (A)   (B)   (C)

12. Mark your answer.   (A)   (B)   (C)

PART 3

Directions: You will hear some conversations between two or more people. You will be asked to answer three questions about what the speakers say in each conversation. Select the best response to each question and mark the letter (A), (B), (C), or (D) on your answer sheet. The conversations will not be printed in your test book and will be spoken only one time.

13. What is the purpose of Gina's call to Kenneth?

(A) To inform him she is going out of town
(B) To urge him to pay for further research
(C) To thank him for meeting with her
(D) To notify him she mailed a report to him

14. What department does Gina most likely work in?

(A) Corporate archive
(B) Sales
(C) Research
(D) Public relations

15. What does Gina plan to do?

(A) Make revisions to her report
(B) Send Kenneth more money
(C) Take some time off work
(D) Give Kenneth some advice

16. Where does the woman work?

(A) At an accounting firm
(B) At a travel agency
(C) At a health clinic
(D) At a beauty salon

17. What does the man say he will be doing next month?

(A) Leading a seminar
(B) Starting to work at a different company
(C) Taking a holiday overseas
(D) Writing a handbook for tourists

18. What does the man imply when he says, "I work until four o'clock on Mondays"?

(A) He desires to be working full-time.
(B) He needs a later appointment.
(C) He would rather come in during the weekend.
(D) He is scheduled to leave early for an event.

Seminar Schedule	
Topic	*Time*
Leadership	10 - 11 A.M.
Teamwork	11 A.M. - Noon
LUNCH	Noon - 1 P.M.
Market Trends	1 - 2 P.M.
Sales Techniques	2 - 3 P.M.

정답 고르고 나서 바로 22-24번 읽기

19. Where most likely is the conversation taking place?

(A) At an electronics shop
(B) At a company office
(C) At a conference room
(D) At a public park

20. What does the woman plan to do?

(A) Give a keynote presentation
(B) Rent a larger venue
(C) Post videos online
(D) Review a marketing proposal

21. Look at the graphic. According to the woman, which session will now be held last?

(A) Leadership
(B) Teamwork
(C) Market Trends
(D) Sales Techniques

Directions: You will hear some talks given by a single speaker. You will be asked to answer three questions about what the speaker says in each talk. Select the best response to each question and mark the letter (A), (B), (C), or (D) on your answer sheet. The talks will not be printed in your test book and will be spoken only one time.

22. Why did people gather at the Carrington Center this morning?

(A) To visit a plant exhibit
(B) To attend an open-air concert
(C) To enroll in a gardening class
(D) To listen to an art lecture

23. What is said about the new building?

(A) It is bordered by water.
(B) It makes use of solar energy.
(C) It has a rooftop café.
(D) It has a sculpture garden.

24. Why was Jay Patel chosen?

(A) He put forth the lowest bid.
(B) He presented the best designs.
(C) He can commence immediately.
(D) He resides in the area.

25. What are listeners asked to provide?

(A) A monthly charge
(B) A production schedule
(C) A computer access code
(D) A form of identification

26. What special feature is mentioned about a new digital key?

(A) It can unlock all the building doors.
(B) It is simple to find a replacement for it.
(C) It can track who enters a building.
(D) It is compatible with an older style of lock.

27. What does the speaker mean when she says, "make sure to check that out"?

(A) Employees should keep a door locked.
(B) Employees should verify their ID.
(C) Employees should read a document.
(D) Employees should rent certain equipment.

Program	
Speaker	**Time**
Ms. Taylor	9:00-9:50
Mr. Davis	9:55-10:45
BREAK	10:45-11:00
Mr. Kim	11:00-11:50
Ms. Chen	11:55-12:45

28. Where most likely is the speaker?

(A) At an award banquet
(B) At a musical performance
(C) At a retirement party
(D) At a training workshop

29. What are listeners asked to do?

(A) Remain seated during the break
(B) Carry their valuables with them
(C) Return all borrowed equipment
(D) Share handouts with others

30. Look at the graphic. Who will be the final speaker?

(A) Ms. Taylor
(B) Mr. Davis
(C) Mr. Kim
(D) Ms. Chen

Day
02

●● 장면을 상상하면서 큰 소리로 여러 번 따라 읽으세요.

유형 16 손으로 눌러 짜고 있다 squeezing   🎧 02_01

The woman's squeezing a plastic bottle.
플라스틱 병을 손으로 짜고 있다.

유형 17 버튼을 누르고 있다 pushing, pressing   🎧 02_02

She's pushing a button on a keypad. 키패드의 버튼을 누르고 있다.
She's pressing a button on a device. 장치의 버튼을 누르고 있다.
The man is ringing the bell at the door. 초인종을 누르고 있다.

유형 18 손짓이나 몸짓하는 장면의 키워드는 gesture   🎧 02_03

A man is gesturing as he talks. 말하면서 손짓하고 있다.

유형 19 박수 치고 있다 applauding, clapping hands   🎧 02_04

어휘 applaud 박수를 치다. 박수갈채를 보내다

They are applauding. 박수갈채를 보내고 있다.
Some people are clapping their hands. 박수 치고 있다.

유형 20 페이지를 넘기고 있다   🎧 02_05

She's turning the pages of a catalog. 카탈로그의 페이지를 넘기고 있다.

유형 21 **악수하는 장면** 거의 대부분 shaking hands나 greeting each other가 들리는 문장이 정답!   🎧 02_06

A woman is shaking hands with a visitor. 방문객과 악수하고 있다.

The men are greeting each other. 서로 인사 나누고 있다.

유형 22 **불을 붙이고 있다** lighting   🎧 02_07

She's lighting the candle with a match. 성냥으로 양초에 불을 붙이고 있다.

유형 23 **(펜으로) 쓰는 장면에서는** writing, jotting, taking notes가 들리는 문장이 정답!   🎧 02_08

• 어휘 jot down ~을 (재빨리) 쓰다, 적다 notepad (떼어 낼 수 있는) 메모지 take notes 메모하다, 기록하다

The man is writing on a sheet of paper. 종이에 쓰고 있다.

She's jotting down some notes on a notepad. 메모지에 메모를 적고 있다.

They're having a pen and paper ready for taking notes. 기록하기 위해 펜과 종이를 준비하고 있다.

She is signing a paper. 서류에 서명하고 있다.

유형 24 **타이핑하고 있다** typing   🎧 02_09

One of the women is typing on a laptop. 노트북 컴퓨터로 타이핑하고 있다.

유형 25 **그리고 있다** painting, drawing, sketching   🎧 02_10

She's painting a picture. (물감으로) 그림을 그리고 있다.

White lines are painted on the road. 도로에 흰색 선이 그려져 있다.

The man is drawing a graph on a presentation board. 프레젠테이션 보드에 그래프를 그리고 있다.

A man is sketching the woman in front of him. 앞에 있는 여자를 스케치하고 있다.

유형 26 페인트칠 하는 장면 painting

🎧 02_11

어휘 doorway 출입구 apply (페인트를) 칠하다, (크림, 약을) 바르다, (라벨을) 붙이다 apply makeup 화장을 하다 shelving unit 선반

The man is painting the wall above a doorway. 출입구 위의 벽에 페인트를 칠하고 있다.

Paint is being applied to a wall. 벽에 페인트를 칠하고 있다.

cf. A man is applying makeup to a woman's face. 남자가 여자의 얼굴에 화장을 해주고 있다.

Labels have been applied to shelving units. 선반에 라벨이 붙어 있다.

유형 27 새기고 있다 carving

🎧 02_12

He is carving a piece of wood. 목재 조각을 새기고 있다.

유형 28 (둥글게) 말고[감고] 있다 rolling up

🎧 02_13

어휘 roll (up) (둥글게) 말다, 감다 rug 깔개, 양탄자 under one's arm 겨드랑이에 (끼고)

She's rolling up a poster. 포스터를 둘둘 말고 있다.

A rug is being rolled up. 깔개를 둥글게 말고 있다.

A patient's sleeve has been rolled[pushed] up. 환자의 소매가 걷어 올려져 있다.

She has a rolled mat under her arm. 둥글게 감긴 매트를 옆구리에 끼고 있다.

유형 29 묶고 있다 tying

🎧 02_14

어휘 shoelace 구두끈, 신발끈

She's tying her shoelaces. 신발끈을 묶고 있다.

유형 30 짐 싸는 장면은 packing이 들리면 정답!

🎧 02_15

She's packing a suitcase. 여행 가방을 싸고 있다.

She's packing a book into a box. 상자에 책을 싸고 있다.

들어 올리다 lift, raise, elevate 02_16

어휘 rear end 후부, 후미 plank 널빤지, 나무판자 checkpoint 검문소 barrier 차단기

They're lifting a chair off the floor. 의자를 바닥에서 들어올리고 있다.

One of the men is lifting a wooden plank. 나무판자를 들어올리고 있다.

The rear end of a car is raised off the ground. 자동차 뒷부분을 땅에서 들어올려놨다.

A checkpoint barrier has been raised. 검문소 차단기가 올려져 있다.

The car has been elevated for repairs. 자동차를 수리를 위해 들어올려 놨다.

유형 32 **picking (up)의 다양한 용법** 02_17

The woman is picking up the document. 서류를 집어 올리고 있다.

The man is picking vegetables in his garden. 텃밭에서 채소를 따고 있다.

A customer is picking up some clothing at a dry cleaner's. 세탁소에서 옷을 찾고 있다.

유형 33 **들고 있다 / 잡고 있다** holding * 매우 자주 출제 02_18

어휘 paddle (작은 보트의) 노 fishing rod[pole] 낚싯대 rail[railing/handrail] 난간, 울타리 test tube 시험관 cardboard box 판지 상자 electric cord 전기 코드, 전선 fuel pump handle 연료 펌프 손잡이 booklet 소책자 steering wheel (자동차의) 핸들, 운전대 watering can 물뿌리개 coil (밧줄, 전선을) 감은 것, 고리, 사리 stack 무더기, 더미 sideways 옆으로 grasp[grab/grip] 움켜잡다 broomstick 빗자루 secure (단단히) 고정시키다 strap (가죽, 천) 끈 briefcase 서류 가방 lap (앉았을 때 양 허벅지 부분) 무릎 forehead 이마

She's holding a paddle. 노를 들고 있다.

She's holding the machine lid[cover] open. 기계 뚜껑을 열어서 잡고 있다. (복사하는 장면 She's making copies.)

The man is holding a fishing rod[pole]. 낚싯대를 들고 있다.

He's holding onto the rail[railing/handrail]. 난간을 붙들고 있다.

He's holding up a test tube. 시험관을 들고 있다.

He's holding a cardboard box. 판지 상자를 들고 있다.

One man is holding the back of his chair. 의자 뒷부분을 잡고 있다.

He's holding an electric(al) cord. 전기 코드를 들고 있다.

He's holding up a board. 판자를 들고 있다.

He's holding a fuel pump handle. 연료 펌프 손잡이를 들고 있다.

One of the women is holding a booklet. 소책자를 들고 있다.

He's holding the steering wheel. 운전대를 잡고 있다.

She's holding a bowl. 그릇을 들고 있다.

She's holding a watering can with both hands. 양손으로 물뿌리개를 들고 있다.

The man is holding a coil of rope. 밧줄 한 사리를 들고 있다.

A salesperson is holding a stack of boxes. 상자 한 더미를 들고 있다.

A ladder is being held sideways. 사다리를 옆으로 들고 있다.

A man is grasping[grabbing/gripping] a broomstick. 빗자루를 잡고 있다.

A man is securing the base of a ladder. 사다리 아랫부분을 단단히 붙들고 있다.

The man has a box in his hands. 손에 상자를 가지고 있다.

A woman has the strap of a bag in her hand. 손에 가방끈을 잡고 있다.

One of the women has a briefcase on her lap. 무릎에 서류 가방을 올려 놓고 있다.

The man has a bag over his shoulder. 어깨에 가방을 메고 있다.

He has his hand on his forehead. 이마에 손을 짚고 있다.

A man has his hand on the back of a chair. 의자 뒷부분에 손을 짚고 있다.

Exercise

🎧 02_19

📖 Workbook p.15   ✏️ 정답 및 해설 p.17

1.   a   b   c   d

2.   a   b   c   d

문제 풀이에 있어서 가장 중요한 원칙 두 가지를 절대 잊지 말자.

1. 질문 앞부분에 집중하라!
2. 오답을 잘 골라낼수록 고수가 된다!

모든 문제를 이 두 가지 원칙에 입각하여 풀면 LC 점수가 급상승하는 것을 경험하게 될 것이다.
이제 부가적인 원칙 몇 가지를 익혀보자.

1. "몰라"라고 대답하면 거의 항상 정답이다

🎯 기출 문제   🎧 02_21

Q. Have we changed our paper supplier?   우리 종이 납품업체를 바꿨나요?
A. I'm not sure.   ≫≫ 잘 모르겠어요.

Q. Who was selected to work on the advertising 광고 프로젝트 담당자로 누가 선발되었나요?
project?
A. I haven't heard.   ≫≫ 저는 못 들었어요.

Q. Should we go ahead with the project or   프로젝트를 진행할까요, 연기할까요?
postpone it?
A. Let's check the budget first.   ≫≫ 우선 예산을 확인해 봅시다.

Q. How much does this tea kettle cost?   이 찻주전자 가격이 얼마인가요?
A. Oh, you should ask a sales associate.   ≫≫ 아, 판매 사원에게 물어보세요.

Q. How do I find the office manager?   사무실 매니저는 어떻게 찾나요?
A. The receptionist would know.   ≫≫ 접수처 직원이 알 겁니다.

Q. When will Dr. Gao give her speech?   Gao 박사는 언제 연설하나요?
A. The conference schedule hasn't been   ≫≫ 학회 일정이 확정되지 않았어요.
finalized.

Q. Who was hired to replace Mr. Tang?   Mr. Tang의 후임자로 누가 채용되었나요?
A. They haven't made a decision yet.   ≫≫ 아직 결정하지 못했습니다.

Q. Didn't Daniel accept the job offer? Daniel이 일자리 제안을 수락하지 않았나요?
A. He'll let us know tomorrow. >>> 내일 알려줄 겁니다.

모른다는 말은 거의 모든 질문에 대한 자연스러운 대답이 된다. 보통 매회 한두 문제 정도는 "몰라"라는 대답이 정답으로 출제되므로 수험자는 질문을 잘 못 알아들었을 때도 이 대답을 선택하면 거의 다 정답을 맞힐 수 있다. 다양한 표현을 모른다는 뜻으로 사용할 수 있는데, 그중 시험에 자주 정답으로 사용된 것들을 암기해 두자.

●● 매일 한 번씩 큰 소리로 따라 읽으세요. 굵은 글씨로 된 문장은 더 자주 출제된다. 🎧 02_22

- **I[We] don't know.** 모르겠어요.
- **I have no idea.** 모르겠어요.
- I wish I knew. 모르겠어요.
- I can't tell. 판단이 서지 않는군요.
- It's too soon[early] to tell. 지금 판단하기는 이르죠.
- **I'm not sure.** 확실히는 모르겠습니다.
- **I don't remember.** 기억이 안 나네요.
- **I can't recall.** 기억이 안 나네요.
- I forgot ~. 잊어버렸어요.
- It's on the tip of my tongue.
  허끝에서 맴도는데.
- It slipped my mind. 잊어버렸어요.
- I really haven't noticed. 정말 눈치 못 챘어요.
- I didn't see anyone.
  (Who 의문문에서) 아무도 못 봤는데요.
- Nobody I've heard of.
  (Who 의문문에서) 아무 이름도 못 들었습니다.
- **I haven't heard yet.** 아직 못 들었어요.
- **I haven't been told yet.** 아직 못 들었어요.
- I haven't been notified[informed].
  통지 못 받았습니다.
- They didn't give an exact date[time].
  (When 의문문, What time 유형에서) 정확한 날짜[시간]은 말해 주지 않더군요.
- She didn't give a reason.
  (Why 의문문에서) 이유를 알려주지 않았어요.
- He didn't say about it. 아무 말도 없던데요.
- I can't give you exact figures.
  (How many[much] 유형에서) 정확한 수치는 말씀드릴 수 없습니다.

- **The schedule hasn't been confirmed yet.** 일정이 확정되지 않았습니다.
- I was too busy to go. 바빠서 못 갔어요.
- I haven't met her yet. 아직 못 만나봤어요.
- I haven't checked. 확인 못 했습니다.
- I'll go check. 가서 알아볼게요.
- Let me check ~. ~을 확인해 볼게요.
- I'll have to check ~. ~을 확인해 봐야 합니다.
- I'll see if ~. ~인지 알아보겠습니다.
- Let's look[check] ~. ~을 한번 알아봅시다.
- **Check with + 사람** ~에게 확인해 보세요.
- **Check + 사물** ~을 확인해 보세요.
- I'll call ~. ~에게 전화해 볼게요.
- I'll find out ~. ~을 알아보겠습니다.
- I'll have to ask ~. ~에게 물어봐야겠어요.
- I'll ask ~. ~에게 물어볼게요.
- I was going to ask ~. ~에게 물어보려고 했어요.
- I will let you know later. 나중에 알려드리죠.
- You should ask ~. ~에게 물어보셔야죠.
- **Ask + 사람** ~에게 물어보세요.
- **사람 + might[probably/should/would] know ~.** ~라면 알 거예요.
- **I[We; They] haven't decided yet.**
  아직 결정을 못했어요.
- **We still haven't decided.**
  아직 결정을 못했어요.
- They're still discussing. 아직 의논 중입니다.
- We're still uncertain. 아직 확실하지 않습니다.
- **It hasn't been decided yet.**
  아직 결정되지 않았습니다.

- A decision hasn't been made yet.
  아직 결정되지 않았습니다.
- There are several options.
  몇 가지 선택 사항이 있습니다.
- I can't decide ~. 결정을 못하겠군요.
- I'm not in charge. 제 담당이 아닙니다.
- That's a difficult question.
  그거 어려운 질문이군요.
- I'm still thinking it over. 아직 숙고 중입니다.
- It's not my decision. 제가 결정할 사항이 아닙니다.
- It's up to you. 당신에게 달려 있어요.
- I'll leave it up to you. 당신에게 맡기겠습니다.
- **It depends on ~.** ~에 따라 다릅니다.
- **It depends.** 그때그때 달라요.

2. Yes, and[but] / (No), but

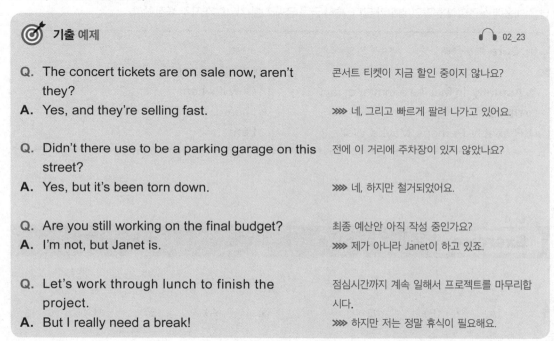

🎯 **기출 예제**   🎧 02_23

Q. The concert tickets are on sale now, aren't they?

콘서트 티켓이 지금 할인 중이지 않나요?

A. Yes, and they're selling fast.

≫≫ 네, 그리고 빠르게 팔려 나가고 있어요.

Q. Didn't there use to be a parking garage on this street?

전에 이 거리에 주차장이 있지 않았나요?

A. Yes, but it's been torn down.

≫≫ 네, 하지만 철거되었어요.

Q. Are you still working on the final budget?

최종 예산안 아직 작성 중인가요?

A. I'm not, but Janet is.

≫≫ 제가 아니라 Janet이 하고 있죠.

Q. Let's work through lunch to finish the project.

점심시간까지 계속 일해서 프로젝트를 마무리합시다.

A. But I really need a break!

≫≫ 하지만 저는 정말 휴식이 필요해요.

질문이 일반 의문문이나 평서문일 때 대답이 **Yes, and / Yes, but / No, but / But**으로 시작하면 항상 정답이다. 매회 한두 문제 정도가 이런 식으로 출제될 수 있으므로 기억하고 있다가 들리기만 하면 거저먹도록 하자.

3. 찍더라도 아무거나 찍지 말라!

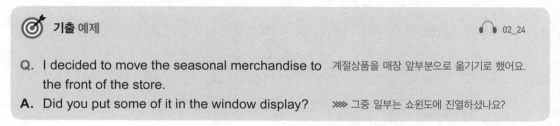

🎯 **기출 예제**   🎧 02_24

Q. I decided to move the seasonal merchandise to the front of the store.

계절상품을 매장 앞부분으로 옮기기로 했어요.

A. Did you put some of it in the window display?

≫≫ 그중 일부는 쇼윈도에 진열하셨나요?

Q. Shall I contact you by e-mail or by phone?
A. Actually, I'll be seeing you tomorrow.

연락을 이메일로 드릴까요, 전화로 드릴까요?
>>> 사실은 제가 내일 당신을 만나러 갈 겁니다.

Q. Isn't the museum closed now?
A. Well, it is after nine.

지금 박물관 문 닫혀 있지 않나요?
>>> 음, 9시가 넘었는데요.

Q. Are you riding your bike to work today?
A. Only if the weather's nice.

오늘 자전거 타고 출근하실 건가요?
>>> 날씨만 좋다면요.

정답을 도저히 알 수 없어서 찍을 수밖에 없다면, 확률이 가장 높은 것을 찍어야 한다. 아래 키워드로 시작하는 대답은 내용에 상관없이 정답인 경우가 많다. 특히 굵은 글씨로 된 키워드가 자주 등장한다.

(1) *Sure. (마법의 키워드 – 매우 자주 출제, 단, 의문사 의문문이 아닌 경우)
(2) **Actually**, In fact, As a matter of fact
(3) **반문**하는 대답
(4) Probably, Perhaps, Maybe, Well
(5) Just
(6) I'd rather[prefer]
(7) Only if[when]
(8) I heard
(9) Let's

Exercise

🎧 02_25

📖 Workbook p.16   ✏️ 정답 및 해설 p.17

1. (A) (B) (C)
2. (A) (B) (C)
3. (A) (B) (C)
4. (A) (B) (C)
5. (A) (B) (C)
6. (A) (B) (C)
7. (A) (B) (C)
8. (A) (B) (C)
9. (A) (B) (C)
10. (A) (B) (C)

Part 3, 4는 일단 미리 잘 읽어두기만 하면 웬만한 문제는 다 해결할 수 있다. 여기에 문제 풀이에 도움이 되는 몇 가지 팁도 기억해 두자.

1. 대화나 담화마다 딸려 있는 세 문제 중 첫 문제로 대화나 담화의 주제, 목적, 화자의 **직업**, 담화의 **대상**, 말하고 있는 **장소**를 묻는 문제가 자주 출제된다. 이것들은 대부분 대화나 담화의 첫 한두 문장에서 정답을 알아낼 수 있다. 첫 문장부터 정답을 선택할 수 있도록 준비하고 있어야 한다.

2. **but, no, actually, so**로 시작하는 문장에는 대부분 정답의 키워드가 들어 있다. but, no, actually, so가 들릴 때 더 집중해보자.

3. **next**로 끝나는 문제(Ex. ~ do next? / ~ happen next? / ~ hear next?)의 정답은 항상 대화나 담화의 마지막 문장에서 나타나므로 끝까지 듣고 정답을 선택하자. 만약 중간에 어떤 키워드가 들린다면 함정일 가능성이 있으므로 속지 않도록 조심해야 한다.

Q **PART 3 Sample Questions**　　　 Workbook p.18　 02_27

1. Who most likely is the man?

(A) An actor
(B) A stage designer
(C) A director
(D) A tailor

2. What problem does the man mention?

(A) He is having trouble finding some papers.
(B) He has a conflicting work obligation.
(C) Some promotional materials are not prepared yet.
(D) An audition has been rescheduled.

3. What does the man offer to do next Tuesday?

(A) Introduce a guest speaker
(B) Obtain a script
(C) Take some photographs
(D) Meet with a designer

W | Br

Hello, this is Martha Benjamin, the director of the Edner Theater. [1]I loved your audition and would like to offer you a role in our upcoming play, "The Lion's Tale." [2][3]Rehearsals begin next Tuesday.

M | Cn

That's wonderful, but I wasn't aware rehearsals would be starting so early. [2]I'm already performing in another theater production, so I won't be available until the end of next week.

W | Br

Well, we can manage without you for the first few days, [3]but I do need your measurements so I can give them to our costume designer. [3]That usually happens on the first day of rehearsals.

M | Cn

That's not a problem at all. [3]I can drop by earlier in the day and meet with the costume designer then.

1. Who most likely is the man?

(A) An actor
(B) A stage designer
(C) A director
(D) A tailor

2. What problem does the man mention?

(A) He is having trouble finding some papers.
(B) He has a conflicting work obligation.
(C) Some promotional materials are not prepared yet.
(D) An audition has been rescheduled.

3. What does the man offer to do next Tuesday?

(A) Introduce a guest speaker
(B) Obtain a script
(C) Take some photographs
(D) Meet with a designer

해설 1번 문제처럼 화자의 직업을 묻는 질문은 대부분 첫 한두 문장에서 정답을 알 수 있다. 여자의 대사 I loved your audition and would like to offer you a role in our upcoming play, "The Lion's Tale."을 들으면 남자가 연극배우라는 것을 알 수 있다. 이 문장이 나오자마자 정답을 빨리 골라야 한다. 바로 이어 나오는 Rehearsals begin next Tuesday.를 놓치면 2번과 3번 문제를 풀 수 없다. 또한 2번은 남자의 대사가 패러프레이즈 되어 있는 것도 간파해야 풀 수 있다. Edner 극장의 연습은 화요일에 시작되지만, 이미 다른 연극 작품에 출연하고 있기 때문에(I'm already performing in another theater production.) 주말까지는 시간을 낼 수 없다고(so I won't be available until the end of next week.), 즉 양쪽 업무의 일정이 겹치고 있다고 말하고 있다. 이와 같이 so로 시작하는 문장은 대부분 정답을 알려주는 부분이다. 계속 듣다 보면 여자가 남자의 치수가 필요하다는 말을 하고 있고(but I do need your measurements), 이어서 그 치수 재는 일을 연습 첫날, 즉 화요일에 해야 한다고 말하고 있다(That usually happens on the first day of rehearsals). 이에 대해 남자는 화요일에 일찍 들러서 의상 디자이너를 만나 치수를 재고 가겠다고 제안하고 있으므로(I can drop by earlier in the day and meet with the costume designer then.) 여기서 3번 문제의 정답을 알 수 있다.

PART 3

1. Where do the speakers work?

(A) At a hotel
(B) At a shopping center
(C) At a restaurant
(D) At a call center

2. What does the man ask about?

(A) How many people have requested a promotion
(B) If a director is in the lobby
(C) Whether a position is available
(D) When new shifts will be assigned

3. What does the woman say the man should be prepared to do?

(A) Address customer complaints
(B) Work within a tight budget
(C) Build relationships with local clients
(D) Work evening hours

PART 4

4. Why is the woman calling?

(A) To express her gratitude
(B) To solicit a favor
(C) To converse about an assignment
(D) To share some good news

5. What does the woman imply when she says, "You have got to tell me where you found the recipe"?

(A) She wonders if some ingredients are sourced locally.
(B) She would like to make the dish herself.
(C) She needs a recommendation for a restaurant.
(D) She cannot find a recipe in a cookbook.

6. Why is the woman looking forward to Wednesday?

(A) She is going to see a performance.
(B) She will be treating a friend to lunch.
(C) Some results will be announced.
(D) A new project will start.

 02_31

●● Actual Test를 풀기 전에 이 단어들을 따라 읽으며 암기하자.

properly 제대로, 적절히	instructor 강사
maintenance (department) 시설관리부	experienced 경험이 풍부한
overnight mail 익일 우편	definitely 분명히, 틀림없이
on short notice 예고 없이, 촉박하게	recognize (공로를) 인정하다, 표창하다
nightly 밤마다 하는	president (대학의) 총장, 학장
newscast 뉴스 프로	present 수여하다
availability 시간을 낼 수 있는지의 여부	token 표시, 징표
film crew 촬영 팀	gratitude 고마움, 감사
frequently 자주, 빈번히	give away 공짜로 나누어 주다
on assignment 임무를 맡아	functional 가동되는
with little warning 예고 없이	in contact with ~와 접촉하는
job requirement 직무 자격 요건	release 발매하다, 공개하다
flexible 마음대로 바꿀 수 있는	feature 특징, 특색
make progress 진전을 보이다[이루다]	resistance 저항성
I know. 맞아, 그래	operation 운영, 경영
view 경치, 전망	main office 본사, 본점
spectacular 장관인, 볼 만한	on sale 할인 중인
make good money 많은 돈을 벌다	pedestal fan 스탠드형 선풍기
enlargement 확대, 확장	recliner (젖혀지는) 안락의자
vocal 성악의	for sure 확실히, 틀림없이

Actual Test

PART 1	1-3
PART 2	4-12
PART 3	13-21
PART 4	22-30

Part 3, 4 '미리 잘 읽기' 전략

LC Directions 시간:	16-18번 읽기
Part 1 Directions 시간:	19-21번 읽기
Part 2 Directions 시간:	28-30번 읽기
Part 3 Directions 시간:	13-15번 읽기
19-21번 문제 읽어주는 시간:	22-24번 읽기
Part 4 Directions 시간:	25-27번 읽기

📖 Workbook p.21   ✏️ 정답 및 해설 p.22

LISTENING TEST

지금 16-18번 읽기

In the Listening test, you will be asked to demonstrate how well you understand spoken English. The entire Listening test will last approximately 45 minutes. There are four parts, and directions are given for each part. You must mark your answers on the separate answer sheet. Do not write your answers in your test book.

PART 1

지금 19-21번 읽기

Directions: For each question in this part, you will hear four statements about a picture in your test book. When you hear the statements, you must select the one statement that best describes what you see in the picture. Then find the number of the question on your answer sheet and mark your answer. The statements will not be printed in your test book and will be spoken only one time.

1.

ⓐ ⓑ ⓒ ⓓ

2.

ⓐ ⓑ ⓒ ⓓ

3.

ⓐ ⓑ ⓒ ⓓ

PART 2

Directions: You will hear a question or statement and three responses spoken in English. They will not be printed in your test book and will be spoken only one time. Select the best response to the question or statement and mark the letter (A), (B), or (C) on your answer sheet.

4.   Mark your answer.   (A)   (B)   (C)

5.   Mark your answer.   (A)   (B)   (C)

6.   Mark your answer.   (A)   (B)   (C)

7.   Mark your answer.   (A)   (B)   (C)

8.   Mark your answer.   (A)   (B)   (C)

9.   Mark your answer.   (A)   (B)   (C)

10.   Mark your answer.   (A)   (B)   (C)

11.   Mark your answer.   (A)   (B)   (C)

12.   Mark your answer.   (A)   (B)   (C)

Directions: You will hear some conversations between two or more people. You will be asked to answer three questions about what the speakers say in each conversation. Select the best response to each question and mark the letter (A), (B), (C), or (D) on your answer sheet. The conversations will not be printed in your test book and will be spoken only one time.

13. Where do the interviewers most likely work?

(A) At an employment agency
(B) At a television station
(C) At an electronics store
(D) At a movie theater

14. What job requirement do the speakers discuss?

(A) Having a professional certificate
(B) Owning the necessary equipment
(C) Possessing managerial experience
(D) Having a flexible schedule

15. What does the man agree to do next?

(A) Show a video
(B) Submit references
(C) Take a tour of a facility
(D) Meet with a manager

16. What is the conversation mainly about?

(A) An enlargement of office space
(B) A move into a new market
(C) A growth in the number of employees
(D) A transition in company leadership

17. Why does the woman say, "I can't believe it"?

(A) She is in strong opposition.
(B) She is seeking an explanation.
(C) She is experiencing disappointment.
(D) She is pleasantly surprised.

18. What does the man imply about the company?

(A) It was founded not long ago.
(B) It is considering adjusting salaries.
(C) It is in a good financial condition.
(D) It has offices in multiple countries.

Applicant	Interview Time	Instrument
Sofia Ochoa	10:00 A.M.	Violin
Soo-Jin Yun	11:00 A.M.	Vocal
James Dixon	1:00 P.M.	Flute
Ted Bailey	2:00 P.M.	Vocal

정답 고르고 나서 바로 22-24번 읽기

19. According to the man, what did the music school do last month?

(A) It moved to a different location.
(B) It held a dedication ceremony.
(C) It appointed a new director.
(D) It sponsored a community program.

20. Why does the woman ask the man to attend some interviews?

(A) Because she needs assistance with taking notes
(B) Because she is unavailable to attend
(C) Because he has endorsed a candidate
(D) Because he is an experienced instructor

21. Look at the graphic. Who will the man help interview today?

(A) Sofia Ochoa
(B) Soo-Jin Yun
(C) James Dixon
(D) Ted Bailey

PART 4

Directions: You will hear some talks given by a single speaker. You will be asked to answer three questions about what the speaker says in each talk. Select the best response to each question and mark the letter (A), (B), (C), or (D) on your answer sheet. The talks will not be printed in your test book and will be spoken only one time.

22. Who is speaking?

(A) A foreign ambassador
(B) A teaching assistant
(C) A company executive
(D) A university official

23. Where does Dr. Waheed work?

(A) At a government institution
(B) At an employment agency
(C) At a research company
(D) At a financial institution

24. What will probably happen next?

(A) An award will be given.
(B) A meeting will be arranged.
(C) A shipment will be received.
(D) A plan will be devised.

25. According to the speaker, what is happening today?

(A) An advertising campaign is being launched.
(B) A new branch is being inaugurated by a company.
(C) A new product is being released in stores.
(D) A clearance sale is being initiated.

26. What does the speaker mean when he says, "From the look of it, you'd think they were giving the phones away"?

(A) The store's advertisement is misleading.
(B) Some products are currently unavailable.
(C) There are a lot of customers waiting at the store.

(D) There are many great bargains at the store.

27. According to the speaker, what feature of the Shadowspeak 7C is most attractive?

(A) Its water resistance
(B) Its reasonable price
(C) Its colorful accessories
(D) Its sleek design

To buy:		
• Wooden bookcase	-	$99 ON SALE
• Vinyl chair	-	$53 ON SALE
• Pedestal fan	-	$85 full-price
• Recliner	-	$169 full-price

28. Where is the woman calling from?

(A) An office building
(B) A furniture shop
(C) An airport
(D) A hotel

29. Look at the graphic. What price is now incorrect?

(A) $99
(B) $53
(C) $85
(D) $169

30. What most likely will happen on Thursday?

(A) Staff training sessions will commence.
(B) Meeting with clients will take place.
(C) A renovation project will conclude.
(D) A job application deadline will pass.

Day

03

●● 장면을 상상하면서 큰 소리로 여러 번 따라 읽으세요.

유형 34 물건을 운반하는 장면 carrying, moving, transporting 🎧 03_01

어휘 earth 흙 dirt 흙 a load of 한 짐의 brick 벽돌 sack 부대, 마대 자루 rearrange 재배열하다, 재배치하다

She's carrying a package under her arm. 꾸러미를 옆구리에 끼고 운반하고 있다.

A woman's carrying a jacket over her arm. 재킷을 팔에 걸치고 있다.

They're carrying bags up some stairs. 계단 위로 가방을 옮기고 있다.

A container is being carried by a man. 용기를 운반하고 있다.

They're helping each other carry something. 서로 도와서 무언가를 옮기고 있다.

The machine is moving the earth[dirt]. 기계가 흙을 운반하고 있다.

One truck is transporting a load of bricks. 한 트럭이 벽돌 한 짐을 운반하고 있다.

Some sacks are being transported by a vehicle. 한 차량이 자루 몇 개를 운반하고 있다.

They are rearranging some furniture. 가구를 재배치하고 있다.

유형 35 바퀴 달린 물건을 운반하는 장면 🎧 03_02
pushing, pulling, wheeling, rolling

어휘 stroller 유모차 wheeled 바퀴 달린 aisle 통로 wheel (바퀴 달린 것을) 밀다, 끌다 roll 굴러가게 하다 gather up 주워[끌어] 모으다

A woman is pushing a stroller. 유모차를 밀고 있다.

She's pulling some wheeled luggage. 바퀴 달린 여행 가방을 끌고 있다.

A cart is being pulled down an aisle by a shopper. 쇼핑객이 통로를 따라 카트를 끌고 가고 있다.

A man is wheeling a baggage cart. 수하물 수레를 끌고 있다.

Some people are rolling suitcases down a park.

공원에서 여행 가방을 끌고 가고 있다.

cf. He's pulling[gathering up] a rope. 밧줄을 끌어 감고 있다.

cf. He's dragging a bag. (쓰레기) 봉투를 끌고 있다.

유형 36 ~을 ~에 놓고 있다

두다/놓다 put, place, position, arrange(정리하다, 배열하다), lay, rest

[어휘] help oneself to ~을 마음껏[자유로이] 먹다 snack 간단한 식사, 간식 compartment (보관용) 칸 dough 밀가루 반죽
pallet (운반용) 판 chin 턱 belongings 소지품

He's putting food on a plate. 접시에 음식을 담고 있다. (뷔페 식당)
(=He's helping himself to a snack. 음식을 마음껏 접시에 담고 있다.)
They are placing documents in compartments. 서류를 칸에 넣고 있다.
Circles of dough are being placed on a wooden pallet.
나무판에 둥글게 자른 밀가루 반죽을 놓고 있다.
She's positioning a sheet of paper on the glass. (복사기) 유리 위에 종이를 놓고 있다.
Flowers are being arranged in vases. 꽃병에 꽃을 꽂고 있다.
He's laying bricks. 벽돌을 놓고 있다.
She's resting her chin on her hand. 손에 턱을 올려놓고[괴고] 있다.
cf. A man has placed his belongings on a wall. 벽에 소지품을 올려놓았다.

유형 37 게시하다 post

03_04

[어휘] notice 게시문, 안내문 pin 핀으로 꽂다 bulletin board 게시판 tack 압정으로 고정하다

The man is posting some information. 정보를 게시하고 있다.
Information has been posted near an entrance. 정보가 출입구 근처에 게시되어 있다.
Some notices are pinned to a bulletin board. 게시문들이 게시판에 핀으로 고정되어 있다.
Papers have been tacked to a bulletin board. 문서가 게시판에 압정으로 고정되어 있다.

유형 38 정리[분류]하고 있다

03_05

[어휘] file (서류를) 철하여 정리하다 staple 스테이플러로 고정하다 organize 정리하다 sort 분류하다 sort through (찾거나 정리하기 위해)
~을 자세히 살펴보다 filing cabinet 서류 캐비닛

He's filing a document. 문서를 철하여 정리하고 있다.
She is stapling a document. 문서를 스테이플러로 고정하고 있다.
Some documents are being organized on a counter. 카운터 위에서 문서를 정리하고 있다.
A man is sorting papers at a desk. 책상에서 서류를 분류하고 있다.
Fruit has been sorted into baskets. 과일을 분류해서 바구니에 담아 놓았다.

Employees are sorting through documents in a filing cabinet.
파일 캐비닛 안에 있는 문서들을 자세히 살펴보고 있다.

유형 39 짐을 싣거나 내리는 장면 load / unload 🎧 03_06

어휘 load ~을 싣다, ~에 짐을 싣다 material 재료, 자재 unload ~을 내리다, ~에서 짐을 내리다 load A with B A에 B를 싣다
luggage 짐, 수하물

He's loading a vehicle. 차에 짐을 싣고 있다.
Workers are loading some materials onto a truck. 트럭에 자재를 싣고 있다.
He's unloading some packages. 몇 개의 짐을 (차에서) 내리고 있다.
A bicycle has been loaded onto a truck. 자전거가 트럭에 실려 있다.
A cart has been loaded with luggage. 카트에 짐이 실려 있다.

유형 40 물건을 건네주는 장면 passing, handing, giving 🎧 03_07

어휘 brochure 안내책자

The woman is passing a notebook to the man. 여자가 남자에게 공책을 건네주고 있다.
A plate is being passed in a kitchen. 주방에서 접시를 건네주고 있다.
A man is handing a woman a brochure. 남자가 여자에게 안내책자를 건네주고 있다.
One of the women is giving some papers to the other. 여자 중 한 명이 다른 한 명에게 서류를 주고 있다.
She is delivering the mail. 우편물을 배달하고 있다.

유형 41 물건에 손만 댔다 하면 모두 handling 🎧 03_08

어휘 handle (손으로) 만지다, 들다, 옮기다 jewelry 보석(류)

Some women are handling a piece of jewelry. 보석 한 점을 들고 있다.
They're handling boxes. 상자를 운반하고 있다.
They're handling a package. 꾸러미를 건네주고 있다.

유형 42 사용하고 있다 🎧 03_09

어휘 cash register 금전 등록기 shovel 삽; 삽으로 퍼내다 power tool 전동 공구 ramp 경사로, 비탈 board ~에 탑승하다
lawn mower 잔디 깎는 기계 calculator 계산기 pole 막대기

She's using a cash register. 금전 등록기를 사용하고 있다.

He's using a shovel to dig a hole. 삽을 이용하여 구덩이를 파고 있다.

The men are shoveling some soil. 삽으로 흙을 퍼내고 있다.

The man is using a hammer. 망치를 사용하고 있다.

She's hammering a nail into a wall. 벽에 못을 박고 있다.

A worker is using a power tool on a piece of wood. 목재에 전동 공구를 사용하고 있다.

Some people are using a ramp to board a boat.

경사로를 이용하여 배에 타고 있다.

A man is using a lawn mower to cut the grass.

잔디 깎는 기계를 이용하여 잔디를 깎고 있다.

A pole is being used to clean a window.

막대기를 이용하여 창문을 청소하고 있다.

유형 43   버리고 있다   03_10

어휘 dispose of ~을 없애다, 처리하다 litter 쓰레기 throw out 버리다 bucket 양동이 wheelbarrow 외바퀴 손수레

The woman is disposing of some litter. 쓰레기를 버리고 있다.

She's throwing something into the trash can. 무언가를 쓰레기통에 던져 넣고 있다.

A piece of paper is being thrown out. 종이 한 장을 버리고 있다.

A man is emptying a bucket into a wheelbarrow. 양동이를 외바퀴 손수레에 비우고 있다.

유형 44   청소하는 장면   03_11

어휘 sidewalk 보도, 인도 vacuum 진공청소기로 청소하다 mop 대걸레로 닦다, 대걸레질하다 walkway 통로, 보도 scrub 문질러 씻다
dust ~의 먼지를 털다[닦다] wipe 닦다, 훔치다 debris 쓰레기 window pane 창유리 rug 깔개, 양탄자 clear away ~을 치우다
polish 윤[광]을 내다 polish to a shine 광이 나도록 닦다

He's sweeping the sidewalk. 보도를 쓸고 있다.

She's vacuuming the floor. 바닥을 진공청소기로 청소하고 있다.

They're mopping the floor. 바닥을 대걸레질하고 있다.

The walkway is being mopped. 통로를 대걸레로 닦고 있다.

She's scrubbing a pan with a brush. 솔로 팬을 문지르고 있다.

She's washing a pot in a sink. 싱크대에서 냄비를 씻고 있다.

The car is being washed. 자동차를 씻고 있다.

A woman is dusting a television screen. 텔레비전 스크린의 먼지를 털어내고 있다.

He's wiping the table. 테이블을 닦고 있다.

He's cleaning up some debris. 쓰레기를 치우고 있다.

Workers are cleaning large window panes. 큰 창유리들을 청소하고 있다.

A rug is being cleaned near a window. 창문 근처에서 깔개를 청소하고 있다.

Snow is being cleared away. 눈을 치우고 있다.

cf. The floor has been polished to a shine. 바닥이 광을 내서 반짝이고 있다.

Exercise

🎧 03_12

📄 Workbook p.28   ✏️ 정답 및 해설 p.33

1.

a   b   c   d

2.

a   b   c   d

DAY 03부터는 유형별로 공부해 보자. Part 2의 유형은 크게 네 가지로 분류할 수 있다.

- 의문사 의문문: 매회 10-12문제
- 일반 의문문 / 평서문: 매회 9-11문제
- 제안/부탁 의문문: 매회 3-4문제
- 선택 의문문: 매회 1-2문제

가장 어려운 선택 의문문을 먼저 공략해 보자.

── 선택 의문문

1. Yes나 No로 시작하는 대답은 기본적으로 오답이다

예를 들어 Coffee or juice?라고 물었는데, Yes/No.라고 대답한다면 당연히 정답이 될 수 없다.

2. A or B, 둘 중 하나를 선택하면 정답

Coffee or juice?라고 물었다면 당연히 Coffee, please. 혹은 Juice, please. 같은 대답이 정답이다. 질문에 나왔던 단어가 반복되는 것을 대부분 오답 장치로 사용되지만, 여기서는 그렇지 않다. A or B에 해당하는 부분이 어딘지 잘 간파하고, 둘 중 하나가 반복되는 것을 정답으로 선택해야 한다. 그러나 A or B가 아닌 다른 부분에 있는 단어가 반복되는 대답은 대부분 오답이다.

3. 둘 중 하나를 선택해서 패러프레이즈하면 정답

Coffee or juice?라는 질문에 대해 Something hot would be better.라고 대답할 수도 있다. 커피를 선택한 대답 이므로 정답이다. 고득점을 위해서는 이 문제를 해결하기 위한 노력이 필요하다.

4. C, 제 3의 선택을 하면 정답

A도 아니고 B도 아닌 C, 즉 제 3의 선택을 할 수도 있다. Coffee or juice?라고 물었을 때 Just water, please.라고 대답해도 정답이 된다.

5. 마법의 키워드가 들리면 무조건 정답으로 선택하자!

(1) Either, Whichever, Whatever, Whenever, Any ~ (Anything, Any time, Anywhere 등) 아무거나
사실 일상생활에서 선택을 요구받은 사람이 가장 많이 하는 대답은 "아무거나"이다. Either의 미국식 발음은 [이더], 영국식 발음은 [아이더]이다. 발음이 두 가지이므로 단어가 두 개라고 생각하고 기억하자.

(2) Both, Each 둘 다, 각각
"둘 중 어느 것을 드릴까요?"라고 물었을 때 "둘 다 주세요."나 "각각 하나씩 주세요."라고 대답할 수도 있다.

(3) Neither 둘 다 아니에요

"A와 B 중 어느 것이 맞나요?"라고 물었을 때 "둘 다 틀렸어요."라고 대답할 수도 있다. 미국식으로는 [니더], 영국식으로는 [나이더]라고 읽는다.

(4) It doesn't matter. 상관없어요.
   I have no preference. 특별히 선호하는 건 없어요.
   특별히 선호하는 게 없거나 선택을 상대방에게 미루고 싶을 때도 있다.

(5) (The) one(s)
   (The) one(s)이라는 키워드가 들리면 무조건 정답으로 선택하면 된다.

(6) 몰라
   "모른다"는 아무 질문에 대해서나 정답이 될 수 있으므로 Day 01에 정리되어 있는 표현들을 잘 기억해 두자.

🎯 **기출 예제**   🎧 03_14

Q. Do you want me to take the highway or Parker Avenue?

고속도로로 갈까요, Parker가(街)로 갈까요?

A. Wouldn't the highway be faster?

≫≫≫ 고속도로가 더 빠르지 않을까요?

Q. Has the date been set for the merger with Peterson's Supply Company or is it still under discussion?

Peterson's Supply Company와의 합병 날짜가 정해졌나요, 아니면 아직 논의 중인가요?

A. We're still talking it over.

≫≫≫ 아직 그것에 대해 이야기하고 있습니다.

Q. Are you going to submit the budget report on Friday, or will you need more time?

예산 보고서를 금요일에 제출하실 건가요, 아니면 시간이 더 필요하신가요?

A. I handed it in already.

≫≫≫ 이미 제출했습니다.

Q. Should we hire an accountant or an analyst?

회계사를 채용할까요, 분석 담당자를 뽑을까요?

A. Either would be useful.

≫≫≫ 어느 쪽이든 유용할 겁니다.

Q. Are you going to send a report or give a presentation to our clients?

고객들에게 보고서를 보낼 건가요, 프레젠테이션을 할 건가요?

A. I'll probably do both.

≫≫≫ 둘 다 할 것 같아요.

Q. Is today's meeting about communication or planning?

오늘 회의가 커뮤니케이션에 관한 것인가요, 기획에 관한 건가요?

A. Neither. It's about strategy.

≫≫≫ 둘 다 아니에요. 전략에 관해서입니다.

Q.	Would you rather have sugar or honey with your tea?	차에 설탕 넣어 드릴까요, 꿀을 넣을까요?
A.	It doesn't matter to me.	>>> 저는 상관없습니다.
Q.	Are you going on vacation this month or next month?	휴가를 이번 달에 가실 건가요, 다음 달에 가실 건가요?
A.	We're still deciding.	>>> 아직 생각 중이에요.

Exercise

📱 03_15

📖 Workbook p.29   ✏️ 정답 및 해설 p.33

1.	(A)	(B)	(C)		**6.**	(A)	(B)	(C)
2.	(A)	(B)	(C)		**7.**	(A)	(B)	(C)
3.	(A)	(B)	(C)		**8.**	(A)	(B)	(C)
4.	(A)	(B)	(C)		**9.**	(A)	(B)	(C)
5.	(A)	(B)	(C)		**10.**	(A)	(B)	(C)

— 순발력 훈련

Part 3, 4 문제를 풀 때는 키워드가 들렸을 때 한 치의 망설임 없이 정답을 선택하는 순발력이 중요하다. 잠깐 머뭇거리는 동안 다음 문제의 키워드가 지나가 버리는 경우가 허다하기 때문이다.

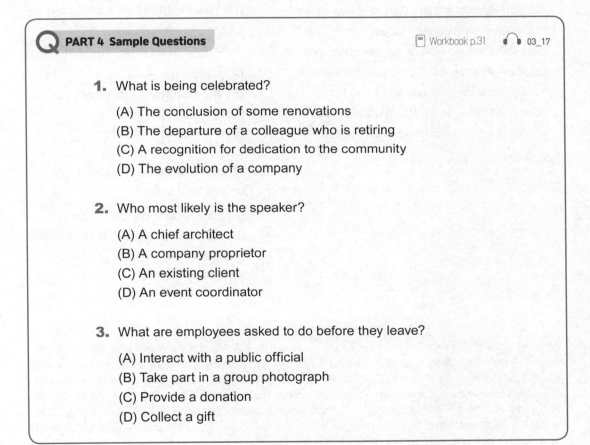

Q PART 4 Sample Questions   Workbook p.31   03_17

1. What is being celebrated?

(A) The conclusion of some renovations
(B) The departure of a colleague who is retiring
(C) A recognition for dedication to the community
(D) The evolution of a company

2. Who most likely is the speaker?

(A) A chief architect
(B) A company proprietor
(C) An existing client
(D) An event coordinator

3. What are employees asked to do before they leave?

(A) Interact with a public official
(B) Take part in a group photograph
(C) Provide a donation
(D) Collect a gift

해설 p.36

Questions 1 through 3 refer to the following conversation.

W Am Good evening! [1]I'm so glad you all could make it tonight to commemorate our company's expansion. [2]When I first started this greeting card company, it was only a small team of five people struggling to make our business work. Currently, we employ thirty full-time staff members, our distribution has grown, and we have moved into a new, significantly larger office. [3]So please, when you leave the banquet, pick up your gift bag. It's my personal token of appreciation to thank all of you for your hard work and dedication that has contributed to our company's success.

1. What is being celebrated?
   (A) The conclusion of some renovations
   (B) The departure of a colleague who is retiring
   (C) A recognition for dedication to the community
   (D) The evolution of a company

2. Who most likely is the speaker?
   (A) A chief architect
   (B) A company proprietor
   (C) An existing client
   (D) An event coordinator

3. What are employees asked to do before they leave?
   (A) Interact with a public official
   (B) Take part in a group photograph
   (C) Provide a donation
   (D) Collect a gift

해설 1번 문제는 첫 문장에서 to commemorate our company's expansion을 듣고 이 부분이 패러프레이즈 되어 있는 표현을 정답으로 선택해야 한다. 그런데 이 문제를 푸는 데 중요한 점은 단지 정답만을 고르는 것이 아니라 '순발력'이 필요하다는 사실이다. 키워드가 나왔을 때 정답 고르기를 조금이라도 머뭇거리면 2번 문제의 키워드가 휙 지나가 버린다. 2번 문제는 바로 이어지는 When I first started this greeting card company를 듣고 화자가 이 회사 소유주임을 간파하고 정답을 선택해야 한다. 이렇게 두 문제의 키워드가 틈을 주지 않고 이어지는 경우가 매우 많으므로, 수험자는 순발력 있게 정답을 고르는 연습을 충분히 해서 습관으로 만들어 놓아야 한다. 3번 문제는 So please, when you leave the banquet, pick up your gift bag.을 들으면서 어렵지 않게 정답을 알 수 있다.

PART 3

1. Who most likely is the man?

(A) A building maintenance employee
(B) A truck operator
(C) A real estate agent
(D) A customer service representative

2. What does the man mean when he says, "That is a problem"?

(A) He should seek advice from a specialist.
(B) He deems another issue to be more critical.
(C) He agrees that the issue demands attention.
(D) He is familiar with this type of problem.

3. What does the woman say about the recent weather?

(A) It has been hot and humid.
(B) It has been raining heavily.
(C) There has been a lot of wind.
(D) There have been snowfalls.

PART 4

4. What does Plexton Enterprises produce?

(A) Television shows
(B) An electronics magazine
(C) Sporting goods
(D) Video games

5. What are listeners invited to do?

(A) Nominate candidates
(B) Submit ideas
(C) Try out products
(D) Write testimonials

6. According to the speaker, what prize will be awarded?

(A) A complimentary journey to an exhibition
(B) A meal accompanied by a celebrity
(C) Electronic appliances
(D) A television appearance

 03_21

●● Actual Test를 풀기 전에 이 단어들을 따라 읽으며 암기하자.

rent 임차하다	in person 직접, 몸소
dine in 식당에서 식사하다	for a change 여느 때와 달리
way (전치사, 부사 강조) 큰 차이로, 훨씬	bustling 부산한, 북적거리는
staff lounge 직원 휴게실	unload 짐을 내리다
boardroom 중역 회의실, 이사회실	attention (안내 방송에서) 알립니다
print media 인쇄 매체	temporarily 일시적으로
supplies 용품, 비품	assembly floor 조립 작업장
flyer 전단지	regarding ~에 관하여
right away 곧바로, 즉시	adjustment 조정, 수정
in terms of ~ 면에서, ~에 관하여	day shift 주간 근무조
frequent 잦은, 빈번한	update 최신 정보
rental 임대의, 대여의	Here's the thing. 그런데 문제는 이겁니다.
manual 수동의	compensate (보수를) ~에게 지불하다
transmission (자동차) 변속기	go through ~을 살펴보다
gift-wrap 선물용으로 포장하다	bother 신경 쓰이게 하다, 괴롭히다
total 총액	bring up (화제를) 꺼내다
malfunction 오작동	organize (어떤 일을) 준비하다, 조직하다
conduct (특정한 활동을) 하다	make a photocopy of ~을 복사하다
face to face 얼굴을 마주 대하고, 대면하여	lyrics 가사
come over 들르다	commemorate 기념하다
for once 이번 한 번만은	expiration date 만기일, 만료일
video conference 화상 회의	duplicate 복사하다, 복제하다

Actual Test

PART 1	1-3
PART 2	4-12
PART 3	13-21
PART 4	22-30

Part 3, 4 '미리 잘 읽기' 전략

LC Directions 시간:	16-18번 읽기
Part 1 Directions 시간:	19-21번 읽기
Part 2 Directions 시간:	28-30번 읽기
Part 3 Directions 시간:	13-15번 읽기
19-21번 문제 읽어주는 시간:	22-24번 읽기
Part 4 Directions 시간:	25-27번 읽기

Actual Test

Workbook p.34   정답 및 해설 p.38

LISTENING TEST

지금 16-18번 읽기

In the Listening test, you will be asked to demonstrate how well you understand spoken English. The entire Listening test will last approximately 45 minutes. There are four parts, and directions are given for each part. You must mark your answers on the separate answer sheet. Do not write your answers in your test book.

PART 1

지금 19-21번 읽기

Directions: For each question in this part, you will hear four statements about a picture in your test book. When you hear the statements, you must select the one statement that best describes what you see in the picture. Then find the number of the question on your answer sheet and mark your answer. The statements will not be printed in your test book and will be spoken only one time.

1.

a   b   c   d

2.

a   b   c   d

3.

a   b   c   d

PART 2

지금 28-30번 읽기

Directions: You will hear a question or statement and three responses spoken in English. They will not be printed in your test book and will be spoken only one time. Select the best response to the question or statement and mark the letter (A), (B), or (C) on your answer sheet.

4. Mark your answer. (A) (B) (C)

5. Mark your answer. (A) (B) (C)

6. Mark your answer. (A) (B) (C)

7. Mark your answer. (A) (B) (C)

8. Mark your answer. (A) (B) (C)

9. Mark your answer. (A) (B) (C)

10. Mark your answer. (A) (B) (C)

11. Mark your answer. (A) (B) (C)

12. Mark your answer. (A) (B) (C)

Directions: You will hear some conversations between two or more people. You will be asked to answer three questions about what the speakers say in each conversation. Select the best response to each question and mark the letter (A), (B), (C), or (D) on your answer sheet. The conversations will not be printed in your test book and will be spoken only one time.

13. Where does this conversation take place?

(A) At a dining establishment
(B) At a garment shop
(C) At a bookshop
(D) At a florist's shop

14. What does the woman want to do with her purchase?

(A) Retrieve it at a later time
(B) Make use of it immediately
(C) Have it wrapped as a gift
(D) Have it delivered to her residence

15. Why is the woman unable to use her credit card?

(A) She forgot to bring her card with her.
(B) Credit cards are not accepted at the business.
(C) The price of her purchase is not high enough.
(D) There is damage to the card.

16. Why is the woman calling the man?

(A) To report an equipment malfunction
(B) To confirm an agenda
(C) To inquire about employee information
(D) To ask about a missing object

17. What does the woman mean when she says, "I'm interviewing someone in here in ten minutes."?

(A) She is in urgent need of help.
(B) She does not want to be disturbed.
(C) She is discontented with an assignment.
(D) She will not attend another meeting.

18. What does the woman say is unusual about the interview?

(A) It will be videorecorded.
(B) It will take place over a weekend.
(C) It will be conducted face-to-face.
(D) It will last for less than half an hour.

Today's Deliveries	
Lindenbrook Bakery	
Customer	**Address**
Franklyn Supermarket	1800 State St
Dinh Industries	360 Hillside St
Tuckman Department Store	45 Jefferson St

정답 고르고 나서 바로 22-24번 읽기

19. Look at the graphic. What street is the man on?

(A) Lindenbrook
(B) State
(C) Hillside
(D) Jefferson

20. What is the man asking about?

(A) How to collect a payment
(B) Where he can park his vehicle
(C) When to make a delivery
(D) Whom he should ask for

21. What does the woman say she will do?

(A) Open a door
(B) Make a phone call
(C) Forward an e-mail
(D) Buy some food

PART 4

Directions: You will hear some talks given by a single speaker. You will be asked to answer three questions about what the speaker says in each talk. Select the best response to each question and mark the letter (A), (B), (C), or (D) on your answer sheet. The talks will not be printed in your test book and will be spoken only one time.

22. Where most likely is this announcement being made?

(A) At a site of construction project
(B) At a production facility
(C) At an auto dealership
(D) At an office supply store

23. What problem does the speaker mention?

(A) Some components are missing.
(B) A manager has yet to show up.
(C) Inclement weather is expected.
(D) Some equipment is not functioning.

24. What will employees be informed about this evening?

(A) Results of an inspection
(B) Alterations in safety procedures
(C) Updates on work schedules
(D) Conditions of roads

25. What bothers the man about Warmson Advertising?

(A) Their lack of punctuality
(B) Their staffing difficulties
(C) Their request to alter a contract
(D) Their focus on cost cutting

26. What does the man mean when he says, "Here's the thing"?

(A) He will showcase a product.
(B) He cannot recall a word.
(C) He has found what he was searching for.
(D) He will bring up a point for discussion.

27. What are the listeners asked to look at?

(A) A design concept
(B) A business contract
(C) A commercial
(D) A budget

Bliss Restaurant
15% off (groups of 20+)
Book rooms for 4 hours!

expires:	Offer good at
July 1st	all locations

28. Why is an event being held?

(A) To celebrate a promotion
(B) To commemorate a retirement
(C) To mark a special occasion
(D) To announce a corporate merger

29. Look at the graphic. Why is the speaker unable to use the coupon for the event?

(A) The group does not have enough people.
(B) The length of the event is excessive.
(C) All of the locations in the area are fully booked.
(D) The event will take place after the expiration date.

30. What does the speaker ask the listener to do?

(A) Select a menu
(B) Distribute invitations
(C) Duplicate song lyrics
(D) Contract a band

Day

04

●● 장면을 상상하면서 큰 소리로 여러 번 따라 읽으세요.

유형 45 무언가를 자르거나 깎거나 다듬는 장면
cutting, trimming, mowing

🎧 04_01

어휘 have one's hair cut 머리를 깎다. 이발하다 hairstylist 미용사. 헤어 디자이너 trim 다듬다. 손질하다 mow (잔디를) 깎다 lawn 잔디밭 saw 톱질하다. 톱으로 켜다 slice (얇게) 썰다 chop (장작 등을) 패다

A man is cutting a tree into pieces. 나무를 여러 조각으로 자르고 있다.

One of the men is having his hair cut. 이발하고 있다.

A hairstylist is trimming a man's hair. 미용사가 남자의 머리를 다듬고 있다.

The man is mowing the lawn. 잔디를 깎고 있다.

A worker is sawing a wooden board. 나무판자를 톱으로 자르고 있다.

A chef is slicing some food into pieces. 음식을 여러 조각으로 얇게 썰고 있다.

Wood has been chopped into pieces.

목재가 여러 조각으로 잘라져 있다.

유형 46 물을 뿌리는 장면 water, spray, sprinkle

🎧 04_02

어휘 water 물을 주다 vase 꽃병 fountain 분수 spray 뿌리다. 뿜어대다 sprinkle 뿌리다

He's watering some flowers in the vase. 꽃병 안의 꽃에 물을 주고 있다.

Plants are being watered in a garden. 정원에서 식물에 물을 주고 있다.

The fountain is spraying water into the air. 분수대에서 공중으로 물이 뿜어져 나오고 있다.

Some plants are being sprayed with water. 화단에 물을 뿌리고 있다.

Plants are being sprinkled with a hose. 호스로 화단에 물을 뿌리고 있다.

유형 47 음악을 연주하는 장면
play music, play instrument, perfom(ance)가 들리는 문장이 정답!

🎧 04_03

어휘 musical piece 악곡 conductor 지휘자 give a performance 공연하다. 연주하다 entertain 즐겁게 해주다

She's playing some music. 음악을 연주하고 있다.

The orchestra is playing a musical piece. 오케스트라가 악곡을 연주하고 있다.

The conductor is leading the orchestra. 지휘자가 오케스트라를 지휘하고 있다.

The musicians are playing different instruments. 각자 다른 악기를 연주하고 있다.

Some women are practicing their instruments. 악기를 연습하고 있다.

A band is performing outdoors. 밴드가 야외에서 연주하고 있다.

A band is giving an outdoor performance. 밴드가 야외 공연을 하고 있다.

Some performers are entertaining an audience. 연주가들이 청중을 즐겁게 해주고 있다.

유형 48 사진 찍는 장면　　🎧 04_04

어휘 photograph ~의 사진을 찍다　pose 포즈를 취하다　portrait 초상화, 인물 사진　subject 피사체

The man is taking a picture[photo] of the people. 사람들의 사진을 찍고 있다.

A photograph is being taken. 사진을 찍고 있다.

He's photographing some model buildings. 모형 건물의 사진을 찍고 있다.

An instrument is being photographed. 악기의 사진을 찍고 있다.

People are having their picture taken. (다른 사람에게 부탁하여) 사진을 찍고 있다.

A woman is posing for a portrait. 초상화를 위해 포즈를 취하고 있다.

The photographer is concentrating on her subject. 사진작가가 피사체에 집중하고 있다.

유형 49 ~에 서 있다 *위치 표현에 집중할 것　　🎧 04_05

어휘 shallow 얕은　stepladder 발판 사다리　podium 연단, 연설대　baggage trolley 수하물 카트　railing 난간　checkout counter 계산대　apart from ~에서 떨어져서　walkway 보도　rise (rose-risen) 일어나다　step up to ~에 다가가다

He's standing in shallow water. 얕은 물에 들어가 서 있다.

A man is standing in the back of the truck. 트럭 짐칸에 서 있다.

She's standing on a stepladder. 발판 사다리 위에 서 있다.

A woman is standing behind the podium. 연단 뒤에 서 있다.

Some people are standing by a display of books. 진열되어 있는 책들 옆에 서 있다.

(= The people are visiting a bookstore. 서점을 방문하고 있다.)

She's standing next to a baggage trolley.

수하물 카트 옆에 서 있다.

The women are standing by a wooden railing.

나무 난간 옆에 서 있다.

A customer is standing by a checkout counter. 계산대 옆에 서 있다.

One person is standing apart from the crowd. 한 사람이 무리로부터 떨어져 서 있다.

The men have stopped on a walkway. 보도 위에 멈춰 서 있다.

A band member has risen from his seat. 밴드 멤버 한 명이 자리에서 일어서 있다.

Some customers have stepped up to the counter. 손님들이 카운터에 다가서 있다.

유형 50 　카운터에 서 있을 때는 help나 assist가 들리면 100% 정답!　🎧 04_06

어휘 wait on (구매하도록 고객을) 돕다　collaborate 협력하다

A salesperson is helping a customer select merchandise.
판매 직원이 손님이 물건을 선택하도록 도와주고 있다.

A man's assisting a customer in a shop. 상점에서 손님을 돕고 있다.

Some people are being helped at a counter. 카운터에서 도움을 받고 있다.

A woman is waiting on a customer. 손님을 도와주고 있다.

cf. They are collaborating on a project. 어떤 프로젝트에 대해 협력하고 있다.

유형 51 　~에 앉아 있다 be seated[sitting] *위치 표현에 집중할 것　🎧 04_07

어휘 patio 테라스　diner (식당의) 식사하는 사람[손님]　near the curb 길가에　stool (등받이와 팔걸이가 없는) 의자, 스툴　stand 가판대, 좌판
opposite (마주 보는) 건너편의　workstation (사무실 등의 작업자의) 공간, 자리

People are sitting at an outdoor patio. 야외 테라스에 앉아 있다.

Customers are seated in a dining area. 식사 공간에 앉아 있다.

Diners are seated near the curb. 식당 손님들이 길가에 앉아 있다.

Some customers are sitting on stools. 스툴에 앉아 있다.

Some women are seated next to a market stand. 시장 좌판 옆에 앉아 있다.

Some people are sitting at opposite workstations.

서로 맞은편 자리에 앉아 있다.

유형 52 　앉아 있는 자세를 나타내는 표현　🎧 04_08

어휘 squat 쪼그리고 앉다　crouch 쪼그리고 앉다　kneel 무릎을 꿇다　wheel 바퀴

A woman is squatting while watering some plants. 화초에 물을 주면서 쪼그리고 앉아 있다.

A man is crouching down next to a wall. 벽 옆에 쪼그리고 앉아 있다.

A person is kneeling by the wheel of the truck. 트럭 바퀴 옆에 무릎을 꿇고 앉아 있다.

04_09

유형 53 몸을 숙이고 있는 장면에서는
leaning이나 bending이 들리면 정답!

어휘 lean (몸을) 숙이다 bend 굽히다, 숙이다 work 일거리

A man is leaning over to pick up a bottle. 병을 집어 들기 위해 몸을 숙이고 있다.

She is bending over her work. 일거리 위로 몸을 숙이고 있다.

04_10

유형 54 사람이나 물건이 모여 있는 장면에서는
gather나 group이 들리면 정답!

어휘 gather 모이다, 모으다 seating area 앉는 장소 pile 무더기, 더미 street vendor 노점상 armchair 팔걸이의자 group 모이다, 모으다 assemble 모이다 canopy 그늘막 텐트

A small group is gathered in a seating area. 앉는 장소에 모여 있다.

Some leaves are being gathered into a pile. 나뭇잎을 모아서 한 더미로 쌓고 있다.

Some people have gathered around a street vendor's stand. 노점상 좌판 주위에 모여 있다.

Armchairs have been grouped around the tables. 팔걸이의자들이 테이블 주위에 모여 있다.

Performers have assembled beneath a canopy.
연주자들이 그늘막 텐트 아래에 모여 있다.

The workers are sharing the same office space.
직원들이 같은 사무실 공간을 공유하고 있다.

They're spending time together. 함께 시간을 보내고 있다.

04_11

유형 55 흩어 놓다, 펼치다 scatter, spread

어휘 scatter 흩어 놓다 object 물건, 물체 spread 늘어놓다; 펼치다 on top of ~의 위에

Some papers are scattered on the table's surface. 테이블 표면에 종이가 흩어져 있다.

Various objects are spread on top of a desk. 다양한 물건들을 책상 위에 늘어놓았다.

They're spreading out a net. 그물을 펼치고 있다.

He's spreading cement with a shovel. 삽으로 시멘트를 개고[펴고] 있다.

유형 56 걸어가는 장면 walking, strolling, marching, approaching 04_12

어휘 archway 아치형 입구 arm in arm 팔짱을 끼고 stroll 거닐다, 산책하다 water's edge 물가 hike 하이킹[도보 여행]을 하다
formation 대형, 진형 doorway 출입구 walk (동물을) 걷게 하다, 산책시키다; 걷기, 산책

He's walking toward an archway. 아치형 입구를 향해 걸어가고 있다.

They're walking past a seating area. 앉는 장소를 지나서 걷고 있다.

They are walking arm in arm. 팔짱을 끼고 걷고 있다.

They're strolling along the water's edge. 물가를 따라 산책하고 있다.

She's hiking on an outdoor path. 야외 산책로를 따라 하이킹을 하고 있다.

They are marching in formation. 대형을 이루어서 행진하고 있다.

Some people are approaching a doorway. 출입구에 접근하고 있다.

They're entering the building. 건물에 들어가고 있다.

cf. A woman is walking her dog along the shore. 해변을 따라 개를 산책시키고 있다.

cf. Some dogs are out for a walk. 개들이 산책하러 밖에 나와 있다.

유형 57 계단을 올라가거나 내려가는 장면 04_13
계단이라는 뜻의 단어 stairs, steps, stairway, staircase를 기억하자

어휘 ascend 오르다, 올라가다 descend 내려오다, 내려가다 level (건물, 땅의) 층 partway 도중까지

He's climbing some stairs. 계단을 올라가고 있다.

Some people are ascending[descending] some stairs. 계단을 올라가고[내려가고] 있다.

People are walking up[down] the steps. 계단을 올라가고[내려가고] 있다.

They're going up[down] the stairs. 계단을 올라가고[내려가고] 있다.

A woman is taking some stairs to a lower level. 계단을 타고 아래층으로 내려오고 있다.

The people are going up to the next floor. 다음 층으로 올라가고 있다.

cf. He has climbed partway up a ladder. 사다리 중간까지 올라가 있다.

cf. They have climbed onto a roof. 지붕 위에 올라가 있다.

cf. Smoke is rising into the air. 연기가 공중으로 올라가고 있다.

📖 Workbook p.41 ✏️ 정답 및 해설 p.49

1.

[a] [b] [c] [d]

2.

[a] [b] [c] [d]

Part 2의 유형은 크게 네 가지로 분류할 수 있다.

- 의문사 의문문: 매회 10-12문제
- 일반 의문문 / 평서문: 매회 9-11문제
- 제안/부탁 의문문: 매회 3-4문제
- 선택 의문문: 매회 1-2문제

Day 03에서는 가장 어려운 선택 의문문을 공부했다. DAY 04에서는 제안/부탁 의문문을 공부해 보자.
우선 주로 출제되는 제안하거나 부탁하는 질문의 형식을 알아보자.

제안/부탁 의문문

1. 제안하는 질문

(1) Why don't we ~? 우리 ~ 할까요?
Why don't you ~? ~ 하지 않겠어요?
Why don't I ~? 제가 ~ 해드릴까요?
Why not ~? ~ 하는 게 어때요?

(2) How[What] about ~? ~ 하는 게 어때요?
What if ~?
How would you like to-V ~?

(3) Would you like + N ~? ~ 드릴까요?
Would you care for + N ~?
Would you like to-V ~? ~ 하실래요?
Would you care to-V ~?
Would you like me to-V ~?
　　　　　　　　제가 ~ 해드릴까요?

(4) Do[Don't] you want + N ~? ~ 드릴까요?
Do[Don't] you want to-V ~? ~ 하실래요?
Do[Don't] you want me to-V ~?
　　　　　　　　제가 ~ 해드릴까요?

(5) Do you need help[assistance] with ~?
~ 도와드릴까요?

(6) ┌ Can ┐
　　│ Can't │ we ~? 우리 ~ 하면 안 될까요?
　　│ Could │
　　└ Couldn't ┘

(7) ┌ Should ┐┌ I ┐ 제가 ~ 해드릴까요?
　　└ Shouldn't ┘└ we ┘ 우리 ~ 할까요?
Shouldn't you ~? ~ 해야 하지 않나요?
Shouldn't you consider ~?
　　~을 생각해야 하지 않나요?
Don't you think we should ~?
　　우리 ~ 해야 하지 않나요?
* should가 들어 있는 질문은 거의 다 제안이다.

(8) Let's ~. ~ 합시다.

2. 부탁하는 질문

(1)
```
    ┌ Can  ┐  ┌ I   ┐  ~? 제가 ~해도 될까요?
    │ Could│  └ you ┘     ~ 해주시겠어요?
    │ Will │
    └ Would┘
    May I ~?
```
(2) Please ~. ~ 해주세요.

3. 자주 출제되는 정답

제안이나 부탁을 받으면 동의나 거절하는 대답을 해야 자연스러운 대화가 된다. 시험에 자주 출제되는 동의 및 거절 표현들을 암기해 두면 많은 문제를 쉽게 해결할 수 있다.

●● 큰 소리로 여러 번 따라 읽으면서 암기하세요. 굵은 글씨로 된 표현은 더 자주 출제된다.

(1) 자주 사용되는 동의 표현

🎧 04_16

사회생활을 원만하게 하려면 웬만한 제안이나 부탁은 거절하지 않는다.
그래서 동의하는 표현이 거절 표현보다 훨씬 더 많다.

- **Sure.**
- **Of course.**
- **Certainly.**
- **Absolutely.**
- **Definitely.**
- **You bet.**
- **Without a doubt.**
- **No problem.**
- **That's a good idea.**
- That's an excellent idea.
- That sounds like a great idea.
- That sounds like a good plan[choice].
- Sounds like fun.
- **That sounds good.**
- That sounds interesting.
- **That would be great!**
- **That would be nice.**
- That would be fantastic.
- That would be very helpful.
- That would help me a lot.
- That would save me some time.
- That would work out well for me.
- You're right.
- I'd like that.
- I'd be delighted to.

- I'd be pleased to.
- **I'd be happy to.**
- **I'd be glad to.**
- I'd be honored to.
- I'd love to.
- **Thanks, ~.**
- **Okay, ~.**
- I will.
- I probably should.
- We can do that.
- **Yes, I would.**
- It's okay[fine] with me.
- **I was planning to.**
- I think I might.
- That's what I was going to do.
- That's what I would suggest.
- That's what I was thinking.
- Help yourself.
- Suit yourself.
- Be my guest.
- By all means.
- Go ahead.
- There's one in[at/on] + 장소
  – 어떤 물건을 부탁받았을 때
- Here you are. – 어떤 물건을 부탁받았을 때

- You'll have to **wait until** next week.
  – 무언가 해달라는 부탁을 받았을 때 문장 중간에 wait until 이 들리면 거의 다 정답이다.
- I can help.
- **Wait a minute.**
- **I'll be right there.**
- **(Yes), if ~.**
- **I'm willing if ~.**
- **I'd appreciate that.**

- **Yes, please.**
- I don't mind if I do.
- That's very generous of you.
- It's so kind of you.
- If you don't[wouldn't] mind.
- Yes, if you insist.
- I'll try my best.
- I'll give it my best shot.

(2) 자주 사용되는 거절 표현

04_17

- **~ don't have time ~**
- **~ too busy ~**
- **~ too much work ~**
- I **already** have one, thanks.
  – already가 들리면 대부분 거절하는 대답이다.
- I'll do it later.
- I'll do it myself.
- No, thanks.
- I can't.
- Thanks, but ~.

- I'd prefer ~.
- I'd rather ~.
- I'd like to ~.
- **I was planning to ~.**
- **That's not necessary.**
- I've had **enough.**
- I wish I could, but ~.
- I'd like to, but ~.
- **I have other plans.**
- **I have a previous appointment.**
  – 선약이 있어요.
- I'm afraid ~.

(3) 누군가가 부재중이라는 대답은 거의 다 거절이다

04_18

She's **out of the office** today.

I'll be **out of town.**

I will be in Greenville that week.

I'm afraid **I won't be able to go.**

(4) 역으로 제안하는 대답은 거의 100% 동의나 거절이다

Let's ~　　　　　　　**How about ~**　　　　　　　Can[Can't] we ~

(5) Do[Would] you mind ~?의 정답 패턴

① 허락 (대부분 허락하는 대답이 정답)

| **Not at all.** | No, I don't. | **Sure.** |
| **Of course.** | Certainly. | No problem. |

② 거절

I'm afraid ~.

Q. Can you give me a hand with these boxes?
A. Sure, I'll be right there.

이 상자들 옮기는 것을 도와주실 수 있겠어요?
≫ 물론이죠, 금방 갈게요.

Q. Could I borrow your scissors for a minute?
A. Of course, here you go.

가위 좀 빌릴 수 있을까요?
≫ 물론이죠, 여기 있어요.

Q. Could I see some sample floral arrangements before I order?
A. Certainly, I have some right here.

주문하기 전에 꽃꽂이 견본을 좀 볼 수 있을까요?
≫ 그럼요, 바로 여기 있습니다.

Q. Can you please submit the receipts from your trip?
A. Absolutely, I'll send them to you now.

출장 때 받으신 영수증들을 제출해 주시겠어요?
≫ 물론이죠, 지금 보내 드릴게요.

Q. Would you be interested in a magazine subscription?
A. Definitely, how much is it?

잡지 구독에 관심 있으십니까?
≫ 그럼요, 얼마인가요?

Q. Can you please turn up the lights so I can take a photograph?
A. Sure, no problem.

사진을 찍을 수 있게 조명을 더 밝게 해 주시겠어요?
≫ 그럼요, 문제없습니다.

Q. You should include an image on each page of the book.
A. Yes, that's a good idea.

책의 각 페이지마다 이미지를 포함시키는 게 좋겠어요.
≫ 네, 좋은 생각입니다.

Q. Can you organize a party for So-Hee's last day?
A. Yes, I'd be happy to.

So-Hee의 마지막 날을 위해 파티를 준비해 주시겠어요?
≫ 네, 기꺼이 하겠습니다.

Q. Why don't I confirm the meeting time with Ms. Moreno?
A. Thanks, that would be great.

제가 Ms. Moreno와 회의 시간을 확정할까요?
≫ 고마워요, 그게 좋겠어요.

Q. How about stopping at that new coffee shop on our way to work tomorrow?
A. OK, I've heard good things about it.

내일 출근길에 저 새로 생긴 커피숍에 들르는 거 어때요?
≫ 좋아요, 저곳에 대해 좋은 얘기를 들었어요.

Q. Would you like me to type up the proposal for you?

A. That would be very helpful.

제가 대신 제안서를 타이핑해 드릴까요?

>>> 그렇게 해주시면 큰 도움이 될 것 같아요.

Q. Let's post the sales report to our team's Web page.

A. I can do that.

우리 팀 웹 페이지에 영업 보고서를 게재합시다.

>>> 제가 할게요.

Q. Should I pick up the food order for Ms. Santos?

A. Yes, if you have the time.

Ms. Santos를 위해 주문한 음식 제가 찾아올까요?

>>> 네, 시간이 되시면요.

Q. Would you like a ride to work tomorrow?

A. I'd appreciate that.

내일 직장까지 태워줄까요?

>>> 그렇게 해 주시면 감사하죠.

Q. Can you give me a tour of the property this afternoon?

A. Sorry. I won't have time until tomorrow.

오늘 오후에 건물을 구경시켜 주실 수 있나요?

>>> 죄송하지만, 내일까지는 시간이 없어요.

Q. Why don't we take a quick break?

A. I can't. I've got too much to do.

잠깐 쉬는 거 어때요?

>>> 안 돼요. 할 일이 너무 많아요.

Q. Why don't we create a video tour of the convention space?

A. I thought you already did that.

전시회 장소의 동영상 투어를 만드는 게 어떨까요?

>>> 그건 당신이 이미 한 줄 알았는데요.

Q. Shouldn't we discuss the advertising campaign now?

A. No, we have other priorities.

이제 광고 캠페인에 대해 의논해야 하지 않을까요?

>>> 아니요, 다른 우선 사항들이 있어요.

Q. Please put in a request for Mona to get access to the database.

A. The IT specialist is out of the office this week.

Mona가 데이터베이스에 접속할 수 있도록 신청서를 제출해 주세요.

>>> 이번 주에는 IT 담당자가 사무실에 없어요.

Q. Would you like me to turn on the air conditioner?

A. No, let's open the windows.

에어컨을 켜 드릴까요?

>>> 아니요, 창문을 열죠.

Q. Let's take our clients to the theater.

A. How about a restaurant instead?

고객들을 극장에 데려갑시다.

>>> 그보다는 식당이 어때요?

Workbook p.42   정답 및 해설 p.49

1.   (A)   (B)   (C)   6.   (A)   (B)   (C)

2.   (A)   (B)   (C)   7.   (A)   (B)   (C)

3.   (A)   (B)   (C)   8.   (A)   (B)   (C)

4.   (A)   (B)   (C)   9.   (A)   (B)   (C)

5.   (A)   (B)   (C)   10.   (A)   (B)   (C)

두 문제의 키워드가 동시에 들리거나 순서가 바뀌는 문제

대화나 담화를 듣고 있으면 대부분 문제 번호 순서대로 키워드가 귀에 들린다. 그러나 가끔은 두 문제의 키워드가 한 문장 속에 동시에 나타나거나, 순서가 바뀌어서 들리는 경우가 있다. Part 3, 4에서 각각 매회 한 번 정도 이런 경우가 있는데, 예제를 통해 공략법을 익혀보자.

Q PART 3 Sample Questions Workbook p.44 04_22

1. What are the speakers mainly discussing?

(A) An internship opportunity
(B) A university course
(C) A due date for a project
(D) A news article

2. What type of business is Patel & Partners?

(A) A medical practice
(B) A staffing firm
(C) A building company
(D) A law firm

3. What does the man ask about?

(A) The outcomes of an investigation
(B) The levels of customer satisfaction
(C) The likelihood of full-time employment
(D) The cost of hiring a professional

W | Am [1][2]Mr. Burgess, I see from your résumé that you're interested in a law internship here at Patel & Partners.

M | Cn Yes, I'm eager to acquire as much knowledge as possible about working in legal services. Plus, I'm looking forward to putting the knowledge I've gained at university into practice.

W | Am Well, if you're selected, you'll work alongside a mentor on a variety of major cases. The work is challenging, but most interns find it very rewarding.

M | Cn That sounds great. I've always admired the work of Patel & Partners. [3]In fact, I'd really like to get a full-time position here someday. Is it common for interns to be employed following their internship periods?

1. What are the speakers mainly discussing?

(A) **An internship opportunity**
(B) A university course
(C) A due date for a project
(D) A news article

2. What type of business is Patel & Partners?

(A) A medical practice
(B) A staffing firm
(C) A building company
(D) **A law firm**

3. What does the man ask about?

(A) The outcomes of an investigation
(B) The levels of customer satisfaction
(C) **The likelihood of full-time employment**
(D) The cost of hiring a professional

해설 우선 1번 문제는 대화 주제를 묻고 있기 때문에 첫 문장에서 정답을 찾을 것이라고 예상할 수 있다. 그런데 첫 문장이 1번 문제의 정답뿐만 아니라, 2번 문제의 키워드까지 알려주고 있다. 수험자는 여기서 1번과 2번의 정답을 동시에 골라야 하므로, 1번 문제를 보면서도 2번 문제의 내용을 생각해야 한다. 어느 문제가 이렇게 두 문제의 키워드를 동시에 들려줄지, 혹은 순서를 바꿔서 들려줄지 알 수 없으므로, 수험자는 모든 문제를 미리 읽을 때 암기하겠다는 생각으로 주의 깊게 읽어야 한다. 물론 대화를 계속 듣다 보면 Patel & Partners가 법률 사무소임을 알려주는 단서가 계속 등장하기는 하지만, 모든 문제가 그렇게 친절하게 여러 번 키워드를 들려주는 것은 아니다. 되도록 첫 번째 기회가 왔을 때 두 문제의 정답을 동시에 고를 수 있도록 문제 내용을 암기하기 위해 노력하자. 3번 문제의 정답은 남자의 대사 마지막 두 문장에서 알 수 있다. 자기와 같은 인턴사원이 정직원으로 채용될 가능성을 궁금해하고 있으므로, 이 부분이 패러프레이즈 되어 있는 문장을 정답으로 선택해야 한다.

PART 3

1. Who most likely is the woman?

  (A) A news reporter
  (B) A store owner
  (C) A real estate agent
  (D) A photographer

2. What is the woman pleased about?

  (A) A contract with a new client
  (B) A recently published article
  (C) A property's location
  (D) A draft of an advertisement

3. What does the man offer to do?

  (A) Rearrange some furniture
  (B) Expedite a service request
  (C) Generate an invoice
  (D) Enlarge some words

PART 4

4. What is the purpose of the telephone message?

  (A) To purchase clothing items
  (B) To offer an apology to a customer
  (C) To reschedule an appointment
  (D) To inquire about a location

5. What problem does the speaker mention?

  (A) Some material is damaged.
  (B) A machine is out of order.
  (C) A shipment is behind schedule.
  (D) Some items are out of stock.

6. What does the speaker say he will do?

  (A) Confirm some specifications
  (B) Consult with a supervisor
  (C) Provide a sample
  (D) Send a replacement

 04_26

●● Actual Test를 풀기 전에 이 단어들을 따라 읽으며 암기하자.

photocopier 복사기
hopefully 바라건대
treat A to B A에게 B를 대접하다
analyst 분석가
connection (교통) 연결 편
make it to ～에 도착하다
in time 시간 맞춰, 늦지 않게
proceed (특정 방향으로) 나아가다, 이동하다
newspaper (agency) 신문사
reference 추천서
fulfill 이행하다, 수행하다
put together (행사)를 준비하다, 계획을 짜다
outing 야유회
eatery 식당
recognition (공로 등의) 인정, 표창
diner (식당에서) 식사하는 사람[손님]
(new) hire 신입 사원
off (근무, 일을) 쉬는; ～에서 할인하여

in advance 미리, 사전에
grant 승인하다, 허락하다
extra 추가의
retain 유지하다, 보유하다
existing 기존의
communicate 전달하다
on a regular basis 정기적으로
extensive 광범위한, 대규모의
tour 순회하다
refurbish 새로 꾸미다, 재단장하다
inspection 시찰, 순시
luncheon 오찬
reassure 안심시키다
pro shop 프로 숍(골프, 테니스 등의 클럽하우스의 스포츠
용품 판매점)
come out on top (시합에서) 이기다
valid 유효한

Actual Test

PART 1	1-3
PART 2	4-12
PART 3	13-21
PART 4	22-30

Part 3, 4 '미리 잘 읽기' 전략

LC Directions 시간:	16-18번 읽기
Part 1 Directions 시간:	19-21번 읽기
Part 2 Directions 시간:	28-30번 읽기
Part 3 Directions 시간:	13-15번 읽기
19-21번 문제 읽어주는 시간:	22-24번 읽기
Part 4 Directions 시간:	25-27번 읽기

 Workbook p.47   정답 및 해설 p.54

LISTENING TEST

지금 16-18번 읽기

In the Listening test, you will be asked to demonstrate how well you understand spoken English. The entire Listening test will last approximately 45 minutes. There are four parts, and directions are given for each part. You must mark your answers on the separate answer sheet. Do not write your answers in your test book.

PART 1

지금 19-21번 읽기

Directions: For each question in this part, you will hear four statements about a picture in your test book. When you hear the statements, you must select the one statement that best describes what you see in the picture. Then find the number of the question on your answer sheet and mark your answer. The statements will not be printed in your test book and will be spoken only one time.

1.

3.

2.

PART 2

Directions: You will hear a question or statement and three responses spoken in English. They will not be printed in your test book and will be spoken only one time. Select the best response to the question or statement and mark the letter (A), (B), or (C) on your answer sheet.

4.   Mark your answer.   (A)   (B)   (C)

5.   Mark your answer.   (A)   (B)   (C)

6.   Mark your answer.   (A)   (B)   (C)

7.   Mark your answer.   (A)   (B)   (C)

8.   Mark your answer.   (A)   (B)   (C)

9.   Mark your answer.   (A)   (B)   (C)

10.   Mark your answer.   (A)   (B)   (C)

11.   Mark your answer.   (A)   (B)   (C)

12.   Mark your answer.   (A)   (B)   (C)

PART 3

Directions: You will hear some conversations between two or more people. You will be asked to answer three questions about what the speakers say in each conversation. Select the best response to each question and mark the letter (A), (B), (C), or (D) on your answer sheet. The conversations will not be printed in your test book and will be spoken only one time.

13. What is the woman's problem?

(A) She misplaced her luggage.
(B) She didn't make it to her flight in time.
(C) She left behind her airplane ticket.
(D) She has no idea where the gate is.

14. Where is the woman's final destination?

(A) San Diego
(B) Seoul
(C) Los Angeles
(D) San Francisco

15. What does the man tell the woman to do?

(A) Present her identification
(B) Consult a travel agent
(C) Look through her baggage
(D) Proceed to an airport gate

16. Where do the speakers work?

(A) At a television station
(B) At an advertising agency
(C) At an electronics store
(D) At a newspaper

17. Why did Activa Media contact the speakers' workplace?

(A) To provide a training seminar
(B) To introduce some new products
(C) To inquire about some photographs
(D) To request a reference

18. What does the woman imply when she says, "I never actually worked with him"?

(A) She cannot fulfill a request.
(B) She would rather work by herself.

(C) She is surprised a colleague is leaving.
(D) She is dissatisfied with an assignment.

LUNCH SPECIALS	
Valencia Fish Soup	$7
Healthy Greek Pita Sandwich	$9
Crispy Mediterranean Salad	$7
Gourmet Provence Sampler	$10

정답 고르고 나서 바로 22-24번 읽기

19. What type of event is the man organizing?

(A) A business seminar
(B) A client luncheon
(C) A retirement party
(D) A department outing

20. What does the woman mention about the café?

(A) Large groups can be hosted in an outdoor patio.
(B) Cancellations must be made with at least 24 hours notice.
(C) It gained recognition among local diners.
(D) The menu varies according to the season.

21. Look at the graphic. What menu item does not contain meat?

(A) The soup
(B) The sandwich
(C) The salad
(D) The sampler

Directions: You will hear some talks given by a single speaker. You will be asked to answer three questions about what the speaker says in each talk. Select the best response to each question and mark the letter (A), (B), (C), or (D) on your answer sheet. The talks will not be printed in your test book and will be spoken only one time.

22. What is the main topic of the anouncement?

(A) Updating the company Web site
(B) Granting new hires extra days off
(C) Offering advanced training to managers
(D) Enhancing the flexibility of work schedules

23. According to the speaker, why is a change being made?

(A) To retain existing staff members
(B) To comply with a company regulation
(C) To enhance communication
(D) To implement improved safety procedures

24. What are the listeners reminded to do?

(A) Update the contact information for clients
(B) Refer to their department handbook
(C) Communicate company policies to their employees
(D) Change their passwords on a regular basis

25. Why is the CEO coming for a visit?

(A) A project has been completed.
(B) A facility has been acquired.
(C) A new manager has joined the company.
(D) A sales goal has been met.

26. Why does the speaker say, "this isn't a formal inspection"?

(A) To dispute a claim
(B) To reassure employees
(C) To acknowledge a positive result

(D) To question a procedure

27. What event have the listeners been invited to?

(A) A farewell party
(B) A groundbreaking ceremony
(C) A welcome reception
(D) A fashion show

**Masayuki's
Tennis Club
50% Off
Select classes**

---

28. What is Mr. Hirano known for?

(A) He is the proprietor of several tennis clubs.
(B) He came out on top in tennis competitions.
(C) He promotes a brand of tennis gear.
(D) He exclusively instructs novice students.

29. Look at the graphic. What classes is the coupon valid for?

(A) Child classes
(B) Adult classes
(C) Advanced classes
(D) Weekend classes

30. What recently changed at Masayuki's Tennis Club?

(A) The size of a store
(B) The types of classes
(C) The surface of a court
(D) The date of a tournament

Day
05

●● 장면을 상상하면서 큰 소리로 여러 번 따라 읽으세요.

유형 58 달리는 장면

🎧 05_01

He's running on the street. 달리고 있다.
They're jogging together. 함께 조깅하고 있다.

유형 59 길이나 다리를 건너는 장면 crossing이 들리면 무조건 정답!

🎧 05_02

어휘 pedestrian 보행자

Pedestrians are crossing the street. 보행자들이 길을 건너고 있다.
Some trucks are crossing a bridge. 트럭들이 다리를 건너고 있다.

유형 60 교통수단 등장 장면

어휘 be about to-V 막 ~ 하려고 하다 aircraft 항공기 direct (길을) 안내하다 away from ~에서 떠나서 rider (자전거, 오토바이를) 탄 사람

(1) 탑승하고 있다 / 내리고 있다

🎧 05_03

> 타다 - board, get on, get into, step into, step onto
> 내리다 - exit, get off, get out of, disembark from
> *disembark from은 비행기나 배에서 내릴 때 사용

People are boarding a train. 기차에 타고 있다.
They're getting into a vehicle. 차에 타고 있다.
A passenger is about to step onto the train. 막 기차에 타려고 한다.
People are exiting through a door. 문을 통해 내리고 있다.
A passenger is getting out of a car. 차에서 내리고 있다.
Passengers are disembarking from an aircraft. 항공기에서 내리고 있다.

Passengers have arrived at the station. 승객들이 역에 도착했다. (기차에서 내리는 장면)

Children are being directed away from the bus. (내리는) 아이들을 버스에서 멀어지는 방향으로 안내하고 있다.

cf. Some of the riders have gotten off their motorcycles. 오토바이에서 내려 서 있다.

(2) 사람이 교통수단을 타고 가는 장면 riding이 들리면 정답!

🎧 05_04

어휘 ahead of ~ 앞에 parallel to ~과 평행으로 carriage 마차 row 노[배]를 젓다 paddle 노를 젓다 pier 부두 cruise 유람선 여행

Some people are riding bicycles by the water. 물가에서 자전거를 타고 있다.

One of the riders is ahead of the other. 자전거 탄 둘 중 한 명이 다른 한 명 앞에 있다.

A motorcyclist is riding parallel to a truck. 오토바이 운전자가 트럭과 나란히 달리고 있다.

Some people are riding on an open carriage. 지붕 없는 마차를 타고 있다.

Some people are riding an escalator. 에스컬레이터를 타고 있다.

They're riding in a boat. 배를 타고 있다.

He's rowing a boat in the water. 배를 저어 가고 있다.

A group is paddling a boat near a pier. 부두 근처 배에서 노를 젓고 있다.

Some people are taking a boat ride[trip]. 배를 타고 있다.

Some people are taking a cruise. 유람선 여행을 하고 있다.

(3) 교통수단이 이동하는 장면

🎧 05_05

어휘 steering wheel (자동차의) 핸들 behind the steering wheel 운전 중인 cliff 절벽 travel 이동하다 track (기차) 선로 sail 항해하다

A worker's driving a vehicle. 차량을 운전하고 있다.

The woman is behind the steering wheel. 운전 중이다.

Cars are being driven across a bridge. 차를 운전해서 다리를 건너고 있다.

Boats are passing between the cliff walls. 배들이 절벽 사이를 지나가고 있다.

A train is traveling on the track. 기차가 선로 위를 이동하고 있다.

Numerous boats are sailing on the water. 많은 배들이 물 위에서 항해하고 있다.

(4) 지나간 자취가 남아 있다

🎧 05_06

어휘 track 지나간 자취, 바큇자국

Tracks have been left in the sand. 모래에 바큇자국이 남아 있다.

Machines are making tracks on the ground. 기계가 땅에 지나간 자취를 남기고 있다.

(5) 주차되어 있다 be parked[left] *위치 표현에 집중할 것

어휘 multi-level 여러 층의 structure 구조물 mechanic's garage 자동차 정비소 aircraft 항공기 rack 자전거 주차대 by a curb 길가에 wheelbarrow 외바퀴 손수레 pile 쌓아 놓은 것, 더미 unattended 방치된, 지켜보는 사람이 없는 airstrip 활주로 tractor 트랙터 service station 주유소 tow 견인하다

Vehicles are parked in multi-level structures. 다층 구조로 주차되어 있다.

A van is parked in a mechanic's garage. 밴이 정비소에 주차되어 있다.

The airplanes are parked on the ground. 비행기가 땅에 주차되어 있다.

Some aircraft are parked in front of a terminal. 항공기들이 터미널 앞에 주차되어 있다.

Bicycles are parked in a rack. 자전거들이 주차대에 주차되어 있다.

A motorcycle is parked by a curb. 오토바이가 길가에 주차되어 있다.

A wheelbarrow has been left next to a pile of rocks. 외바퀴 손수레가 돌무더기 옆에 놓여 있다.

Some carts have been left unattended. 카트 몇 대가 방치되어 있다.

The helicopters have landed on the grass[an airstrip]. 헬리콥터가 잔디밭에[활주로에] 착륙해 있다.

cf. The airplanes have taken off. 비행기들이 이륙했다.

A tractor has stopped near some plants. 트랙터가 수풀 근처에 멈추어 서 있다.

A car has stopped at a service station. 차가 주유소에 멈추어 서 있다.

The car is being towed. 차가 견인되고 있다.

(6) 주유소 장면

05_08

어휘 fill 채우다 gas 휘발유 pump (펌프로) 퍼 올리다

The man is filling the car with fuel. 차에 연료를 채우고 있다.

Gas is being pumped into the vehicle. 차에 휘발유가 들어가고 있다.

(7) 기차[버스]가 역[정류장]으로[에서] 들어오는[나가는] 장면

05_09

어휘 pull into (열차가 역에) 들어오다 pull out of (열차가 역에서) 떠나다

The train is pulling into the station. 기차가 역에 들어오고 있다.

The train is pulling out of the station. 기차가 역에서 나가고 있다.

The bus is approaching the bus stop. 버스가 정류장에 접근하고 있다.

The train has pulled into the station. 기차가 역에 들어와 있다.

A train has arrived at a platform. 기차가 플랫폼에 도착했다.

The travelers are waiting with their suitcases. 여행객들이 여행 가방을 가지고 기다리고 있다.

(8) 배가 정박해 있는 장면

어휘 dock 부두에 대다; 부두 harbor 항구, 항만 anchor 닻을 내리다, 정박하다 port 항구 tie up (보트를 말뚝 등에) 묶다 offshore 육지에서 떨어진 곳에, 앞바다에 float (물에) 뜨다 shore 해안, 해변

Many boats are docked in a harbor. 많은 배들이 항만에 정박해 있다.

A ship is anchored at port. 배가 항구에 정박해 있다.

The boat is tied up offshore. 배가 앞바다에 묶여 있다.

Some boats are floating by a dock. 배들이 부두 옆에 떠 있다.

cf. The boats have been taken out of the water. 배들을 물 밖으로 꺼내어 놓았다.

cf. Some small boats have been pulled onto the shore. 작은 배 몇 척을 해변으로 끌어 올려놓았다.

Exercise

Workbook p.55   정답 및 해설 p.64

1.

a   b   c   d

2.

a   b   c   d

> **일반 의문문/ 평서문**
>
> 의문사 의문문은 Yes나 No로 시작하는 대답이 들리면 오답인 반면, 일반 의문문이나 평서문에서는 Yes/No가 자연스러운 대답이다. Yes/No를 대신할 수 있는 표현들이 들리면 대부분 정답이다. 큰 소리로 여러 번 따라 읽으면서 암기해 두자.

➡ Yes/No를 대신하는 표현 🎧 05_13

(1) Yes를 대신하는 표현

Sure. 물론이죠.
Of course.
Certainly.
Absolutely.
Definitely.
You bet.
Without a doubt.

I think so. 그런 것 같아요.
I thought so.
I think she did.
I believe so.
I believe she has.
I hope so.
I guess so.
I suppose so.

All right. 좋아요.
OK.

You're right. 맞아요.
That's right.
That's true.

That's the forecast I heard.
제가 들은 예보로는 그래요.
That's what the memo says.
단체 메일에 그렇게 쓰여 있더군요.
That's what I heard. 제가 듣기로는 그래요.
That's what they told me.

(2) No를 대신하는 표현

Not yet. 아직 아니에요.
Not quite yet.
Not quite.

I don't think so. 아닌 것 같은데요.
I don't think we have.
I don't think she's in today.
I didn't think he was, either.
I don't think he is.

Never. 절대 아니에요.
I never did.

Not at all. 전혀 그렇지 않아요.

I'm sorry ~ 미안하지만 ~
I'm afraid ~ 유감이지만 ~

Not that I know of. 제가 아는 한은 아닙니다.
Not that I'm aware of.

(3) 애매한 대답

Not really. / Not necessarily. 꼭 그런 건 아니에요.

Q. Are you free to meet the new staff members today?
A. Sure, bring them by after lunch.

오늘 신입 직원들 만날 시간 되세요?
≫≫ 그럼요, 점심시간 후에 보내 주세요.

Q. The gymnastics class was really fun, wasn't it?
A. Absolutely, I really enjoyed myself.

체조 수업 정말 재미있었죠?
≫≫ 물론이죠, 정말 재미있었어요.

Q. Isn't the development workshop going well?
A. I think it is.

개발 워크숍은 잘 진행되고 있지 않나요?
≫≫ 그럴 거예요.

Q. Are you going to see Fabien when you visit Lyon?
A. I hope so.

Lyon을 방문하시면 Fabien을 만나실 건가요?
≫≫ 그러기를 바라요.

Q. That photocopy machine is broken, isn't it?
A. You're right, it needs to be replaced.

복사기가 고장 났죠?
≫≫ 맞아요, 교체가 필요해요.

Q. It's supposed to be warmer tomorrow, isn't it?
A. That's the forecast I heard.

내일은 더 따뜻하겠죠?
≫≫ 제가 들은 예보는 그래요.

Q. Will our gym memberships renew automatically?
A. That's what I was told.

헬스클럽 회원권이 자동으로 갱신되나요?
≫≫ 그렇다고 들었어요.

Q. Won't they be here by eight?
A. That's what they told me.

그들이 8시까지 오는 거 아닌가요?
≫≫ 그들이 그렇게 말했죠.

Q. Have the machines on the factory floor been cleaned?
A. No, not yet.

공장 작업장의 기계들은 청소가 되었나요?
≫≫ 아니요, 아직 안 되었습니다.

Q. They're ready to leave, aren't they?
A. No, not quite yet.

그분들 출발할 준비 되신 거죠?
≫≫ 아니요, 아직 안 되셨어요.

Q. I don't believe we've met before.
A. No, I don't think we have.

전에 만난 적이 없는 것 같네요.
≫≫ 네, 뵌 적이 없는 것 같아요.

Q. Should I go over my report with Ms. Carey before presenting it?

A. I don't think she's in today.

제 보고서를 발표하기 전에 Ms. Carey와 함께 검토할까요?

>>> 그녀는 오늘 출근하시지 않은 것 같은데요.

Q. The sales associate wasn't very helpful, was he?

A. I didn't think he was, either.

그 영업 사원이 그리 도움이 되지는 않았죠?

>>> 저도 그렇게 생각해요.

Q. Would you mind if I borrow one of your staplers?

A. Not at all, there's one on my desk.

스테이플러 하나 빌릴 수 있을까요?

>>> 그럼요, 제 책상에 있어요.

Q. Does this pasta come with a side salad?

A. No, I'm afraid not.

이 파스타에는 사이드 샐러드가 같이 나오나요?

>>> 죄송하지만 그렇지는 않습니다.

Q. Do you think the new law will help to reduce crime?

A. Not necessarily.

새 법률이 범죄를 줄이는 데 도움이 될 것이라고 생각하시나요?

>>> 반드시 그럴 것 같지는 않습니다.

문제를 풀 때는 가장 중요한 풀이 원칙을 절대 잊지 말자.

1. 질문 앞부분에 집중하라!
2. 오답을 잘 골라낼수록 고수가 된다!

📄 Workbook p.56　　✏️ 정답 및 해설 p.64

1.	(A)	(B)	(C)	**6.**	(A)	(B)	(C)
2.	(A)	(B)	(C)	**7.**	(A)	(B)	(C)
3.	(A)	(B)	(C)	**8.**	(A)	(B)	(C)
4.	(A)	(B)	(C)	**9.**	(A)	(B)	(C)
5.	(A)	(B)	(C)	**10.**	(A)	(B)	(C)

PART 3&4

→ **키워드가 패러프레이즈 되는 문제 1**

Part 3, 4에서 몇 문제는 미리 읽어 둔 키워드가 그대로 들리지 않고, 패러프레이즈 된 상태로 등장한다. LC 만점을 위해 이 유형의 문제들을 정복하도록 최선을 다하자.

Q **PART 3 Sample Questions**   Workbook p.58   05_17

1. Where do the speakers most likely work?

(A) At a dining establishment
(B) At an exercise facility
(C) At an athletic arena
(D) At a lodging establishment

2. What are the speakers discussing?

(A) Attending a sporting event
(B) Preparing for extra customers
(C) Organizing a remodeling project
(D) Expanding to a new location

3. What will the woman ask Ramon to do?

(A) Provide some directions
(B) Ask for a price quote
(C) Work an extra shift
(D) Present a demonstration

Questions 1 through 3 refer to the following conversation. ✎ 해설 p.66

W | Am [1]It looks like we'll have to arrange for extra wait staff for next Saturday. [2]There's a volleyball game in the stadium next door, and we'll have a big dinner crowd after it's over.

M | Au Definitely, we should have at least three servers here for dinner.

W | Am Well, Akiko and Henry are already scheduled, [3]but Ramon is working the day shift. I'll see if he can work some extra hours.

1. Where do the speakers most likely work?

(A) At a dining establishment
(B) At an exercise facility
(C) At an athletic arena
(D) At a lodging establishment

2. What are the speakers discussing?

(A) Attending a sporting event
(B) Preparing for extra customers
(C) Organizing a remodeling project
(D) Expanding to a new location

3. What will the woman ask Ramon to do?

(A) Provide some directions
(B) Ask for a price quote
(C) Work an extra shift
(D) Present a demonstration

해설 1번 문제가 대화 장소를 묻고 있기 때문에 첫 한두 문장에서 정답을 알아낼 것이라고 예상할 수 있다. 여자의 첫 대사 It looks like we'll have to arrange for extra wait staff for next Saturday.를 들으면서 여기가 식당임을 알아내고 정답을 고르자. 2번 문제도 보통 첫 한두 문장에서 정답을 알려주는 대화 주제를 묻는 문제다. 1번에서 정답 고르기를 조금이라도 머뭇거리면 키워드를 놓칠 수 있으므로 항상 순발력이 필요하다는 사실을 잊지 말자. 이어지는 문장에 들어 있는 big dinner crowd가 선택지에는 extra customers로 바뀌어 있다. 저녁 시간에 몰려올 인파를 대비하기 위해 서빙 직원들이 더 필요하다는 내용이므로 (B) Preparing for extra customers가 정답이다. 3번 문제의 키워드는 but으로 시작하는 대사에 들어 있다. but, no, actually, so로 시작하는 문장이 정답을 알려줄 확률이 높다는 사실도 기억하자. I'll see if he can work some extra hours.라는 마지막 문장을 듣고 이 부분이 패러프레이즈 되어 있는 선택지를 정답으로 선택해야 한다. 어휘력 향상과 받아쓰기, 따라 읽기 같은 청취력 훈련을 통해 키워드가 지문 속에서 패러프레이즈 되는 문제를 정복해서 LC 만점에 도전해 보자.

Workbook p.59 정답 및 해설 p.67

PART 3

---

1. In what department does the man most likely work?

(A) Human Resources
(B) Product Development
(C) Technical Support
(D) Building Maintenance

2. What does the woman give the man?

(A) An employee handbook
(B) A job application
(C) A training schedule
(D) A feedback questionnaire

3. What does the woman suggest the man to do?

(A) Secure a conference room
(B) Discuss plans with a colleague
(C) Reschedule a workshop
(D) Update a software program

PART 4

---

4. What kind of business does the speaker work for?

(A) A restaurant
(B) A grocery store
(C) A furniture store
(D) A gym

5. Why does the speaker assign extra work to the listeners?

(A) A deadline is fast approaching.
(B) One of the employees is unwell.
(C) A large number of customers are expected.
(D) Equipment needs to be unpacked.

6. What does the speaker ask listeners to tell customers about?

(A) Changed business hours
(B) Membership cards
(C) A special dish
(D) A holiday sale

Today's Vocabulary

 05_21

● ● Actual Test를 풀기 전에 이 단어들을 따라 읽으며 암기하자.

beside a curb 길가에

waterfront 해안가

professional development 전문성 개발

nomination 지명, 추천

room 공간, 여유

reserve 예약하다

shortly 얼마 안 가서, 곧

sample 맛보다, 시식하다

unusually 이례적으로

slow 부진한, 경기가 나쁜

lower 내리다, 낮추다

fund-raising 기금 마련

address 고심하다, 다루다

frustrate 좌절감을 주다, 불만스럽게 만들다

on time 시간을 어기지 않고, 정각에

nervous 불안한, 초조한, 긴장한

figure out ~을 이해하다, 알아내다

make up for ~에 대해 보상하다

inconvenience 불편, 애로

fund-raiser 기금 마련 행사

bring up (화제를) 꺼내다

present 참석한, 출석한

end up V–ing 결국 ~하게 되다

incomplete 불완전한, 불충분한

place an order for ~을 주문하다

make use of ~을 이용하다, 활용하다

vendor 판매 회사

blend (차, 담배 등의) 블렌드, 혼합 (제품)

grab ~을 손에 넣다

wholesome 건강에 좋은

treat 간식, 군것질거리

fiber 섬유(질)

content 함유량, 함량

ample 충분한, 풍부한

protein 단백질

substitute 대용품

head (특정 방향으로) 가다, 향하다

sort 종류, 유형

glitch (작은) 문제, 결함

to one's surprise 놀랍게도

mistaken 잘못 알고[판단하고] 있는

appreciate (진가를) 알아보다, 인정하다

feature (상품의 특징적) 기능

alert 알림

specific 특정한

malfunction 제대로 작동하지 않다

investigate 조사하다

Actual Test

PART 1	1-3
PART 2	4-12
PART 3	13-21
PART 4	22-30

Part 3, 4 '미리 잘 읽기' 전략

LC Directions 시간:	16-18번 읽기
Part 1 Directions 시간:	19-21번 읽기
Part 2 Directions 시간:	28-30번 읽기
Part 3 Directions 시간:	13-15번 읽기
19-21번 문제 읽어주는 시간:	22-24번 읽기
Part 4 Directions 시간:	25-27번 읽기

📘 Workbook p.61 ✏️ 정답 및 해설 p.69

LISTENING TEST

지금 16-18번 읽기

In the Listening test, you will be asked to demonstrate how well you understand spoken English. The entire Listening test will last approximately 45 minutes. There are four parts, and directions are given for each part. You must mark your answers on the separate answer sheet. Do not write your answers in your test book.

PART 1

지금 19-21번 읽기

Directions: For each question in this part, you will hear four statements about a picture in your test book. When you hear the statements, you must select the one statement that best describes what you see in the picture. Then find the number of the question on your answer sheet and mark your answer. The statements will not be printed in your test book and will be spoken only one time.

1.

 a b c d

3.

 a b   c d

2.

 a b c d

Directions: You will hear a question or statement and three responses spoken in English. They will not be printed in your test book and will be spoken only one time. Select the best response to the question or statement and mark the letter (A), (B), or (C) on your answer sheet.

4. Mark your answer.   (A)   (B)   (C)

5. Mark your answer.   (A)   (B)   (C)

6. Mark your answer.   (A)   (B)   (C)

7. Mark your answer.   (A)   (B)   (C)

8. Mark your answer.   (A)   (B)   (C)

9. Mark your answer.   (A)   (B)   (C)

10. Mark your answer.   (A)   (B)   (C)

11. Mark your answer.   (A)   (B)   (C)

12. Mark your answer.   (A)   (B)   (C)

PART 3

Directions: You will hear some conversations between two or more people. You will be asked to answer three questions about what the speakers say in each conversation. Select the best response to each question and mark the letter (A), (B), (C), or (D) on your answer sheet. The conversations will not be printed in your test book and will be spoken only one time.

13. What problem does the woman mention?

(A) Business is unusually slow.
(B) A restaurant received negative feedback.
(C) There is a shortage of employees.
(D) There has been no renewal of the lease.

14. What does the man suggest?

(A) Providing outdoor dining
(B) Relocating to a larger space
(C) Lowering prices
(D) Catering for business functions

15. What does the woman ask the man to do?

(A) Recruit an assistant
(B) Organize a training session
(C) Prepare for an inspection
(D) Create some food samples

16. What does the woman imply when she says, "I volunteered last year"?

(A) She can aid in the training of other volunteers.
(B) She takes pride in her volunteer work.
(C) She did not have a good time at the event last year.
(D) She has no plans to be present at the event.

17. What is the woman nervous about?

(A) Delivering a speech
(B) Responding to customer complaints
(C) Translating a complex document
(D) Assuming a new position

18. What does the man say he will do tomorrow?

(A) Reassign certain tasks
(B) Discuss an issue at a meeting
(C) Get ready to provide some feedback
(D) Conduct some preliminary research

RALTON HOME FURNISHINGS
Order #45709

Quantity	Description	Total Price
5	Dinner Plate	$25
7	Soup Bowl	$42
4	Coffee Mug	$16
2	Teapot	$50

정답 고르고 나서 바로 22-24번 읽기

19. What does the woman say happened when she moved?

(A) She was overcharged for a service.
(B) A carton was misplaced.
(C) A shipment was delivered to an incorrect location.
(D) Some items were damaged.

20. Why does the woman need assistance?

(A) She is not pleased with her purchase.
(B) She is unable to access a Web site.
(C) She received an incomplete order.
(D) She lost a copy of an invoice.

21. Look at the graphic. How much money will the woman be refunded?

(A) $25
(B) $42
(C) $16
(D) $50

PART **4**

Directions: You will hear some talks given by a single speaker. You will be asked to answer three questions about what the speaker says in each talk. Select the best response to each question and mark the letter (A), (B), (C), or (D) on your answer sheet. The talks will not be printed in your test book and will be spoken only one time.

22. Where does the speaker say the company is considering?

(A) Contracting with a new vendor
(B) Extending the lunch hour
(C) Establishing an intern program
(D) Refurbishing company kitchens

23. What can listeners receive for free tomorrow?

(A) A coffee mug
(B) A clothing item
(C) A notebook
(D) A beverage

24. Why should listeners visit Marlene's office?

(A) To acquire training materials
(B) To participate in a project
(C) To be awarded a prize
(D) To submit a form

25. What product is being advertised?

(A) A seasoning
(B) A liquid refreshment
(C) A snack
(D) A vitamin supplement

26. According to the speaker, what is the advantage of Dr. Yummy?

(A) It is highly nutritious.
(B) It is reasonably priced.
(C) It is sold in packs of six.
(D) It appeals to children.

27. What does the speaker mean when she says, "You won't be able to get enough"?

(A) There are not enough items in stock.
(B) You will want plenty of these products.
(C) You cannot buy these goods in bulk.
(D) There is a diverse range of flavors to enjoy.

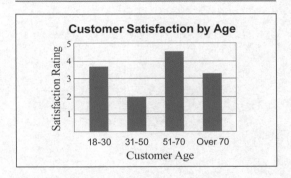

28. What does the speaker say she was wrong about?

(A) Increase in online sales
(B) A Web site malfunctioning
(C) The level of demand for a product
(D) The cost of enhancing a service

29. What does the speaker say is a popular Web site feature?

(A) Automated payment processing
(B) Reviews from customers
(C) Discounts on shipping
(D) E-mail notifications

30. Look at the graphic. What age group does the speaker ask Jeremy to investigate?

(A) 18-30   (B) 31-50
(C) 51-70   (D) Over 70

Day

06

●● 장면을 상상하면서 큰 소리로 여러 번 따라 읽으세요.

유형 61 **식당 장면** 🎧 06_01

🔹**어휘** cafeteria 카페테리아(셀프 서비스식 식당) help oneself to ~을 마음대로 집어먹다. 자유로이 먹다 pitcher 주전자 make a toast 건배하다 sip 홀짝거리다. 조금씩 마시다 water fountain (분수식) 식수대 set the table 식탁을 차리다 arrange 정리하다. 배열하다 lay out (가지런히) ~을 늘어놓다 platter (큰 서빙용) 접시 take a bite of ~을 한 입 먹다 cattle (집합적) 소 graze 풀을 뜯다 pasture 초원, 목초지 feed ~에게 먹이를 주다

A man is getting some food from a cafeteria. 카페테리아에서 음식을 받고 있다.

He's putting food on a plate. 접시에 음식을 담고 있다.

She's helping herself to a snack. 음식을 마음껏 접시에 담고 있다.

The customer is ordering some food. 음식을 주문하고 있다.

A server is taking an order. 주문을 받고 있다.

He's pouring liquid from a pitcher. 주전자에서 액체를 따르고 있다.

The man is pouring a mixture into a cup. 컵에 혼합물을 따르고 있다.

Someone is filling a cup. 컵을 채우고 있다.

The cup is being filled with a beverage. 컵에 음료를 채우고 있다.

They are making a toast. 건배하고 있다.

A woman is sipping a beverage. 음료를 조금씩 마시고 있다.

She's sipping from a cup of coffee. 커피 한 잔을 조금씩 마시고 있다.

She is drinking from a water fountain. 식수대에서 마시고 있다.

A waiter is serving some customers. 손님에게 음식을 제공하고 있다.

Beverages are being served to some customers. 손님에게 음료를 제공하고 있다.

The waiter is setting the table. 테이블을 차리고 있다.

A table has been set for a meal. 식사를 위해 식탁이 차려져 있다.

The meal has been arranged on the table. 식탁에 식사가 준비되어 있다.

Some food has been laid out on platters.

큰 서빙용 접시에 음식이 가지런히 놓여 있다.

A dining area is prepared for a meal. 식사를 위한 식사 공간이 준비되어 있다.

She's eating in a picnic area. 피크닉장에서 식사하고 있다.

One of the men is dining alone. 혼자 식사하고 있다.

They're having a conversation over a meal. 식사하면서 대화하고 있다.

She's taking a bite of her sandwich. 샌드위치를 한입 먹고 있다.

cf. The cattle are grazing in the pasture. 소떼가 초원에서 풀을 뜯고 있다.

The child is feeding the birds. 새들에게 모이를 주고 있다.

유형 62 주방 장면

 06_02

어휘 slice (얇게) 썰다 stir 젓다 grill 석쇠 do the dishes 설거지를 하다

A chef is slicing some food into pieces. 음식을 여러 조각으로 잘게 썰고 있다.

He's stirring something in the bowl. 그릇 안에 무언가를 젓고 있다.

He's cooking some food on a grill. 석쇠 위에 음식을 요리하고 있다.

Some food is being cooked on a grill. 석쇠 위에 음식을 요리하고 있다.

The chef is preparing something to eat. 먹을 것을 준비하고 있다.

She's doing the dishes. 설거지하고 있다.

유형 63 쇼핑하는 장면

 06_03

어휘 open-air 야외의, 노천의 vendor 판매상 offer 권하다 weigh 무게를 달다 scale 저울

Customers are shopping in an open-air market. 노천 시장에서 쇼핑하고 있다.

He is shopping for groceries. 식료품 쇼핑을 하고 있다.

A salesperson is showing the woman some shoes. 여자에게 신발을 보여주고 있다.

A vendor is offering some items to a customer. 손님에게 물건을 권하고 있다.

A man's selling flowers. 꽃을 팔고 있다.

Some plants are being sold in an outdoor market. 야외 시장에서 일부 식물을 팔고 있다.

He's weighing some fruit on the scale. 저울로 과일의 무게를 달고 있다.

계산대 장면

 06_04

pay for, purchase, cash register, pay the cashier가 들리면 정답!

어휘 cash register 금전 등록기 cashier 출납원 serve (상점에서 손님의) 구매를 돕다

He is making a purchase. 물건을 구입하고 있다.

A purchase is being made. 구매가 이루어지고 있다.

A customer is purchasing some merchandise. 상품을 구입하고 있다.

The customer is paying for his purchase. 구입품의 값을 지불하고 있다.

A customer is paying at a cash register. 계산대에서 돈을 내고 있다.

The man is ready to pay the cashier. 출납원에게 돈을 지불하려고 한다.

An employee is serving the customer. 손님의 구매를 돕고 있다.

유형 65 **여가를 즐기는 장면**

06_05

어휘 bend over 몸을 앞으로 숙이다 lift 들어올리다 weight 역기 hang 매달리다 bar 철봉 slope (산)비탈, 경사면 work out (건강, 몸매 등을 위해) 운동하다 riverbank 강둑, 강기슭 swing 그네

He's about[ready] to hit the ball. 막 공을 치려고 한다. (골프)

He's bending over to hit the ball. 공을 치기 위해 몸을 숙이고 있다. (골프)

They're lifting weights. 역기를 들어 올리고 있다.

The girl is hanging from a bar. 철봉에 매달려 있다.

The skier is moving down the slope. 스키 탄 사람이 비탈을 내려오고 있다.

The couples are dancing. 커플들이 춤추고 있다.

A man is kicking a ball up in the air. 공을 공중으로 차고 있다.

People are skating in a city park. 도심 공원에서 스케이트를 타고 있다.

They're stretching by the water. 물가에서 스트레칭 하고 있다.

She's playing a sport. 운동하고 있다.

She's doing an exercise. 운동하고 있다.

She's working out indoors. 실내에서 운동하고 있다.

People are fishing on a riverbank. 강둑에서 낚시하고 있다.

The men are playing a game. 게임하고 있다.

A game's being played on a table. 테이블에서 게임하고 있다.

The child is playing on the swing. 그네를 타고 있다.

어휘 in progress 진행 중인 put up (건물 등을) 세우다, 짓다 structure 구조물, 건축물 scaffolding (건축 공사장의) 비계, 발판 erect 세우다, 건설하다 exterior 외부의 walkway 보도, 통로 resurface(=repave) (도로를) 재포장하다 flatten 평평하게 만들다 smooth 평탄하게 하다, 고르다 roadway 도로, 차도 lane 차선 maintenance 유지 보수 measure 측정하다, 재다 board 널빤지, 판자 take a measurement 치수를 재다 ditch 도랑, 배수로 dig up 파내다, 파헤치다 rake 갈퀴질을 하다 drill (드릴로) 구멍을 뚫다 light bulb 백열전구 weld 용접하다 sliding door 미닫이문 portion 일부, 부분 unfinished 미완성의

The building is under construction. 건물이 공사 중이다.

The construction of the building is in progress. 건물의 공사가 진행 중이다.

The building is being constructed. 건물을 짓고 있다.

He's building a rock wall. 돌벽을 만들고 있다.

They're putting up a new structure. 새 구조물을 세우고 있다.

Scaffolding has been erected next to an exterior wall. 외벽 옆에 발판이 세워져 있다.

A walkway is being resurfaced[repaved]. 보도를 재포장하고 있다.

The surface of the road is being flattened[smoothed]. 도로 표면에 평탄화 작업을 하고 있다.

The men are improving the roadway. 도로의 개선 작업을 하고 있다.

A lane has been blocked for maintenance work. 보수 작업을 위해 한 차선을 막아 놓았다.

The man is measuring a board. 판자 길이를 재고 있다.

A piece of wood is being measured. 목재의 길이를 재고 있다.

A woman is taking a measurement. 길이를 재고 있다.

The machine is digging a ditch. 기계로 도랑을 파고 있다.

A road is being dug up by some workers. 인부들이 도로를 파헤치고 있다.

Some workers are raking the soil. 흙에 갈퀴질을 하고 있다.

He's hammering a nail. 못에 망치질하고 있다.

A man is drilling a hole in some wood. 드릴로 목재에 구멍을 뚫고 있다.

The woman is changing a light bulb. 백열전구를 갈고 있다.

A man is welding a pipe. 파이프를 용접하고 있다.

A man is installing a sliding door. 미닫이문을 설치하고 있다.

They're installing a roof on a house. 집에 지붕을 설치하고 있다.

A portion of the roof is unfinished. 지붕 일부가 완성되지 않았다.

Exercise

📖 Workbook p.69 ✏️ 정답 및 해설 p.80

1.

  a   b   c   d

2.

  a   b   c   d

> **의문사 의문문**
>
> 선택 의문문과 제안/부탁 의문문, 일반 의문문/평서문을 모두 공부했고, 이제 남은 유형은 의문사 의문문뿐이다. 의문사 의문문은 다른 유형에 비해 쉽지만, 매회 가장 많은 수가 출제되고, 의문사의 종류도 다양하기 때문에 충분한 시간을 들여 공부할 필요가 있다.

●● 기본 공략법

(1) 의문사별 분류

사실 의문사 의문문은 질문 맨 앞에 있는 의문사만 알아들어도 해결할 수 있는 경우가 많다. 각 의문사마다 정답의 패턴이 있기 때문이다. 예를 들어, Who 의문문이라면 사람 이름이 들릴 때 정답을 선택하면 된다. Where 의문문이면 장소 표현이, When 의문문이면 시간 표현이 들리는 대답이 정답이다. 일단 문제를 쉽게 풀기 위해 앞으로 소개될 각 의문사 의문문의 정답 패턴을 암기해 두자.

(2) 문제 번호에 따른 분류

7-31번 문제로 구성된 Part 2를 풀다 보면, 보통 22, 23번쯤이 기점이 되어 난이도가 올라가기 시작한다. 이 번호 앞부분에서 출제되는 문제들은 의문사별 정답 패턴을 익혀 두면 쉽게 해결되는 것들이 많지만, 이후에 출제되는 문제들은 일반적인 패턴에서 벗어나는 고난도 문제일 수 있다. 이 문제들을 해결하기 위해서는 Part 2에서 가장 중요한 풀이 방식인 '질문 앞부분에 집중하기'와 가장 중요한 기술인 '오답 골라내기'를 성실하고 적극적으로 사용해야 하며, 동시에 청취력을 완성하기 위한 받아쓰기 훈련도 열심히 해야 한다.

우선 Why 의문문부터 공부해 보자.

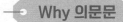

→ Why 의문문

(1) 항상 정답이 되는 어형과 문형

① To-V ~ 하기 위해
② For + 명사 ~를 위해
③ So (that) + S + can[may/will] + V ~ 하기 위해
④ Due to / Because (of) ~ 때문에

 기출 예제 06_09

Q. Why did she call the library?
A. To reserve a book.

그녀가 도서관에 왜 전화했나요?
≫≫ 책을 예약하려고요.

Q. Why are you moving to Madrid?
A. For a new job.

왜 마드리드로 이사 가나요?
>>>> 새 직장을 위해서요.

Q. Why were so many people invited to this meeting?
A. So everyone can meet the new staff members.

이번 회의에는 왜 이렇게 많은 사람들이 초대되었나요?
>>>> 모두가 신입 직원들을 만나게 하려고요.

Q. Why did the flight from Hong Kong arrive so late?
A. Probably because of the weather.

홍콩에서 오는 비행편은 왜 그렇게 늦게 도착했나요?
>>>> 아마 날씨 때문이겠죠.

(2) 항상 정답이 되는 내용

① 날씨 - weather, rain, storm, flooded
② 공사 - construction, renovation, remodeling, fixing cracks, painting, repaving
③ 교통 - traffic, missed the bus
④ 기계적 결함 - system is down, virus, mechanical problem, broken, not working, paper jam

🎯 기출 예제　　　　　　　　　　🎧 06_10

Q. Why is the ceremony being moved indoors?
A. Because there's rain in the forecast.

행사를 왜 실내로 옮기나요?
>>>> 비가 예보되어서요.

Q. Why are all the windows closed?
A. A storm is coming.

창문이 왜 다 닫혀 있나요?
>>>> 폭풍이 다가오고 있거든요.

Q. Why will the locker room be closed next week?
A. They're doing renovations.

다음 주에 라커룸은 왜 폐쇄되나요?
>>>> 개조 공사를 할 거예요.

Q. Why is the street closed?
A. Because they're doing repair work.

도로가 왜 폐쇄되었나요?
>>>> 수리 작업을 하고 있어서요.

Q. Why was Thomas so late?
A. Because his train was delayed.

Thomas는 왜 그렇게 늦었나요?
>>>> 기차가 연착되어서요.

Q. Why haven't the books I ordered arrived yet?
A. There was a problem with the truck.

제가 주문한 책이 왜 아직 도착하지 않고 있죠?
>>>> 트럭에 문제가 생겼습니다.

Q. Why are production numbers so low this month?
A. Because some machines were down for repairs.

이번 달에는 생산 수치가 왜 이렇게 낮죠?
>>>> 일부 기계가 수리 때문에 작동하지 않았습니다.

(3) 반복적으로 출제되는 문제

🎧 06_11

🎯 **기출 예제**

Q. Why did they reschedule the interview?
A. Mr. Potter couldn't be there.

면접 일정을 왜 다시 잡았나요?
»» Mr. Potter가 못 오셔서요.

Q. Why was the annual meeting cancelled?
A. The director was away.

연례 회의가 왜 취소되었나요?
»» 이사님이 안 계셔서요.

Q. Why hasn't the mural in the lobby been painted yet?
A. Because the artist is out of town.

로비 벽화는 왜 아직 그려져 있지 않은 거죠?

»» 미술가가 다른 지역에 가 있습니다.

Q. Why was the engineering lecture rescheduled?
A. The speaker was delayed.

엔지니어링 강연 일정이 왜 변경되었나요?
»» 강사가 늦게 오게 되어서요.

Q. Why was tonight's business dinner canceled?
A. Because our client's flight is late.

오늘 저녁 비즈니스 만찬은 왜 취소되었나요?
»» 고객의 비행편이 늦어서요.

Q. Why hasn't the performance started yet?
A. An actor is late.

공연이 왜 아직도 시작되지 않았어요?
»» 배우 한 명이 늦어서요.

Q. Why hasn't the meeting started yet?
A. Ms. Ming is speaking with her client.

회의가 왜 아직도 시작되지 않나요?
»» Ms. Ming이 고객과 대화 중이거든요.

일정 변경의 이유를 묻는 질문이 자주 출제되는데, 정답은 "항상 누군가의 부재"이다.

기출 예제를 여러 번 따라 읽으면서 정답의 패턴을 익혀 두자. 일반적인 패턴에서 벗어나는 문제도 모두 해결하기 위해 질문 앞부분에 집중하고 오답을 골라내는 기술을 성실히 연마하는 한편 청취력 향상을 위한 받아쓰기 연습도 열심히 해 두자.

1. (A)   (B)   (C)   6.   (A)   (B)   (C)

2. (A)   (B)   (C)   7.   (A)   (B)   (C)

3. (A)   (B)   (C)   8.   (A)   (B)   (C)

4. (A)   (B)   (C)   9.   (A)   (B)   (C)

5. (A)   (B)   (C)   10. (A)   (B)   (C)

 키워드가 패러프레이즈 되는 문제 2

LC 만점을 위해 키워드가 패러프레이즈 되는 문제들을 더 연습해 보자.

Exercise
 06_14

 Workbook p.72 ✏ 정답 및 해설 p.83

PART 3

1. Why does the woman call the man?

    (A) To verify an e-mail address
    (B) To reschedule an appointment
    (C) To respond to a message
    (D) To give directions to a place

2. What problem does the man mention?

    (A) He is unable to locate his keys.
    (B) He cannot remember his
        password.
    (C) He will not arrive on time for an
        appointment.
    (D) He was not given some
        instructions.

3. What does the man say he will do
   tomorrow?

    (A) Visit the bank
    (B) Contact a client
    (C) Work remotely
    (D) Dine with a colleague

PART 4

4. What kind of business does the
   speaker work in?

    (A) A financial institution
    (B) A travel bureau
    (C) A staffing firm
    (D) An insurance provider

5. According to the speaker, what
   advantage does the new location have?

    (A) It has more spacious offices.
    (B) It is close to a variety of cafés.
    (C) It is easily accessible by public transit.
    (D) It has exquisitely landscaped gardens.

6. What policy change does the speaker
   mention?

    (A) Staff members will receive
        additional vacation time.
    (B) The company will offer
        telecommuting as an option.
    (C) Attendance at weekly meetings will
        be compulsory.
    (D) The sharing of office spaces will
        be mandatory.

●● Actual Test를 풀기 전에 이 단어들을 따라 읽으며 암기하자.

sidewalk 인도, 보도

hectic 정신없이 바쁜, 빡빡한

freezer 냉동고

at the moment 지금은, 현재

mean to-V ~할 셈이다

inspection 점검

exposition 박람회, 전시회

due (발생할) 예정인

line 제품군; (전화) 회선

focus group 포커스 그룹 (테스트할 상품에 대해 토의하는 소비자 그룹)

moderator 사회자

launch 출시

charity 자선

terrific 아주 좋은, 훌륭한

thus far 지금까지

take over 인계받다

pharmacology 약리학

on track 제대로 진행되고 있는

double-check 재확인하다

list 명단에 포함하다

credits 크레디트 (제작진, 출연진 명단)

be involved in ~에 관여하다

pharmaceutical 제약

unveil (신제품을) 공개하다, 발표하다

terminate 끝내다, 종료하다

charge (요금을) 부과하다

transfer 전근시키다

relocate 이전하다

proceed with ~을 진행하다

get to ~에 착수하다

hesitate 망설이다, 주저하다

call in 전화를 하다

bring out ~을 출간하다

set to-V ~할 준비가 된

in print 인쇄된

convince 납득시키다, 확신시키다

contemporary 현대의, 당대의

set (견해, 생각이) 고정된

maintain 유지하다, 지속하다

approach 접근법

crucial 중대한

content 만족하는

feasible 실현 가능한

constraint 제약, 제한

can afford to-V (시간, 금전적으로) ~할 여유가 있다

contact 연락을 주고받는 사람

pass on ~을 넘겨주다, 전달하다

diverse 다양한

concern 관심사

refer 소개하다

so (that) + S + can[may/will] + V ~하기 위해서

Actual Test

PART 1	1-3
PART 2	4-12
PART 3	13-21
PART 4	22-30

Part 3, 4 '미리 잘 읽기' 전략

LC Directions 시간:	16-18번 읽기
Part 1 Directions 시간:	**19-21번 읽기**
Part 2 Directions 시간:	**28-30번 읽기**
Part 3 Directions 시간:	**13-15번 읽기**
19-21번 문제 읽어주는 시간:	**22-24번 읽기**
Part 4 Directions 시간:	**25-27번 읽기**

📖 Workbook p.74   ✏ 정답 및 해설 p.85

LISTENING TEST

지금 16-18번 읽기

In the Listening test, you will be asked to demonstrate how well you understand spoken English. The entire Listening test will last approximately 45 minutes. There are four parts, and directions are given for each part. You must mark your answers on the separate answer sheet. Do not write your answers in your test book.

PART **1**

지금 19-21번 읽기

Directions: For each question in this part, you will hear four statements about a picture in your test book. When you hear the statements, you must select the one statement that best describes what you see in the picture. Then find the number of the question on your answer sheet and mark your answer. The statements will not be printed in your test book and will be spoken only one time.

1.

ⓐ   ⓑ   ⓒ   ⓓ

2.

ⓐ   ⓑ   ⓒ   ⓓ

3.

ⓐ   ⓑ   ⓒ   ⓓ

PART 2

Directions: You will hear a question or statement and three responses spoken in English. They will not be printed in your test book and will be spoken only one time. Select the best response to the question or statement and mark the letter (A), (B), or (C) on your answer sheet.

4.   Mark your answer.   (A)   (B)   (C)

5.   Mark your answer.   (A)   (B)   (C)

6.   Mark your answer.   (A)   (B)   (C)

7.   Mark your answer.   (A)   (B)   (C)

8.   Mark your answer.   (A)   (B)   (C)

9.   Mark your answer.   (A)   (B)   (C)

10. Mark your answer.   (A)   (B)   (C)

11. Mark your answer.   (A)   (B)   (C)

12. Mark your answer.   (A)   (B)   (C)

PART 3

지금 13-15번 읽기

Directions: You will hear some conversations between two or more people. You will be asked to answer three questions about what the speakers say in each conversation. Select the best response to each question and mark the letter (A), (B), (C), or (D) on your answer sheet. The conversations will not be printed in your test book and will be spoken only one time.

13. What are the speakers discussing?

(A) Securing financial backing
(B) Negotiating a company merger
(C) Making travel arrangements
(D) Handing over a project's leadership

14. What does Frank advise the woman to do?

(A) Conduct negotiations in person
(B) Forward confirmation e-mails
(C) Lower overhead costs
(D) Modify a budget

15. What does Frank say he is excited about?

(A) Collaborating with new colleagues
(B) Receiving a pay raise
(C) Hiring an support staff member
(D) Working in foreign country

16. What industry do the speakers most likely work in?

(A) Pharmaceutical
(B) Banking
(C) Marketing
(D) Information technology

17. What does the woman say will happen this year?

(A) Some research will receive additional funding.
(B) A new product will be unveiled.
(C) There will be a merger of two companies.
(D) An award ceremony will take place.

18. What does the woman imply when she says, "Wasn't Akira involved in this project"?

(A) Certain findings are not ready yet.
(B) A project requires additional personnel.
(C) There is a lack of information on a slide.
(D) The man must meet with a researcher

Contract Length	Cost per Month
3 months	$50.00
6 months	$40.00
1 year	$30.00
2 years	$20.00

정답 고르고 나서 바로 22-24번 읽기

19. According to the woman, when is an extra fee charged?

(A) When a customer transfers to a new location
(B) When a payment is overdue
(C) When new application is installed
(D) When a contract is canceled early

20. What does the man say he will do next year?

(A) Relocate abroad
(B) Complete an internship program
(C) Purchase another device
(D) Renew a contract

21. Look at the graphic. How much has the man agreed to pay per month?

(A) $50.00   (B) $40.00
(C) $30.00   (D) $20.00

PART 4

Directions: You will hear some talks given by a single speaker. You will be asked to answer three questions about what the speaker says in each talk. Select the best response to each question and mark the letter (A), (B), (C), or (D) on your answer sheet. The talks will not be printed in your test book and will be spoken only one time.

22. What is Ms. Lin's area of expertise?

(A) Management of nonprofit organizations
(B) Professional advice on career choices
(C) Event planning and coordination
(D) Individual financial planning

23. What are listeners encouraged to do?

(A) Share their opinions over the phone
(B) Update their résumés
(C) Participate in a workshop
(D) Keep track of household spending

24. What does the speaker say will happen next month?

(A) An educational session will be conducted.
(B) A schedule will be altered.
(C) An interview is scheduled to take place.
(D) A book will become available.

25. What did the speaker discuss with Tara Goldberg?

(A) A hiring policy
(B) A product design
(C) An order for supplies
(D) An itinerary for a trip

26. What does the speaker imply when he says, "she's the head of the department"?

(A) He wants to introduce a new executive.
(B) He lacks the authority to make the final decision.
(C) A job title has been incorrectly printed.
(D) A colleague has achieved great success.

27. What will the speaker most likely do next?

(A) Set up a meeting
(B) Refer to a catalog
(C) Fill out a form
(D) Meet with a client

Survey Results

Expanded swimming facility – 40%
Extended operating hours – 20%
Updated exercise equipment – 10%
Diverse classes – 30%

---

28. According to the speaker, what is the center's main concern?

(A) Satisfying current members
(B) Complying with industry standards
(C) Minimizing operating expenses
(D) Developing successful marketing campaigns

29. Look at the graphic. What survey result does the speaker want to address?

(A) Expanded swimming facility
(B) Extended operating hours
(C) Updated exercise equipment
(D) Diverse classes

30. What does the speaker ask the listeners to do?

(A) Perform safety assessments
(B) Enroll in a certification program
(C) Refer potential employees
(D) Tour a construction site

Day
07

●● 장면을 상상하면서 큰 소리로 여러 번 따라 읽으세요.

유형 67 **기계를 다루는 장면** 07_01

어휘 plug in ~의 플러그를 꽂다[전원을 연결하다] plug A into B A를 B에 연결하다 power cord 전원 코드 outlet 콘센트 operate (기계를) 가동하다. 조작하다 heavy machinery 중장비 farm machinery 농기계 sewing machine 재봉틀 maneuver 조종하다 adjust 조정하다. 조절하다 window shade 차양 sail 돛

She's plugging in a fan. 선풍기의 플러그를 꽂고 있다.

A woman is plugging a power cord into an outlet. 전원 코드를 콘센트에 연결하고 있다.

He's inserting a plug into an outlet. 플러그를 콘센트에 끼우고 있다.

A power cord has been plugged into the outlet. 전원 코드가 콘센트에 연결되어 있다.

He's operating heavy machinery. 중장비를 가동하고 있다.

He is operating farm machinery. 농기계를 가동하고 있다.

The woman is operating a sewing machine. 재봉틀을 가동하고 있다.

A man is maneuvering a machine. 기계를 조종하고 있다.

She's adjusting a window shade. 차양을 조정하고 있다.

The sail of a boat is being adjusted. 배의 돛을 조정하고 있다.

유형 68 **수리하는 장면** checking, fixing, repairing 07_02

어휘 mechanic 정비공 rooftop 옥상 streetlamp 가로등 inflate (공기나 가스로) 부풀리다

The mechanic is checking the car's engine. 자동차 엔진을 점검하고 있다.

The rooftop of a home is being fixed. 어떤 집 지붕을 고치고 있다.

A streetlamp is being repaired. 가로등을 수리하고 있다.

A man is making a repair with a hammer. 망치로 수리 작업을 하고 있다.

cf. The man's inflating a tire. 타이어에 공기를 넣고 있다.

일하고 있다 working * 매우 자주 출제 ⌒ 07_03

🔸어휘 station 배치하다 underground 지하에서

(1) 사무실 장면

He's working on a laptop computer. 노트북 컴퓨터로 일하고 있다.

He's working with an electronic device. 전자 기기로 일하고 있다.

She's doing some paperwork. 서류 작업을 하고 있다.

He's taking care of some paperwork. 서류 작업을 처리하고 있다.

An employee is stationed at a service window. 서비스 창구에 직원이 배치되어 있다.

(2) 공사/수리 장면

They are working at a construction site. 공사 현장에서 일하고 있다.

They're working on a construction project. 공사 프로젝트를 진행하고 있다.

Some men are working on a roof. 지붕에서 일하고 있다.

Some people are working underground. 지하에서 일하고 있다.

The man is working on a motorbike. 오토바이를 수리하고 있다.

(3) 기타

Technicians are working in a laboratory. 기술자들이 실험실에서 일하고 있다.

Some people are working in a field. 들판에서 일하고 있다. (농사)

The woman is working on a painting. 그림 작업을 하고 있다.

They're working on sewing projects. 꿰매는 일을 하고 있다.

She's sewing some fabric. 직물을 꿰매고 있다.

유형 **70** **마법의 키워드** concentrating ⌒ 07_04
어떤 동작을 하고 있든 concentrating이 들리면 정답이다!

🔸어휘 subject 피사체

The photographer is concentrating on her subject. 사진작가가 피사체에 집중하고 있다.

A worker is concentrating on cutting a piece of wood. 목재를 자르는 데 집중하고 있다.

They're concentrating on a game. 게임에 집중하고 있다.

The woman's concentrating on her task. 업무에 집중하고 있다.

유형 71 휴식을 취하는 장면 relaxing, resting, taking a break, lying 🎧 07_05

어휘 fountain 분수대 at the bottom of ~의 맨 아래에 step 계단 on top of ~의 위에 lap (앉았을 때 허벅지 부분) 무릎 lawn 잔디밭

People are relaxing around a fountain. 분수대 둘레에서 쉬고 있다.

The woman is resting at the bottom of the steps. 계단 맨 아래에서 쉬고 있다.

A man is resting with the newspaper on his lap. 무릎에 신문을 놓고 쉬고 있다.

They're taking a break on the lawn. 잔디밭에서 쉬고 있다.

They're lying on a beach. 해변에 누워 있다.

유형 72 방향을 나타내는 표현   07_06

어휘 face ~을 마주보다, 향하다 head (특정 방향으로) 가다, 향하다 presenter 발표자 back 등, (등)허리

Some vehicles are facing a low wall. 차량들이 낮은 벽을 향하고 있다.

A fan has been turned to face a wall. 선풍기를 벽을 향하도록 돌려놓았다.

> 같은 방향으로 - in the same direction
> 서로 반대[다른] 방향으로 - in opposite[different] directions

They're both heading in the same direction. 두 사람 모두 같은 방향을 향하고 있다.

People are moving in different directions. 다른 방향으로 이동하고 있다.

The trucks are facing in opposite directions. 트럭들이 서로 반대 방향을 향하고 있다.

> ~을 향하고 있다 - be turned to[toward]
> ~을 등지고 있다 - have turned away from
>   one's back is turned to
>   have one's back to

The women are turned toward the presenter. 발표자를 향하고 있다.

She's turned away from the pictures on the wall. 벽에 있는 그림으로부터 돌아서 있다.

The man's back is turned to the window. 창문을 등지고 있다.

One of the men has his back to a group of people. 사람들을 등지고 있다.

유형 73 복장을 묘사하는 문장

어휘 have *sth* on ~을 착용하고 있다 long-sleeved[short-sleeved] shirt 긴팔[반팔] 셔츠 veil 베일, (여성용) 덮어 가리는 것 identical 동일한, 똑같은 alike 똑같이 dressed (특정한 양식으로) 옷을 입은 wristwatch 손목시계 hard hat 안전모 lab coat 실험실 가운 smock 작업복, 덧옷 protective clothing 보호복 safety gear 안전 장비 barefoot 맨발의 try on (옷 따위를) 입어[신어] 보다 pull on 잡아당겨 입다[신다, 끼다] fasten 매다, 고정시키다

● 복장을 묘사할 때는 **wearing**을 사용하는 문장이 정답이다. 입거나 벗는 동작을 나타내는 putting on, removing, taking off가 들리는 문장은 거의 대부분 오답이다. Day 01 **주의 3**의 내용을 기억하자.

A guitarist is wearing glasses. 안경을 쓰고 있다.

The woman has her glasses on. 안경을 쓰고 있다.

They have long-sleeved[short-sleeved] shirts on. 긴팔[반팔] 셔츠를 입고 있다.

A woman has a veil[cover] over her hair. ──────

머리에 베일을 쓰고 있다.

A woman has covered her hair. 무언가로 머리를 덮었다.

They're wearing identical uniforms. 똑같은 유니폼을 입고 있다.

They are dressed alike. 같은 옷을 입고 있다.

He's dressed formally. 정장을 입고 있다.

The girls are wearing backpacks. 배낭을 메고 있다.

The man is wearing a wristwatch. 손목시계를 차고 있다.

He's wearing a hard hat. 안전모를 쓰고 있다.

The man is wearing a lab coat. 실험실 가운을 입고 있다.

A customer is wearing a protective smock. ──────

보호용 덧옷을 입고 있다.

The men are wearing work vests. 작업 조끼를 입고 있다.

He's wearing protective clothing. 보호복을 입고 있다.

The man is wearing safety gear. 안전 장비를 착용하고 있다.

She's barefoot on the beach. 해변에서 맨발로 있다.

● 매우 드물기는 하지만 착용하는 동작이 출제될 수도 있다.

One woman is trying on hats. 모자를 써 보고 있다.

She's pulling on protective gloves. 보호 장갑을 잡아당겨 끼고 있다.

He's putting on his jacket. 재킷을 입고 있다.

The women are fastening their aprons. 앞치마를 매고 있다.

Exercise

07_08

Workbook p.83   정답 및 해설 p.96

1.

2.

a   b   c   d

How 의문문

How 뒤에 붙는 형용사나 부사에 따라 여러 가지 유형으로 분류할 수 있다. 우선 각 유형의 전형적인 정답 패턴을 익힌 후, 패턴에서 벗어나는 고난도 문제도 함께 연습하도록 하자.

(1) How long ~?

➡ **(for) + 기간, since + 과거 시점**

대부분 '기간' 표현이 정답의 키워드다.

🎯 **기출 예제** 🎧 07_10

Q. How long was Mr. Park out sick?   Mr. Park은 얼마 동안 아파서 결근하셨죠?
A. Only a few days.   ≫ 딱 며칠만요.

Q. How long have you been employed at this   이 회사에서 얼마 동안 근무하셨습니까?
company?
A. Since it was established.   ≫ 설립되었을 때부터요.

---

(2) How many + 명사 ~ ?

➡ **숫자, many, (a) few, several, every, each, more than I can count**(셀 수 없을 만큼 많이)

거의 대부분 '숫자'를 듣고 정답을 선택하면 되지만, 다른 키워드를 통해 정답을 알아내야 하는 경우도 있다.

🎯 **기출 예제** 🎧 07_11

Q. How many computers and printers have been   컴퓨터와 프린터 몇 대를 주문했나요?
ordered?
A. Three of each.   ≫ 각각 세 대요.

Q. How many people have signed up for the   온라인 교육 프로그램에 몇 명이 등록했나요?
online training program?
A. About a dozen so far.   ≫ 지금까지 10여 명이요.

Q. How many boxes should I order?   상자 몇 개를 주문할까요?
A. We need quite a few.   ≫ 꽤 많이 필요해요.

Q. How many applications have we received so far?

A. There have been several.

지금까지 몇 개의 지원서를 받았나요?

>>>> 몇 개 있었어요.

Q. How many employees are expected to show up at the training course?

A. Everyone from the research department.

교육에는 몇 명의 직원들이 올 것으로 예상됩니까?

>>>> 연구부서 전원이요.

Q. How many orders did we receive today?

A. More than I can count.

오늘 몇 건의 주문을 받았나요?

>>>> 셀 수 없을 정도로 많아요.

(3) How ~ get[go/commute/travel] to ~? How ~ be transported[delivered]?

➡ 교통수단, 길 이름, 계단(stairs, steps, stairway, staircase), elevator, escalator, walk, on foot(걸어서), 길[장소] 안내

대부분 '교통수단'이나 '길 이름'이 정답의 키워드다. 계단이나 엘리베이터를 이용하거나 걸어간다는 대답도 정답이 될 수 있으며, 최근에는 '길 안내'나 '장소 안내'도 정답으로 출제된다.

🎯 **기출 예제**   🎧 07_12

Q. How will you get to the restaurant tonight?

A. I'll take the bus.

오늘 저녁에 식당까지 어떻게 갈 건가요?

>>>> 버스를 타려고요.

Q. How will you get to the airport tomorrow morning?

A. A friend of mine will give me a ride.

내일 아침에 공항에 어떻게 가실 건가요?

>>>> 제 친구가 태워 줄 거예요.

Q. Excuse me, how do I get to the train station from here?

A. Take Hill Street to Park Avenue.

실례지만, 여기서 기차역까지 어떻게 갑니까?

>>>> Hill Street를 타고 Park Avenue가 나올 때까지 가세요.

Q. How do I get to the second floor?

A. Take the stairs at the end of the hallway.

2층에 어떻게 가요?

>>>> 복도 끝에서 계단을 이용하세요.

Q. How do I get to the mailroom?

A. It's at the end of this hallway.

우편실에 어떻게 가나요?

>>>> 이 복도 끝에 있어요.

Q. How can I get to the nearest bank?

A. Turn left at the next corner.

가장 가까운 은행까지는 어떻게 가죠?

>>>> 다음 모퉁이에서 좌회전하세요.

(4) How did you learn[find out/hear] ~?

➡️ **~ told me, 각종 통신 매체(TV, 라디오, 신문, 인터넷 등), advertisement**

told me의 발음을 연습해 두자. d 발음이 탈락하고 '토우ㄹ미'라고 읽어야 한다. advertisement는 미국 발음과 영국 발음이 다르다. 미국식으로는 강세를 첫 음절에 주면서 '앤버ㄹ타이즈먼트'라고 읽고, 영국이나 호주 식으로는 강세를 두 번째 음절에 주면서 '얻버(ㄹ)티스먼트'라고 한다.

🎯 **기출 예제** 🎧 07_13

Q. How did you learn about our organization?   저희 기관에 대해 어떻게 알게 되셨나요?
A. A colleague told me.   ≫≫ 동료가 알려줬습니다.

Q. How did you hear about the change in personnel?   인사 변동에 대해 어떻게 들으셨어요?
A. Through the company Web site.   ≫≫ 회사 웹 사이트를 통해서요.

Q. How did you find out about this job opening?   이 공석에 대해 어떻게 알게 되셨습니까?
A. I saw an advertisement.   ≫≫ 광고를 봤습니다.

(5) How + be동사 + S ?

➡️ **형용사**

"어떠니?"라고 물었을 때 "어떻다"라고 대답하며, "어떻다"로 주로 사용하는 단어가 형용사다.

🎯 **기출 예제** 🎧 07_14

Q. How's your new job?   새 직장이 어떠세요?
A. It's very challenging.   ≫≫ 정말 힘들어요.

Q. How was the marketing meeting?   마케팅 회의는 어땠나요?
A. It was very productive.   ≫≫ 매우 생산적이었어요.

(6) How do you like[enjoy/feel about] ~?

➡️ **형용사, 부사**

의견을 물었을 때는 대부분 형용사나 부사를 사용하는 대답이 자연스럽다.

🎯 **기출 예제** 🎧 07_15

Q. How do you like the new vice president?   새 부사장님에 대해 어떻게 생각하세요?
A. He's very friendly.   ≫≫ 매우 친절하세요.

> **Q.** How do you like the new software?
> **A.** It's working well so far.
>
> 새 소프트웨어가 어떤가요?
> ≫≫ 지금까지는 잘 작동합니다.

(7) How much ~? How big[large] ~?
➡ 숫자

금액이나, 양, 규모 등을 묻는 질문의 대답에는 '숫자'가 들어가는 것이 자연스럽다.

🎯 **기출 예제**　　　　　　　　　　　🎧 07_16

Q. How much was our travel budget increased this year?
A. It's almost doubled.

올해 우리 출장 예산은 얼마나 증액되었나요?
≫≫ 거의 두 배가 되었습니다.

Q. How much will the budget increase next year?
A. About ten percent.

내년에는 예산이 얼마나 늘어날까요?
≫≫ 약 10퍼센트요.

Q. How big is the main conference room?
A. Big enough for three hundred people.

대회의장 규모가 얼마나 되나요?
≫≫ 300명이 들어갈 만큼 충분히 큽니다.

(8) How often ~?
➡ ~ times a week[month/quarter/year], every ~, whenever ~

🎯 **기출 예제**　　　　　　　　　　　🎧 07_17

Q. How often do you take business trips?
A. About once a quarter.

출장을 얼마마다 한 번씩 가시나요?
≫≫ 분기마다 한 번 정도요.

Q. How often do you travel abroad for work?
A. Every couple of months.

해외 출장을 얼마마다 한 번씩 가시나요?
≫≫ 두세 달에 한 번씩이요.

Q. How often does your company have employee training sessions?
A. Whenever it's necessary.

당신 회사는 직원 교육 모임을 얼마마다 한 번씩 갖습니까?
≫≫ 필요할 때마다요.

(9) How soon[quickly/late] ~?
➡ When 의문문과 같은 패턴

"얼마나 빨리[늦게까지] ~?"라고 묻는 것은 사실상 "언제?"라고 묻는 것과 같다. 그러므로 이 유형은 When 의문문이라고 생각하고 풀면 된다.

기출 예제

Q. How soon will you be able to get the budget proposal ready?
A. By next week, I think.

예산 기획안을 얼마나 빨리 준비해 줄 수 있겠어요?

>>> 제 생각에는 다음 주까지요.

Q. How late is the museum open?
A. Until five P.M.

박물관은 얼마나 늦게까지 개방합니까?

>>> 오후 5시까지요.

Q. How late is your shop open tonight?
A. We close at nine.

당신 가게는 오늘 밤 얼마나 늦게까지 문을 엽니까?

>>> 9시에 문 닫습니다.

(10) How ~ go(ing)?

➡ **형용사, 부사**

이 유형은 일의 경과를 묻는 질문이다. 형용사나 부사를 사용해서 대답하면 정답이 된다.

기출 예제 07_19

Q. How did the planning meeting go this morning?
A. Good. We addressed a lot of issues.

오전에 기획 회의는 어떻게 됐나요?

>>> 좋았어요. 많은 사안을 다루었죠.

Q. How did your presentation for the board of directors go?
A. It went well.

이사회를 위한 프레젠테이션은 어떻게 되었나요?

>>> 잘 됐어요.

(11) How far ~ ?

➡ **kilometers, miles, blocks, Not that far[Not much further](별로 안 멀어요), 걸리는 시간**

kilometers, miles, blocks 같은 거리 단위가 들리면 정답으로 선택하자. Not that far나 Not much further(별로 안 멀어요) 같은 참 성의 없는 대답도 정답으로 꾸준히 출제되어 왔다. 최근에는 직접적으로 거리를 말하는 대신 걸리는 시간을 알려주는 대답이 정답으로 나오기도 한다.

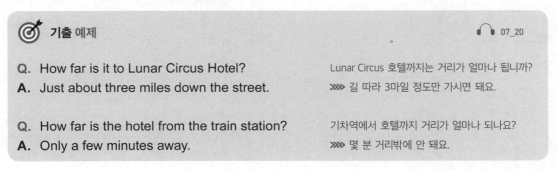

기출 예제 07_20

Q. How far is it to Lunar Circus Hotel?
A. Just about three miles down the street.

Lunar Circus 호텔까지는 거리가 얼마나 됩니까?

>>> 길 따라 3마일 정도만 가시면 돼요.

Q. How far is the hotel from the train station?
A. Only a few minutes away.

기차역에서 호텔까지 거리가 얼마나 되나요?

>>> 몇 분 거리밖에 안 돼요.

Q.	How far is it from downtown to the airport?	시내에서 공항까지 거리는 얼마나 되죠?
A.	It's about a forty-minute ride by taxi.	⋙ 택시로 40분 정도 가면 됩니다.

(12) How + 조동사/be동사 + 주어 + 일반 동사 ~ ?
➡ 명령문, By + 동명사

질문이 "어떻게 ~하죠?"이므로 "~하세요."나 "~함으로써"가 자연스러운 대답이 된다.

🎯 기출 예제　　　　　　　　　　　　　　　　🎧 07_21

Q.	How could I request more office supplies?	추가 사무용품은 어떻게 요청하나요?
A.	Call the purchasing department.	⋙ 구매 부서에 전화하세요.
Q.	How can I set up for automatic bill payment?	자동 이체는 어떻게 설정하죠?
A.	By filling out a form.	⋙ 양식을 작성하시면 돼요.

Exercise　　　　　　　　　　　　　　　　🎧 07_22

📖 Workbook p.84　　✏ 정답 및 해설 p.96

1.	(A)	(B)	(C)	6.	(A)	(B)	(C)
2.	(A)	(B)	(C)	7.	(A)	(B)	(C)
3.	(A)	(B)	(C)	8.	(A)	(B)	(C)
4.	(A)	(B)	(C)	9.	(A)	(B)	(C)
5.	(A)	(B)	(C)	10.	(A)	(B)	(C)

화자의 의도 파악 문제 1

화자의 의도를 파악하는 문제는 대화나 담화의 맥락을 고려하여 주어진 문장의 속뜻을 유추해야 한다. 생각할 시간이 필요하기 때문에 정답을 고르는 데 약간 시간이 걸린다. 의도 파악 문제의 정답 선택이 너무 지체되면 다음 문제를 푸는 데 지장을 주므로 되도록 지체 없이 정답을 고르기 위해 선택지들의 내용을 기억하고 있어야 한다. 명심하자. 화자의 의도 파악 문제를 풀 때는 선택지의 내용을 암기하도록 노력해야 한다.

Q PART 3 Sample Questions   Workbook p.86   07_24

1. What does the woman say she did in high school?

(A) She founded a club.
(B) She developed a Web site.
(C) She participated in a musical group.
(D) She took online lessons.

2. What is available on the store Web site?

(A) Promotional discounts
(B) Instructional videos
(C) Interactions with musicians
(D) A schedule of store events

3. What does the woman imply when she says, "Oh, that sounds good"?

(A) An e-mail address is easy to remember.
(B) A lesson appears reasonably priced.
(C) An instrument is in tune.
(D) She is able to join a mailing list.

Questions 1 through 3 refer to the following conversation.

🖊 해설 p.98

W Br Hi, I saw a television advertisement for cello lessons at your shop, and I'd like to sign up.

M Cn Excellent. Do you have any experience with the cello?

W Br ¹Well, I played a little in my high school orchestra.

M Cn OK, it seems like the intermediate class would be a good fit for you. The classes are scheduled to start next week.

W Br Great.

M Cn ² ³In the meantime, you have the option to view tutorial videos on our Web site by subscribing to our weekly e-mails. ³Are you interested in becoming a member?

W Br [Oh, that sounds good.] ³My e-mail address is elsa785@mailexchange.com.

M Cn All right, you're all set, and the first lesson is scheduled for next Monday at 7 P.M. See you there!

1. What does the woman say she did in high school?

(A) She founded a club.
(B) She developed a Web site.
(C) She participated in a musical group.
(D) She took online lessons.

2. What is available on the store Web site?

(A) Promotional discounts
(B) Instructional videos
(C) Interactions with musicians
(D) A schedule of store events

3. What does the woman imply when she says, "Oh, that sounds good"?

(A) An e-mail address is easy to remember.
(B) A lesson appears reasonably priced.
(C) An instrument is in tune.
(D) She is able to join a mailing list.

해설 1번 문제는 키워드 high school이 들어 있는 문장 I played a little in my high school orchestra.가 패러프레이즈 되어 있는 선택지가 정답이다. 2번 문제 역시 키워드 Web site가 들어 있는 문장 you have the option to view tutorial videos on our Web에서 정답을 알 수 있다. tutorial videos가 문제에서는 Instructional videos로 바뀌어 있다. 이 문제의 정답을 고를 때는 순발력이 필요하다. 바로 이어지는 문장을 잘 듣고 3번 문제를 풀어야 하기 때문이다. 개별 지도 동영상을 보려면 주간 이메일을 구독해야 한다고 말하면서(by subscribing to our weekly e-mails) 가입을 권유하고 있다(Are you interested in becoming a member?). Oh, that sounds good.은 이 권유를 수락하는 대답이다. 게다가 이어지는 문장에서 이메일 주소를 알려주고 있으므로, 여자의 의도는 메일링 리스트에 가입하겠다고 말하는 것이다. 대화의 맥락을 고려하여 정답을 고르는 시간이 너무 길어지면 다음 문제를 푸는 데 지장이 있다. 소요 시간을 최소화하려면 선택지의 내용을 모두 기억하기 위해 노력해야 한다는 사실을 잊지 말자.

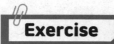

PART 3

1. What department do the speakers work in?

   (A) Product development
   (B) Human resources
   (C) Accounting
   (D) Marketing

2. Why does the woman say, "That's a substantial rise from last year"?

   (A) To suggest that some news is good
   (B) To deny a proposed budget adjustment
   (C) To indicate that a fee is appropriate
   (D) To correct some inaccurate information

3. According to the man, what do the department managers plan to do?

   (A) Purchase new equipment
   (B) Organize a conference
   (C) Recruit some more employees
   (D) Diversify a product range

PART 4

4. Why does the man say, "it's the holiday season"?

   (A) To express his thrill
   (B) To turn down a request
   (C) To express dissatisfaction with a schedule
   (D) To show appreciation to a colleague

5. What has the company recently done?

   (A) Adjusted a product price
   (B) Updated a policy
   (C) Established a new facility
   (D) Recruited temporary workers

6. What will the man most likely do next?

   (A) Return some paperwork
   (B) Post some photographs
   (C) Revise a manual
   (D) Lead an orientation

●● Actual Test를 풀기 전에 이 단어들을 따라 읽으며 암기하자.

exterior 외부, 바깥 면

quarter to ten 10시 15분 전

price tag 가격표

missing 없어진

control panel (기계, 장치의) 제어판

post 게시하다, 게재하다

announcement 알림, 공고

significant 상당한

store 보관하다

commute 통근 (거리)

book 예약하다

treat A to B A에게 B를 대접하다

cruise ship 유람선

riverfront 강변 지대

look into ~을 조사하다

cruise 유람선 여행

inventory 재고(품)

perform (기계가) 작동하다, 돌아가다

endorse 승인하다

vacuum cleaner 진공청소기

floor polisher 바닥 광택기

check in 반납하다

due 반납 기일이 되는

locally-grown 이 지역에서 재배한

lettuce 상추

comment 의견을 말하다

flavor 풍미, 맛

dine 식사하다

establishment 기관, 시설

source 구입하다, 조달하다

reflect on ~을 되돌아보다

firm 회사

co-found 공동 창업하다

acquire 취득하다

share 몫, 지분

stock (한 기업의) 주식 자본

thrilled 크게 기뻐하는, 흥분된

rapid 빠른, 급속한

ferry (카)페리, 연락선

swiftly 신속하게, 재빨리

clear (눈, 비 등이) 그치다

in time for ~하는 시간에 맞춰

inclement (날씨가) 궂은, 사나운

dress 옷을 입다

Actual Test

PART 1	1-3
PART 2	4-12
PART 3	13-21
PART 4	22-30

Part 3, 4 '미리 잘 읽기' 전략

LC Directions 시간:	16-18번 읽기
Part 1 Directions 시간:	19-21번 읽기
Part 2 Directions 시간:	28-30번 읽기
Part 3 Directions 시간:	13-15번 읽기
19-21번 문제 읽어주는 시간:	22-24번 읽기
Part 4 Directions 시간:	25-27번 읽기

📖 Workbook p.89   ✏️ 정답 및 해설 p.101

LISTENING TEST

지금 16-18번 읽기

In the Listening test, you will be asked to demonstrate how well you understand spoken English. The entire Listening test will last approximately 45 minutes. There are four parts, and directions are given for each part. You must mark your answers on the separate answer sheet. Do not write your answers in your test book.

PART ❶

지금 19-21번 읽기

Directions: For each question in this part, you will hear four statements about a picture in your test book. When you hear the statements, you must select the one statement that best describes what you see in the picture. Then find the number of the question on your answer sheet and mark your answer. The statements will not be printed in your test book and will be spoken only one time.

1.

ⓐ ⓑ ⓒ ⓓ

3.

ⓐ ⓑ ⓒ ⓓ

2.

ⓐ ⓑ ⓒ ⓓ

Directions: You will hear a question or statement and three responses spoken in English. They will not be printed in your test book and will be spoken only one time. Select the best response to the question or statement and mark the letter (A), (B), or (C) on your answer sheet.

4. Mark your answer.   (A)   (B)   (C)

5. Mark your answer.   (A)   (B)   (C)

6. Mark your answer.   (A)   (B)   (C)

7. Mark your answer.   (A)   (B)   (C)

8. Mark your answer.   (A)   (B)   (C)

9. Mark your answer.   (A)   (B)   (C)

10. Mark your answer.   (A)   (B)   (C)

11. Mark your answer.   (A)   (B)   (C)

12. Mark your answer.   (A)   (B)   (C)

Directions: You will hear some conversations between two or more people. You will be asked to answer three questions about what the speakers say in each conversation. Select the best response to each question and mark the letter (A), (B), (C), or (D) on your answer sheet. The conversations will not be printed in your test book and will be spoken only one time.

13. What problem does the man mention?

(A) A reservation is not accurate.
(B) A business trip has been deferred.
(C) An event is sold out.
(D) Credit card payments are not permitted.

14. What does the woman suggest offering their colleagues?

(A) A meal on a boat
(B) A room upgrade at a hotel
(C) Admission to a sporting event
(D) Gift certificates for a store

15. What does the man ask the woman to do?

(A) Contact a travel agent
(B) Research pricing information
(C) Make a payment beforehand
(D) Coordinate transportation

16. What problem does the woman mention?

(A) An error occurred during a research.
(B) Some project deadlines have expired.
(C) A department lacks adequate financial resources.
(D) Some staff members are inexperienced.

17. What does the woman mean when she says, "Now that's an idea"?

(A) She is seeking additional advice.
(B) The man has come up with a useful suggestion.
(C) The existing plan is overly complicated.
(D) A change is occurring at the right time.

18. What will the speakers most likely do next?

(A) Discuss a proposal
(B) Offer a promotion
(C) Arrange an interview
(D) Examine a report

Item #	Date Checked Out	Date Due
343	April 15	April 17
228	April 16	April 17
216	April 18	April 19
326	April 19	April 21

정답 고르고 나서 바로 22-24번 읽기

19. What did the business recently purchase?

(A) Some software
(B) Several trucks
(C) Office furniture
(D) Safety eyewear

20. What type of business do the speakers most likely work for?

(A) A laundry service
(B) An electronics store
(C) A cleaning company
(D) A courier service

21. Look at the graphic. When is the conversation taking place?

(A) On April 15
(B) On April 17
(C) On April 19
(D) On April 21

Directions: You will hear some talks given by a single speaker. You will be asked to answer three questions about what the speaker says in each talk. Select the best response to each question and mark the letter (A), (B), (C), or (D) on your answer sheet. The talks will not be printed in your test book and will be spoken only one time.

22. Where does the speaker most likely work?

(A) On a vegetable farm
(B) In a grocery store
(C) At a dining establishment
(D) At a publishing company

23. What do customers like about fresh vegetables?

(A) The appearance
(B) The price
(C) The size
(D) The taste

24. What does the speaker recommend?

(A) Increasing vegetable intake
(B) Cultivating one's own vegetables
(C) Requesting a discount from large wholesalers
(D) Sourcing more vegetables from local farms

25. What type of company is Vega, Incorporated?

(A) Media and advertising
(B) Academic software
(C) Medical equipment
(D) Environmental consulting

26. What does the speaker imply when he says, "Now, we have over four hundred people on staff"?

(A) A training program needs to be expanded.
(B) A company has experienced rapid growth.
(C) A department requires reorganization.
(D) An office building is overcrowded.

27. What is being announced?

(A) Employees will be able to invest in the company.
(B) Solar panels are scheduled for installation.
(C) A product is being discontinued.
(D) A board member will step down next year.

Ostar Island Ferry

Departures	Arrivals
10:00 A.M.	10:30 A.M.
12:00 P.M.	12:30 P.M.
5:30 P.M.	6:00 P.M.
7:30 P.M.	8:00 P.M.

28. What has caused a cancellation?

(A) Inclement weather
(B) Mechanical problems
(C) An unwell crew member
(D) Insufficient number of passengers

29. Look at the graph. What time will the ferry leave?

(A) 10:00 A.M.   (B) 12:00 P.M.
(C) 5:30 P.M.   (D) 7:30 P.M.

30. What does the speaker say listeners may want to do?

(A) Travel the following day
(B) Retain a receipt
(C) Grab a bite to eat
(D) Dress in warm layers

Day

08

●● 장면을 상상하면서 큰 소리로 여러 번 따라 읽으세요.

유형 74 ～가 ～에 있다 매달 출제, 위치 표현 중요

(1) 사람/사물 + is/are + 위치 표현 🎧 08_01

어휘 rider (말, 자전거, 오토바이를) 탄 사람 transparent 투명한 conveyor 컨베이어 벨트 carrousel (공항의) 수하물 컨베이어 벨트 multiple 많은, 다수의 level (건물의) 층 exterior 외부, 외면

The riders are on both sides of the road. 길 양옆에 자전거를 탄 사람들이 있다.

He's at the edge of a platform. 플랫폼 가장자리에 있다.

They're at the site of a construction project. 공사 현장에 있다.

They're on opposite sides of a transparent partition. 서로 투명 칸막이가 맞은편에 있다.

The suitcases are on the conveyor[carrousel]. 옷가방들이 컨베이어 벨트 위에 있다.

The cars are on multiple levels. 차들이 여러 층에 (주차되어) 있다.

A clock is on the exterior of the building. 건물 외벽에 시계가 있다.

A row of wheelchairs is in front of the window. ———

휠체어들이 창문 앞에 일렬로 있다.

(2) There is/are + 사물 + 위치 표현 🎧 08_02

어휘 tram 전차 alleyway 골목, 골목길 grassy 풀로 덮인 saucer (커피 잔의) 받침 접시 cupboard 찬장 serving dish 서빙용 큰 접시 diagram 도표, 도해 fireplace 벽난로 knob (문, 서랍에 달린 동그란) 손잡이 stand 가판대, 좌판 walkway 보도, 통로

There is a tram on the street. 거리에 전차가 있다.

There's no car traffic in the alleyway. 골목길에 자동차가 없다.

There are cars parked along the street. 길을 따라 주차된 차들이 있다.

There are trees on the opposite shore. ———

맞은편 물가에 나무들이 있다.

There is a grassy area beside the park. 공원 옆에 잔디밭이 있다.

There are a lot of saucers in the cupboard. 찬장에 접시가 많이 있다.

There's a gap between the tables. 테이블 사이에 간격이 있다.

There's some food on the serving dishes. 서빙용 접시에 음식이 있다.

There are diagrams on the blackboard. 칠판에 도표가 그려져 있다.

There's a fireplace in the living room. 거실에 벽난로가 있다.

There are knobs on the desk drawers. 책상 서랍에 손잡이가 있다.

There's a mobile food stand on a walkway.

보도에 이동식 식품 가판대가 있다.

(3) 사물 + is/are[have/has been] + 두다/놓다-ed + 위치 표현
가장 많이 출제

어휘 ledge (창문 밑) 선반 vertical 수직의 beam 기둥 stool (등받이와 팔걸이가 없는) 의자 upside down (아래위가) 거꾸로, 뒤집혀 bedding 침구 make the[one's] bed (자고 나서) 잠자리를 정돈하다 traffic cone 원뿔형 교통 표지 patterned 무늬가 있는 rug 깔개 canal 운하. 수로 athletic field 운동장 pottery 도자기 arrange 배열하다. 정렬시키다 potted plant 화분에 심은 화초 border 가장자리 patio 테라스 semi-circle 반원 symmetrically 대칭으로 trench 도랑 statue 조각상 pedestal (동상의) 받침대 on top of ~의 위에 pitcher 주전자 mount 설치하다. 올려놓다 light fixture 조명 기구 store 보관하다 cookware 취사도구 stove 가스레인지 portable 들고 다닐 수 있는 staircase 계단

A plant has been put on a ledge.

창문 밑 선반에 식물이 놓여 있다.

Chairs have been placed around the base of a tree. 나무 밑동 둘레에 의자들이 놓여 있다.

A ladder has been placed next to a vertical beam. 수직 기둥 옆에 사다리가 놓여 있다.

Some traffic cones have been placed near the truck. 트럭 근처에 원뿔형 교통 표지들이 놓여 있다.

Some chairs have been placed along a canal. 수로를 따라 의자들이 놓여 있다.

A tray of food has been placed on a counter. 카운터에 음식 한 접시가 놓여 있다.

Some stools have been placed upside down. 등받이 없는 의자들이 뒤집혀서 놓여 있다.

Bedding has been folded and placed on a mattress. 침구가 개어져서 매트리스 위에 놓여 있다.

cf. One of the beds has not been made. 침대 중 하나가 정돈되지 않았다.

A patterned rug's been placed over a floor. 바닥에 무늬가 있는 깔개가 놓여 있다.

Chairs are positioned on opposite sides of the room.

의자들이 서로 방 맞은편에 놓여 있다.

Some boats are positioned at the river's edge. 강가에 배들이 있다.

Desks are positioned one in front of the other.

책상들이 앞뒤로 놓여 있다.

152 | 토익 마법 2주의 기적 990 LC

An athletic field is located near some trees. 나무들 근처에 운동장이 있다.

A large piece of pottery is situated in the corner. 큰 도자기 한 점이 구석에 있다.

Potted plants have been arranged along the border of the patio.
테라스 가장자리를 따라서 화분에 심은 화초들이 정렬되어 있다.

The windows are arranged symmetrically. 창문이 대칭으로 배치되어 있다.

The seats are arranged in a semi-circle. 좌석이 반원형으로 배열되어 있다.

Pipes have been laid in the trench.
파이프가 도랑에 놓여 있다.

A statue is set on a pedestal.
조각상이 받침대 위에 놓여 있다.

A lamp has been set on top of a counter.
카운터 위에 램프가 있다.

Some metal pitchers have been set on a shelf.
선반 위에 금속 주전자들이 놓여 있다.

Bulletin boards have been mounted to the wall. 벽에 게시판이 설치되어 있다.

Some light fixtures are mounted on the walls. 벽에 조명 기구들이 설치되어 있다.

Files are being stored on multiple shelves. 파일들이 여러 개의 선반에 보관되어 있다.

* 진행 시제 수동태이지만 예외적으로 동작이 아니라 상태를 나타낸다.

Some cookware has been left on a stove. 가스레인지 위에 취사도구가 놓여 있다.

A couch has been pushed to one side of the room.
소파가 방 한쪽으로 밀어져 있다.

A portable staircase has been brought up to the door.
이동식 계단을 문 앞에 가져다 놓았다.

(4) 사물 + stand/sit/lie/rest + 위치 표현

08_04

어휘 structure 구조물, 건축물 an assortment of 여러 가지의 rug 깔개 lie 가로놓여 있다 cord 코드, 전깃줄 rest ~에 기대다, 받치다

A stone structure stands above the town.
석조 건축물이 마을 위에 서 있다.

An assortment of items sits on a counter. 카운터 위에 다양한 물건들이 있다.

A clock is sitting on a shelf. 선반 위에 시계가 있다.

A rug is lying in front of the door. 문 앞에 깔개가 가로놓여 있다.

Some cords are lying across the top of a counter. 전기 코드들이 카운터 위에 가로질러 놓여 있다.

A pair of scissors is resting in a cup. 컵 안에 가위 하나가 기대어 있다.

His arms are resting on a desk. 팔을 책상 위에 올려놓고 있다.

(5) 사물 + be + visible[seen] + 위치 표현

08_05

어휘 pointed 뾰족한 in the distance 먼 곳에, 저 멀리에 skyline (건물, 언덕이) 하늘과 맞닿은 윤곽선, 스카이라인

A city skyline is visible in the distance. 먼 곳에 도시의 스카이라인이 보인다.

Mountains can be seen from an outdoor pool. 야외 수영장에서 산을 볼 수 있다.

A pointed roof is visible in the distance. 저 멀리에 뾰족한 지붕이 보인다.

(6) 장소/사물 + have[hold] + 사물

08_06

어휘 story (건물의) 층 light-colored 옅은[밝은] 색의

The building has many stories. 건물이 여러 층으로 이루어져 있다.

Most of the windows have light-colored frames. 대부분의 창문에 밝은 색깔의 창틀이 있다.

A car has a flat tire. 자동차 바퀴가 바람이 빠져 있다.

An island has several buildings on it. 섬에 건물이 몇 채 있다.

A glass vase holds some flowers. 유리 화병에 꽃이 몇 송이 있다.

유형 75　~을 내려다보고 있다 overlook　08_07

어휘 domed 둥근 지붕의　overlook (건물 등이) 내려다보다　pier 부두　monument 기념물, 기념비　deck 데크(평평한 목재 바닥)
face ~에 면하다　lawn 잔디밭

Some domed buildings overlook a pier. 둥근 지붕의 건물들이 부두를 내려다보고 있다.

A public monument is overlooking a walkway. 기념비가 보도를 내려다보고 있다.

There's a deck overlooking a lake. 호수를 내려다보는 데크가 있다.

Some of the buildings face the lawn. 건물들이 잔디에 면해 있다.

유형 76　길, 난간, 계단, 다리 등이 뻗어 있다 extend, lead, run, span　08_08

어휘 footbridge 보행자 전용 다리　extend 뻗다　awning 차양　ramp 경사로, 비탈　lead ~로 이어지다　steps 계단　run ~로 이어지다,
뻗다　railing 난간　curved 곡선의, 약간 굽은　handrail 난간　span 가로지르다, ~에 걸쳐 있다　waterway 수로　a body of water
(바다, 강, 호수의) 수역　cross 가로지르다　suspend 띄우다　stream 개울, 시내　protrude 튀어나오다, 돌출되다　wooded 나무가 우거진
into the distance 저 멀리

A footbridge extends across the water. 보행자용 다리가 물 위에 뻗어 있다.

Windows extend from the floor to the ceiling.
바닥부터 천장까지 유리창이 뻗어 있다.

A hose has been extended from a vehicle.
호스가 차에서 뻗어 나와 있다.

An awning extends over a shop entrance. 상점 입구 위에 차양이 뻗어 있다.

A ramp leads into the back of a truck. 경사로가 트럭 짐 싣는 부분으로 뻗어 있다.

Stone steps lead down to the water. 돌계단이 물 쪽으로 뻗어 내려가고 있다.

A fence runs along the edge of the road. 도로를 따라 울타리가 뻗어 있다.

There's a handrail running up the middle of the steps. ────────

계단 한 가운데를 뻗어 올라가는 난간이 있다.

A railing runs along the top of the curved wall. ────────

난간이 곡선 모양의 벽 윗부분을 따라 뻗어 있다.

A bridge with arches spans a waterway. ────────

아치가 있는 다리가 수로 위에 걸쳐 있다.

A bridge spans a body of water.

다리가 호수[강] 위에 가로질러 놓여 있다.

A bridge crosses over a waterway. 다리가 수로 위에 가로질러 놓여 있다.

A bridge is suspended over a stream. 시내 위에 다리가 있다.

A walkway protrudes into the water. 통로가 물 쪽으로 돌출해 있다. ────

The road passes by a wooded area. 나무가 우거진 지역 옆에 길이 나 있다.

The road curves into the distance. 길이 저 멀리 휘어 있다.

Exercise

08_09

Workbook p.98   정답 및 해설 p.112

1.

a   b   c   d

2.

a   b   c   d

What 의문문

What 의문문도 How 의문문만큼이나 다양한 유형으로 출제된다. 각 유형의 전형적인 정답 패턴을 익히고, 고난도 문제도 함께 연습해 보자.

(1) What + 명사 ~?
   What kind[type/form] of + 명사
   ➡ ① **What 바로 뒤에 나오는 명사만 알아들으면 해결할 수 있다.**
      ② **(the) one(s)이 들리면 정답이다.**
      ③ **something (that)이 들리면 정답이다.**

🎯 **기출 예제** 🎧 08_11

Q. What material is this shirt made of? 이 셔츠는 어떤 재료로 만들어졌나요?
A. It's a light cotton fabric. ⟫⟫⟫ 가벼운 면직물입니다.

Q. What kind of decoration would you like on the tables? 테이블에는 어떤 종류의 장식물을 놓고 싶으세요?
A. Just some flower arrangements. ⟫⟫⟫ 약간의 꽃꽂이면 되겠어요.

Q. What documents should I bring on my first day of work? 근무 첫날에 어떤 서류를 가져가야 하나요?
A. The ones in the welcome packet. ⟫⟫⟫ 환영 자료집에 있는 것들이요.

Q. What type of shoes are you looking for? 어떤 유형의 신발을 찾으시나요?
A. Something suitable for running. ⟫⟫⟫ 달리기에 적합한 거요.

---

(2) What time ~ ?
   ➡ **When 의문문과 같은 패턴**
   반드시 '몇 시 몇 분'이라고 대답하는 것은 아니다.

기출 예제

Q. What time do you usually get to work?
A. Between seven thirty and eight.

보통 몇 시에 출근하시나요?
≫ 7시 30분에서 8시 사이에요.

Q. What time is the conference supposed to begin?
A. It starts in about an hour.

회의는 몇 시에 시작하기로 되어 있나요?
≫ 약 한 시간 후에 시작합니다.

Q. What time are you leaving the office today?
A. As soon as I'm done with this report.

오늘은 몇 시에 퇴근하시나요?
≫ 이 보고서가 끝나자마자 하려고요.

(3) What's the price[charge/fee/fare/rate/cost/budget/estimate] of ~?
 '돈'이 들리면 정답

기출 예제

Q. What's the hourly pay rate?
A. It's thirty dollars.

시급이 얼마인가요?
≫ 30달러입니다.

Q. What is the shipping charge?
A. Four dollars per kilo.

운송 요금은 얼마입니까?
≫ 킬로당 4달러입니다.

Q. What's the projected budget for the trip to New York?
A. I'd estimate it's about six thousand dollars.

예상되는 뉴욕 여행의 예산은 얼마인가요?
≫ 약 6,000 달러일 것으로 예상해요.

Q. What's the total cost of the repair work?
A. It's free because of the warranty.

수리 작업의 총 비용은 얼마인가요?
≫ 품질 보증서가 있어서 무료입니다.

(4) What's ~ like?
➡ 형용사

'How + be동사 + S ~?'와 같은 의미의 질문이다. 정답도 똑같이 형용사를 사용하는 대답이다.

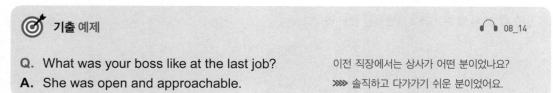

기출 예제

Q. What was your boss like at the last job?
A. She was open and approachable.

이전 직장에서는 상사가 어떤 분이었나요?
≫ 솔직하고 다가가기 쉬운 분이었어요.

(5) What's ~ about? / What ~ discuss ~? / What's the topic of ~?
→ **명사(구)**

주어, 동사가 갖춰진 완전한 문장이 정답인 경우가 거의 없고, 대부분 명사(구)로만 구성된 단답형 대답이 정답이다.

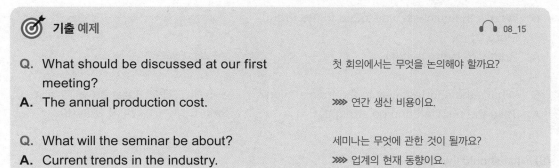

🎯 **기출 예제**　　　　　　　　　　　　　🎧 08_15

Q. What should be discussed at our first meeting?　　　첫 회의에서는 무엇을 논의해야 할까요?

A. The annual production cost.　　　≫ 연간 생산 비용이요.

Q. What will the seminar be about?　　　세미나는 무엇에 관한 것이 될까요?

A. Current trends in the industry.　　　≫ 업계의 현재 동향이요.

(6) What's your opinion[impression] of ~?
What do you think of[about] ~?
→ **형용사, 부사**

How do you like[enjoy/feel about] ~?도 의견을 묻는 질문이다. How 의문문이나 What 의문문처럼 의견을 묻는 질문에는 형용사나 부사를 이용하는 대답이 매우 자주 정답으로 출제된다.

🎯 **기출 예제**　　　　　　　　　　　　　🎧 08_16

Q. What do you think of the company's new logo?　　　회사의 새 로고에 대해 어떻게 생각하시나요?

A. It represents our image perfectly.　　　≫ 우리의 이미지를 완벽하게 나타내고 있군요.

Q. What's your impression of our new uniforms?　　　새 유니폼에 대해 어떤 인상을 받으셨나요?

A. They look very comfortable.　　　≫ 아주 편안해 보입니다.

(7) What's the fastest[best/quickest/shortest] way to ~?
→ **교통수단, 길 이름, 길 안내**

🎯 **기출 예제**　　　　　　　　　　　　　🎧 08_17

Q. What's the fastest way to the convention center?　　　컨벤션 센터까지 가는 가장 빠른 방법이 뭘까요?

A. Drive down Hill Street.　　　≫ 차를 몰고 Hill 가(街)를 따라 가세요.

Q. What's the best way for us to get to the trade fair?	우리가 무역 박람회에 가는 가장 좋은 방법은 뭘까요?
A. Let's take a look at the train schedule.	≫≫ 기차 일정표를 봅시다.
Q. What's the quickest way to get to the Proud Mary Café?	Proud Mary 카페까지 가는 가장 빠른 방법은 뭐죠?
A. Route 26 is the fastest.	≫≫ 26번 국도가 가장 빠르죠.
Q. What's the shortest way to the train station?	기차역까지 가는 가장 짧은 길은 어디입니까?
A. Take the next left and go straight.	≫≫ 다음 길에서 좌회전해서 직진하세요.

(8) What should I[we] do ~?
➡ 명령문

"어떻게 해야 하죠?"라고 물었으니 "어떻게 하세요."라고 명령문으로 대답하는 것이 자연스럽다.

 기출 예제 🎧 08_18

| Q. What should I do if I miss a training session? | 교육 세션을 놓치면 어떻게 해야 하나요? |
| A. Speak to the instructor. | ≫≫ 강사에게 말씀하세요. |

(9) What do you do (for a living)?
What kind[type/sort/line] of work do you do (for a living)?
➡ 직업 이름, 업종

 기출 예제 🎧 08_19

Q. What do you do at the laboratory?	연구소에서 어떤 일을 하시죠?
A. I'm a technician.	≫≫ 기술자에요.
Q. What sort of work do you do?	어떤 일을 하시나요?
A. Construction, mostly.	≫≫ 대개는 건설업이죠.

1. (A) (B) (C)   6. (A) (B) (C)

2. (A) (B) (C)   7. (A) (B) (C)

3. (A) (B) (C)   8. (A) (B) (C)

4. (A) (B) (C)   9. (A) (B) (C)

5. (A) (B) (C)   10. (A) (B) (C)

→ 화자의 의도 파악 문제 2

화자의 의도 파악 문제를 더 연습해 보자. 대화나 담화의 맥락을 고려하여 주어진 문장의 속뜻을 유추할 때, 시간이 오래 걸리지 않도록 선택지들의 내용을 기억하는 것이 중요하다는 점을 잊지 말자.

Exercise

 08_22

 Workbook p.101 ✎ 정답 및 해설 p.115

PART 3

1. What are the speakers mainly discussing?

   (A) An employee assessment
   (B) A sales promotion
   (C) A new patron
   (D) An itinerary for a trip

2. Why does the man say, "the company doesn't have a policy in place for this"?

   (A) To defer an announcement
   (B) To grant approval to the woman
   (C) To offer an explanation
   (D) To propose a policy modification

3. Why is the manager unavailable?

   (A) She is delivering a speech at a conference.
   (B) She is training new hires.
   (C) She is finishing a sales report.
   (D) She is meeting some clients.

PART 4

4. What is the purpose of the announcement?

   (A) To scrutinize a budget proposal
   (B) To discuss an upcoming merger
   (C) To interpret some survey results
   (D) To welcome new staff members

5. What does the woman mean when she says, "And why wouldn't we"?

   (A) She endorses a decision.
   (B) She hopes to be transferred.
   (C) She seeks input from the listeners.
   (D) She is worried about a shipment.

6. What does the woman ask listeners to do?

   (A) Participate in a training session
   (B) Complete some documents
   (C) Compile a set of questions
   (D) Review some information online

Today's Vocabulary

●● Actual Test를 풀기 전에 이 단어들을 따라 읽으며 암기하자.

cover story 표지 기사

further 더 이상의, 추가의

stitch 바느질하다, 꿰매다

schedule *sth* for + 날짜/요일 ~로 ~의 일정을 잡다

approval 승인

rent 임대, 임차

head (특정 방향으로) 가다, 향하다

hire 빌리다, 세내다

venue 장소

investigate 조사하다

pleasant 쾌적한

alternative 대안의, 대신의

word count 총 단어 수

piece (신문, 잡지의) 기사

forward 보내다, 전달하다

lengthen 길게 하다, 늘이다

corporate 기업의, 회사의

face 직면하다

try out ~을 시험해 보다

skeptical 의심이 많은, 회의적인

trail (산속의) 작은 길, 산길

partially 부분적으로

unavailable 이용할 수 없는

maintenance 유지 보수

halfway through 중간쯤에서

trek 트레킹

apply (화장품을) 바르다

sunscreen 자외선 차단제

Actual Test

PART 1	1-3
PART 2	4-12
PART 3	13-21
PART 4	22-30

Part 3, 4 '미리 잘 읽기' 전략

LC Directions 시간:	16-18번 읽기
Part 1 Directions 시간:	19-21번 읽기
Part 2 Directions 시간:	28-30번 읽기
Part 3 Directions 시간:	13-15번 읽기
19-21번 문제 읽어주는 시간:	22-24번 읽기
Part 4 Directions 시간:	25-27번 읽기

Actual Test

Workbook p.103   정답 및 해설 p.117

LISTENING TEST

지금 16-18번 읽기

In the Listening test, you will be asked to demonstrate how well you understand spoken English. The entire Listening test will last approximately 45 minutes. There are four parts, and directions are given for each part. You must mark your answers on the separate answer sheet. Do not write your answers in your test book.

PART 1

지금 19-21번 읽기

Directions: For each question in this part, you will hear four statements about a picture in your test book. When you hear the statements, you must select the one statement that best describes what you see in the picture. Then find the number of the question on your answer sheet and mark your answer. The statements will not be printed in your test book and will be spoken only one time.

1.

ⓐ   ⓑ   ⓒ   ⓓ

3.

ⓐ   ⓑ   ⓒ   ⓓ

2.

ⓐ   ⓑ   ⓒ   ⓓ

PART 2

Directions: You will hear a question or statement and three responses spoken in English. They will not be printed in your test book and will be spoken only one time. Select the best response to the question or statement and mark the letter (A), (B), or (C) on your answer sheet.

4. Mark your answer. (A) (B) (C)

5. Mark your answer. (A) (B) (C)

6. Mark your answer. (A) (B) (C)

7. Mark your answer. (A) (B) (C)

8. Mark your answer. (A) (B) (C)

9. Mark your answer. (A) (B) (C)

10. Mark your answer. (A) (B) (C)

11. Mark your answer. (A) (B) (C)

12. Mark your answer. (A) (B) (C)

Directions: You will hear some conversations between two or more people. You will be asked to answer three questions about what the speakers say in each conversation. Select the best response to each question and mark the letter (A), (B), (C), or (D) on your answer sheet. The conversations will not be printed in your test book and will be spoken only one time.

13. According to the man, what will happen next year?

(A) A new product will be launched.
(B) Additional perks will be provided.
(C) Several employees will be hired.
(D) Some offices will be renovated.

14. What does Yaping suggest?

(A) Using online advertisements
(B) Supplementing details to a contract
(C) Hiring a venue for meetings
(D) Developing orientation materials

15. What does Yuko agree to do?

(A) Investigate a location
(B) Interact with a client
(C) Complete a transaction
(D) Edit a document

16. What event are the speakers discussing?

(A) A company dinner
(B) An inauguration ceremony
(C) A product launch
(D) An annual reunion

17. What does the man imply when he says, "The recent weather has been quite pleasant, though"?

(A) He feels disappointed at a decision.
(B) He is reluctant to plan an outdoor function.
(C) He wishes for an increase in his vacation allowance.
(D) He anticipates a shift in the weather tonight.

18. What does the woman suggest?

(A) Postponing a dinner appointment
(B) Setting up video equipment outdoors
(C) Serving some food at an alternative place
(D) Offering a markdown

Article	Deadline
"Exploring Naples"	September 14
"Cheeses of Italy"	September 14
"Affordable Tour Packages"	October 17
"Copenhagen by Bicycle"	November 12

정답 고르고 나서 바로 22-24번 읽기

19. What does the man ask the woman to do?

(A) Extend an agreement
(B) Arrange a meeting for an interview
(C) Lengthen an article
(D) Proofread a document

20. Look at the graphic. Which article's deadline will be changed?

(A) "Exploring Naples"
(B) "Cheeses of Italy"
(C) "Affordable Tour Packages"
(D) "Copenhagen by Bicycle"

21. What does the woman say she will send the man?

(A) An itinerary for a tour
(B) An expense report
(C) Meeting minutes
(D) Ideas for upcoming articles

PART 4

Directions: You will hear some talks given by a single speaker. You will be asked to answer three questions about what the speaker says in each talk. Select the best response to each question and mark the letter (A), (B), (C), or (D) on your answer sheet. The talks will not be printed in your test book and will be spoken only one time.

22. What is wrong with the camera?

(A) It is missing a component.
(B) It is an outdated model.
(C) It weighs too much.
(D) It has been damaged.

23. Where does the speaker want to go this afternoon?

(A) To a warehouse
(B) To an electronics store
(C) To a real estate agency
(D) To a post office

24. Why does the speaker request a return call?

(A) To cancel an order
(B) To inquire about a rental
(C) To verify a location
(D) To give driving directions

25. What is Tina Brownstein's area of expertise?

(A) Online marketing
(B) Customer service
(C) Corporate accounting
(D) Business laws

26. What is C3VR?

(A) A digital camera brand
(B) An electronic reading device
(C) An automatic payment method
(D) A software program

27. Why does the speaker say, "Only her employees had the opportunity to try out the product before its official release"?

(A) To explain why some experts are skeptical about a product
(B) To confirm whether testing on a product had to be terminated
(C) To inquire about the number of employees in a company
(D) To encourage the audience to test some merchandise

Morrista National Park Trail Map

28. Who most likely are the listeners?

(A) Park rangers
(B) Bus operators
(C) Maintenance workers
(D) Tourists

29. Look at the graphic. Where will the listeners be unable to go today?

(A) The North Pond
(B) The Picnic Area
(C) The Honeybee Garden
(D) The Visitor Center

30. What does the woman encourage the listeners to do?

(A) Study the park trail map
(B) Listen to the weather report
(C) Secure their belongings
(D) Use sun protection

Day

09

●● 장면을 상상하면서 큰 소리로 여러 번 따라 읽으세요.

유형 77 물건이 진열, 전시되어 있는 장면 🎧 09_01
display, lay out, arrange, stock, exhibit, organize, set out

어휘 garment 의복, 옷 clothing 의복, 옷 rack 선반, 걸이 flower arrangement 꽃꽂이 on display 전시된, 진열된 reading material 읽을거리 hallway 복도 lay out (가지런히) ~을 늘어놓다, 펼쳐놓다 arrange 정리하다, 배열하다 stock A with B A를 B로 채워놓다 supplies 용품, 비품 artifact (인공) 유물 exhibit 전시하다 refreshments (행사의) 다과, (가벼운) 음식 organize 정리하다 set out ~을 정리하다, 진열하다

Some food items are displayed for sale. 식품이 판매를 위해 진열되어 있다.

Garments are being displayed. 의복이 진열되어 있다.

* 진행 수동태의 예외적인 사용 - display는 진행 수동태로 표현해도 '상태'를 나타낸다. 따라서 사람이 '없을' 때에도 정답이 될 수 있다.

Some clothing is being displayed on racks. 옷걸이에 옷이 진열되어 있다.

Flower arrangements are on display. 꽃꽂이가 진열되어 있다.

Reading material is on display in a hallway. 복도에 읽을거리가 전시되어 있다.

Different kinds of bread are laid out for sale.
여러 종류의 빵이 판매를 위해 진열되어 있다.

Some vegetables have been arranged on wooden platforms.
채소가 나무 진열대 위에 정리되어 있다.

Display shelves are stocked with products. 진열 선반이 상품으로 채워져 있다.

A cabinet has been stocked with supplies. 캐비닛이 비품으로 채워져 있다.

Some artifacts are exhibited in a case. 유물들이 케이스에 전시되어 있다.

Some refreshments have been organized in a display case.
진열장에 다과가 정리되어 있다.

Some products have been set out under tents. 천막 아래에 상품이 진열되어 있다.

The bags are available for purchase.

가방을 구매할 수 있게 해 놓았다.(구매를 위해 진열해 놓았다.)

장식되어 있다 장식물의 이름을 알아야 한다 🎧 09_02

어휘 window box (창가의) 화분, 화단 pavement 포장 도로 geometric 기하학적인 ornamental 장식용의 carpet ~에 카펫을 깔다

A house is decorated with window boxes. 화단으로 집을 장식해 놓았다.

A graphic design decorates the building's roof. 그래픽 디자인으로 건물의 지붕을 장식해 놓았다.

The pavement is decorated with geometric design. 포장도로를 기하학적인 디자인으로 장식해 놓았다.

Cabinets have been decorated with ornamental handles. 장식용 손잡이로 캐비닛을 장식해 놓았다.

A floral arrangement decorates each table. 꽃꽂이로 각 테이블을 장식해 놓았다.

The stairs have been carpeted. 계단에 카펫을 깔아놓았다.

Some floor tiles are in a pattern. 바닥 타일들이 같은 무늬로 되어 있다.

유형 79 **설치되어 있다** set up, built, assembled 🎧 09_03

어휘 computer station 컴퓨터 set up ~을 설치하다; 세우다, 놓다 pavilion (공원 등의) 정자 archway 아치 길; 아치형 입구 assemble 조립하다

A computer station has been set up on a desk. 책상 위에 컴퓨터가 설치되어 있다.

Some chairs have been set up under a pavilion. 정자 아래에 의자들이 설치되어 있다.

Tents are being set up in a field. 들판에서 텐트를 설치하고 있다.

There are chairs set up in front of a building. ──────

건물 앞에 의자들이 놓여 있다.

An archway has been built over the path. 길 위에 아치형 통로가 지어져 있다.

A set of drums has been assembled. 드럼 한 세트가 조립되어 있다.

유형 80 **벽이나 천장에 걸려 있거나 매달려 있는 장면** 🎧 09_04
hang(ing), hung, suspend

어휘 storefront 매장 전면, 가게 앞 (공간) hang 걸다, 매달다; 걸리다, 매달리다; (아래로) 늘어지다 hook 고리, 걸이 light fixture 조명 기구 suspend 매달다, 걸다

Handbags are hanging near a storefront. ──────

핸드백들이 가게 앞에 걸려 있다.

Some cables are hanging off the desk. 전선들이 책상에서 늘어져 있다.

Some clothes have been hung from hooks. 옷이 옷걸이에 걸려 있다.

Some pictures are being hung on a wall. 벽에 그림이 걸려 있다.

* 진행 수동태의 예외적인 사용 – hang은 진행 수동태로 표현해도 '상태'를 나타낸다.

따라서 사람이 '없을' 때에도 정답이 될 수 있다.

A light fixture is suspended above a dining area. 식사 공간 위로 조명 기구가 매달려 있다.

cf. He's hanging a clock. 시계를 걸고 있다.

유형 81　붙어 있다　attached

🎧 09_05

어휘 shelving unit 선반

A balcony is attached to every apartment. 아파트마다 발코니가 있다.

Labels have been attached to shelving units. 선반에 라벨이 붙어 있다.

유형 82　매여 있다　secured

🎧 09_06

어휘 secure (단단히) 고정시키다, 잡아매다　post 기둥

Some bicycles have been secured to metal posts.

자전거가 금속 기둥에 매여 있다.

Packages have been secured by some rope.

꾸러미가 밧줄로 매여 있다.

유형 83　줄지어 있는 장면　line, row

🎧 09_07

어휘 line 줄; 줄을 세우다, ~을 따라 늘어서다　line up ~을 일렬로 배열하다　locker 사물함　corridor 복도, 회랑　space ~ 사이에 간격을 두고 배치하다　organize 정리하다

Some boats are lined up in rows. 배들이 여러 줄로 늘어서 있다.

Lockers are lined up in a hallway. 복도에 사물함들이 줄지어 있다.

A corridor is lined with arches. 복도에 아치들이 줄지어 있다.

Lamps are spaced in a row on a tabletop. 램프들이 테이블 위에 간격을 두고 놓여 있다.

They are waiting in line. 줄서서 기다리고 있다.

Trees line both sides of the street. 나무가 길 양옆을 따라 늘어서 있다.

There are some vehicles lining the side of a street. 차량들이 길가를 따라 줄지어 있다.

Products have been organized into rows. 상품들이 여러 줄로 정리되어 있다.

A row of lights is above the edge of the platform.
플랫폼 가장자리 위에 조명이 일렬로 있다.

유형 84 나란히 side by side, next[close] to each other 🎧 09_08

어휘 planter box 화분 carton 판지 상자

Some people are walking side by side. 나란히 걷고 있다.

Some wooden planter boxes have been set next to each other. 나무 화분이 나란히 놓여 있다.

Some cartons have been placed close to each other. 상자들이 나란히 놓여 있다.

유형 85 물건이 쌓여 있는 장면 stack, pile, heap 🎧 09_09

어휘 crate (운송용 대형) 상자 stack[pile] 쌓다; 더미 on top of each other (위아래로) 차곡차곡 plate 접시, 그릇 utensil (주방용, 식사용) 기구, 도구 bin 통, 상자 heap (아무렇게나) 쌓다; 더미 wheelbarrow 외바퀴 손수레

Some of the crates are stacked on top of each other. 상자가 차곡차곡 쌓여 있다.

Plates have been stacked next to some utensils. 접시가 식기류(또는 조리 기구) 옆에 쌓여 있다.

Some fruit has been stacked in a bin. 과일이 상자 안에 쌓여 있다.

Stacks of paper have been left on a desk. 여러 더미의 종이가 책상 위에 놓여 있다.

The boxes have been placed in stacks. 상자가 여러 더미로 쌓여 있다.

Some vegetables are piled in heaps on the table. 채소가 테이블 위에 여러 더미로 쌓여 있다.

A wheelbarrow has been left next to a pile of rocks. 돌 더미 옆에 외바퀴 손수레가 놓여 있다.

Vegetables are arranged in piles. 채소가 여러 더미로 놓여 있다.

유형 86 기대어 있다 leaning, propped 🎧 09_10

어휘 lean 기대다 prop 기대어 세우다 column 기둥 support 떠받치다, 받치다 porch 현관

The chairs are leaning against the tables. 의자들이 테이블에 기대어 있다.

A man is leaning on a countertop. 카운터에 기대어 서 있다.

Ladders of various heights are propped up against the building.
다양한 높이의 사다리가 건물에 기대어 있다.

cf. Columns support a porch roof. 기둥들이 현관 지붕을 받치고 있다.

어휘 stand 관중석 spectator 관중

A bookshelf has been filled with reading materials. 책꽂이가 읽을거리로 가득 차 있다.

The stands are filled with spectators. 관중석이 관중들로 꽉 차 있다.

The drawer is full of folders. 서랍이 폴더로 가득 차 있다.

The outdoor café is crowded with customers. 야외 카페가 손님들로 북적거린다.

Exercise
 09_12

📄 Workbook p.112   ✏️ 정답 및 해설 p.128

1.

ⓐ ⓑ ⓒ ⓓ

2.

ⓐ ⓑ ⓒ ⓓ

Where / When 의문문

Where / When 의문문은 Part 2 앞부분에서 전형적인 패턴에 따라 출제되면 쉽게 풀 수 있다.
뒷부분에서 어렵게 출제되는 경우를 대비한 연습을 철저히 해 두자.

1. Where 의문문

① in / at / on + 장소 ← 90% 이상 출제됨
② 장소 전치사 + 장소: beside / by / next to, across (from), to, near[close] to, from, in front of, outside 등
③ try / check + 장소
④ 장소 부사: (over) there, down the street, down the hall, (a)round the corner, online, downstairs, nearby 등
⑤ 장소 명칭: apartment, post office, Gate 36-B, Platform 2, Track 7, Seat 16-C, Aisle 5 등
⑥ 거리, 가는 데 걸리는 시간

🎯 **기출 예제**　　　　　　　　　　🎧 09_14

Q. Where are the best seats available for tomorrow's performance?　　　내일 공연 때 비어 있는 가장 좋은 좌석은 어디인가요?
A. There are a few left in the third row.　　　⋙ 세 번째 줄에 몇 자리 남아 있습니다.

Q. Where is the parking area?　　　주차장이 어디에 있나요?
A. At the rear of the building.　　　⋙ 건물 뒤편에요.

Q. Where did you post the schedule?　　　일정표를 어디에 게시했나요?
A. I hung a copy on the conference room door.　　　⋙ 회의실 문에 한 부 붙여 놓았어요.

Q. Where can I catch the train to the city center?　　　시내로 가는 기차는 어디에서 탈 수 있습니까?
A. The station's across the street.　　　⋙ 길 건너에 역이 있어요.

Q. Where should we set up the new packaging machine?　　　새 포장 기계는 어디에 설치할까요?
A. By the loading dock.　　　⋙ 하역장 옆에요.

Q. Where's this shipment of parts being sent?
A. To the assembly plant in Dublin.

이번에 운송되는 부품들은 어디로 보낼 건가요?
≫≫ Dublin에 있는 조립 공장으로요.

Q. Where are you planning to open your next store?
A. Near the city center.

다음 매장은 어디에 열 계획인가요?
≫≫ 도심 근처에요.

Q. Where should I meet you at the theater?
A. In front of the box office.

극장 어디에서 만날까요?
≫≫ 매표소 앞에서요.

Q. Where did these oranges come from?
A. From a supplier in California.

이 오렌지들은 어디에서 왔죠?
≫≫ 캘리포니아의 납품업체로부터요.

Q. Where can I rent a commercial property downtown?
A. Check the Burnside Building.

시내 어디에서 상업용 부동산을 임대할 수 있나요?
≫≫ Burnside 빌딩을 확인해 보세요.

Q. Where's the book you and Patrick were talking about?
A. Over there on the table.

당신과 Patrick이 얘기하던 책이 어디 있나요?
≫≫ 저쪽 테이블 위에요.

Q. Where is the nearest coffee shop?
A. It's right down the street.

가장 가까운 커피숍은 어디 있나요?
≫≫ 바로 길 아래에 있어요.

Q. Where's the nearest subway station?
A. Just (a)round the corner.

가장 가까운 지하철역이 어디입니까?
≫≫ 바로 길모퉁이에요.

Q. Where can I attend an evening course?
A. The college has some night classes.

야간 수업을 어디서 들을 수 있죠?
≫≫ 대학교에 야간 수업이 몇 개 있죠.

Q. Where's the post office?
A. Two hundred meters from here.

우체국이 어디에 있나요?
≫≫ 여기서 200미터 가시면 돼요.

Q. Where does our company have its headquarters?
A. It's about thirty minutes from here.

우리 회사 본사는 어디인가요?
≫≫ 여기서 30분 정도만 가시면 돼요.

Q. Where does John usually store the extra supplies?
A. You'd better ask him.

John은 남는 비품들을 보통 어디에 보관하나요?
≫≫ 그에게 물어보시는 게 좋겠어요.

2. When 의문문

(1) 현재 / 미래 시제

① in + 시간

② next week[month / year]

③ sometime, someday, anytime, any day

④ at 6 o'clock, at around 4:30

10 past 5 5시 10분, **5 to 11** 11시 5분 전, **quarter to 6** 6시 15분 전, **half past 4** 4시 반

every hour on the hour 매시 정각에, **(every hour) on the half hour** 매시 30분에

⑤ at[by] the end of the day[week / month / quarter / year]

⑥ at the next board[staff] meeting

⑦ 요일, 날짜, 달 이름, 계절, 년도

⑧ 시간 + from now[today]

⑨ between + 시간

⑩ within + 시간

⑪ 시간 부사: soon, now, today, tomorrow, the day after tomorrow, this afternoon, this evening, tonight 등

(2) 과거 시제

last, ago, yesterday, this morning, recently, earlier today, just now 등

(3) 시제와 관계없이 정답인 표현 아래 접속사나 전치사로 시작하는 문장은 100% 정답!

① Not until, Not before, Not for

② When, While, As soon as

③ Before, After

🎯 **기출 예제**　　　　　　　　　　　　　　　　　🎧 09_15

Q. When will you hear back about your interview?　면접 결과는 언제 알게 되나요?

A. In a week or so.　》》》 한 일주일 정도 후에요.

Q. When will the accounting team meet?　회계팀은 언제 모여요?

A. Sometime next week.　》》》 다음 주 중에요.

Q. When do you usually leave the office?　보통 언제 퇴근하나요?

A. Around half past eight.　》》》 한 8시 반쯤이에요.

Q. When is the hiring committee making a final decision?　채용 위원회가 언제 최종 결정을 내릴까요?

A. By the end of the month.　》》》 월말까지요.

Q. When are we distributing the employee survey?　직원 설문조사는 언제 배부할 건가요?

A. Maybe at the end of the quarter.　》》》 아마 분기 말에요.

Q. When does Ms. Hines send orders for office supplies?

A. On the first day of every month.

Ms. Hines가 사무용품 주문서를 언제 보냅니까?

>>> 매달 1일에요.

Q. When can we expect the product?

A. Within forty-eight hours.

제품을 언제 받을 수 있나요?

>>> 48시간 이내에요.

Q. When is the company outing?

A. Two weeks from now.

회사 야유회는 언제 있습니까?

>>> 지금으로부터 2주 후에요.

Q. When will we receive the specifications for the new model of laptop computer?

A. We should be hearing from the supplier soon.

새 노트북 컴퓨터 모델의 사양은 언제 받게 됩니까?

>>> 곧 공급업체로부터 연락이 있을 겁니다.

Q. When did Helen buy the piano?

A. Last week, I think.

Helen이 피아노를 언제 샀죠?

>>> 제 생각에는 지난주에요.

Q. When did Keito start working here?

A. I think it was two years ago.

Keito는 언제 여기서 일하기 시작했죠?

>>> 2년 전일 걸요.

Q. When will the order be delivered?

A. Not until Wednesday afternoon.

주문품은 언제 배달되나요?

>>> 수요일 오후는 되어야 와요.

Q. When will I receive a confirmation e-mail for my reservation?

A. As soon as it is finalized.

제 예약의 확인 이메일은 언제 받게 됩니까?

>>> 완료되는 대로요.

Q. When do I get reimbursed for my travel expenses?

A. Right after the form's been approved.

제 출장비는 언제 환급받게 됩니까?

>>> 서식이 승인된 직후에요.

Q. When does the modern painting exhibit open?

A. Let me check the calendar.

현대회화 전시회는 언제 열리나요?

>>> 제가 일정표를 확인해 볼게요.

Q. When are we going to release the updated car model?

A. It's too soon to tell.

신차 모델은 언제 공개하게 되죠?

>>> 지금 말하기는 너무 이릅니다.

Q. When does the computer update go into effect?

A. Mr. Kang might know.

컴퓨터 업데이트의 효력이 언제 발생되나요?

>>> Mr. Kang이 아실 겁니다.

Workbook p.113   정답 및 해설 p.128

1. (A)   (B)   (C)

2. (A)   (B)   (C)

3. (A)   (B)   (C)

4. (A)   (B)   (C)

5. (A)   (B)   (C)

6. (A)   (B)   (C)

7. (A)   (B)   (C)

8. (A)   (B)   (C)

9. (A)   (B)   (C)

10. (A)   (B)   (C)

그래픽 문제 1

아래 예제를 풀어 보자. 3번 문제에서 남자가 주문할 스크린의 크기를 묻고 있는데, 선택지에 있는 크기를 언급하면서 "몇 인치짜리를 주문할 것이다."라고 말하지는 않을 것이다. 그래픽을 보면서 풀어야 하는데, 대화에서 스크린 크기는 언급되지 않고 가격 정보만 들려줄 것이라고 예상할 수 있다. 이 유형은 항상 간접적으로 정보를 알려준다.

Q PART 3 Sample Questions   Workbook p.115   09_18

Screen Size	System Price
11 inches	$999
13 inches	$1,099
15 inches	$1,199
17 inches	$1,299

1. What does the woman ask the man to do?

(A) Order some equipment
(B) Search for a new vendor
(C) Repair a laptop computer
(D) Contact a potential employee

2. What problem does the man mention?

(A) A graphic designer has left the company.
(B) A supplier has increased its prices.
(C) A software program has been discontinued.
(D) A departmental budget has been lowered.

3. Look at the graphic. What size screen will the man order?

(A) 11 inches
(B) 13 inches
(C) 15 inches
(D) 17 inches

W Br Mike, a new graphic designer will be joining us next month, ¹so we'll need to set him up with a laptop and additional monitor. Can you place orders for those?

M Cn Sure. ²You're aware that our vendor has raised their prices, right?

W Br Really?

M Cn Yes. I just took a look at the catalog a few minutes ago, and their latest models are more expensive now.

W Br Right. ³Well, our budget per work area is twelve hundred dollars maximum. So let's order the system with the largest screen that falls within that price.

M Cn ³OK. I'll take another look at the prices and then place the order.

Screen Size	System Price
11 inches	$999
13 inches	$1,099
³15 inches	³$1,199
17 inches	$1,299

1. What does the woman ask the man to do?

(A) Order some equipment
(B) Search for a new vendor
(C) Repair a laptop computer
(D) Contact a potential employee

2. What problem does the man mention?

(A) A graphic designer has left the company.
(B) A supplier has increased its prices.
(C) A software program has been discontinued.
(D) A departmental budget has been lowered.

3. Look at the graphic. What size screen will the man order?

(A) 11 inches   (B) 13 inches
(C) 15 inches   (D) 17 inches

해설 여자가 새로 오는 그래픽 디자이너에게 노트북 컴퓨터와 모니터를 마련해 주어야 한다고 말하면서(so we'll need to set him up with a laptop and additional monitor.) 남자에게 주문을 부탁하고 있다(Can you place orders for those?). 여기서 1번 문제의 정답을 고르자. 정답을 고를 때는 언제나 순발력이 필요하다는 사실을 잊어서는 안 된다. 바로 이어지는 문장 You're aware that our vendor has raised their prices, right?을 듣고 패러프레이즈 된 문장을 2번 문제의 정답으로 선택해야 한다. 여자의 말에 따르면 회사에서 업무 공간 하나에 할당되는 예산은 최대 1,200달러이다(our budget per work area is twelve hundred dollars maximum). 그래서 여자는 이 가격을 넘어가지 않는 시스템 중 모니터가 가장 큰 것으로 주문하자고 제안했고(So let's order the system with the largest screen that falls within that price.), 남자는 여기에 동의했다(OK). 표를 보면 1,200달러가 안 되는 시스템 중 스크린이 가장 큰 것은 15인치 제품이다. 이렇게 간접적으로 제시되는 단서를 통해 정답을 찾아내야 한다.

PART 3

Options	
Seafood platter	$1,000
Steak platter	$850
Chicken platter	$700
Vegetarian platter	$550

PART 4

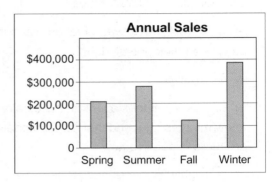

1. What type of event is being organized?

(A) A trade fair
(B) A managers' meeting
(C) A tour
(D) A party

2. Look at the graphic. What option will the man most likely select?

(A) Seafood platter
(B) Steak platter
(C) Chicken platter
(D) Vegetarian platter

3. What information does the man still have to provide?

(A) A purchase order number
(B) Some payment information
(C) The location of a business
(D) A list of guests

4. What type of product does the business sell?

(A) Apparel
(B) Footwear
(C) Electronic appliances
(D) Computer programs

5. Look at the graphic. In what season did the business relocate?

(A) Spring
(B) Summer
(C) Fall
(D) Winter

6. What did the business do after it relocated?

(A) It diversified its range of merchandise.
(B) It increased its workforce.
(C) It placed some advertisements.
(D) It organized an inauguration event.

Today's Vocabulary

 09_22

Actual Test를 풀기 전에 이 단어들을 따라 읽으며 암기하자.

set up ~을 설치하다

photo shoot 사진 촬영

psychologist 심리학자

check-up (건강) 검진

in a while 한동안

greet 인사하다, 맞이하다

left over from (쓰고 난 뒤) 남은

trade fair 무역 박람회

seek out ~을 찾아내다

customize 맞춤 제작을 하다

directory 인명부

misspell ~의 철자를 잘못 쓰다

spot 발견하다, 알아채다

incorrectly 부정확하게

light fixture 조명 기구

architecture 건축학

inn 소규모 호텔, 식당, 술집

state-of-the-art 최첨단의, 최신식의

energy-efficient 에너지 효율이 좋은

non-polluting 무공해의

architect 건축가

environmentally friendly 환경 친화적인

go through ~을 살펴보다

favor 선호하다

contemporary 현대의

reach out 연락을 취하다

disapproval 반감, 승인하지 않음

consult 상의하다

run (길이) 뻗다, 이어지다

block off (도로나 출입구를) 차단하다, 봉쇄하다

allow (시간, 돈을 어림하여) 잡다, 정하다, 할당하다

travel 이동

Actual Test

PART 1	1-3
PART 2	4-12
PART 3	13-21
PART 4	22-30

Part 3, 4 '미리 잘 읽기' 전략

LC Directions 시간:	16-18번 읽기
Part 1 Directions 시간:	19-21번 읽기
Part 2 Directions 시간:	28-30번 읽기
Part 3 Directions 시간:	13-15번 읽기
19-21번 문제 읽어주는 시간:	22-24번 읽기
Part 4 Directions 시간:	25-27번 읽기

📖 Workbook p.118 ✏ 정답 및 해설 p.134

LISTENING TEST

지금 16-18번 읽기

In the Listening test, you will be asked to demonstrate how well you understand spoken English. The entire Listening test will last approximately 45 minutes. There are four parts, and directions are given for each part. You must mark your answers on the separate answer sheet. Do not write your answers in your test book.

PART ①

지금 19-21번 읽기

Directions: For each question in this part, you will hear four statements about a picture in your test book. When you hear the statements, you must select the one statement that best describes what you see in the picture. Then find the number of the question on your answer sheet and mark your answer. The statements will not be printed in your test book and will be spoken only one time.

1.

2.

a b c d

3.

a b c d

PART 2

Directions: You will hear a question or statement and three responses spoken in English. They will not be printed in your test book and will be spoken only one time. Select the best response to the question or statement and mark the letter (A), (B), or (C) on your answer sheet.

4.   Mark your answer.   (A)   (B)   (C)

5.   Mark your answer.   (A)   (B)   (C)

6.   Mark your answer.   (A)   (B)   (C)

7.   Mark your answer.   (A)   (B)   (C)

8.   Mark your answer.   (A)   (B)   (C)

9.   Mark your answer.   (A)   (B)   (C)

10.   Mark your answer.   (A)   (B)   (C)

11.   Mark your answer.   (A)   (B)   (C)

12.   Mark your answer.   (A)   (B)   (C)

Directions: You will hear some conversations between two or more people. You will be asked to answer three questions about what the speakers say in each conversation. Select the best response to each question and mark the letter (A), (B), (C), or (D) on your answer sheet. The conversations will not be printed in your test book and will be spoken only one time.

13. What will happen on Monday?

(A) Some landscaping work will begin.
(B) A news conference will take place.
(C) Some clients will visit the company.
(D) An internship period will start.

14. What did the woman forget to do?

(A) Revise a schedule
(B) Seek out some volunteers
(C) Update a list of contacts
(D) Serve refreshments

15. What does the man say is available?

(A) Some notepads
(B) Cleaning products
(C) Customized clothing
(D) New flooring

---

16. What are the speakers mainly talking about?

(A) Creating a product catalog
(B) Ordering some visitor badges
(C) Updating a company's Web site
(D) Organizing a welcome reception

17. What problem does the woman notice?

(A) A report has not been filed.
(B) An identification badge is malfunctioning.
(C) A telephone number has been omitted.
(D) A name has been incorrectly spelled.

18. Why does the woman say, "It's easy to miss"?

(A) To express her understanding
(B) To clarify her responsibilities in a project
(C) To detail the steps involved in a process
(D) To inform the man of a detour

Item	Quantity	Total Price
Suit jackets	7	€175
Dresses	9	€270
Scarves	11	€33
Hats	17	€38
		Order Total = €516

정답 고르고 나서 바로 22-24번 읽기

19. Where do the speakers most likely work?

(A) At a travel bureau
(B) At a theater
(C) At a clothier
(D) At a tailor's shop

20. Look at the graphic. Which quantity will be changed?

(A) 7   (B) 9
(C) 11   (D) 17

21. What does the woman say she will do next?

(A) Hang some light fixtures
(B) Apply paint to the ceiling
(C) Sanitize a piece of equipment
(D) Take measurements of the actors

PART **4**

Directions: You will hear some talks given by a single speaker. You will be asked to answer three questions about what the speaker says in each talk. Select the best response to each question and mark the letter (A), (B), (C), or (D) on your answer sheet. The talks will not be printed in your test book and will be spoken only one time.

22. Where is the talk taking place?

(A) At an art museum
(B) At a construction site
(C) At a hotel
(D) At a power plant

23. Who most likely are the listeners?

(A) Architects
(B) Engineering students
(C) Hoteliers
(D) Event coordinators

24. What is mentioned about the materials used?

(A) They are manufactured locally.
(B) They are reasonably priced.
(C) They are environmentally friendly.
(D) They are hard to come by.

25. What industry does the speaker work in?

(A) Publishing
(B) Paper production
(C) Advertising
(D) Food service

26. Why does the speaker say, "It isn't what I was expecting"?

(A) To explain the exceptional nature of a project.
(B) To express disapproval for a design
(C) To suggest that a project's deadline be adjusted
(D) To indicate surprise at a surge in sales

27. What does the speaker suggest the listener do?

(A) Seek career advancement
(B) Organize a press conference
(C) Take some time off
(D) Consult with a colleague

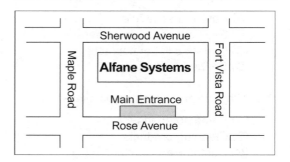

28. What will take place tomorrow morning?

(A) A road improvement project
(B) A competition
(C) A street performance
(D) An employee training session

29. Look at the graphic. Which street will be closed?

(A) Sherwood Avenue
(B) Fort Vista Road
(C) Rose Avenue
(D) Maple Road

30. What does the speaker suggest?

(A) Arriving at the workplace in the afternoon
(B) Attending a corporate function
(C) Exploring certain study materials
(D) Allowing extra time for travel

Day

10

●● 장면을 상상하면서 큰 소리로 여러 번 따라 읽으세요.

유형 88 무언가가 열려 있는 장면 open 10_01

어휘 overhead storage compartment (비행기, 기차의) 상부 짐칸 umbrella 우산, 파라솔 arched 아치 모양의 opening 통로, 틈, 구멍 patio 테라스

Some balcony doors have been opened. 발코니 문이 열려 있다.

Some people have opened their umbrellas. 사람들이 우산을 펼쳤다.

Some overhead storage compartments are open. 상부 짐칸이 열려 있다.

A drawer has been left open. 서랍이 열려 있다.

There's an open umbrella over a dining area. 식사 공간 위로 파라솔이 펼쳐져 있다.

A building has arched openings. 건물에 아치 모양의 통로가 있다. ————

(cf.) She's opening a package. 소포를 열고 있다.

(cf.) Patio[Tabletop] umbrellas have been closed. 테라스 파라솔들이 접혀 있다.

(cf.) The blinds are drawn. 블라인드가 닫혀 있다.

유형 89 자리가 차 있거나 비어 있는 장면
자리가 차 있을 때 occupied
비어 있을 때 unoccupied, empty, vacant, available 10_02

어휘 occupied 사용 중인 workstation (한 사람의) 작업 공간[자리] unoccupied 비어 있는 vacant 비어 있는 hanger 옷걸이 intersection 교차로 deserted 텅 빈, 인적이 없는

Most of the tables are occupied. 대부분의 테이블이 차 있다.

The parking lot is fully occupied. 주차장이 꽉 차 있다.

A workstation is unoccupied. 사무실 자리가 비어 있다.

A picnic area is empty. 피크닉 구역이 비어 있다.

Seating space is vacant beside the man. 남자 옆에 앉을 자리가 비어 있다.

Some hangers are available for use. 옷걸이 몇 개가 이용할 수 있게 비어 있다.

* 어떤 공간에 사람이 아무도 없을 때는 deserted가 사용되기도 한다.

The intersection is deserted. 교차로가 텅 비어 있다.

유형 90 둘러싸여 있는 장면 surround, border 🎧 10_03

어휘 railing 난간 surround 둘러싸다, 에워싸다 border ~의 가장자리를 이루다, ~을 둘러싸다 a body of water (바다, 강, 호수의) 수역
parkway 공원 도로 (공원 안의 승용차 전용 도로) board ~에 판자를 대다, ~을 판자로 둘러싸다

A railing surrounds the top deck. 난간이 위층 갑판을 둘러싸고 있다.
Railings border a body of water. 난간이 수역을[호수를] 둘러싸고 있다.

cf. A wall borders a walking path. 산책로 가장자리에 벽이 세워져 있다.
cf. The parkway is boarded by a wall. 공원 도로 가장자리에 판자벽이 세워져 있다.

유형 91 덮여 있는 장면 cover 🎧 10_04

어휘 tablecloth 식탁보 partially 부분적으로 rug 깔개 plastic sheet 비닐 시트 frame (건물의) 뼈대 rear window (자동차의) 뒷창문

The tables are covered with tablecloths. 테이블들이 식탁보로 덮여 있다.
The floor is partially covered by a rug. 바닥 일부분이 깔개로 덮여 있다.
Plastic sheets cover a building frame. 비닐 시트가 건물 뼈대를 덮고 있다. (비닐하우스)
Leaves are covering a car's rear window. 나뭇잎들이 자동차 뒷창문을 덮고 있다.

유형 92 구역이 나뉘어 있는 장면 divide, separate 🎧 10_05

어휘 stairway 계단 handrail 난간 partition 칸막이 lawn 잔디밭 walkway 통로, 보도 artifact (인공) 유물 rope off ~에 밧줄[로프]을
쳐서 차단하다 link 연결하다

A stairway is divided by a handrail. 계단이 난간으로 나누어져 있다.
Two workstations are separated by a partition. 두 자리가 칸막이로 분리되어 있다.
A lawn separates two walkways. 잔디밭이 두 개의 통로를 가르고 있다.

An artifact has been roped off. 유물이 밧줄로 차단되어 있다.
cf. The boats are linked together by a rope. 배들이 밧줄로 한데 연결되어 있다.
cf. The train cars are connected. 기차의 객차들이 연결되어 있다.

유형 93   사물이 거울, 물 등에 반사되는 장면 reflect(ion)

 10_06

어휘 scenery 경치, 풍경

The scenery is reflected on the surface of the water. 경치가 물 표면에 비치고 있다.

A woman is looking at her reflection in a mirror. 거울에 비친 자기 모습을 보고 있다.

유형 94   자연 경관을 묘사하는 문장

10_07

어휘 pot 화분 plant 심다; (식물로) 덮다, 가꾸다 weed 잡초 vine 포도나무, 덩굴 crop 농작물 in bloom[blooming] 꽃이 활짝 핀[만발한] rocky 바위투성이의, 돌투성이의 stream 흘러나오다 at the rear of ~ 뒤쪽에 faucet 수도꼭지 tap water 수돗물

Some bushes are being planted. 관목을 심고 있다.

Small trees have been planted in individual pots. 각각의 화분에 작은 나무들이 심겨 있다.

A garden has been planted outside of a building. 건물 바깥에 정원이 가꾸어져 있다.

A tree is growing against the building. 나무가 건물에 붙어서 자라고 있다.

Some weeds are growing next to a wall. 잡초가 담벼락 옆에서 자라고 있다.

Fruit is growing on a vine. 과일(포도)이 덩굴에서 자라고 있다.

Crops are growing in a field. 농작물이 들판에서 자라고 있다.

The trees are full of leaves. 나무에 잎이 무성하다.

Trees have lost their leaves. 나무에서 잎이 떨어져 있다.

Some leaves have fallen from the trees. 나무에서 잎이 떨어져 있다.

Flowers are in bloom around the building. 건물 주변에 꽃이 활짝 피어 있다.

The pots are filled with blooming plants. 화분들이 꽃이 활짝 핀 식물로 가득 차 있다.

The landscape in this area is dry and rocky. 이 지역의 풍경은 건조하고 돌이 많다.

Sunlight is streaming through the clouds. 구름 사이로 햇빛이 흘러나오고 있다.

Light is coming from the window at the rear of the room. 방 뒤편 창문으로 빛이 들어오고 있다.

Water is flowing from an outdoor faucet. 야외 수도꼭지에서 물이 흘러나오고 있다.

Tap water is flowing into a sink. 물이 싱크대로 흘러 들어가고 있다.

The water is very calm. 물이 매우 잔잔하다.

유형 95 · 조명이 켜져 있는 장면

10_08

어휘 illuminate (~에 불을) 비추다

Some lights have been turned on. 조명이 켜져 있다.

A sitting area is illuminated by floor lamps. 플로어 스탠드가 휴식 공간을 비추고 있다.

유형 96 · 그늘이나 그림자가 드리워진 장면

10_09

어휘 shade 그늘; 그늘지게 하다, (빛이나 열로부터) 가리다 cast (그림자를) 드리우다 shield 보호하다, 가리다 vendor 행상인, 노점상
shelter 보호하다, 지키다

Some trees are shading a walkway. 나무들이 통로에 그늘을 드리우고 있다.

Some trees are providing shade for a picnic area. 나무들이 피크닉 구역에 그늘을 제공하고 있다.

The chairs are shaded by umbrellas. 의자들이 파라솔에 가려져 있다.

A motorcycle is casting a shadow. 오토바이가 그림자를 드리우고 있다.

Shadows are being cast on the sand. 모래 위에 그림자가 드리워져 있다.

A hat is shielding a vendor's face from the sun.

모자가 상인의 얼굴을 햇빛으로부터 가려주고 있다.

Some shoppers are sheltered by an umbrella.

쇼핑객들이 파라솔 아래에 있다.

유형 97 · 모양을 나타내는 형용사

10_10

어휘 clock face 시계 문자판 striped 줄무늬가 있는 centerpiece (테이블 중앙의) 장식물 floral 꽃으로 만든, 꽃무늬의

The clock faces are round. 시계 문자판이 둥글다.

The table has a square base. 테이블 받침대가 사각형이다.

Some of the hats are striped. 모자 몇 개에 줄무늬가 있다.

The centerpiece is floral. 식탁 가운데 장식물이 꽃으로 만들어져 있다.

어휘 globe 지구본 prop 기대어 세우다

One of the buildings is larger than all of the others. 건물들 중 하나가 다른 것들보다 더 크다.

The globes are different sizes. 지구본들의 크기가 다르다.

Ladders of various heights are propped up against the building.
다양한 높이의 사다리가 건물에 기대어 있다.

The buildings are built in a similar style. 건물들이 유사한 양식으로 지어져 있다.

There are different styles of railings on the balconies. 발코니에 서로 다른 모양의 난간들이 있다.

Exercise 🎧 10_12

📄 Workbook p.127   ✏️ 정답 및 해설 p.144

1.

[a] [b] [c] [d]

2.

[a] [b] [c] [d]

Who / Which 의문문

Part 2에서 가장 쉬운 유형이다. 정답 패턴을 잘 기억해 두고, 고난도 문제를 대비한 훈련도 철저히 해서 한 문제도 틀리지 않도록 해 보자.

1. Who 의문문의 정답 패턴 ← 90%는 ①과 ②로 출제된다

① 사람 이름
② 직함, 신분 - manager, director, accountant 등
③ 관계 - colleague, client, father, sister 등
④ Someone from[in]으로 시작하는 문장(매우 자주), anyone, no one, nobody가 들어 있는 문장
⑤ 회사 이름, 부서 이름

🎯 기출 예제   🎧 10_14

Q. Who should write the press release?
A. Michael can take care of that.

보도 자료를 누가 써야 할까요?
⋙ 그건 마이클이 맡아서 할 수 있어요.

Q. Who's going to stock the shelves in Aisle three?
A. The overnight workers are supposed to do it.

3번 통로의 선반들은 누가 채울 건가요?
⋙ 야간 근무자들이 하기로 되어 있습니다.

Q. Who was that woman I saw with Mr. Hall?
A. I think she's our new colleague.

Mr. Hall과 함께 있었던 그 여자는 누구였나요?
⋙ 그녀가 우리의 새 동료인 것 같은데요.

Q. Who's the new public relations manager?
A. Someone from the London branch.

새 홍보부장은 누구인가요?
⋙ 런던 지사에서 온 사람이요.

Q. Who's supposed to attend the training workshop?
A. Anyone who's interested.

교육 워크숍에는 누가 참석하게 되어 있죠?
⋙ 관심 있는 사람은 누구든지요.

Q. Who's developing the new processing equipment?
A. The Voltrin Engineering Company.

새 가공 장비는 누가 개발하고 있나요?
⋙ Voltrin Engineering 사(社)요.

Q. Who do I submit the reimbursement request form to?

A. The payroll department.

환급 신청서는 누구에게 제출합니까?

>>> 경리부요.

Q. Who supplies your copy paper?

A. Check with the office manager.

당신들의 복사용지는 누가 공급합니까?

>>> 사무실 매니저에게 확인해 보세요.

Q. Who is attending the sales conference in Montreal?

A. It hasn't been decided yet.

몬트리올에서 하는 영업 회의에는 누가 참석합니까?

>>> 아직 결정되지 않았습니다.

2. Which 의문문의 정답 패턴

① (The) one(s)이 들리면 무조건 정답!

② Which 바로 뒤에 붙는 명사만 알아들으면 해결할 수 있다.

🎯 **기출 예제**　　　　　🎧 10_15

Q. Which spaces are designated for visitor parking?

A. The ones with yellow signs.

어느 공간이 방문객 주차장으로 지정되어 있나요?

>>> 노란 표지판이 있는 곳들이요.

Q. Which water pipe comes out of the kitchen sink?

A. The grey plastic one.

주방 싱크대에서 어느 수도관이 나오죠?

>>> 회색 플라스틱 관이요.

Q. Which attendees are missing from the guest list?

A. The new hires still have to be added.

어느 참석자가 초대 손님 명단에서 빠졌나요?

>>> 아직 신입직원들을 추가해야 합니다.

Q. Which client did you meet with this morning?

A. The Glendale Company representative.

오늘 오전에 어느 고객을 만나셨나요?

>>> Glendale 사(社) 대표요.

Q. Which of these paint colors would look best in the hallway?

A. My preference is the yellow.

이 페인트 색상 중 어느 것이 복도에 가장 잘 어울릴까요?

>>> 제가 선호하는 건 노란색이에요.

Q. Which hotel did you stay at?

A. I can't recall the name.

어느 호텔에 묵으셨나요?

>>> 이름이 기억이 안 나네요.

3. 간접 의문문

일반 의문문 중 중간에 의문사가 들어 있는 간접 의문문이 출제될 수 있다. 의문사를 놓치지 않아야 문제를 해결할 수 있다.

Q. I haven't heard who the board chose as a chairperson.

이사회가 의장으로 누구를 선택했는지 듣지 못했어요.

A. I believe it was Mr. Peterson.

≫≫ Mr. Peterson일 겁니다.

Q. Have you decided which laptop computer to buy?

어느 노트북 컴퓨터를 살지 결정하셨나요?

A. Yes, the one on the left seems quite good.

≫≫ 네, 왼쪽에 있는 게 꽤 좋아 보이는군요.

Q. Do you know which customer ordered the pasta dish?

어느 손님이 파스타 요리를 주문했는지 아세요?

A. The woman at table three.

≫≫ 3번 테이블의 여자분이요.

Q. Could you tell me where I can find Room thirty-five?

35호실을 어디서 찾을 수 있는지 말씀해 주시겠어요?

A. It's on the third floor at the end of the hall.

≫≫ 3층 복도 끝에 있어요.

Q. Do you know when the new product demonstration begins?

신제품 시연회가 언제 시작되는지 아시나요?

A. In about thirty minutes.

≫≫ 한 30분 후에요.

Q. Do you know how to get to the movie theater?

극장까지 어떻게 가는지 아세요?

A. The 605 bus goes straight there.

≫≫ 605번 버스가 그리로 곧장 갑니다.

Q. Can you show me how to submit a tech help ticket?

기술 지원 신청서 제출하는 법을 알려주시겠어요?

A. Let me send you the link.

≫≫ 링크를 보내 드릴게요.

Q. Do you know why Mr. Cruz is coming tomorrow?

Mr. Cruz가 내일 왜 오는지 아세요?

A. I'll ask Jane about that.

≫≫ 그건 Jane에게 물어볼게요.

📑 Workbook p.128   ✏️ 정답 및 해설 p.144

1. (A)   (B)   (C)   6. (A)   (B)   (C)

2. (A)   (B)   (C)   7. (A)   (B)   (C)

3. (A)   (B)   (C)   8. (A)   (B)   (C)

4. (A)   (B)   (C)   9. (A)   (B)   (C)

5. (A)   (B)   (C)   10. (A)   (B)   (C)

PART 3&4

그래픽 문제 2

지난 시간에 이어 고난도 그래픽 문제를 더 연습해서 LC 만점에 도전해 보자.

Exercise　　　　　🎧 10_19

📖 Workbook p.130　　✏️ 정답 및 해설 p.147

PART 3

Office Directory
1st FL: OE Furniture Company
2nd FL: Gold Coast Imagination, Inc.
3rd FL: Batista Construction
4th FL: Brown & Sons

1. Who most likely are the speakers?

(A) Carpet weavers

(B) Hair stylists

(C) Cleaning staff

(D) Construction workers

2. Look at the graphic. Where is the man currently working?

(A) On the first floor

(B) On the second floor

(C) On the third floor

(D) On the fourth floor

3. What are the speakers probably going to do next?

(A) Rearrange a table

(B) Repair a machine

(C) Review some plans

(D) Conduct a conference call

PART 4

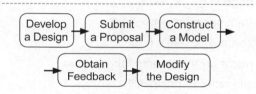

4. What does the speaker say about the company's kitchen appliances?

(A) They sold well in the previous quarter.

(B) They achieved success in a design contest.

(C) They are priced lower than competing products.

(D) They were featured in a trade magazine.

5. Look at the graphic. According to the speaker, which step was recently added?

(A) Submit a proposal

(B) Construct a model

(C) Obtain feedback

(D) Modify the Design

6. What concern does the speaker mention?

(A) Raw materials are in short supply.

(B) More appliances are being purchased online.

(C) Employees' time has been used inefficiently.

(D) A production deadline has been adjusted.

 10_21

●● Actual Test를 풀기 전에 이 단어들을 따라 읽으며 암기하자.

pick up ~를 차로 데리러 가다

exhibit 작품을 전시하다, 전시회를 열다

supplier 공급(업)자, 공급업체

directions 길 안내

around the corner (시간적으로) 아주 가까이, 임박하여

good to go 준비가 다 된

transportation 교통수단, 차량

sort out ~을 처리하다

make arrangements for ~을 준비하다

slip one's mind 잊어버리다

incomplete 불완전한, 미완성의

handcrafted 수공예품인

be fond of ~을 좋아하다

give away ~을 선물로 주다

on schedule 예정대로

encounter 맞닥뜨리다

the rest 나머지

run 운행하다

scrutinize 세심히 살피다

gratitude 감사, 고마움

management 경영진

reward 보상하다

resources 재원, 자금

tie up (돈을 쉽게 쓸 수 없도록) 묶어 두다

elsewhere 다른 곳에서

identify 찾다, 발견하다

implement 시행하다

set aside (돈, 시간을) 따로 떼어 두다

individually 개별적으로, 각각 따로

departmental 부서의

reserve 따로 남겨[떼어] 두다

conduct 실시하다, 수행하다

one-on-one 일대일의

rank (등급, 순위를) 매기다

take note of ~에 주목하다

rapid 빠른

surpass 능가하다, 뛰어넘다

attribute A to B A를 B의 결과로[덕분으로] 보다

surge 급증, 급등

innovative 획기적인

try out ~을 시험적으로 사용해 보다

existing 기존의

adopt 채택하다

strategy 전략

Actual Test

PART 1	1-3
PART 2	4-12
PART 3	13-21
PART 4	22-30

Part 3, 4 '미리 잘 읽기' 전략

LC Directions 시간:	16-18번 읽기
Part 1 Directions 시간:	19-21번 읽기
Part 2 Directions 시간:	28-30번 읽기
Part 3 Directions 시간:	13-15번 읽기
19-21번 문제 읽어주는 시간:	22-24번 읽기
Part 4 Directions 시간:	25-27번 읽기

LISTENING TEST

지금 16-18번 읽기

In the Listening test, you will be asked to demonstrate how well you understand spoken English. The entire Listening test will last approximately 45 minutes. There are four parts, and directions are given for each part. You must mark your answers on the separate answer sheet. Do not write your answers in your test book.

PART 1

지금 19-21번 읽기

Directions: For each question in this part, you will hear four statements about a picture in your test book. When you hear the statements, you must select the one statement that best describes what you see in the picture. Then find the number of the question on your answer sheet and mark your answer. The statements will not be printed in your test book and will be spoken only one time.

1.

ⓐ　ⓑ　ⓒ　ⓓ

3.

ⓐ　ⓑ　ⓒ　ⓓ

2.

ⓐ　ⓑ　ⓒ　ⓓ

Directions: You will hear a question or statement and three responses spoken in English. They will not be printed in your test book and will be spoken only one time. Select the best response to the question or statement and mark the letter (A), (B), or (C) on your answer sheet.

4.   Mark your answer.   (A)   (B)   (C)

5.   Mark your answer.   (A)   (B)   (C)

6.   Mark your answer.   (A)   (B)   (C)

7.   Mark your answer.   (A)   (B)   (C)

8.   Mark your answer.   (A)   (B)   (C)

9.   Mark your answer.   (A)   (B)   (C)

10. Mark your answer.   (A)   (B)   (C)

11. Mark your answer.   (A)   (B)   (C)

12. Mark your answer.   (A)   (B)   (C)

Directions: You will hear some conversations between two or more people. You will be asked to answer three questions about what the speakers say in each conversation. Select the best response to each question and mark the letter (A), (B), (C), or (D) on your answer sheet. The conversations will not be printed in your test book and will be spoken only one time.

13. What are the speakers mainly discussing?

(A) Strategies for minimizing a travel budget
(B) Attractions in Edmonton
(C) Potential venues for a conference
(D) Preparations for an upcoming business trip

14. What problem do the speakers have?

(A) Their business cards are yet to be delivered.
(B) Their reservations are for the incorrect dates.
(C) Their transportation arrangements are incomplete.
(D) Their client in Edmonton is currently unavailable

15. What does the woman suggest they do?

(A) Cancel an order
(B) Communicate with a hotel
(C) Arrange to deliver a speech
(D) Defer making a decision

16. What does the woman say is special about the scarves?

(A) They are made by hand.
(B) They are exported overseas.
(C) They are made from velvet.
(D) They are sold only in designated stores.

17. What does man imply when he says, "I get paid only once a month"?

(A) He used to be paid more frequently.
(B) He lacks the funds to make a purchase.

(C) He has to collect his paycheck today.
(D) He is planning to ask for a pay increase.

18. Why does the woman say she no longer wears her scarf?

(A) She misplaced it.
(B) She tore it.
(C) She returned it.
(D) She gave it away.

Name	Comment
Kevin Lee	Unclean seating
Jean Villiers	No price reduction
Anthony Choi	Web site inaccessible
Robin Jarvela	Running behind schedule

정답 고르고 나서 바로 22-24번 읽기

19. Where do the speakers most likely work?

(A) At a cargo company
(B) At a car manufacturer
(C) At a taxi service company
(D) At an airport

20. Look at the graphic. Which customer are the speakers discussing?

(A) Kevin Lee
(B) Jean Villiers
(C) Anthony Choi
(D) Robin Jarvela

21. What will the speakers do next?

(A) Examine fuel prices
(B) Scrutinize customer feedback
(C) Revise staffing schedules
(D) Organize training sessions

Directions: You will hear some talks given by a single speaker. You will be asked to answer three questions about what the speaker says in each talk. Select the best response to each question and mark the letter (A), (B), (C), or (D) on your answer sheet. The talks will not be printed in your test book and will be spoken only one time.

22. Who are the listeners?

(A) Company stakeholders
(B) Sales associates
(C) Marketing experts
(D) Software developers

23. Why does the speaker thank the listeners?

(A) For working extended hours
(B) For organizing a fundraiser
(C) For decreasing expenditures
(D) For assisting clients

24. What will the listeners receive?

(A) An invitation to a banquet
(B) Some extra time off work
(C) Some additional money
(D) A state-of-the-art device

---

25. What does the speaker imply when she says, "Who knows when that will be"?

(A) She is unable to comprehend a demand.
(B) She expects her staff to quicken their pace.
(C) She is uncertain when a project will be completed.
(D) She wants to receive feedback from the audience.

26. What is the topic of the meeting?

(A) Hiring an accountant
(B) Promoting a product
(C) Lowering costs
(D) Planning a trade fair

27. What does the speaker say she will reserve time to do?

(A) Conduct one-on-one meetings
(B) Analyze data from a questionnaire
(C) Contact potential clients
(D) Draft a written contract

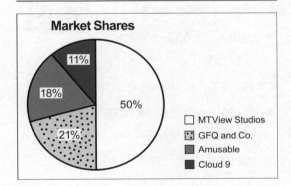

Market Shares

MTView Studios
GFQ and Co.
Amusable
Cloud 9

28. What industry does the speaker work in?

(A) Interior design
(B) News reporting
(C) Film production
(D) Game development

29. Look at the graphic. What company does the speaker work for?

(A) MTView Studios
(B) GFQ and Co.
(C) Amusable
(D) Cloud 9

30. According to the speaker, what will the company do in the next quarter?

(A) Restructure a division
(B) Decrease production costs
(C) Negotiate a contract
(D) Adopt a new business strategy

DAY별 음원 듣기

- 본 책 각 DAY 첫 페이지 왼쪽 상단에 있는 QR코드로 접속하면
  DAY별 전체 음원을 바로 들을 수 있습니다.

 홈페이지에서 전체 음원 다운받기

스마트폰으로 접속하기

➜ 오른쪽 QR 코드로 접속하기

➜ 오른쪽 상단의 🔵를 클릭하여
   회원 가입하기

➜ QR 코드로 다시 접속하여 로그인 하기

➜ 게시판이 나오고 Link 아래 [**토익마법 2주의
   기적 990LC.zip**] 버튼 클릭하기

➜ 전체 음원 다운로드 하기

PC로 접속하기

➜ 성안당 홈페이지 접속하기: https://cyber.co.kr

➜ 우측 상단의 [자료실] 클릭하기

➜ 중간에 [외국어자료실] 클릭하기

➜ 게시판의 [토익마법 2주의 기적 990 LC 음원]
   클릭하기

➜ 내용이 나오면 오른쪽 상단의 [회원가입] 후
   다시 접속하기

➜ Link에 있는 음원 다운로드 하기

 저자 선생님과 함께 공부하기

- 우측 QR코드로 접속해서 저자 선생님이 올려 주신 부가학습 자료와 질문 코너를
  이용해 보세요.
- 단어 시험지, 추가 어휘 문제 등을 다운받을 수 있습니다.
- 저자에게 질문하는 코너를 통해 교재에서 궁금했던 내용을 바로 질문하고 답변 받을
  수 있습니다.

저자
질문코너

단어시험지

청취력 향상
받아쓰기

추가
어휘 문제

▮ 이교희

2009년에 강남에서 강의를 시작하며 정기 토익에서 10회 만점을 달성했다. 가장 효율적인 문제 풀이 방식을 제시하는 깔끔한 강의로 수강생들의 호응을 얻었으며, 각종 인터넷 강의로도 수많은 수험생들과 만났다. 강사이자 저자로서 끊임 없이 축적해 온 연구의 결실을 '토익 마법－2주의 기적 990'을 통해 함께 즐겨보자.

약력

● **학원**

광주광역시 제제 외국어학원 대표 강사
파고다 외국어학원 토익 일타 강사(신촌, 종로)
현, 안산 이지어학원 토익 대표 강사

● **인터넷 강의**

ujeje.com
Cracking TOEIC
파고다스타 '이교희의 탑토익 족보공개'

● **저서**

토익 마법 2주의 기적 990 RC (2024)
토익 마법 2주의 기적 990 LC (2024)
토익 마법 2주의 기적 RC (2022)
토익 마법 2주의 기적 LC (2022)
시나공 토익 950 실전 모의고사 (2012)
파고다 외국어학원 월간 모의고사 해설

토익 마법 2주의 기적 990 LC

2024. 10. 23. 초 판 1쇄 인쇄
2024. 10. 30. 초 판 1쇄 발행

지은이 | 이교희
펴낸이 | 이종춘
펴낸곳 | BM (주)도서출판 **성안당**

주소 | 04032 서울시 마포구 양화로 127 첨단빌딩 3층(출판기획 R&D 센터)
　　　10881 경기도 파주시 문발로 112 파주 출판 문화도시(제작 및 물류)
전화 | 02) 3142-0036
　　　031) 950-6300
팩스 | 031) 955-0510
등록 | 1973. 2. 1. 제406-2005-000046호
출판사 홈페이지 | www.cyber.co.kr
ISBN | 978-89-315-5864-7 (13740)
정가 | 19,800원

이 책을 만든 사람들
책임 | 최옥현
진행 | 김은주
편집·교정 | 김은주, 김수민
영문 검수 | Thomas Giammarco
본문 디자인 | 신인남
표지 디자인 | 박원석
홍보 | 김계향, 임진성, 김주승, 최정민
국제부 | 이선민, 조혜란
마케팅 | 구본철, 차정욱, 오영일, 나진호, 강호묵
마케팅 지원 | 장상범
제작 | 김유석

■ 도서 A/S 안내

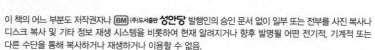

성안당에서 발행하는 모든 도서는 저자와 출판사, 그리고 독자가 함께 만들어 나갑니다.
좋은 책을 펴내기 위해 많은 노력을 기울이고 있습니다. 혹시라도 내용상의 오류나 오탈자 등이 발견되면 "좋은 책은 나라의 보배"로서 우리 모두가 함께 만들어 간다는 마음으로 연락주시기 바랍니다. 수정 보완하여 더 나은 책이 되도록 최선을 다하겠습니다.
성안당은 늘 독자 여러분들의 소중한 의견을 기다리고 있습니다. 좋은 의견을 보내주시는 분께는 성안당 쇼핑몰의 포인트(3,000포인트)를 적립해 드립니다.
잘못 만들어진 책이나 부록 등이 파손된 경우에는 교환해 드립니다.

케임브리지 대학 출판부의 베스트셀러 문법 교재 <GRAMMAR IN USE> 시리즈!

초급 Basic Grammar in use 4/e

전 세계 수백만 명의 학습자가 사용하는 영문법 교재입니다. 이 책의 구성은 스스로 공부하는 학생과 영어 수업의 필수 참고서로 적합한 교재입니다. 학습가이드를 통하여 영문법을 익히고 연습문제를 통하여 심화학습 할 수 있습니다. 쉽고 간결한 구성으로 Self-Study를 원하는 학습자와 강의용으로 사용하는 모두에게 알맞은 영어교재입니다.

❚ Book with answers and Interactive eBook 978-1-316-64673-1
❚ Book with answers 978-1-316-64674-8

초급 Basic Grammar in use 한국어판

한국의 학습자들을 위하여 간단 명료한 문법 해설과 2페이지 대면 구성으로 이루어져 있습니다. 미국식 영어를 학습하는 초급 단계의 영어 학습자들에게 꼭 필요한 문법을 가르치고 있습니다. 또한 쉽게 따라 할 수 있는 연습문제는 문법 학습을 용이하도록 도와줍니다. 본 교재는 Self-Study 또는 수업용 교재로 활용이 가능합니다.

❚ Book with answers 978-0-521-26959-9

초급 Essential Grammar in use 4/e

영어 초급 학습자를 위한 필수 문법교재 입니다. 학습가이드와 연습문제를 제공하며 Self-Study가 가능하도록 구성되어 있습니다.

❚ Book with answers and Interactive eBook 978-1-107-48053-7
❚ Book with answers 978-1-107-48055-1

중급 Grammar in use Intermediate 4/e

미국식 영어학습을 위한 중급 문법교재입니다. 간단한 설명과 명확한 예시, 이해하기 쉬운 설명과 연습으로 구성되어 Self-Study와 강의용 교재 모두 사용 가능합니다.

❚ Book with answers and interactive eBook 978-1-108-61761-1
❚ Book with answers 978-1-108-44945-8

BM (주)도서출판 성안당 | CAMBRIDGE | 도서문의 031-950-6394

중급 **Grammar in use Intermediate 한국어판**

이해하기 쉬운 문법 설명과 실제 생활에서 자주 쓰이는 예문이 특징인 \<Grammar in use Intermediate 한국어판\>은 미국 영어를 배우는 중급 수준의 학습자를 위한 문법 교재입니다. 총 142개의 Unit로 구성되어 있는 이 교재는, Unit별로 주요 문법 사항을 다루고 있으며, 각 Unit은 간단명료한 문법 설명과 연습문제가 대면 방식의 두 페이지로 구성되어 있습니다. 문법과 전반적인 영어를 공부하고 하는 사람은 물론 TOEIC, TOEFL, IELTS 등과 같은 영어능력 시험을 준비하는 학습자에게도 꼭 필요한 교재입니다.

Book with answers 978-0-521-14786-6

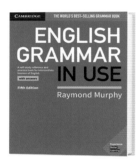

중급 **English Grammar in use 5/e**

최신판으로 중급 학습자를 위한 첫 번째 선택이며, 해당 레벨에서 필요한 모든 문법을 학습할 수 있는 교재입니다. \<IN USE\> 시리즈는 전 세계 누적 판매 1위의 영문법 교재로 사랑받고 있습니다. 145개의 Unit으로 이루어져 있으며, Study guide를 제공하여 Self-Study에 적합하며 강의용 교재로 활용할 수 있습니다.

Book with answers and Interactive eBook 978-1-108-58662-7
Book with answers 978-1-108-45765-1

고급 **Advanced Grammar in use 4/e**

영어 심화 학습자를 위한 영문법 교재입니다. Study planner를 제공하여 자율학습을 용이하게 합니다. 포괄적인 문법 범위와 친숙한 구성으로 고급레벨 학습자에게 적합합니다. 이미 학습한 언어 영역을 다시 확인할 수 있는 Grammar reminder 섹션을 제공합니다. Cambridge IELTS를 준비하는 학생들에게 이상적인 교재입니다.

Book with Online Tests and eBook 978-1-108-92021-6
eBook with Audio and Online Tests 978-1-009-36801-8

BM (주)도서출판 성안당 | CAMBRIDGE | 도서문의 031-950-6394

당신이 찾던 토익책!

LISTENING

토익마법
2주의 기적
990

워크북 & 해설집

BM (주)도서출판 성안당

DOWNLOAD SAMPLE CONTENT

www.cambridge.org/unlock

비판적 사고력을 키워 주는 스킬북, Unlock 시리즈!

Unlock 시리즈는 학업에 필요한 스킬과 언어를 강화하는 코스입니다.
초기 언어 학습부터 학문적 맥락의 비판적 사고까지 기를 수 있도록 안내합니다.

- **Critical Thinking Skills** 목표 측정과 자기 평가를 통한 비판적 사고 기술 습득
- **Video Content** 학문, 시사 및 일반 상식 등 다양한 주제의 동영상 콘텐츠로 흥미 유발
- **Cambridge English Corpus** 수십억 개의 단어로 구성된 캠브리지 코퍼스로 실생활에 쓰이는 언어를 제공하여 최신 언어 학습 가능
- **Cambridge One** 캠브리지 학습관리 플랫폼인 Cambridge One에서 추가 학습 가능
  - eBook, Class audio, Video, Digital Workbook with videos, Digital Classroom Material
  - 대체 읽기 및 듣기 자료, 통합 워크시트, 추가 읽기 및 대학 수업용 자료, 테스트

The digital resources

Powered by
Cambridge One

Presentation
Plus

eBook
with Audio
and Video

Video

Downloadable
Audio

Teacher Training
cambridge.org/training

BM (주)도서출판 성안당 | CAMBRIDGE | 도서문의 031-950-6394

LISTENING

토익마법
2주의 기적
990
WORKBOOK

BM (주)도서출판 성안당

PART 1 Exercise

🎧 **Vocabulary** 따라 읽으면서 **암기**하세요   🎧 01_17

organize 정리하다	peer into 자세히 들여다보다, 유심히 보다
cash register 금전 등록기	position 놓다, 두다
an article of clothing 의복 한 벌	rearrange 재배열하다, 재배치하다
stock (~에 상품을) 채우다, 갖추다	countertop 작업대
wrap up ~을 싸다, 포장하다	

🎧 **Dictation**

1. [M|Cn] 🎧 01_16_01

    (A) Products have been _____ a _____.

    (B) People are _____ an _____ of _____.

    (C) Store clerks are _____ a _____.

    (D) A salesperson is _____.

2. [W|Am] 🎧 01_16_02

    (A) Some scientists are _____.

    (B) A woman is _____ a piece of _____ to a man.

    (C) Some pieces of _____ on a countertop.

    (D) A piece of _____.

PART 2 Exercise

🎧 **Vocabulary** 따라 읽으면서 **암기**하세요   🎧 01_20

refile (서류 등을) 다시 철하여 정리하다	relocate 전근하다; 이동하다, 이전하다
electrician 전기 기사[기술자]	instructions 설명
power outlet 전기 콘센트	medication 약, 약물
intersection 교차로	take (약을) 먹다, 복용하다
compliment 칭찬, 찬사	diagram 도표, 도해
catering 출장 뷔페	outdated 구식의, 시대에 뒤떨어진
out of order 고장 난	be supposed to-V ~하기로 되어 있다, ~해야 한다
deserve ~을 받을 만하다[누릴 자격이 있다]	in pairs 둘씩 짝을 지어
recognition (공로 등에 대한) 인정, 표창	place of origin 원산지

1. [M | Cn] [M | Au] 🎧 01_19_01

You _____ these _____, didn't you?

(A) _____ they should be _____.

(B) I'll make the _____.

(C) At the _____ the _____.

2. [W | Br] [M | Au] 🎧 01_19_02

The _____ is _____ today, isn't he?

(A) Yes, to _____ the _____.

(B) No, the _____'s in October.

(C) The _____.

3. [M | Au] [W | Br] 🎧 01_19_03

_____ Elizabeth _____ on our proposal yet?

(A) She _____'d _____ this afternoon.

(B) Maybe at the _____.

(C) That's _____!

4. [M | Cn] [W | Am] 🎧 01_19_04

I _____ to you on Wednesday.

(A) I don't _____ 've _____.

(B) They're _____.

(C) Right _____ the _____.

5. [M | Cn] [M | Au] 🎧 01_19_05

Ms. Kim _____ three times _____!

(A) Only the _____ materials.

(B) She _____ the _____.

(C) _____ would be enough.

6. W|Br, (M|Cn) 🎧 01_19_06

The _____ about next year's budget.

(A) I _____ they _____ .

(B) She's _____ .

(C) It's _____ .

7. W|Am M|Cn 🎧 01_19_07

Dr. Rossi _____ for your _____, didn't he?

(A) He _____ .

(B) To the Prescott M_____ C_____ .

(C) I _____ .

8. W|Br M|Cn 🎧 01_19_08

_____ 's _____ on page forty-eight.

(A) Don't _____ it.

(B) Mr. Peterson _____ .

(C) OK, I'll _____ .

9. W|Br M|Au 🎧 01_19_09

_____ today, didn't we?

(A) Our _____ is _____ .

(B) The store _____ four years _____ .

(C) Yes, it was a _____ .

10. M|Cn W|Am 🎧 01_19_10

_____ can we _____ the _____ to be _____ ?

(A) Yes, you're supposed to _____ .

(B) The _____ is on the _____ .

(C) They _____ with it.

Vocabulary 따라 읽으면서 **암기**하세요 01_22

look over ~을 살펴보다	shot 사진, 장면
aerial photo 항공 사진	ID(identification) number 식별 번호
brochure 안내 책자	high-resolution 고해상도의

Dictation

Questions 1 through 3 refer to the following conversation. 01_21

[M Cn] Hi, this is Ezra Goldman from the city tourism office. Your photos were recommended to me by one of my colleagues. 've _____ your Web site, and 'd _____ _____ of the city. We'd like to _____ _____.

[W Am] Great! I have _____. Could you tell me the _____ next to the photograph?

[M Cn] Sure, it's 78231.

[W Am] OK. Um... you can go ahead and _____ _____, and then 'll _____ with the _____ - _____ of the picture.

1. Who most likely is the woman?
   (A) A photographer
   (B) A city tourism official
   (C) An airline representative
   (D) A travel journalist

2. What information does the woman request?
   (A) A cost estimate
   (B) An identification number
   (C) An mailing address
   (D) A tour itinerary

3. What does the woman say she will do?
   (A) Revise an invoice
   (B) Look over a brochure
   (C) Make a recommendation
   (D) Send a file

✚ Vocabulary 따라 읽으면서 **암기**하세요 🎧 01_24

check out ~을 살펴보다	component (구성) 요소
lower (가치·정도 등을) 낮추다, 떨어뜨리다	profitable 수익성이 있는, 이익이 많은
property 건물, 부동산	dependable 믿을[신뢰할] 수 있는
appealing 매력적인, 흥미로운	switch 전환하다, 바꾸다
concern 걱정, 우려	guarantee 보장하다, 약속하다
furnace 보일러	reliable 믿을[신뢰할] 수 있는
in good shape 상태가 좋은	competitor 경쟁자, 경쟁업체
leave A with B A를 B한 상태에 처하게 하다	take one's word for it ~의 말을 곧이곧대로 받아들이다

✚ Dictation

📝 **Questions 1 through 3** refer to the following conversation with three speakers. 🎧 01_23_01

[M|Au] Welcome, Keith and Susan. I'm so _____ you _____ to _____ and _____ the house. As I mentioned, the seller has _____ the _____ _____.

[W|Br] Yes, the _____ to us, but we do have some concerns.

[M|Cn] We're _____ about the _____ _____. Like the _____; do you know _____?

[M|Au] Yes, just last year, and _____ the _____ ___. Everything here is _____.

[M|Cn] After _____ that was _____ _____, it's quite _____ the _____ _____ to _____.

[M|Au] Well, she _____ _____. So, she was _____ _____.

1. Who most likely are Keith and Susan?
   (A) Property managers
   (B) Maintenance workers
   (C) Building inspectors
   (D) Potential home buyers

2. What are Keith and Susan concerned about?
   (A) The placement of smoke detectors
   (B) The measurement of a property
   (C) The cost of major repairs
   (D) The number of occupants

3. What is mentioned about the current owner?
   (A) She has decided to take on a new job.
   (B) She owns multiple properties.
   (C) She can recommend skilled workers.
   (D) She is available only in the afternoon.

Questions 4 through 6 refer to the following advertisement.

🎧 01_23_02

M | Cn One of _____

_____ is a _____

_____ . That's why so many customers are

switching to Chiefa Online. At Chiefa, we _____

that our Internet service is _____

_____ any of our _____ . But don't just take our

word for it. Go onto our Web site at chiefaonline.net

to _____

_____ . Join our list of satisfied customers.

---

4. What is being advertised?
   (A) A cleaning service
   (B) A computer shop
   (C) An Internet service provider
   (D) An accounting firm

5. What does the speaker emphasize about the service?
   (A) Its reliability
   (B) Its reasonable prices
   (C) Its speed
   (D) Its user-friendliness

6. According to the speaker, what is available on the Web site?
   (A) Discount codes
   (B) Promotional videos
   (C) Software applications
   (D) Customer testimonials

PART 1

🎧 01_27

Vocabulary 따라 읽으면서 **암기**하세요

put away (다 쓴 물건을) 치우다	adjust 조정하다, 조절하다
collect 받다, 수령하다	pull on (장갑을) 잡아당겨 끼다
discard 버리다	tear down (- tore - torn) (건물·담 등을) 허물다, 헐다
diner (식당의) 식사하는 사람[손님]	in the distance 먼 곳에서
address 연설(하다); ~에게 말을 걸다[하다]	draw one's attention (- drew - drawn) ~의 주목을 끌다

Dictation

1. M Cn 🎧 01_26_01

   (A) One of the women is _____.

   (B) A _____ is _____.

   (C) One of the women is _____.

   (D) Some diners are _____.

2. W Br 🎧 01_26_02

   (A) Some people are _____.

   (B) A speaker is _____.

   (C) A projector _____.

   (D) Documents _____ to the attendees.

3. M Cn 🎧 01_26_03

   (A) Some paintings _____.

   (B) One of the women is _____.

   (C) A _____ in the distance.

   (D) Some _____ have _____.

Vocabulary 따라 읽으면서 **암기**하세요 🎧 01_28

dining car (기차의) 식당차
organize 정리하다
in alphabetical order 알파벳순으로
renewable 재생 가능한

let *sb* in ~를 들어오게 하다
contractor 하청업자, 도급업자
initial 성명의 첫 글자[머리글자]를 표시하다
with + N + 형용사[분사] ~가 ~인 채로

Dictation

4. [W | Br] [M | Cn] 🎧 01_26_04

_____ the _____?
(A) No, _____.
(B) I _____ in the _____.
(C) You can _____.

5. [M | Au] [W | Am] 🎧 01_26_05

Did you _____ for the printer?
(A) _____ dollars.
(B) They're _____ now.
(C) Thirty _____.

6. [M | Cn] [W | Br] 🎧 01_26_06

Please _____ when you're _____ the _____.
(A) Sure, ____'ll _____ minutes.
(B) For the new _____.
(C) No, they're _____ in _____.

7. [M | Au] [W | Am] 🎧 01_26_07

_____ Ms. Freeman's _____ this _____?
(A) _____, __'ll _____ her to do it.
(B) The _____.
(C) _____ in the _____.

8. [W|Am] [M|Cn] 🎧 01_26_08

_____ will the _____ the office building?

(A) The _____ can _____.

(B) They're _____ the _____.

(C) The work will be _____.

9. [M|Cn] [W|Br] 🎧 01_26_09

Why is the _____ this afternoon?

(A) I _____ you _____ to come.

(B) You have to _____.

(C) At least _____.

10. [M|Cn] [M|Au] 🎧 01_26_10

Do you _____ for a _____?

(A) Don't you _____?

(B) I _____.

(C) _____ my ball?

11. [W|Br] [W|Am] 🎧 01_26_11

_____ laptop _____ already _____?

(A) I _____ new _____ set.

(B) No, you have to _____.

(C) _____ usually _____ Tuesdays.

12. [W|Br] [M|Au] 🎧 01_26_12

Don't you want to _____ with you?

(A) No problem, ___'ll _____.

(B) _____ a break.

(C) No, I _____.

Vocabulary 따라 읽으면서 **암기**하세요 🎧 01_29

interoffice 사내의	browse 둘러보다
be willing to-V ~할 의향이 있다	staff forum (온라인) 직원 토론 게시판
typo 오타	upcoming 다가오는, 곧 있을
content 내용	rent 빌리다
draft (글, 원고의) 초고, 초안	conference room 회의실
revision 수정, 정정	post 게시하다
vaccination 예방 접종	presenter 발표자
make it (시간 맞춰) 가다	

 Questions 13 through 15 refer to the following conversation. 🎧 01_26_13

M|Au Hello. Kenneth Cook speaking.

W|Am This is Gina Masterson. I'm calling _____ _____ I've ____ my research _____. You should have it by the end of the day. I _____ you're still _____ for me.

M|Au Absolutely! I'll be _____ on business over the next few days, but I'll _____ _____. I've also _____ your _____ additional _____ _____.

W|Am Thank you very much. Don't worry about the _____. The report will be sent to an editor. But please _____ some _____. It's just the _____ and I'm going to _____ _____. I'm really looking forward to your feedback.

13. What is the purpose of Gina's call to Kenneth?
(A) To inform him she is going out of town
(B) To urge him to pay for further research
(C) To thank him for meeting with her
(D) To notify him she mailed a report to him

14. What department does Gina most likely work in?
(A) Corporate archive
(B) Sales
(C) Research
(D) Public relations

15. What does Gina plan to do?
(A) Make revisions to her report
(B) Send Kenneth more money
(C) Take some time off work
(D) Give Kenneth some advice

[W | Br] Thank you for calling Hamilton M_____
C_____. This is Natalie speaking. How can I help you?
[M | Cn] Hello, my name is Jeffrey Hines. I'm planning
to _____ and
I have to get some _____. Do you have _____
_____ at your office?
[W | Br] I think we can find time for you, Mr. Hines.
Let me check our calendar. Well, it looks like we
have _____ next Monday. Does
_____?
[M | Cn] I work until four o'clock on Mondays.
[W | Br] OK, how about four-thirty? Will you be able
to _____ by that time?
[M | Cn] That'll _____. Thanks and see
you then.

16. Where does the woman work?
    (A) At an accounting firm
    (B) At a travel agency
    (C) At a health clinic
    (D) At a beauty salon

17. What does the man say he will be
    doing next month?
    (A) Leading a seminar
    (B) Starting to work at a different
        company
    (C) Taking a holiday overseas
    (D) Writing a handbook for tourists

18. What does the man imply when he
    says, "I work until four o'clock on
    Mondays"?
    (A) He desires to be working full-
        time.
    (B) He needs a later appointment.
    (C) He would rather come in during
        the weekend.
    (D) He is scheduled to leave early
        for an event.

[M | Cn] Hi, Yolanda. I was testing a company
computer _____ my _____, and _____
_____ online staff forum, and ...
[W | Br] Ah, how does it look?
[M | Cn] It looks great. And it _____ there's
a lot of _____.
Will we need additional space? We could _____
_____, or ...
[W | Br] We'll be all right. I'm planning to _____
digital _____ of all the presentations _____
_____.
[M | Cn] Good idea.
[W | Br] Oh, and ... we've made a switch. The _____
_____ the _____ and _____
_____. So the day's _____ will be ...
Sales Techniques. We _____ change because
Ms. Park, the _____, has to _____
lunch.

Seminar Schedule

Topic	Time
Leadership	10 - 11 A.M.
Teamwork	11 A.M. - Noon
LUNCH	Noon - 1 P.M.
Market Trends	1 - 2 P.M.
Sales Techniques	2 - 3 P.M.

19. Where most likely is the conversation
    taking place?
    (A) At an electronics shop
    (B) At a company office
    (C) At a conference room
    (D) At a public park

20. What does the woman plan to do?
    (A) Give a keynote presentation
    (B) Rent a larger venue
    (C) Post videos online
    (D) Review a marketing proposal

21. Look at the graphic. According to the
    woman, which session will now be
    held last?
    (A) Leadership
    (B) Teamwork
    (C) Market Trends
    (D) Sales Techniques

Vocabulary 따라 읽으면서 **암기**하세요 01_30

alike (앞에 언급한 두 사람[사물]이) 둘 다, 똑같이	**exterior** 외부의
view 보다	**obtain** 입수하다, 획득하다
exhibit 전람회, 전시회	**employee ID badge** 사원증
unveil 처음 공개하다	**exclusively** 독점적으로, 오로지 (~만)
feature 특별히 포함하다	**monitor** 모니터하다, 감시하다
a wide selection of 다양하게 엄선해 놓은	**newsletter** 소식지, 회보
on display 전시된, 진열된	**make sure to-V** 반드시 ~하도록 하다
through (~을 포함하여) ~까지	**feel free to-V** 자유롭게[마음 놓고] ~하다
dedication 전념, 헌신	**department head** 부서장
preservation 보존, 보호, 유지	**cover** 다루다
architect 건축가	**go over** ~을 점검하다, 검토하다
power 동력을 공급하다, 작동시키다	**administrative** 관리의, 행정의
solar panel 태양 전지판	**halfway through** (기간, 행사의) 중간쯤에
board of directors 이사회	**it has come to one's attention that** ~가 ~을 알게 되었다
present 제시하다, 제출하다	**so (that) + S + can[may/will] + V** ~하기 위해서

 Questions 22 through 24 refer to the following news report. 01_26_16

M | Au Today, _____
_____ gathered at the Carrington Center to _____ the
latest _____ that was _____ this morning.
The exhibit, _____ T _____ P _____ International E_____,
_____ a _____ of _____
and will be on display through the end of the month.
As most of you are aware, the Carrington Center is
_____ its _____ to _____
_____. They recently _____
Jay Patel to ____ a new visitors' center _____
_____ that the new building be _____
_____. The
center's board of directors was _____ with
the _____ by Mr. Patel, stating that his
designs were the _____ they had seen.

22. Why did people gather at the Carrington Center this morning?
(A) To visit a plant exhibit
(B) To attend an open-air concert
(C) To enroll in a gardening class
(D) To listen to an art lecture

23. What is said about the new building?
(A) It is bordered by water.
(B) It makes use of solar energy.
(C) It has a rooftop café.
(D) It has a sculpture garden.

24. Why was Jay Patel chosen?
(A) He put forth the lowest bid.
(B) He presented the best designs.
(C) He can commence immediately.
(D) He resides in the area.

W | Br Attention, Keller Grace employees. Starting next month, all of the _____ will _____ new _____. Everyone _____ a new, um, digital key. _____ your _____ _____ so the guard can make a new key for you. The new keys will be _____ your employee ID, _____ us to _____ the _____ and _____ in the building. There's _____ available about the upcoming security changes _____, so make sure to check that out. _____ _____ it, feel free to _____ _____ any questions you may have. Thanks.

25. What are listeners asked to provide?
  (A) A monthly charge
  (B) A production schedule
  (C) A computer access code
  (D) A form of identification

26. What special feature is mentioned about a new digital key?
  (A) It can unlock all the building doors.
  (B) It is simple to find a replacement for it.
  (C) It can track who enters a building.
  (D) It is compatible with an older style of lock.

27. What does the speaker mean when she says, "Make sure to check that out"?
  (A) Employees should keep a door locked.
  (B) Employees should verify their ID.
  (C) Employees should read a document.
  (D) Employees should rent certain equipment.

W | Br We're happy to see you all at _____ _____ this morning. We have _____ useful information _____. But before we start, let's go over a few _____. There will be one _____, h _____. L_____ can be _____ when you leave the room - there will always be someone in here - but do _____ your _____ and _____ or ... uh ... other small _____. D_____ them at the . _____. And it has _____ our _____ that there's an _____ your printed _____: there will be a change - a _____ - _____. Ms. Chen has to _____ today.

Program	
Speaker	Time
Ms. Taylor	9:00-9:50
Mr. Davis	9:55-10:45
BREAK	10:45-11:00
Mr. Kim	11:00-11:50
Ms. Chen	11:55-12:45

28. Where most likely is the speaker?
  (A) At an award banquet
  (B) At a musical performance
  (C) At a retirement party
  (D) At a training workshop

29. What are listeners asked to do?
  (A) Remain seated during the break
  (B) Carry their valuables with them
  (C) Return all borrowed equipment
  (D) Share handouts with others

30. Look at the graphic. Who will be the final speaker?
  (A) Ms. Taylor
  (B) Mr. Davis
  (C) Mr. Kim
  (D) Ms. Chen

✛ Vocabulary 따라 읽으면서 **암기**하세요 🎧 02_20

glass pane 유리판	be about to-V 막 ~하려는 참이다
put up (건물 등을) 세우다, 짓다	roll (up) (둥글게) 말다, 감다
apply (페인트를) 칠하다	on a curb 길가에
(window) frame 창틀	curb (인도와 차도 사이의) 연석, 도로 경계석

✛ Dictation

1. **W│Am** 🎧 02_19_01

   (A) A glass _____ in the frame.

   (B) A house _____.

   (C) Paint _____ to a window frame.

   (D) A window _____.

2. **M│Au** 🎧 02_19_02

   (A) He's _____ a vehicle.

   (B) He's walking _____.

   (C) He has a _____.

   (D) He has _____.

✛ Vocabulary 따라 읽으면서 **암기**하세요 🎧 02_26

go well 잘 진행되다	paperwork 서류
aisle seat 통로 쪽 좌석	patio 테라스
run (버스 · 기차 등이) 운행하다	set a place 자리를 마련하다
behind schedule 일정보다 늦게	place an order for ~을 주문하다
material 자료	reach (~에 손이) 닿다
round-trip 왕복(여행)의	mailroom 우편실
warranty 품질 보증(서)	closet 벽장
expire 만료되다, 만기가 되다	look around 둘러보다

1. [W|Am] [M|Au] 🎧 02_25_01

Charlie, _____ to the _____?

(A) Oh, _____?

(B) It was _____!

(C) It _____.

2. [M|Cn] [W|Am] 🎧 02_25_02

Does the _____ Platform _____ or Platform _____?

(A) An _____.

(B) _____.

(C) No, it's _____.

3. [W|Br] [M|Au] 🎧 02_25_03

I think we should _____ Jay _____.

(A) _____ A.

(B) Everyone was _____.

(C) But Mariko _____.

4. [M|Cn] [W|Br] 🎧 02_25_04

I'm _____ more _____ your _____.

(A) _____ with two _____.

(B) Sure, _____ a few _____.

(C) Seven _____.

5. [M|Au] [W|Br] 🎧 02_25_05

Laura _____, didn't she?

(A) My new _____.

(B) _____ the test.

(C) 'll _____.

6. W|Am M|Cn 🎧 02_25_06

_____ does the _____ of your television _____?

(A) I _____ when I moved.

(B) The _____.

(C) I _____ on Friday.

7. W|Br W|Am 🎧 02_25_07

_____ in this area?

(A) We _____.

(B) I'm _____.

(C) An outdoor _____ is available.

8. M|Cn W|Am 🎧 02_25_08

Don't we need to _____ at the table?

(A) Ms. Dunn _____.

(B) I've _____ one.

(C) Yes, it's a _____.

9. M|Au M|Cn 🎧 02_25_09

_____ that box on the top shelf.

(A) I think _____.

(B) Yes, I have some _____.

(C) There may be a _____.

10. M|Au W|Am 🎧 02_25_10

Are you going to _____ night?

(A) I've _____ online.

(B) No, this is my _____.

(C) Well, it is _____.

➕ Vocabulary | 따라 읽으면서 **암기**하세요   🎧 02_28

rehearsal 리허설, 예행연습	manage 어떻게든 해내다
theater 연극	measurement 치수
production 창작품	costume (연극, 영화 등의) 의상
available 시간이 있는	drop by (~에) 들르다

➕ Dictation

🖼️ **Questions 1 through 3** refer to the following conversation.   🎧 02_27

[W | Br] Hello, this is Martha Benjamin, the director of the Edner Theater. I _____ and _____ _____, "The Lion's Tale." _____ next Tuesday.

[M | Cn] That's wonderful, but I _____ _____ so early. I'm already _____ _____, so I _____ _____.

[W | Br] Well, we can manage _____ _____, but I _____ _____ them to our costume designer. That usually _____ _____.

[M | Cn] That's not a problem at all. I can _____ _____ and _____ _____ then.

1. Who most likely is the man?
   (A) An actor
   (B) A stage designer
   (C) A director
   (D) A tailor

2. What problem does the man mention?
   (A) He is having trouble finding some papers.
   (B) He has a conflicting work obligation.
   (C) Some promotional materials are not prepared yet.
   (D) An audition has been rescheduled.

3. What does the man offer to do next Tuesday?
   (A) Introduce a guest speaker
   (B) Obtain a script
   (C) Take some photographs
   (D) Meet with a designer

+ Vocabulary 따라 읽으면서 **암기**하세요 02_30

work 근무하다; 담당하다	**managerial** 관리의, 운영의
shift 교대 근무; 교대조	**chance** 가능성
for a while 당분간, 한동안	**though** (문장 끝에서) 그렇지만, 하지만
cover for ~ 대신 일하다	**set up** (for) ~을 준비하다
supervisor 관리자	**spicy** 매운
replacement 후임자	**have got to-V** (구어) ~해야 한다
opening 공석, 결원	**get started** 시작하다
take on (일 등을) 맡다	

+ Dictation

Questions 1 through 3 refer to the following conversation. 02_29_01

M Au Oh, hi, Paula. I didn't expect to see you at the front desk this late. Don't you usually _____ _____ in the morning?

W Am Actually, I'll be _____ _____. I'm _____ _____ who recently got promoted, but only until the hotel _____.

M Au Oh, so there's an _____ a front desk supervisor _____? I've been looking for a chance to _____. Are _____?

W Am Yes, and if you _____ _____, I think you have a _____ _____. I'd contact the human resources director right now, though - she's starting interviews this week.

1. Where do the speakers work?
   (A) At a hotel
   (B) At a shopping center
   (C) At a restaurant
   (D) At a call center

2. What does the man ask about?
   (A) How many people have requested a promotion
   (B) If a director is in the lobby
   (C) Whether a position is available
   (D) When new shifts will be assigned

3. What does the woman say the man should be prepared to do?
   (A) Address customer complaints
   (B) Work within a tight budget
   (C) Build relationships with local clients
   (D) Work evening hours

W Am Yolanda! I appreciate your help in _____ _____ after last night's _____ _____. I _____ _____, and the spicy _____ _____ was _____! You have got to tell me where you found the recipe! Everyone really _____, and it _____ _____. Anyway, I guess I'll see you Wednesday. I think we have _____ for James Roland's _____. I'm really _____ _____.

4. Why is the woman calling?
   (A) To express her gratitude
   (B) To solicit a favor
   (C) To converse about an assignment
   (D) To share some good news

5. What does the woman imply when she says, "You have got to tell me where you found the recipe"?
   (A) She wonders if some ingredients are sourced locally.
   (B) She would like to make the dish herself.
   (C) She needs a recommendation for a restaurant.
   (D) She cannot find a recipe in a cookbook.

6. Why is the woman looking forward to Wednesday?
   (A) She is going to see a performance.
   (B) She will be treating a friend to lunch.
   (C) Some results will be announced.
   (D) A new project will start.

PART 1

🔌 **Vocabulary**   따라 읽으면서 **암기**하세요   🎧 02_33

work site 작업 현장	secure (단단히) 고정하다
plank 널빤지	column 기둥
tool belt 공구 벨트	erect 짓다, 세우다
rest 쉬다, 휴식을 취하다	travel 이동하다, 나아가다
veranda 베란다	strap (가죽, 천으로 된) 끈

🔌 **Dictation**

1. [W | Br] 🎧 02_32_01

   (A) A ladder _____ a work site.

   (B) Construction workers are _____.

   (C) Some men have _____.

   (D) _____ of the workers is _____.

2. [W | Am] 🎧 02_32_02

   (A) _____ along the platform.

   (B) A train is _____.

   (C) A man _____.

   (D) People are _____.

3. [M | Cn] 🎧 02_32_03

   (A) Some workers are _____.

   (B) One man is _____.

   (C) One man is _____.

   (D) People are _____ outside the shop.

✚ Vocabulary 따라 읽으면서 **암기**하세요 🎧 02_34

somewhere 어딘가, 어떤 곳	make a right turn 우회전하다
view 경관, 경치	breathtaking 숨이 멎을 듯한[정도로 아름다운]
away 떨어져 있는	entrée 앙트레(식당이나 만찬의 주요리)
open (시간이) 비어 있는	count *sb* in (활동에) ~를 포함시키다, 끼워 주다
crew 팀, 조, 반	proposal 기획안, 제안서
properly 제대로, 적절히	on time 제시간에
maintenance (department) 시설관리부	overnight mail 익일 우편
down the hall 복도 끝에서	

✚ Dictation

4. [W│Br] [M│Cn] 🎧 02_32_04

_____ would you recommend?

(A) I _____.

(B) _____ a fine _____ of woods.

(C) The _____.

5. [W│Am] [M│Au] 🎧 02_32_05

There are _____ Watertown today, are there?

(A) Watertown is _____.

(B) _____, _____ you can take a _____.

(C) _____ the city.

6. [M│Cn] [W│Br] 🎧 02_32_06

We can _____ on Wednesday.

(A) We _____ at a discount.

(B) _____ do you have _____?

(C) Your _____.

7. [M│Cn] [W│Am] 🎧 02_32_07

_____ in your office?

(A) We _____.

(B) I _____ 'll _____ there.

(C) She _____.

8. [W|Am] [M|Au] 🎧 02_32_08

_____ 've _____ in the hotel room.

(A) You should make a _____ actually.

(B) I _____ at the Wakeson H_____.

(C) It's _____ today anyway.

9. [M|Cn] [W|Br] 🎧 02_32_09

_____ scheduled for _____ today?

(A) I _____ - it's a breathtaking _____.

(B) There is a very _____.

(C) Yes, there are _____ this afternoon.

10. [M|Cn] [W|Br] 🎧 02_32_10

_____ the client dinner?

(A) It's been _____.

(B) At an Italian _____.

(C) A selection of _____.

11. [W|Am] [M|Au] 🎧 02_32_11

Shall I show you _____ to make the _____?

(A) It _____.

(B) Absolutely, _____ me _____!

(C) Thank you for the _____.

12. [M|Cn] [W|Br] 🎧 02_32_12

Will our proposal _____ the town council _____?

(A) In the Banbury S_____.

(B) A five-percent _____.

(C) It was _____.

+ Vocabulary 따라 읽으면서 **암기**하세요 02_35

on short notice 예고 없이, 급하게	I know 맞아, 그래
nightly 밤마다 하는	spectacular 장관인, 볼 만한
newscast 뉴스 프로	division 부서
camera operator 촬영 기사, 촬영 감독	accounting 회계 (업무)
availability 시간을 낼 수 있음	make good money 많은 돈을 벌다
film crew 촬영 팀	vocal 성악의
frequently 자주, 빈번히	instructor 강사
on assignment 업무를 맡아	experienced 경험이 풍부한
with little warning 예고 없이	make-up class 보충 수업
video clip 짧은 동영상	definitely 분명히, 틀림없이
make progress 진전을 보이다[이루다]	copy (문서) 한 부

Questions 13 through 15 refer to the following conversation with three speakers. 02_32_13

[W|Am] Thanks for interviewing _____ _____, Mr. McLane. I'm Susie Park, H_____ H_____ R_____ C_____.

[W|Br] And I'm Valerie Fairchild. I _____ _____.

[M|Cn] Nice to meet you both.

[W|Br] After reviewing your résumé, it's clear that you are highly qualified for the camera operator position. But we're _____ _____, since our _____ _____.

[M|Cn] I understand that I would _____ _____. That's no problem.

[W|Am] OK, so, why don't we take a look at some of your work? You said you _____ _____. Can you _____?

[M|Cn] Sure, the files are right here on my laptop.

13. Where do the interviewers most likely work?
(A) At an employment agency
(B) At a television station
(C) At an electronics store
(D) At a movie theater

14. What job requirement do the speakers discuss?
(A) Having a professional certificate
(B) Owning the necessary equipment
(C) Possessing managerial experience
(D) Having a flexible schedule

15. What does the man agree to do next?
(A) Show a video
(B) Submit references
(C) Take a tour of a facility
(D) Meet with a manager

M Au Have you two taken a look at the _____ _____ on the ____ _____ ? It _____ ____ !

W Am _____ ! I can't believe it! And the _____ of the city _____ are _____ .

M Cn I'm curious to see which division will go up there once it's done.

W Am I heard it's the accounting department.

M Au Ah, because they have the most people.

W Am Probably. I'd be so happy to work in an office on that floor, though.

M Cn Yeah. Well, the _____ _____ if they're adding more space!

M Au I _____ , there!

16. What is the conversation mainly about?
(A) An enlargement of office space
(B) A move into a new market
(C) A growth in the number of employees
(D) A transition in company leadership

17. Why does the woman say, "I can't believe it"?
(A) She is in strong opposition.
(B) She is seeking an explanation.
(C) She is experiencing disappointment.
(D) She is pleasantly surprised.

18. What do the men imply about the company?
(A) It was founded not long ago.
(B) It is considering adjusting salaries.
(C) It is in a good financial condition.
(D) It has offices in multiple countries.

M Au Hi, Rebecca. I _____ to see you since we _____ . How's it going?

W Am I've been busy hiring more music teachers now that we have the larger space to offer additional classes. By the way, we're _____ _____ today. Since you're our _____ , I'd _____ .

M Au Well, I scheduled a _____ for a _____ who _____ her _____ last week, so I'm _____ . But if you have any _____ , _____ .

W Am That's great. Here's a copy of the interview schedule. We'll be meeting in the Peterson Hall.

Applicant	Interview Time	Instrument
Sofia Ochoa	10:00 A.M.	Violin
Soo-Jin Yun	11:00 A.M.	Vocal
James Dixon	1:00 P.M.	Flute
Ted Bailey	2:00 P.M.	Vocal

19. According to the man, what did the music school do last month?
(A) It moved to a different location.
(B) It held a dedication ceremony.
(C) It appointed a new director.
(D) It sponsored a community program.

20. Why does the woman ask the man to attend some interviews?
(A) Because she needs assistance with taking notes
(B) Because she is unavailable to attend
(C) Because he has endorsed a candidate
(D) Because he is an experienced instructor

21. Look at the graphic. Who will the man help interview today?
(A) Sofia Ochoa   (B) Soo-Jin Yun
(C) James Dixon   (D) Ted Bailey

Vocabulary 따라 읽으면서 **암기**하세요 🎧 02_36

occasion 경우, 행사	in contact with ~와 접촉하는
recognize (공로를) 인정하다, 표창하다	operation 운영, 경영
innovative 혁신적인	main office 본사, 본점
substance 물질	on one's way to ~로 가는 도중인
hydrogen 수소	staff lounge 직원 휴게실
vegetable oil 식물성 기름	flyer (광고 · 안내용) 전단
president (대학의) 총장, 학장	on sale 할인 중인
token 표시, 징표	pedestal fan 스탠드형 선풍기
gratitude 고마움, 감사	recliner (젖혀지는) 안락의자
give away (사은품으로) 나누어 주다	for sure 확실히, 틀림없이
significant 커다란, 중요한, 의미 있는	set up ~을 설치하다
functional 가동되는, 기능하는	right away 즉시, 곧바로

 Questions 22 through 24 refer to the following introduction. 🎧 02_32_16

W | Br Good evening. Thank you for _____ _____. We are here to _____ and _____ Dr. Omar Waheed for _____ _____. Dr. Waheed has _____ international _____ his _____ in _____ using substances like hydrogen and vegetable oil. We are fortunate that he has also _____ _____ with the valuable _____ to _____ at _____, OW Global Solutions. As the _____ of National University of Science and Technology, _____ _____, Dr. Waheed, for _____ _____ for our students. We _____ _____ _____.

22. Who is speaking?
(A) A foreign ambassador
(B) A teaching assistant
(C) A company executive
(D) A university official

23. Where does Dr. Waheed work?
(A) At a government institution
(B) At an employment agency
(C) At a research company
(D) At a financial institution

24. What will probably happen next?
(A) An award will be given.
(B) A meeting will be arranged.
(C) A shipment will be received.
(D) A plan will be devised.

🎧 02_32_17

[M | Au] This is Adam Brennan from Channel 15 News. I'm standing outside Lifeline Electronics this morning, where _____ _____ Shadowspeak 7C _____ - _____. Some began waiting in line as early as four A.M. From the look of it, you'd think they were giving the phones away. Now, the Shadowspeak 7C is a significant improvement from earlier phone models, but _____ _____ is its _____ _____. The new phone's design _____ that it _____ _____.

25. According to the speaker, what is happening today?
   (A) An advertising campaign is being launched.
   (B) A new branch is being inaugurated by a company.
   (C) A new product is being released in stores.
   (D) A clearance sale is being initiated.

26. What does the speaker mean when he says, "From the look of it, you'd think they were giving the phones away"?
   (A) The store's advertisement is misleading.
   (B) Some products are currently unavailable.
   (C) There are a lot of customers waiting at the store.
   (D) There are many great bargains at the store.

27. According to the speaker, what feature of the Shadowspeak 7C is most attractive?
   (A) Its water resistance
   (B) Its reasonable price
   (C) Its colorful accessories
   (D) Its sleek design

Questions 28 through 30 refer to the following telephone message and list.

🎧 02_32_18

[W | Br] Hi, Shawn. This is Maria _____ O _____. I'm guessing you're on your way to West Elm Furniture. Listen, I have a copy of your "to buy" list of things for our second-floor staff lounge, and there's good news. According to the _____ this morning, _____ _____ - it's _____. But we'll _____ _____. When you get back, we'll need to set up the furniture right away since the _____, and _____ 'll _____ in that room. OK. See you soon then.

To buy:
• Wooden bookcase	-	$99 ON SALE
• Vinyl chair	-	$53 ON SALE
• Pedestal fan	-	$85 full-price
• Recliner	-	$169 full-price

28. Where is the woman calling from?
   (A) An office building
   (B) A furniture shop
   (C) An airport
   (D) A hotel

29. Look at the graphic. What price is now incorrect?
   (A) $99   (B) $53
   (C) $85   (D) $169

30. What most likely will happen on Thursday?
   (A) Staff training sessions will commence.
   (B) Meeting with clients will take place.
   (C) A renovation project will conclude.
   (D) A job application deadline will pass.

PART 1 Exercise

➜ Vocabulary　따라 읽으면서 **암기**하세요　🎧 03_13

put up 세우다, 짓다	container 그릇, 용기
load ~을 싣다, ~에 짐을 싣다	storekeeper 가게 주인
brick 벽돌	bag 봉지[가방]에 넣다
wheelbarrow 외바퀴 손수레	pick (과일 등을) 따다
sort 분류하다	orchard 과수원

➜ Dictation

1. **M | Au** 🎧 03_12_01

   (A) A man is _____ a fence.

   (B) A man is _____ a building.

   (C) A cart _____ with bricks.

   (D) A wheelbarrow _____ at a work site.

2. **W | Br** 🎧 03_12_02

   (A) The _____ to a shop has been _____.

   (B) Fruit has been _____.

   (C) A _____ is _____ some groceries.

   (D) A worker is _____ fruit at an _____.

PART 2 Exercise

➜ Vocabulary　따라 읽으면서 **암기**하세요　🎧 03_16

trade show 무역 박람회	flower arrangement 꽃꽂이
try on ~을 입어 보다	brass 놋쇠, 황동
offer to-V (기꺼이) ~해 주겠다고 제안하다	hardware 철물
pack (짐을) 싸다	used 중고의
stairs 계단	fit (모양, 크기가) ~에 맞다
turn out (일, 상황이) ~게 되다	down the street 길 아래로
pick up ~을 찾다, 찾아오다	settle (주어야 할 돈을) 지불하다, 계산하다

1. [W | Br] [W | Am] 🎧 03_15_01

   Should we _____ or _____ first?
   (A) _____ at the _____.
   (B) Let me _____ to you.
   (C) _____.

2. [M | Au] [W | Br] 🎧 03_15_02

   Did you _____ or _____?
   (A) I _____.
   (B) Do you have this _____?
   (C) Yes, the _____.

3. [W | Am] [M | Cn] 🎧 03_15_03

   Is it _____ during the afternoon meeting or can we just
   _____?
   (A) She _____ there.
   (B) It'd be _____.
   (C) At two thirty every day.

4. [M | Cn] [M | Au] 🎧 03_15_04

   Should _____ the discussion, or would _____ like to _____?
   (A) I _____.
   (B) Our _____.
   (C) No, it isn't.

5. [W | Br] [W | Am] 🎧 03_15_05

   Are you _____, or are you _____?
   (A) The _____ yesterday.
   (B) Our _____.
   (C) Did Francois _____ for me?

6. [M | Au] [W | Br] 🎧 03_15_06

Should we _____ or in the _____ ?

(A) On the _____ would be best.

(B) This _____ really _____ .

(C) Some people have to _____ .

7. [M | Au] [M | Cn] 🎧 03_15_07

_____ Ms. Ming _____ her order, or _____ it?

(A) She _____ this morning.

(B) That's all right. I _____ .

(C) A _____ .

8. [M | Au] [W | Am] 🎧 03_15_08

Are you using the _____ or the _____

_____ ?

(A) I've _____ in the kitchen.

(B) Were we _____ ?

(C) Yes, she _____ .

9. [M | Au] [W | Am] 🎧 03_15_09

Are you interested in _____ or just _____ ?

(A) I _____ .

(B) It _____ .

(C) There is a _____ .

10. [W | Am] [M | Au] 🎧 03_15_10

Would you like to have _____ , or are you _____

_____ ?

(A) Her _____ were _____ .

(B) I'll have _____ .

(C) At the _____ by the Wangu Tower.

Vocabulary 따라 읽으면서 **암기**하세요 03_18

make it 참석하다	distribution 유통, 판매망
commemorate 기념하다	significantly 상당히, 크게
greeting card (생일 등의) 인사[축하] 카드	banquet 연회
struggle 몸부림치다, 허우적[버둥]거리다	token 표시, 징표
work (제대로) 돌아가다	dedication 헌신
full-time 정규직의	

Dictation

 Questions 1 through 3 refer to the following speech. 03_17

W Am Good evening! I'm so glad you all _____ _____ tonight to _____ _____. When I _____ _____, it was only a small team of five people _____ _____. Currently, we employ thirty full-time staff members, our distribution has grown, and we have moved into a new, significantly larger office. So please, when you leave the banquet, _____ _____. It's my personal _____ to thank all of you for your _____ and _____ _____ that has _____ _____.

1. What is being celebrated?
   (A) The conclusion of some renovations
   (B) The departure of a colleague who is retiring
   (C) A recognition for dedication to the community
   (D) The evolution of a company

2. Who most likely is the speaker?
   (A) A chief architect
   (B) A company proprietor
   (C) An existing client
   (D) An event coordinator

3. What are employees asked to do before they leave?
   (A) Interact with a public official
   (B) Take part in a group photograph
   (C) Provide a donation
   (D) Collect a gift

Vocabulary 따라 읽으면서 **암기**하세요 ∩ 03_20

make it to ~에 시간 맞춰 가다	investigate 조사하다
on short notice 갑자기, 급하게	issue 문제, 걱정거리
drip (액체가) 뚝뚝 떨어지다	attendee 참석자
awful 끔찍한, 지독한	convention 컨벤션, 전시회
leak 누출	sponsor 후원 업체
puddle 물웅덩이, 액체가 고인 곳	trade show 무역 박람회
heavy rain 폭우	seek 청하다, 구하다
lately 최근에, 요즈음	plot 구성, 줄거리
at this moment 지금[현재]으로서는	winner 수상 작품
as good as ~나 다름없는[마찬가지인]	arrange 마련하다, 준비하다, 주선하다
opening 구멍	with + 명사 + 형용사[분사] ~가 ~인 채로[~하면서]

Dictation

Questions 1 through 3 refer to the following conversation. ∩ 03_19_01

W|Br Thank you for _____ my apartment _____, Colin. Come in - I'll show you where the _____'s _____. It looks _____.

M|Au Ah, I see. That is a problem. When _____ _____?

W|Br Well, I _____ on the bathroom floor when I _____ this morning, so it must've started in the middle of the night. I'm _____ it's _____ all this _____ _____'ve _____ or by a broken pipe.

M|Au At this moment, _____ _____. I'm sorry, but I will need to _____ _____ in your ceiling to _____.

1. Who most likely is the man?
   (A) A building maintenance employee
   (B) A truck operator
   (C) A real estate agent
   (D) A customer service representative

2. What does the man mean when he says, "That is a problem"?
   (A) He should seek advice from a specialist.
   (B) He deems another issue to be more critical.
   (C) He agrees that the issue demands attention.
   (D) He is familiar with this type of problem.

3. What does the woman say about the recent weather?
   (A) It has been hot and humid.
   (B) It has been raining heavily.
   (C) There has been a lot of wind.
   (D) There have been snowfalls.

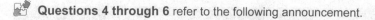

M Cn Hello and a warm welcome to all attendees of the tenth annual Video Game Convention. My name is Sanjay Patel, and I'm the president of Plexton Enterprises, one of the official sponsors of this year's trade show. I'm here to introduce you to an exciting opportunity. We are _____ _____ and are _____! _____ _____ of the upcoming Plexton adventure game. If your idea is _____, we'll _____ to Yokohama, _____ _____, for next year's Video Game Convention.

4. What does Plexton Enterprises produce?
   (A) Television shows
   (B) An electronics magazine
   (C) Sporting goods
   (D) Video games

5. What are listeners invited to do?
   (A) Nominate candidates
   (B) Submit ideas
   (C) Try out products
   (D) Write testimonials

6. According to the speaker, what prize will be awarded?
   (A) A complimentary journey to an exhibition
   (B) A meal accompanied by a celebrity
   (C) Electronic appliances
   (D) A television appearance

PART 1

show (장소로) 안내하다, 인도하다	garbage 쓰레기
deck (배의) 갑판	traffic light 신호등
ramp 경사로, 비탈	chimney 굴뚝
doorway 출입구	broom 빗자루
crew 승무원 (전원)	prop against ~에 받쳐[괴어] 놓다
toss 던지다	windowsill 창턱
anchor 닻	

➔ **Dictation**

1. [M | Au] 🎧 03_22_01

   (A) Passengers _____ on the _____.

   (B) People are _____ a ship.

   (C) A sign has been _____.

   (D) A crew member is _____ into the water.

2. [M | Cn] 🎧 03_22_02

   (A) Some people are _____ at a truck.

   (B) Some people are _____ on the street.

   (C) Vehicles are _____.

   (D) The back of the truck _____.

3. [W | Am] 🎧 03_22_03

   (A) She's _____ up some _____.

   (B) She's _____ some patio _____.

   (C) A brick _____.

   (D) A broom has been _____.

Vocabulary 따라 읽으면서 **암기**하세요

rent 임차하다
set up ~을 설립하다
place 거처, 살 곳, 집
dine in (포장하지 않고) 식당에서 식사하다
way (전치사, 부사 강조) 훨씬, 너무
demonstrate (능력, 자질을) 보여주다, 발휘하다
repaint 다시 칠하다
staff lounge 직원 휴게실
boardroom 중역 회의실, 이사회실
closet 벽장
more than enough 충분하고도 남는
can afford to-V (시간이나 금전에서) ~할 여유가 있다
print media 인쇄 매체

find out ~을 알아내다
supplies 용품, 비품
supply closet 비품 창고
flyer 전단지
right away 곧바로, 즉시
in terms of ~ 면에서, ~에 관하여
up and running 완전히 제대로 작동되는
available for purchase 구입할 수 있는
frequent 잦은, 빈번한
rental 임대의, 대여의
manual 수동의
transmission (자동차) 변속기

Dictation

4. W|Am M|Cn 🎧 03_22_04

Does the company _____ or _____ its office building?

(A) To _____.

(B) I'm _____.

(C) I believe they're _____.

5. M|Au W|Br 🎧 03_22_05

Are you planning to _____, or would you like to _____?

(A) Yes, it was absolutely _____.

(B) Just _____.

(C) I think I should _____.

6. M|Cn W|Am 🎧 03_22_06

Is the staff lunch being held at the _____ or at a _____?

(A) Our _____.

(B) John _____ good _____.

(C) Yes, we'll have to _____.

7. ⬚M|Cn⬚ ⬚W|Br⬚ 🎧 03_22_07

Shall we _____ the _____ or the _____?

(A) There may be _____.

(B) There's _____ in here.

(C) We can _____.

8. ⬚W|Am⬚ ⬚M|Au⬚ 🎧 03_22_08

Will we focus on _____ or _____?

(A) The customers are _____.

(B) Yes, it looks _____.

(C) Let's _____.

9. ⬚M|Au⬚ ⬚W|Br⬚ 🎧 03_22_09

Should I _____ the supplies _____, or _____?

(A) _____ eighty-five dollars.

(B) Actually, I've _____.

(C) They're in the _____.

10. ⬚M|Au⬚ ⬚W|Br⬚ 🎧 03_22_10

Are the _____ going to be _____, or do you _____ to finish them?

(A) I'll _____.

(B) I have no idea who is _____.

(C) His _____ will be late.

11. ⬚M|Au⬚ ⬚W|Br⬚ 🎧 03_22_11

In terms of office equipment, should we invest in _____ computers or _____?

(A) The Web site is _____ now.

(B) They're _____ at any store.

(C) _____ are _____.

12. ⬚W|Am⬚ ⬚M|Cn⬚ 🎧 03_22_12

Does the rental vehicle have _____ or _____?

(A) It's _____ in the office.

(B) Maureen will be _____.

(C) The _____ turn on _____.

Vocabulary 따라 읽으면서 **암기**하세요 03_25

gift-wrap 선물용으로 포장하다
kind of 약간, 어느 정도
total 총액
come over 들르다
in that case 그렇다면
for once 이번 한 번만은
video conference 화상 회의
in person 직접, 몸소
for a change 여느 때와 달리

just about 거의 (다)
bustling 부산한, 북적거리는
unload 짐을 내리다
oversight 실수, 간과
first-time 처음으로 해 보는
head over (to) ~로 가다, 향하다
run behind schedule 예정보다 늦다
delivery stop 배송지

 Questions 13 through 15 refer to the following conversation. 03_22_13

[M | Au] _____'ll _____ thirty dollars. Would you like _____?

[W | Am] Oh, I'm purchasing them for my own use. You know, I _____'ll _____. It's kind of cold out there. Do you _____?

[M | Au] Yes, but _____. Your _____.

[W | Am] Alright, then I'll _____.

13. Where does this conversation take place?
(A) At a dining establishment
(B) At a garment shop
(C) At a bookshop
(D) At a florist's shop

14. What does the woman want to do with her purchase?
(A) Retrieve it at a later time
(B) Make use of it immediately
(C) Have it wrapped as a gift
(D) Have it delivered to her residence

15. Why is the woman unable to use her credit card?
(A) She forgot to bring her card with her.
(B) Credit cards are not accepted at the business.
(C) The price of her purchase is not high enough.
(D) There is damage to the card.

W | Br Hi Leo, it's Amirah from Human Resources. I just _____ that the _____ _____ in Meeting Room 4B _____.

M | Au Oh, I'm sorry, I can _____ and _____.

W | Br Right now? Uh... I'm interviewing someone in here in ten minutes. And I _____ _____. So, if you could wait...

M | Au Oh, OK, in that case, I'll come over when you're finished. Is _____ _____?

W | Br Yeah, thanks. _____ I'm interviewing someone who _____, so there's _____. It'll be nice to _____.

16. Why is the woman calling the man?
(A) To report an equipment malfunction
(B) To confirm an agenda
(C) To inquire about employee information
(D) To ask about a missing object

17. What does the woman mean when she says, "I'm interviewing someone in here in ten minutes."?
(A) She is in urgent need of help.
(B) She does not want to be disturbed.
(C) She is discontented with an assignment.
(D) She will not attend another meeting.

18. What does the woman say is unusual about the interview?
(A) It will be videorecorded.
(B) It will take place over a weekend.
(C) It will be conducted face-to-face.
(D) It will last for less than half an hour.

M | Cn Hi, I'm _____ with the _____ for today, but I'm having _____ _____ Dinh Industries. I've _____ _____, but the _____, and there's _____.

W | Am I apologize for the _____, as Dinh Industries is a _____ and I forgot to include the parking information on the delivery schedule. They have a parking area behind the building.

M | Cn OK, I'll _____ now. I'm _____ _____, though. I hope my next delivery stop will still be open.

W | Am It _____, so I'll _____ and let them know you'll be arriving a bit late.

Today's Deliveries

Lindenbrook Bakery	
Customer	Address
Franklyn Supermarket	1800 State St
Dinh Industries	360 Hillside St
Tuckman Department Store	45 Jefferson St

19. Look at the graphic. What street is the man on?
(A) Lindenbrook
(B) State
(C) Hillside
(D) Jefferson

20. What is the man asking about?
(A) How to collect a payment
(B) Where he can park his vehicle
(C) When to make a delivery
(D) Whom he should ask for

21. What does the woman say she will do?
(A) Open a door
(B) Make a phone call
(C) Forward an e-mail
(D) Buy some food

Vocabulary 따라 읽으면서 **암기**하세요 03_26

attention (안내 방송에서) 알립니다	commercial (텔레비전, 라디오의) 광고 (방송)
observe 보다, (보고) 알다	admit 인정하다, 시인하다
temporarily 일시적으로	rather than ~보다는
maintenance 유지 보수, 정비	Here's the thing. 그런데 문제는 이겁니다.
crew 팀, 조, 반	compensate A for B A에게 B에 대해 보상하다
in the meantime 그 동안[사이]에	go through ~을 살펴보다
personnel 직원들	stipulation 계약 조건[조항]
report to (도착을) 알리다, 보고하다	arrange an agreement 계약을 맺다
assignment 임무, 업무	might want to-V ~하는 게 좋겠다
assembly floor 조립 작업장[현장]	someplace 어딘가에서
regarding ~에 관하여	make a photocopy of ~을 복사하다
adjustment 조정, 수정	sing along 함께 노래를 따라 부르다
day shift 주간 근무조	

Questions 22 through 24 refer to the following introduction. 03_22_16

W | Am _____ :

As you may have observed, the _____

_____. The _____

to the belt is expected to _____ a minimum of a

_____, according to the maintenance

crew. The _____ will stay _____ until

this is complete. _____, all production

line personnel are required to _____

_____ for special assignments. You

can _____ later tonight from an _____

_____ regarding any _____

_____ for tomorrow's _____.

22. Where most likely is this announcement being made?
(A) At a site of construction project
(B) At a production facility
(C) At an auto dealership
(D) At an office supply store

23. What problem does the speaker mention?
(A) Some components are missing.
(B) A manager has yet to show up.
(C) Inclement weather is expected.
(D) Some equipment is not functioning.

24. What will employees be informed about this evening?
(A) Results of an inspection
(B) Alterations in safety procedures
(C) Updates on work schedules
(D) Conditions of roads

M | Au So the _____ is to _____
_____ with Warmson Advertising and make
a _____ whether... uhm... whether to _____
_____.
Yesterday, I had a conversation with their team and
I must admit, I'm feeling _____. It _____
_____ rather
than producing high-quality commercials for us.
Here's the thing. If we decide to _____
_____, we will have to _____
_____ that has _____. Let's quickly
_____ together. You'll find that's a
_____ in the _____.

25. What bothers the man about Warmson Advertising?
(A) Their lack of punctuality
(B) Their staffing difficulties
(C) Their request to alter a contract
(D) Their focus on cost cutting

26. What does the man mean when he says, "Here's the thing"?
(A) He will showcase a product.
(B) He cannot recall a word.
(C) He has found what he was searching for.
(D) He will bring up a point for discussion.

27. What are the listeners asked to look at?
(A) A design concept
(B) A business contract
(C) A commercial
(D) A budget

W | Br Hi. It's Valerie, and I'm calling with some
information about _____
_____ Monica's _____. Now, um... you and I
_____.
And, I'm really glad to hear that thirty-five people
from the office are coming. But, unfortunately, it
looks like we _____ from Bliss
Restaurant _____. We _____
_____. Also, Anwei agreed
to _____ Monica's _____
during the party. Do you think you could _____
_____ so that _____ can
_____?

Bliss Restaurant	
15% off (groups of 20+)	
Book rooms for 4 hours!	
expires:	Offer good at all
July 1st	locations

28. Why is an event being held?
(A) To celebrate a promotion
(B) To commemorate a retirement
(C) To mark a special occasion
(D) To announce a corporate merger

29. Look at the graphic. Why is the speaker unable to use the coupon for the event?
(A) The group does not have enough people.
(B) The length of the event is excessive.
(C) All of the locations in the area are fully booked.
(D) The event will take place after the expiration date.

30. What does the speaker ask the listener to do?
(A) Select a menu
(B) Distribute invitations
(C) Duplicate song lyrics
(D) Contract a band

+ Vocabulary 따라 읽으면서 **암기**하세요 🎧 04_15

curved 곡선의
file (서류 등을) 철하여 정리하다
patio 테라스

overlook (건물, 산 등이) 내려다보다
railing 난간
stream 흘러나오다

+ Dictation

1. M Cn 🎧 04_14_01

   (A) Some employees are standing _____ .

   (B) Some employees are _____ some documents.

   (C) A technician is _____ a software program.

   (D) A worker is _____ a sign.

2. W Am 🎧 04_14_02

   (A) Some chairs _____ .

   (B) A mountain _____ .

   (C) A person is standing _____ .

   (D) Sunlight is _____ .

+ Vocabulary 따라 읽으면서 **암기**하세요 🎧 04_21

fill out ~을 작성하다
price tag 가격표
put *sth* on display ~을 진열하다
All sales are final. 교환이나 환불이 안 됩니다.
minutes 회의록
projector 영사기
invite 요청하다, 청하다
trade fair 무역 박람회
in writing 서면으로

change 동전, 잔돈
be supposed to-V ~하기로 되어 있다
projection 예상, 추정
accounts receivable 외상 매출금, 미수금
occasionally 가끔
keynote speaker 기조 연설자
conference 회의, 학회
charge 부과하다, 청구하다
thoroughly 대단히, 완전히

1. [W|Am] [M|Au] 🎧 04_20_01

Do you mind _____?

(A) Actually, I _____.

(B) A _____ in another city.

(C) No, _____'s _____.

2. [M|Au] [M|Cn] 🎧 04_20_02

Should I _____ to the new merchandise before _____

_____?

(A) Yes, _____, thanks.

(B) I'm sorry, but _____.

(C) It's next to the _____.

3. [W|Am] [M|Au] 🎧 04_20_03

Would you _____ from our staff meeting earlier today?

(A) Sure, I'll _____ by the end of the day.

(B) There are _____, too.

(C) _____ in the office.

4. [M|Cn] [W|Br] 🎧 04_20_04

____'d _____ you've recently submitted.

(A) Our _____ was that _____.

(B) _____, it seems.

(C) _____ tomorrow?

5. [W|Br] [M|Au] 🎧 04_20_05

Should we _____ to attend the trade fair?

(A) We're _____ her.

(B) I _____.

(C) From Boston to Melbourne.

6. [W|Am] [M|Au] 🎧 04_20_06

Should we get the _____?

(A) Sorry, I don't _____.

(B) That _____.

(C) I'll _____ another day.

7. [M|Cn] [M|Au] 🎧 04_20_07

Should we _____ Ms. Colley to _____?

(A) I'm _____ here.

(B) _____ for the second quarter.

(C) But the _____.

8. [W|Br] [W|Am] 🎧 04_20_08

Would you like me to _____?

(A) _____.

(B) I _____ them _____.

(C) I'll have the salmon salad.

9. [W|Am] [M|Cn] 🎧 04_20_09

Could you _____?

(A) Where did you _____?

(B) Ms. Carson was the _____.

(C) The doors _____.

10. [M|Au] [W|Br] 🎧 04_20_10

_____ the conference until August?

(A) The hotel _____.

(B) Take it to the _____.

(C) I _____ the conference.

Vocabulary | 따라 읽으면서 **암기하세요** 🎧 04_23

acquire 습득하다, 얻다
plus 더욱이, 게다가
put *sth* into practice ~을 실행하다
alongside ~와 함께
case 소송 사건

challenging 힘든, 까다로운
rewarding 보람 있는
admire 감탄하며 바라보다
following ~ 후에

Dictation

 Questions 1 through 3 refer to the following conversation. 🎧 04_22

W|Am Mr. Burgess, I see _____ that you're _____ here at Patel & Partners.

M|Cn Yes, I'm _____ _____ about working in legal services. Plus, I'm looking forward to _____ _____.

W|Am Well, if you're selected, you'll _____ _____ a variety of _____. The work is _____, but most interns ___ _____.

M|Cn That sounds great. I've always _____ _____ Patel & Partners. In fact, I'd really like to _____ here someday. Is it _____ _____?

1. What are the speakers mainly discussing?
   (A) An internship opportunity
   (B) A university course
   (C) A due date for a project
   (D) A news article

2. What type of business is Patel & Partners?
   (A) A medical practice
   (B) An staffing firm
   (C) A building company
   (D) A law firm

3. What does the man ask about?
   (A) The outcomes of an investigation
   (B) The levels of customer satisfaction
   (C) The likelihood of full-time employment
   (D) The cost of hiring a professional

Vocabulary 따라 읽으면서 **암기**하세요 04_25

first draft 초안	fabric 직물, 천
come along (원하는 대로) 되어 가다	tear 찢다 (tore–torn)
appreciate ~에 대해 감사하다	collect 수거하다
point 의견, 주장	drop off (사람, 짐 등을) 내려주다
ultimately 궁극적으로, 결국	shipment 수송품
primary 주된, 주요한	grateful 고마워하는, 감사하는
relocation 이전	patronage 애용
encounter 부딪히다, 맞닥뜨리다	

Dictation

Questions 1 through 3 refer to the following conversation. 04_24_01

[M | Cn] Hello, Ms. Sapra. It's Walter Lee. Have you _____ the _____ the design I _____ for your _____?

[W | Br] Thanks for calling, Walter. Yes, I think the design is _____. I really _____ how you _____ _____ instead of just the logo.

[M | Cn] I'm happy you like that idea. Should I _____ _____ " ____ 've _____ !" _____ ?

[W | Br] Yes, good point. Ultimately, the _____ _____ is to _____ about the _____'s _____.

1. Who most likely is the woman?
(A) A news reporter
(B) A store owner
(C) A real estate agent
(D) A photographer

2. What is the woman pleased about?
(A) A contract with a new client
(B) A recently published article
(C) A property's location
(D) A draft of an advertisement

3. What does the man offer to do?
(A) Rearrange some furniture
(B) Expedite a service request
(C) Generate an invoice
(D) Enlarge some words

[M｜Au] Hello Ms. Ellington. I _____

_____ about the _____

_____ with some of the _____

_____ to your company two days ago. I _____

_____ that was delivered. We are

more than happy to visit your factory to collect the

fabric that you cannot use and _____

_____ .

We apologize once more for any _____

_____ . We are _____

for your _____ and for your continued

_____ .

4. What is the purpose of the telephone message?
   (A) To purchase clothing items
   (B) To offer an apology to a customer
   (C) To reschedule an appointment
   (D) To inquire about a location

5. What problem does the speaker mention?
   (A) Some material is damaged.
   (B) A machine is out of order.
   (C) A shipment is behind schedule.
   (D) Some items are out of stock.

6. What does the speaker say he will do?
   (A) Confirm some specifications
   (B) Consult with a supervisor
   (C) Provide a sample
   (D) Send a replacement

→ Vocabulary 따라 읽으면서 **암기**하세요 🎧 04_28

scaffolding (건축 공사장의) 비계
prune 가지치기하다

bush 관목
structure 구조물, 건축물

→ Dictation

1. [M | Cn] 🎧 04_27_01

   (A) Some people are _____ in a garden.

   (B) A woman is _____ while _____.

   (C) A _____ in a garden.

   (D) Some people are _____.

2. [W | Br] 🎧 04_27_02

   (A) He's standing _____.

   (B) He's _____ next to a building.

   (C) He's _____.

   (D) He's _____ with a shovel.

3. [M | Au] 🎧 04_27_03

   (A) Some dogs are _____.

   (B) The man is _____ at something _____.

   (C) One of the women is _____.

   (D) They're _____.

✚ Vocabulary 따라 읽으면서 **암기**하세요 🎧 04_29

receptionist 접수 담당자
in that case 그런 경우에는
welcome reception 환영 리셉션
track 추적하다; 선로
quarterly 분기별의
organization committee 조직 위원회
go well 잘 진행되다
couldn't agree more 전적으로 동감이다
outstanding 뛰어난, 걸출한

photocopier 복사기
overnight delivery 익일 배송
hopefully 바라건대
double-sided 양면의
treat A to B A에게 B를 대접하다
analyst 분석가
(new) recruit 신입 사원
fit (~에 들어가기에) 맞다

✚ Dictation

4. [M|Cn] [W|Am] 🎧 04_27_04

Why don't we hire another _____?

(A) In that case, try _____.

(B) _____ to our manager.

(C) There'll be a _____ for her.

5. [W|Am] [M|Cn] 🎧 04_27_05

_____ that _____ this quarter?

(A) Yeah, I'll _____.

(B) A _____.

(C) _____ thirty-seven.

6. [W|Am] [M|Cn] 🎧 04_27_06

_____ joining the organization committee?

(A) Yes, ___'d _____.

(B) _____ evening.

(C) I _____ interesting article _____.

7. [M|Au] [W|Br] 🎧 04_27_07

_____ holding a _____ on the new database?

(A) I think _____.

(B) ___'ve_____ there before.

(C) I _____!

8. [W|Br] [W|Am] 🎧 04_27_08

_____ go to the _____ on Saturday evening?

(A) Sorry, I'll be _____.

(B) I _____, it was _____.

(C) His _____ work.

9. [M|Au] [M|Cn] 🎧 04_27_09

Why don't we _____ for the dinner?

(A) ___'ve_____ there several times.

(B) It may be _____ the menu.

(C) Yes, _____ first.

10. [W|Am] [W|Br] 🎧 04_27_10

___'d_____ to repair the photocopier.

(A) Yes, we offer _____.

(B) _____ too long.

(C) Ten _____ copies, please.

11. [M|Au] [W|Am] 🎧 04_27_11

I would like to _____ next Friday.

(A) We _____ twenty minutes _____.

(B) We _____ in the budget this quarter.

(C) Does this _____?

12. [M|Cn] [W|Br] 🎧 04_27_12

_____ hire an analyst.

(A) That's _____.

(B) Several _____.

(C) It _____ to _____ in the _____.

Vocabulary 따라 읽으면서 **암기**하세요 04_30

connection (교통) 연결 편	if you don't mind 괜찮다면
direct flight 직항 편	get in touch with ~와 연락하다
be willing to-V 기꺼이 ~하다	typical 일반적인
connect (교통편을) 갈아타다	put together (행사를) 준비하다, 계획을 짜다
name 이름을 지어주다	outing 야유회
newspaper (agency) 신문사	café 카페, 식당
list 목록에 포함시키다	vote (투표로) 선출하다
staff 전속의	eatery 식당

 Questions 13 through 15 refer to the following conversation. 04_27_13

[W | Br] Is there _____ _____ to San Diego? My flight from Seoul _____, so I _____ _____.

[M | Cn] Let's see... I don't have any direct flights, but if you're willing to _____ Los angeles, there is a flight leaving in about twenty minutes.

[W | Br] _____ San Diego, I'll _____. My name's Tanya Bryant.

[M | Cn] Here's your ticket, Ms. Bryant. Please _____ _____ G _____ E _____.

---

13. What is the woman's problem?
(A) She misplaced her luggage.
(B) She didn't make it to her flight in time.
(C) She left behind her airplane ticket.
(D) She has no idea where the gate is.

14. Where is the woman's final destination?
(A) San Diego
(B) Seoul
(C) Los Angeles
(D) San Francisco

15. What does the man tell the woman to do?
(A) Present her identification
(B) Consult a travel agent
(C) Look through her baggage
(D) Proceed to an airport gate

Questions 16 through 18 refer to the following conversation with three speakers. 🎧 04_27_14

[W Am] Sorry to _____ you, but I'm wondering if _____ remember _____ César Villa. He _____ at the newspaper _____ _____.

[M Au] That name _____ to me. Why?

[W Am] Someone from Activa Media _____ today. César _____ for a job there, and he _____ _____ as his _____ _____. They _____ a recommendation, but I never actually worked with him.

[M Cn] César Villa? I remember César. He _____ _____ with us for about a year. He _____.

[W Am] Could you please provide the recommendation, if you don't mind?

[M Cn] Sure, I'd be happy to, but I _____ _____ one of us directly. That's the typical procedure.

16. Where do the speakers work?
(A) At a television station
(B) At an advertising agency
(C) At an electronics store
(D) At a newspaper

17. Why did Activa Media contact the speakers' workplace?
(A) To provide a training seminar
(B) To introduce some new products
(C) To inquire about some photographs
(D) To request a reference

18. What does the woman imply when she says, "I never actually worked with him"?
(A) She cannot fulfill a request.
(B) She would rather work by herself.
(C) She is surprised a colleague is leaving.
(D) She is dissatisfied with an assignment.

[W|Am] Dana's Café. May I help you?

[M|Cn] Hi, I'm calling from Synergy Software. I'm _____ a lunch _____ for my _____. Can you _____ for thirty people?

[W|Am] Yes. _____ are you interested in?

[M|Cn] Next Wednesday, from noon to two o'clock?

[W|Am] OK.

[M|Cn] Also, _____ staff members _____ _____. Will they be able to eat at your café?

[W|Am] Sure. If you _____ menu, you'll _____ _____ that _____ "healthy" in their name. Those meals _____ _____. In fact, we were _____ _____ on PinevilleRestaurants.com.

[M|Cn] Great. Let me _____ and _____ you.

LUNCH SPECIALS

Valencia Fish Soup	$7
Healthy Greek Pita Sandwich	$9
Crispy Mediterranean Salad	$7
Gourmet Provence Sampler	$10

19. What type of event is the man organizing?
(A) A business seminar
(B) A client luncheon
(C) A retirement party
(D) A department outing

20. What does the woman mention about the café?
(A) Large groups can be hosted in an outdoor patio.
(B) Cancellations must be made with at least 24 hours notice.
(C) It gained recognition among local diners.
(D) The menu varies according to the season.

21. Look at the graphic. What menu item does not contain meat?
(A) The soup
(B) The sandwich
(C) The salad
(D) The sampler

PART 4

 Vocabulary 따라 읽으면서 **암기**하세요 🎧 04_31

wrap up ~을 마무리짓다	**refurbish** 새로 꾸미다, 재단장하다
management 경영진, 운영진	**luncheon** 오찬
time off 휴식, 휴가	**availability** 시간을 낼 수 있음
dissatisfaction 불만	**instruction** 가르침, 지도
seek 찾다, 구하다	**advanced** 고급의, 상급의
(new) hire 신입 사원	**pro shop** 프로 숍(골프나 테니스 클럽하우스의 스포츠용품 판매점)
off (근무, 일을) 쉬는	**feature** 특별히 포함하다
ensure 반드시 ~하게[이게] 하다	**a wide range of** 매우 다양한
in advance 미리, 사전에	**apparel** 의류
conclude 끝내다, 마치다	**gear** (특정 활동의) 장비, 복장
extensive 광범위한, 대규모의	**check out** ~을 살펴보다
in line with 보조를 같이 하는	**exclusive** 독점적인, 전용의
corporate 회사의, 기업의	**buy-one-get-one-free** 원 플러스 원의
initiative 계획	**guest pass** 비회원 입장권
modernize 현대화하다	**get off** ~에서 떠나다
tour 순회하다	**bleacher** 관람석, 관중석

 Questions 22 through 24 refer to the following announcement. 🎧 04_27_16

W Br Before we _____ this _____, I have an important update _____ _____ to share with you. As you know, new employees are _____ _____ during _____ here. Many of our employees have _____ with this policy _____ after only a few months. This means that the company _____ _____ new staff. So, in order to _____ the company, we'll be _____ beginning next year. Please _____ that your employees are _____ and remind them ____ _____ to _____ you _____ if they _____.

22. What is the main topic of the announcement?
(A) Updating the company Web site
(B) Granting new hires extra days off
(C) Offering advanced training to managers
(D) Enhancing the flexibility of work schedules

23. According to the speaker, why is a change being made?
(A) To retain existing staff members
(B) To comply with a company regulation
(C) To enhance communication
(D) To implement improved safety procedures

24. What are the listeners reminded to do?
(A) Update the contact information for clients
(B) Refer to their department handbook
(C) Communicate company policies to their employees
(D) Change their passwords on a regular basis

[M | Au] Before we _____ today's managers' meeting, I have an important announcement to make. I _____ that Elsa Shadler, our chief executive officer, will be visiting next Tuesday. As you know, the _____ _____ were _____ to _____ all the department stores in our chain. The CEO has been _____ _____, and _____ is coming up next. Now, this isn't a formal inspection, so you _____ _____. But _____ 'll _____ for Ms. Shadler that day, and ___ 'd if you could _____. Please _____ your _____ by Friday.

25. Why is the CEO coming for a visit?
   (A) A project has been finished.
   (B) A facility has been acquired.
   (C) A new manager has joined the company.
   (D) A sales goal has been met.

26. Why does the speaker say, "this isn't a formal inspection"?
   (A) To dispute a claim
   (B) To reassure employees
   (C) To acknowledge a positive result
   (D) To question a procedure

27. What event have the listeners been invited to?
   (A) A farewell party
   (B) A groundbreaking ceremony
   (C) A welcome reception
   (D) A fashion show

[W | Br] Come to Masayuki's Tennis Club and _____ your forehand and backhand swings with _____ Masayuki Hirano. Mr. Hirano has fifteen years of instruction experience and is _____ _____, so _____ _____ students can _____ from him. Explore our _____ featuring an _____ tennis rackets and apparel, ensuring you find the _____ _____ for your game! Don't forget to check out the *Syracuse Shopping Magazine* for _____ _____, such as buy-one-get-one-free lessons for kids, _____, and free _____ for members over the weekend. So _____ _____ today!

Masayuki's
Tennis Club

50% Off
Select classes

28. What is Mr. Hirano known for?
   (A) He is the proprietor of several tennis clubs.
   (B) He came out on top in tennis competitions.
   (C) He promotes a brand of tennis gear.
   (D) He exclusively instructs novice students.

29. Look at the graphic. What classes is the coupon valid for?
   (A) Child classes
   (B) Adult classes
   (C) Advanced classes
   (D) Weekend classes

30. What recently changed at Masayuki's Tennis Club?
   (A) The size of a store
   (B) The types of classes
   (C) The surface of a court
   (D) The date of a tournament

Vocabulary 따라 읽으면서 **암기**하세요 🎧 05_12

bus station 버스 터미널	dump truck 덤프트럭
line up 일렬로 세우다	earth 흙
intersection 교차로	

Dictation

1. [M Cn] 🎧 05_11_01

   (A) Many passengers are _____.

   (B) Some of the riders have _____.

   (C) Motorcycles are _____.

   (D) Fuel is being _____.

2. [W Br] 🎧 05_11_02

   (A) A dump truck is _____ on the ground.

   (B) Trucks are _____.

   (C) Workers are _____ on a roadway.

   (D) Vehicles have been _____.

Vocabulary 따라 읽으면서 **암기**하세요 🎧 05_16

come with ~이 같이 나오다[제공되다]	be done with ~을 다 처리하다
Iranian 이란의	to go (식당에서 먹지 않고) 가지고 갈
distributor 유통업체	give *sb* a ride ~를 차에 태워 주다
distribution 분배	lab (=laboratory) 실습실
informative 유익한	sales figures 매출액
textile printing 날염	line 제품군
rating 평점, 등급	assessment 평가
would rather A (than B) (B하기 보다는 차라리) A 하겠다[하고 싶다]	down the street 길 아래쪽의
	start over 다시 시작하다

1. [W|Am] [M|Cn] 05_15_01

This meal _____, doesn't it?

(A) Would you like to _____?

(B) _____.

(C) It was _____.

2. [M|Au] [W|Br] 05_15_02

Ellen _____ back from the _____, has she?

(A) To ensure an _____.

(B) I _____, no.

(C) Can you _____ these boxes?

3. [W|Am] [M|Au] 05_15_03

Have the _____ since we _____?

(A) An informative _____.

(B) The _____ policy.

(C) _____.

4. [M|Cn] [W|Am] 05_15_04

_____ the textile printing _____ again?

(A) That's an _____.

(B) _____, but almost.

(C) No, _____.

5. [M|Cn] [W|Br] 05_15_05

_____ Conference Room 2A?

(A) ____ usually _____.

(B) A four-o'clock _____.

(C) It _____.

6. [W | Br] [W | Am] 🎧 05_15_06

_____ after we're done with this paperwork.

(A) Could I _____, please?

(B) Sorry, I have _____.

(C) The _____'s _____.

7. [W | Am] [M | Cn] 🎧 05_15_07

_____ is the _____ so _____?

(A) For _____.

(B) I'll give you a _____.

(C) Should we _____?

8. [W | Br] [M | Au] 🎧 05_15_08

_____ to log on to the computer?

(A) Now we have a _____.

(B) Yes, but I _____ it.

(C) She's in the _____.

9. [M | Cn] [W | Am] 🎧 05_15_09

I _____ when the design workshop is.

(A) _____ Mr. Wayne.

(B) It's extremely _____.

(C) About this _____'s _____.

10. [W | Br] [M | Au] 🎧 05_15_10

The _____ for _____ is _____, isn't it?

(A) The _____.

(B) The _____ down the street.

(C) The studio _____.

+ Vocabulary 따라 읽으면서 **암기**하세요 🎧 05_18

arrange for 준비하다, 계획을 짜다 wait staff (식당) 종업원	shift 교대 근무

+ Dictation

Questions 1 through 3 refer to the following conversation. 🎧 05_17

W | Am It looks like we'll have to _____ _____ for next Saturday. There's a volleyball game in the stadium next door, and we'll have a ____ _____ after it's over.

M | Au Definitely, we _____ _____ here for dinner.

W | Am Well, Akiko and Henry are already scheduled, but Ramon is _____. I'll _____ _____.

1. Where do the speakers most likely work?
   (A) At a dining establishment
   (B) At an exercise facility
   (C) At an athletic arena
   (D) At a lodging establishment

2. What are the speakers discussing?
   (A) Attending a sporting event
   (B) Preparing for extra customers
   (C) Organizing a remodeling project
   (D) Expanding to a new location

3. What will the woman ask Ramon to do?
   (A) Provide some directions
   (B) Ask for a price quote
   (C) Work an extra shift
   (D) Present a demonstration

Vocabulary 따라 읽으면서 **암기**하세요 🎧 05_20

supervisor 관리자	briefly 잠시
hands-on 실습의	overview 개념, 개관
session (특정한 활동을 위한) 시간	terrific 멋진, 훌륭한
meet (모임 등이) 열리다	understaffed 인원이 부족한
look over ~을 살펴보다	in charge of ~을 맡은[담당하는]
coordinate 조화시키다	assorted 여러 가지의, 갖은
module 교과목	grilled (그릴에) 구운

Dictation

 Questions 1 through 3 refer to the following conversation. 🎧 05_19_01

[M | Cn] Hi, Margot. _____
_____ just reminded me about the new employee orientation next week. I'm still responsible for _____, correct?

[W | Br] That's correct.

[M | Cn] And _____ the afternoon?

[W | Br] Right. Here's the _____
_____ - take a minute to look it over.

[M | Cn] Sure thing.

[W | Br] Great. Just one more thing - you'll want to _____ your _____ with the morning _____ Ms. Cho. It might be helpful to _____ to _____.

[M | Cn] Terrific. I'll get it done today.

1. In what department does the man most likely work?
(A) Human Resources
(B) Product Development
(C) Technical Support
(D) Building Maintenance

2. What does the woman give the man?
(A) An employee handbook
(B) A job application
(C) A training schedule
(D) A feedback questionnaire

3. What does the woman suggest the man do?
(A) Secure a conference room
(B) Discuss plans with a colleague
(C) Reschedule a workshop
(D) Update a software program

W Am OK, before you _____, I need to inform you that the restaurant is _____ tonight. Rajesh called me this afternoon to let me know that he _____. So I'm _____ _____ to be _____ _____ tonight. Please also remember to _____ _____, which features a rice dish with _____. I believe it'll _____ since many of our customers have been asking for more vegetarian options. That's it for tonight.

4. What kind of business does the speaker work for?

(A) A restaurant
(B) A grocery store
(C) A furniture store
(D) A gym

5. Why does the speaker assign extra work to the listeners?

(A) A deadline is fast approaching.
(B) One of the employees is unwell.
(C) A large number of customers are expected.
(D) Equipment needs to be unpacked.

6. What does the speaker ask listeners to tell customers about?

(A) Changed business hours
(B) Membership cards
(C) A special dish
(D) A holiday sale

PART 1

→ **Vocabulary** 따라 읽으면서 **암기**하세요   🎧 05_23

beside a curb 길가에	dive (물 속으로) 뛰어들다
trim (깎아) 다듬다, 손질하다	waterfront 해안가
crop (농)작물	

→ **Dictation**

1. [M|Au] 🎧 05_22_01

   (A) A car is _____ .

   (B) A motorcycle has been _____ .

   (C) Bushes _____ in the garden.

   (D) _____ in the field.

2. [W|Am] 🎧 05_22_02

   (A) A man is _____ a boat _____ .

   (B) Some small boats are _____ on the water.

   (C) Some small boats have been _____ .

   (D) Some boats are _____ .

3. [M|Cn] 🎧 05_22_03

   (A) _____ is _____ on the dock.

   (B) A swimmer is _____ into the water.

   (C) A group is _____ a boat _____ .

   (D) Several boats are _____ .

➕ **Vocabulary** 따라 읽으면서 **암기**하세요 🎧 05_24

past (위치상으로 ~을) 지나서
lost and found 분실물 보관소
sell out 다 팔리다, 매진되다
attract 끌어들이다
automate 자동화하다
checkout counter 계산대
professional development 전문성 개발

nomination 지명, 추천
room 여유; 공간
cover 떠맡다, 책임지다; 덮개
logistics 물류 관리
unnecessarily 불필요하게, 쓸데없이
overtime 초과 근무
shortly 얼마 안 가서, 곧

➕ **Dictation**

4. W|Am M|Au 🎧 05_22_04

_____ if I can't attend the conference, right?

(A) _____.

(B) _____, on the right.

(C) Have you _____?

5. W|Br W|Am 🎧 05_22_05

That theater is _____, isn't it?

(A) I _____.

(B) Our _____.

(C) True, so let's _____.

6. W|Am M|Cn 🎧 05_22_06

I don't think we _____ the store renovations yet.

(A) That's _____ Mateo _____.

(B) Yes, it's _____ more _____.

(C) The _____.

7. M|Cn W|Am 🎧 05_22_07

I _____ the professional development _____ was really _____.

(A) I'd be happy to _____.

(B) That was _____, _____.

(C) Sure, let me _____ it.

8. [M | Cn] [M | Au] 🎧 05_22_08

_____ the employee awards _____?

(A) The _____ deadline has _____.

(B) That _____'s _____.

(C) Three hundred people _____.

9. [W | Am] [M | Au] 🎧 05_22_09

The _____ for our magazine has _____ recently.

(A) There's _____ in the budget _____.

(B) The monthly _____ is twenty dollars.

(C) There are _____ on the table.

10. [W | Br] [M | Au] 🎧 05_22_10

Can you _____ on Tuesday?

(A) The _____ department.

(B) This _____'s _____ large.

(C) I'm _____.

11. [W | Br] [M | Cn] 🎧 05_22_11

I think I _____ this conference room _____.

(A) _____ did it _____?

(B) I'm so sorry. I'll be _____.

(C) A hotel in the _____.

12. [W | Am] [W | Br] 🎧 05_22_12

_____ at the Freiburg warehouse.

(A) Only _____ the main highway.

(B) Yes, we can _____ on Friday.

(C) I actually _____ Offenburg.

PART 3

 Vocabulary 따라 읽으면서 **암기**하세요

dining 식사	confidence 신뢰; 확신
entrée 앙트레(식당이나 만찬의 주요리)	challenge 과제, 난제
come up with (해답을) 찾아내다, 내놓다	fund-raiser 기금 마련 행사
sample 맛보다, 시식하다	bring up (화제를) 꺼내다
fund-raising 기금 마련	packing slip 운송 전표
address 고심하다, 다루다	end up V-ing 결국 ~하게 되다
frustrate 좌절감을 주다, 불만스럽게 만들다	place an order for ~을 주문하다
on time 시간을 어기지 않고, 정각에	pattern 무늬, 도안
nervous 불안한, 초조한, 긴장한	discontinue 단종하다, 생산을 중단하다
figure out ~을 이해하다, 알아내다	complimentary 무료의
make up for ~에 대해 보상하다	

Questions 13 through 15 refer to the following conversation.   05_22_13

[W | Br] OK, Ahmed, here's the problem. Over the last month, we _____ _____. We must find solutions to attract more people to the restaurant. Could you share any _____ _____?

[M | Au] Well, how about _____ _____ where all _____ are offered at a _____? I'll _____ for dishes that are not too expensive to make.

[W | Br] That's a good idea. Please _____ _____ those, but I'd like to _____ _____ before we make a decision about including them on the menu.

13. What problem does the woman mention?
(A) Business is unusually slow.
(B) A restaurant received negative feedback.
(C) There is a shortage of employees.
(D) There has been no renewal of the lease.

14. What does the man suggest?
(A) Providing outdoor dining
(B) Relocating to a larger space
(C) Lowering prices
(D) Catering for business functions

15. What does the woman ask the man to do?
(A) Recruit an assistant
(B) Organize a training session
(C) Prepare for an inspection
(D) Create some food samples

M Au Linda! You're still at your desk? I _____ you were _____ company's _____ event today.

W Am Well, I volunteered last year, and now I'm _____ _____ this month.

M Au Oh, I'm sorry to hear that. Can you tell me what happened?

W Am A group of _____ that they _____ their translations _____, and I'm feeling _____ about _____ _____.

M Au I understand. Well, I have confidence in your ability to handle this. You've _____ _____ in the past. I have to _____ _____ now, but I'll _____ _____ tomorrow so that it doesn't happen again.

16. What does the woman imply when she says, "I volunteered last year"?
- (A) She can aid in the training of other volunteers.
- (B) She takes pride in her volunteer work.
- (C) She did not have a good time at the event last year.
- (D) She has no plans to be present at the event.

17. What is the woman nervous about?
- (A) Delivering a speech
- (B) Responding to customer complaints
- (C) Translating a complex document
- (D) Assuming a new position

18. What does the man say he will do tomorrow?
- (A) Reassign certain tasks
- (B) Discuss an issue at a meeting
- (C) Get ready to provide some feedback
- (D) Conduct some preliminary research

M Cn I can help the next customer.

W Br Hi. I moved to a new house recently, and _____ a few dishes _____.
I _____ through your online store, and they were delivered yesterday. The problem is, I _____ _____ I requested.

M Cn I apologize for the inconvenience. May I take a look at your packing slip?

W Br Yes, here it is.

M Cn Hmm... Unfortunately, this particular dish _____'s _____. The three bowls you received are the last ones we had with that design. As a solution, I can _____ _____, and you can also _____ you received _____ gift.

W Br Thanks a lot! I appreciate that.

RALTON HOME FURNISHINGS

Order #45709

Quantity	Description	Total Price
5	Dinner Plate	$25
7	Soup Bowl	$42
4	Coffee Mug	$16
2	Teapot	$50

19. What does the woman say happened when she moved?
 (A) She was overcharged for a service.
 (B) A carton was misplaced.
 (C) A shipment was delivered to an incorrect location.
 (D) Some items were damaged.

20. Why does the woman need assistance?
 (A) She is not pleased with her purchase.
 (B) She is unable to access a Web site.
 (C) She received an incomplete order.
 (D) She lost a copy of an invoice.

21. Look at the graphic. How much money will the woman be refunded?
 (A) $25
 (B) $42
 (C) $16
 (D) $50

PART 4

 Vocabulary 따라 읽으면서 **암기**하세요 🎧 05_26

make use of ~을 이용하다, 활용하다	**sort** 종류, 유형
vendor 판매 회사	**glitch** 작은 문제[결함]
blend (차, 담배 등의) 블렌드, 혼합 (제품)	**to one's surprise** 놀랍게도
grab ~을 손에 넣다	**mistaken** 잘못 알고[판단하고] 있는
fill out ~을 기입하다, 작성하다	**so far** 지금까지
leave 맡기다, 위탁하다	**encounter** 맞닥뜨리다
complete 작성하다	**appreciate** ~의 진가를 알아보다, 인정하다
short on ~이 부족한	**feature** (상품의 특징적) 기능
burst 폭발, 터뜨림	**alert** 알림
consumer goods 소비재	**out-of-stock** (일시적으로) 재고가 떨어진
wholesome 건강에 좋은	**restock** 다시 채우다
treat 간식, 군것질거리	**perceive** ~을 (~로) 여기다
feel full and satisfied 포만감을 느끼다	**age group** 연령대
fiber 섬유(질)	**outcome** 결과
content 함유량, 함량	**depict** 묘사하다, 그리다
ample 충분한, 풍부한	**specific** 특정한
protein 단백질	**hopefully** 원하건대, (일이) 잘 되면
substitute 대용품	**boost** 신장시키다, 북돋우다
head (특정 방향으로) 가다, 향하다	

 Questions 22 through 24 refer to the following excerpt from meeting. 🎧 05_22_16

M Cn As you know, _____ _____ the coffee services provided in the company kitchens throughout the day. We're _____, and so tomorrow, _____ will be offering different coffee blends in the lobby. Feel free to _____ _____ that suits your taste. We just ask that you _____ on the coffee by giving us some feedback. It should take only five minutes to _____, and you can _____ Marlene in Office B-14.

22. What does the speaker say the company is considering?
(A) Contracting with a new vendor
(B) Extending the lunch hour
(C) Establishing an intern program
(D) Refurbishing company kitchens

23. What can listeners receive for free tomorrow?
(A) A coffee mug
(B) A clothing item
(C) A notebook
(D) A beverage

24. Why should listeners visit Marlene's office?
(A) To acquire training materials
(B) To participate in a project
(C) To be awarded a prize
(D) To submit a form

Questions 25 through 27 refer to the following advertisement. 05_22_17

W |Am| _____ time for a meal? Need a _____ _____? ! The Canadian _____ that brought you Hercules Grains Cereal is now offering a new product. Dr. Yummy is a _____ that will help you _____. With its _____, low _____, and _____ _____ this healthy snack is a _____ _____ junk food. You won't be able to get enough! Dr. Yummy is _____, so _____ today!

25. What product is being advertised?
(A) A seasoning
(B) A liquid refreshment
(C) A snack
(D) A vitamin supplement

26. According to the speaker, what is the advantage of Dr. Yummy?
(A) It is highly nutritious.
(B) It is reasonably priced.
(C) It is sold in packs of six.
(D) It appeals to children.

27. What does the speaker mean when she says, "You won't be able to get enough"?
(A) There are not enough items in stock.
(B) You will want plenty of these products.
(C) You cannot buy these goods in bulk.
(D) There is a diverse range of flavors to enjoy.

 Questions 28 through 30 refer to the following excerpt from and chart. 05_22_18

W |Am| As most of you know, I was _____ that our new Web site _____, but _____, I was _____. So far we _____, and the majority of our customers are pleased with the new services we're providing. They _____ _____ of receiving _____ _____ when _____ _____. I'm surprised, though, by _____ _____ by various age groups. The _____ _____ on this graph are, um, different from what I anticipated. Jeremy, could you please research why _____ shows the _____ _____ with the site? Using that information, we can hopefully _____ _____.

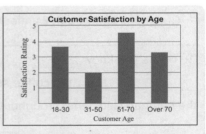

28. What does the speaker say she was wrong about?
(A) Increase in online sales
(B) A Web site malfunctioning
(C) The level of demand for a product
(D) The cost of enhancing a service

29. What does the speaker say is a popular Web site feature?
(A) Automated payment processing
(B) Reviews from customers
(C) Discounts on shipping
(D) E-mail notifications

30. Look at the graphic. What age group does the speaker ask Jeremy to investigate?
(A) 18-30   (B) 31-50
(C) 51-70   (D) Over 70

Day 06

PART 1 Exercise

✚ Vocabulary 따라 읽으면서 **암기**하세요   🎧 06_08

cashier 출납원	stare into ~을 응시하다
remove (옷 등을) 벗다	distance 먼 곳

✚ Dictation

1. M | Au 🎧 06_07_01

    (A) A man is _____ food items _____.

    (B) A sales clerk is _____ an item _____.

    (C) A woman is _____ on a wall.

    (D) A customer is ready to _____.

2. M | Cn 🎧 06_07_02

    (A) The man is _____.

    (B) The woman is _____.

    (C) A _____'s _____ on a table.

    (D) The family is _____.

PART 2 Exercise

✚ Vocabulary 따라 읽으면서 **암기**하세요   🎧 06_13

first thing (아침에) 제일 먼저	assistant 조수, 비서
supply closet 비품 창고	tour 둘러보다
accounting 회계 (업무)	ship 수송하다, 운송하다
memo 단체 메일, 회람	stock 재고(품)
guidelines 지침	packing 포장
complicated 복잡한	deplete 고갈시키다
simplify 간단하게[단순하게] 하다	sporting goods 스포츠 용품
copy (책, 신문 등의) 한 부	typically 보통, 일반적으로
webinar 웨비나(인터넷상의 세미나)	or so ~ 정도 ~쯤
suit ~에게 어울리다	stairs 계단

1. ☐ W|Am ☐ M|Cn 🎧 06_12_01

Why do we have to _____ the event?

(A) Maybe at the _____.

(B) I'll do it _____ tomorrow morning.

(C) I'm sorry, my _____'s _____.

2. ☐ M|Au ☐ W|Am 🎧 06_12_02

Why _____ my computer _____?

(A) There have been some _____.

(B) _____ at the stop sign.

(C) The computer _____ are in the _____.

3. ☐ W|Am ☐ M|Cn 🎧 06_12_03

Why _____ memo?

(A) You _____?

(B) I'm _____ they _____.

(C) Directly to Mr. Benjamin.

4. ☐ M|Cn ☐ W|Am 🎧 06_12_04

Why are _____?

(A) Thanks for _____ today.

(B) ___'ve _____ Chris _____ them.

(C) There are _____ for everyone.

5. ☐ W|Am ☐ W|Br 🎧 06_12_05

Why was the _____?

(A) A magazine _____.

(B) Mr. De Luca _____.

(C) I _____.

6. W | Br   M | Au   🎧 06_12_06

Why is the _____ from your lunch menu today?

(A) It _____ perfectly.

(B) _____ of water.

(C) We're _____ .

7. W | Br   M | Cn   🎧 06_12_07

Why does Dr. Houston _____ ?

(A) I _____ she _____ one.

(B) _____ two years' _____ .

(C) Yes, we _____ the new lab.

8. W | Br   M | Cn   🎧 06_12_08

Why _____ such a _____ in _____ these orders?

(A) _____ the next forty-eight hours.

(B) Our _____ has been _____ .

(C) _____ .

9. M | Au   M | Cn   🎧 06_12_09

Why _____ Ms. Lim _____ in the office all week?

(A) No, I _____ her.

(B) _____ until five o'clock _____ .

(C) You'll have to _____ .

10. M | Au   W | Am   🎧 06_12_10

Why _____ Steven _____ to the office?

(A) Take the _____ to your _____ .

(B) I _____ to two o'clock.

(C) _____ are at the _____ .

Vocabulary 따라 읽으면서 **암기**하세요 🎧 06_15

customer service representative 고객 서비스 직원	merge 합병하다
follow up on ~에 대응하여 조치하다	consolidation 합병, 통합
get back to ~에게 (나중에) 다시 연락하다	transition 이동, 변화
transaction 거래	advantageous 이로운, 유리한
drop by (=stop by) 잠깐 들르다	commute 통근하다
walk A through B A에게 B를 하나하나 보여주다[가르쳐주다]	be entitled to ~에 대한 자격을[권리를] 부여받다
personally 직접, 몸소	

Dictation

📝 **Questions 1 through 3** refer to the following conversation. 🎧 06_14_01

[W|Am] Hello. This is Mary Ying, customer service _____ at Doylestown Bank. I _____ _____ the message you _____ _____.

[M|Au] Yes, thank you for getting back to me. I recently opened a checking account, but the _____ _____.

[W|Am] I'm happy to assist you with that. Just provide me with your e-mail, and I'll send you a _____ _____ on how to _____. Alternatively, you can _____ tomorrow, and I can _____ personally.

[M|Au] That sounds good to me. I work in the neighborhood, so _____ during my lunch break _____. I'll see you at one o'clock.

1. Why does the woman call the man?
   (A) To verify an e-mail address
   (B) To reschedule an appointment
   (C) To respond to a message
   (D) To give directions to a place

2. What problem does the man mention?
   (A) He is unable to locate his keys.
   (B) He cannot remember his password.
   (C) He will not arrive on time for an appointment.
   (D) He was not given some instructions.

3. What does the man say he will do tomorrow?
   (A) Visit the bank
   (B) Contact a client
   (C) Work remotely
   (D) Dine with a colleague

M Au I called this meeting to announce officially
that _____ with Stratton
B _____ .
The _____ will result in a
positive impact on all of you as our employees. The
_____ is our _____
_____ . This new building's _____
_____ , which will be _____ for
those of you _____ . In
addition, we will follow Stratton Bank's vacation
policy, so all employees will be _____
_____ each year. Does anyone
have any questions?

4. What kind of business does the
   speaker work in?
   (A) A financial institution
   (B) A travel bureau
   (C) A staffing firm
   (D) An insurance provider

5. According to the speaker, what
   advantage does the new location
   have?
   (A) It has more spacious offices.
   (B) It is close to a variety of cafés.
   (C) It is easily accessible by public
       transit.
   (D) It has exquisitely landscaped
       gardens.

6. What policy change does the speaker
   mention?
   (A) Staff members will receive
       additional vacation time.
   (B) The company will offer
       telecommuting as an option.
   (C) Attendance at weekly meetings
       will be compulsory.
   (D) The sharing of office spaces will
       be mandatory.

PART 1

➕ **Vocabulary** ────── 따라 읽으면서 **암기**하세요 ────────────────── 🎧 06_18

pedestrian 보행자	portion 일부, 부분
sidewalk 인도, 보도	unfinished 완성되지 않은
resurface (도로를) 다시 포장하다	roofing 지붕 공사
safety cone 안전 원뿔형 표지	crane 기중기, 크레인
direct traffic 교통정리를 하다	window box (창가의) 화초 상자
dig up (땅을) 파내다, 파헤치다	lie 가로놓여 있다

➕ **Dictation** ────────────────────────────────────

1. ⬚W|Br⬚ 🎧 06_17_01

(A) A vehicle has been _____.

(B) _____ are _____ a street.

(C) Workers are _____.

(D) A sidewalk _____.

2. ⬚W|Am⬚ 🎧 06_17_02

(A) Some safety cones _____ from a work site.

(B) Some helmets have been _____.

(C) Some workers are _____.

(D) A road _____ by some workers.

3. ⬚W|Am⬚ 🎧 06_17_03

(A) A _____ of the roof is _____.

(B) Some _____.

(C) A house is _____ with _____.

(D) A ladder is _____ across a _____.

Vocabulary

따라 읽으면서 **암기**하세요   🎧 06_19

estimate 견적서	due (특정일까지 발생할) 예정인
anyhow 아무튼, 어쨌든	choreographer 안무가
hectic 정신없이 바쁜, 빡빡한	beautifully 멋지게, 훌륭하게
freezer 냉동고	dress rehearsal 총연습
at the moment 지금은, 현재	yet (의문문에서) 벌써, 이제; (최상급과 함께) 이제[지금]까지
mean to-V ~하려고 하다	moderator 사회자
stack 쌓다	launch 출시
against ~에 붙여	charity 자선
inspection 점검	sign up 등록하다
supplier 공급(업)자, 공급업체	in advance 미리, 사전에
exposition 박람회, 전시회	

Dictation

4. [W|Am] [M|Au] 🎧 06_17_04

Why has the seminar been _____?

(A) About thirty _____.

(B) In R_____ F_____.

(C) Because _____.

5. [M|Cn] [W|Br] 🎧 06_17_05

Why did Jeong-Won _____?

(A) She will _____ in October.

(B) Anyhow, they _____.

(C) _____ of how _____ is?

6. [W|Br] [M|Au] 🎧 06_17_06

Why did you _____ delivered this morning _____?

(A) It's not _____.

(B) I _____.

(C) Shall we begin _____ soon?

7. [W|Am] [W|Br] 🎧 06_17_07

Why are we _____?
(A) Just _____ the books _____ wall.
(B) I will be _____ if necessary.
(C) Haven't you _____?

8. [M|Cn] [W|Br] 🎧 06_17_08

Why has our _____ decided to _____?
(A) I'll _____.
(B) Sure, last week.
(C) How many would you like?

9. [M|Cn] [W|Br] 🎧 06_17_09

I'd like to know _____'s _____ the _____.
(A) Try _____ to the left.
(B) Registrations _____ next Friday.
(C) There are _____ at B_____.

10. [W|Br] [M|Au] 🎧 06_17_10

Cynthia Stroman is the _____ of this musical, isn't she?
(A) Yes, and it's _____.
(B) No, I _____ music.
(C) There will be a _____ this evening.

11. [M|Cn] [W|Br] 🎧 06_17_11

Have the _____ of the new skincare line's testing _____ yet?
(A) A _____ discussion _____.
(B) They _____.
(C) The _____ has been _____.

12. [M|Cn] [W|Am] 🎧 06_17_12

_____ the charity event, can't you?
(A) Don't forget to _____.
(B) The _____ have _____ been _____.
(C) _____ was the _____ yet.

→ Vocabulary | 따라 읽으면서 **암기하세요** 06_20

terrific 아주 좋은, 훌륭한	double-check 재확인하다
thus far 지금까지	credits 크레디트 (제작진, 출연진 명단)
take over 인계받다	Hold on. 기다려, 멈춰
keep *sth* in mind ~을 명심하다, 유념하다	be involved in ~에 관여하다
in writing 서면으로	in search of ~을 찾고 있는
make sure (that) 반드시 (~하도록) 하다	plan 요금제
in person 직접, 몸소	competitive 경쟁력 있는
get it 이해하다	rate 요금
pharmacology 약리학	terminate 끝내다, 종료하다
trial 임상 시험	transfer 전근시키다
promising 조짐이 좋은	commit to ~을 확실히 약속하다
on track 제대로 진행되고 있는	proceed with ~을 진행하다
at the moment 바로 지금	get to ~에 착수하다

Questions 13 through 15 refer to the following conversation with three speakers. 06_17_13

M Au Thank you both for attending this meeting regarding the Dover building project. It was a _____.

W Am Absolutely, Frank's _____ with the project _____, and I'm really looking forward to _____ from this point.

M Au Frank, is there any other information that Mina _____?

M Cn One more detail to _____ - the client requires _____. So make sure you _____ any discussions _____.

W Am Got it. So Frank, I've heard you'll be _____ _____.

M Cn Yeah, 've _____ Morocco before, so I'm really excited about my next building project in Marrakesh.

13. What are the speakers discussing?
(A) Securing financial backing
(B) Negotiating a company merger
(C) Making travel arrangements
(D) Handing over a project's leadership

14. What does Frank advise the woman to do?
(A) Conduct negotiations in person
(B) Forward confirmation e-mails
(C) Lower overhead costs
(D) Modify a budget

15. What does Frank say he is excited about?
(A) Collaborating with new colleagues
(B) Receiving a pay raise
(C) Hiring an support staff member
(D) Working in foreign country

[M | Cn] Jennifer. So, about my _____

_____ ...

[W | Br] So sorry! I _____ 've _____ to you

earlier.

[M | Cn] That's fine. I know you've been concentrating

on the _____.

[W | Br] Yeah, but the _____.

We're _____

_____.

[M | Cn] Excellent! So would you like to see some

slides at the moment?

[W | Br] Sure.

[M | Cn] All right, I just _____ if I

_____ on the credits

slide.

[W | Br] OK, let me see... hmm... yeah... Hold on.

Wasn't Akira involved in this project...?

[M | Cn] Oh, you're right! I'm _____.

16. What industry do the speakers most
likely work in?
(A) Pharmaceutical
(B) Banking
(C) Marketing
(D) Information technology

17. What does the woman say will
happen this year?
(A) Some research will receive
additional funding.
(B) A new product will be unveiled.
(C) There will be a merger of two
companies.
(D) An award ceremony will take
place.

18. What does the woman imply when
she says, "Wasn't Akira involved in
this project"?
(A) Certain findings are not ready
yet.
(B) A project requires additional
personnel.
(C) There is a lack of information on
a slide.
(D) The man must meet with a
researcher.

[M | Cn] Hi, I'm _____ Internet provider, so I _____ 'd _____ about your service plans.

[W | Am] Of course. We offer the _____ _____ in this area. _____ on this chart, the _____ your contract period, the _____ your monthly cost.

[M | Cn] But what happens if I need to _____ _____ before its completion?

[W | Am] Well... we do _____ for that.

[M | Cn] Umm... I'm _____ _____, so I'm _____ _____ the two-year plan. But I _____ _____ possible price.

[W | Am] In that case, the one-year plan seems like the _____ option. Shall we _____ _____ the contract?

[M | Cn] Sure, let's _____.

Contract Length	Cost per Month
3 months	$50.00
6 months	$40.00
1 year	$30.00
2 years	$20.00

19. According to the woman, when is an extra fee charged?

(A) When a customer transfers to a new location
(B) When a payment is overdue
(C) When new application is installed
(D) When a contract is canceled early

20. What does the man say he will do next year?

(A) Relocate abroad
(B) Complete an internship program
(C) Purchase another device
(D) Renew a contract

21. Look at the graphic. How much has the man agreed to pay per month?

(A) $50.00
(B) $40.00
(C) $30.00
(D) $20.00

Vocabulary 따라 읽으면서 **암기**하세요 06_21

outline ~의 개요를 서술하다	contemporary 현대의, 당대의
strategy 전략	be set on ~에 대해 (견해, 생각이) 확고한, 고정된
profession 직업	maintain 유지하다, 지속하다
towards ~ 무렵에	approach 접근법
hesitate 망설이다, 주저하다	go over ~을 점검하다, 검토하다
call in 전화를 하다	crucial 중대한
line (전화) 회선	content 만족하는
It has come to one's attention that ~을 알게 되다	feasible 실현 가능한
bring out ~을 출간하다	constraint 제약, 제한
set to-V ~할 준비가 된	can afford to-V (시간, 금전적으로) ~할 여유가 있다
in print 인쇄된	contact 연락을 주고받는 사람
convince 납득시키다, 확신시키다	pass on ~을 넘겨주다, 전달하다

 Questions 22 through 24 refer to the following broadcast. 06_17_16

W|Br Good morning, RKZ Radio listeners! Today on the Chester Business Show, we _____ Janet Lin _____ _____. O _____, Ms. Lin will _____ for discovering a profession that matches your skills, interests, and personality. _____ the show, we would love to _____, so _____ when the lines are open and _____. Well, let me start off by saying welcome, Ms. Lin. It has _____ you're _____ _____ on this topic, _____ next month.

22. What is Ms. Lin's area of expertise?
(A) Management of nonprofit organizations
(B) Professional advice on career choices
(C) Event planning and coordination
(D) Individual financial planning

23. What are listeners encouraged to do?
(A) Share their opinions over the phone
(B) Update their résumés
(C) Participate in a workshop
(D) Keep track of household spending

24. What does the speaker say will happen next month?
(A) An educational session will be conducted.
(B) A schedule will be altered.
(C) An interview is scheduled to take place.
(D) A book will become available.

M | Au Hi, Shawn. I've just finished _____ Tara Goldberg _____. She _____ the company's upcoming _____, but she's _____ _____ than what we originally suggested. I _____ _____ her that a _____ _____ was needed, but she was _____ a traditional approach. There _____ _____. You know... she's the head of the department. Anyway, I'm back at my desk now, so I'm going to _____ on our calendars tomorrow when we can _____ and _____ _____.

25. What did the speaker discuss with Tara Goldberg?

(A) A hiring policy
(B) A product design
(C) An order for supplies
(D) An itinerary for a trip

26. What does the speaker imply when he says, "she's the head of the department"?

(A) He wants to introduce a new executive.
(B) He lacks the authority to make the final decision.
(C) A job title has been incorrectly printed.
(D) A colleague has achieved great success.

27. What will the speaker most likely do next?

(A) Set up a meeting
(B) Refer to a catalog
(C) Fill out a form
(D) Meet with a client

[W|Br] Let's start the staff meeting by going over the results of the member survey our fitness center recently completed. It's _____ to _____ that our _____, which is why these _____. Here are the top four answers to the question, "What _____ would you _____?" While _____ a desire for a larger pool, it is _____ due to financial _____. However, we _____ ____ a couple of new staff members so we can _____. If you have any _____ who are qualified and might be interested in a position here, please _____ _____.

Survey Results	
Expanded swimming facility	40%
Extended operating hours	20%
Updated exercise equipment	10%
Diverse classes	30%

설문 조사 결과	
수영 시설 확장	40%
운영 시간 연장	20%
운동 장비 교체	10%
다양한 수업	30%

28. According to the speaker, what is the center's main concern?
    (A) Satisfying current members
    (B) Complying with industry standards
    (C) Minimizing operating expenses
    (D) Developing successful marketing campaigns

29. Look at the graphic. What survey result does the speaker want to address?
    (A) Expanded swimming facility
    (B) Extended operating hours
    (C) Updated exercise equipment
    (D) Diverse classes

30. What does the speaker ask the listeners to do?
    (A) Perform safety assessments
    (B) Enroll in a certification program
    (C) Refer potential employees
    (D) Tour a construction site

Day 07

Vocabulary 따라 읽으면서 **암기**하세요 · 07_09

try on (옷을) 입어 보다. (신발을) 신어 보다	**polish** (윤이 나도록) 닦다
apron 앞치마	**corridor** 복도
cash register 금전 등록기	**set** (특정한 위치에) 놓다
artwork 미술품	**reach** (손, 팔을 ~쪽으로) 뻗다, 내밀다
hang (hung-hung) 걸다, 매달다	

Dictation

1. ⟦M | Cn⟧ · 07_08_01

   (A) Some people are _____.

   (B) Customers are waiting _____.

   (C) Artworks are being _____.

   (D) Some artists are _____.

2. ⟦W | Am⟧ · 07_08_02

   (A) Some workers are _____.

   (B) Pieces of tile _____ into a floor.

   (C) The people are _____.

   (D) One of the women is _____.

Vocabulary 따라 읽으면서 **암기**하세요 · 07_23

regarding ~에 관하여[대하여]	**turnout** 참가자 수
exceptional 탁월한, 특출한	**librarian** (도서관의) 사서
cover letter 자기소개서	**check out** (도서관에서) 대출하다
mail carrier 우편집배원	**fly** 비행기를 타고 가다
stop by 잠시 들르다	**projector** 영사기
photocopier 복사기	**sign up (for)** ~을 신청하다, 등록하다
application 앱, 애플리케이션	**off** 할인하여
frequently 자주, 흔히	**showcase** 진열하다
mechanical engineering 기계 공학	**new arrival** 신착 상품
shipment 수송품	**storefront** 매장 앞쪽

1. [M | Au] [W | Am] 🎧 07_22_01

   How soon can I _____ my job application?

   (A) No, it's _____.

   (B) An _____ résumé and _____.

   (C) We'll call you in two weeks.

2. [M | Br] [W | Br] 🎧 07_22_02

   _____ my e-mail account on my tablet?

   (A) The _____ by soon.

   (B) On the table next to the _____.

   (C) _____ the e-mail _____.

3. [W | Am] [M | Au] 🎧 07_22_03

   _____ your new job _____?

   (A) I can _____.

   (B) A _____.

   (C) My brother _____ me _____.

4. [W | Br] [M | Au] 🎧 07_22_04

   _____ are you from the clinic?

   (A) I'm _____.

   (B) I'll make an _____.

   (C) That clinic is _____.

5. [W | Am] [M | Au] 🎧 07_22_05

   _____ are we expecting today?

   (A) It was an _____.

   (B) I can _____ if you _____.

   (C) No, it _____ than that.

6. [M | Au] [W | Am] 🎧 07_22_06

_____ one of the meeting rooms at the library?

(A) Let me _____ .

(B) They _____ A.M.

(C) That _____ 's _____ .

7. [M | Cn] [W | Br] 🎧 07_22_07

How often do you _____ Boston _____ ?

(A) My _____ .

(B) We usually _____ .

(C) Yes, it's one of my _____ !

8. [W | Br] [M | Cn] 🎧 07_22_08

_____ the project deadline?

(A) It _____ we'll _____ .

(B) Can you _____ ?

(C) The meeting _____ .

9. [W | Am] [M | Cn] 🎧 07_22_09

_____ the additional discount coupons?

(A) I _____ online.

(B) Usually _____ .

(C) No, the package _____ .

10. [M | Cn] [W | Am] 🎧 07_22_10

How do you want to _____ ?

(A) Let's _____ .

(B) They're _____ .

(C) You _____ .

🎧 07_25

➜ **Vocabulary** 따라 읽으면서 **암기**하세요

intermediate 중급의	tutorial 개별 지도
good fit 잘 맞는 것	set 준비가 된
in the meantime 그 동안[사이]에	

➜ **Dictation**

🖼️ **Questions 1 through 3** refer to the following conversation.　🎧 07_24

W | Br　Hi, I _____

for cello lessons at your shop, and I'd like to sign

up.

M | Cn　Excellent. Do you _____

with the cello?

W | Br　Well, I _____ in my high school

orchestra.

M | Cn　OK, it _____ the _____

would be a _____ for you. The classes are

scheduled to start next week.

W | Br　Great.

M | Cn　_____, you have the option

to _____ on our Web site by

_____. Are you

interested in becoming a member?

W | Br　Oh, that sounds good. My e-mail address is

elsa785@mailexchange.com.

M | Cn　All right, you're _____, and the first lesson

is scheduled for next Monday at 7 P.M. See you

there!

1. What does the woman say she did in high school?
    (A) She founded a club.
    (B) She developed a Web site.
    (C) She participated in a musical group.
    (D) She took online lessons.

2. What is available on the store Web site?
    (A) Promotional discounts
    (B) Instructional videos
    (C) Interactions with musicians
    (D) A schedule of store events

3. What does the woman imply when she says, "Oh, that sounds good"?
    (A) An e-mail address is easy to remember.
    (B) A lesson appears reasonably priced.
    (C) An instrument is in tune.
    (D) She is able to join a mailing list.

Vocabulary 따라 읽으면서 **암기**하세요 🎧 07_27

bring up (화제를) 꺼내다	wrap up 마무리짓다
workload 업무량	time off 휴가
company director 대표 이사	shipping 운송, 수송
allocate 할당하다	volume 양, 분량
substantial 상당한	help 도우미, 일꾼
give one's approval for ~을 승인하다	send in ~을 제출하다
beneficial 유익한	update 갱신하다

Dictation

 Questions 1 through 3 refer to the following conversation. 🎧 07_26_01

W | Br Evan, _____
this morning? You were going to _____
_____ and _____,
right?

M | Au Yes! The company director has agreed to

_____

_____ to our marketing department's budget.

W | Br That's a substantial rise from last year! Do
you have any details on _____
_____?

M | Au Well, the department managers have _____
_____ for _____ to
_____ two new staff members. _____
_____ artist and a digital advertising specialist to
our team would be _____
_____.

1. What department do the speakers work in?
   (A) Product development
   (B) Human resources
   (C) Accounting
   (D) Marketing

2. Why does the woman say, "That's a substantial rise from last year"?
   (A) To suggest that some news is good
   (B) To deny a proposed budget adjustment
   (C) To indicate that a fee is appropriate
   (D) To correct some inaccurate information

3. According to the man, what do the department managers plan to do?
   (A) Purchase new equipment
   (B) Organize a conference
   (C) Recruit some more employees
   (D) Diversify a product range

M | Au To _____, I need to _____
_____ . A number of drivers _____
_____ the end of this
month... but you know it's the holiday season. _____
_____ by forty percent
over the next four weeks. And in fact, we're going
to be so busy that we _____
_____ . So, for those of you who _____
_____, If you're considering taking _____
_____, I'll be _____
_____ to you so you can update them with new
dates.

4. Why does the man say, "it's the holiday season"?
   (A) To express his thrill
   (B) To turn down a request
   (C) To express dissatisfaction with a schedule
   (D) To show appreciation to a colleague

5. What has the company recently done?
   (A) Adjusted a product price
   (B) Updated a policy
   (C) Established a new facility
   (D) Recruited temporary workers

6. What will the man most likely do next?
   (A) Return some paperwork
   (B) Post some photographs
   (C) Revise a manual
   (D) Lead an orientation

PART 1

back 등; (등)허리	**carry** 휴대하다, 들고 다니다
take off (옷 등을) 벗다	**lean** ~에 기대다
fasten 동여매다, 고정시키다	**safety gear** 안전 장구
exterior 외부, 바깥 면	

➕ **Dictation**

1. ⟨ M｜Au ⟩ 🎧 07_29_01

   (A) One of the women is _____ at something on the board.

   (B) One of the men is _____ the room.

   (C) One of the women _____.

   (D) One of the men is _____ a folder.

2. ⟨ W｜Br ⟩ 🎧 07_29_02

   (A) The man is _____ a bicycle _____.

   (B) The man is _____ his helmet.

   (C) The man is _____ his bike to the _____ of a vehicle.

   (D) The man is _____ a bicycle to the _____.

3. ⟨ M｜Cn ⟩ 🎧 07_29_03

   (A) The man is _____ a bucket with water.

   (B) The man is _____ a helmet.

   (C) The man is _____ a wall.

   (D) The man is _____.

Vocabulary 따라 읽으면서 **암기**하세요 🎧 07_31

quarter to ten 10시 15분 전
price tag 가격표
missing 없어진
owe 빚지고 있다
control panel (기계, 장치의) 제어판
rate 요금
post 게시하다, 게재하다
announcement 알림, 공고
significant 상당한
store 보관하다

outing 야유회
staff (모든) 직원
knowledgeable 아는 것이 많은
commute 통근 (거리)
headquarters 본사
commercial 상업의, 이윤을 목적으로 한
away 자리에 없는
confirm 확정하다
tremendous 엄청난, 대단한

Dictation

4. [M|Cn] [W|Br] 🎧 07_29_04

How much _____?

(A) _____ these days.

(B) It's _____.

(C) Is the _____?

5. [W|Br] [M|Au] 🎧 07_29_05

_____ the projector screen?

(A) I _____ for dinner.

(B) The _____ 's _____ the door.

(C) _____?

6. [W|Br] [M|Au] 🎧 07_29_06

How can we _____ for the marketing team?

(A) These are the _____.

(B) I'll _____ for them.

(C) Let's _____ on campus.

7. [W | Br] [M | Au] 🎧 07_29_07

How can we _____?
(A) It's on the _____.
(B) I _____.
(C) We use a _____ for printing.

8. [M | Cn] [W | Am] 🎧 07_29_08

_____ these photographs?
(A) Rachel is _____.
(B) From the company _____.
(C) Yes, the staff is very _____.

9. [W | Am] [W | Br] 🎧 07_29_09

Does this job candidate have _____?
(A) Here's a _____.
(B) The _____ at 5 P.M.
(C) A very _____.

10. [W | Am] [M | Au] 🎧 07_29_10

_____ to be working on this research project?
(A) She's with another _____.
(B) I'm going to _____ for exercise.
(C) Their _____.

11. [W | Am] [M | Cn] 🎧 07_29_11

_____ to drive to the headquarters.
(A) A _____'s _____.
(B) Sorry, I'm _____.
(C) I'll be _____.

12. [W | Br] [W | Am] 🎧 07_29_12

Has the cleaning service _____?
(A) The event was a _____!
(B) I _____ my e-mail yet.
(C) Because it was _____.

+ Vocabulary 따라 읽으면서 **암기**하세요  🎧 07_32

book 예약하다	hands-on 실무형의, 직접 관여하는
riverfront 강변 지대	dedicated to ∼을 전담하는
city landscape 도시 전경	professional development 전문성 개발
be supposed to-V (일반적으로) ∼라고 한다	productivity 생산성
spectacular 장관인, 볼 만한	inventory 재고(품)
look into ∼을 조사하다	perform (기계가) 작동하다, 돌아가다
impressed 인상 깊게 생각하는	endorse 승인하다
talented 재능 있는	keep track of ∼에 대해 계속 알다[파악하다]
manage to-V (어려움에도) 해내다	vacuum cleaner 진공청소기
recruit 모집하다	floor polisher 바닥 광택기
give *sth* thought 곰곰이 생각하다	misplaced 잃어버린
identify 찾다, 발견하다	refer to ∼을 보다, 참조하다
sharp 예리한, 명석한	monitor 감독하다, 주시하다
up-and-coming 전도유망한	status 상태, 상황
in need of ∼이 필요한	check in 반납하다
quality 양질의	

 Questions 13 through 15 refer to the following conversation. 🎧 07_29_13

M|Cn Hi, Carly. I _____ for the play we _____ Taipei ___, but there _____. Do you have any other ideas for activities we can do instead?

W|Br Oh, that's unfortunate. Well, the weather is _____ this weekend. Have you considered _____ at Port View Restaurant? It's located on a _____ _____, and I've brought guests there before.

M|Cn 've _____ that ship, and the _____ from the river is supposed to be _____. Could you please _____ of the dinner cruise?

13. What problem does the man mention?
(A) A reservation is not accurate.
(B) A business trip has been deferred.
(C) An event is sold out.
(D) Credit card payments are not permitted.

14. What does the woman suggest offering their colleagues?
(A) A meal on a boat
(B) A room upgrade at a hotel
(C) Admission to a sporting event
(D) Gift certificates for a store

15. What does the man ask the woman to do?
(A) Contact a travel agent
(B) Research pricing information
(C) Make a payment beforehand
(D) Coordinate transportation

W | Br I'm really _____ by how many _____ _____ we've _____ recently, but I'm also _____ _____ the kind of _____ we need for these upcoming projects.

M | Au I've been _____ as well. We've _____ some of the _____ _____ in the industry, but they're _____. We _____ to the department, especially one _____ _____.

W | Br Now that's an idea. The _____ the _____ _____ to the new employees, the _____ their _____ will be. How about we _____ _____ this to the vice president?

16. What problem does the woman mention?
(A) An error occurred during a research.
(B) Some project deadlines have expired.
(C) A department lacks adequate financial resources.
(D) Some staff members are inexperienced.

17. What does the woman mean when she says, "Now that's an idea"?
(A) She is seeking additional advice.
(B) The man has come up with a useful suggestion.
(C) The existing plan is overly complicated.
(D) A change is occurring at the right time.

18. What will the speakers most likely do next?
(A) Discuss a proposal
(B) Offer a promotion
(C) Arrange an interview
(D) Examine a report

W | Br _____'s the new inventory-control _____ _____? It's been a month since I _____ your _____ for it.

M | Au This software is really helpful. It _____ _____, vacuum cleaners, floor polishers, and everything else. You may remember that I got it after _____ _____ last year.

W | Br Indeed. So every piece of equipment is _____ with this new software. And then it _____ into the system whenever it's _____?

M | Au That's correct. I can _____ to _____ of all the items in use. Look, two items are _____ _____ today.

Item #	Date Checked Out	Date Due
343	April 15	April 17
228	April 16	April 17
216	April 18	April 19
326	April 19	April 21

19. What did the business recently purchase?
(A) Some software
(B) Several trucks
(C) Office furniture
(D) Safety eyewear

20. What type of business do the speakers most likely work for?
(A) A laundry service
(B) An electronics store
(C) A cleaning company
(D) A courier service

21. Look at the graphic. When is the conversation taking place?
(A) On April 15
(B) On April 17
(C) On April 19
(D) On April 21

Vocabulary 따라 읽으면서 **암기**하세요 🎧 07_33

locally-grown 이 지역에서 재배한	**reflect on** ~을 되돌아보다
lettuce 상추	**co-found** 공동 창업하다
comment on ~에 대해 의견을 말하다	**unparalleled** 비할[견줄] 데 없는
costly 많은 비용이 드는	**wastewater** 폐수, 하수
compared to ~와 비교하여	**in recognition of** ~을 인정하여
distributor 유통업체	**acquire** 취득하다
well worth ~할 가치가 충분히 있는	**share** 몫, 지분
flavor 풍미, 맛	**stock** (한 기업의) 주식 자본
personally 직접, 개인적으로	**ferry** (카)페리, 연락선
pick out ~을 고르다, 선택하다	**rest assured (that)** ~라는 것에 대해 안심하다
produce 농산물, 농작물	**though** (문장 끝에서) 그렇지만, 하지만
make up ~을 보충하다	**swiftly** 신속하게, 재빨리
boost 증가	**clear** (눈, 비 등이) 그치다
review 논평, 비평	**in time for** ~하는 시간에 맞춰
press conference 기자 회견	**accommodate** 수용하다
founder 창립자, 설립자	**chilly** 쌀쌀한, 추운
Incorporated(Inc.) (회사명 뒤에서) 주식회사	**inconvenience** 불편

 Questions 22 through 24 refer to the following talk. 🎧 07_29_16

W Am The purpose of this meeting is to _____
_____. I believe it's
time we _____
_____. Since we began
using _____ lettuce and tomatoes
in our salads, our customers have _____
_____. While I understand that
these vegetables can be more _____
____ those _____ from a major distributor, I believe
they're _____. Because the
vegetables are fresher, they have _____,
and our chefs have the opportunity to _____
_____ by visiting the
farms. And besides, we'll probably _____
_____ by seeing a _____ in
customer numbers and _____ restaurant
reviews.

22. Where does the speaker most likely work?
(A) On a vegetable farm
(B) In a grocery store
(C) At a dining establishment
(D) At a publishing company

23. What do customers like about fresh vegetables?
(A) The appearance
(B) The price
(C) The size
(D) The taste

24. What does the speaker recommend?
(A) Increasing vegetable intake
(B) Cultivating one's own vegetables
(C) Requesting a discount from large wholesalers
(D) Sourcing more vegetables from local farms

[M | Au] I want to express my _____ to the _____ for being _____ at today's _____. I'm Girolamo Vega, _____ and CEO of Vega, Incorporated. It's truly _____ to _____ environmental consulting firm, which I _____ with a small group of friends only _____, has been _____. Now, we have over four hundred people on staff. And they are _____ in the industry. It's because of their _____ that _____ some of the _____ _____ has been such a success. _____ this, I'm announcing that employees will now have the _____ to _____ in the company. I'm thrilled to offer this _____ _____ to our staff.

25. What type of company is Vega, Incorporated?
(A) Media and advertising
(B) Academic software
(C) Medical equipment
(D) Environmental consulting

26. What does the speaker imply when he says, "Now, we have over four hundred people on staff"?
(A) A training program needs to be expanded.
(B) A company has experienced rapid growth.
(C) A department requires reorganization.
(D) An office building is overcrowded.

27. What is being announced?
(A) Employees will be able to invest in the company.
(B) Solar panels are scheduled for installation.
(C) A product is being discontinued.
(D) A board member will step down next year.

W Am Attention, all passengers waiting for the five-thirty P.M. ferry to Ostar Island. Please _____ _____ the ferry has been cancelled due to a _____ _____ . R _____ , _____ , the storm is moving _____ and is expected to _____ _____ the final departure of the day. In order to _____ all the extra passengers on the final ferry trip, we will be using the _____ _____ . It can get _____ up there, so _____'d _____ a sweater or jacket if you have one with you. We appreciate your patience and apologize for any inconvenience.

Departures	Arrivals
10:00 A.M.	10:30 A.M.
12:00 P.M.	12:30 P.M.
5:30 P.M.	6:00 P.M.
7:30 P.M.	8:00 P.M.

28. What has caused a cancellation?
(A) Inclement weather
(B) Mechanical problems
(C) An unwell crew member
(D) Insufficient number of passengers

29. Look at the graphic. What time will the ferry leave?
(A) 10:00 A.M.
(B) 12:00 P.M.
(C) 5:30 P.M.
(D) 7:30 P.M.

30. What does the speaker say listeners may want to do?
(A) Travel the following day
(B) Retain a receipt
(C) Grab a bite to eat
(D) Dress in warm layers

✦ Vocabulary 따라 읽으면서 **암기**하세요 🎧 08_10

skyscraper 고층 건물	cord 코드, 전깃줄
ferryboat 연락선, 페리보트	lie 가로놓여 있다
dock (배를) 부두에 대다	plug 플러그를 꽂다
pier 부두	plug A into B A를 B에 연결하다
cityscape 도시 경관	power outlet 전기 콘센트
coastal 해안의, 연안의	aim 겨누다
rack 선반, 꽂이	flashlight 손전등

✦ Dictation

1. M|Au 🎧 08_09_01

   (A) Some _____ are _____.
   (B) Some ferryboats are _____.
   (C) The cityscape is _____ of the water.
   (D) A line of vehicles are _____.

2. M|Cn 🎧 08_09_02

   (A) Some equipment _____.
   (B) Some cords are _____.
   (C) A man is _____ a device _____.
   (D) A man is _____ a flashlight _____ to find something.

✦ Vocabulary 따라 읽으면서 **암기**하세요 🎧 08_21

conference call 전화 회의	brochure 안내 책자
customer service representative 고객 서비스 상담원	invoice 송장(送狀), 청구서
keep V-ing ~을 계속하다, 반복하다	on foot 걸어서, 도보로
definitely 확실히	building directory 건물 안내판
native art 민속 예술	pass along ~을 전달하다
guidebook 여행[관광] 안내서	shortly 곧, 얼마 안 있어
promotional 홍보의, 판촉의	momentarily 곧, 금방

1. [M|Cn] [W|Am] 🎧 08_20_01

   What _____ the conference call?

   (A) Only with customer service _____.

   (B) _____ the customer satisfaction survey.

   (C) The discussion _____.

2. [W|Br] [M|Au] 🎧 08_20_02

   What _____ would you prefer for your new office?

   (A) That's a _____.

   (B) I'll just _____.

   (C) It _____ week.

3. [W|Br] [M|Cn] 🎧 08_20_03

   _____ to the city last weekend?

   (A) Definitely the N_____ A____ C_____ !

   (B) Thanks, but I already _____.

   (C) Yes, the _____ useful.

4. [M|Au] [W|Br] 🎧 08_20_04

   What should I do with the _____?

   (A) She was _____ to manager.

   (B) _____ to the subscribers on our mailing list.

   (C) _____.

5. [M|Cn] [M|Au] 🎧 08_20_05

   What's the _____ for this item?

   (A) I saw a television _____.

   (B) Batteries are _____ in the package.

   (C) All the _____.

6. [M | Cn] [W | Am] 🎧 08_20_06

What time _____ come?

(A) I'm _____ .

(B) A _____ ticket.

(C) It's on F_____-F_____ Street.

7. [M | Cn] [M | Au] 🎧 08_20_07

What _____ is Spellman Technologies on?

(A) There's a _____ you.

(B) _____ machine _____ .

(C) Yes, that's _____ located.

8. [M | Cn] [W | Am] 🎧 08_20_08

What did you do _____ yesterday?

(A) _____ everyone _____ .

(B) I _____ to whoever _____ .

(C) We're _____ to leave _____ .

9. [M | Au] [W | Am] 🎧 08_20_09

What's the _____ for Langford Restaurant?

(A) It's _____ .

(B) Steak or pasta?

(C) Our supervisor _____ .

10. [W | Br] [M | Au] 🎧 08_20_10

_____ tonight?

(A) At the corner of Jefferson Street and Elm Avenue.

(B) _____ tables are _____ .

(C) Your _____ .

Vocabulary 따라 읽으면서 **암기**하세요 🎧 08_23

division (조직의) 부서	merger 합병
performance appraisal 인사 고과, 고과 평가	namely 말하자면, 이를테면
evaluation 평가	take advantage of ~을 이용하다, 활용하다
in place 시행 중인	elevate 높이다
chance 가능성	cutting-edge 최첨단의
overlook 못 보고 넘어가다, 간과하다	editorial 편집의, 편집과 관련된
be away on business 출장 중이다	be poised to-V ~할 준비가 되어 있다
potential client 잠재 고객	unparalleled 비할[견줄] 데 없는
to begin with 우선, 먼저	grant (권리, 권한을) 부여하다
editor-in-chief 편집 주간	publication 출판물, 간행물
thrilled 크게 기뻐하는, 흥분된	familiarize oneself with ~에 익숙해지다

Dictation

📝 **Questions 1 through 3** refer to the following conversation with three speakers. 🎧 08_22_01

W|Br Hi, Oliver and Lydia. You _____ in the sales division for several months before your _____ _____, right?

M|Cn Yes, that sounds right.

W|Am It took four months for me to have my first evaluation. Why?

W|Br 've _____ for four months, but no one has _____ _____ to me yet. I'm wondering _____ _____.

M|Cn Well, the company doesn't have a policy in place for this.

W|Am That's true. It's a _____ that your supervisor _____. You know _____ _____ on business for the last week. She's having meetings with some _____ in Tokyo.

W|Br Well, _____ she returns, _____.

1. What are the speakers mainly discussing?
   (A) An employee assessment
   (B) A sales promotion
   (C) A new patron
   (D) An itinerary for a trip

2. Why does the man say, "the company doesn't have a policy in place for this"?
   (A) To defer an announcement
   (B) To grant approval to the woman
   (C) To offer an explanation
   (D) To propose a policy modification

3. Why is the manager unavailable?
   (A) She is delivering a speech at a conference.
   (B) She is training new hires.
   (C) She is finishing a sales report.
   (D) She is meeting some clients.

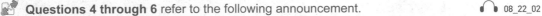
W Br Welcome to this month's all-staff meeting.

_____, I have some exciting news. As

the _____ *Global Commerce*

magazine, I am _____ to announce the completion

of our company's _____ with Jenson Publishing.

This means many great things for us, _____ that

we can _____ Jenson's _____

technology department _____ the

quality of the online version of our magazine. And

why wouldn't we? With Jenson's _____

technology and our _____ expertise, we

are _____ to create an _____ digital

experience for our readers. Now, Jenson has

already _____

publications. So, please _____ over the

next few weeks to _____

____ Web sites.

4. What is the purpose of the announcement?

(A) To scrutinize a budget proposal
(B) To discuss an upcoming merger
(C) To interpret some survey results
(D) To welcome new staff members

5. What does the woman mean when she says, "And why wouldn't we"?

(A) She endorses a decision.
(B) She hopes to be transferred.
(C) She seeks input from the listeners.
(D) She is worried about a shipment.

6. What does the woman ask listeners to do?

(A) Participate in a training session
(B) Complete some documents
(C) Compile a set of questions
(D) Review some information online

PART 1

Vocabulary 따라 읽으면서 **암기**하세요   🎧 08_26

plaza 광장	canal 운하, 수로
broom 빗자루	span 가로지르다, ~에 걸쳐 있다
domed 둥근 지붕의	waterway 수로
structure 구조물, 건축물	a flight of stairs (두 층 사이에) 한 줄로 이어진 계단
open-air 야외의, 노천의	fasten 단단히 고정시키다
pedestrian 보행자	column 기둥
line up ~을 일렬[한 줄]로 세우다[배열하다]	awning 차양

Dictation

1. M | Cn   🎧 08_25_01

   (A) Some people are _____ the plaza with _____.

   (B) A _____ is _____.

   (C) An _____ is _____ despite the rain.

   (D) A pedestrian is _____ the rain _____.

2. W | Br   🎧 08_25_02

   (A) Some statues _____ on a bridge.

   (B) Trees are _____ the _____.

   (C) A _____ a waterway.

   (D) A _____ are _____ to a _____.

3. W | Am   🎧 08_25_03

   (A) A woman's standing _____.

   (B) An _____ over a shop entrance.

   (C) A group of people is _____.

   (D) A brick patio _____.

→ Vocabulary 따라 읽으면서 **암기**하세요 🎧 08_27

cover story 표지 기사	stitch 바느질하다, 꿰매다
issue (간행물의) 호; 문제, 걱정거리	schedule *sth* for + **날짜/요일** ~로 ~의 일정을 잡다
paragraph 단락, 절	a while ago 조금 전에
further 더 이상의, 추가의	summarize 요약하다
upstairs 위층에서	projection 예상, 추정
entrance hall 현관 홀, 입구 홀	

→ Dictation

4. [M|Cn] [W|Am] 🎧 08_25_04

_____ for this month's _____?

(A) The _____ later today to make a decision.

(B) July, August, and September.

(C) No, Shelley's having a computer issue.

5. [M|Au] [W|Am] 🎧 08_25_05

_____ of the _____ in this document?

(A) I think they _____.

(B) You can find some _____.

(C) The _____ in this room is very good.

6. [W|Br] [M|Cn] 🎧 08_25_06

What _____?

(A) _____ days ago, I think.

(B) I _____.

(C) The floor _____.

7. [M|Au] [W|Am] 🎧 08_25_07

What _____ for the marketing workshop?

(A) A _____.

(B) _____ Miguel _____ everything?

(C) That _____.

8. [W | Br] [M | Au] 🎧 08_25_08

Do you know _____ one hundred percent _____?

(A) Please _____ for display.

(B) _____ by seventy percent.

(C) There _____.

9. [W | Br] [M | Cn] 🎧 08_25_09

_____ the heating system _____ today?

(A) Elizabeth _____.

(B) _____ on the shelf.

(C) I _____ the hotel.

10. [M | Au] [W | Am] 🎧 08_25_10

Why don't we _____ the training session _____?

(A) It _____.

(B) I _____ 'll _____ of the building.

(C) _____ for me.

11. [M | Cn] [W | Br] 🎧 08_25_11

_____ to _____?

(A) No, because it's _____ thirty dollars.

(B) We _____ here.

(C) An _____.

12. [W | Am] [M | Au] 🎧 08_25_12

Why don't you _____ some of the interns to _____ on the project?

(A) A _____ sales _____.

(B) I really _____ the internship.

(C) I _____.

✚ Vocabulary 따라 읽으면서 **암기**하세요 08_28

item 항목, 사항	pleasant 쾌적한
agenda 의제, 안건	arrange 배열하다, 배치하다
extensive 대규모의	set-up 구성, 배열
host 주최하다	word count 총 단어 수
reference ~에 대해 언급하다	plenty 많은 양[수]
own 소유하다	cover 다루다, 포함시키다
rent 임대, 임차	assignment 임무, 수행 업무
head (특정 방향으로) 가다, 향하다	on another note 그건 그렇고
ponder 숙고하다, 곰곰이 생각하다	compile (자료를 수집하여) (목록, 보고서 등을) 작성하다, 정리하다
contact 연락을 주고받는 사람, 연락 담당자	piece (신문, 잡지의) 기사
make sense 타당하다	forward 보내다, 전달하다

Questions 13 through 15 refer to the following conversation with three speakers. 08_25_13

[M | Au] The _____ is the office renovations _____ next year, which are expected to be _____. As a result, we _____ client meetings here during that period. Does anyone have any suggestions to offer?

[W | Am] Yaping and I were discussing this earlier and she _____ in this morning's newspaper. _____, Yaping?

[W | Br] Well, there seems to be a place not too far from here called Get Space Solutions. They _____ and they have meeting rooms _____. I believe _____ ___ for our needs.

[M | Au] OK. Could you _____ this afternoon and _____?

[W | Br] Of course, I'll _____.

13. According to the man, what will happen next year?
(A) A new product will be launched.
(B) Additional perks will be provided.
(C) Several employees will be hired.
(D) Some offices will be renovated.

14. What does Yaping suggest?
(A) Using online advertisements
(B) Supplementing details to a contract
(C) Hiring a venue for meetings
(D) Developing orientation materials

15. What does Yuko agree to do?
(A) Investigate a location
(B) Interact with a client
(C) Complete a transaction
(D) Edit a document

M | Au Hey, Yuko. I've been _____ - our outdoor dining area is available tonight. Do you think we could have the Dully Manufacturing dinner outside?

W | Am Well, 've _____ _____ at the company, and they informed me about a video presentation that will be _____ _____. It's not possible to hold it outdoors.

M | Au I guess _____. The recent weather has been _____, though!

W | Am Yeah. You know, I think it'd be nice to _____ _____ on the _____.

M | Au That sounds like a good plan! We can _____ _____ a few tables and chairs out there. It _____.

16. What event are the speakers discussing?
(A) A company dinner
(B) An inauguration ceremony
(C) A product launch
(D) An annual reunion

17. What does the man imply when he says, "The recent weather has been quite pleasant, though"?
(A) He feels disappointed at a decision.
(B) He is reluctant to plan an outdoor function.
(C) He wishes for an increase in his vacation allowance.
(D) He anticipates a shift in the weather tonight.

18. What does the woman suggest?
(A) Postponing a dinner appointment
(B) Setting up video equipment outdoors
(C) Serving some food an alternative place
(D) Offering a markdown

[M | Au] Hi, Fatima. This is Larry, your editor at *Euro Directions* magazine. Is _____?

[W | Br] Yes, I _____.

[M | Au] Great. Would you be able to _____ _____ your "Exploring Naples" article to two thousand words?

[W | Br] OK, there's _____ on the topic. But I _____ that same day.

[M | Au] Ah, I see that on your assignment chart. _____ _____ by seven days. This will allow you to focus on Naples.

[W | Br] Thanks, I appreciate it. On another note, I've been _____ some _____ this winter. I'll _____ to you later today for your feedback.

Article	Deadline
"Exploring Naples"	September 14
"Cheeses of Italy"	September 14
"Affordable Tour Packages"	October 17
"Copenhagen by Bicycle"	November 12

19. What does the man ask the woman to do?
(A) Extend an agreement
(B) Arrange a meeting for an interview
(C) Lengthen an article
(D) Proofread a document

20. Look at the graphic. Which article's deadline will be changed?
(A) "Exploring Naples"
(B) "Cheeses of Italy"
(C) "Affordable Tour Packages"
(D) "Copenhagen by Bicycle"

21. What does the woman say she will send the man?
(A) An itinerary for a tour
(B) An expense report
(C) Meeting minutes
(D) Ideas for upcoming articles

PART 4

Vocabulary 따라 읽으면서 **암기**하세요 08_29

representative 대표(자), 대리인	face ~에 직면하다
replacement 교체물, 대체물	try out ~을 시험해 보다
ship 수송하다, 운송하다	commercial break (TV, 라디오의) 중간광고 시간
corporate 기업의, 회사의	trail (산속의) 작은 길, 산길
release 발매하다; 발매, 출시	partially 부분적으로
enhance 향상시키다	unavailable 이용할 수 없는
interactive 대화형의, 쌍방향의	maintenance 유지 보수
involve 수반하다, 포함하다	halfway through 중간쯤에서
interact 소통하다	trek 트레킹
simulated 모의의, 모조의	sunscreen 자외선 차단제

 Questions 22 through 24 refer to the following telephone message. 08_25_16

W Am Hello, this is Josephine Chen. I wanted to inform you that the _____ from your online store _____ when it arrived. I want to _____ at the post office this afternoon, but I'd like to have a _____ from your company before I send it. You see, I'm moving to a new house next week, so the replacement will need to be _____. Please call me back so I can be _____ that the camera will be _____ by your shipping department.

---

22. What is wrong with the camera?
(A) It is missing a component.
(B) It is an outdated model.
(C) It weighs too much.
(D) It has been damaged.

23. Where does the speaker want to go this afternoon?
(A) To a warehouse
(B) To an electronics store
(C) To a real estate agency
(D) To a post office

24. Why does the speaker request a return call?
(A) To cancel an order
(B) To inquire about a rental
(C) To verify a location
(D) To give driving directions

[M | Au] Welcome to Business Tips and Tricks on WJNK Radio. On today's show, I'll be talking with Tina Brownstein, who is a _____ _____ around the country. But that's _____. She's also the _____ known as C3VR, which was _____. Customer service representatives can _____ _____ through this _____ _____ that _____ simulated, computer-generated customers. However, Ms. Brownstein's most recent training software has _____ from some technology experts. Only her employees had the opportunity to try out the product before its official release. Therefore, there is _____ ... _____ this _____.

25. What is Tina Brownstein's area of expertise?
(A) Online marketing
(B) Customer service
(C) Corporate accounting
(D) Business laws

26. What is C3VR?
(A) A digital camera brand
(B) An electronic reading device
(C) An automatic payment method
(D) A software program

27. Why does the speaker say, "Only her employees had the opportunity to try out the product before its official release"?
(A) To explain why some experts are skeptical about a product
(B) To confirm whether testing on a product had to be terminated
(C) To inquire about the number of employees in a company
(D) To encourage the audience to test some merchandise

W Am Hello, _____ the V _____ C _____ at Morrista National Park. I'm Sylvia, your _____ today's hike. _____ 'd _____ the Zion Trail to the Picnic Area, but it's _____ this week due to _____ _____ . So instead, we've decided to _____ the Zion Trail and _____ the La Quinta Trail _____ , _____ here on the map. Our lunch break will be _____ the La Quinta Trail, _____ 'll _____ the Mary's Rock Trail _____ . It's supposed to be sunny today, so it's a good idea to _____ _____ by _____ and wearing a hat.

Morrista National Park Trail Map

28. Who most likely are the listeners?
(A) Park rangers
(B) Bus operators
(C) Maintenance workers
(D) Tourists

29. Look at the graphic. Where will the listeners be unable to go today?
(A) The North Pond
(B) The Picnic Area
(C) The Honeybee Garden
(D) The Visitor Center

30. What does the woman encourage the listeners to do?
(A) Study the park trail map
(B) Listen to the weather report
(C) Secure their belongings
(D) Use sun protection

PART 1 Exercise

Vocabulary 따라 읽으면서 **암기**하세요　　　　　　　　🎧 09_13

adjust 조정하다, 조절하다	drape 걸치다
angle 각, 각도	shopkeeper 가게 주인
lace 끈, 줄	reach 손을 뻗다
shawl 숄, 어깨걸이	refrigerated display case 냉장 진열장

Dictation

1. [W|Am] 🎧 09_12_01

    (A) One of the women is _____.

    (B) An employee is _____ into a pair of shoes.

    (C) Many pairs of shoes _____ along a wall.

    (D) One of the women _____ shoulders.

2. [M|Cn] 🎧 09_12_02

    (A) The shopkeeper is _____.

    (B) Some customers are standing _____.

    (C) Some bottles are _____.

    (D) Refreshments have been _____.

PART 2 Exercise

Vocabulary 따라 읽으면서 **암기**하세요　　　　　　　　🎧 09_17

loading dock 하역장	publishing house 출판사
overnight shipping 익일 배송	publicity 홍보, 광고
find out ~을 알게 되다	officer 간부, 중역
win a contract 계약을 따내다	out of order 고장 난
no later than 늦어도 ~까지는	send out (많은 사람들에게) ~을 발송하다
public relations 홍보 (활동)	launch 출시하다
just round the corner 아주 가까운	behind schedule 예정보다 늦게
a significant amount of 상당량의, 상당한 금액의	floor plan 평면도
florist 꽃집	

1. [W｜Am] [W｜Br] 🎧 09_16_01

   Where can I get some _____ ?

   (A) _____'ll _____ .

   (B) Yes, an _____ shipping.

   (C) She doesn't live there.

2. [M｜Au] [M｜Cn] 🎧 09_16_02

   _____ if I won the contract?

   (A) _____ Thursday.

   (B) The _____ team.

   (C) _____ it?

3. [W｜Am] [W｜Br] 🎧 09_16_03

   Where will your new office be located?

   (A) A _____ today.

   (B) _____'ll _____ .

   (C) I don't think she's here today.

4. [M｜Cn] [M｜Au] 🎧 09_16_04

   When was the _____ to the Port Franklin Museum?

   (A) A _____ money.

   (B) Three or four years ago.

   (C) He's a _____ .

5. [W｜Br] [W｜Am] 🎧 09_16_05

   _____ fresh flowers _____ ?

   (A) Nine thirty this morning.

   (B) Yes, in March and April.

   (C) _____ S ____ A _____ .

6. ⬚M|Cn⬚ ⬚W|Am⬚ 🎧 09_16_06

When was your _____?

(A) 've _____ working here.

(B) The _____

(C) On Sullivan Street.

7. ⬚M|Cn⬚ ⬚W|Am⬚ 🎧 09_16_07

_____ of tomorrow's schedule?

(A) Just a _____ .

(B) Every Tuesday and Thursday.

(C) The _____'s _____ .

8. ⬚W|Am⬚ ⬚M|Au⬚ 🎧 09_16_08

_____ the results of the customer survey?

(A) _____ questions.

(B) She's _____ customer.

(C) We _____ this morning.

9. ⬚W|Br⬚ ⬚M|Cn⬚ 🎧 09_16_09

_____ the mobile phone application?

(A) Thanks, but I _____ .

(B) We're _____ .

(C) Because I _____ previously.

10. ⬚W|Br⬚ ⬚M|Au⬚ 🎧 09_16_10

_____ the new file cabinets _____?

(A) Ms. Martin _____ .

(B) Just the _____ , please.

(C) I _____ last month.

Vocabulary 따라 읽으면서 **암기**하세요 🎧 09_19

set A up with B A에게 B를 제공하다 vendor 판매업체	fall within ~의 범위에 들어가다

Dictation

📝 **Questions 1 through 3** refer to the following conversation and list. 🎧 09_18

[W|Br] Mike, a new graphic designer will be joining us next month, so we'll need to _____ laptop and additional monitor. Can you _____ _____?

[M|Cn] Sure. You're _____ _____, right?

[W|Br] Really?

[M|Cn] Yes. I _____ the catalog a few minutes ago, and their latest models are more expensive now.

[W|Br] Right. Well, our _____ is _____ maximum. So _____ _____ _____ that price.

[M|Cn] OK. I'll _____ the prices and then place the order.

Screen Size	System Price
11 inches	$999
13 inches	$1,099
15 inches	$1,199
17 inches	$1,299

1. What does the woman ask the man to do?
   (A) Order some equipment
   (B) Search for a new vendor
   (C) Repair a laptop computer
   (D) Contact a potential employee

2. What problem does the man mention?
   (A) A graphic designer has left the company.
   (B) A supplier has increased its prices.
   (C) A software program has been discontinued.
   (D) A departmental budget has been lowered.

3. Look at the graphic. What size screen will the man order?
   (A) 11 inches
   (B) 13 inches
   (C) 15 inches
   (D) 17 inches

+ Vocabulary 따라 읽으면서 **암기**하세요   09_21

cater ~에 출장 뷔페를 제공하다	considering ~을 고려하면, 감안하면
have *sth* in mind ~을 염두에 두다[생각하다]	neighborhood (도시 내의) 지역, 동네
farewell 작별	relocation 이전
no more than 겨우 ~, 불과 ~	lead to ~로 이어지다
meet the requirements 조건에 맞다	record 기록하다; 기록적인
browse through ~을 살펴보다, 열람하다	quarter 분기, 사분기
proceed with ~을 계속 진행하다	unaware of ~을 알지[눈치 채지] 못하는
deposit 보증금, 계약금	presence 있음, 존재
summarize 요약하다	pick up 회복되다, 개선되다
sales figures 매출액	towards ~즈음에, 무렵에
find ~라고 여기다, 생각하다	commercial 광고 (방송)
intriguing 아주 흥미로운	put out ~을 내보내다, 방송하다

+ Dictation

 Questions 1 through 3 refer to the following conversation and list.   09_20_01

M | Au Hi, I'm calling to gather some information about _____ .

W | Am Sure. Could you tell me the _____ _____ and the _____ _____ ?

M | Au We're organizing a _____ for one of our managers. We expect around thirty guests, and we're working with a _____ _____ .

W | Am We do offer a _____ _____ . On our Web site, if you click on the Options tab, you can _____ _____ there.

M | Au Oh, OK, you do have _____ 'll for us. I'd like to _____ .

W | Am Sure, I'll just need a _____ to _____ .

Options	
Seafood platter	$1,000
Steak platter	$850
Chicken platter	$700
Vegetarian platter	$550

1. What type of event is being organized?
   (A) A trade fair
   (B) A managers' meeting
   (C) A tour
   (D) A party

2. Look at the graphic. What option will the man most likely select?
   (A) Seafood platter
   (B) Steak platter
   (C) Chicken platter
   (D) Vegetarian platter

3. What information does the man still have to provide?
   (A) A purchase order number
   (B) Some payment information
   (C) The location of a business
   (D) A list of guests

W Am There's one more _____
during the staff meeting today. I've just distributed
a _____ the yearly _____
_____ . And, well... I _____
_____ , especially _____ to a
different neighborhood this year. As anticipated,
the relocation _____ in our
sales at first. We recorded the _____ of
the entire year _____ .
That was largely because the new community
was _____ . However,
business _____ quickly _____
_____ as a result of the _____
_____ , leading to a record
number of sales.

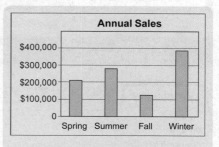

Annual Sales

$400,000
$300,000
$200,000
$100,000
0

Spring   Summer   Fall   Winter

4. What type of product does the
   business sell?
   (A) Apparel
   (B) Footwear
   (C) Electronic appliances
   (D) Computer programs

5. Look at the graphic. In what season
   did the business relocate?
   (A) Spring
   (B) Summer
   (C) Fall
   (D) Winter

6. What did the business do after it
   relocated?
   (A) It diversified its range of
       merchandise.
   (B) It increased its workforce.
   (C) It placed some advertisements.
   (D) It organized an inauguration
       event.

PART 1

column 기둥	board up (문, 창문 등을) 판자로 막다
suspend 매달다, 걸다	apply (페인트, 크림 등을) 바르다
pavement 포장 도로	prop 기대어 세우다
geometric 기하학적인	

➕ **Dictation**

1. M｜Au 🎧 09_23_01

    (A) Some _____.

    (B) People are attending a _____.

    (C) _____ are _____ the display.

    (D) People are working at an _____.

2. W｜Br 🎧 09_23_02

    (A) A park is _____ with _____.

    (B) A row of trees _____ the plaza.

    (C) People are sitting in an outdoor _____.

    (D) The _____ is decorated with _____ design.

3. W｜Am 🎧 09_23_03

    (A) They're _____ the windows of a building.

    (B) Paint _____ to a balcony.

    (C) _____ different _____ the house.

    (D) A paint can _____ from the roof.

Vocabulary 따라 읽으면서 **암기**하세요

set up ~을 설치하다	account 거래 (계약)
photo shoot 사진 촬영	misplace 어딘가에 두고 잊어버리다
psychologist 심리학자	section (조직의) 부서, 과
director 책임자, 관리자	in a while 한동안
downstairs 아래층에	opening 빈자리, 공석

Dictation

4. [M｜Cn] [W｜Br] 🎧 09_23_04

_____ the equipment for the photo shoot?

(A) _____ for next week.

(B) _____ in Brussel.

(C) I _____ the electronics store.

5. [M｜Au] [W｜Am] 🎧 09_23_05

_____'s the lecture _____?

(A) Next week is fine with me.

(B) A _____.

(C) Oh, I _____.

6. [M｜Cn] [W｜Br] 🎧 09_23_06

_____'s the new department director _____?

(A) It's _____.

(B) Ms. Watson _____ for several weeks.

(C) No, _____'s _____.

7. [M｜Au] [W｜Br] 🎧 09_23_07

_____ can I _____?

(A) Because it _____ ten o'clock.

(B) No, you _____.

(C) What _____ is it?

8. [W|Br] [M|Cn] 🎧 09_23_08

When do you think _____'ll _____'ve _____ the Barclays _____?

(A) I _____ my _____ manual.

(B) One of _____.

(C) Ms. Pavlova _____.

9. [M|Cn] [W|Br] 🎧 09_23_09

_____ appointment for a check-up?

(A) _____.

(B) I _____ my train ticket.

(C) _____'ve _____ a new section _____.

10. [W|Am] [M|Cn] 🎧 09_23_10

Do I have to _____?

(A) When did you _____?

(B) I know a nice _____.

(C) The elevator's _____.

11. [W|Br] [M|Au] 🎧 09_23_11

_____ Juan _____ an apartment in the city?

(A) I _____ to him _____.

(B) Those _____ need to be _____.

(C) The _____ at nine P.M.

12. [M|Au] [W|Am] 🎧 09_23_12

_____ on your company's graphic design team?

(A) The new design is very _____.

(B) We're _____ eight o'clock.

(C) You're _____.

PART 3

set-up 배치	trade fair 무역 박람회
put together (이것저것을 모아) 만들다, 준비하다	directory 인명부
information packet 자료집	so far 지금까지
greet 인사하다, 맞이하다	hold on (명령문으로) 기다려, 멈춰
willing to-V ~할 의향이 있는	misspell ~의 철자를 잘못 쓰다
spot 발견하다, 알아채다	reuse 재사용하다
double-check 재확인하다	production (연극, 영화, 방송) 작품
costume (연극, 영화 등에서) 의상	the rest 나머지
send off ~을 발송하다	suspend 매달다, 걸다
do 적절하다, 충분하다	bracket 버팀대, 받침대

 Questions 13 through 15 refer to the following conversation.   09_23_13

M Cn Fatima, is everything ready _____ _____ on Monday?

W Br Yes, their _____, and I've just _____.

M Cn And... don't forget to _____ _____ on Monday to _____ as they arrive.

W Br Oh, thanks for reminding me. I'm sure I'll be able to find some people _____ ____. But how will the interns _____ _____?

M Cn How about providing volunteers with a _____ _____? We _____ _____ for our last trade fair. Let me go get them for you now.

13. What will happen on Monday?
(A) Some landscaping work will begin.
(B) A news conference will take place.
(C) Some clients will visit the company.
(D) An internship period will start.

14. What did the woman forget to do?
(A) Revise a schedule
(B) Seek out some volunteers
(C) Update a list of contacts
(D) Serve refreshments

15. What does the man say is available?
(A) Some notepads
(B) Cleaning products
(C) Customized clothing
(D) New flooring

[M|Au] Soo-mi, I'm ready to _____ to the employee directory _____.
Would you _____ it before I _____ _____?

[W|Br] Hmm... it seems good so far, but, uh... hold on, there's an issue here. The vice president's name has been _____. Actually, her name _____ only one L.

[M|Au] Wow, I can't believe I _____.
Thank you for _____.

[W|Br] It's easy to miss. Once you make that change, it should be ready to upload. Let me know if you need any more help.

16. What are the speakers mainly talking about?
(A) Creating a product catalog
(B) Ordering some visitor badges
(C) Updating a company's Web site
(D) Organizing a welcome reception

17. What problem does the woman notice?
(A) A report has not been filed.
(B) An identification badge is malfunctioning.
(C) A telephone number has been omitted.
(D) A name has been incorrectly spelled.

18. Why does the woman say, "It's easy to miss"?
(A) To express her understanding
(B) To clarify her responsibilities in a project
(C) To detail the steps involved in a process
(D) To inform the man of a detour

Item	Quantity	Total Price
Suit jackets	7	€175
Dresses	9	€270
Scarves	11	€33
Hats	17	€38
		Order Total = €516

M | Cn　Donna, we've _____ _____ of the upcoming season. Could you please _____ before I _____?

W | Am　Of course. Let's take a look... Alright... Alright... um, we don't really _____ hats. _____ will do. We can reuse the ones from the spring production.

M | Cn　OK, I'll _____. Anything else?

W | Am　No issues with the rest. You go ahead and submit the order, and I'll _____ _____ the new ceiling lights. They're going to be _____ we _____.

M | Cn　Oh, _____ 'll _____ nice. Brighter is better.

19. Where do the speakers most likely work?
(A) At a travel bureau
(B) At a theater
(C) At a clothier
(D) At a tailor's shop

20. Look at the graphic. Which quantity will be changed?
(A) 7
(B) 9
(C) 11
(D) 17

21. What does the woman say she will do next?
(A) Hang some light fixtures
(B) Apply paint to the ceiling
(C) Sanitize a piece of equipment
(D) Take measurements of the actors

Vocabulary 따라 읽으면서 **암기**하세요 🎧 09_27

architecture 건축학
inn 소규모 호텔, 식당, 술집
state-of-the-art 최첨단의, 최신식의
energy-efficient 에너지 효율이 좋은
non-polluting 무공해의
lodge 산장
access 접근
surrounding 인근의, 주위의
host (주인으로서) 접대하다
architect 건축가
cost-effective 비용 효율[효과]이 높은
utilize 활용하다, 이용하다

architectural 건축의
favor 선호하다
contemporary 현대의
reach out 연락을 취하다
attention (안내 방송에서) 알립니다, 주목하세요
run (길이) 뻗다, 이어지다
block off (도로나 출입구를) 차단하다, 봉쇄하다
accordingly 그에 맞춰
neighboring 이웃한, 인근의
accessible 접근[입장/이용] 가능한
no matter which *sth* 어느 ~이든 상관없이
vicinity 부근, 인근

 Questions 22 through 24 refer to the following talk. 🎧 09_23_16

W Am Hello everyone, and welcome to the _____ taking place at the East Wind Eco I____. This hotel was constructed last year using _____ and ____ _____ materials. Additionally, the lodge provides _____ _____ that the region is well-known for. We are pleased to be _____ _____. I'm sure you'll have _____ about _____ _____ the materials ____ 've _____ are, and why you should consider using them in your _____ _____.

22. Where is the talk taking place?
   (A) At an art museum
   (B) At a construction site
   (C) At a hotel
   (D) At a power plant

23. Who most likely are the listeners?
   (A) Architects
   (B) Engineering students
   (C) Hoteliers
   (D) Event coordinators

24. What is mentioned about the materials used?
   (A) They are manufactured locally.
   (B) They are reasonably priced.
   (C) They are environmentally friendly.
   (D) They are hard to come by.

W Am Hey Stan, it's Min-hee. I'm going through the _____ _____ for Clark Restaurant, and I wanted to _____ with you. It isn't what I was expecting. Clark Restaurant has always _____ very _____ advertisements, and _____ _____ is quite _____. I apologize for _____ the client's _____ earlier. I understand this is your first project with them. You know, why don't you _____ Shinji for assistance? He has _____ Clark Restaurant before. Thanks, Stan. I'll speak to you later.

25. What industry does the speaker work in?
(A) Publishing
(B) Paper production
(C) Advertising
(D) Food service

26. Why does the speaker say, "It isn't what I was expecting"?
(A) To explain the exceptional nature of a project.
(B) To express disapproval for a design
(C) To suggest that a project's deadline be adjusted
(D) To indicate surprise at a surge in sales

27. What does the speaker suggest the listener do?
(A) Seek career advancement
(B) Organize a press conference
(C) Take some time off
(D) Consult with a colleague

M | Au Attention, all employees of Alfane Systems. Please be reminded that the city's _____ _____ will take place tomorrow, _____ the _____ _____ to be _____ from six A.M. until ten A.M. So you'll need to _____. The _____ _____ will remain _____. No matter which route you choose to take to work, _____ as there will be a _____ due to the race.

28. What will take place tomorrow morning?
   (A) A road improvement project
   (B) A competition
   (C) A street performance
   (D) An employee training session

29. Look at the graphic. Which street will be closed?
   (A) Sherwood Avenue
   (B) Fort Vista Road
   (C) Rose Avenue
   (D) Maple Road

30. What does the speaker suggest?
   (A) Arriving at the workplace in the afternoon
   (B) Attending a corporate function
   (C) Exploring certain study materials
   (D) Allowing extra time for travel

PART 1 Exercise

➕ **Vocabulary** 따라 읽으면서 **암기**하세요 🎧 10_13

umbrella 우산, 파라솔	occupied 사용 중인
face ~에 면하다, ~을 향하다	pile 쌓다
lawn 잔디밭	vacant 비어 있는
tear down (tore-torn) (건물, 담 등을) 허물다, 헐다	

➕ **Dictation**

1. [W | Am] 🎧 10_12_01

    (A) _____ have been _____.

    (B) Some of the buildings _____.

    (C) A brick wall _____.

    (D) Most of the tables are _____.

2. [M | Au] 🎧 10_12_02

    (A) Chairs _____ in a corner.

    (B) People are _____ around the room.

    (C) Some of the seats are _____.

    (D) Plants are _____.

PART 2 Exercise

➕ **Vocabulary** 따라 읽으면서 **암기**하세요 🎧 10_18

organized 계획성 있는, 체계적인	handbook 편람, 안내서
assignment 임무, 업무	supervisor 감독(자), 관리자
coordinator 진행자, 책임자	involved in ~에 관여하는, 관련된
along with ~와 함께	admission 들어감, 입장
assign 배정하다	inventory 재고(품)
committed 헌신적인, 열성적인	warehouse 창고
advisory committee 자문 위원회	come up with ~을 생각해내다, 내놓다
report to ~에 도착을 보고하다; ~의 밑에서 일하다	go well 잘 진행되다

1. [W|Am] [W|Br] 🎧 10_17_01

   _____ is Satoshi's?

   (A) Sure, I can do that for you.

   (B) It's _____.

   (C) She's very _____.

2. [M|Cn] [W|Am] 🎧 10_17_02

   Who informed the _____ of the _____?

   (A) The _____ of the program.

   (B) Just a couple of minor _____.

   (C) Along with the _____.

3. [M|Au] [M|Cn] 🎧 10_17_03

   _____ are meeting tomorrow?

   (A) She's very _____ to the project.

   (B) No, it was _____ yesterday.

   (C) Only the _____ committee.

4. [M|Au] [W|Am] 🎧 10_17_04

   _____ should I _____ today?

   (A) The times should be _____ in the _____.

   (B) I _____'d _____.

   (C) _____?

5. [W|Br] [M|Au] 🎧 10_17_05

   Who's supposed to _____ the _____?

   (A) She _____ recently.

   (B) The _____.

   (C) Several _____.

6. ⬚W | Br⬚ ⬚M | Cn⬚ 🎧 10_17_06

_____'s _____ in _____ the annual town _____?

(A) Parking, admission and activities are _____.

(B) It's _____ morning.

(C) Oh, are you _____ out?

7. ⬚W | Am⬚ ⬚M | Au⬚ 🎧 10_17_07

_____ the new _____ management software?

(A) I was _____ me.

(B) No, he _____.

(C) At the F   S _____.

8. ⬚M | Au⬚ ⬚W | Am⬚ 🎧 10_17_08

_____ the office library?

(A) I _____.

(B) I _____ Mr. Park.

(C) Six new books.

9. ⬚W | Br⬚ ⬚M | Cn⬚ 🎧 10_17_09

_____'s _____ the bookstore _____?

(A) _____ history and ___ books.

(B) At nine A.M.

(C) I _____ the staff schedule.

10. ⬚W | Am⬚ ⬚W | Br⬚ 🎧 10_17_10

_____ our updated slogan?

(A) I _____ pretty well.

(B) This elevator is going down.

(C) _____ the marketing team.

✦ **Vocabulary** 따라 읽으면서 **암기**하세요 10_20

check in (일의 진행을) 확인하다	Well done! 잘 했어!, 훌륭했어!
vacuum 진공청소기로 청소하다	construct 제작하다, 조립하다
stain 얼룩	executive board 이사회
shampoo (카펫 등을 세제로) 빨다	move forward with ~을 진행하다, 추진하다
a hand 도움(의 손길)	prototype 시제품
right away 즉시, 곧바로	lately 최근에
flowchart 플로 차트, 작업 순서도	arise 생기다, 발생하다
exceptional 탁월한, 특출한	excessive 지나친, 과도한
line 제품군	enhance 높이다, 향상시키다
kitchen appliance 주방용품	efficiency 효율(성)
outsell ~보다 더 많이 팔리다	productivity 생산성

✦ **Dictation**

 Questions 1 through 3 refer to the following conversation and sign. 🎧 10_19_01

W Am Hi, Baolin. I'm just _____. How's everything _____? Have you _____ _____ the Batista Construction offices yet?

M Au No, it's taking _____ _____. I vacuumed the carpet, but there are a lot of _____. So I made the decision to _____ it. But then I had to _____ to get the steam-cleaning machine and _____.

W Am Well, before you start shampooing, could you _____ again? I _____ moving a large table in one of the conference rooms.

M Au Sure, I'll _____. This is a _____ for me from working on these carpets, anyway.

Office Directory
1st FL: OE Furniture Company
2nd FL: Gold Coast Imagination, Inc.
3rd FL: Batista Construction
4th FL: Brown & Sons

1. Who most likely are the speakers?
   (A) Carpet weavers
   (B) Hair stylists
   (C) Cleaning staff
   (D) Construction workers

2. Look at the graphic. Where is the man currently working?
   (A) On the first floor
   (B) On the second floor
   (C) On the third floor
   (D) On the fourth floor

3. What are the speakers probably going to do next?
   (A) Rearrange a table
   (B) Repair a machine
   (C) Review some plans
   (D) Conduct a conference call

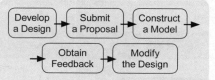

M | Au Let's begin the meeting with some wonderful news - thanks to the _____ created by this team, our line of kitchen appliances _____ on the market last quarter. Well done! Now I want to discuss the _____ _____. As you can see from this flowchart, ___'ve _____ "Develop a Design" and "Construct a Model". This new step means you'll have to be _____ from the executive board _____ _____. Lately, some _____ has _____ about the _____ _____ on _____ that _____ _____. The introduction of this new process is intended to _____ our team's _____ and _____.

4. What does the speaker say about the company's kitchen appliances?
   (A) They sold well in the previous quarter.
   (B) They achieved success in a design contest.
   (C) They are priced lower than competing products.
   (D) They were featured in a trade magazine.

5. Look at the graphic. According to the speaker, which step was recently added?
   (A) Submit a proposal
   (B) Construct a model
   (C) Obtain feedback
   (D) Modify the Design

6. What concern does the speaker mention?
   (A) Raw materials are in short supply.
   (B) More appliances are being purchased online.
   (C) Employees' time has been used inefficiently.
   (D) A production deadline has been adjusted.

Actual Test

PART 1

plastic sheet 비닐 시트	illuminate (~에 불을) 비추다
frame (건물의) 뼈대; 액자에 넣다	refreshments 다과
vertical 수직의	couch 소파
beam 기둥	fireplace 벽난로
erect (건물, 동상 등을) 세우다	carton 판지 상자
mow (잔디를) 깎다	railing 난간

➔ Dictation

1. M | Cn   🎧 10_22_01

   (A) A tank has been _____.

   (B) _____.

   (C) _____ have been _____ on a construction site.

   (D) A _____ around the building.

2. W | Br   🎧 10_22_02

   (A) A _____ is _____ by lamps.

   (B) _____ have been left on a table.

   (C) A _____ is _____ the fireplace.

   (D) Some pictures _____ for display.

3. W | Am   🎧 10_22_03

   (A) All of the _____ have been left _____.

   (B) There is a fence around the _____.

   (C) _____ are in a row on the ground.

   (D) There are _____ on the balconies.

Vocabulary 따라 읽으면서 **암기**하세요 🎧 10_24

pick up ∼을 차로 데리러 가다
one-way 편도의
exhibit 작품을 전시하다, 전시회를 열다
supplier 공급(업)자, 공급업체
dairy product 유제품
(every) now and then 때때로, 이따금씩
supply room 비품실
breathtaking 숨이 멎을 정도로 멋진[놀라운]

directions 길 안내
complimentary 무료의
accounting office 경리실
dumpling 만두
left-handed 왼손잡이의
supply drawer 비품 서랍
setback 차질

Dictation

4. [W｜Am] [M｜Cn] 🎧 10_22_04

   _____ Mr. Hendrix from the airport?

   (A) I don't have a car.

   (B) It's a _____ ticket.

   (C) No, it's _____.

5. [M｜Cn] [M｜Au] 🎧 10_22_05

   _____ in the Rattigan A___G_____ next month?

   (A) Yes, it _____ six P.M.

   (B) My _____Arshad_____, too.

   (C) It's a _____ Korean artists.

6. [M｜Au] [M｜Cn] 🎧 10_22_06

   _____ do you use for _____?

   (A) _____.

   (B) In the _____.

   (C) The one on Lombard Street.

7. [M｜Cn] [W｜Am] 🎧 10_22_07

   _____ to the client's office?

   (A) I _____ take _____ there.

   (B) _____ tomorrow, maybe.

   (C) Wow, the view here is _____!

8. [W | Br] [W | Am] 🎧 10_22_08

I _____ the convention center from the train station.

(A) Wayne's _____.

(B) A _____ lunch.

(C) Five hundred _____.

9. [W | Am] [M | Au] 🎧 10_22_09

Do you know _____ the _____ office is _____?

(A) The _____ for November.

(B) They've _____, so I'm not sure.

(C) The lights _____.

10. [W | Br] [M | Cn] 🎧 10_22_10

_____ Chinese restaurant in town.

(A) Samantha is _____ in October.

(B) It's _____.

(C) Fried rice and dumplings.

11. [W | Am] [M | Cn] 🎧 10_22_11

_____'ve _____ the Bayside Center before, right?

(A) _____.

(B) I'm actually _____.

(C) Mr. Mendez ____.

12. [M | Au] [W | Br] 🎧 10_22_12

You _____ the financial report _____ this week, didn't you?

(A) No, she _____ for it.

(B) The _____.

(C) _____, _____ there's been a _____.

➡ Vocabulary 따라 읽으면서 **암기**하세요 🎧 10_25

around the corner (시간적으로) 아주 가까이, 임박하여	a while ago 얼마 전에
I know (동의, 공감의) 맞아, 그래	handcrafted 수공예품인
big-name 유명한, 저명한	weaver 직공, 방직공
good to go 준비가 다 된	one of a kind 독특핸[유례를 찾기 힘든] 것
transportation 교통수단, 차량	impressed 인상 깊게 생각하는
sort out ~을 처리하다	recall 기억해 내다
make arrangements for ~을 준비하다	be fond of ~을 좋아하다
slip one's mind 잊어버리다	dissatisfied 불만스러워 하는
preoccupied with ~에 정신이 팔린[사로잡힌]	far from 전혀[결코] ~이 아닌
organize 정리하다, 구성하다	on schedule 예정대로
materials 자료	encounter 맞닥뜨리다
stress out 스트레스를 받다	might want to-V ~ 하는 게 좋을 것 같다
courtesy bus (호텔, 전시장 등의) 무료 셔틀버스	impact 영향을 주다
fabulous 기막히게 좋은[멋진]	concern 우려, 걱정

🖥 **Questions 13 through 15** refer to the following conversation with three speakers. 🎧 10_22_13

M Au I _____ the Edmonton convention is _____!

W Am I know. It should be fantastic, especially with _____. Are we _____ with _____?

M Cn Uh, the _____ have already been _____, and you _____ for the _____ while we're there, right, Arvind?

M Au Oh, no! It _____ to reserve the car! I've been _____ organizing my workshop materials!

M Cn All right... We're only _____ _____. Getting a car now might be a challenge!

W Am Let's not _____. I read about a _____ to and from the hotel. _____ and find out.

13. What are the speakers mainly discussing?
(A) Strategies for minimizing a travel budget
(B) Attractions in Edmonton
(C) Potential venues for a conference
(D) Preparations for an upcoming business trip

14. What problem do the speakers have?
(A) Their business cards are yet to be delivered.
(B) Their reservations are for the incorrect dates.
(C) Their transportation arrangements are incomplete.
(D) Their client in Edmonton is currently unavailable.

15. What does the woman suggest they do?
(A) Cancel an order
(B) Communicate with a hotel
(C) Arrange to deliver a speech
(D) Defer making a decision

[M｜Au] Eun-Jung, look at these scarves!

[W｜Br] I know - _____! I got one _____ _____. They're _____ by local _____, making each scarf _____- a total original.

[M｜Au] I'm impressed. I'd like to _____ _____. She has a birthday coming up. But... uhh... I only get paid once a month.

[W｜Br] Oh, I'd be happy to _____ today. You can pay me back whenever you can.

[M｜Au] Thank you very much! But... I _____ ever _____ before.

[W｜Br] Actually, I _____ one time, and she _____ _____.

16. What does the woman say is special about the scarves?
   (A) They are made by hand.
   (B) They are exported overseas.
   (C) They are made from velvet.
   (D) They are sold only in designated stores.

17. What does the man imply when he says, "I get paid only once a month"?
   (A) He used to be paid more frequently.
   (B) He lacks the funds to make a purchase.
   (C) He has to collect his paycheck today.
   (D) He is planning to ask for a pay increase.

18. Why does the woman say she no longer wears her scarf?
   (A) She misplaced it.
   (B) She tore it.
   (C) She returned it.
   (D) She gave it away.

[W|Br] I've been informed that there have been some _____ lately.

[M|Cn] Yes, I'm afraid that's right. In fact, I've _____ _____ with one of them.

[W|Br] Oh. Well, uh, _____ from the customer?

[M|Cn] She was _____. Our driver _____, but _____ _____ on the way to the airport, and she _____.

[W|Br] Hmm. We might want to _____ _____ in the area. It could be _____ _____ than we thought.

[M|Cn] Right. And we have some _____ _____ as well. Take a look at _____ _____. We'll need to decide how to respond to them.

Name	Comment
Kevin Lee	Unclean seating
Jean Villiers	No price reduction
Anthony Choi	Web site inaccessible
Robin Jarvela	Running behind schedule

19. Where do the speakers most likely work?
(A) At a cargo company
(B) At a car manufacturer
(C) At a taxi service company
(D) At an airport

20. Look at the graphic. Which customer are the speakers discussing?
(A) Kevin Lee
(B) Jean Villiers
(C) Anthony Choi
(D) Robin Jarvela

21. What will the speakers do next?
(A) Examine fuel prices
(B) Scrutinize customer feedback
(C) Revise staffing schedules
(D) Organize training sessions

PART 4

Vocabulary 따라 읽으면서 **암기**하세요 · 10_26

communicate (정보 등을) 전달하다	identify 찾다, 발견하다
exceed 초과하다, 넘다	set aside (돈, 시간을) 따로 떼어 두다
initial 최초의, 초기의	individually 개별적으로, 각각 따로
gratitude 감사, 고마움	breakdown (통계적) 분석, 분류
management 경영진	(market) share 시장 점유율
reward 보상하다	rank (등급, 순위를) 매기다
reflect 반영하다, 나타내다	take note of ~에 주목하다
paycheck 급여(로 받는 수표)	rapid 빠른
outstanding 뛰어난, 걸출한	surpass 능가하다, 뛰어넘다
performance 실적, 성과	keep up 뒤처지지 않다, 따라가다
departmental 부서의	attribute A to B A를 B를 결과로[덕분으로] 보다
head 책임자	surge 급증, 급등
primary 주된, 주요한	innovative 획기적인
budget 예산을 세우다	for free 무료로
come along (원하는 대로) 되어 가다	implement 시행하다
release 발매, 출시	approach 접근법, 처리 방법
push back 미루다, 연기하다	try out ~을 시험해 보다
resources 재원, 자금	existing 기존의
tie up (돈을 쉽게 쓸 수 없도록) 묶어 두다	explore 탐구하다, 타진하다
for the time being 당분간	current 현재의
elsewhere 다른 곳에서	

Questions 22 through 24 refer to the following excerpt from a meeting. · 10_22_16

[W][Am] Hello, I've called this _____ _____ to communicate some good news. Our _____ for the new software _____, and I'd like to express my _____ for the _____ _____ to design such a great product. So, the management has _____ _____ with a bonus, which will be _____ in your upcoming paycheck. Thank you again for your _____!

22. Who are the listeners?
(A) Company stakeholders
(B) Sales associates
(C) Marketing experts
(D) Software developers

23. Why does the speaker thank the listeners?
(A) For working extended hours
(B) For organizing a fundraiser
(C) For decreasing expenditures
(D) For assisting clients

24. What will the listeners receive?
(A) An invitation to a banquet
(B) Some extra time off work
(C) Some additional money
(D) A state-of-the-art device

W Am Thanks for joining us at this _____ _____. Our primary focus for today is _____. Our new video game is _____, but the _____ _____. This means a _____ _____ will be _____ until this project is finished, but who knows when that will be. _____ _____, we must _____. So I request each of you to _____ in your department where you can _____ _____. I'm prepared to _____ to _____ on reviewing your _____. Let me know your _____ for this.

25. What does the speaker imply when she says, "Who knows when that will be"?
(A) She is unable to comprehend a demand.
(B) She expects her staff to quicken their pace.
(C) She is uncertain when a project will be completed.
(D) She wants to receive feedback from the audience.

26. What is the topic of the meeting?
(A) Hiring an accountant
(B) Promoting a product
(C) Lowering costs
(D) Planning a trade fair

27. What does the speaker say she will reserve time to do?
(A) Conduct one-on-one meetings
(B) Analyze data from a questionnaire
(C) Contact potential clients
(D) Draft a written contract

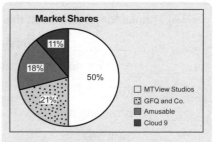

Market Shares

11%
18%
50%
21%

☐ MTView Studios
▨ GFQ and Co.
▨ Amusable
■ Cloud 9

W | Br Alright everyone, let me _____ _____ of this year's video-game market shares. While we're still _____ _____ companies, we should _____ GFQ's _____ - they _____. Although we're _____ with an eighteen percent share, we need to _____. Our market _____ _____ GFQ's _____ to its _____ _____, where they offer their games _____, with consumers _____ within the game. We believe _____ _____ may _____ new users, so we're going to _____ with some of our _____ in the upcoming quarter to _____ of growing _____ our current eighteen-percent market share.

28. What industry does the speaker work in?

(A) Interior design
(B) News reporting
(C) Film production
(D) Game development

29. Look at the graphic. What company does the speaker work for?

(A) MTView Studios
(B) GFQ and Co.
(C) Amusable
(D) Cloud 9

30. According to the speaker, what will the company do in the next quarter?

(A) Restructure a division
(B) Decrease production costs
(C) Negotiate a contract
(D) Adopt a new business strategy

PART 1 Exercise

1 (B)　　**2** (A)

1. M|Cn

(A) Products have been organized near a cash register.
(B) People are examining an article of clothing.
(C) Store clerks are stocking a display case.
(D) A salesperson is wrapping up a sweater.

어휘 organize 정리하다　cash register 금전 등록기
examine (자세히) 살펴보다　an article of clothing 의복
한 벌　stock (~에 상품을) 채우다. 갖추다　wrap up 싸다.
포장하다

해석 (A) 금전 등록기 근처에 상품들이 정리되어 있다.
(B) 옷 한 벌을 살펴보고 있다.
(C) 상점 직원들이 진열장을 채우고 있다.
(D) 판매원이 스웨터를 포장하고 있다.

해설 an article of clothing이라는 어구가 낯설지 않도록 기
억해 두자. 옷을 살펴보고 있으므로 동사 examining이
들리는 문장을 정답으로 선택해야 한다. 사진에 금전
등록기(a cash register)가 보이지 않으므로 (A)는 오답
이다. 진열장에 물건을 채워 넣거나(stocking) 스웨터를
포장하고(wrapping up) 있지도 않으므로 (C)와 (D)도
오답임을 알 수 있다.

2. W|Am

(A) Some scientists are peering into microscopes.
(B) A woman is passing a piece of equipment to a man.
(C) Some pieces of scientific equipment are being positioned on a countertop.
(D) A piece of furniture is being rearranged.

어휘 peer into ~을 자세히 들여다보다. 유심히 보다　position
놓다. 두다　countertop 작업대　rearrange 재배열하다.
재배치하다

해석 (A) 과학자들이 현미경을 들여다보고 있다.
(B) 여자가 남자에게 장비 한 점을 건네주고 있다.
(C) 과학 장비 몇 점이 작업대 위에 놓이고 있다.
(D) 가구가 재배치되고 있다.

해설 '자세히 들여다보다'라는 뜻의 동사구 peering into가
들릴 때 곧장 정답을 선택하면 된다. passing은 '건네
주고 있다'는 뜻이므로 (B)는 오답이다. (C)와 (D)는 진
행 시제 수동태 문장이므로 물건을 진열대 위에 놓고
있거나(are being positioned) 가구를 재배치하는(is
being rearranged) 동작을 하고 있어야 정답이 될 수
있다.

PART 2 Exercise

1 (A)	**2** (A)	**3** (A)	**4** (A)	**5** (B)
6 (A)	**7** (A)	**8** (C)	**9** (C)	**10** (C)

1. M|Cn M|Au

You wanted these charts copied, didn't you?

(A) And then they should be refiled.
(B) I'll make the coffee.

(C) At the bottom of the chart.

어휘 refile (서류 등을) 다시 철하여 정리하다

해석 이 도표들을 복사해 달라고 하셨죠?
(A) 그러고 나서 다시 정리해야 합니다.
(B) 제가 커피를 내릴게요.
(C) 도표 하단에요.

해설 질문에 들어 있는 단어가 대답에서 반복되거나 발음이 비슷한 단어가 들리면 거의 다 오답이다. copied − coffee라는 유사 발음과 반복되는 단어 chart를 통해 (B)와 (C)를 오답으로 골라내자.

---

2. W|Br M|Au

The electrician is coming today, isn't he?

(A) Yes, to fix the lights.
(B) No, the election's in October.
(C) The power outlet.

어휘 electrician 전기 기사[기술자] power outlet 전기 콘센트

해석 오늘 전기 기사가 오는 거죠?
(A) 네, 조명 고치러요.
(B) 아니요, 선거는 10월에 있습니다.
(C) 전기 콘센트요.

해설 질문 앞부분 The electrician is coming(전기 기사가 오는 거죠?)에만 집중하고 있으면 자연스러운 대답이 (A) 임을 알 수 있다. (B)는 electrician과 발음이 비슷한 election으로, (C)는 연상되는 단어 power outlet으로 오답을 유도하고 있다.

---

3. M|Au W|Br

Hasn't Elizabeth commented on our proposal yet?

(A) She said she'd look at it this afternoon.
(B) Maybe at the next intersection.
(C) That's such a lovely compliment!

어휘 intersection 교차로 compliment 칭찬, 찬사

해석 Elizabeth가 아직 우리 제안에 대해 의견을 말하지 않았나요?
(A) 오늘 오후에 보겠다고 했어요.
(B) 아마 다음 교차로에서요.
(C) 정말 기분 좋은 칭찬이네요!

해설 질문 앞부분 Hasn't Elizabeth commented(Elizabeth가 의견을 말하지 않았나요?)에 집중하면 (A)가 자연스러운 대답임을 알 수 있다. (C)는 질문의 commented와 발음이 비슷한 compliment를 이용하여 오답을 유도하고 있다.

---

4. M|Cn W|Am

I sent the catering order to you on Wednesday.

(A) I don't think we've received it.
(B) They're out of order.
(C) Right around the corner.

어휘 catering 출장 뷔페 out of order 고장 난

해석 수요일에 당신에게 출장 뷔페 주문서를 보냈습니다.
(A) 못 받은 것 같은데요.
(B) 고장 났어요.
(C) 모퉁이 돌면 바로 있어요.

해설 질문 맨 앞의 I sent(보냈습니다.)만 알아들어도 (A)가 정답인 것을 알 수 있다. (B)에서는 질문에 나왔던 order가 반복되고 있고, (C)에서는 발음이 비슷한 corner가 오답 장치다.

---

5. M|Cn M|Au

Ms. Kim was promoted three times in just two years!

(A) Only the promotional materials.
(B) She deserves the recognition.
(C) Four of those would be enough.

어휘 deserve ~을 받을 만하다[누릴 자격이 있다] recognition (공로 등에 대한) 인정, 표창

해석 Ms. Kim은 단 2년 만에 세 번이나 승진했어요!
(A) 홍보 자료만요.
(B) 인정받을 만하죠.
(C) 그 네 개면 충분할 겁니다.

해설 질문 앞부분 Ms. Kim was promoted(Ms. Kim은 승진했어요!)에 대한 자연스러운 대답 (B)가 정답이다. (A)는 promoted − promotional의 유사 발음을 통해, (C)는 질문에 들어 있는 숫자 three, two에서 연상되는 단어 Four로 오답을 유도하고 있다.

---

6. W|Br M|Cn

The committee is making a decision about next year's budget.

(A) I hope they approve it.
(B) She's decided to relocate.
(C) It's almost full.

어휘 relocate 전근하다; 이동하다, 이전하다

해석 위원회가 내년도 예산안에 대해 결정을 내릴 거예요.
(A) 승인을 해줬으면 좋겠네요.
(B) 그녀는 전근하기로 했어요.
(C) 거의 다 찼습니다.

해설 질문 앞부분 The committee is making a decision(위원회가 결정을 내릴 거예요.)에 대한 자연스러운 대답 (A)를 정답으로 선택하자. (B)는 decision – decided의 유사 발음을 통한 오답 장치이다.

---

7. [W|Am] [M|Cn]

Dr. Rossi gave you instructions for your medication, didn't he?

(A) He said to take it twice a day.
(B) To the Prescott Medical Center.
(C) I felt rather tired.

어휘 give *sb* instructions ~에게 설명하다
take medication 약을 먹다, 복용하다
say to-V ~하라고 말하다

해석 Rossi 선생님이 약에 대해 설명해 주셨죠?
(A) 하루에 두 번 먹으라고 하셨어요.
(B) Prescott 병원으로요.
(C) 조금 나른한데요.

해설 질문 앞부분 Dr. Rossi gave you instructions(Rossi 선생님이 설명해 주셨죠?)에 집중하여 자연스러운 대답을 정답으로 선택하자. (B)와 (C)는 모두 질문에 있는 Dr.나 medication에서 연상되는 대답으로 오답을 유도하고 있다. 내용을 알아듣기 어려울 때, 연상되는 표현이 들리는 대답은 절대 정답으로 선택하지 말자.

---

8. [W|Br] [M|Cn]

There's a helpful diagram on page forty-eight.

(A) Don't mention it.
(B) Mr. Peterson did.
(C) OK, I'll take a look.

어휘 diagram 도표, 도해

해석 48페이지에 도움이 될 만한 도표가 있어요.
(A) 별말씀을요.
(B) Mr. Peterson이 했습니다.
(C) 알겠습니다. 한 번 볼게요.

해설 질문 앞부분 There's a helpful diagram(도움이 될 만한 도표가 있어요)에 대한 자연스러운 대답을 선택하면 된다.

---

9. [W|Br] [M|Au]

We sold eighteen laptop computers today, didn't we?

(A) Our desktop computer is outdated.
(B) The store opened four years ago.
(C) Yes, it was a good day.

어휘 outdated 구식의, 시대에 뒤진

해석 우리가 오늘 노트북 컴퓨터를 18대 팔았죠?
(A) 우리 데스크톱 컴퓨터는 구식이죠.
(B) 그 상점은 4년 전에 문을 열었습니다.
(C) 네, 수지맞은 날이었어요.

해설 질문 앞부분 We sold eighteen laptop computers(우리가 노트북 컴퓨터를 18대 팔았죠?)에 집중하면 자연스러운 대답이 어느 것인지 알 수 있다. (A)는 질문에 있는 단어 computer를 다시 들려주면서 오답을 유도하고 있다.

---

10. [M|Cn] [W|Am]

When can we expect the labeling machine to be repaired?

(A) Yes, you're supposed to work in pairs.
(B) The place of origin is on the label.
(C) They still don't know what's wrong with it.

어휘 be supposed to-V ~하기로 되어 있다, ~해야 한다
in pairs 둘씩 짝을 지어 place of origin 원산지

해석 상표 부착기가 언제 수리될 것으로 예상하면 될까요?
(A) 네, 여러분은 둘씩 짝지어 일해야 합니다.
(B) 원산지는 라벨에 있습니다.
(C) 아직 뭐가 잘못된 건지도 몰라요.

해설 질문과 대답의 내용을 완벽하게 알아듣는다면 (C)가 자연스러운 대답이라는 것을 알 수 있지만, 제대로 알아듣지 못해도 반드시 정답은 맞히도록 하자. 의문사 의문문이므로 Yes로 시작하는 (A)는 오답이다. (B)는 질문에 나왔던 label이 반복되는 것을 듣고 오답으로 골라낼 수 있다.

PART 3 Sample Questions

1-3번 문제는 다음 편지에 관한 것입니다.

남: 안녕하세요, 시 관광청의 Ezra Goldman입니다. 제 동료 중 한 명이 당신의 사진을 추천했어요. 당신 홈페이지를 살펴보고 있는데요, 당신이 찍은 시의 항공 사진을 구입하고 싶습니다. 관광 안내 책자에 넣고 싶거든요.
여: 좋죠! 여러 다양한 사진들이 몇 장 있어요. 사진 옆에 있는 식별 번호를 불러주시겠어요?
남: 네, 782311이요.
여: 알겠습니다. 음... 계속 진행하셔서 제 홈페이지에서 결제하시면 됩니다. 그러면 제가 고해상도 버전의 사진 파일을 이메일로 보내드리겠습니다.

어휘 look over ~을 살펴보다 aerial photo 항공 사진 brochure 안내 책자 shot 사진, 장면 ID(identification)) number 식별 번호 high-resolution 고해상도의

---

1. 여자는 누구이겠는가?

(A) 사진작가
(B) 시 관광 담당 공무원
(C) 항공사 직원
(D) 여행 기자

---

2. 여자는 어떤 정보를 요청하는가?

(A) 비용 견적
(B) 식별 번호
(C) 우편 주소
(D) 관광 일정

---

3. 여자는 무엇을 할 것이라고 말하는가?

(A) 청구서를 수정한다
(B) 안내 책자를 살펴본다
(C) 추천을 한다
(D) 파일을 보낸다

PART 3 & 4 Exercise

1 (D) **2** (C) **3** (A) **4** (C) **5** (A) **6** (D)

Questions 1 through 3 refer to the following conversation with three speakers.

[M｜Au] Welcome, Keith and Susan. [1]I'm so glad you decided to come and check out the house. As I mentioned, the seller has just lowered the price.

[W｜Br] Yes, the property is appealing to us, [2]but we do have some concerns.

[M｜Cn] We're worried about the cost of major renovations. Like the roof; do you know if it's been replaced?

[M｜Au] Yes, just last year, and so was the furnace. Everything here is in good shape.

[M｜Cn] After all the work that was done on the house, it's quite surprising the owner decided to move.

[M｜Au] [3]Well, she just accepted a job out of the city. So, she was left with no other option.

1-3번 문제는 다음 3인 대화에 관한 것입니다.

> **남1:** Keith, Susan, 어서 오세요. 두 분이 오셔서 집을 보시겠다고 하시니 정말 기쁩니다. 말씀드렸다시피 파는 분이 지금 막 가격을 낮추셨어요.
> **여:** 네, 건물이 저희에게 매력적이에요. 하지만 걱정도 조금 있어요.
> **남2:** 큰 보수 공사 비용이 걱정이거든요. 지붕 같은 거요. 혹시 교체되었는지 아시나요?
> **남1:** 네, 바로 작년에요. 보일러도 마찬가지고요. 여기는 모든 것이 상태가 좋습니다.
> **남2:** 집주인이 집에 그 모든 작업을 해놓고 나서 이사를 가기로 했다는 게 참 놀랍군요.
> **남1:** 아, 최근에 외지에서 일자리를 수락했거든요. 그러니까 당연히 다른 선택의 여지가 없었던 거죠.

어휘 check out 살펴보다 lower (가치·정도 등을) 낮추다, 떨어뜨리다 property 건물, 부동산 appealing 매력적인, 흥미로운 concern 걱정, 우려 replace 대체하다 furnace 보일러 in good shape 상태가 좋은 leave A with B A를 B한 상태에 처하게 하다

---

1. Who most likely are Keith and Susan?

(A) Property managers
(B) Maintenance workers
(C) Building inspectors
(D) Potential home buyers

해석 Keith와 Susan은 누구이겠는가?
(A) 부동산 관리인
(B) 시설 관리 직원
(C) 건축 감리사
(D) 잠재 주택 구매자

---

2. What are Keith and Susan concerned about?

(A) The placement of smoke detectors
(B) The measurement of a property
(C) The cost of major repairs
(D) The number of occupants

해석 Keith와 Susan은 무엇에 대해 걱정하는가?
(A) 연기 탐지기의 배치
(B) 건물의 크기
(C) 큰 수리 작업 비용
(D) 입주자 수

---

3. What is mentioned about the current owner?

(A) She has decided to take on a new job.
(B) She owns multiple properties.
(C) She can recommend skilled workers.
(D) She is available only in the afternoon.

해석 현 소유주에 대해 무엇이 언급되는가?
(A) 새 일자리를 맡기로 했다.
(B) 다수의 부동산을 소유하고 있다.
(C) 숙련된 인부들을 추천해 줄 수 있다.
(D) 오후에만 만날 시간이 있다.

해설 부동산 중개업자의 첫 대사 I'm so glad you decided to come and check out the house. As I mentioned, the seller has just lowered the price.에서 Keith와 Susan은 집을 사기 위해 보러 다니는 사람들이라는 것을 추론할 수 있으므로 여기서 1번 문제의 정답을 선택하자. 2번은 대화 중 여자의 대사 but we do have some concerns.에 이어 남자가 We're worried about the cost of major renovations.라고 말하는 것을 들으면 거의 똑같은 말이 쓰여 있는 선택지가 있으므로 쉽게 정답을 알 수 있다. 3번은 중개업자가 마지막에 말하는 Well, she just accepted a job out of the city.를 듣고 이 부분이 패러프 레이즈 되어 있는 문장을 정답으로 선택해야 한다.

Questions 4 through 6 refer to the following advertisement.

[M | Cn] ⁴One of the essential components of a profitable business is a dependable Internet connection. That's why so many customers are switching to Chiefa Online. ⁵At Chiefa, we guarantee that our Internet service is ten times more reliable than any of our competitors'. But don't just take our word for it. ⁶Go onto our Web site at chiefaonline. net to read what our customers have written about our service. Join our list of satisfied customers.

4-6번 문제는 다음 광고에 관한 것입니다.

남: 수익성이 있는 사업의 필수 요소 중 하나는 신뢰할 만한 인터넷 연결입니다. 그 점 때문에 이렇게 많은 고객 들이 Chiefa Online으로 전환하고 계십니다. Chiefa에서 는 우리의 인터넷 서비스가 어느 경쟁업체들의 서비스보 다도 열 배 더 신뢰할 수 있음을 보장합니다. 단지 저희의 말을 곧이곧대로 믿기만 하지는 마세요. 저희 홈페이지 chiefaonline.net으로 가셔서 고객들이 저희 서비스에 대해 써놓은 것을 읽어보시기 바랍니다. 저희의 만족하신 고 객 중 한 분이 되어보세요.

어휘 component (구성) 요소 profitable 수익성이 있는, 이익이 많은 dependable 믿을[신뢰할] 수 있는 switch to ~로 전환하다, 바꾸다 guarantee 보장하다, 약속하다 reliable 믿을[신뢰할] 수 있는 competitor 경쟁자, 경쟁업체 take one's word for it ~의 말을 곧이곧대로 받아들이다

4. What is being advertised?

(A) A cleaning service
(B) A computer shop
(C) An Internet provider
(D) An accounting firm

해석 무엇을 광고하고 있는가?
(A) 청소 서비스
(B) 컴퓨터 상점
(C) 인터넷 서비스 제공업체
(D) 회계법인

5. What does the speaker emphasize about the service?

(A) Its reliability
(B) Its reasonable prices
(C) Its speed
(D) Its user-friendliness

해석 화자는 서비스에 대해 무엇을 강조하는가?
(A) 신뢰성
(B) 저렴한 가격
(C) 속도
(D) 사용자 친화성

6. According to the speaker, what is available on the Web site?

(A) Discount codes
(B) Promotional videos
(C) Software applications
(D) Customer testimonials

해석 화자의 말에 따르면 홈페이지에서 무엇을 이용할 수 있 는가?
(A) 할인 코드
(B) 홍보용 동영상
(C) 소프트웨어 앱
(D) 고객이 쓴 추천의 글

해설 첫 문장 One of the essential components of a profitable business is a dependable Internet connection. 을 들으면 인터넷 서비스 제공업체의 광고라는 것을 알 수 있으므로 바로 1번 문제의 정답을 고르자. 2번의 정답은 At Chiefa, we guarantee that our Internet service is ten

Actual Test

1 (D)	**2** (B)	**3** (D)	**4** (A)	**5** (B)
6 (A)	**7** (B)	**8** (A)	**9** (A)	**10** (C)
11 (B)	**12** (C)	**13** (D)	**14** (C)	**15** (A)
16 (C)	**17** (C)	**18** (B)	**19** (B)	**20** (C)
21 (A)	**22** (A)	**23** (B)	**24** (B)	**25** (D)
26 (C)	**27** (C)	**28** (D)	**29** (B)	**30** (C)

* 정답을 맞힌 문제도 해설을 읽어보세요.

Part 1

1. ☐ M | Cn ☐

(A) One of the women is putting away a bag.
(B) A cashier is collecting a payment.
(C) One of the women is discarding a brochure.
(D) Some diners are seated across from each other.

🔹**어휘** put away (다 쓰고 난 물건을) 치우다 collect 받다, 수령하다 payment 지불액 discard 버리다 brochure 안내 책자 diner (식당의) 식사하는 사람[손님]

🔹**해석** (A) 여자들 중 한 명이 가방을 치우고 있다.
(B) 계산원이 지불금을 받고 있다.
(C) 여자들 중 한 명이 안내 책자를 버리고 있다.
(D) 손님들이 서로 맞은편에 앉아 있다.

🔹**해설** 물건을 치우거나(putting away) 버리는(discarding) 장면이 아니므로 (A)와 (C)는 오답이다. 사진 속에 계산원으로 보이는 사람도 없으므로 (B)도 오답이다. 사람들이 탁자를 사이에 두고 마주보는 장면에서 전치사 across가 들리는 문장은 항상 정답이다.

---

2. ☐ W | Br ☐

(A) Some people are watching a movie.
(B) A speaker is addressing a group.
(C) A projector is being adjusted.
(D) Documents are being distributed to the attendees.

🔹**어휘** address 연설(하다); ~에게 말을 걸다[하다] adjust 조정 하다, 조절하다

🔹**해석** (A) 사람들이 영화를 보고 있다.
(B) 화자가 한 그룹에게 말하고 있다.
(C) 프로젝터를 조정하고 있다.
(D) 참석자들에게 문서가 배포되고 있다.

🔹**해설** 영화를 보고 있지 않으므로 (A)가 오답인 것은 쉽게 알 수 있다. 진행 시제 수동태는 동작을 나타내므로 (C)나 (D)가 정답이 되려면 영사기를 조정하거나(adjust) 문서를 배포하는(distribute) 동작을 하고 있어야 한다. 한 남자가 그룹에게 말하고 있는 장면이므로 동사 addressing이 들리는 문장을 정답으로 선택하자.

---

3. ☐ M | Cn ☐

(A) Some paintings are being taken off a wall.
(B) One of the women is pulling on her gloves.
(C) A bridge is being torn down in the distance.

(D) Some artworks have drawn the women's attention.

어휘 take A off B B에서 A를 떼어내다 pull on (장갑을) 잡아당겨 끼다 tear down (– tore – torn) (건물·담 등을) 허물다, 헐다 in the distance 먼 곳에서 draw one's attention (– drew – drawn) ~의 주목을 끌다

해석 (A) 벽에서 그림들을 떼어내고 있다.
(B) 여자들 중 한 명이 장갑을 잡아당겨 끼고 있다.
(C) 먼 곳에서 다리가 철거되고 있다.
(D) 미술 작품들이 여자들의 주목을 끌었다.

해설 진행 시제 수동태는 동작을 나타내므로 (A)나 (C)가 정답이 되려면 그림을 벽에서 떼어내거나(take off) 교량을 철거하고(tear down) 있어야 한다. 장갑을 끼는 동작도 아니므로 (B)도 오답이다. 여자들이 미술 작품을 감상하고 있으므로 "미술 작품들이 여자들의 주목을 끌었다"고 말하는 문장이 정답이다.

Part 2

4. [W｜Br] [M｜Cn]

Aren't we taking the same train?

(A) No, one leaves later.
(B) I ate in the dining car.
(C) You can take both of them.

어휘 dining car (기차의) 식당차

해석 우리가 같은 열차를 타는 거 아닌가요?
(A) 아니요, 한 명은 나중에 출발해요.
(B) 식당차에서 먹었어요.
(C) 둘 다 가지셔도 됩니다.

해설 Aren't는 수험생들이 알아듣기 어려워하는 단어 중 하나다. 질문을 따라 읽어보자. 영국 발음이므로 Aren't에서 r은 발음하지 않고, t 발음도 불편하기 때문에 생략한다. "안 위 테이킹 더 세임 츄레인?" 함께 출발하는 줄 알고 있는 여자에게 둘 중 한 명은 나중에 출발한다고 알려주는 (A)가 정답이다. (B)는 질문의 train에서 연상되는 단어 dining car로, (C)는 동사 take를 반복시켜서 오답을 유도하고 있으므로, 질문과 (A)를 제대로 이해하지 못해도 정답인 것을 알 수 있다. 오답을 잘 골라낼수록 고수가 된다!

5. [M｜Au] [W｜Am]

Did you find the replacement parts for the printer?

(A) Under sixty dollars.
(B) They're being installed now.
(C) Thirty pages a minute.

어휘 replacement 교체 part 부품

해석 프린터 교체 부품을 찾으셨나요?
(A) 60달러 이하요.
(B) 지금 설치하고 있어요.
(C) 분당 30페이지요.

해설 질문 앞부분 Did you find the replacement parts(교체 부품을 찾으셨나요?)에 집중하면 자연스러운 대답을 알아낼 수 있다. (C)는 질문의 printer에서 연상되는 대답으로 오답을 유도하고 있다.

6. [M｜Cn] [W｜Br]

Please let me know when you're finished with the label maker.

(A) Sure, it'll only take a couple minutes.
(B) For the new filing cabinet.
(C) No, they're organized in alphabetical order.

어휘 organize 정리하다 in alphabetical order 알파벳순으로

해석 상표 부착기 다 쓰시면 알려주세요.
(A) 네, 몇 분밖에 안 걸릴 거예요.
(B) 새 서류 캐비닛에 쓰려고요.
(C) 아니요, 알파벳순으로 정리되어 있습니다.

해설 질문 앞부분 Please let me know(알려주세요)에 집중하면 Sure라고 대답하는 (A)가 가장 자연스러운 대답이다. (B)와 (C)는 모두 질문의 label maker에서 연상되는 대답으로 오답을 유도하고 있다.

7. [M｜Au] [W｜Am]

What was Ms. Freeman's group asked to work on this month?

(A) Sure, I'll ask her to do it.
(B) The report on renewable resources.
(C) Later in the month.

어휘 renewable 재생 가능한

해석 Ms. Freeman의 그룹은 이번 달에 어떤 일을 해달라고 요청받았나요?
(A) 물론이죠, 그녀에게 하라고 요청할게요.
(B) 재생 가능한 자원에 대한 보고서요.
(C) 이달 하순에요.

해설 질문이 의문사 의문문이므로 Yes나 No로 시작하는 대답은 오답이다. Sure는 Yes라고 말하는 것과 같으므로 (A)는 오답이다. (C)는 질문에 나온 month를 반복하면서 오답을 유도하고 있다. 오답을 잘 골라낼수록 고수가 된다!

8. [W｜Am] [M｜Cn]

How will the construction workers get into the office building?

(A) The security guard can let them in.
(B) They're renovating the fifth floor.
(C) The work will be done by Thursday.

▶ 어휘 let *sb* in ~를 들어오게 하다

▶ 해석 공사 인부들이 사무실 건물에 어떻게 들어가나요?
(A) 경비원이 들어가게 해줄 겁니다.
(B) 5층을 개조할 거예요.
(C) 작업은 목요일까지 완료될 겁니다.

▶ 해설 공사 인부들이 건물에 들어가는 방법을 적절하게 설명하고 있는 (A)가 정답이다. (B)는 질문의 construction이나 building에서 연상되는 대답으로 오답을 유도하고 있으며, (C)는 When 의문문에 알맞은 대답이다. 오답을 잘 골라낼수록 고수가 된다!

---

9. [M｜Cn] [W｜Br]

Why is the contractor coming in this afternoon?

(A) I thought you asked him to come.
(B) You have to initial each page.
(C) At least four weeks.

▶ 어휘 contractor 하청업자, 도급업자 initial 첫 글자[머리글자]들을 표시하다

▶ 해석 오늘 오후에 하청업자가 왜 오나요?
(A) 당신이 오라고 한 줄 알았는데요.
(B) 각 페이지에 이름 첫 글자를 써야 합니다.
(C) 최소 4주요.

▶ 해설 자연스러운 대답이 되는 (A)를 따라 읽어보자. asked는 원래 영국 발음으로 '아스크트'라고 읽어야 하지만 뒤에 him이 붙으면서 발음이 불편해진다. 그래서 asked him은 k 발음을 빼고 두 단어를 연음시키면서 '아스팀'이라고 읽는다(아이 쏱 유 아스팀 투 컴). (B)에서 말하는 각 페이지마다 이름 첫 글자를 쓰는 것은 계약서를 쓸 때의 관행이므로, 질문의 contractor와 발음이 비슷한 contract에서 연상되는 대답으로 오답을 유도하는 것이다. (C)는 기간을 말하고 있으므로 How long ~? 에 대한 대답으로 알맞다. 오답을 잘 골라낼수록 고수가 된다!

---

10. [M｜Cn] [M｜Au]

Do you have time for a quick football game?

(A) Don't you remember that one?
(B) I haven't seen them play.
(C) Should I bring my ball?

▶ 해석 잠깐 축구 경기 할 시간 있어요?
(A) 저거 생각 안 나세요?
(B) 그들이 경기하는 것은 못 봤습니다.
(C) 제 공을 가져갈까요?

▶ 해설 축구 경기를 함께 하자는 제안에 대해 "제 공을 가져갈까요?"라고 말하는 것은 제안을 수락하겠다는 뜻이므로 자연스러운 대답이 된다.

---

11. [W｜Br] [W｜Am]

Doesn't the laptop come with that program already installed?

(A) I bought a new television set.
(B) No, you have to download it from the Internet.
(C) She usually comes on Tuesdays.

▶ 어휘 with + N + 형용사[분사] ~가 ~인 채로

▶ 해석 노트북이 그 프로그램이 이미 설치된 채로 나오지 않나요?
(A) 새 텔레비전 세트를 샀어요.
(B) 아니요, 인터넷에서 다운로드하셔야 합니다.
(C) 그녀는 보통 화요일에 와요.

▶ 해설 'with + N + 형용사[분사]'는 토익 모든 파트에서 매우 빈번하게 사용되는 표현이므로 반드시 기억하고 알아들어야 한다. 노트북에 어떤 프로그램이 내장되어 있지 않은지 확인하는 질문에 대해 인터넷에서 따로 다운로드해야 한다는 대답이 정답이다.

---

12. [W｜Br] [M｜Au]

Don't you want to take your umbrella with you?

(A) No problem, I'll be there.
(B) He wants to take a break.
(C) No, I shouldn't need it.

▶ 해석 우산 안 가져가실 건가요?
(A) 문제없어요, 갈게요.
(B) 그는 쉬고 싶어 합니다.
(C) 네, 필요 없을 거예요.

▶ 해설 비가 올까 봐 우산을 챙겨갈 것을 권하는 질문에 대해 우산이 필요 없을 것이라고 대답하면 자연스러운 대화가 된다.

Part 3

Questions 13 through 15 refer to the following conversation.

> [M | Au] Hello. Kenneth Cook speaking.
>
> [W | Am] This is Gina Masterson. ¹³ ¹⁴I'm calling to let you know I've put my research report in the interoffice mail. You should have it by the end of the day. I hope you're still willing to review it for me.
>
> [M | Au] Absolutely! I'll be out of town on business over the next few days, but I'll bring it with me. ¹⁴I've also received your request for additional funding to continue your research.
>
> [W | Am] Thank you very much. Don't worry about the typos. The report will be sent to an editor. But please make some suggestions about the content. It's just the first draft and ¹⁵I'm going to make revisions. I'm really looking forward to your feedback.

13-15번 문제는 다음 대화에 관한 것입니다.

> 남: 여보세요. Kenneth Cook입니다.
> 여: Gina Masterson입니다. 연구 보고서를 사내 우편으로 보냈다고 알려드리려고 전화 드렸어요. 오늘 퇴근하시기 전에 받아 보시게 될 거예요. 여전히 검토해 볼 의향이 있으시면 좋겠네요.
> 남: 물론이죠! 앞으로 며칠 동안 업무차 다른 지역에 있을 건데, 그것을 가져갈게요. 그리고 연구를 계속하기 위해 추가 자금을 요청한 것도 잘 받았어요.
> 여: 정말 고맙습니다. 오타에 대해서는 신경 쓰지 마세요. 보고서를 편집자에게 보낼 겁니다. 하지만 내용에 대해서는 제안을 좀 해주시기를 부탁드립니다. 이건 그냥 초안이고 수정을 할 거니까요. 피드백 기대하겠습니다.

[어휘] interoffice 사내의 be willing to-V ~할 의향이 있다 typo 오타 content 내용 draft (글, 원고의) 초고, 초안 revision 수정, 정정

13. What is the purpose of Gina's call to Kenneth?

(A) To inform him she is going out of town

(B) To urge him to pay for further research

(C) To thank him for meeting with her

(D) To notify him she mailed a report to him

[어휘] urge 강력히 권고[촉구]하다 notify 알리다

[해석] Gina가 Kenneth에게 전화를 건 목적은 무엇인가?
(A) 외지로 나갈 것이라고 알리기 위해
(B) 추가 연구 비용을 지급해 달라고 촉구하기 위해
(C) 만나준 것에 대해 감사를 표하기 위해
(D) 보고서를 우편으로 보냈다고 알리기 위해

14. What department does Gina most likely work in?

(A) Corporate archive
(B) Sales
(C) Research
(D) Public relations

[어휘] corporate 기업의, 회사의 archive 기록 보관소

[해석] Gina는 어느 부서에서 일하겠는가?
(A) 회사 기록 보관소
(B) 영업부
(C) 연구부
(D) 홍보부

15. What does Gina plan to do?

(A) Make revisions to her report
(B) Send Kenneth more money
(C) Take some time off work
(D) Give Kenneth some advice

[어휘] off work 근무하지 않는

[해석] Gina는 무엇을 할 계획인가?
(A) 보고서를 수정한다
(B) Kenneth에게 추가로 돈을 보낸다
(C) 잠깐 일을 쉰다
(D) Kenneth에게 조언을 한다

[해설] 대화의 주제나 목적은 보통 첫 한두 문장에 드러난다. I'm calling to let you know I've put my research report in the interoffice mail.이 나올 때 13번 문제의 정답을 선택하자. 이 문장에서 my research report라는 키워드를 포착하면 Gina가 일하는 부서도 짐작할 수 있다. 그리고 뒤에 나오는 남자의 대사 I've also received your request for additional funding to continue your research.를 들으면 Gina가 연구 업무에 종사하는 사람임을 더 확실히 알 수 있으므로 여기서 14번 정답을 고르자. 15번의 정답은 대화

거의 마지막에 나오는 여자의 대사 I'm going to make revisions.에서 쉽게 알아낼 수 있다.

Questions 16 through 18 refer to the following conversation.

W Br ¹⁶Thank you for calling Hamilton Medical Clinic. This is Natalie speaking. How can I help you?

M Cn Hello, my name is Jeffrey Hines. ¹⁷I'm planning to travel overseas on holiday next month and I have to get some vaccinations. ¹⁸Do you have any appointments available at your office?

W Br I think we can find time for you, Mr. Hines. Let me check our calendar. Well, it looks like we have several openings next Monday. ¹⁸Does three P.M. work for you?

M Cn [I work until four o'clock on Mondays.]

W Br ¹⁸OK, how about four-thirty? Will you be able to make it here by that time?

M Cn That'll work for me. Thanks and see you then.

16–18번 문제는 다음 대화에 관한 것입니다.

여: Hamilton 병원에 전화 주셔서 고맙습니다. 저는 Natalie입니다. 어떻게 도와드릴까요?
남: 안녕하세요, 제 이름은 Jeffrey Hines입니다. 다음 달에 휴가차 해외로 여행을 가려고 하고요 예방 접종을 해야 합니다. 그쪽 병원에서 예약을 할 수 있을까요?
여: 시간을 잡아드릴 수 있을 거예요, Mr. Hines. 일정표를 확인해 볼게요. 음, 다음 주 월요일에 비는 시간이 좀 있는 것 같아요. 오후 3시 괜찮으세요?
남: 월요일에는 제가 4시까지 일해요.
여: 알겠습니다. 4시 30분은 어떠세요? 그 시간까지 여기로 오실 수 있겠어요?
남: 그게 괜찮겠어요. 고맙습니다. 그때 봬요.

어휘 vaccination 예방 접종 appointment (진찰) 예약 opening 빈 자리 make it (시간 맞춰) 가다 work for ~에게 문제없다, 좋다

---

16. Where does the woman work?

(A) At an accounting firm
(B) At a travel agency
(C) At a health clinic

(D) At a beauty salon

해석 여자는 어디에서 일하는가?
(A) 회계 법인
(B) 여행사
(C) 병원
(D) 미용실

---

17. What does the man say he will be doing next month?

(A) Leading a seminar
(B) Starting to work at a different company
(C) Taking a holiday overseas
(D) Writing a handbook for tourists

해석 남자는 다음 달에 무엇을 할 것이라고 말하는가?
(A) 세미나를 진행한다
(B) 다른 회사에서 근무를 시작한다
(C) 해외에서 휴가를 보낸다
(D) 관광객들을 위한 안내서를 쓴다

---

18. What does the man imply when he says, "I work until four o'clock on Mondays"?

(A) He desires to be working full-time.
(B) He needs a later appointment.
(C) He would rather come in during the weekend.
(D) He is scheduled to leave early for an event.

어휘 would rather (차라리) ~하겠다[하고 싶다]

해석 남자는 "월요일에는 제가 4시까지 일해요."라고 말할 때 무엇을 암시하는가?
(A) 정규직으로 일하기를 바란다.
(B) 더 늦은 예약이 필요하다.
(C) 차라리 주말에 가겠다.
(D) 행사 때문에 일찍 떠날 예정이다.

해설 화자가 일하는 장소는 거의 대부분 첫 한두 문장에서 알아낼 수 있다. 여자의 첫 대사 Thank you for calling Hamilton Medical Clinic.을 듣자마자 16번 문제의 정답을 선택하자. 17번 문제의 정답은 키워드 next month가 들어 있는 문장에서 쉽게 알아낼 수 있다. I'm planning to travel overseas on holiday next month가 나올 때 정답을 고르자. 18번에서 주어진 문장은 Does three P.M. work for you?라는 여자의 질문에 대한 대답(I work until four o'clock on Mondays.)이므로 3시보다는 늦은 시간으로 예약을 잡아달라는 요청을 암시한다.

Questions 19 through 21 refer to the following conversation and schedule.

M Cn Hi, Yolanda. ¹⁹I was testing a company computer here in my office, ²⁰and browsed around our online staff forum, and ...

W Br Ah, how does it look?

M Cn It looks great. And it seems like there's a lot of interest in our upcoming seminars. Will we need additional space? We could rent a conference room, or ...

W Br We'll be all right. ²⁰I'm planning to create digital videos of all the presentations and post them on our staff forum.

M Cn Good idea.

W Br Oh, and ... we've made a switch. ²¹The times for the first and last sessions have been switched. So the day's first topic will be ... Sales Techniques. We made that change because Ms. Park, the presenter, has to leave before lunch.

19–21번 문제는 다음 대화와 일정표에 관한 것입니다.

남: 안녕, Yolanda. 여기 내 사무실에서 회사 컴퓨터를 테스트하고 있었어요. 그러면서 우리 회사 온라인 직원 토론 게시판을 둘러보고 있었는데 말이죠. ...

여: 아, 어때 보여요?

남: 훌륭해 보여요. 그리고 다가오는 세미나에 관심이 많은 것 같아 보이네요. 추가 공간이 필요할까요? 회의실을 빌릴 수도 있고요, 아니면 ...

여: 괜찮을 거예요. 내가 모든 프레젠테이션의 디지털 동영상을 만들어서 직원 토론 게시판에 올릴 계획이거든요.

남: 좋은 생각이에요.

여: 아, 그리고 ... 변경된 게 하나 있어요. 첫 번째와 마지막 모임의 시간이 서로 바뀌었어요. 그러니까 그날의 첫 주제는 .... '영업 기법'이 될 거예요. 발표자 Ms. Park이 점심시간 전에 가셔야 해서 그렇게 변경했어요.

🔑어휘 browse 둘러보다 staff forum (온라인) 직원 토론 게시판 upcoming 다가오는, 곧 있을 rent 빌리다 conference room 회의실 post 게시하다 switch 변경; 서로 바꾸다 presenter 발표자

Seminar Schedule	
Topic	*Time*
Leadership	10 – 11 A.M.
Teamwork	11 A.M. – Noon
LUNCH	Noon – 1 P.M.
Market Trends	1 – 2 P.M.
Sales Techniques	2 – 3 P.M.

세미나 일정	
주제	*시간*
리더십	오전 10 – 11시
팀워크	오전 11시 – 정오
점심	정오 – 오후 1시
시장 동향	오후 1 – 2시
영업 기법	오후 2 – 3시

19. Where most likely is the conversation taking place?

(A) At an electronics shop
(B) At a company office
(C) At a conference room
(D) At a public park

🔑해석 대화는 어디에서 이루어지고 있겠는가?
(A) 전자 제품 매장
(B) 회사 사무실
(C) 회의실
(D) 공원

20. What does the woman plan to do?

(A) Give a keynote presentation
(B) Rent a larger venue
(C) Post videos online
(D) Review a marketing proposal

🔑어휘 keynote presentation[speech/address/lecture] 기조 발표[연설/강연] venue 장소 proposal 기획안, 제안서
🔑해석 여자는 무엇을 할 계획인가?
(A) 기조 발표를 한다
(B) 더 큰 장소를 빌린다
(C) 온라인에 동영상을 게재한다
(D) 마케팅 기획안을 검토한다

21. Look at the graphic. According to the woman, which session will now be held last?

(A) **Leadership**
(B) Teamwork
(C) Market Trends
(D) Sales Techniques

🔲**해석** 그래픽을 보라. 여자의 말에 따르면 어느 모임이 마지막에 열릴 것인가?
(A) 리더십
(B) 팀워크
(C) 시장 동향
(D) 영업 기법

🔲**해설** 19번 같은 장소에 관한 질문은 거의 항상 첫 한두 문장에 정답의 키워드가 있다. 남자의 첫 대사 I was testing a company computer here in my office.에서 이곳이 사무실이라고 분명히 말하고 있다. 20번 문제는 키워드 plan to가 또렷이 들리는 문장 I'm planning to create digital videos of all the presentations and post them on our staff forum.에서 정답을 알 수 있다. 21번은 여자의 마지막 대사에 들어 있는 The times for the first and last sessions have been switched.를 듣고 정답을 선택하자. 첫 번째와 마지막 모임의 시간이 서로 바뀌었다고 했으므로 마지막 세미나 주제는 '리더십'이다.

Part 4

Questions 22 through 24 refer to the following news report.

M | Au ²²Today, tourists and residents alike gathered at the Carrington Center to view the latest exhibit that was unveiled this morning. The exhibit, called Tropical Plant International Expo, features a wide selection of tropical plants and will be on display through the end of the month. As most of you are aware, the Carrington Center is well-known for its dedication to environmental preservation. ²³ ²⁴They recently hired architect Jay Patel to design a new visitors' center with the requirement that the new building be powered primarily by energy from solar panels. The center's board of directors was impressed with the portfolio presented by Mr. Patel, ²⁴stating that his designs were the strongest they had seen.

22-24번 문제는 다음 뉴스 보도에 관한 것입니다.

남: 오늘 관광객들과 주민들이 다 같이 오전에 처음 공개된 최신 전시회를 보기 위해 Carrington 센터에 모였습니다. '국제 열대식물 박람회'라고 불리는 이 전시회는 다양하게 엄선된 열대식물을 포함하고 있으며 이달 말까지 진행됩니다. 대부분 아시다시피 Carrington 센터는 환경 보존에 대한 헌신으로 잘 알려져 있습니다. 최근에는 건축가 Jay Patel을 고용하여 새 방문객 센터를 설계하게 했는데, 새 건물이 주로 태양 전지판에서 얻는 에너지로 동력이 공급되어야 한다는 요구 조건이 있었습니다. 센터 이사회는 Mr. Patel이 제출한 포트폴리오에 깊은 인상을 받았으며 그의 설계가 그들이 본 것 중 가장 훌륭했다고 말했습니다.

🔲**어휘** alike (앞에 언급한 두 사람[사물]이) 둘 다, 똑같이 view 보다 exhibit 전람회, 전시회 unveil 처음 공개하다 feature 특별히 포함하다 a wide selection of 다양하게 엄선해 놓은 on display 전시된, 진열된 through (~을 포함하여) ~까지 aware 알고 있는 dedication 헌신, 전념 preservation 보존, 보호, 유지 architect 건축가 requirement 요구 조건 power 동력을 공급하다, 작동시키다 primarily 주로 solar panel 태양 전지판 board of directors 이사회 present 제출하다, 제시하다

22. Why did people gather at the Carrington Center this morning?

(A) **To visit a plant exhibit**
(B) To attend an open-air concert
(C) To enroll in a gardening class
(D) To listen to an art lecture

🔲**어휘** open-air 야외의 enroll in ~에 등록하다

🔲**해석** 오늘 오전에 사람들이 왜 Carrington 센터에 모여들었는가?
(A) 식물 전시회를 방문하기 위해
(B) 야외 콘서트에 참석하기 위해
(C) 원예 수업에 등록하기 위해
(D) 미술 강연을 듣기 위해

23. What is said about the new building?

(A) It is bordered by water.
(B) **It makes use of solar energy.**
(C) It has a rooftop café.
(D) It has a sculpture garden.

🔲**어휘** border ~와 접하다, 둘러싸다 make use of ~을 이용하다, 활용하다

(A) 물로 둘러싸여 있다.
(B) 태양열 에너지를 사용한다.
(C) 옥상 카페가 있다.
(D) 조각 공원이 있다.

---

24. Why was Jay Patel chosen?

(A) He put forth the lowest bid.
(B) He presented the best designs.
(C) He can commence immediately.
(D) He resides in the area.

어휘 put forth 제시하다 bid 입찰(가) commence 시작하다
immediately 즉시 reside 살다, 거주하다

해석 왜 Jay Patel이 선택되었는가?
(A) 가장 낮은 입찰가를 제시했다.
(B) 최고의 설계안을 제출했다.
(C) 즉시 시작할 수 있다.
(D) 그 지역에 거주한다.

해설 첫 두 문장에서 22번의 정답을 알아낼 수 있다. 사람들이 오전에 시작된 전시회를 보기 위해 Carrington 센터에 모여들었다고(Today, tourists and residents alike gathered at the Carrington Center to view the latest exhibit that was unveiled this morning.) 말하는데 이어 이 전시회는 열대식물 박람회라고 소개하고 있다(The exhibit, called Tropical Plant International Expo, features a wide selection of tropical plants). 23번은 최근에 새 건물을 짓기 위해 건축가를 모집하면서 내건 조건이 주 에너지원으로 태양열을 사용하는 건물이어야 함을 말하는 데서(They recently hired architect Jay Patel to design a new visitors' center with the requirement that the new building be powered primarily by energy from solar panels.) 정답을 알 수 있다. Jay Patel이 선정된 이유를 묻는 24번의 정답은 stating that his designs were the strongest they had seen. 이라고 말하는 마지막 문장에서 알 수 있다.

Questions 25 through 27 refer to the following announcement.

[W | Br] Attention, Keller Grace employees. Starting next month, all of the exterior doors will have new digital locks installed. Everyone must obtain a new, um, digital key. ²⁵Bring your employee ID badge to the security desk so the guard can make a new key for you. The new keys will be linked exclusively to your employee ID, ²⁶enabling us to monitor the entry and exit times of individuals in the building. ²⁷There's more information available about the upcoming security changes in the company newsletter, so [make sure to check that out.] Once you have reviewed it, feel free to ask your department head any questions you may have. Thanks.

25-27번 문제는 다음 공지에 관한 것입니다.

여: Keller Grace 직원 여러분 주목해 주세요. 다음 달부터 시작해서 모든 외부 출입문에 새 디지털 잠금 장치가 설치됩니다. 모든 분들이 새, 어, 디지털 열쇠를 받으셔야 합니다. 사원증을 보안 데스크로 가져다 주셔서 보안 요원이 새 열쇠를 만들 수 있게 해주시기 바랍니다. 새 열쇠는 여러분의 사원증에만 연결되어 건물 내 개인의 출입 시간을 모니터할 수 있습니다. 사보에 곧 있을 보안상의 변경 사항에 대해 보실 수 있는 정보가 더 있으니 반드시 살펴보시기 바랍니다. 일단 검토하고 나서 궁금한 점이 있으면 부서장에게 자유롭게 물어보세요. 고맙습니다.

어휘 exterior 외부의 obtain 얻다, 입수하다 employee ID badge 사원증 so (that) + S + can[may/will] + V ~가 ~하기 위해서 exclusively 독점적으로, 오로지 (~만) enable ~할 수 있게 하다 monitor 모니터하다, 감시하다 entry and exit 출입 newsletter 소식지, 회보 make sure to-V 반드시 ~하도록 하다 check out 살펴보다 feel free to-V 자유롭게[마음 놓고] ~하다 department head 부서장

---

25. What are listeners asked to provide?

(A) A monthly charge
(B) A production schedule
(C) A computer access code
(D) A form of identification

어휘 identification 신분증

해석 청자들은 무엇을 제공하라고 요구받는가?
(A) 월 요금
(B) 생산 일정
(C) 컴퓨터 접속 코드
(D) 어떤 형태의 신분증

---

26. What special feature is mentioned about a new digital key?

(A) It can unlock all the building doors.
(B) It is simple to find a replacement for it.
(C) It can track who enters a building.
(D) It is compatible with an older style of lock.

---

27. What does the speaker mean when she says, "make sure to check that out"?

(A) Employees should keep a door locked.
(B) Employees should verify their ID.
(C) Employees should read a document.
(D) Employees should rent certain equipment.

Questions 28 through 30 refer to the following talk and program.

W | Br [28]We're happy to see you all at this workshop this morning. We have plenty of useful information to cover. But before we start, let's go over a few administrative details. There will be one break, halfway through the morning. Laptops can be left here when you leave the room - there will always be someone in here - [29]but do keep your money and phones or ... uh ... other small electronic devices with you. Don't leave them at the tables. And it has come to our attention that there's an error in your printed program: [30]there will be a change - a switch - in times for the last two speakers. Ms. Chen has to leave a little early today.

Program	
Speaker	**Time**
Ms. Taylor	9:00–9:50
Mr. Davis	9:55–10:45
BREAK	10:45–11:00
Mr. Kim	11:00–11:50
Ms. Chen	11:55–12:45

프로그램	
발표자	**시간**
Ms. Taylor	9:00–9:50
Mr. Davis	9:55–10:45
휴식	10:45–11:00
Mr. Kim	11:00–11:50
Ms. Chen	11:55–12:45

---

28. Where most likely is the speaker?

(A) At an award banquet
(B) At a musical performance
(C) At a retirement party
(D) At a training workshop

해석 화자는 어디에 있겠는가?
(A) 시상식 연회
(B) 음악 공연
(C) 은퇴 파티
(D) 교육 워크숍

29. What are listeners asked to do?

(A) Remain seated during the break
(B) Carry their valuables with them
(C) Return all borrowed equipment
(D) Share handouts with others

어휘 carry 휴대하다, 가지고 다니다 valuables 귀중품
equipment 장비 handout 유인물

해석 청자들은 무엇을 하도록 요구받는가?
(A) 휴식 시간에 계속 앉아 있다
(B) 귀중품을 지니고 다닌다
(C) 빌린 장비는 모두 반납한다
(D) 유인물을 다른 사람들과 함께 본다

30. Look at the graphic. Who will be the final speaker?

(A) Ms. Taylor
(B) Mr. Davis
(C) Mr. Kim
(D) Ms. Chen

해석 그래픽을 보라. 마지막 발표자는 누가 될 것인가?
(A) Ms. Taylor
(B) Mr. Davis
(C) Mr. Kim
(D) Ms. Chen

해설 28번 같은 담화의 장소를 묻는 질문은 거의 항상 첫 한두 문장에 정답이 드러난다. 첫 문장에서 this workshop이라는 키워드만 들리면 바로 정답을 알 수 있다. 29번 문제의 정답은 담화 중간에 방에서 나갈 때 노트북은 놔두고 가도 되지만 돈이나 전화기, 전자 기기 등은 반드시 지니고 있으라고 말하는 부분에서 알 수 있다(but do keep your money and phones or ... uh ... other small electronic devices with you). 그래픽을 보면 마지막 두 명의 발표자인 Mr. Kim과 Ms. Chen에게 배정된 시간이 서로 바뀐다는 말이 나온다(there will be a change – a switch – in times for the last two speakers). 그러므로 30번 문제에서 묻는 마지막 발표자는 Mr. Kim이 된다.

PART 1 Exercise

1 (C)   **2** (C)

1. ⬚W ⬚Am

(A) A glass pane is being put in the frame.
(B) A house is being put up.
(C) Paint is being applied to a window frame.
(D) A window is being washed.

🔹어휘 glass pane 유리판 put up (건물 등을) 세우다, 짓다 apply (페인트를) 칠하다 (window) frame 창틀 apply (페인트를) 칠하다

🔹해석 (A) 유리판을 창틀에 끼워 넣고 있다.
(B) 집을 짓고 있다.
(C) 창틀에 페인트를 칠하고 있다.
(D) 창문을 닦고 있다.

🔹해설 창틀에 유리판을 끼워 넣거나(is being put) 집을 짓거나(is being put up) 물로 씻는(is being washed) 동작이 아니므로 (A), (B), (D)는 모두 오답이다. 페인트를 칠한다는 뜻으로 동사 apply를 사용한다는 사실을 알고 있어야 한다.

2. ⬚M ⬚Au

(A) He's about to get in a vehicle.
(B) He's walking toward a building entrance.
(C) He has a rolled mat in his bag.
(D) He has parked his car on a curb.

🔹어휘 be about to-V 막 ~하려는 참이다 roll (up) (둥글게) 말다, 감다 on a curb 길가에 curb (인도와 차도 사이의) 연석, 도로 경계석

🔹해석 (A) 막 차에 타려고 한다.
(B) 건물 입구를 향해 걸어가고 있다.
(C) 가방에 둥글게 감은 매트를 가지고 있다.
(D) 길가에 차를 세웠다.

🔹해설 지금 막 차에 타려고 하는 것인지(A), 건물 입구를 향해 걷고 있는 것인지(B), 길가에 차를 세워놨는지는(D) 모두 사진을 통해 판단하기 어려운 내용이다. 둥글게 말려 있는 매트가 가방에 들어 있는 것은 사진에서 확실히 알 수 있다.

PART 2 Exercise

1 (A)   **2** (B)   **3** (C)   **4** (B)   **5** (C)
6 (A)   **7** (B)   **8** (A)   **9** (C)   **10** (C)

1. ⬚W ⬚Am ⬚M ⬚Au

Charlie, are you driving to the client meeting?

(A) Oh, would you like a ride?
(B) It was great meeting you!
(C) It went very well.

🔹어휘 go well 잘 진행되다

🔹해석 Charlie, 고객과 만날 때 차로 갈 건가요?
(A) 아, 태워드릴까요?
(B) 만나서 정말 반가웠어요!
(C) 매우 잘 진행되었습니다.

🔹해설 질문 앞부분 are you driving(차로 갈 건가요?)에 집중하면 자연스러운 대답을 알 수 있다. (B)는 질문에 나왔던 meeting을 반복하면서, (C)는 질문의 the client meeting에서 연상되는 대답으로 오답을 유도하고 있다. 도저히 정답을 알 수 없는 문제를 만났을 때는 (A)처럼 반문하는 대답이 정답일 확률이 매우 높다는 사실을 기억하자.

2. M|Cn W|Am

Does the train leave from Platform twenty-three or Platform twenty-four?

(A) An aisle seat.
(B) Let's check our tickets.
(C) No, it's running behind schedule.

어휘 aisle seat 통로 쪽 좌석 run (버스·기차 등이) 운행하다
behind schedule 일정보다 늦게

해석 기차가 출발하는 게 23번 플랫폼인가요, 24번 플랫폼인가요?
(A) 통로 쪽 좌석이요.
(B) 티켓을 확인해 보죠.
(C) 아니요, 일정보다 늦게 운행하고 있습니다.

해설 Let's check[look]이나 Let me check 같은 말은 모른다는 뜻으로 매우 자주 사용되는 표현이다. 모른다는 대답은 거의 항상 정답이 되므로 표현들을 잘 암기해 두자. (A)는 질문의 train, Platform 같은 단어에서 연상되는 대답으로 오답을 유도하고 있다. (C)는 No로 시작하고 있는데, 선택 의문문은 Yes나 No가 들리면 오답이다.

---

3. W|Br M|Au

I think we should let Jay give the presentation.

(A) Conference room A.
(B) Everyone was given a present.
(C) But Mariko knows the material better.

어휘 conference room 회의실 material 자료

해석 제 생각에는 Jay에게 프레젠테이션을 시키는 게 좋겠어요.
(A) A 회의실이요.
(B) 모든 사람이 선물을 받았습니다.
(C) 하지만 Mariko가 자료에 대해 더 잘아요.

해설 (A)는 질문의 give the presentation에서 연상되는 대답으로, (B)는 질문의 presentation과 발음이 비슷한 present를 들려주면서 오답을 유도하고 있다. 일반 의문문이나 평서문은 Yes, and[but]이나 (No), but으로 대답하면 모두 정답이다.

---

4. M|Cn W|Br

I'm interested in learning more about your upcoming tours.

(A) Last October with two colleagues.
(B) Sure, here are a few brochures.
(C) Seven round-trip tickets.

어휘 upcoming 다가오는, 곧 있을 brochure 안내책자
round-trip 왕복(여행)의

해석 곧 있을 당신들의 투어에 대해 더 알아보고 싶습니다.
(A) 작년 10월에 동료 두 명과 함께요.
(B) 네, 여기 안내책자가 몇 권 있습니다.
(C) 왕복 티켓 7장이요.

해설 곧 있을 투어(your upcoming tours)에 대해 문의하고 있으므로 (A)에서 작년 10월(Last October)이라는 말이 들리는 순간 오답인 것을 알 수 있다. (C)는 질문의 tours에서 연상되는 대답으로 오답을 유도하고 있다. (B)가 자연스러운 대답인데, 도저히 정답을 모르겠다면, Sure는 Part 2에서 매우 자주 정답으로 사용되는 마법의 키워드라는 사실을 기억해서 정답 확률을 높이도록 하자.

---

5. M|Au W|Br

Laura tested the program, didn't she?

(A) My new computer.
(B) Right after the test.
(C) I'll ask her.

해석 Laura가 프로그램을 테스트했죠?
(A) 저의 새 컴퓨터요.
(B) 테스트 직후에요.
(C) 물어볼게요.

해설 (A)는 질문의 tested the program에서 연상되는 대답으로, (B)는 질문에 나왔던 test를 반복시키면서 오답을 유도하고 있다. "몰라."라는 대답은 거의 항상 정답이며, '(I'll) ask + 사람' 같은 대답은 매우 자주 시험에 등장하고 있다. (C)는 읽는 연습도 해두자. 영국 발음이기 때문에 ask는 '아스크'라고 읽어야 하며, her에서는 r 발음이 탈락된다. 연음되는 부분을 익혀 두자. "아일라 스커."라고 읽어야 한다.

---

6. W|Am M|Cn

When does the warranty of your television expire?

(A) I lost all that paperwork when I moved.
(B) The recently added show.
(C) I met with her on Friday.

어휘 warranty 품질 보증(서) expire 만료되다, 만기가 되다
paperwork 서류

해석 당신 텔레비전의 품질 보증은 언제 만료되나요?
(A) 이사하면서 그 서류를 모두 잃어버렸어요.
(B) 최근에 추가된 프로그램이요.
(C) 금요일에 그녀와 만났습니다.

---

7. W|Br W|Am

What are the best seafood restaurants in this area?

(A) We close in an hour.
(B) I'm not the best person to ask.
(C) An outdoor patio is available.

어휘 patio 테라스

해석 이 지역에서 가장 좋은 해산물 식당은 어디인가요?
(A) 저희는 한 시간 후에 문 닫습니다.
(B) 저는 물어보기에 적당한 사람이 아닌 것 같은데요.
(C) 야외 테라스를 이용할 수 있습니다.

해설 동사 ask가 들어가는 문장은 대부분 "몰라." 유형의 대답이라는 사실을 기억하면 문장을 완벽하게 알아듣지 못해도 정답을 알아낼 수 있다. (A)와 (C)는 모두 질문의 restaurants에서 연상되는 대답으로 오답을 유도하고 있다. 연상되는 표현은 오답 장치라는 사실을 절대 잊지 말자.

---

8. M|Cn W|Am

Don't we need to set another place at the table?

(A) Ms. Dunn won't be coming.
(B) I've already placed an order for one.
(C) Yes, it's a lovely restaurant.

어휘 set a place 자리를 마련하다 place an order for ~을 주문하다

해석 테이블에 자리를 하나 더 마련해야 하지 않나요?
(A) Ms. Dunn이 안 올 거예요.
(B) 제가 이미 하나 주문했습니다.
(C) 네, 정말 훌륭한 식당이에요.

해설 won't는 수험생들이 잘 못 알아듣는 단어 중 하나이므로 발음을 잘 익혀두자. t 발음이 탈락되면서 "미즈 던 워운비 커밍."이라고 읽어야 한다. Ms. Dunn이 오지 않을 것이라는 말이 자리를 하나 더 마련할 필요는 없다는 뜻이므로 자연스러운 대답이다. (B)는 질문에 나왔던 place를 반복시키면서, (C)는 질문에서 연상되는 대답으로 오답을 유도하고 있다. 오답을 잘 골라낼수록 고수가 된다!

---

9. M|Au M|Cn

I can't reach that box on the top shelf.

(A) I think it's in the mailroom.
(B) Yes, I have some extra space.
(C) There may be a ladder in the closet.

어휘 reach (~에 손이) 닿다 mailroom 우편실 closet 벽장

해석 맨 위 선반에 있는 저 상자에 손이 닿지 않네요.
(A) 우편실에 있을 것 같은데요.
(B) 네, 저에게 남는 공간이 조금 있어요.
(C) 벽장 안에 사다리가 있을 거예요.

해설 질문 앞부분 I can't reach(손이 닿지 않네요.)에만 집중하고 있으면 자연스러운 대답을 알아낼 수 있다.

---

10. M|Au W|Am

Are you going to rent that apartment you looked around last night?

(A) I've purchased the part online.
(B) No, this is my first time.
(C) Well, it is quite expensive.

어휘 rent 빌리다 look around 둘러보다 purchase 구입하다 part 부품

해석 어제 저녁에 둘러본 저 아파트를 빌릴 건가요?
(A) 부품을 온라인으로 구입했어요.
(B) 아니요, 이번이 처음입니다.
(C) 어, 거기는 상당히 비싸잖아요.

해설 (A)는 질문의 that apartment와 발음이 비슷한 the part를 들려주면서, (B)는 질문의 that에서 연상되는 단어 this와 last에서 연상되는 단어 first를 통해 오답을 유도하고 있다. 질문 앞부분 Are you going to rent(빌릴 건가요?)만 알아들으면 자연스러운 대답이 (C)라는 것을 파악할 수 있다. 알아듣기에 약간 까다로운 질문이므로 읽는 연습을 해두자. rent that apartment you looked around 부분을 연음시키면서 읽어야 한다. "아 유 고잉 투 렌더러팔먼튜룩터라운 라스 나잇?" 도저히 정답을 알 수 없을 때는 Well로 시작하는 대답이 정답일 확률이 높다는 사실을 기억하자.

1-3번 문제는 다음 대화에 관한 것입니다.

여: 안녕하세요, 저는 Edner 극장 연출가 Martha Benjamin입니다. 당신의 오디션이 정말 마음에 들어서 다가오는 우리 연극 '사자 이야기'에 역할을 제안하고 싶어요. 연습은 다음 주 화요일에 시작합니다.

남: 너무 잘 됐습니다. 그런데 연습이 그렇게 일찍 시작되는 줄은 몰랐네요. 제가 이미 다른 연극 작품에 출연하고 있어서요, 다음 주말까지는 시간을 못 냅니다.

여: 어, 처음 며칠 동안은 당신 없이도 그럭저럭 할 수 있어요. 하지만 의상 디자이너에게 주기 위해서 당신의 치수가 필요해요. 그게 보통 연습 첫 날에 있어요.

남: 그건 전혀 문제가 안 되죠. 제가 그날 일찍 들러서 그때 의상 디자이너와 만나면 돼요.

어휘 upcoming 다가오는, 곧 있을 rehearsal 리허설, 예행연습 theater 연극 production 창작품 available 시간이 있는 manage 어떻게든 해내다 measurement 치수 so (that) + S + can[may/will] + V ~하기 위해서 costume (연극, 영화 등의) 의상 drop by (~에) 들르다

1. 남자는 누구이겠는가?
 (A) 배우
 (B) 무대 디자이너
 (C) 연출가
 (D) 재단사

2. 남자는 어떤 문제를 언급하는가?
 (A) 어떤 문서를 찾는 데 어려움이 있다.
 (B) 겹치는 업무가 있다.
 (C) 어떤 홍보 자료가 아직 준비되지 않았다.
 (D) 오디션 일정이 다시 잡혔다.

어휘 conflict (시간, 계획이) 겹치다 obligation 의무, 책무 promotional material 홍보 자료

3. 남자는 다음 주 화요일에 무엇을 하겠다고 제안하는가?
 (A) 초청 강사를 소개한다
 (B) 대본을 입수한다
 (C) 사진을 찍는다
 (D) 디자이너와 만난다

1 (A) **2** (C) **3** (D) **4** (A) **5** (B) **6** (D)

Questions 1 through 3 refer to the following conversation.

M | Au Oh, hi, Paula. [1]I didn't expect to see you at the front desk this late. Don't you usually work at the hotel in the morning?

W | Am Actually, I'll be working the evening shift for a while. I'm covering for a front desk supervisor who recently got promoted, but only until the hotel finds a permanent replacement.

M | Au [2]Oh, so there's an opening for a front desk supervisor position? I've been looking for a chance to take on a managerial role. [2]Are applications still being accepted?

W | Am [3]Yes, and if you don't mind working evening hours, I think you have a good chance at the job. I'd contact the human resources director right now, though - she's starting interviews this week.

1-3번 문제는 다음 대화에 관한 것입니다.

남: 어, 안녕, Paula. 이렇게 늦은 시간에 프런트에서 당신을 볼게 될 거라고는 생각하지 못했어요. 보통 오전에 호텔에서 근무하는 거 아닌가요?

여: 실은 제가 당분간 저녁 근무를 맡게 됐거든요. 최근에 승진한 프런트 관리자 대신 근무하는 건데, 호텔 측에서 상임 후임자를 찾을 때까지만이에요.

남: 아, 그러니까 프런트 관리자 자리가 공석이라는 거죠? 제가 관리직을 맡을 기회를 찾고 있었거든요. 아직도 지원을 받고 있나요?

여: 네, 그리고 저녁 시간을 담당하는 것이 괜찮다면, 제 생각에는 그 자리에는 당신이 가능성이 높아요. 하지만 저라면 지금 당장 인사 담당자에게 연락하겠어요. 이번 주에 면접을 시작하거든요.

어휘 work 근무하다; 담당하다 shift 교대 근무; 교대조 for a while 당분간, 한동안 cover for ~ 대신 일하다 supervisor 관리자 permanent 영구적인, 상임의 replacement 후임자 opening 공석, 결원 take on (일 등을) 맡다 managerial 관리의, 운영의 don't mind ~하든지 상관없다, 괜찮다 chance 가능성 though (문장 끝에서) 그렇지만, 하지만

1. Where do the speakers work?

(A) At a hotel
(B) At a shopping center
(C) At a restaurant
(D) At a call center

해석 화자들은 어디에서 일하는가?
(A) 호텔에서
(B) 쇼핑센터에서
(C) 식당에서
(D) 콜센터에서

2. What does the man ask about?

(A) How many people have requested a promotion
(B) If a director is in the lobby
(C) Whether a position is available
(D) When new shifts will be assigned

어휘 promotion 승진 assign 배정하다, 맡기다, 할당하다

해석 남자는 무엇에 관하여 묻는가?
(A) 몇 명이 승진을 신청했는지
(B) 담당자가 로비에 있는지
(C) 자리가 비어 있는지
(D) 새 교대조가 언제 배정될 것인지

3. What does the woman say the man should be prepared to do?

(A) Address customer complaints
(B) Work within a tight budget
(C) Build relationships with local clients
(D) Work evening hours

어휘 address 다루다, 해결하려 하다 complaint 불평, 불만 사항 tight 빠듯한, 빡빡한 budget 예산 relationship 관계

해석 여자는 남자가 무엇을 할 준비를 해야 한다고 말하는가?
(A) 고객의 불만 사항을 다룰 준비
(B) 빠듯한 예산으로 일할 준비
(C) 지역 고객들과 관계를 구축할 준비
(D) 저녁 시간을 담당할 준비

해설 1번 문제처럼 장소를 묻는 문제는 대부분 첫 한두 문장에서 정답을 알 수 있다. 대화가 시작되자마자 남자의 대사 I didn't expect to see you at the front desk this late.에서 프런트를 통해 장소가 어디인지 짐작할 수 있는데, 이어지는 문장 Don't you usually work at the hotel in the morning?을 들으면 두 사람의 근무 장소가 호텔임을 확신할 수 있다. 2번 문제의 정답은 남자의 대사가 패러프 레이즈 되어 있는 문장이다. so there's an opening

for a front desk supervisor position?과 Are applications still being accepted?를 통해 관리자 자리가 비어 있는지 묻고 있다. 3번 문제는 여자의 대사가 패러프레이즈 된 문장이 정답이다. 저녁에 근무하는 게 싫지 않다면 회사 측에서 당신을 뽑을 가능성이 높다는 것은(if you don't mind working evening hours, I think you have a good chance at the job.) 저녁 근무를 할 수 있도록 준비해 보라는 제안이다.

Questions 4 through 6 refer to the following telephone message.

[W | Am] Yolanda! ⁴I appreciate your help in setting up for the party after last night's theater performance. ⁴I couldn't have done it without you, ⁵and the spicy dish you brought was incredibly delicious! [You have got to tell me where you found the recipe!] Everyone really liked it, ⁵and it didn't seem too complicated. ⁶Anyway, I guess I'll see you Wednesday. I think we have rehearsal together for James Roland's new play. I'm really excited to get started.

4-6번 문제는 다음 전화 메시지에 관한 것입니다.

여: Yolanda! 어제 저녁 연극 공연 후에 파티 준비할 때 도와줘서 정말 고마워요. 당신이 없었다면 할 수 없었을 거예요. 그리고 가져온 그 매운 요리가 엄청나게 맛있었어요! 조리법을 어디서 찾았는지 꼭 말해 주셔야 해요! 모든 사람이 좋아하던데, 그리 복잡해 보이지도 않더라고요. 그나저나, 제 생각에는 우리가 수요일에 만날 것 같네요. James Roland의 새 연극 연습을 함께 할 것 같아요. 시작하게 되어 정말 기대가 커요.

어휘 set up (for) ~을 준비하다 theater 연극 spicy 매운 incredibly 엄청나게, 정말 have got to-V ~해야 한다 complicated 복잡한 rehearsal 예행연습 get started 시작하다

4. Why is the woman calling?

(A) To express her gratitude
(B) To solicit a favor
(C) To converse about an assignment
(D) To share some good news

어휘 gratitude 고마움, 감사 solicit 간청하다, 요청하다 favor 청, 부탁 converse 대화를 나누다 assignment 과제, 임무

해석 여자는 왜 전화하고 있는가?
(A) 감사를 표하기 위해
(B) 부탁을 하기 위해
(C) 업무에 대해 대화하기 위해
(D) 좋은 소식을 공유하기 위해

5. What does the woman imply when she says, "You have got to tell me where you found the recipe"?

(A) She wonders if some ingredients are sourced locally.
(B) She would like to make the dish herself.
(C) She needs a recommendation for a restaurant.
(D) She cannot find a recipe in a cookbook.

어휘 imply 암시하다 source 공급하다 locally 현지에서

해석 여자는 "조리법을 어디서 찾았는지 꼭 말해주셔야 해요!"라고 말할 때 무엇을 암시하는가?
(A) 어떤 재료가 현지에서 공급된 것인지 궁금하다.
(B) 요리를 직접 만들어보고 싶다.
(C) 식당 추천이 필요하다.
(D) 요리책에서 조리법을 찾을 수 없다.

6. Why is the woman looking forward to Wednesday?

(A) She is going to see a performance.
(B) She will be treating a friend to lunch.
(C) Some results will be announced.
(D) A new project will start.

어휘 treat A to B A에게 B를 대접하다

해석 여자는 왜 수요일이 기대되는가?
(A) 공연을 볼 예정이다.
(B) 친구에게 점심을 살 것이다.
(C) 어떤 결과가 발표될 것이다.
(D) 새 프로젝트가 시작될 것이다.

해설 1번 문제와 같이 주제나 목적을 물어보는 문제는 첫 문장에서 정답을 고를 수 있게 준비하고 있자. 도와줘서 고맙다고 직접적으로 말하고 있다(I appreciate your help). 게다가 이어지는 문장 I couldn't have done it without you도 감사를 표하기 위해 하는 말이다. 5번 문제는 주어진 문장 앞뒤의 내용을 살펴보자. "가져온 그 매운 요리가 엄청나게 맛있었어요(the spicy dish you brought was incredibly delicious)!"와 "그리 복잡해 보이

지도 않더라고요(it didn't seem too complicated)."는 청자로부터 조리법을 얻어 음식을 직접 만들어 보고자 하는 의향을 나타낸다. 6번 문제는 키워드 Wednesday 이후에 나오는 마지막 두 문장에서 정답을 알 수 있다. 수요일에 새 연극 연습이 있고(I think we have rehearsal together for James Roland's new play.), 시작하는 게 설렌다고 말하고 있다(I'm really excited to get started). 수요일에 새 프로젝트가 시작되는 게 기대된다는 뜻이다.

Actual Test

1 (B)	**2** (C)	**3** (C)	**4** (A)	**5** (B)
6 (B)	**7** (A)	**8** (C)	**9** (C)	**10** (A)
11 (A)	**12** (C)	**13** (B)	**14** (D)	**15** (A)
16 (A)	**17** (D)	**18** (C)	**19** (A)	**20** (D)
21 (B)	**22** (D)	**23** (C)	**24** (A)	**25** (C)
26 (C)	**27** (A)	**28** (A)	**29** (D)	**30** (B)

* 정답을 맞힌 문제도 해설을 읽어보세요.

Part 1

1. W | Br

(A) A ladder is being carried across a work site.
(B) Construction workers are lifting a wooden plank.
(C) Some men have climbed onto a roof.
(D) Each of the workers is wearing a tool belt.

어휘 work site 작업 현장 plank 널빤지 tool belt 공구 벨트

해석 (A) 작업 현장을 가로질러 사다리를 운반하고 있다.
(B) 공사 인부들이 나무판자를 들어올리고 있다.
(C) 몇몇 남자들이 지붕 위로 올라가 있다.
(D) 인부들이 각자 공구 벨트를 차고 있다.

해설 (A)는 운반하고 있는 물건이 사다리(A ladder)가 아니므로 오답. (C)는 남자들이 서 있는 곳이 지붕 위(onto a roof)가 아니므로 오답. (D)는 공구 벨트를 차고 있는

(wearing a tool belt) 인부는 한 명뿐이므로 오답이다. '들어올리다'라는 뜻으로 lift, raise, elevate를 기억하자.

---

2. W Am

(A) Columns are being erected along the platform.
(B) A train is traveling on the track.
(C) A man has the straps of a bag in his hand.
(D) People are exiting through a door.

어휘 column 기둥 erect 짓다, 세우다 travel 이동하다, 나아가다 strap (가죽, 천으로 된) 끈

해석 (A) 플랫폼을 따라 기둥들이 세워지고 있는 중이다.
(B) 기차가 선로를 따라 이동하고 있다.
(C) 남자가 손에 가방끈을 잡고 있다.
(D) 사람들이 문을 통해 나오고 있다.

해설 진행 시제 수동태는 동작을 나타내므로 (A)가 정답이 되려면 기둥을 세우는(erect) 공사를 하는 중이어야 한다. 기차가 서 있으므로 이동한다고 말하는(traveling) (B)는 오답이며, 내리는(exiting) 사람도 보이지 않으므로 (D)도 오답이다. 가방끈(the straps of a bag)을 손에 들고 있는 남자를 보면서 정답을 선택하자.

---

3. M Cn

(A) Some workers are painting the frame

of a window.
(B) One man is resting on a veranda.
(C) One man is securing the base of a ladder.
(D) People are standing in line outside the shop.

어휘 rest 쉬다, 휴식을 취하다 veranda 베란다 secure (단단히) 고정하다

해석 (A) 인부들이 창틀에 페인트를 칠하고 있다.
(B) 한 남자가 베란다에서 쉬고 있다.
(C) 한 남자가 사다리 아래 부분을 잡고 있다.
(D) 사람들이 상점 바깥에 줄 서 있다.

해설 페인트를 칠하거나(painting) 휴식을 취하거나(resting) 줄 서 있는(standing in line) 장면이 아니다. 동사 secure의 의미만 알고 있으면 정답을 선택할 수 있다.

Part 2

4. W Br M Cn

What security software would you recommend?

(A) I forgot what it's called.
(B) Somewhere with a fine view of woods.
(C) The front entrance is locked.

어휘 somewhere 어딘가, 어떤 곳 view 경관, 경치

해석 어느 보안 소프트웨어를 추천하시겠어요?
(A) 그게 이름이 뭐였는지 잊어버렸네요.
(B) 숲 경치가 좋은 어딘가요.
(C) 정문이 잠겨 있습니다.

해설 "모른다"는 대답은 거의 모든 질문에서 정답이 된다. I don't remember. / I can't recall. / I forgot ~. / It's on the tip of my tongue. / It slipped my mind. 같은 표현들을 기억해 두자. (B)는 질문의 software와 발음이 비슷한 Somewhere로, (C)는 질문의 security에서 연상되는 대답으로 오답을 유도하고 있다.

---

5. W Am M Au

There are no more trains to Watertown today, are there?

(A) Watertown is ten miles away.
(B) No, but you can take a bus instead.
(C) Three more stops before the city.

어휘 away 떨어져 있는

해석 오늘은 Watertown으로 가는 열차가 더 이상 없죠?
(A) Watertown은 10마일 떨어져 있습니다.
(B) 네, 하지만 대신 버스를 타셔도 돼요.
(C) 그 도시까지는 세 정거장 더요.

해설 (A)는 질문의 Watertown을 반복하면서, (C)는 more를 반복하면서 오답을 유도하고 있다. 일반 의문문이나 평서문에서 Yes, and[but]이나 (No), but으로 시작하는 대답은 모두 정답이다.

---

6. M | Cn W | Br

We can come and do the repair on Wednesday.

(A) We bought the tools at a discount.
(B) What other days do you have open?
(C) Your crew did a great job.

어휘 open (시간이) 비어 있는 crew 팀, 조, 반

해석 저희가 수요일에 가서 수리해 드릴 수 있어요.
(A) 우리는 도구들을 할인가로 샀습니다.
(B) 다른 요일에는 언제 시간이 비나요?
(C) 당신의 팀이 일을 참 잘 했습니다.

해설 문장을 알아듣기 어려울 때는 반문하는 대답이 정답일 확률이 높다는 사실을 기억하자.

---

7. M | Cn W | Am

Is the Internet working properly in your office?

(A) We just called maintenance.
(B) I think I'll walk there.
(C) She works down the hall.

어휘 properly 제대로, 적절히 maintenance (department) 시설관리부 down the hall 복도 끝에서

해석 당신 사무실에서 인터넷 제대로 되나요?
(A) 지금 막 시설관리부에 전화했어요.
(B) 거기에 걸어서 갈 것 같아요.
(C) 그녀는 복도 끝 쪽에서 일합니다.

해설 질문 앞부분 Is the Internet working properly(인터넷이 제대로 되나요?)에 집중하면 자연스러운 대답을 알아낼 수 있다. (B)와 (C)는 모두 질문에 들어 있는 working과 발음이 비슷한 단어를 사용하거나 반복시키면서 오답을 유도하고 있다. 오답을 잘 골라낼수록 고수가 된다는 사실을 잊지 말자.

---

8. W | Am M | Au

I must've left my umbrella in the hotel room.

(A) You should make a right turn actually.
(B) I prefer to stay at the Wakeson Hotel.
(C) It's expected to be sunny today anyway.

어휘 make a right turn 우회전하다

해석 호텔 방에 우산을 놓고 온 게 틀림없어요.
(A) 실은 우회전 하셔야 해요.
(B) 저는 Wakeson 호텔에 묵는 걸 선호해요.
(C) 어차피 오늘은 화창할 것으로 예상되어요.

해설 (A)는 질문의 left에서 연상되는 단어 right를 들려주면서 오답을 유도하고 있다. left – right 오답 장치는 토익 시험에 매우 자주 사용되는 함정이다. (B)는 질문에 나왔던 hotel을 반복시키면서 오답을 유도하고 있다. 오답을 잘 골라내면 (C)를 들을 필요가 없다. 또한 질문 앞부분 I must've left my umbrella(우산을 놓고 온 게 틀림없어요)에 집중하면 자연스러운 대답을 파악할 수 있기도 하다.

---

9. M | Cn W | Br

Are there any other candidates scheduled for interviews today?

(A) I agree - it's a breathtaking view.
(B) There is a very interesting article about it.
(C) Yes, there are two more to meet this afternoon.

어휘 breathtaking 숨이 멎을 듯한[정도로 아름다운]

해석 오늘 면접 일정이 잡혀 있는 다른 지원자가 있나요?
(A) 동의해요. 숨이 멎을 것 같이 아름다운 경치예요.
(B) 그것에 대해 매우 흥미로운 기사가 있습니다.
(C) 네, 오늘 오후에 만날 사람이 두 명 더 있어요.

해설 (A)는 질문의 interviews에 포함된 view를 반복시키면서, (B)는 질문의 interviews에서 연상되는 단어 article을 들려주면서 오답을 유도하고 있다. 질문 앞부분 Are there any other candidates(다른 지원자가 있나요?)에 집중하면 자연스러운 대답을 알아낼 수 있다.

---

10. M | Cn W | Br

Who's planning the client dinner?

(A) It's been canceled.
(B) At an Italian restaurant.
(C) A selection of entrées.

어휘 a selection of 엄선된, 다양한 entrée 앙트레(식당이나 만찬의 주요리)

해설 고객과의 식사는 누가 계획하고 있나요?
(A) 그거 취소됐습니다.
(B) 이탈리아 식당에서요.
(C) 엄선된 주요리들이요.

해설 고객과의 식사가 취소되었기 때문에 누구도 계획을 잡을 필요가 없다고 대답하는 (A)가 정답이다. (B)는 Where 의문문의 대답으로 알맞은 문장이고, (C)는 질문의 dinner에서 연상되는 대답으로 오답을 유도하고 있다. 오답을 잘 골라낼수록 고수가 된다!

---

11. W|Am M|Au

Shall I show you how to make the font size larger?

(A) It is hard to read at this size.
(B) Absolutely, count me in!
(C) Thank you for the letter.

어휘 count *sb* in ~를 포함시키다, 끼워 주다

해석 폰트 크기를 더 크게 하는 방법을 알려드릴까요?
(A) 이 크기로는 정말 읽기 어렵겠네요.
(B) 물론이죠! 저도 끼워 주세요.
(C) 편지 고맙습니다.

해설 질문이 사실은 폰트 크기가 너무 작다는 불만을 말하는 문장이므로, 이 불만을 수긍하는 (A)가 정답이다. 읽는 연습을 해보자. hard to read at this size를 모두 연음시켜서 "잇 이z 하투리댓디사이z."라고 읽어야 한다. (B)는 질문의 font를 fun으로 잘못 알아들었을 때 고를 수 있는 대답이고, (C)는 letter에 '글자, 문자'라는 뜻이 있기 때문에 font에서 연상되는 대답으로 오답을 유도하고 있는 것이다.

---

12. M|Cn W|Br

Will our proposal get to the town council on time?

(A) In the Banbury Square.
(B) A five-percent increase.
(C) It was sent by overnight mail.

어휘 proposal 기획안, 제안서 on time 제시간에 overnight mail 익일 우편

해석 우리 기획안이 시 의회에 제때 도착할까요?
(A) Banbury 광장에서요.
(B) 5퍼센트 인상이요.
(C) 익일 우편으로 보냈어요.

해설 기획안을 익일 우편으로 보냈으므로 제때 도착할 것이니 걱정하지 말라고 대답하는 (C)가 정답이다. 읽는 연습을 해보자. sent에서 t 발음이 탈락한다. "잇 워z 센빠이 오우버나잇 메일."이라고 읽어야 한다.

Part 3

Questions 13 through 15 refer to the following conversation with three speakers.

W|Am Thanks for interviewing on such short notice, Mr. McLane. ¹³I'm Susie Park, Head of Human Resources at Channel 14.

W|Br And I'm Valerie Fairchild. ¹³I produce the nightly newscast.

M|Cn Nice to meet you both.

W|Br After reviewing your résumé, it's clear that you are highly qualified for the camera operator position. ¹⁴But we're curious about your availability, since our film crews frequently go out on assignment with little warning.

M|Cn ¹⁴I understand that I would need to be available on short notice. That's no problem.

W|Am OK, so, why don't we take a look at some of your work? ¹⁵You said you brought some video clips. Can you show us?

M|Cn ¹⁵Sure, the files are right here on my laptop.

13-15번 문제는 다음 3인 대화에 관한 것입니다.

여1: 급하게 면접에 응해 주셔서 고맙습니다. Mr. McLane. 저는 Channel 14의 인사팀장 Susie Park입니다.
여2: 저는 Valerie Fairchild이고요. 심야 뉴스 프로를 제작하고 있습니다.
남: 두 분 모두 만나서 반갑습니다.
여2: 이력서를 검토해 보니 촬영 감독 자리를 위한 자격을 충분히 갖추신 게 분명합니다. 하지만 당신이 시간을 내실 수 있는지의 여부가 궁금합니다. 저희 촬영 팀이 자주 예고 없이 업무를 맡아 나가거든요.
남: 촉박한 통보에도 시간을 낼 수 있어야 한다는 거 알고 있습니다. 문제없어요.
여1: 좋습니다, 그럼 당신의 작업물을 좀 볼까요? 동영상을 가져왔다고 하셨는데요. 보여주시겠어요?
남: 물론입니다. 파일이 여기 제 노트북에 있습니다.

어휘 on short notice 예고 없이, 급하게 produce (방송 프로를) 제작하다 nightly 밤마다 하는 newscast 뉴스 프로 review 검토하다 be qualified for ~에 자격이 있다 camera operator 촬영 기사, 촬영 감독 availability 시간을 낼 수 있음 film crew 촬영 팀 frequently 자주, 빈번히 on assignment 업무를 맡아 with little warning 예고 없이 available 시간이 있는 video clip 짧은 동영상

13. Where do the interviewers most likely work?

(A) At an employment agency
(B) At a television station
(C) At an electronics store
(D) At a movie theater

> **해석** 면접관들은 어디에서 일하겠는가?
> (A) 직업소개소에서
> (B) 텔레비전 방송국에서
> (C) 전자 제품 매장에서
> (D) 영화관에서

14. What job requirement do the speakers discuss?

(A) Having a professional certificate
(B) Owning the necessary equipment
(C) Possessing managerial experience
(D) Having a flexible schedule

> **어휘** job requirement 직무 요건 certificate 자격증 managerial 관리의, 경영의 flexible 마음대로 바꿀 수 있는
> **해석** 화자들은 어떤 직무 자격 요건을 논하는가?
> (A) 전문 자격증을 소지할 것
> (B) 필요한 장비를 소유할 것
> (C) 관리직 경력을 보유할 것
> (D) 스케줄을 바꾸기 쉬울 것

15. What does the man agree to do next?

(A) Show a video
(B) Submit references
(C) Take a tour of a facility
(D) Meet with a manager

> **어휘** reference 추천서 facility 시설
> **해석** 남자는 이후에 무엇을 하는 데 동의하는가?
> (A) 동영상을 보여준다
> (B) 추천서를 제출한다
> (C) 시설을 둘러본다
> (D) 매니저와 만난다

> **해설** 13번은 장소를 묻고 있으므로 첫 한두 문장에서 정답을 알아내겠다는 생각으로 집중해야 한다. 'Channel 14의 인사팀장(Head of Human Resources at Channel 14)'과 '심야 뉴스 방송 제작(I produce the nightly newscast.)' 등의 자기소개를 들으면 이곳이 텔레비전 방송국임을 알 수 있다. 14번은 영국 여자와 남자의 대사를 모두 알아들어야 한다. 남자가 시간을 낼 수 있는지

궁금하다고 말하면서(But we're curious about your availability) 그 이유로 촬영 업무가 예고 없이 이루어지는 경우가 많다는 점을 들고 있다(since our film crews frequently go out on assignment with little warning). 이에 대해 남자는 자신도 촉박하게 시간을 내서 일할 수 있어야 한다는 사실을 알고 있다고 대답하고 있다(I understand that I would need to be available on short notice). 대화를 종합하면 이 일자리의 요건은 일정을 바꾸기 쉬워야 한다는 점을 추론할 수 있다. 15번은 남자가 무엇에 동의하는지(the man agree to do) 묻고 있으므로 우선 여자의 제안이 무엇인지 잘 들은 후에 남자의 동의하는 대답을 듣고 정답을 선택해야 한다. 미국 여자가 You said you brought some video clips. Can you show us?라고 묻자 Sure라고 대답하고 있으므로 남자는 동영상을 보여주는 데 동의하고 있다.

Questions 16 through 18 refer to the following conversation with three speakers.

> [M Au] **16**Have you two taken a look at the progress they've made upstairs on the office expansion? **17**It looks wonderful!
>
> [W Am] **17**I know! [I can't believe it!] And the views of the city from the offices up there are quite spectacular.
>
> [M Cn] I'm curious to see which division will go up there once it's done.
>
> [W Am] I heard it's the accounting department.
>
> [M Au] Ah, because they have the most people.
>
> [W Am] Probably. I'd be so happy to work in an office on that floor, though.
>
> [M Cn] Yeah. **18**Well, the company must be making good money if they're adding more space!
>
> [M Au] **18**I guess you're right, there!

16-18번 문제는 다음 3인 대화에 관한 것입니다.

> **남1:** 두 사람 위층에서 사무실 확장 공사 진행된 상황 봤어요? 아주 근사해 보여요!
> **여:** 맞아요! 믿을 수 없을 정도예요! 그 사무실들에서 보이는 도시 전망도 꽤 볼 만해요.
> **남2:** 다 되고 나면 어느 부서가 거기로 올라가는 건지 궁금하네요.
> **여:** 회계부서라고 들었어요.
> **남1:** 아, 거기가 사람이 제일 많으니까 그렇겠죠.

여: 아마도요. 하지만 저도 그 층 사무실에서 일하게 된다면 참 좋겠어요.

남2: 그렇죠. 그나저나, 증축하는 걸 보니 회사가 틀림없이 돈을 잘 벌고 있는 것 같아요.

남1: 당신 말이 맞는 것 같아요!

어휘 make progress 진전을 보이다[이루다] expansion 확장 I know 맞아, 그래 view 경치, 전망 spectacular 장관인, 볼 만한 division 부서 accounting 회계 (업무) though 하지만 make good money 많은 돈을 벌다

---

16. What is the conversation mainly about?

(A) An enlargement of office space
(B) A move into a new market
(C) A growth in the number of employees
(D) A transition in company leadership

어휘 enlargement 확대, 확장 transition 변화

해석 대화는 주로 무엇에 관한 것인가?
(A) 사무실 공간의 확대
(B) 새로운 시장 진출
(C) 직원 수의 증가
(D) 회사 지도부의 변화

---

17. Why does the woman say, "I can't believe it"?

(A) She is in strong opposition.
(B) She is seeking an explanation.
(C) She is experiencing disappointment.
(D) She is pleasantly surprised.

어휘 in opposition 반대하는 seek 청하다, 구하다 experience 겪다, 느끼다

해석 여자는 왜 "믿을 수 없을 정도예요!"라고 말하는가?
(A) 강력히 반대한다
(B) 설명을 청하고 있다
(C) 실망감을 느끼고 있다
(D) 기분 좋게 놀랐다

---

18. What do the men imply about the company?

(A) It was founded not long ago.
(B) It is considering adjusting salaries.
(C) It is in good financial condition.
(D) It has offices in multiple countries.

어휘 found 설립하다 adjust 조정하다, 조절하다 multiple 다수의

해석 남자들은 회사에 관해 무엇을 암시하는가?
(A) 설립된 지 오래 되지 않았다.
(B) 급여 조정을 고려하고 있다.
(C) 재무 상태가 좋다.
(D) 여러 나라에 지점이 있다.

해석 16번 문제와 같이 주제를 묻는 질문은 대부분 첫 한두 문장에서 정답을 알 수 있다. Have you two taken a look at the progress they've made upstairs on the office expansion?을 듣고 the office expansion이 패러프레이즈 되어 있는 선택지를 정답으로 선택하자. 17번은 주어진 문장의 앞뒤 내용을 통해 여자의 의도를 유추해야 한다. 앞에서는 It looks wonderful!이라는 남자의 감탄에 대해 I know!라고 동감을 표하고 있으며, 뒤에서는 확장되고 있는 사무실이 전망까지 좋다며 부연 설명까지 하고 있다(And the views of the city from the offices up there are quite spectacular). 앞뒤의 내용을 종합해 볼 때 여자의 대사 I can't believe it!은 기분 좋게 놀랐음을 나타내는 말이다. 18번은 남자들의 마지막 대사에 집중해서 정답을 추론해 보자. 캐나다 남자가 회사가 많은 돈을 벌고 있는 것 같다고 추측하자(the company must be making good money) 호주 남자가 I guess you're right, there!라는 말로 동의를 나타내고 있다. 남자들은 지금 회사가 탄탄한 재무 상태에 있다고 생각한다.

Questions 19 through 21 refer to the following conversation and schedule.

M | Au Hi, Rebecca. **19**I haven't had the chance to see you since we moved the music school into this building last month. How's it going?

W | Am I've been busy hiring more music teachers now that we have the larger space to offer additional classes. **20**By the way, we're interviewing some vocal instructors today. Since you're our most experienced vocal teacher, I'd really like you to be there.

M | Au Well, I scheduled a make-up class for a student who missed her lesson last week, **21**so I'm not available this afternoon. But if you have any morning interviews scheduled, I could definitely be there.

W | Am That's great. Here's a copy of the interview schedule. We'll be meeting in Peterson Hall.

19-21번 문제는 다음 대화와 일정표에 관한 것입니다.

> 남: 안녕, Rebecca. 지난달에 음악 학교를 이 건물로 옮긴 이후로 만날 기회가 없었네요. 어떻게 지내요?
>
> 여: 이제 더 넓어진 공간으로 수업을 추가로 제공할 수 있게 되었기 때문에 음악 선생님들을 더 채용하느라 바빴어요. 그건 그렇고, 오늘 성악 강사들 몇 명을 면접 보려고 하거든요. 당신이 가장 경험이 풍부한 성악 선생님이니까 꼭 좀 와줬으면 좋겠어요.
>
> 남: 어, 지난주 레슨에 못 들어온 학생을 위해 보충 수업을 잡아놔서요, 오늘 오후에는 시간을 낼 수 없어요. 하지만 일정 잡혀 있는 오전 면접이 있다면 그건 꼭 갈게요.
>
> 여: 그거 잘 됐네요. 여기 면접 일정표예요. Peterson 홀에서 모일 거예요.

어휘 vocal 성악의 instructor 강사 experienced 경험이 풍부한 schedule ~의 일정을 잡다 make-up class 보충 수업 available 시간이 있는 definitely 분명히, 틀림없이 copy (문서) 한 부

Applicant	Interview Time	Instrument
Sofia Ochoa	10:00 A.M.	Violin
Soo-Jin Yun	11:00 A.M.	Vocal
James Dixon	1:00 P.M.	Flute
Ted Bailey	2:00 P.M.	Vocal

지원자	면접 시간	악기
Sofia Ochoa	오전 10:00	바이올린
Soo-Jin Yun	오전 11:00	성악
James Dixon	오후 1:00	플루트
Ted Bailey	오후 2:00	성악

19. According to the man, what did the music school do last month?

(A) It moved to a different location.
(B) It held a dedication ceremony.
(C) It appointed a new director.
(D) It sponsored a community program.

어휘 hold 열다, 개최하다 dedication 개소식, 개관식 appoint 임명하다 sponsor 후원하다

해석 남자의 말에 따르면 음악 학교가 지난달에 무엇을 했는가?
(A) 다른 장소로 옮겼다.
(B) 개관식을 치렀다.
(C) 새 원장을 임명했다.
(D) 지역 공동체 프로그램을 후원했다.

20. Why does the woman ask the man to attend some interviews?

(A) Because she needs assistance with taking notes
(B) Because she is unavailable to attend
(C) Because he has endorsed a candidate
(D) Because he is an experienced instructor

어휘 take notes 메모하다, 기록하다 unavailable 시간이 없는 endorse 지지하다

해석 여자는 왜 남자에게 면접에 참석해 달라고 요구하는가?
(A) 기록하는 데 도움이 필요하기 때문에
(B) 자신은 참석할 수 없기 때문에
(C) 그가 어떤 지원자를 지지했기 때문에
(D) 그가 경험이 풍부한 강사이기 때문에

21. Look at the graphic. Who will the man help interview today?

(A) Sofia Ochoa
(B) Soo-Jin Yun
(C) James Dixon
(D) Ted Bailey

해석 그래픽을 보라. 남자는 오늘 누구의 면접을 도울 것인가?
(A) Sofia Ochoa
(B) Soo-Jin Yun
(C) James Dixon
(D) Ted Bailey

해설 19번 문제는 첫 문장에 the music school과 last month라는 키워드가 모두 들어 있기 때문에(I haven't had the chance to see you since we moved the music school into this building last month.) 잘 집중하면 어렵지 않게 정답을 알 수 있다. 20번도 오늘 성악 강사 면접이 있다는 진술(we're interviewing some vocal instructors today)과 남자가 그 자리에 와주기를 바란다는 부탁(I'd really like you to be there.) 사이에 Since you're our most experienced vocal teacher가 있으므로 키워드를 듣고 정답을 알아낼 수 있다. 21번은 남자의 대사 중 so와 but으로 시작하는 문장을 잘 듣고 정답을 추론하자. 오후에는 시간이 없지만 오전 면접이 있다면 거기에는 반드시 참석하겠다고 했다(so I'm not available this afternoon. But if you have any morning interviews scheduled, I could definitely be there). 그리고 20번 문제를 풀면서 남자가 성악 강사라는 사실도 확인했으므로, 남자는 오전 11시에 있는 Soo-Jin Yun의 면접에 참석할 것이다.

Part 4

Questions 22 through 24 refer to the following introduction.

> W | Br Good evening. Thank you for joining us on this special occasion. ²²We are here to recognize and thank Dr. Omar Waheed for his contribution to our university. Dr. Waheed has gained international recognition for his research in developing innovative fuels using substances like hydrogen and vegetable oil. ²³We are fortunate that he has also provided many of our students with the valuable opportunity to work as interns at his research company, OW Global Solutions. ²²As the president of National University of Science and Technology, I would like to thank you, Dr. Waheed, for all you have done for our students. ²⁴We would now like to present you with this small token of our gratitude.

22-24번 문제는 다음 소개에 관한 것입니다.

> **여:** 안녕하세요. 이 특별한 행사에 저희와 함께해 주셔서 고맙습니다. 우리는 Omar Waheed 박사께서 우리 대학교에 하신 공헌에 대해 그에게 표창과 감사를 드리려고 이 자리에 모였습니다. Waheed 박사는 수소와 식물성 기름과 같은 물질을 사용하여 혁신적인 연료를 개발하는 연구로 국제적인 인정을 받으셨습니다. 그가 우리 학생들 중 상당수에게 자신의 연구업체 OW Global Solutions에서 인턴으로 일할 소중한 기회를 제공하신 것은 우리에게 행운입니다. 국립과학기술대학교의 총장으로서, Waheed 박사님, 우리 학생들을 위해 해주신 모든 일에 대해 감사드리고 싶습니다. 이제 박사님께 우리의 작은 감사의 표시를 드리고자 합니다.

어휘 occasion 행사 recognize (공로를) 인정하다, 표창하다 contribution 공헌, 기여 recognition (공로에 대한) 인정, 표창 innovative 혁신적인 substance 물질 hydrogen 수소 vegetable oil 식물성 기름 president (대학의) 총장, 학장 present A with B A에게 B를 token 표시, 징표 gratitude 고마움, 감사

22. Who is speaking?

(A) A foreign ambassador
(B) A teaching assistant
(C) A company executive
(D) A university official

어휘 ambassador 대사 official 임원

해석 누가 연설하고 있는가?
(A) 외국 대사
(B) 조교
(C) 회사 중역
(D) 대학교 임원

23. Where does Dr. Waheed work?

(A) At a government institution
(B) At an employment agency
(C) At a research company
(D) At a financial institution

어휘 institution 기관, 단체

해석 Waheed 박사는 어디에서 일하는가?
(A) 정부 기관
(B) 직업소개소
(C) 연구업체
(D) 금융 기관

24. What will probably happen next?

(A) An award will be given.
(B) A meeting will be arranged.
(C) A shipment will be received.
(D) A plan will be devised.

어휘 arrange 준비하다, 마련하다 shipment 배송품 devise 고안하다

해석 이후에 어떤 일이 있겠는가?
(A) 상이 주어진다.
(B) 회의가 준비된다.
(C) 배송품을 받는다.
(D) 계획이 짜여진다.

해설 22번과 같이 화자가 누구인지 묻는 문제는 대부분 첫 한두 문장으로 정답을 알 수 있다. 행사에서 We are here to recognize and thank Dr. Omar Waheed for his contribution to our university.와 같은 말을 할 사람은 대학교 임원밖에 없다. 게다가 연설 뒷부분에 가면 As the president of National University of Science and Technology, I would like to thank you, Dr. Waheed에서 자신이 이 대학교 총장이라고 직접적으로 말하고 있다. 23번은 연설 중간에 나오는 키워드 his research company, OW Global Solutions를 통해 정답을 알 수 있다. Waheed 박사는 연구업체를 운영하고 있다. 24번은 next 문제인데 이 유형은 언제나 마지막 대사로 정답을 알려준다. We would now like to present you with this small token of our gratitude.를 들으면 이제 Waheed 박사가 앞으로 나와 상을 받을 것임을 짐작할 수 있다.

Questions 25 through 27 refer to the following news report.

M | Au This is Adam Brennan from Channel 15 News. I'm standing outside Lifeline Electronics this morning, ²⁵ ²⁶where hundreds of people have spent hours waiting to buy the new Shadowspeak 7C mobile phone - available starting today. Some began waiting in line as early as four A.M. [From the look of it, you'd think they were giving the phones away.] Now, the Shadowspeak 7C is a significant improvement from earlier phone models, ²⁷but what excites consumers the most is its water-protective coating. The new phone's design ensures that it remains fully functional even when in contact with water.

25-27번 문제는 다음 뉴스 보도에 관한 것입니다.

남: Channel 15 뉴스 Adam Brennan입니다. 저는 오늘 아침, Lifeline 전자 밖에 서 있는데요, 여기서는 수백 명의 사람들이 오늘부터 구입할 수 있는 새로 나온 Shadowspeak 7C 휴대폰을 사기 위해 기다리면서 몇 시간을 보내고 있습니다. 어떤 사람들은 새벽 4시부터 줄 서서 기다리기 시작했습니다. 보시면 전화기를 공짜로 나누어 주고 있나 생각하실 겁니다. 자, Shadowspeak 7C는 이전 전화기 모델로부터 크게 개선된 제품인데요, 그중 소비자들을 가장 흥분시키는 것은 방수 코팅입니다. 새 전화기의 디자인은 물과 접촉했을 때에도 완전히 기능을 유지하도록 보장합니다.

어휘 electronics 전자 as early as (벌써) ~부터 give away (사은품으로) 나누어 주다 significant 커다란, 중요한, 의미 있는 functional 가동되는, 기능하는 in contact with ~와 접촉하는

---

25. According to the speaker, what is happening today?

(A) An advertising campaign is being launched.
(B) A new branch is being inaugurated by a company.
(C) A new product is being released in stores.
(D) A clearance sale is being initiated.

어휘 launch 시작하다, 개시하다 branch 지점, 지사 inaugurate ~의 시업식[개관식·발족식·개소식]을 하다 release 발매하다, 공개하다 clearance sale 재고 정리

세일 initiate 시작하다, 개시하다

해석 화자에 따르면 오늘 어떤 일이 있는가?
(A) 광고 캠페인이 시작된다.
(B) 어떤 회사의 새 지점 시업식이 있다.
(C) 매장에서 신제품이 발매된다.
(D) 재고 정리 세일이 시작된다.

---

26. What does the speaker mean when he says, "From the look of it, you'd think they were giving the phones away"?

(A) The store's advertisement is misleading.
(B) Some products are currently unavailable.
(C) There are a lot of customers waiting at the store.
(D) There are many great bargains at the store.

어휘 misleading 오해의 소지가 있는 currently 현재, 지금 bargain 할인 상품

해석 화자는 "보시면 전화기를 공짜로 나누어 주고 있나 생각하실 겁니다."라고 말할 때 무엇을 의미하는가?
(A) 상점 광고에 오해의 소지가 있다.
(B) 현재 어떤 상품을 이용할 수 없다.
(C) 상점에서 기다리는 고객들이 많다.
(D) 상점에 매우 싸게 파는 상품이 많다.

---

27. According to the speaker, what feature of the Shadowspeak 7C is most attractive?

(A) Its water resistance
(B) Its reasonable price
(C) Its colorful accessories
(D) Its sleek design

어휘 feature 특징, 특색 resistance (외부 요인에 대한) 내성 reasonable (가격이) 적정한, 너무 비싸지 않은 sleek (모양이) 매끈한, 날렵한

해석 화자에 따르면 Shadowspeak 7C의 어떤 특징이 가장 매력적인가?
(A) 내수성(耐水性)
(B) 적정한 가격
(C) 다채로운 액세서리
(D) 매끈한 디자인

해설 where hundreds of people have spent hours waiting to buy the new Shadowspeak 7C mobile phone – available starting today.에서 25번과 26번의 정답을 모두 알 수 있다. 우선 available starting today가 25번 문제의 정답을 알려준다. 26번의 정답도 이 문장에서 알 수 있는데, '물건을 공짜로 나누어 주고 있나?'는 보통 많은 사람들이 줄 서 있을 때 할 수 있는 생각이다. 27번 문제의 정답은 but으로 시작하는 문장이 알려주고 있다. but what excites consumers the most is its water-protective coating.에서 키워드가 패러프레이즈 된 선택지를 정답으로 선택하면 된다. 전화기가 물에 닿았을 때 완전히 기능을 한다고 말하는 마지막 문장(The new phone's design ensures that it remains fully functional even when in contact with water.)도 정답을 확인시켜 주고 있다.

Questions 28 through 30 refer to the following telephone message and list.

[W｜Br] Hi, Shawn. ²⁸This is Maria calling from Operations here at the main office. I'm guessing you're on your way to West Elm Furniture. Listen, I have a copy of your "to buy" list of things for our second-floor staff lounge, and there's good news. ²⁹According to the flyer I got this morning, every item on the list is on sale except for that pedestal fan - it's still full price. But we'll pay less for the recliner for sure. When you get back, we'll need to set up the furniture right away ³⁰since the clients are coming on Thursday, and we'll be holding some of the meetings in that room. OK. See you soon then.

28-30번 문제는 다음 전화 메시지와 목록에 관한 것입니다.

여: 안녕하세요, Shawn. 여기 본사 운영 팀의 Maria예요. 당신은 지금 West Elm Furniture로 가는 도중일 것 같군요. 들어보세요. 당신이 작성한 2층 직원 휴게실을 위한 '살 것' 목록 사본을 갖고 있는데요, 좋은 소식이 있어요. 오늘 오전에 받은 전단지에 따르면, 그 스탠드형 선풍기만 제외하고 목록에 있는 모든 물건이 할인 중이에요. 선풍기는 여전히 정상가네요. 하지만 리클라이너는 확실히 돈을 덜 내게 될 거예요. 당신이 돌아오면 가구를 즉시 설치해야 할 거예요. 목요일에 고객들이 올 건데, 회의를 중 일부는 그 방에서 할 것이기 때문이죠. 자, 그럼 곧 만나요.

어휘 operation 운영, 경영 main office 본사, 본점 on one's way to ~로 가는 도중인 staff lounge 직원 휴게실 flyer (광고·안내용) 전단 on sale 할인 중인 pedestal fan 스탠드형 선풍기 recliner (젖혀지는) 안락의자 for sure

확실히, 틀림없이 **set up** ~을 설치하다 **right away** 즉시, 곧바로

To buy:
- Wooden bookcase – $99 ON SALE
- Vinyl chair – $53 ON SALE
- Pedestal fan – $85 full-price
- Recliner – $169 full-price

살 것:
- 목재 책장 – 99달러 할인 중
- 비닐 의자 – 53달러 할인 중
- 스탠드형 선풍기 – 85달러 정상가
- 리클라이너 – 169달러 정상가

어휘 bookcase 책장 vinyl 비닐

28. Where is the woman calling from?
(A) An office building
(B) A furniture shop
(C) An airport
(D) A hotel

해설 여자는 어디에서 전화하고 있는가?
(A) 사무실 건물
(B) 가구 매장
(C) 공항
(D) 호텔

29. Look at the graphic. What price is now incorrect?
(A) $99
(B) $53
(C) $85
(D) $169

해설 그래픽을 보라. 지금은 어느 가격이 맞지 않는가?
(A) 99달러
(B) 53달러
(C) 85달러
(D) 169달러

30. What most likely will happen on Thursday?
(A) Staff training sessions will commence.
(B) Meetings with clients will take place.
(C) A renovation project will conclude.

(D) A job application deadline will pass.

어휘 training session 교육 (과정) **commence** 시작되다
take place (행사, 회의가) 열리다 **conclude** 끝나다

해석 목요일에는 어떤 일이 있겠는가?

(A) 직원 교육이 시작될 것이다.

(B) 고객과의 회의가 있을 것이다.

(C) 개조 프로젝트가 끝날 것이다.

(D) 입사 지원 마감 기한이 지날 것이다.

해설 28번은 장소를 묻는 문제이므로 첫 한두 문장에서 정답이 나올 것이라고 예측할 수 있다. This is Maria calling from Operations here at the main office.를 들으면서 바로 정답을 선택하자. 29번은 여자가 전단지 내용을 설명하는 부분을 잘 들어야 한다. 목록에서 스탠드형 선풍기를 제외한 모든 품목이 할인 중이며(every item on the list is on sale except for that pedestal fan – it's still full price.), 리클라이너는 더 싼 가격에 살 수 있게 되었다고 설명하고 있으므로(But we'll pay less for the recliner for sure.), 이제 목록에서 리클라이너는 full-price가 아니라 ON SALE로 표시되어야 한다. 즉, 리클라이너의 가격 $169는 더 이상 맞지 않는 수치가 된다. 30번은 client와 Thursday, meeting 같은 키워드가 들리는 부분에서 어렵지 않게 정답을 알 수 있다(since the clients are coming on Thursday, and we'll be holding some of the meetings).

Day 03

PART 1 Exercise

1 (D) **2** (B)

1. M | Au

(A) A man is putting up a fence.
(B) A man is entering a building.
(C) A cart is being loaded with bricks.
(D) A wheelbarrow is being pushed at a work site.

어휘 put up 세우다, 짓다 load A with B A에 B를 싣다 brick 벽돌 wheelbarrow 외바퀴 손수레

해석 (A) 펜스를 세우고 있다.
(B) 건물에 들어가고 있다.
(C) 수레에 벽돌을 싣고 있다.
(D) 작업장에서 외바퀴 손수레를 밀고 있다.

해설 펜스를 세우고 있지도, 건물에 들어가고 있지도, 수레에 벽돌을 싣고 있지도 않다. 바퀴 달린 물건을 이동시킬 때 사용하는 동사 pushing, pulling, wheeling, rolling을 기억하고 정답을 선택하자.

2. W | Br

(A) The entrance to a shop has been closed.
(B) Fruit has been sorted into containers.
(C) A storekeeper is bagging some groceries.
(D) A worker is picking fruit at an orchard.

어휘 sort 분류하다 container 그릇, 용기 storekeeper 가게 주인 bag 봉지[가방]에 넣다 pick (과일 등을) 따다 orchard 과수원

해석 (A) 가게 입구가 닫혀 있다.
(B) 과일이 분류되어 용기들에 들어 있다.
(C) 가게 주인이 식료품을 봉투에 넣고 있다.
(D) 과수원에서 과일을 따고 있다.

해설 상점 입구가 닫혀 있지 않으므로 (A)는 오답이다. bagging은 봉투에 넣고 있다는 뜻이고, picking은 과일을 따고 있다는 뜻이므로 (C)와 (D)도 모두 오답이다. 과일을 분류하여 상자들에 넣어 놓았으므로 동사 sort를 사용하는 문장이 정답이다.

PART 2 Exercise

1 (C)	**2** (A)	**3** (B)	**4** (A)	**5** (B)
6 (C)	**7** (A)	**8** (B)	**9** (A)	**10** (B)

1. W | Br   W | Am

Should we go straight to the trade show or stop at the office first?

(A) Left at the second light.
(B) Let me show them to you.
(C) Whatever you prefer.

어휘 trade show 무역 박람회

해석 무역박람회장으로 바로 갈까요, 사무실에 먼저 들를까요?
(A) 두 번째 신호등에서 좌회전이요.
(B) 그것들을 보여드릴게요.
(C) 당신이 좋으실 대로요.

해설 (A)는 질문에 나오는 go straight에서 연상되는 대답으로, (B)는 show를 반복시키면서 오답을 유도하고 있다. 선택 의문문은 '아무거나(either, whichever, whatever, whenever, any ~)'라는 대답이 들리면 항상 정답이다.

2. M|Au W|Br

Did you buy the shirt online or from a shop?

(A) I never buy clothes without trying them on.
(B) Do you have this in a larger size?
(C) Yes, the line isn't very long.

어휘 try on ~을 입어 보다

해석 셔츠를 인터넷으로 사셨나요, 가게에서 사셨나요?
(A) 저는 옷을 입어 보지 않고는 사지 않아요.
(B) 이거 더 큰 사이즈로 있나요?
(C) 네, 줄이 그리 길지 않습니다.

해설 입어 보지 않고는 옷을 사지 않는다는 말은 가게에 가서 샀다는 뜻이므로 질문의 buy the shirt .... from a shop을 패러프레이즈 한 (A)가 정답이다. (C)는 Yes가 들리는 순간 오답임을 알 수 있다.

---

3. W|Am M|Cn

Is it necessary to offer food during the afternoon meeting or can we just serve drinks?

(A) She offered to drive me there.
(B) It'd be nice to buy some snacks.
(C) At two thirty every day.

어휘 offer to-V (기꺼이) ~해 주겠다고 제안하다

해석 오후 회의 때 음식을 제공해야 할까요, 아니면 그냥 음료만 내놓으면 될까요?
(A) 그녀가 저를 그곳에 태워주겠다고 했어요.
(B) 간식을 사오는 게 좋겠어요.
(C) 매일 2시 30분이에요.

해설 (A)는 질문에 나오는 offer를 다시 들려주면서, (C)는 질문의 the afternoon meeting에서 연상되는 대답으로 오답을 유도하고 있다. offer food가 buy some snacks로 패러프레이즈 되어 있음을 간파하고 정답을 선택하자.

---

4. M|Cn M|Au

Should I begin the discussion, or would you like to take the first turn?

(A) I don't have much to say.
(B) Our plans for the upcoming year.
(C) No, it isn't.

어휘 upcoming 다가오는, 곧 있을 take the first turn 처음 순서에 하다

해석 제가 논의를 시작할까요, 당신이 먼저 하시겠어요?

(A) 저는 할 말이 많지 않아요.
(B) 우리의 내년 계획이요.
(C) 아니요, 그렇지 않습니다.

해설 할 말이 별로 없다는 대답이 상대방에게 발언의 우선권을 넘긴다는 뜻이므로 정답이다. (B)는 논의(the discussion)의 주제가 무엇인지 물었을 때 할 만한 대답이고, (C)는 No만 듣고도 오답임을 알 수 있다.

---

5. W|Br W|Am

Are you ready to leave, or are you still packing?

(A) The package arrived yesterday.
(B) Our flight isn't until seven.
(C) Did Francois leave anything for me?

어휘 pack (짐을) 싸다

해석 출발할 준비가 됐나요, 아직도 짐 싸고 있나요?
(A) 소포가 어제 도착했어요.
(B) 비행기는 7시는 되어야 출발하잖아요.
(C) Francois가 저에게 남겨둔 것 있나요?

해설 (A)는 질문의 packing과 발음이 비슷한 package를 들려주면서, (C)는 leave를 반복시키면서 오답을 유도하고 있다. 오답을 잘 골라낼수록 고수가 된다는 사실을 잊지 말자. 비행기 출발 시간이 아직 많이 남아 서두를 필요가 없어서 아직 짐을 싸는 중이라고 대답하는 (B)가 정답이다.

---

6. M|Au W|Br

Should we take a group photo now or in the afternoon?

(A) On the stairs near the entrance would be best.
(B) This picture really turned out well.
(C) Some people have to leave before noon.

어휘 stairs 계단 turn out (일, 상황 등이) ~게 되다

해석 단체 사진을 지금 찍을까요, 오후에 찍을까요?
(A) 출입구 근처 계단이 가장 좋겠어요.
(B) 이 사진 정말 잘 나왔네요.
(C) 어떤 분들은 정오 전에 가셔야 해요.

해설 (A)와 (B)는 모두 질문의 a group photo에서 연상되는 대답으로 오답을 유도하고 있다. 오답을 잘 골라낼수록 고수가 된다. 몇 명은 오전 중에 떠나야 하므로 단체 사진 촬영을 오후가 아닌 지금 하자고 대답하고 있는 (C)가 정답이다.

7. M | Au   M | Cn

Will Ms. Ming pick up her order, or should we deliver it?

(A) She picked it up this morning.
(B) That's all right. I don't need any.
(C) A flower arrangement.

어휘 pick up ~을 찾다. 찾아오다 flower arrangement 꽃꽂이

해석 Ms. Ming이 주문한 물건을 찾아가실 건가요, 아니면 우리가 배달해 드려야 하나요?
(A) 오전에 찾아 가셨어요.
(B) 괜찮습니다. 필요하지 않아요.
(C) 꽃꽂이요.

해설 Ms. Ming이 주문품을 찾아갈 예정인 것도 아니고, 배달해 주어야 하는 것도 아니고, 이미 물건을 찾아갔다고 말하는 (A)가 정답이다. 제3의 선택이 정답이 되는 경우다. 문장 읽는 연습을 해보자. picked it up은 "픽티럽"이라고 읽어야 한다.

8. M | Au   W | Am

Are you using the older version of the software or the one that was just released?

(A) I've decided to use brass hardware in the kitchen.
(B) Were we supposed to update the program?
(C) Yes, she bought a used computer.

어휘 release 발매하다. 출시하다 brass 놋쇠, 황동 hardware 철물 be supposed to-V ~하기로 되어 있다. ~해야 한다 used 중고의

해석 예전 버전의 소프트웨어를 사용하고 계신가요, 아니면 막 출시된 것인가요?
(A) 주방에 황동 철물을 사용하기로 했어요.
(B) 프로그램을 업데이트했어야 하는 건가요?
(C) 네, 그녀는 중고 컴퓨터를 샀어요.

해설 (A)는 질문에 나오는 use를 반복시키고 software와 발음이 비슷한 hardware를 들려주면서 오답을 유도하고 있다. (C)는 Yes를 듣는 순간 오답으로 골라낼 수 있다. 오답을 잘 골라낼수록 고수가 된다. (B)가 자신이 예전 버전의 소프트웨어를 사용하고 있음을 암시하는 대답이므로 정답이다. 도저히 알아들을 수 없을 때는 (B)처럼 반문하는 대답이 정답일 확률이 높다는 사실을 기억하자.

9. M | Au   W | Am

Are you interested in joining a fitness class or just using the pool?

(A) I don't like to swim.
(B) It fits perfectly.
(C) There is a gym down the street.

어휘 fit (모양, 크기가) ~에 맞다 down the street 길 아래로

해석 피트니스 수업을 듣고 싶으신가요, 그냥 수영장만 이용하실 건가요?
(A) 저는 수영을 좋아하지 않아요.
(B) 완벽하게 맞습니다.
(C) 길 아래에 헬스 클럽이 있어요.

해설 수영을 좋아하지 않는다는 대답이 수영장은 이용하지 않고 피트니스 수업에만 참여하겠다는 뜻이므로 정답이다. (B)는 질문의 fitness와 발음이 비슷한 fits를 들려주면서, (C)는 질문에서 연상되는 대답으로 오답을 유도하고 있다.

10. W | Am   M | Au

Would you like to have another beverage, or are you ready to settle the bill?

(A) Her test scores were well above average.
(B) I'll have another cup of coffee.
(C) At the top of the hill by the Wangu Tower.

어휘 settle (주어야 할 돈을) 지불하다, 계산하다

해석 음료를 한 잔 더 드릴까요, 아니면 계산하시겠습니까?
(A) 그녀의 시험 점수는 평균보다 훨씬 높았어요.
(B) 커피 한 잔 더 마실게요.
(C) 언덕 꼭대기 Wangu 타워 옆에요.

해설 have another beverage를 have another cup of coffee로 살짝 바꿔 놓은 (B)가 정답이다. (A)는 질문에 있는 beverage와 발음이 비슷한 average를, (C)는 bill과 발음이 비슷한 hill을 들려주면서 오답을 유도하고 있다. 오답을 잘 골라낼수록 고수가 된다!

PART 4 Sample Questions

1-3번 문제는 다음 연설에 관한 것입니다.

여: 안녕하세요! 오늘 저녁 우리 회사의 성장을 기념하기 위해 여러분이 모두 와 주셔서 정말 기쁩니다. 제가 이 카드 회사를 처음 시작했을 때는 사업이 돌아가게 만드느라 버둥거리는 겨우 다섯 명의 작은 팀이었죠. 현재 우리는 30명의 정규직 직원들을 채용하고 있고, 판매망은 넓어졌으며, 훨씬 더 큰 새 사무실로 이사까지 했습니다. 자, 연회장에서 나가실 때는 선물 가방을 가지고 가시기 바랍니다. 우리 회사의 성공에 이바지한 여러분 모두의 성실과 헌신에 대해 감사드리기 위한 저의 개인적인 감사의 표시입니다.

어휘 make it 참석하다 commemorate 기념하다 greeting card 인사[축하] 카드 struggle 몸부림치다, 허우적[버둥]거리다 work (제대로) 돌아가다 currently 현재 full-time 정규직의 distribution 유통, 판매망 significantly 상당히, 크게 banquet 연회 token 표시, 징표 appreciation 감사 dedication 헌신

---

1. 무엇을 기념하고 있는가?
(A) 몇몇 개조 공사의 마무리
(B) 은퇴하는 동료의 새 출발
(C) 지역 사회 헌신에 대한 표창
(D) 회사의 발전

어휘 celebrate 기념하다, 축하하다 conclusion 마무리 renovation 개조, 보수 departure 출발 recognition 인정, 표창 evolution 발전, 진전

---

2. 화자는 누구이겠는가?
(A) 수석 건축가
(B) 회사 소유주
(C) 기존 고객
(D) 행사 진행자

어휘 architect 건축가 proprietor 소유주 existing 기존의 coordinator 진행자

---

3. 직원들에게 떠나기 전에 무엇을 하라고 요청하는가?
(A) 공무원과 소통한다
(B) 단체 사진에 참여한다
(C) 기부금을 제공한다
(D) 선물을 받는다

어휘 interact 소통하다 public official 공무원 collect (상 등을) 받다, 타다

PART 3 & 4 Exercise

1 (A) **2** (C) **3** (B) **4** (D) **5** (B) **6** (A)

Questions 1 through 3 refer to the following conversation.

W Br Thank you for making it to my apartment on such short notice, Colin. Come in – [1]I'll show you where the water's dripping down from the ceiling. [2]It looks pretty awful.

M Au Ah, I see. [That is a problem.] When did you say the leak began?

W Br Well, I discovered a puddle of water on the bathroom floor when I woke up this morning, so it must've started in the middle of the night. [3]I'm not sure if it's caused by all this heavy rain we've been getting lately or by a broken pipe.

M Au At this moment, your guess is as good as mine. I'm sorry, but I will need to create an opening in your ceiling to investigate the issue.

1-3번 문제는 다음 대화에 관한 것입니다.

여: 그렇게 급하게 연락드렸는데도 제 아파트에 와 주셔서 고마워요, Colin. 들어오세요. 천장에서 물이 떨어지는 곳이 어딘지 알려드릴게요. 아주 심해 보여요.
남: 아, 알겠어요. 정말 문제네요. 누가 언제 시작됐다고 하셨죠?
여: 어, 오늘 아침에 일어났을 때 욕실 바닥에 물이 고여 있는 걸 발견했거든요. 그러니까 한밤중에 시작된 게 틀림없어요. 이게 요즘에 있었던 이 모든 폭우가 원인이 된 건지 아니면 망가진 파이프 때문인 건지 모르겠네요.
남: 지금으로서는 제 추측도 당신 생각과 다를 게 없어요. 미안하지만, 천장에 구멍을 내서 문제를 조사해 봐야겠어요.

어휘 make it to ~에 시간 맞춰 가다 on short notice 갑자기, 급하게 drip (액체가) 뚝뚝 떨어지다 awful 끔찍한, 지독한 leak 누출 puddle 물웅덩이, 액체가 고인 곳 heavy rain 폭우 lately 최근에, 요즈음 at this moment 지금[현재]으로서는 as good as ~나 다름없는[마찬가지인] opening 구멍 investigate 조사하다 issue 문제, 걱정거리

---

1. Who most likely is the man?

   (A) A building maintenance employee
   (B) A truck operator
   (C) A real estate agent
   (D) A customer service representative

해석 남자는 누구이겠는가?
   (A) 건물 시설관리 직원
   (B) 트럭 운전기사
   (C) 부동산 중개업자
   (D) 고객서비스 직원

---

2. What does the man mean when he says, "That is a problem"?

   (A) He should seek advice from a specialist.
   (B) He deems another issue to be more critical.
   (C) He agrees that the issue demands attention.
   (D) He is familiar with this type of problem.

어휘 seek 청하다, 구하다 specialist 전문가 deem (~로) 여기다, 생각하다 critical 대단히 중요한

해석 남자는 "정말 문제네요."라고 말할 때 무엇을 의미하는가?
   (A) 전문가로부터 조언을 구해야 한다.
   (B) 다른 문제를 더 중요한 것으로 여긴다.
   (C) 이 문제가 주목을 요한다는 점에 동의한다.
   (D) 이러한 유형의 문제에 익숙하다.

---

3. What does the woman say about the recent weather?

   (A) It has been hot and humid.
   (B) It has been raining heavily.
   (C) There has been a lot of wind.
   (D) There have been snowfalls.

어휘 humid 습한 snowfall 강설

해석 여자는 최근의 날씨에 대해 무엇이라고 말하는가?
   (A) 덥고 습했다.
   (B) 비가 매우 많이 왔다.
   (C) 바람이 많이 불었다.
   (D) 눈이 왔다.

해설 1번과 같이 화자의 직업을 묻는 문제는 대부분 첫 한두 문장에서 정답을 알 수 있다. 두 번째 문장에서 여자가 천장에서 물이 떨어지는 곳이 어딘지 알려주겠다고 말하고 있으므로(I'll show you where the water's dripping down from the ceiling.), 남자는 천장 누수 문제를 해결하러 온 사람, 즉 건물 시설관리 직원이다. 여기서 정답을 고를 때 가장 중요한 점은 '순발력'이다. 해당 문장을 듣고 정답 고르기를 조금이라도 머뭇거리면 다음 문제의 키워드가 순식간에 지나가 버린다. 이어지는 문장에서 여자가 "이건 정말 심한 것 같아요(It looks pretty awful)."라고 말했고 이에 대한 대답으로 남자가 That is a problem.이라고 말하고 있다. is를 강조해서 말하고 있으므로 "그거 정말 문제군요."라는 뜻이다. 즉, 남자는 여자가 말한 It looks pretty awful.에 동의하는 대답을 하고 있는 것이다. 3번 문제의 정답은 상대적으로 쉽게 알아낼 수 있다. all this heavy rain we've been getting lately라는 키워드를 들으면서 선택하자.

Questions 4 through 6 refer to the following announcement.

M | Cn Hello and a warm welcome to all attendees of the tenth annual Video Game Convention. My name is Sanjay Patel, and I'm the president of Plexton Enterprises, one of the official sponsors of this year's trade show. I'm here to introduce you to an exciting opportunity. [4]We are creating a new video game and [5]are seeking your story ideas! Send us an e-mail describing your vision for the plot of the upcoming Plexton adventure game. [6]If your idea is selected as the winner, we'll arrange for you to travel to Yokohama, with all expenses paid, for next year's Video Game Convention.

4-6번 문제는 다음 발표문에 관한 것입니다.

남: 안녕하세요. 제10회 연례 비디오 게임 컨벤션에 오신 모든 분들께 따뜻한 환영을 전하는 바입니다. 제 이름은 Sanjay Patel이며, 올 무역 박람회의 공식 후원사 중 하나인 Plexton Enterprises의 회장입니다. 여러분께 흥미진진한 기회를 소개해 드리고자 나왔습니다. 저희가 새 비디오 게임을 만들고 있는데 여러분의 스토리 아이디어를 구합니다! 다가오는 Plexton 어드벤처 게임의 줄거리에 대한 여러분의 비전을 설명하는 이메일을 보내주세요. 아이디어가 수상작으로 선정되면, 모든 경비는 저희 부담으로 내년도 비디오 게임 컨벤션을 보실 수 있게 요코하마로 가는 여행을 마련해 드리겠습니다.

어휘 attendee 참석자 convention 컨벤션, 전시회 sponsor 후원 업체 trade show 무역 박람회 seek 청하다, 구하다 describe 설명하다 plot 구성, 줄거리 upcoming 다가오는, 곧 있을 winner 수상 작품 arrange 마련하다, 준비하다, 주선하다 with + 명사 + 형용사[분사] ~가 ~인 채로 [~하면서] expense 경비

---

4. What does Plexton Enterprises produce?

(A) Television shows
(B) An electronics magazine
(C) Sporting goods
(D) Video games

해석 Plexton Enterprises는 무엇을 생산하는가?
(A) 텔레비전 쇼
(B) 전자 제품 잡지
(C) 스포츠 용품
(D) 비디오 게임

---

5. What are listeners invited to do?

(A) Nominate candidates
(B) Submit ideas
(C) Try out products
(D) Write testimonials

어휘 nominate 지명하다, 추천하다 try out ~을 시험해 보다 testimonial 추천의 글
해석 청차들에게 무엇을 하도록 청하는가?
(A) 후보를 추천한다
(B) 아이디어를 제출한다
(C) 상품을 사용해 본다
(D) 추천의 글을 쓴다

---

6. According to the speaker, what prize will be awarded?

(A) A complimentary trip to an exhibition
(B) A meal accompanied by a celebrity
(C) Electronic appliances
(D) A television appearance

어휘 award 주다, 수여하다 complimentary 무료의 accompany ~에 함께하다 celebrity 유명 인사 appearance 출연
해석 화자의 말에 따르면 어떤 상이 주어질 것인가?
(A) 전시회에 가는 무료 여행
(B) 유명 인사와 함께하는 식사
(C) 전자 제품
(D) 텔레비전 출연

해설 4번 문제의 정답은 We are creating a new video game을 들으면서 쉽게 알아낼 수 있다. 문제는 이 문제의 정답을 빨리 골라야 한다는 점이다. 바로 이어지는 말이 and are seeking your story ideas!와 Send us an e-mail describing your vision for the plot of the upcoming Plexton adventure game.이다. 개발 중인 게임 스토리에 대한 아이디어를 이메일로 보내달라고 요청하고 있으므로 여기서 5번 문제의 정답을 선택해야 한다. 이 문제에서도 계속 순발력이 필요하다. 이어지는 마지막 문장에 집중해서 전체적으로 알아듣고 6번의 정답을 선택해야 하기 때문이다. 제출한 아이디어가 수상작으로 선정되면(If your idea is selected as the winner), 경비는 회사가 부담한 채(with all expenses paid), 내년도 비디오 게임 전시회를 볼 수 있도록(for next year's Video Game Convention) 여행을 마련해주겠다고 했다(we'll arrange for you to travel to Yokohama). 이 발표문은 전체적으로 후반부에 세 문제 모두의 키워드가 몰려 있기 때문에 다른 담화문에 비해 더욱 순발력을 발휘해야 한다.

Actual Test

1 (B)	**2** (A)	**3** (A)	**4** (C)	**5** (C)
6 (A)	**7** (C)	**8** (C)	**9** (B)	**10** (A)
11 (C)	**12** (B)	**13** (B)	**14** (B)	**15** (C)
16 (A)	**17** (B)	**18** (C)	**19** (C)	**20** (B)
21 (B)	**22** (B)	**23** (D)	**24** (D)	**25** (D)
26 (D)	**27** (B)	**28** (B)	**29** (D)	**30** (C)

* 정답을 맞힌 문제도 해설을 읽어보세요.

Part 1

1. M | Au

(A) Passengers are being shown to their seats on the deck of a ship.
(B) People are using a ramp to board a ship.

(C) A sign has been posted above a doorway.
(D) A crew member is tossing an anchor into the water.

어휘 show (장소로) 안내하다. 인도하다 deck 갑판 ramp 경사로, 비탈 board 탑승하다 post 게시하다 doorway 출입구 crew 승무원 (전원) toss 던지다 anchor 닻

해석 (A) 배 갑판에서 승객들이 좌석으로 안내받고 있다.
(B) 경사로를 이용하여 배에 타고 있다.
(C) 출입구 위에 표지판이 게시되어 있다.
(D) 승무원이 닻을 물에 던지고 있다.

해설 Part 1에서 자주 들을 수 없는 문장들이지만, 확실히 알아듣기 어려워도 겁먹지 말자. seats(좌석), doorway(출입구), anchor(닻) 같은 단어들만 알아들으면 오답을 걸러낼 수 있다. 사진에 보이지 않는 사물이 단 하나라도 들리면 무조건 오답이기 때문이다. 경사로를 이용하여 배에 탑승하는 장면이므로 (B)가 정답이다.

2. **M | Cn**

(A) **Some people are disposing of their garbage at a truck.**
(B) Some people are picking up litter on the street.
(C) Vehicles are stopped at a traffic light.
(D) The back of the truck is being closed.

어휘 dispose of ~을 없애다. 처리하다 garbage 쓰레기 litter 쓰레기 traffic light 신호등

해석 (A) 트럭에 쓰레기를 처리하고 있다.
(B) 길에서 쓰레기를 줍고 있다.
(C) 차량들이 신호등에 멈춰 있다.
(D) 트럭 뒷부분이 닫히고 있다.

해설 '처리하다, 없애다'라는 뜻으로 dispose of를 알고 있으면 정답을 파악할 수 있다. picking up이나 is being closed 같은 동사가 들리면 (B)와 (D)는 오답이라는 것을 알 수 있다. 사진에 신호등(traffic light)이 없으므로 (C)도 오답이다.

3. **W | Am**

(A) **She's cleaning up some debris.**
(B) She's installing some patio tiles.
(C) A brick chimney is being painted.
(D) A broom has been propped against a windowsill.

어휘 debris 쓰레기 patio 테라스 brick 벽돌 chimney 굴뚝 broom 빗자루 prop against ~에 받쳐[괴어] 놓다 windowsill 창턱

해석 (A) 쓰레기를 치우고 있다.
(B) 테라스 타일을 설치하고 있다.
(C) 벽돌 굴뚝에 페인트를 칠하고 있다.
(D) 빗자루를 창턱에 받쳐 놓았다.

해설 정확하게 알아듣고 정답을 선택할 수 있게 debris의 발음을 알아두자. s는 묵음이며 붙어 단어처럼 '드브리'라고 읽어야 한다. 동사 installing과 is being painted를 듣고 (B)와 (C)는 오답으로 골라내야 한다. (D)도 오답인데, prop against(~에 받쳐 놓다) 같은 표현은 가끔 정답으로 출제되므로 기억해두는 게 좋다.

Part 2

4. **W | Am** **M | Cn**

Does the company own or rent its office building?

(A) To set up a business.
(B) I'm searching for a two-bedroom place.
(C) **I believe they're renting.**

어휘 rent 임차하다 set up ~을 설립하다 place 거처, 살 곳, 집

해석 회사가 사무실 건물을 소유하고 있나요, 빌려 쓰고 있나요?
(A) 사업을 차리려고요.
(B) 침실 두 개짜리 집을 찾고 있습니다.
(C) 빌려 쓰고 있을 거예요.

해설 (A)와 (B)는 질문에 나오는 rent와 building에서 연상되는 대답으로 오답을 유도하고 있다. own or rent 중 하나를 선택하는 대답이 정답이다.

5. M Au W Br

Are you planning to dine in, or would you like to take your food with you?

(A) Yes, it was absolutely delicious.
(B) Just a little later.
(C) I think I should get back to the office.

어휘 dine in (포장하지 않고) 식당에서 식사하다

해석 음식을 여기서 드시겠어요, 아니면 가져가고 싶으신가요?
(A) 네, 정말 맛있었어요.
(B) 조금만 나중에요.
(C) 사무실로 돌아가야 할 것 같아요.

해설 (A)는 Yes가 들리는 순간 오답임을 알 수 있다. 이 질문은 식당에서 들을 수 있는 표현으로, (B)도 식당에서 할 수 있는 "(주문을) 조금만 있다가 할게요."라는 대답으로 오답을 유도하고 있다. 사무실로 돌아가야 한다는 말이 음식을 포장해서 가져가겠다는 뜻이므로 (C)가 정답이다.

6. M Cn W Am

Is the staff lunch being held at the office or at a restaurant?

(A) Our conference room is way too small.
(B) John demonstrated good leadership.
(C) Yes, we'll have to hire more staff.

어휘 way (전치사, 부사 강조) 훨씬, 너무 demonstrate (능력, 자질을) 보여주다, 발휘하다

해석 점심 회식을 사무실에서 할 건가요, 식당으로 갈 건가요?
(A) 회의실은 너무 많이 작잖아요.
(B) John은 훌륭한 리더십을 보여줬어요.
(C) 네, 우리는 직원을 더 채용해야 해요.

해설 회의실이 너무 작아서 회사 내에서는 회식을 할 수 없으니 식당으로 가자는 뜻인 (A)가 정답이다. (B)는 질문의 staff와 office에서 연상되는 대답으로 오답을 유도하고 있으며, (C)는 Yes를 듣고 오답으로 골라내야 한다.

7. M Cn W Br

Shall we repaint the staff lounge or the boardroom?

(A) There may be some in the closet.

(B) There's more than enough room in here.
(C) We can afford to do both.

어휘 repaint 다시 칠하다 staff lounge 직원 휴게실 boardroom 중역 회의실, 이사회실 closet 벽장 more than enough 충분하고도 남는 can afford to-V (시간이나 금전에서) ~할 여유가 있다

해석 직원 휴게실을 다시 칠할까요, 중역 회의실을 칠할까요?
(A) 아마 벽장 안에 조금 있을 거예요.
(B) 여기서는 공간이 충분하고도 남아요.
(C) 둘 다 할 수 있는 여유가 있잖아요.

해설 (A)는 질문에 나오는 repaint와 발음이 비슷한 paint에서 연상되는 대답으로, (B)는 질문의 boardroom에 들어 있는 room을 반복시키면서 오답을 유도하고 있다. (B)는 또한 질문에 등장하는 staff lounge나 boardroom 같은 공간에서 연상되는 대답이기도 하다. 선택 의문문에서는 대답에서 both나 each가 들리면 주저 말고 정답으로 선택하자.

8. W Am M Au

Will we focus on advertising in print media or online?

(A) The customers are waiting in line.
(B) Yes, it looks fantastic.
(C) Let's find out what the team thinks.

어휘 print media 인쇄 매체 find out ~을 알아내다

해석 인쇄 매체 광고에 집중할 건가요, 아니면 온라인인가요?
(A) 고객들이 줄 서서 기다리고 있습니다.
(B) 네, 기막히게 좋아 보이네요.
(C) 팀원들은 어떻게 생각하는지 알아봅시다.

해설 (A)는 질문에 나왔던 online과 발음이 비슷한 in line이 들릴 때, (B)는 Yes가 나오자마자 오답임을 알 수 있다. 오답을 잘 골라낼수록 고수가 된다!

9. M Au W Br

Should I order the supplies today, or wait until next week?

(A) A total of eighty-five dollars.
(B) Actually, I've already sent the order.
(C) They're in the supply closet.

어휘 supplies 용품, 비품 supply closet 비품 창고

해석 비품을 오늘 주문할까요, 다음 주까지 기다릴까요?
(A) 총 85달러입니다.

(C) 비품 창고에 있어요.

해설 이미 주문서를 보냈기 때문에 오늘 주문할 필요도, 다음 주까지 기다려야 할 필요도 없다고 말하는 (B)가 정답이다. 가끔 제3의 선택이 정답이 된다는 사실을 기억하자. (A)는 질문의 order the supplies에서 연상되는 대답으로, (C)는 supply를 반복시키면서 오답을 유도하고 있다. 도저히 정답을 알 수 없을 때는 Actually가 들리는 대답이 정답일 확률이 높다는 점을 활용하자.

---

10. M|Au W|Br

Are the flyers going to be ready today, or do you need more time to finish them?

(A) I'll start working on them right away.
(B) I have no idea who is going.
(C) His flight will be late.

어휘 flyer 전단지 right away 곧바로, 즉시

해석 전단지가 오늘 준비될까요, 아니면 끝마치는 데 시간이 더 필요하신가요?
(A) 당장 작업을 시작하겠습니다.
(B) 누가 갈 건지 모르겠어요.
(C) 그의 비행편은 늦을 겁니다.

해설 당장 작업을 시작하겠다는 대답이 전단지가 오늘 준비될 것이라는 뜻인지, 시간을 더 달라는 말인지 확실하지는 않지만, 어쨌든 자연스러운 대답이다. 대화를 알아듣기 어려워도 오답을 잘 걸러내서 정답을 맞혀야 한다. (B)는 질문에 나오는 going을 반복시키면서, (C)는 flyers와 발음이 비슷한 flight를 들려주면서 오답을 유도하고 있다.

---

11. M|Au W|Br

In terms of office equipment, should we invest in desktop computers or laptops?

(A) The Web site is up and running now.
(B) They're available for purchase at any store.
(C) Many of our staff members are frequent travelers.

어휘 in terms of ~ 면에서, ~에 관하여 up and running 완전히 제대로 작동되는 available for purchase 구입할 수 있는 frequent 잦은, 빈번한

해석 사무 장비에 관해서요, 데스크톱 컴퓨터에 돈을 쓸까요, 노트북에 할까요?
(A) 홈페이지는 지금 완전히 제대로 작동하고 있습니다.
(B) 아무 매장에서나 구입할 수 있습니다.
(C) 우리 직원들 중 상당수는 자주 출장을 다니죠.

해설 질문에 들어 있는 단어에서 연상되는 대답이 대부분 오답 장치라는 사실을 절대 잊지 말자. (A)와 (B)가 모두 질문의 computers에서 연상되는 대답으로 오답을 유도하고 있다. 노트북 컴퓨터를 사는 것이 좋겠다는 내용을 출장이 잦은 직원들이 많다는 대답으로 패러프레이즈 한 (C)가 정답이다.

---

12. W|Am M|Cn

Does the rental vehicle have automatic or manual transmission?

(A) It's on the top shelf in the office.
(B) Maureen will be driving the vehicle.
(C) The smart lights turn on automatically.

어휘 rental 임대의, 대여의 manual 수동의 transmission (자동차) 변속기

해석 렌터카 변속기가 자동인가요, 수동인가요?
(A) 사무실 맨 위 선반에 있어요.
(B) Maureen이 차를 운전할 거예요.
(C) 스마트 조명이 자동으로 켜집니다.

해설 형용사 manual의 의미를 모르면 명사로 생각해서 (A)를 정답으로 짐작할 수 있다. (C)는 질문에 나오는 automatic을 반복시키면서 오답을 유도하고 있다. 운전할 사람이 따로 있으니 그에게 물어보라고 말하는 "몰라" 유형의 대답 (B)가 정답이다.

Part 3

Questions 13 through 15 refer to the following conversation.

M|Au [13]That'll be thirty dollars. Would you like these gloves gift-wrapped?

W|Am Oh, I'm purchasing them for my own use. [14]You know, I think I'll wear them home. It's kind of cold out there. [15]Do you accept credit cards?

M|Au [15]Yes, but only for amounts over thirty-two dollars. Your total is less than that.

W|Am Alright, then I'll settle this with cash.

해석 여자는 왜 신용 카드를 사용할 수 없는가?
(A) 카드 가져오는 것을 잊어버렸다.
(B) 사업체에서 신용 카드를 받지 않는다.
(C) 구입품의 가격이 충분히 높지 않다.
(D) 카드에 손상이 있다.

해설 13번 문제는 장소를 묻고 있으므로 정답을 첫 한두 문장에서 알려줄 것이라고 기대할 수 있다. 남자의 첫 대사 That'll be thirty dollars. Would you like these gloves gift-wrapped?를 들으면서 정답을 선택하자. 정답을 알아내는 것 자체는 별로 어렵지 않지만, 여기서 중요한 것은 순발력이다. 머뭇거리고 있으면 여자의 대사 You know, I think I'll wear them home.을 놓칠 수 있다. 여기서 14번의 정답을 골라야 한다. 이 문제도 정답을 빨리 골라야 다음 문제를 놓치지 않을 수 있다. 여자가 곧바로 Do you accept credit cards?라고 묻는데, 남자가 "신용 카드를 받기는 하지만 구입 금액이 32달러에 못 미치기 때문에 지금은 사용할 수 없다(Yes, but only for amounts over thirty-two dollars. Your total is less than that.)"고 대답하고 있으므로 여기서 15번의 정답을 알아내야 한다.

Questions 16 through 18 refer to the following conversation.

[W | Br] Hi Leo, it's Amirah from Human Resources. [16]I just wanted to let you know that the computer in Meeting Room 4B is not working.

[M | Au] Oh, I'm sorry, [17]I can come over right away and take a look at it.

[W | Br] [17]Right now? Uh... [I'm interviewing someone in here in ten minutes.] And I don't need the computer to do that. So, if you could wait...

[M | Au] Oh, OK, in that case, I'll come over when you're finished. Is everything else you need in the room set up?

[W | Br] Yeah, thanks. [18]For once I'm interviewing someone who already lives in the area, so there's no need for a video conference. It'll be nice to talk to someone in person for a change.

13-15번 문제는 다음 대화에 관한 것입니다.

남: 30달러입니다. 이 장갑을 선물용으로 포장해 드릴까요?
여: 아, 그거 제가 쓰려고 사는 거예요. 그러니까, 집까지 끼고 갈 생각이에요. 밖이 조금 춥거든요. 신용카드 받으시나요?
남: 네, 하지만 32달러가 넘는 금액에 대해서만요. 손님의 총액은 그보다 적습니다.
여: 알겠어요, 그렇다면 이건 현금으로 계산할게요.

어휘 gift-wrap 선물용으로 포장하다 kind of 약간, 어느 정도 total 총액 settle 지불하다, 계산하다

---

13. Where does this conversation take place?

(A) At a dining establishment
(B) At a garment shop
(C) At a bookshop
(D) At a florist's shop

해석 이 대화는 어디에서 일어나는가?
(A) 음식점
(B) 옷가게
(C) 서점
(D) 꽃가게

---

14. What does the woman want to do with her purchase?

(A) Retrieve it at a later time
(B) Make use of it immediately
(C) Have it wrapped as a gift
(D) Have it delivered to her residence

어휘 retrieve 되찾다, 회수하다 make use of ~을 이용하다, 활용하다 wrap 포장하다 residence 거주지

해석 여자는 구입한 물건으로 무엇을 하고 싶은가?
(A) 나중에 되찾는다
(B) 즉시 이용한다
(C) 선물로 포장한다
(D) 자기 거주지로 배달시킨다

---

15. Why is the woman unable to use her credit card?

(A) She forgot to bring her card with her.
(B) Credit cards are not accepted at the business.
(C) The price of her purchase is not high enough.

16-18번 문제는 다음 대화에 관한 것입니다.

> **여:** 안녕, Leo. 인사부의 Amirah예요. 4B 회의실 컴퓨터가 작동하지 않는다고 알려드리려고요.
>
> **남:** 아, 미안해요. 즉시 건너가서 볼게요.
>
> **여:** 지금 당장이요? 어... 제가 10분 후에 여기서 누구 면접을 보거든요. 그리고 그걸 하는 데는 컴퓨터가 필요 없고요. 그러니까 기다리실 수 있다면...
>
> **남:** 아, 알겠어요. 그렇다면 일이 끝나면 들를게요. 그밖에 회의실에서 필요한 것들은 다 설치되어 있나요?
>
> **여:** 네, 고마워요. 이번만큼은 이미 이 지역에 살고 있는 사람을 면접 보거든요. 그래서 화상 회의를 할 필요가 없어요. 여느 때와 달리 직접 누군가와 대화하는 것도 즐거울 거예요.

어휘 come over 들르다 right away 즉시, 곧바로 in that case 그렇다면 set up 설치하다 for once 이번 한 번만은 video conference 화상 회의 in person 직접, 몸소 for a change 여느 때와 달리

---

16. Why is the woman calling the man?

(A) **To report an equipment malfunction**

(B) To confirm an agenda

(C) To inquire about employee information

(D) To ask about a missing object

어휘 malfunction 오작동 confirm 확정하다 agenda 의제, 안건 inquire about ~에 대해 문의하다

해석 여자는 왜 남자에게 전화하고 있는가?
(A) 장비 오작동을 알리기 위해
(B) 안건을 확정하기 위해
(C) 직원 정보에 대해 문의하기 위해
(D) 누락된 물건에 대해 묻기 위해

---

17. What does the woman mean when she says, "I'm interviewing someone in here in ten minutes."?

(A) She is in urgent need of help.

(B) **She does not want to be disturbed.**

(C) She is discontented with an assignment.

(D) She will not attend another meeting.

어휘 in need of ~이 필요한 urgent 긴급한 discontented 불만[불평]을 품은 assignment 업무

해석 여자는 "제가 10분 후에 여기서 누구 면접을 보거든요."라고 말할 때 무엇을 의미하는가?
(A) 긴급하게 도움이 필요하다.
(B) 방해받고 싶지 않다.
(C) 어떤 업무에 불만이 있다.
(D) 다른 회의에는 참석하지 않을 것이다.

---

18. What does the woman say is unusual about the interview?

(A) It will be videorecorded.

(B) It will take place over a weekend.

(C) **It will be conducted face to face.**

(D) It will last for less than half an hour.

어휘 unusual 이례적인 conduct (특정한 활동을) 하다 face to face 얼굴을 마주 대하고, 대면하여 last 지속되다

해석 여자는 면접에 관하여 무엇이 이례적이라고 말하는가?
(A) 녹화될 것이다.
(B) 주말 동안 있을 것이다.
(C) 대면하여 실시될 것이다.
(D) 30분이 안 되게 지속될 것이다.

해석 16번처럼 대화의 주제나 목적을 묻는 문제가 보이면 첫 문장을 놓치지 않도록 집중해야 한다. 여자가 I just wanted to let you know that the computer in Meeting Room 4B is not working.이라고 했으므로 장비의 오작동을 알리는 것이 통화 목적이다. 여기서는 정답을 빨리 고르는 것이 매우 중요하다. 바로 이어지는 문장을 놓치면 17번 문제를 풀 수 없게 된다. 남자가 즉시 가서 살펴보겠다고 말하자(I can come over right away and take a look at it.) 여자가 10분 후에 이곳에서 면접이 있다는 말을 하고 있으며(I'm interviewing someone in here in ten minutes.), 면접에는 컴퓨터가 필요 없다는 부연 설명까지 하고 있다(And I don't need the computer to do that). 여자는 남자가 컴퓨터를 수리하러 와서 면접을 방해하지 않기를 바라고 있다. 16번을 풀 때 순발력을 발휘하지 않으면 17번이 어려워진다. 18번은 여자의 마지막 대사를 이해해야 한다. for once(이번 한 번만은), in person(직접, 몸소), for a change(여느 때와 달리) 같은 표현들을 알아야 한다. 이것들이 문제에서 unusual(이례적인), face to face(얼굴을 마주 대하고)와 같은 단어들로 바뀌어 있다.

Questions 19 through 21 refer to the following conversation and schedule.

M Cn ¹⁹Hi, I'm just about finished with the deliveries for today, but I'm having trouble with the one for Dinh Industries. I've reached the office building, ²⁰but the street is bustling, and there's no available parking for unloading.

W Am I apologize for the oversight, as Dinh Industries is a first-time customer and I forgot to include the parking information on the delivery schedule. They have a parking area behind the building.

M Cn OK, I'll head over there now. I'm running behind schedule, though. I hope my next delivery stop will still be open.

W Am It might not be, ²¹so I'll give them a call and let them know you'll be arriving a bit late.

19–21번 문제는 다음 대화와 일정표에 관한 것입니다.

남: 안녕하세요. 오늘 배달은 거의 다 끝났는데요, Dinh Industries에 할 배달에 문제가 있어요. 사무실 건물에 도착하기는 했는데, 도로가 북적거리고 있고요 짐을 내리기 위해 이용할 수 있는 주차 공간이 없어요.

여: 실수에 대해 사과드립니다. Dinh Industries는 처음 거래하는 고객사인데 깜빡 잊고 배달 일정표에 주차 정보를 포함하지 않았어요. 건물 뒤편에 주차장이 있어요.

남: 알겠어요. 지금 그리로 갈게요. 그런데 제가 예정보다 늦고 있거든요. 다음 배송지가 계속 영업 중이면 좋겠네요.

여: 아닐지도 몰라요. 제가 전화해서 당신이 약간 늦게 도착할 거라고 알려줄게요.

어휘 just about 거의 (다) have trouble with ~에 문제가 있다 bustling 부산한, 북적거리는 unload 짐을 내리다 oversight 실수, 간과 first-time 처음으로 해 보는 head over (to) ~로 가다, 향하다 run behind schedule 예정보다 늦다 though (문장 끝에서) 그렇지만, 하지만 delivery stop 배송지

Today's Deliveries **Lindenbrook Bakery**	
Customer	**Address**
Franklyn Supermarket	1800 State St
Dinh Industries	360 Hillside St
Tuckman Department Store	45 Jefferson St

오늘의 배송 **Lindenbrook 베이커리**	
고객	**주소**
Franklyn 슈퍼마켓	1800 State St
Dinh Industries	360 Hillside St
Tuckman 백화점	45 Jefferson St

19. Look at the graphic. What street is the man on?

(A) Lindenbrook
(B) State
(C) Hillside
(D) Jefferson

해석 그래픽을 보라. 남자는 어느 도로에 있는가?
(A) Lindenbrook
(B) State
(C) Hillside
(D) Jefferson

20. What is the man asking about?

(A) How to collect a payment
(B) Where he can park his vehicle
(C) When to make a delivery
(D) Whom he should ask for

해석 남자는 무엇에 대해 묻고 있는가?
(A) 대금을 징수하는 법
(B) 차량을 주차할 수 있는 장소
(C) 배달할 시간
(D) 찾아야 할 사람

21. What does the woman say she will do?

(A) Open a door
(B) Make a phone call
(C) Forward an e-mail
(D) Buy some food

해석 여자는 무엇을 하겠다고 말하는가?
(A) 문을 연다
(B) 전화를 건다
(C) 이메일을 전달한다
(D) 음식을 산다

해설 남자의 첫 대사에서 19번 문제의 정답을 알 수 있다. 오늘 배달은 거의 끝나 가는데, Dinh Industries에 할 배달에 문제가 있다고 하면서(I'm just about finished with the deliveries for today, but I'm having trouble with the one for Dinh Industries.) 지금 그 회사 앞에 와 있다고 말하고 있다(I've reached the office building). 배달 일정표를 보면 Dinh Industries의 주소는 360 Hillside St이다. 남자의 대사와 그래픽 정보를 종합하여 정답을 선택하면 되는데, 이때 필요한 것이 순발력이다. 바로 이어지는 문장 but the street is bustling, and there's no available parking for unloading.을 듣고 20번의 정답을 골라야 하기 때문이다. but, no, actually, so로 시작하는 문장에는 정답의 키워드가 들어 있을 확률이 크다는 사실도 기억하자. 여자의 마지막 대사도 so로 시작하는 문장으로 끝나는데(so I'll give them a call), 여기서 21번의 정답을 알아내야 한다.

Part 4

Questions 22 through 24 refer to the following announcement.

W Am ²²Attention to all production line employees: ²³As you may have observed, the main conveyor belt is temporarily out of order. The repair to the belt is expected to take a minimum of a couple of hours, according to the maintenance crew. The production line will stay closed until this is complete. In the meantime, all production line personnel are required to report to your manager's office for special assignments. ²⁴You can expect a call later tonight from an assembly floor supervisor regarding any potential schedule adjustments for tomorrow's day shift.

22-24번 문제는 다음 공지에 관한 것입니다.

여: 모든 생산 라인 직원 여러분께 알립니다. 아마 보셔서 아시겠지만, 메인 컨베이어 벨트가 일시적으로 고장나 있습니다. 정비팀에 따르면 벨트 수리는 최소 두세 시간은 걸릴 것으로 예상됩니다. 이 작업이 완료될 때까지 생산 라인은 폐쇄됩니다. 그 동안 모든 생산 라인 직원 여러분은 특별 업무를 위해 각 매니저의 사무실에 보고하시기 바랍니다. 내일 주간 근무조에 대한 잠재적인 일정 조정에 관해서는 오늘 저녁에 조립 현장 관리자로부터 전화를 받을 수 있습니다.

> **어휘** attention (안내 방송에서) 알립니다 observe 보다, (보고) 알다 temporarily 일시적으로 out of order 고장난 maintenance 유지 보수, 정비 crew 팀, 조, 반 in the meantime 그 동안[사이]에 personnel 직원들 report to (도착을) 알리다, 보고하다 assignment 임무, 업무 assembly floor 조립 작업장[현장] supervisor 감독관, 관리자 regarding ~에 관하여 adjustment 조정, 수정 day shift 주간 근무조

22. Where most likely is this announcement being made?

(A) At a site of construction project
(B) At a production facility
(C) At an auto dealership
(D) At an office supply store

> **해석** 이 공지는 어디에서 이루어지고 있겠는가?
> (A) 건설 프로젝트 현장에서
> (B) 생산 시설에서
> (C) 자동차 대리점에서
> (D) 사무용품 매장에서

23. What problem does the speaker mention?

(A) Some components are missing.
(B) A manager has yet to show up.
(C) Inclement weather is expected.
(D) Some equipment is not functioning.

> **어휘** component 부품 show up (예정된 곳에) 나타나다 inclement (날씨가) 좋지 못한, 궂은
> **해석** 화자는 어떤 문제점을 언급하는가?
> (A) 일부 부품이 누락되었다.
> (B) 관리자가 아직 나타나지 않았다.
> (C) 악천후가 예상된다.
> (D) 일부 장비가 작동하지 않고 있다.

24. What will employees be informed about this evening?

(A) Results of an inspection
(B) Alterations in safety procedures
(C) Updates on work schedules
(D) Conditions of roads

> **어휘** inspection 점검, 검사 alteration 변경 update 최신 정보
> **해석** 오늘 저녁에 직원들은 무엇에 대한 통지를 받을 것인가?
> (A) 검사 결과

(B) 안전 절차의 변경
(C) 업무 일정에 대한 최신 정보
(D) 도로 사정

해설 22번과 같이 말하고 있는 장소를 묻는 문제는 대부분 첫 한두 문장에서 정답을 알 수 있으므로 첫 문장부터 놓치지 않도록 집중하자. Attention to all production line employees를 듣자마자 정답을 알 수 있다. 그러나 정답을 알아내는 것보다 더 중요한 것은 순발력이다. 그야말로 0.1초만에 정답을 골라야 다음 문장을 놓치지 않고 23번 문제의 정답을 선택할 수 있다. the main conveyor belt is temporarily out of order.를 들으면서 정답을 고르자. 24번 문제의 정답은 안내방송 끝부분에서 알 수 있다. 내일 주간 근무조에 일정 변경이 생기면 오늘 저녁에 전화로 알려주겠다고 했다(You can expect a call later tonight from an assembly floor supervisor regarding any potential schedule adjustments for tomorrow's day shift).

Questions 25 through 27 refer to the following excerpt from a meeting.

M | Au So the purpose of this meeting is to review our contract with Warmson Advertising and make a decision on whether... uhm... whether to keep using their services for our TV commercials. Yesterday, I had a conversation with their team ²⁵and I must admit, I'm feeling a bit worried. It seems like their primary focus is on cutting their costs rather than producing high-quality commercials for us. [Here's the thing.] ²⁶If we decide to end this business relationship, we will have to compensate them for any work that has already been done. ²⁷Let's quickly go through this contract together. You'll find that's a stipulation in the agreement we arranged.

25-27번 문제는 다음 회의 발췌문에 관한 것입니다.

남: 자, 이번 회의 목적은 Warmson Advertising과의 계약을 검토해서 우리의 TV 광고를 만드는 데 그들의 서비스를, 어... 계속 사용할지 말지를 결정하는 것입니다. 어제 제가 그 팀과 대화를 나누었는데, 조금 걱정이 되는 것은 사실입니다. 그들의 주안점은 우리에게 고품질의 광고를 제작하는 것보다는 자신들의 비용을 절감하는 데 있는 것으로 보입니다. 그런데 문제는 이겁니다. 만약 우리가 이 거래 관계를 끝내기로 결정한다면, 이미 이루어진 작업물에 대해 그들에게 보상해 줘야 한다는 거죠. 잠깐 이 계약서를 함께 살펴보시죠. 그게 우리가 맺은 계약의 조항이라는 것을 알게 될 겁니다.

어휘 so 자, 그래 commercial (텔레비전, 라디오의) 광고 (방송) admit 인정하다, 시인하다 rather than ~보다는 Here's the thing. 그런데 문제는 이겁니다. compensate A for B A에게 B에 대해 보상하다 go through ~을 살펴보다 stipulation 계약 조건[조항] arrange an agreement 계약을 맺다

25. What bothers the man about Warmson Advertising?

(A) Their lack of punctuality
(B) Their staffing difficulties
(C) Their request to alter a contract
(D) Their focus on cost cutting

어휘 bother 신경 쓰이게 하다, 괴롭히다 punctuality 시간 엄수 staffing 인력 수급 alter 변경하다

해석 Warmson Advertising에 관해 무엇이 남자를 신경 쓰이게 하는가?
(A) 시간을 엄수하지 않음
(B) 인력 수급의 어려움
(C) 계약을 변경하자는 요청
(D) 비용 절감에 대한 집중

26. What does the man mean when he says, "Here's the thing."?

(A) He will showcase a product.
(B) He cannot recall a word.
(C) He has found what he was searching for.
(D) He will bring up a point for discussion.

어휘 showcase 소개하다, 선보이다 bring up (화제를) 꺼내다

해석 남자는 "그런데 문제는 이겁니다."라고 말할 때 무엇을 의미하는가?
(A) 상품을 선보일 것이다
(B) 말이 생각나지 않는다
(C) 찾던 물건을 발견했다
(D) 논의할 점을 제기할 것이다

27. What are the listeners asked to look at?

(A) A design concept
(B) A business contract
(C) A commercial
(D) A budget

해석 청자들에게 무엇을 보라고 요구하는가?
(A) 디자인 콘셉트

(B) 사업 계약서
(C) 광고
(D) 예산안

첫 문장을 들으면서 화자가 일을 맡긴 광고 회사를 마음에 들어 하지 않고 있으며 계약을 종료하고 싶어 한다는 뉘앙스를 감지하자(whether to keep using their services for our TV commercials). 그러고 나서 이어지는 문장에 들어 있는 I'm feeling a bit worried.가 25번 질문에서 bothers the man으로 패러프레이즈 되어 있다는 점을 간파하면서 정답 고를 준비를 하자. 이어지는 It seems like their primary focus is on cutting their costs에서 정답을 알 수 있다. 정답을 알아내는 것 자체는 어렵지 않지만 훨씬 더 중요한 것은 순발력이다. 곧바로 이어지는 문장이 Here's the thing.이기 때문이다. 여기서 the thing이 어떤 사물을 가리킨다면 26번의 (A), (B), (C)가 모두 정답일 가능성이 있다. 그러나 다음 문장의 내용을 들어보면 정답은 (D)이다. 지금 계약을 종료하면 금전적인 손해를 감수해야 한다는 점이 문제라고 말하고 있기 때문이다(If we decide to end this business relationship, we will have to compensate them for any work that has already been done). 여기서도 순발력을 발휘해야 27번 문제를 원활하게 해결할 수 있다. 바로 다음 문장에서 함께 계약서를 살펴보자고 말하고 있다(Let's quickly go through this contract together).

Questions 28 through 30 refer to the following telephone message and coupon.

[W] [Br] Hi. It's Valerie, ²⁸and I'm calling with some information about the party that we're organizing for Monica's retirement. ²⁹Now, um... you and I decided that the party would be on July fourth. And, I'm really glad to hear that thirty-five people from the office are coming. ²⁹But, unfortunately, it looks like we can't use the coupon from Bliss Restaurant after all. We might want to make a reservation someplace else... Also, Anwei agreed to play Monica's favorite song on the piano during the party. ³⁰Do you think you could make photocopies of the lyrics so that everyone can sing along?

는 다음 전화 메시지와 쿠폰에 관한 것입니다.

여: 안녕, Valerie예요. Monica의 은퇴를 위해 우리가 준비하고 있는 파티에 대한 정보를 알려드리려고 전화했어요. 자, 음... 당신과 내가 파티를 7월 4일에 하자고 결정했죠. 그리고, 사무실에서 35명의 사람들이 온다고 들어서 정말 기뻐요. 그런데, 안타깝게도, Bliss 식당 쿠폰은 결국 사용할 수 없을 것 같네요. 다른 어딘가에 예약을 하는 게 좋을 것 같아요... 그리고, Anwei가 파티 때 Monica가 가장 좋아하는 노래를 피아노로 연주하기로 했어요. 다 같이 따라 부를 수 있게 가사를 복사해 줄 수 있겠어요?

어휘 organize 준비하다, 조직하다 might want to-V ~하는 게 좋겠다 someplace 어딘가에서 make a photocopy of ~을 복사하다 lyrics 가사 sing along 함께 노래를 따라 부르다 so (that) + S + can[may/will] + V ~하기 위해서

Bliss Restaurant	
15% off (groups of 20+)	
Book rooms for 4 hours!	
²⁹expires:	Offer good at
July 1st	all locations

Bliss 식당	
15% 할인 (20인 이상 단체)	
4시간 동안 방을 예약하세요!	
만료 날짜:	할인은 모든
7월 1일	지점에서 유효함

어휘 off 할인되어 offer 할인 good 유효한

28. Why is an event being held?

(A) To celebrate a promotion
(B) To commemorate a retirement
(C) To mark a special occasion
(D) To announce a corporate merger

어휘 commemorate 기념하다, 축하하다 mark 기념하다, 축하하다 occasion 경우, 때 corporate 기업의, 회사의 merger 합병

해석 행사는 왜 열리는가?
(A) 승진을 축하하기 위해서
(B) 은퇴를 축하하기 위해서
(C) 특별한 때를 기념하기 위해서
(D) 회사 합병을 발표하기 위해서

29. Look at the graphic. Why is the speaker unable to use the coupon for the event?

(A) The group does not have enough people.
(B) The length of the event is excessive.
(C) All of the locations in the area are fully booked.
(D) The event will take place after the expiration date.

어휘 length (시간의) 길이, 기간 excessive 지나친, 과도한 location 장소 expiration date 만기일, 만료일

해석 그래픽을 보라. 화자는 왜 행사에 쿠폰을 사용할 수 없는가?
(A) 단체에 사람이 충분하지 않다.
(B) 행사 시간이 지나치게 길다.
(C) 지역의 모든 지점에서 예약이 다 찼다.
(D) 행사가 만료일 이후에 진행된다.

----

30. What does the speaker ask the listener to do?

(A) Select a menu
(B) Distribute invitations
(C) Duplicate song lyrics
(D) Contract a band

어휘 distribute 배포하다 duplicate 복사하다, 복제하다 contract ~와 계약하다

해석 화자는 청자에게 무엇을 해달라고 요구하는가?
(A) 메뉴를 선정한다
(B) 초대장을 배포한다
(C) 노래 가사를 복사한다
(D) 밴드와 계약한다

해설 첫 문장에서 the party that we're organizing for Monica's retirement라는 구문을 들으면서 28번 문제의 정답을 순발력 있게 골라야 한다. 곧바로 이어지는 문장을 듣고 29번의 정답을 알아내야 하기 때문이다. 파티 날짜를 7월 4일로 정했다고 했는데(you and I decided that the party would be on July fourth.), 쿠폰의 만료 날짜가 7월 1일이다. 30번은 마지막 문장에 나오는 make photocopies of가 Duplicate로 바뀌어 있는 선택지를 정답으로 고르면 된다.

PART 1 Exercise

1 (A)　　**2** (C)

1. M | Cn

(A) **Some employees are standing behind the curved desk.**
(B) Some employees are filing some documents.
(C) A technician is installing a software program.
(D) A worker is hanging up a sign.

어휘 curved 곡선의　file (서류를) 철하여 정리하다　hang up ~을 걸다

해석 (A) 직원들이 곡선형 책상 뒤에 서 있다.
(B) 직원들이 서류를 철하여 정리하고 있다.
(C) 기술자가 소프트웨어 프로그램을 설치하고 있다.
(D) 직원이 표지판을 걸고 있다.

해설 "~에 서 있다"는 위치 표현에 주의해야 한다. curved desk가 연음되어 "커r브데스크"라고 들린다. 읽는 연습을 많이 해서 알아들을 수 있게 해두자. (B)와 (D)는 file, hang up 같은 동사를 알고 있으면 오답으로 골라낼 수 있다. (C)처럼 사진을 통해 확인할 수 없는 내용은 정답이 될 수 없다.

2. W | Am

(A) Some chairs are being moved onto a patio.
(B) A mountain overlooks a lake.
(C) **A person is standing by a wooden railing.**
(D) Sunlight is streaming through the clouds.

어휘 patio 테라스　overlook (건물, 산 등이) 내려다보다　railing 난간　stream 흘러나오다

해석 (A) 의자들을 테라스로 옮기고 있다.
(B) 산이 호수를 내려다보고 있다.
(C) 나무 난간 옆에 서 있다.
(D) 햇빛이 구름 사이로 흘러나오고 있다.

해설 진행 시제 수동태는 동작을 나타내기 때문에 (A)가 정답이 되려면 어떤 사람이 옮기는 동작을 하고 있어야 한다. (B)는 사진에 없는 호수(lake)를 언급하고 있으므로 오답이다. 위치 표현을 잘 듣고 (C)를 정답으로 선택해야 한다.

PART 2 Exercise

1 (A)　　**2** (A)　　**3** (A)　　**4** (C)　　**5** (B)
6 (B)　　**7** (C)　　**8** (B)　　**9** (A)　　**10** (A)

1. W | Am　M | Au

Do you mind filling out an application?

(A) **Actually, I already have.**
(B) A job opening in another city.
(C) No, mine's still full.

어휘 fill out ~을 작성하다

해석 지원서를 작성해 주시겠어요?
(A) 실은 이미 했습니다.
(B) 다른 도시의 공석이요.
(C) 아니요, 제 것은 아직 가득 차 있습니다.

해설 제안/부탁 의문문은 already가 들어 있는 대답이 들리면 거절하는 것으로 알고 정답으로 선택하면 된다. (B)는 질문의 filling out an application에서 연상되는 단어 job opening을, (C)는 fill과 발음이 비슷한 full을 들려주면서 오답을 유도하고 있다. 도저히 정답을 알 수 없을 때는 Actually가 들리는 대답은 정답일 확률이 높다는 사실을 기억하자.

2. M|Au M|Cn

Should I attach the price tags to the new merchandise before putting it on display?

(A) Yes, that would be nice, thanks.
(B) I'm sorry, but all our sales are final.
(C) It's next to the discount table.

🔴어휘 price tag 가격표 put *sth* on display ~을 진열하다
All sales are final. 교환이나 환불이 안 됩니다.

🔴해석 신상품을 진열하기 전에 가격표를 붙일까요?
(A) 네, 그러는 게 좋겠어요. 고마워요.
(B) 죄송하지만, 저희는 교환이나 환불이 안 됩니다.
(C) 할인 상품 테이블 옆에 있습니다.

🔴해설 Should(n't) I[we] ~?는 매우 자주 출제되는 제안하는 질문이며, that would be nice[great]는 매우 자주 출제되는 동의하는 대답이다. (B)는 질문의 price나 merchandise에서 연상되는 표현 all our sales are final을, (C)는 역시 price에서 연상되는 단어 discount를 들려주면서 오답을 유도하고 있다. (C)는 질문의 new merchandise와 on display에서 연상되는 대답이기도 하다.

---

3. W|Am M|Au

Would you type out the minutes from our staff meeting earlier today?

(A) Sure, I'll have them ready by the end of the day.
(B) There are several other types, too.
(C) Nearly all colleagues in the office.

🔴어휘 minutes 회의록

🔴해석 오늘 오전에 한 직원회의 회의록을 작성해 주시겠어요?
(A) 물론이죠, 오늘 중에 준비해 둘게요.
(B) 몇몇 다른 유형도 있습니다.
(C) 사무실의 거의 모든 동료들이요.

🔴해설 Sure는 제안/부탁 의문문에서 정답으로 출제되는 빈도가 가장 높은 대답이다. (B)는 질문에 나왔던 type를 반복해서 들려주면서, (C)는 staff meeting에서 연상되는 대답으로 오답을 유도하고 있다.

---

4. M|Cn W|Br

I'd like to discuss the project you've recently submitted.

(A) Our latest purchase was that projector.
(B) Not very often, it seems.
(C) Could it wait until tomorrow?

🔴어휘 projector 영사기 wait 연기되다, 미뤄지다

🔴해석 최근에 제출하신 프로젝트에 대해 의논하고 싶습니다.
(A) 가장 최근의 구매 상품은 저 영사기입니다.
(B) 그리 자주는 아닌 것 같습니다.
(C) 내일로 미뤄도 괜찮을까요?

🔴해설 (A)는 project와 발음이 비슷한 projector를 들으면서 오답임을 짐작할 수 있고, (B)는 질문 앞부분 I'd like to discuss(의논하고 싶습니다.)에 집중하면 오답인 것을 알 수 있다. 오답을 골라내면 (C)는 들을 필요도 없게 된다. 제안/부탁 의문문은 대답에 wait until이 들어 있으면 정답이다. 도저히 정답을 알 수 없을 때는 (C)처럼 반문하는 대답이 정답일 확률이 가장 높다는 사실을 기억하자.

---

5. W|Br M|Au

Should we invite more staff to attend the trade fair?

(A) We're not sure about hiring her.
(B) I don't think it's necessary.
(C) From Boston to Melbourne.

🔴어휘 invite 요청하다, 청하다 trade fair 무역 박람회

🔴해석 더 많은 직원들에게 무역 박람회에 참석하라고 요청해야 할까요?
(A) 그녀를 채용하는 건 확실하지 않습니다.
(B) 그럴 필요는 없을 것 같아요.
(C) 보스턴에서 멜버른까지요.

🔴해설 Should(n't) I[we] ~?는 매우 자주 출제되는 제안하는 질문이다. 거절하는 대답 That's not necessary.를 기억하고 정답을 선택하자. 질문 앞부분 Should we invite more staff(더 많은 직원들에게 요청해야 할까요?)에 집중하면 (A)와 (C)는 적절한 대답이 아니라는 것도 알 수 있다.

---

6. W|Am M|Au

Should we get the changes to this contract in writing?

(A) Sorry, I don't have any change.
(B) That sounds like a good idea.
(C) I'll write about that another day.

🔴어휘 in writing 서면으로 change 변경; 잔돈

🔴해석 이 계약서의 변경 사항을 서면으로 작성해 두어야겠죠?
(A) 미안합니다. 저는 잔돈이 없어요.
(B) 좋은 생각인 것 같아요.
(C) 그것에 대해서는 다음에 쓰겠습니다.

🔴해설 Should(n't) I[we] ~?는 매우 자주 출제되는 제안하는 질문이며, That sounds like a good idea.는 매우 자주 출제되는 동의하는 대답이다. (A)는 질문에 들어 있는

---

change를, (C)는 write를 반복시키면서 오답을 유도하고 있다.

7. M Cn M Au

Should we remind Ms. Colley to send us the budget report?

(A) I'm supposed to meet the reporter here.
(B) Sales projections for the second quarter.
(C) But the deadline isn't for another week.

➡️**어휘** be supposed to–V ~하기로 되어 있다 projection 예상, 추정

📘**해석** Ms. Colley에게 우리에게 예산 보고서 보내는 거 다시 한 번 알려줄까요?
(A) 여기서 기자와 만나기로 했습니다.
(B) 2사분기 예상 매출액이요.
(C) 마감 일자가 1주일 이상 남았는데요.

📗**해설** (A)는 질문에 있는 report와 발음이 비슷한 reporter를 들려주면서, (B)는 budget report에서 연상되는 단어 Sales projections로 오답을 유도하고 있다. 일반 의문문은 대답을 Yes, and / Yes, but / No, but / But으로 시작하면 항상 정답이다.

8. W Br W Am

Would you like me to place an order for additional business cards?

(A) Accounts receivable.
(B) I only use them occasionally.
(C) I'll have the salmon salad.

➡️**어휘** place an order for ~을 주문하다 accounts receivable 외상 매출금, 미수금 occasionally 가끔

📘**해석** 명함을 추가로 주문할까요?
(A) 미수금이요.
(B) 그건 가끔씩만 써요.
(C) 저는 연어 샐러드로 할게요.

📗**해설** 명함은 자주 사용하지 않기 때문에 추가로 주문할 필요가 없다고 말하는 (B)가 정답이다. (A)는 질문에 있는 order나 business에서 연상되는 단어로, (C)도 질문의 place an order에서 연상되는 대답으로 오답을 유도하고 있다.

9. W Am M Cn

Could you help me find my car keys?

(A) Where did you last put them?

(B) Ms. Carson was the keynote speaker.
(C) The doors lock automatically.

➡️**어휘** keynote speaker 기조 연설자

📘**해석** 제 자동차 열쇠 찾는 것 좀 도와주시겠어요?
(A) 마지막으로 두신 곳이 어딘데요?
(B) Ms. Carson이 기조 연설자였습니다.
(C) 문은 자동으로 잠깁니다.

📗**해설** (B)는 질문에 나오는 key가 반복되는 것을 들으면서, (C)는 연상되는 대답이 나오는 것을 들으면서 오답으로 골라낼 수 있다. 도저히 정답을 모르겠다면 (A)처럼 반문하는 대답이 정답일 확률이 가장 높다.

10. M Au W Br

Couldn't we postpone the conference until August?

(A) The hotel charges cancellation fees.
(B) Take it to the nearest post office.
(C) I thoroughly enjoyed the conference.

➡️**어휘** conference 회의, 학회 charge 부과하다, 청구하다 thoroughly 대단히, 완전히

📘**해석** 학회를 8월로 연기하면 안 될까요?
(A) 호텔 측에서 취소 수수료를 부과할 거예요.
(B) 가장 가까운 우체국으로 가져가세요.
(C) 학회는 정말 즐거웠어요.

📗**해설** 질문 앞부분 Couldn't we postpone(연기하면 안 될까요?)에 집중하면 (A)가 자연스러운 대답이라는 것을 알 수 있다. (B)와 (C)는 각각 질문에 들어 있는 post와 conference를 반복시키면서 오답을 유도하고 있다.

PART 3 Sample Questions

1–3번 문제는 다음 대화에 관한 것입니다.

여: Mr. Burgess, 이력서를 보니 이곳 Patel & Partners에서의 변호사 인턴사원 근무에 관심이 있으시네요.
남: 네, 법률 서비스 분야에서 일하는 것에 대해 되도록 많은 지식을 얻고 싶습니다. 게다가 대학에서 습득한 지식을 실행해 보기를 기대하고 있기도 하고요.
여: 음, 선발되신다면 다양한 주요 사건들을 맡아 멘토와 함께 일하시게 될 거예요. 일은 힘들지만 대부분 인턴사원들은 매우 보람 있게 여긴답니다.
남: 잘 됐네요. 저는 언제나 Patel & Partners가 하는 일을 감탄하며 바라보았거든요. 사실 언젠가는 꼭 여기서 정규직 자리를 얻고 싶습니다. 인턴사원들이 인턴 기간 이후에 채용되는 일이 흔한가요?

어휘 acquire 습득하다, 얻다 **plus** 더욱이, 게다가 **put** *sth* **into practice** ～을 실행하다 **alongside** ～와 함께 **case** 소송, 사건 **challenging** 힘든, 까다로운 **rewarding** 보람 있는 **admire** 감탄하며 바라보다 **following** ～ 후에

---

1. 화자들은 주로 무엇을 논하고 있는가?

(A) 인턴사원 근무 기회
(B) 대학교 과정
(C) 프로젝트 마감일
(D) 뉴스 기사

---

2. Patel & Partners는 어떤 유형의 사업체인가?

(A) 병원
(B) 인재 파견 회사
(C) 건축 회사
(D) 법률 사무소

---

3. 남자는 무엇에 대해 묻는가?

(A) 조사의 결과
(B) 고객 만족도
(C) 정규직 채용의 가능성
(D) 전문가를 고용하는 비용

어휘 outcome 결과 investigation 조사 likelihood 가능성

PART 3 & 4 Exercise

1 (B) **2** (D) **3** (D) **4** (B) **5** (A) **6** (D)

Questions 1 through 3 refer to the following conversation.

[M | Cn] Hello, Ms. Sapra. It's Walter Lee. [2]Have you taken a look at the first draft of the design I prepared for your newspaper advertisement?

[W | Br] Thanks for calling, Walter. [2]Yes, I think the design is coming along nicely. [1]I really appreciate how you included a photo of my shoe store instead of just the logo.

[M | Cn] I'm happy you like that idea. [3]Should I make the words "We've moved!" a bit bigger?

[W | Br] Yes, good point. Ultimately, the primary purpose of the ad is to inform people about the store's relocation.

1-3번 문제는 다음 대화에 관한 것입니다.

남: 안녕하세요, Ms. Sapra. Walter Lee입니다. 제가 신문 광고용으로 준비해 드린 디자인 초안 보셨나요?

여: 전화 주셔서 고마워요, Walter. 네, 디자인이 잘 되어 가고 있는 것 같아요. 단지 로고만 넣지 않고 저희 신발 가게의 사진까지 포함시켜주셔서 정말 감사합니다.

남: 그 아이디어가 마음에 드신다니 기쁩니다. "우리 이사했어요!"라는 문구는 조금 더 크게 해드릴까요?

여: 네, 좋은 의견이에요. 궁극적으로 광고의 주요 목적은 매장이 새 장소로 이전했다는 것을 사람들에게 알리는 것이니까요.

어휘 first draft 초안 come along (원하는 대로) 되어 가다 appreciate ～에 대해 감사하다 point 의견, 주장 ultimately 궁극적으로, 결국 primary 주된, 주요한 relocation 이전

---

1. Who most likely is the woman?

(A) A news reporter
(B) A store owner
(C) A real estate agent
(D) A photographer

해석 여자는 누구이겠는가?
(A) 뉴스 기자
(B) 상점 주인
(C) 부동산 중개업자
(D) 사진작가

---

2. What is the woman pleased about?

(A) A contract with a new client
(B) A recently published article
(C) A property's location
(D) A draft of an advertisement

어휘 publish 게재하다, 싣다 property 부동산, 건물 draft 초안
해석 여자는 무엇에 대해 만족하는가?
(A) 새 고객과의 계약
(B) 최근에 게재된 기사
(C) 건물의 위치
(D) 광고 초안

---

3. What does the man offer to do?

(A) Rearrange some furniture
(B) Expedite a service request
(C) Generate an invoice
(D) Enlarge some words

어휘 rearrange 재배열하다, 재배치하다 expedite 더 신속히 처리하다 generate 만들어 내다 invoice 명세서, 청구서 enlarge 확대하다, 확장하다

해석 남자는 무엇을 해주겠다고 제안하는가?

(A) 일부 가구를 재배치한다
(B) 서비스 요청을 더 신속히 처리한다
(C) 명세서를 작성한다
(D) 일부 문구를 확대한다

해설 1번 문제는 화자의 직업을 묻는 문제이므로 수험자는 첫 문장에서 정답을 알게 될 것이라고 예상하기 쉽다. 그러나 이례적으로 먼저 정답을 알 수 있는 문제는 2번이다. 남자가 신문 광고 디자인 초안을 보았는지 묻자(Have you taken a look at the first draft of the design I prepared for your newspaper advertisement?) 여자가 디자인이 잘 되어 가는 것 같다며(I think the design is coming along nicely.) 광고 초안에 대한 만족감을 표하고 있다. 먼저 1번 문제의 정답을 고를 준비를 하고 있다가도 이 부분이 들릴 때 2번 문제의 내용이 생각나야 한다. 내용을 암기하겠다는 생각으로 미리 읽어야 한다. 또한 정답을 고를 때는 항상 순발력이 필요하다는 사실도 잊지 말자. 바로 이어지는 문장에서 my shoe store라는 키워드를 듣고 1번 문제의 정답을 선택해야 한다. 3번 문제의 정답은 남자의 대사 중 make the words "We've moved!" a bit bigger가 패러프레이즈 되어 있는 선택지이다.

Questions 4 through 6 refer to the following telephone message.

M | Au Hello, Ms. Ellington. I just received your message about the problems you encountered with some of the fabric that we sent to your company two days ago. ⁴ ⁵I apologize for the torn material that was delivered. ⁶We'll be more than happy to visit your factory to collect the fabric that you cannot use and drop off a replacement shipment at no additional cost. We apologize once more for any inconvenience you may have experienced. We are grateful for your understanding and for your continued patronage.

4-6번 문제는 다음 전화 메시지에 관한 것입니다.

남: 안녕하세요, Ms. Ellington. 이틀 전에 저희가 귀사로 보낸 직물 중 일부에서 문제에 부딪혔다는 메시지를 방금 받았습니다. 찢어진 직물이 배송된 것에 대해 사과드립니다. 저희가 기꺼이 공장을 방문해서 사용할 수 없는 직물을 수거하고 교체 상품을 추가 비용 없이 가져다드리도록 하겠습니다. 다시 한번 겪으셨을 불편에 대해 사과드립니다. 양해와 지속적인 애용에 감사드립니다.

어휘 encounter 부딪히다, 맞닥뜨리다 fabric 직물, 천 tear 찢다 (tore-torn) collect 수거하다 drop off (사람, 짐 등을) 내려주다 replacement 대체품 shipment 수송품 grateful 고마워하는, 감사하는 patronage 애용

---

4. What is the purpose of the telephone message?

(A) To purchase clothing items
(B) To offer an apology to a customer
(C) To reschedule an appointment
(D) To inquire about a location

해석 전화 메시지의 목적은 무엇인가?

(A) 의류 제품을 구입하는 것
(B) 고객에게 사과하는 것
(C) 예약을 다시 잡는 것
(D) 어떤 장소에 대해 문의하는 것

---

5. What problem does the speaker mention?

(A) Some material is damaged.
(B) A machine is out of order.
(C) A shipment is behind schedule.
(D) Some items are out of stock.

어휘 out of order 고장 난 behind schedule 예정보다 늦은 out of stock 재고가 떨어진

해석 화자는 어떤 문제를 언급하는가?

(A) 일부 재료가 손상되었다.
(B) 기계가 고장 났다.
(C) 수송이 예정보다 늦었다.
(D) 일부 제품의 재고가 없다.

---

6. What does the speaker say he will do?

(A) Confirm some specifications
(B) Consult with a supervisor
(C) Provide a sample
(D) Send a replacement

어휘 specification 명세 (사항) consult with ～와 상의하다

해석 화자는 무엇을 하겠다고 말하는가?
(A) 명세 사항을 확인한다
(B) 상사와 상의한다
(C) 견본을 제공한다
(D) 교체 상품을 보낸다

해설 4번처럼 담화의 목적을 묻는 문제는 대부분 첫 한 두 문장에서 정답을 알 수 있다. 두 번째 문장 I apologize for the torn material that was delivered.를 들으면 고객에게 사과하기 위해 남긴 메시지임을 알 수 있다. 그런데 여기서 더 중요한 점은 5번 문제의 정답을 동시에 골라야 한다는 것이다. torn material이라는 키워드를 통해 정답을 알아내야 한다. 잊지 말자. 두 문제의 정답을 동시에 고르는 일이 원활히 되려면 읽은 문제의 내용을 기억해야 한다. 또한 모든 문제의 정답을 고를 때는 순발력이 중요하다는 사실도 잊지 말자. 바로 이어지는 문장에서 drop off a replacement shipment at no additional cost.를 듣고 6번 문제의 정답을 선택해야 한다.

Actual Test

1 (B)	**2** (D)	**3** (A)	**4** (B)	**5** (A)
6 (A)	**7** (A)	**8** (A)	**9** (B)	**10** (B)
11 (B)	**12** (A)	**13** (B)	**14** (A)	**15** (D)
16 (D)	**17** (D)	**18** (A)	**19** (D)	**20** (C)
21 (B)	**22** (B)	**23** (A)	**24** (C)	**25** (A)
26 (B)	**27** (C)	**28** (B)	**29** (B)	**30** (A)

* 정답을 맞힌 문제도 해설을 읽어보세요.

Part 1

1. M | Cn

(A) Some people are planting trees in a garden.
(B) A woman is squatting while holding a camera.
(C) A lawn is being mowed in a garden.

(D) Some people are strolling along the path.

어휘 squat 쪼그리고 앉다 lawn 잔디밭 mow (잔디를) 깎다 stroll 거닐다, 산책하다

해석 (A) 정원에서 나무를 심고 있다.
(B) 카메라를 든 채 쪼그리고 앉아 있다.
(C) 정원에서 잔디를 깎고 있다.
(D) 오솔길을 따라 산책하고 있다.

해설 앉아 있는 자세를 나타내는 동사 squat, crouch(쪼그리고 앉다), kneel(무릎을 꿇다)을 기억하고 정답을 선택하자. 나머지 선택지들은 planting, is being mowed, strolling 같은 동사들을 들으면서 오답으로 골라내야 한다.

2. W | Br

(A) He's standing on the scaffolding.
(B) He's pruning a bush next to a building.
(C) He's crossing a river.
(D) He's spreading cement with a shovel.

어휘 scaffolding (건축 공사장의) 비계 prune 가지치기하다 bush 관목 spread 펼치다

해석 (A) 비계 위에 서 있다.
(B) 건물 옆에서 관목을 가지치기하고 있다.
(C) 강을 건너고 있다.
(D) 삽으로 시멘트를 개고 있다.

해설 (A)와 (B), (C)는 각각 위치 표현 on the scaffolding, 동사 pruning, 명사 a river를 듣고 오답임을 알 수 있다. 사진은 관에서 흘러나오는 시멘트를 삽으로 개는 장면이다.

3. M | Au

(A) Some dogs are out for a walk.
(B) The man is pointing at something on the water.
(C) One of the women is photographing a structure.
(D) They're standing in shallow water.

어휘 walk 걷기, 산책 structure 구조물, 건축물 shallow 얕은

해석 (A) 개들이 산책하러 밖에 나와 있다.
(B) 물 위의 무언가를 손가락으로 가리키고 있다.
(C) 어떤 구조물의 사진을 찍고 있다.
(D) 얕은 물에 들어가 서 있다.

해설 walk는 보통 정답의 동사 키워드로 사용되지만, 드물게 명사 키워드로도 사용할 수 있다. (B)는 남자가 손가락으로 가리키는 방향을 잘못 말하고 있으며, (C)는 사진에 없는 a structure를 언급하고 있으므로 오답이다. (D)는 사람들이 서 있는 위치를 잘못 말했다.

Part 2

4. [M|Cn] [W|Am]

Why don't we hire another receptionist?

(A) In that case, try restarting it.
(B) Let's propose it to our manager.
(C) There'll be a welcome reception for her.

어휘 receptionist 접수 담당자 in that case 그런 경우에는 restart 다시 시작하다 welcome reception 환영 리셉션

해석 접수 담당자를 한 명 더 채용하는 게 어떨까요?
(A) 그런 경우에는 다시 시작해 보세요.
(B) 매니저에게 제안합시다.
(C) 그녀를 위한 환영 리셉션이 있을 거예요.

해설 Why don't we와 Let's만 듣고 정답을 알 수 있다. 제안/부탁 의문문은 역으로 제안하는 대답이 들리면 정답이다. (A)와 (C)는 각각 질문의 receptionist와 발음이 비슷한 restarting it, reception을 들려주면서 오답을 유도하고 있다.

5. [W|Am] [M|Cn]

Will you create a chart that tracks our expenses this quarter?

(A) Yeah, I'll do that right now.
(B) A quarterly charge.
(C) Try Track thirty-seven.

어휘 track 추적하다; 선로 quarterly 분기별의

해석 이번 분기 경비를 추적하는 차트를 만들어 주시겠어요?
(A) 네, 지금 바로 해 드릴게요.
(B) 분기별 요금이요.
(C) 37번 선로로 가 보세요.

해설 질문 앞부분 Will you create(만들어 주시겠어요?)에만 집중하면 자연스러운 대답을 선택할 수 있다. (B)와 (C)는 각각 질문에 있는 quarter, track을 반복해서 들려주면서 오답을 유도하고 있다.

6. [W|Am] [M|Cn]

Would you be interested in joining the organization committee?

(A) Yes, I'd be honored to.
(B) Last Thursday evening.
(C) I read an interesting article about it.

어휘 organization committee 조직 위원회

해석 조직 위원회에 참여할 의향이 있으신가요?
(A) 네, 영광입니다.
(B) 지난 주 목요일 저녁이요.
(C) 그것에 대한 흥미로운 기사를 읽었어요.

해설 제안/부탁 의문문에서 I'd be delighted[pleased/happy/glad/honored] to. 같은 대답은 매우 자주 출제되는 동의 표현이다. (C)는 질문의 interested와 발음이 비슷한 interesting을 들려주면서 오답을 유도하고 있다.

7. [M|Au] [W|Br]

How about holding a training session on the new database?

(A) I think we should.
(B) I've never been there before.
(C) I thought it went well!

어휘 training session 강습회 go well 잘 진행되다

해석 새 데이터베이스에 대한 강습회를 여는 게 어때요?
(A) 그래야 할 것 같아요.
(B) 거기는 전에 가본 적이 없습니다.
(C) 잘 진행된 것 같아요.

해설 제안하는 질문이므로 동의하는 대답이 정답이다. (B)와 (C)는 모두 질문에 있는 training session에서 연상되는 대답으로 오답을 유도하고 있다.

8. [W|Br] [W|Am]

Do you want to go to the art gallery opening on Saturday evening?

(A) Sorry, I'll be out of town.

(B) I couldn't agree more, it was outstanding.
(C) His most recent work.

> **어휘** couldn't agree more 전적으로 동감이다 outstanding 뛰어난, 걸출한

> **해석** 토요일 저녁 미술관 개관식에 가시겠어요?
> (A) 미안합니다. 저 출장 가요.
> (B) 전적으로 동감이에요. 훌륭했어요.
> (C) 그의 가장 최근 작품이요.

> **해설** Do[Don't] you want to–V ~?는 매우 자주 출제되는 제안하는 질문이며 out of town[office]은 40여 년 동안 꾸준히 정답으로 사용된 거절하는 표현이다. (B)와 (C)는 모두 질문의 the art gallery에서 연상되는 대답으로 오답을 유도하고 있다.

---

9. [M | Au] [M | Cn]

Why don't we add a vegetarian dish for the dinner?

(A) I've been there several times.
(B) It may be too late to change the menu.
(C) Yes, wash the dishes first.

> **어휘** vegetarian 야채만의, 채식의 dinner 만찬

> **해석** 만찬에 채식 요리를 추가하는 거 어때요?
> (A) 그곳은 몇 번 가 봤어요.
> (B) 메뉴를 바꾸기에는 너무 늦은 것 같은데요.
> (C) 네, 먼저 설거지를 해주세요.

> **해설** (A)는 there가 어디를 가리키는지 전혀 알 수 없고, (C)는 질문에 나왔던 dish를 반복시키면서 오답을 유도하고 있다. 오답을 잘 골라낼수록 고수가 된다!

---

10. [W | Am] [W | Br]

You'd better call the technician to repair the photocopier.

(A) Yes, we offer overnight delivery.
(B) Hopefully it won't take him too long.
(C) Ten double-sided copies, please.

> **어휘** photocopier 복사기 overnight delivery 익일 배송 hopefully 바라건대 double-sided 양면의 copy (문서) 한 부

> **해석** 복사기를 고치려면 기술자를 부르는 게 좋겠어요.
> (A) 네, 저희는 익일 배송을 제공합니다.
> (B) 그가 너무 오래 걸리지 않았으면 좋겠네요.
> (C) 양면으로 열 부 부탁합니다.

> **해설** 질문 앞부분 You'd better call the technician(기술자를 부르는 게 좋겠어요)에 집중하자. "그가 너무 오래 걸리지 않았으면 좋겠네요."는 이 제안에 동의하는 대답이다. 질문 앞부분에 집중하면 (A)는 오답임을 알 수 있으며, (C)는 질문의 –copier와 발음이 비슷한 copies를 들려주면서 오답을 유도하고 있다.

---

11. [M | Au] [W | Am]

I would like to treat our staff to a nice dinner next Friday.

(A) We waited twenty minutes for a table.
(B) We do have some money left in the budget this quarter.
(C) Does this recipe include pork?

> **어휘** treat *sb* to *sth* ~에게 ~을 대접하다

> **해석** 다음 주 금요일에 우리 직원들에게 근사한 저녁을 대접하고 싶어요.
> (A) 자리가 나기를 20분 동안 기다렸어요.
> (B) 이번 분기 예산에 남은 돈이 조금 있기는 하죠.
> (C) 이 조리법에 돼지고기가 포함되나요?

> **해설** 질문에 있는 단어에서 연상되는 표현은 오답 장치라는 사실을 기억하자. (A)와 (C)는 모두 질문의 dinner에서 연상되는 대답으로 오답을 유도하고 있다. 오답을 잘 골라낼수록 고수가 된다!

---

12. [M | Cn] [W | Br]

I think we should hire an analyst.

(A) That's not such a bad idea.
(B) Several new recruits.
(C) It seems to fit in the bottom shelf.

> **어휘** analyst 분석가 (new) recruit 신입 사원 fit in ~에 들어맞다

> **해석** 애널리스트를 고용하는 게 좋겠어요.
> (A) 그리 나쁜 생각은 아니군요.
> (B) 몇 명의 신입 사원들이요.
> (C) 맨 아래 선반에 들어갈 것 같아요.

> **해설** That's not such a bad idea.는 사실상 That's a good idea.라고 말하는 것과 같은 동의하는 대답이다. (B)는 질문의 hire에서 연상되는 대답으로 오답을 유도하고 있으며, (C)는 hire와 발음이 똑 같은 higher에서 연상되는 단어 bottom을 들려주면서 오답을 유도하고 있다.

Part 3

Questions 13 through 15 refer to the following conversation.

> **W Br** **14**Is there any way I can get on the next flight to San Diego? **13**My flight from Seoul didn't arrive on time, so I missed my connection.
>
> **M Cn** Let's see... I don't have any direct flights, but if you're willing to connect in Los angeles, there is a flight leaving in about twenty minutes.
>
> **W Br** **14**As long as it takes me to San Diego, I'll take it. My name's Tanya Bryant.
>
> **M Cn** Here's your ticket, Ms. Bryant. **15**Please hurry to Gate Eleven.

13-15번 문제는 다음 대화에 관한 것입니다.

> **여:** 샌디에이고로 가는 다음 비행 편을 탈 방법이 있을까요? 서울에서 출발한 항공편이 제시간에 도착하지 않아 연결 편을 놓쳤어요.
> **남:** 한 번 보겠습니다... 직항 편은 없지만, 로스앤젤레스에서 갈아타는 게 괜찮다면, 약 20분 후에 출발하는 비행 편이 있네요.
> **여:** 샌디에이고로 데려다주기만 한다면, 탈게요. 제 이름은 Tanya Bryant예요.
> **남:** 티켓 여기 있습니다, Ms. Bryant. 11번 게이트로 서둘러 가세요.

어휘 on time 제 시간에 connection (교통) 연결 편 direct flight 직항 편 be willing to-V 기꺼이 ~하다 connect (교통편을) 갈아타다

---

13. What is the woman's problem?

(A) She misplaced her luggage.
(B) She didn't make it to her flight in time.
(C) She left behind her airplane ticket.
(D) She has no idea where the gate is.

어휘 misplace 제자리에 두지 않다(그래서 찾지 못하다) make it to ~에 도착하다 in time 시간 맞춰, 늦지 않게 leave behind 두고 가다

해석 여자의 문제는 무엇인가?
(A) 짐 둔 곳을 찾지 못했다.
(B) 비행기 시간에 도착하지 못했다.
(C) 항공권을 두고 왔다.
(D) 게이트가 어디 있는지 모른다.

---

14. Where is the woman's final destination?

(A) San Diego
(B) Seoul
(C) Los Angeles
(D) San Francisco

해석 여자의 최종 목적지는 어디인가?
(A) 샌디에이고
(B) 서울
(C) 로스앤젤레스
(D) 샌프란시스코

---

15. What does the man tell the woman to do?

(A) Present her identification
(B) Consult a travel agent
(C) Look through her baggage
(D) Proceed to an airport gate

어휘 present 제시하다, 제출하다 identification 신분증 consult ~와 상담하다 travel agent 여행사 직원 look through ~을 뒤지다 proceed (특정 방향으로) 나아가다, 이동하다

해석 남자는 여자에게 무엇을 하라고 말하는가?
(A) 신분증을 제시한다
(B) 여행사 직원과 상담한다
(C) 짐 가방을 뒤진다
(D) 공항 게이트로 이동한다

해설 첫 문장에서 여자가 샌디에이고로 가는 비행 편에 대해 묻고 있다(Is there any way I can get on the next flight to San Diego?). 이어지는 문장 My flight from Seoul didn't arrive on time, so I missed my connection.까지 들으면 13번과 14번 문제의 정답을 동시에 알 수 있다. 이런 문제를 원활히 해결하려면 문제를 미리 읽을 때 내용을 암기하도록 노력해야 한다. 15번의 정답은 남자의 마지막 대사 Please hurry to Gate Eleven.에서 알 수 있다.

Questions 16 through 18 refer to the following conversation with three speakers.

[W Am] Sorry to bother you, but I'm wondering if either of you remember someone named César Villa. ¹⁶He worked here at the newspaper not too long ago.

[M Au] That name doesn't seem familiar to me. Why?

[W Am] ¹⁷Someone from Activa Media called today. César applied for a job there, ¹⁶and he listed our newspaper agency as his last place of employment. ¹⁷ ¹⁸They asked for a recommendation, [but I never actually worked with him].

[M Cn] César Villa? I remember César. He worked as a staff photographer with us for about a year. He had a lot of talent.

[W Am] Could you please provide the recommendation, if you don't mind?

[M Cn] Sure, I'd be happy to, but I wish he had gotten in touch with one of us directly. That's the typical procedure.

16–18번 문제는 다음 3인 대화에 관한 것입니다.

여: 성가시게 해서 미안하지만, 두 사람 중 누구든 César Villa라는 이름 기억하는지 궁금하네요. 우리 신문사에서 얼마 전에 근무했어요.

남1: 그런 이름은 익숙하지 않는데요. 왜요?

여: 오늘 Activa Media에서 누가 전화를 했어요. César가 그곳 어느 자리에 지원했는데, 우리 신문사를 마지막 근무처로 기재했대요. 추천서를 부탁하는데, 나는 실제로 그와 일해 본 적이 없어서요.

남2: César Villa라고요? César 기억나요. 한 1년 정도 우리와 함께 전속 사진 기자로 일했죠. 재주가 많았어요.

여: 괜찮다면 당신이 추천서를 제공해 주겠어요?

남2: 물론 기꺼이 할게요. 하지만 그가 우리 중 한 명에게 직접 연락했더라면 좋았을 뻔했어요. 그게 일반적인 절차잖아요.

> **어휘** name 이름을 지어주다 newspaper (agency) 신문사 list 목록에 포함시키다 staff 전속의 if you don't mind 괜찮으시다면 get in touch with ~와 연락하다 typical 일반적인

16. Where do the speakers work?

(A) At a television station
(B) At an advertising agency
(C) At an electronics store
(D) At a newspaper

> **해석** 화자들은 어디에서 근무하는가?
> (A) 텔레비전 방송국
> (B) 광고 대행사
> (C) 전자제품 매장
> (D) 신문사

17. Why did Activa Media contact the speakers' workplace?

(A) To provide a training seminar
(B) To introduce some new products
(C) To inquire about some photographs
(D) To request a reference

> **어휘** workplace 직장 reference 추천서
> **해석** Activa Media는 왜 화자들의 직장에 연락했는가?
> (A) 교육 세미나를 제공하기 위해
> (B) 신제품을 소개하기 위해
> (C) 사진에 대해 문의하기 위해
> (D) 추천서를 요청하기 위해

18. What does the woman imply when she says, "I never actually worked with him"?

(A) She cannot fulfill a request.
(B) She would rather work by herself.
(C) She is surprised a colleague is leaving.
(D) She is dissatisfied with an assignment.

> **어휘** fulfill 이행하다, 수행하다 dissatisfied 불만스러워 하는 assignment (할당된) 임무
> **해석** 여자는 "나는 실제로 그와 일해 본 적이 없어요."라고 말할 때 무엇을 암시하는가?
> (A) 요청 사항을 이행할 수 없다.
> (B) 차라리 혼자 일하고 싶다.
> (C) 동료가 그만둔다는 소식에 놀랐다.
> (D) 배정된 업무가 불만스럽다.

16번 문제의 정답은 여자의 대사에 들어 있는 here at the newspaper나 our newspaper agency 같은 키워드를 통해 알 수 있다. 여자가 Someone from Activa Media called today.라고 말할 때 17번의 정답을 고를 수 있게 준비하고 있어야 한다. 이어지는 문장 They asked for a recommendation에서 recommendation의 동의어가 reference라는 것을 알면 정답을 알아낼 수 있다. 그런데 여기서 중요한 점은 이 문장이 18번 정답의 단서가 되기도 한다는 사실이다. but I never actually worked with him.은 추천서를 써 줄 수 없다는 말이다. 문제를 미리 읽을 때 내용을 잘 기억하고 있다가 They asked for a recommendation이 두 문제 모두의 정답을 알려주고 있음을 간파하도록 하자.

Questions 19 through 21 refer to the following conversation and coupon.

W Am Dana's Café. May I help you?

M Cn Hi, I'm calling from Synergy Software. ¹⁹I'm putting together a lunch outing for my department. Can you take a reservation for thirty people?

W Am Yes. What date are you interested in?

M Cn Next Wednesday, from noon to two o'clock?

W Am OK.

M Cn Also, a few of our staff members don't eat meat. Will they be able to eat at your café?

W Am Sure. ²¹If you look at our menu, you'll find some items that have the word "healthy" in their name. Those meals don't have any meat in them. ²⁰In fact, we were voted the area's best vegetarian eatery on PinevilleRestaurants.com.

M Cn Great. Let me talk to my colleagues and get back to you.

19–21번 문제는 다음 대화와 쿠폰에 관한 것입니다.

여: Dana's Café입니다. 도와드릴까요?
남: 안녕하세요. 여기는 Synergy Software입니다. 부서 점심 야유회를 준비하고 있어요. 30명 예약 받으실 수 있나요?
여: 네. 어떤 날짜를 원하시나요?
남: 다음 주 수요일 정오부터 2시?
여: 알겠습니다.

남: 그리고 저희 직원들 중 몇 명은 고기를 먹지 않아요. 그들도 그 식당에서 식사할 수 있을까요?
여: 물론이죠. 저희 메뉴를 보시면, 이름에 '건강'이라는 단어가 들어 있는 항목이 보이실 거예요. 그 음식에는 고기가 전혀 들어가지 않습니다. 사실 저희는 PinevilleRestaurants.com에서 지역 최고의 채식 식당으로 선정되었답니다.
남: 잘됐네요. 저희 동료들과 얘기해 보고 나서 다시 연락드릴게요.

어휘 put together (행사)를 준비하다, 계획을 짜다 outing 야유회 café 카페, 식당 vote (투표로) 선출하다 eatery 식당

LUNCH SPECIALS

Valencia Fish Soup	$7
Healthy Greek Pita Sandwich	$9
Crispy Mediterranean Salad	$7
Gourmet Provence Sampler	$10

점심 특선

발렌시아 생선 수프	7달러
그리스식 건강 피타 샌드위치	9달러
지중해식 크리스피 샐러드	7달러
프로방스 고급 샘플러	10달러

어휘 pita 피타(지중해, 중동 지방의 납작한 빵) crispy 바삭바삭한 Mediterranean 지중해의 gourmet 미식가를 위한 고급의 sampler 모둠 요리

19. What type of event is the man organizing?

(A) A business seminar
(B) A client luncheon
(C) A retirement party
(D) A department outing

어휘 organize (행사를) 준비하다 luncheon 오찬
해석 남자는 어떤 유형의 행사를 준비하고 있는가?
(A) 비즈니스 세미나
(B) 고객 오찬
(C) 은퇴 파티
(D) 부서 야유회

20. What does the woman mention about the café?

(A) Large groups can be hosted in an outdoor patio.

(B) Cancellations must be made with at least 24 hours notice.

(C) It gained recognition among local diners.

(D) The menu varies according to the season.

■ 어휘 host 접대하다 patio 테라스 recognition (공로 등의) 인정 diner (식당에서) 식사하는 사람[손님] vary 서로[각기] 다르다

■ 해석 여자는 식당에 대해 무엇을 언급하는가?

(A) 대규모 단체는 야외 테라스에서 접대할 수 있다.

(B) 취소는 최소 24시간 전에 해야 한다.

(C) 지역 식당 이용객들 사이에서 인정을 받았다.

(D) 메뉴가 계절에 따라 다르다.

21. Look at the graphic. What menu item does not contain meat?

(A) The soup

(B) The sandwich

(C) The salad

(D) The sampler

■ 해석 그래픽을 보라. 어느 메뉴 품목에 고기가 들어 있지 않은가?

(A) 수프

(B) 샌드위치

(C) 샐러드

(D) 모둠 요리

■ 해설 19번 문제의 정답은 남자의 대사 I'm putting together a lunch outing for my department.에서 어렵지 않게 알아낼 수 있다. 주의가 필요한 문제는 20번과 21번 인데, 순서를 바꿔서 정답을 알려주고 있으므로 미리 읽으면서 내용을 기억해야 한다. If you look at our menu, you'll find some items that have the word "healthy" in their name. Those meals don't have any meat in them. 을 들으면서 21번의 정답을 먼저 고르자. 바로 이어지는 문장에서 20번 정답을 골라야 하므로 순발력이 필요하다는 점도 잊지 말자. we were voted the area's best vegetarian eatery on the PinevilleRestaurants.com.을 통해 이 식당이 지역 식당 이용객들의 인정을 받는 곳이라는 점을 파악할 수 있다.

Part 4

Questions 22 through 24 refer to the following announcement.

W | Br Before we wrap up this management meeting, I have an important update regarding the company's time off policy to share with you. [22]As you know, new employees are limited to a one-week vacation during their first year here. Many of our employees have expressed dissatisfaction with this policy and then left after only a few months. This means that the company has had to continuously seek and train new staff. [22] [23]So, in order to prevent new hires from leaving the company, we'll be offering two weeks off beginning next year. [24]Please ensure that your employees are informed of this change and remind them of the company policy to notify you in advance if they intend to be out of the office.

22-24번 문제는 다음 공지에 관한 것입니다.

여: 이번 운영진 회의를 마치기 전에 회사 휴가 정책과 관련하여 여러분과 공유할 중요한 최신 정보가 있습니다. 이 시다시피 신입 직원들은 입사 첫 해 동안 휴가가 1주일로 제한됩니다. 상당수의 우리 직원들이 이 정책에 대해 불만을 표하고 나서는 겨우 몇 달 만에 그만두어 버렸습니다. 이것은 회사가 계속해서 신입 직원들을 찾아서 교육해야 했다는 것을 의미합니다. 그래서 신입 사원들이 회사를 그만두는 것을 방지하기 위해 내년부터는 2주간 휴가를 제공할 예정입니다. 여러분의 직원들이 이 변경 사항을 반드시 알게 해 주시고 외근을 나가려고 하는 경우에는 여러분에게 사전에 알려야 한다는 회사 정책도 상기시켜 주시기 바랍니다.

■ 어휘 wrap up ~을 마무리짓다 management 경영진, 운영진 update 최신 정보 regarding ~에 관하여 time off 휴식, 휴가 dissatisfaction 불만 seek 찾다, 구하다 (new) hire 신입 사원 off (근무, 일을) 쉬는 ensure 반드시 ~하게 [이게] 하다 in advance 미리, 사전에

22. What is the main topic of the announcement?

(A) Updating the company Web site

(B) Granting new hires extra days off

(C) Offering advanced training to managers

(D) Enhancing the flexibility of work schedules

어휘 update 최신화하다 grant 승인하다. 허락하다 extra 추가의 advanced 고급의, 상급의 flexibility 유연성

해석 공지 사항의 주제는 무엇인가?

(A) 회사 웹 사이트 최신화하기

(B) 신입 사원들에게 추가 휴가 승인하기

(C) 관리자들에게 고급 교육 제공하기

(D) 근무 일정의 유연성 향상시키기

---

23. According to the speaker, why is a change being made?

(A) To retain existing staff members

(B) To comply with a company regulation

(C) To enhance communication

(D) To implement improved safety procedures

어휘 retain 유지하다. 보유하다 existing 기존의 comply with ~를 따르다. 준수하다 implement 시행하다

해석 화자의 말에 따르면 왜 변경이 이루어지는가?

(A) 기존 직원들을 유지하기 위해

(B) 회사 규정을 준수하기 위해

(C) 의사소통을 향상시키기 위해

(D) 개선된 안전 수칙을 시행하기 위해

---

24. What are the listeners reminded to do?

(A) Update the contact information for clients

(B) Refer to their department handbook

(C) Communicate company policies to their employees

(D) Change their passwords on a regular basis

어휘 contact information 연락처 refer to ~을 참고하다 handbook 편람, 안내서 communicate 전달하다 on a regular basis 정기적으로

해석 청자들에게 무엇을 하라고 상기시키는가?

(A) 고객들의 연락처를 갱신한다

(B) 부서 편람을 참고한다

(C) 맡고 있는 직원들에게 회사 정책을 전달한다

(D) 정기적으로 비밀번호를 변경한다

해설 이례적으로 담화의 주제가 도입부에서 드러나지 않는 고난도 문제다. 신입 직원들에게 1주일의 휴가만 주는 회사 정책이(new employees are limited to a one-week vacation during their first year here.) 2주간 휴가를 허용하는 것으로 바뀐다는 내용이다(we'll be offering two weeks off beginning next year). 문제 풀이를 더욱 어렵게 하는 것은 화자가 주제를 말하면서 정책이 변경되는 이유도 함께 언급하고 있다는 점이다(in order to prevent new hires from leaving the company). 22번과 23번 문제의 내용을 잘 기억하고 있다가 동시에 정답을 골라야 한다. so로 시작하는 문장에서 정답을 알려줄 확률이 높다는 점도 기억하자. 또한 순발력도 중요하다. 22, 23번 문제의 정답을 빨리 고르지 못하면 마지막 문장을 놓쳐서 24번을 틀릴 수 있다. Please ensure that your employees are informed of this change and remind them of the company policy to notify you in advance if they intend to be out of the office.는 변경 사항 전달과 함께 직원들이 잘 지키지 않는 정책을 상기시킬 것을 부탁하고 있다.

Questions 25 through 27 refer to the following excerpt from a meeting.

M Au Before we conclude today's managers' meeting, I have an important announcement to make. I just learned that Elsa Shadler, our chief executive officer, will be visiting next Tuesday. [25]As you know, the recent extensive renovations we completed were in line with the corporate initiative to modernize all the department stores in our chain. [25]The CEO has been touring the newly refurbished stores, and our turn is coming up next. [26]Now, [this isn't a formal inspection], so you don't need to make any special preparations. [27]But there'll be a luncheon for Ms. Shadler that day, and it'd be great if you could come and give her a warm welcome. Please let me know your availability by Friday.

25-27번 문제는 다음 회의 발췌문에 관한 것입니다.

> **남:** 오늘 관리자 회의를 마치기 전에 중요하게 공지할 사항이 있습니다. 최고 경영자 Elsa Shadler가 다음 주 화요일에 방문한다는 소식을 지금 막 들었습니다. 아시다시피 최근에 끝난 대규모의 개조 공사는 우리 체인 내의 모든 백화점을 현대화한다는 회사의 계획과 보조를 같이 한 것이었습니다. CEO는 새롭게 단장한 매장들을 순회하고 있는데, 우리 차례가 다음번으로 다가오고 있습니다. 자, 이것은 공식 시찰이 아닙니다. 그래서 여러분은 특별한 준비를 할 필요는 없습니다. 하지만 그날 Ms. Shadler를 위한 오찬 행사는 있을 예정인데, 여러분이 오셔서 따뜻하게 환영해 주시면 좋겠습니다. 금요일까지 참석 가능 여부를 알려주시기 바랍니다.

어휘 excerpt 발췌[인용] (부분) conclude 끝내다, 마치다 announcement 공지, 발표 chief executive officer(CEO) 최고 경영자 extensive 광범위한, 대규모의 in line with 보조를 같이 하는 corporate 회사의, 기업의 initiative 계획 modernize 현대화하다 tour 순회하다 refurbish 새로 꾸미다, 재단장하다 inspection 시찰, 순시 luncheon 오찬 availability 시간을 낼 수 있음

25. Why is the CEO coming for a visit?

(A) A project has been finished.
(B) A facility has been acquired.
(C) A new manager has joined the company.
(D) A sales goal has been met.

어휘 acquire 매입하다, 취득하다 meet 충족시키다

해석 CEO는 왜 방문하는가?
(A) 프로젝트가 완료되었다.
(B) 시설을 매입했다.
(C) 새 매니저가 회사에 합류했다.
(D) 영업 목표를 달성했다.

26. Why does the speaker say, "this isn't a formal inspection"?

(A) To dispute a claim
(B) To reassure employees
(C) To acknowledge a positive result
(D) To question a procedure

어휘 dispute 반박하다, 이의를 제기하다 claim 주장 reassure 안심시키다 acknowledge 감사를 표하다 question 의문[이의]을 제기하다

해석 화자는 왜 "이것은 공식 시찰이 아닙니다."라고 말하는가?
(A) 주장에 반박하기 위해
(B) 직원들을 안심시키기 위해

(C) 긍정적인 결과에 감사를 표하기 위해
(D) 절차에 의문을 제기하기 위해

27. What event have the listeners been invited to?

(A) A farewell party
(B) A groundbreaking ceremony
(C) A welcome reception
(D) A fashion show

해석 청자들은 어떤 행사에 초대받았는가?
(A) 송별 파티
(B) 기공식
(C) 환영 리셉션
(D) 패션쇼

해설 세 번째 문장에서 최근에 대규모의 개조 공사를 마무리 지었다고 말하고 있으며(the recent extensive renovations we completed), 그 다음 문장에 의하면 CEO가 개조 프로젝트가 완료된 매장들을 둘러보고 있으며, 우리 백화점이 다음 차례(The CEO has been touring the newly refurbished stores, and our turn is coming up next). 여기서 순발력을 발휘하여 재빨리 25번 문제의 정답을 고르자. 바로 이어지는 문장이 this isn't a formal inspection이다. 특별한 준비는 필요 없다고 설명하고 있으므로(so you don't need to make any special preparations.), this isn't a formal inspection의 속뜻은 "안심해."이다. 여기서 26번 문제의 정답을 고를 때도 순발력이 필요하므로 문제를 미리 읽을 때 선택지의 내용을 암기하려고 노력해야 한다. 바로 이어지는 문장에서 직원들을 오찬 행사(luncheon)에 초대하고 있는데(But there'll be a luncheon for Ms. Shadler that day, and it'd be great if you could come and give her a warm welcome.), luncheon이 27번 문제에서 welcome reception으로 바뀌어 있다.

Questions 28 through 30 refer to the following advertisement and coupon.

> W Br Come to Masayuki's Tennis Club and perfect your forehand and backhand swings with tennis pro Masayuki Hirano. [28]Mr. Hirano has fifteen years of instruction experience and is famous for winning multiple tennis championships, so beginning to advanced students can learn something valuable from him. [30]Explore our newly expanded pro shop featuring an even wider range of tennis rackets and apparel, ensuring you find the perfect gear for your game! [29]Don't forget to

check out the Syracuse Shopping Magazine for exclusive discount coupons, such as buy-one-get-one-free lessons for kids, half-priced adult classes, and free guest passes for members over the weekend. So get off the bleachers and onto the courts today!

28-30번 문제는 다음 광고와 쿠폰에 관한 것입니다.

여: Masayuki 테니스 클럽에 오셔서 테니스 프로 Masayuki Hirano와 함께 포핸드와 백핸드 스윙을 완성해 보세요. Mr. Hirano는 15년의 지도 경력이 있으며 다수의 테니스 선수권 대회에서 우승한 경력이 있기 때문에 초보부터 고급 수준의 학생들까지 누구나 귀중한 것들을 배울 수 있습니다. 새로 확장하여 훨씬 더 다양한 테니스 라켓과 의류가 있는 프로 숍을 둘러보시고 경기하기에 완벽한 장비를 꼭 찾으시기 바랍니다! Syracuse Shopping Magazine에서 아동을 위한 원 플러스 원 레슨, 반값 성인 수업, 주말 회원을 위한 비회원 무료 동반권 같은 독점 할인 쿠폰을 확인하는 것을 잊지 마세요. 자, 오늘 관람석에서 코트로 내려오세요!

어휘 instruction 가르침, 지도 championship 선수권 대회 advanced 고급의, 상급의 pro shop 프로 숍(골프나 테니스 클럽하우스의 스포츠용품 판매점) feature 특별히 포함하다 a wide range of 매우 다양한 apparel 의류 gear (특정 활동의) 장비, 복장 check out ~을 살펴보다 exclusive 독점적인, 전용의 buy-one-get-one-free 원 플러스 원의 guest pass 비회원 입장권 get off ~에서 떠나다 bleacher 관람석, 관중석 court (테니스 등의) 코트

Masayuki's
Tennis Club

50% Off

Select classes

Masayuki's
테니스 클럽

50% 할인

선별 수업

어휘 off ~에서 할인하여 select 엄선된

---

28. What is Mr. Hirano known for?

(A) He is the proprietor of several tennis clubs.

(B) He came out on top in tennis competitions.

(C) He promotes a brand of tennis gear.

(D) He exclusively instructs novice students.

어휘 proprietor 소유주 come out on top (시합에서) 이기다 competition (경연) 대회, 시합 exclusively 오로지 ~만 instruct 가르치다 novice 초보자

해석 Mr. Hirano는 무엇으로 유명한가?
(A) 몇몇 테니스 클럽의 소유주이다.
(B) 테니스 대회에서 우승했다.
(C) 테니스 장비 브랜드를 홍보한다.
(D) 초보 학생들만 가르친다.

---

29. Look at the graphic. What classes is the coupon valid for?

(A) Child classes
(B) Adult classes
(C) Advanced classes
(D) Weekend classes

어휘 valid 유효한

해석 그래픽을 보라. 쿠폰은 어느 수업에 유효한가?
(A) 아동 수업
(B) 성인 수업
(C) 고급반 수업
(D) 주말 수업

---

30. What recently changed at Masayuki's Tennis Club?

(A) The dimensions of a store
(B) The types of classes
(C) The surface of a court
(D) The date of a tournament

어휘 dimensions 넓이, 면적

해석 Masayuki 테니스 클럽에서 최근에 무엇이 변경되었는가?
(A) 상점의 면적
(B) 수업의 유형
(C) 코트의 표면
(D) 토너먼트 날짜

해설 famous for winning multiple tennis championships 라는 키워드가 들릴 때 고민하지 말고 28번의 정답을 선택하자. our newly expanded pro shop만 알아들으면 30번의 정답도 알아낼 수 있는데, 문제는 29번과 30번 문제 정답의 키워드가 순서를 바꿔서 등장하고 있다는 것이다. 문제를 미리 읽을 때 내용을 기억하도록 노력해서 원활하게 해결해 보자. 29번은 키워드 discount coupons와 half-priced adult classes가 들릴 때 그래픽을 보면서 정답을 알아낼 수 있다.

PART 1 Exercise

1 (B)　　**2** (A)

1. [M | Cn]

(A) Many passengers are standing at a bus station.
(B) Some of the riders have gotten off their motorcycles.
(C) Motorcycles are lined up at an intersection.
(D) Fuel is being pumped from a truck.

🔹어휘 bus station 버스 터미널　line up 일렬로 세우다
intersection 교차로　pump (펌프로) 퍼 올리다

🔹해석 (A) 많은 승객들이 버스 터미널에 서 있다.
(B) 일부 운전자들은 오토바이에서 내려 서 있다.
(C) 오토바이들이 교차로에 일렬로 세워져 있다.
(D) 연료가 트럭으로부터 공급되고 있다.

🔹해설 사진의 장소가 버스 터미널(a bus station)도 아니고 교차로(an intersection)도 아니므로 (A)와 (C)는 오답이다. 사진에 트럭이 보이지도 않으므로 (D)도 오답이다. 정답을 알아들을 수 있게 gotten의 발음을 연습해 보자. 미국식으로 읽을 때는 "갓 은"이라고 읽게 된다.

2. [W | Br]

(A) A dump truck is making tracks on the ground.

(B) Trucks are moving the earth.
(C) Workers are painting lines on a roadway.
(D) Vehicles have been parked in a row.

🔹어휘 dump truck 덤프트럭　track 지나간 자취, 바큇자국
earth 흙

🔹해석 (A) 덤프트럭이 땅에 바큇자국을 만들고 있다.
(B) 트럭들이 흙을 나르고 있다.
(C) 인부들이 도로에 차선을 그리고 있다.
(D) 차량들이 일렬로 주차되어 있다.

🔹해설 '지나간 자취, 바큇자국'이라는 뜻의 명사 track만 알면 정답을 선택할 수 있다. (B)는 트럭들이 무엇을 운반하고 있는지 알 수 없으므로 오답이고, (C)는 Workers만 들어도 오답임을 알 수 있다. 사진에 안 보이는 사람을 언급하고 있기 때문이다. 차량들이 주차되어 있지 않으므로 (D)도 오답이다.

PART 2 Exercise

1 (B)　　**2** (B)　　**3** (C)　　**4** (B)　　**5** (C)
6 (B)　　**7** (C)　　**8** (B)　　**9** (A)　　**10** (C)

1. [W | Am] [M | Cn]

This meal comes with a soup and salad, doesn't it?

(A) Would you like to come with me?
(B) That's right.
(C) It was delicious.

🔹어휘 come with ~이 같이 나오다[제공되다]

🔹해석 이 식사에는 수프와 샐러드가 같이 나오죠?
(A) 저와 함께 가시겠어요?
(B) 맞습니다.
(C) 맛있었어요.

🔹해설 (A)는 질문에 나온 come with를 반복시키면서, (C)는 질문의 meal에서 연상되는 단어 delicious를 들려주면서 오답을 유도하고 있다. That's right.은 Yes.라고 대답한 것과 같으므로 정답이다.

2. [M | Au] [W | Br]

Ellen hasn't heard back from the Iranian distributors, has she?

(A) To ensure an equal distribution of funds.

(B) I don't think so, no.

(C) Can you help me move these boxes?

어휘 Iranian 이란의 distributor 유통업체 distribution 분배

해석 Ellen은 이란 유통업체들로부터 답신을 받지 못했죠?

(A) 자금의 균등한 분배를 보장하기 위해서요.

(B) 네, 그런 것 같아요.

(C) 이 상자들 옮기는 것 좀 도와주시겠어요?

해설 (A)는 distributors – distribution의 유사 발음을 이용해서, (C)는 distributors와 관련이 있어 보일 수 있는 move these boxes를 들려주면서 오답을 유도하고 있다. I (don't) think so.라고 대답하면 Yes.나 No.라고 말한 것과 같으므로 정답이다.

---

3. W Am | M Au

Have the budget figures changed since we last discussed it?

(A) An informative discussion.

(B) The financial policy.

(C) Not that I'm aware of.

어휘 informative 유익한

해석 우리가 마지막으로 논의한 이후에 예산 수치가 변경되었나요?

(A) 유익한 논의요.

(B) 금융 정책이요.

(C) 제가 알기로는 아닙니다.

해설 (A)는 질문에 들어 있는 discussed와 발음이 비슷한 discussion을, (B)는 the budget figures에서 연상되는 단어 The financial policy를 들려주면서 오답을 유도하고 있다. 오답을 잘 골라내면 (C)는 들을 필요도 없다. Not that I know of.나 Not that I'm aware of. 같은 대답은 No.를 대신하는 표현으로 일상생활에서도 많이 사용된다.

---

4. M Cn | W Am

Are the textile printing machines operating again?

(A) That's an impressive rating.

(B) Not quite, but almost.

(C) No, I haven't.

어휘 textile printing 날염 rating 평점, 등급

해석 날염 기계가 다시 작동하나요?

(A) 인상적인 평점입니다.

(B) 완전하지는 않지만, 거의 다 됐어요.

(C) 아니요, 저는 안 했습니다.

해설 (A)는 질문에 나온 operating과 발음이 비슷한 rating을 들려주면서 오답을 유도하고 있으며, (C)는 질문이 Are로 시작했다는 것만 기억해도 오답임을 알 수 있다. 일반 의문문에서는 Not yet. / Not quite yet. / Not quite. 같은 No를 대신하는 대답이 들리면 정답으로 선택해야 한다.

---

5. M Cn | W Br

Wouldn't you rather meet in Conference Room 2A?

(A) It usually does.

(B) A four-o'clock meeting.

(C) It would be quieter.

어휘 would rather A (than B) (B하기 보다는 차라리) A 하겠다 [하고 싶다] conference room 회의실

해석 2A 회의실에서 만나시겠어요?

(A) 그게 보통은 그렇습니다.

(B) 4시 회의요.

(C) 거기가 더 조용하겠네요.

해설 질문 앞부분을 놓치지 말자. Wouldn't you로 시작하고 있으므로 (A) It usually does.는 정답이 될 수 없다. (B)는 질문에 들어 있는 meet in과 발음이 비슷한 meeting을 들려주면서 오답을 유도하고 있다. 오답을 잘 골라낼수록 고수가 된다!

---

6. W Br | W Am

Some of us are going out for dinner after we're done with this paperwork.

(A) Could I get this to go, please?

(B) Sorry, I have more work to do.

(C) The newspaper's on your desk.

어휘 be done with ~을 다 처리하다 to go (식당에서 먹지 않고) 가지고 갈

해석 우리 중 몇 명은 이 서류 작업이 끝나고 나서 저녁 먹으러 나갈 거예요.

(A) 이거 포장해서 가져갈 수 있을까요?

(B) 미안해요. 저는 해야 할 일이 더 있어요.

(C) 신문은 당신 책상 위에 있어요.

해설 (A)는 질문에 들어 있는 go를 반복시키고 있기도 하고, dinner에서 연상되는 표현 to go를 통해 오답을 유도하고 있기도 하다. (C)는 this paperwork와 발음이 비슷한 단어 newspaper를 듣고 오답임을 짐작할 수 있다. 오답을 잘 골라낼수록 고수가 된다!

7. W Am M Cn

Why is the train so late?

(A) For about an hour and a half.
(B) I'll give you a ride to the station.
(C) Should we take a bus instead?

🔹어휘 give *sb* a ride ~를 차에 태워 주다

🔹해석 기차가 왜 이렇게 늦죠?
(A) 약 한 시간 반 동안이요.
(B) 제가 역까지 태워 드릴게요.
(C) 대신 버스를 탈까요?

🔹해설 (A)는 기간을 말하고 있으므로 How long ~?에 대한 대답으로 알맞다. (B)는 질문에 들어 있는 train과 late에서 연상되는 대답으로 오답을 유도하고 있다. 오답을 잘 골라낼수록 고수가 된다! 도저히 정답을 알 수 없을 때는 (C)와 같이 반문하는 대답이 가장 확률이 높다는 사실을 기억하자.

8. W Br M Au

Don't we need a password to log on to the computer?

(A) Now we have a new logo.
(B) Yes, but I can't remember it.
(C) She's in the computer lab.

🔹어휘 lab (=laboratory) 실습실

🔹해석 컴퓨터에 로그온 하려면 비밀번호가 있어야 하지 않나요?
(A) 이제는 새 로고가 있습니다.
(B) 네, 하지만 기억이 안 나네요.
(C) 그녀는 컴퓨터 실습실에 있어요.

🔹해설 (A)는 질문의 log on과 발음이 비슷한 logo를, (C)는 computer를 반복시키면서 오답을 유도하고 있다. 일반 의문문은 Yes, and[but] / (No), but으로 시작하는 대답이 들리면 다 정답이다.

9. M Cn W Am

I have no idea when the design workshop is.

(A) Check with Mr. Wayne.
(B) It's extremely attractive.
(C) About this quarter's sales figures.

🔹어휘 sales figures 매출액

🔹해석 디자인 워크숍이 언제인지 모르겠군요.
(A) Mr. Wayne에게 확인해 보세요.
(B) 정말 멋지네요.

(B) 이번 분기 매출액에 대해서요.

🔹해설 어떤 질문이든 모른다고 대답하면 거의 다 정답이다. Day 01에 정리되어 있는 "몰라." 유형의 대답들을 암기하자. 'Check with + 사람'이나 'Let me check ~' 같은 대답은 매우 자주 출제된다. (B)는 질문에 나온 design에서 연상되는 단어 attractive로 오답을 유도하고 있다.

10. W Br M Au

The commercial for our new line of green tea is almost finished, isn't it?

(A) The yearly assessment.
(B) The supermarket down the street.
(C) The studio had to start over.

🔹어휘 commercial 광고 방송 line 제품군 assessment 평가 down the street 길 아래쪽의 start over 다시 시작하다

🔹해석 새 녹차 제품군의 광고는 거의 다 되었죠?
(A) 연례 평가요.
(B) 길 아래에 있는 슈퍼마켓이요.
(C) 스튜디오에서 처음부터 다시 시작했어요.

🔹해설 스튜디오에서 촬영을 처음부터 다시 시작했다는 대답이 끝나려면 아직 멀었다는 뜻이므로 정답이다.

PART 3 Sample Questions

1–3번 문제는 다음 대화에 관한 것입니다.

> **여:** 다음 주 토요일에 서빙할 종업원을 추가로 배치해야 할 것 같아요. 이웃한 경기장에서 배구 시합이 있고, 끝나고 나면 식사하기 위해 큰 인파가 몰려들 거예요.
> **남:** 당연하죠. 저녁 시간에 서빙 할 사람이 최소 세 명은 있어야 해요.
> **여:** 음, Akiko와 Henry는 이미 일정이 잡혀 있는데, Ramon이 주간 근무를 하네요. 초과 근무를 조금 할 수 있을지 알아볼게요.

🔹어휘 arrange for ~을 준비하다, 마련하다 wait staff (식당) 종업원 shift 교대 근무

1. 화자들은 어디에서 일하겠는가?

(A) 음식점
(B) 운동 시설
(C) 운동 경기장
(D) 숙박 시설

2. 화자들은 무엇을 의논하고 있는가?

    (A) 스포츠 행사 참석하기

    (B) 평소보다 많은 고객들 대비하기

    (C) 리모델링 프로젝트 준비하기

    (D) 새 장소로 확장하기

어휘 organize (행사를) 준비하다

---

3. 여자는 Ramon에게 무엇을 하라고 요구할 것인가?

    (A) 지시 사항을 제공한다

    (B) 가격 견적을 요청한다

    (C) 추가 근무를 한다

    (D) 시범 설명을 한다

어휘 directions 명령, 지시 price quote 가격 견적 present 보여주다, 제시하다 demonstration 시범 설명

PART 3 & 4 Exercise

1 (C)　**2** (C)　**3** (B)　**4** (A)　**5** (B)　**6** (C)

Questions 1 through 3 refer to the following conversation.

M Cn Hi, Margot. ¹My supervisor on the technical support team just reminded me about the new employee orientation next week. I'm still responsible for leading the hands-on training, correct?

W Br That's correct.

M Cn And all of my sessions meet in the afternoon?

W Br Right. ²Here's the complete orientation schedule - take a minute to look it over.

M Cn Sure thing.

W Br Great. Just one more thing - ³you'll want to coordinate your hands-on activities with the morning classroom training modules led by Ms. Cho. It might be helpful to meet her briefly to get an overview of the classroom material.

M Cn Terrific. I'll get it done today.

1-3번 문제는 다음 대화에 관한 것입니다.

남: 안녕, Margot. 우리 기술 지원 팀장님이 방금 다음 주에 있을 신입사원 오리엔테이션에 대해 다시 한 번 얘기하더라고요. 실습 교육 진행은 여전히 제가 담당하는 거 맞죠?

여: 맞아요.

남: 제가 맡은 시간은 모두 오후에 열리는 것이고요?

여: 그렇죠. 오리엔테이션 전체 일정표 여기 있어요. 잠깐 시간 내서 살펴보세요.

남: 알겠어요.

여: 좋아요. 한 가지만 더. 실습 활동을 Ms. Cho가 진행하는 오전 강의실 교육 과목과 맞게 조율하고 싶을 거예요. 그녀를 잠깐 만나서 강의 자료에 대한 전체적인 설명을 들어보는 게 도움이 될 것 같네요.

남: 그게 좋겠어요. 오늘 중에 할게요.

어휘 supervisor 관리자 hands-on 실습의 session (특정한 활동을 위한) 시간 meet (모임 등이) 열리다 look over ~을 살펴보다 coordinate 조화시키다 module 교과목 briefly 잠시 overview 개념, 개관 terrific 멋진, 훌륭한

---

1. In what department does the man most likely work?

    (A) Human Resources

    (B) Product Development

    (C) Technical Support

    (D) Building Maintenance

해석 남자는 어느 부서에서 근무하겠는가?

    (A) 인사부

    (B) 제품개발부

    (C) 기술지원부

    (D) 건물관리부

---

2. What does the woman give the man?

    (A) An employee handbook

    (B) A job application

    (C) A training schedule

    (D) A feedback questionnaire

어휘 handbook 편람, 안내서 questionnaire 설문지

해석 여자는 남자에게 무엇을 주는가?

    (A) 직원 편람

    (B) 입사 지원서

    (C) 교육 일정표

    (D) 피드백 설문지

3. What does the woman suggest the man to do?

(A) Secure a conference room
(B) Discuss plans with a colleague
(C) Reschedule a workshop
(D) Update a software program

conference room 회의실 secure 확보하다, 획득하다

여자는 남자에게 무엇을 하라고 제안하는가?
(A) 회의실을 확보한다
(B) 동료와 계획에 대해 의논한다
(C) 워크숍 일정을 다시 잡는다
(D) 소프트웨어 프로그램을 업데이트한다

대화가 시작되자마자 나오는 My supervisor on the technical support team에서 1번 문제의 정답을 알 수 있다. 2번 문제의 정답은 여자의 대사 Here's the complete orientation schedule에서 알 수 있는데, orientation이 선택지에서 training으로 바뀌어 있다. 3번은 고난도 문제다. 여자의 마지막 대사를 이해해야 한다. 오전에 강의실에서 진행되는 수업 내용과 오후에 있을 실습 교육이 조화를 이루어야 하므로(to coordinate your hands-on activities with the morning classroom training modules), Ms. Cho 를 만나서 강의실에서 사용할 자료에 대한 전체적인 설명을 들어보라고 조언하고 있으므로(to meet her briefly to get an overview of the classroom material) 이 부분을 요약하는 (B) Discuss plans with a colleague가 정답이다.

Questions 4 through 6 refer to the following talk.

[W|Am] ⁴OK, before you start serving food, I need to inform you that the restaurant is a bit understaffed tonight. ⁵Rajesh called me this afternoon to let me know that he has a cold. So I'm requesting each of you to be in charge of one additional table tonight. ⁶Please also remember to tell each table of guests about our new menu special, which features a rice dish with assorted grilled vegetables. I believe it'll gain popularity since many of our customers have been asking for more vegetarian options. That's it for tonight.

4-6번 문제는 다음 담화에 관한 것입니다.

여: 자, 음식 서빙을 시작하기 전에, 오늘 저녁에는 식당에 약간 인원이 부족하다는 점을 알려드려야겠습니다. Rajesh가 오후에 전화로 감기에 걸렸다고 알려 왔거든요.

그래서 여러분 각각에게 오늘 저녁에는 테이블을 하나씩 더 맡아 달라고 요청하는 바입니다. 또한 각 테이블의 고객들에게 새 스페셜 메뉴에 대해 말하는 것도 잊지 말기 바랍니다. 스페셜 메뉴에는 갖가지 구운 채소를 곁들인 밥 요리가 포함되죠. 상당수의 고객들이 더 많은 채식 옵션을 요구해 왔기 때문에 인기를 얻을 거로 생각합니다. 오늘 저녁에는 여기까지입니다.

understaffed 인원이 부족한 in charge of ~을 맡은[담당하는] feature 특별히 포함하다 assorted 여러 가지의, 갖은 grilled (그릴에) 구운

4. What kind of business does the speaker work for?

(A) A restaurant
(B) A grocery store
(C) A furniture store
(D) A gym

화자는 어떤 사업체에서 근무하는가?
(A) 식당
(B) 식료품 가게
(C) 가구 매장
(D) 헬스클럽

5. Why does the speaker assign extra work to the listeners?

(A) A deadline is fast approaching.
(B) One of the employees is unwell.
(C) A large number of customers are expected.
(D) Equipment needs to be unpacked.

assign 맡기다, 배정하다 extra 추가의 unwell 몸이 편치 않은 unpack (짐을) 풀다

화자는 왜 청자들에게 추가로 업무를 맡기는가?
(A) 마감 기한이 얼마 남지 않았다.
(B) 직원 중 한 명의 몸이 안 좋다.
(C) 고객 수가 많을 것으로 예상된다.
(D) 장비를 포장에서 꺼내야 한다.

6. What does the speaker ask listeners to tell customers about?

(A) Changed business hours
(B) Membership cards
(C) A special dish
(D) A holiday sale

해석 화자는 청자들이 고객들에게 무엇에 대해 말할 것을 요구하는가?
(A) 바뀐 영업시간
(B) 회원 카드
(C) 특별 요리
(D) 휴일 할인

해설 4번 문제는 화자가 일하는 장소를 묻고 있다. 장소에 관한 질문은 첫 한두 문장만 듣고 정답을 고를 수 있게 준비해야 한다. 첫 문장에서 before you start serving food를 듣자마자 정답을 선택하자. 5번은 requesting each of you to be in charge of one additional table이 질문에서 assign extra work to the listeners로 패러프레이즈 되어 있음을 간파해야 한다. 직원들에게 테이블을 하나씩 더 맡아서 서빙해줄 것을 요구하는 이유로 Rajesh가 감기로 출근할 수 없다는 사실을 언급하고 있는데(he has a cold), 선택지에 있는 unwell이라는 단어의 뜻을 알면 정답을 알 수 있다. 5번 문제의 정답을 고를 때는 순발력이 필요하다. 바로 이어지는 문장 Please also remember to tell each table of guests about our new menu special을 듣고 6번의 정답을 골라야 하기 때문이다.

Actual Test

1 (B)	**2** (C)	**3** (C)	**4** (A)	**5** (C)
6 (A)	**7** (B)	**8** (B)	**9** (A)	**10** (C)
11 (B)	**12** (C)	**13** (A)	**14** (C)	**15** (D)
16 (D)	**17** (B)	**18** (B)	**19** (D)	**20** (C)
21 (B)	**22** (A)	**23** (D)	**24** (D)	**25** (C)
26 (A)	**27** (B)	**28** (B)	**29** (D)	**30** (C)

* 정답을 맞힌 문제도 해설을 읽어보세요.

Part 1

1. M | Au

(A) A car is passing through a gate.
(B) A motorcycle has been parked beside a curb.
(C) Bushes are being trimmed in the garden.
(D) Crops are growing in the field.

어휘 beside a curb 길가에 trim (깎아) 다듬다, 손질하다 crop (농)작물

해석 (A) 자동차가 정문을 통과하고 있다.
(B) 오토바이가 길가에 주차되어 있다.
(C) 정원에서 관목을 다듬고 있다.
(D) 들판에서 농작물이 자라고 있다.

해설 (A)와 (D)는 A car, Crops, the field 같은 사진에 없는 사물이 언급되는 것을 들으면서 오답으로 골라낼 수 있다. (C)는 동작을 나타내는 진행 시제 수동태이므로 사진에 사람이 있어야 정답이 될 수 있다. 정답을 맞히려면 beside a curb(길가에) 같은 위치 표현을 알고 있어야 한다.

2. W | Am

(A) A man is rowing a boat across the water.
(B) Some small boats are floating on the water.
(C) Some small boats have been pulled onto the shore.
(D) Some boats are docked at a pier.

어휘 row 노[배]를 젓다 float (물에) 뜨다 shore 해안, 해변 dock 부두에 대다 pier 부두

해석 (A) 배를 저어 물을 건너고 있다.
(B) 작은 배 몇 척이 물 위에 떠 있다.
(C) 작은 배 몇 척을 해변으로 끌어 올려놓았다.
(D) 배 몇 척이 부두에 정박해 있다.

해설 (A)는 A man만 듣고도 오답으로 골라낼 수 있다. 물론 동사 rowing은 다른 문제의 정답을 맞히기 위해 알고 있어야 한다. (B)에 있는 floating과 (D)에 있는 docked at a pier 같은 표현들도 잘 공부해 두고, 이 문제에서는 오답을 골라내는 데 사용하자.

3. [M｜Cn]

(A) A row of boats is waiting for tourists on the dock.
(B) A swimmer is diving into the water.
(C) A group is paddling a boat along the waterfront.
(D) Several boats are competing in a race.

🔹어휘 dock 부두 dive (물 속으로) 뛰어들다 paddle 노를 젓다
waterfront 해안가

🔹해석 (A) 부두에서 배들이 일렬로 관광객들을 기다리고 있다.
(B) 물속으로 뛰어들고 있다.
(C) 해안가를 따라 배를 저어 가고 있다.
(D) 배 몇 척이 경주를 하고 있다.

🔹해설 (A)와 (B)는 각각 A row of boats, A swimmer를 통해 오답으로 골라낼 수 있다. (D)는 사진으로 판단할 수 없는 내용이므로 오답이다. paddling이 무슨 뜻인지 알고 있으면 정답을 선택할 수 있다.

Part 2

4. [W｜Am] [M｜Au]

I'll lose my registration fee if I can't attend the conference, right?

(A) I'm afraid so.
(B) Just past the bridge, on the right.
(C) Have you checked the lost and found?

🔹어휘 conference 회의, 학회 past (위치상으로 ~을) 지나서
lost and found 분실물 보관소

🔹해석 학회에 참석하지 못하면 등록비는 그냥 버리는 거죠?
(A) 유감스럽지만 그런 것 같습니다.
(B) 바로 다리 지나서 오른쪽이요.
(C) 분실물 보관소는 확인해 보셨어요?

🔹해설 질문 앞부분 I'll lose my registration fee(등록비는 그냥 버리는 거죠?)에 집중하면 자연스러운 대답을 알 수 있다. (B)는 질문 끝에 있는 right을 반복시키면서, (C)는 질문에 나온 lose의 과거형인 lost를 들려주면서 오답을 유도하고 있다.

5. [W｜Br] [W｜Am]

That theater is known for selling out quickly, isn't it?

(A) I prefer musicals.
(B) Our seats were in the front row.
(C) True, so let's get our tickets as soon as possible.

🔹어휘 sell out 다 팔리다, 매진되다

🔹해석 저 극장은 금방 매진되기로 유명하죠?
(A) 저는 뮤지컬을 선호해요.
(B) 우리 좌석은 앞줄에 있었어요.
(C) 맞아요, 그러니까 되도록 빨리 티켓을 구합시다.

🔹해설 (A)와 (B)는 모두 질문에 들어 있는 theater에서 연상되는 대답으로 오답을 유도하고 있다. 일반 의문문은 You're right. / That's right. / That's true. 같은 Yes를 대신하는 표현이 들리면 정답으로 선택하자.

6. [W｜Am] [M｜Cn]

I don't think we can afford to start the store renovations yet.

(A) That's not what Mateo said.
(B) Yes, it's attracting more shoppers.
(C) The automated checkout counters.

🔹어휘 can afford to-V (시간, 금전적으로) ~할 여유가[형편이] 되다 attract 끌어들이다 automate 자동화하다
checkout counter 계산대

🔹해석 아직은 우리가 매장 개조 공사를 시작할 만한 여유가 없는 것 같아요.
(A) Mateo는 그렇게 말하지 않던데요.
(B) 네, 더 많은 쇼핑객들을 끌어들이고 있어요.
(C) 자동화된 계산대요.

🔹해설 본 책에 정리되어 있는 Yes/No를 대신하는 표현들을 열심히 따라 읽어보자. That's what the memo says. 같은 표현을 익혀 두었다면 That's not what Mateo said.도 잘 들릴 것이다. (B)와 (C)는 각각 질문의 store에서 연상되는 단어 shoppers와 checkout counters를 들려주면서 오답을 유도하고 있다.

7. [M｜Cn] [W｜Am]

I thought the professional development workshop was really helpful.

(A) I'd be happy to help out.
(B) That was my experience, too.
(C) Sure, let me take care of it.

🔹어휘 professional development 전문성 개발

해석 전문성 개발 워크숍이 정말 도움이 된 것 같아요.
(A) 기꺼이 도와드리겠습니다.
(B) 저에게도 그랬어요.
(C) 물론이죠, 제가 처리할게요.

해설 (A)는 질문에서 나온 helpful과 발음이 비슷한 help out 을 들려주면서 오답을 유도하고 있다. (C)처럼 Sure로 대답하는 문장이 오답인 경우는 매우 드문데, 이 문제 는 예외적인 경우다. 질문을 이해하지 못한 채 helpful 의 help만 알아들은 수험생이 도와달라는 부탁으로 짐 작하고 선택하라고 만든 대답이다. 고난도 문제도 해결 할 수 있게 받아쓰기 연습을 성실하게 해두자.

---

8. [M | Cn] [M | Au]

Aren't you attending the employee awards banquet tomorrow?

(A) The nomination deadline has passed.
(B) That event's next week.
(C) Three hundred people attended.

어휘 banquet 연회, 만찬 nomination 지명, 추천 deadline 기한

해석 내일 직원 시상식 연회에 참석하지 않으실 건가요?
(A) 후보 추천 기한이 지났습니다.
(B) 그 행사는 다음 주잖아요.
(C) 300명이 참석했습니다.

해설 (A)는 질문에 나오는 employee awards에서 연상되는 단어 nomination으로, (C)는 동사 attend를 반복해서 들 려주면서 오답을 유도하고 있다. 오답을 잘 골라낼수록 고수가 된다!

---

9. [W | Am] [M | Au]

The number of subscribers for our magazine has declined recently.

(A) There's room in the budget for additional advertising.
(B) The monthly membership fee is twenty dollars.
(C) There are seven folders on the table.

어휘 room 여유; 공간

해석 최근에 우리 잡지 구독자 수가 감소했어요.
(A) 예산에 추가 광고를 위한 여유가 있어요.
(B) 월 회비는 20달러입니다.
(C) 테이블에 폴더가 7개 있어요.

해설 (B)는 질문에서 나오는 subscribers for our magazine 에서 연상되는 단어 monthly membership fee를, (C)는 The number of에서 연상되는 단어 seven을 들려주면 서 오답을 유도하고 있다.

---

10. [W | Br] [M | Au]

Can you cover my shift on Tuesday?

(A) The logistics department.
(B) This cover's unnecessarily large.
(C) I'm already working overtime.

어휘 cover 떠맡다, 책임지다; 덮개 shift 교대 근무 logistics 물류 관리 unnecessarily 불필요하게, 쓸데없이 overtime 초과 근무

해석 화요일에 나 대신 근무해 줄 수 있겠어요?
(A) 물류 관리 부서요.
(B) 이 덮개는 불필요하게 크네요.
(C) 저는 이미 초과 근무를 하고 있어요.

해설 Day 04에서 공부한 제안/부탁 의문문의 동의/거절 표 현을 기억하자. already가 들어가는 문장은 다 거절하 는 대답으로 정답이다. (A)는 질문에 나오는 cover my shift에서 연상되는 대답으로, (B)는 cover를 반복해서 들려줌으로서 오답을 유도하고 있다.

---

11. [W | Br] [M | Cn]

I think I have this conference room reserved.

(A) When did it take place?
(B) I'm so sorry. I'll be out shortly.
(C) A hotel in the center of town.

어휘 conference room 회의실 reserve 예약하다 shortly 얼마 안 가서, 곧

해석 이 방은 제가 예약해 놓은 것 같은데요.
(A) 그런 일이 언제 있었죠?
(B) 죄송합니다. 금방 나갈게요.
(C) 시내 중심가에 있는 호텔이요.

해설 (A)와 (C)는 모두 질문에 들어 있는 conference에서 연 상되는 대답으로 오답을 유도하고 있다. 다른 사람이 방을 예약했다는 말을 들었으므로 금방 나가겠다고 대 답하는 게 자연스럽다.

---

12. [W | Am] [W | Br]

There isn't any more space at the Freiburg warehouse.

(A) Only a few kilometers from the main highway.
(B) Yes, we can make a delivery on Friday.
(C) I actually asked about the one in Offenburg.

어휘 warehouse 창고 make a delivery 배달하다

해석 Freiburg 창고에는 더 이상 공간이 없어요.
　　(A) 주요 고속도로에서 겨우 몇 킬로미터 떨어져 있습니다.
　　(B) 네, 금요일에 배송해 드릴 수 있습니다.
　　(C) 실은 제가 Offenburg에 있는 창고에 대해 물었거든요.

해설 질문 앞부분 There isn't any more space(더 이상 공간이 없어요.)에 집중하면 (A)와 (B)는 모두 오답임을 알 수 있다. 또한 (A)는 질문 맨 끝에 나오는 warehouse에서 연상되는 대답으로, (B)는 Freiburg와 발음이 비슷한 Friday를 들려주면서 오답을 유도하고 있기도 하다. 질문 앞부분에 집중하고, 오답을 골라내는 것이 가장 중요한 기술이다.

Part 3

Questions 13 through 15 refer to the following conversation.

[W | Br] ¹³OK, Ahmed, here's the problem. Over the last month, we haven't had as many customers as we had last year at this time. We must find solutions to attract more people to the restaurant. Could you share any suggestions you may have as our head chef?

[M | Au] ¹⁴Well, how about organizing a discount dining week where all entrées are offered at a reduced price? ¹⁵I'll come up with some recipes for dishes that are not too expensive to make.

[W | Br] That's a good idea. ¹⁵Please go ahead and prepare those, but I'd like to sample them first before we make a decision about including them on the menu.

13-15번 문제는 다음 대화에 관한 것입니다.

여: 자, Ahmed, 문제가 있어요. 지난 한 달 동안 작년 이맘때만큼 손님이 많지 않았어요. 식당에 더 많은 사람들을 끌기 위한 해결책을 찾아야 해요. 주방장으로서 제안이 있으면 공유해 주겠어요?
남: 음, 모든 앙트레 메뉴가 할인가로 제공되는 할인 식사 주간을 준비해 보면 어떨까요? 만들기가 너무 비싸지 않은 요리로 조리법을 생각해 볼게요.

여: 좋은 생각이에요. 진행해서 준비해 보세요. 하지만 메뉴에 포함시키는 것에 대해서는 결정하기 전에 먼저 맛을 좀 보고 싶어요.

어휘 attract 끌어들이다 organize 조직하다, 준비하다 dining 식사 entrée 앙트레(식당이나 만찬의 주요리) come up with (해답을) 찾아내다, 내놓다 sample 맛보다, 시식하다

13. What problem does the woman mention?

　(A) **Business is unusually slow.**
　(B) A restaurant received negative feedback.
　(C) There is a shortage of employees.
　(D) There has been no renewal of the lease.

어휘 unusually 이례적으로 slow 부진한, 경기가 나쁜 shortage 부족 renewal 갱신 lease 임대차 계약

해석 여자는 어떤 문제를 언급하는가?
　(A) 사업이 이례적으로 부진하다.
　(B) 식당이 부정적인 피드백을 받았다.
　(C) 직원이 부족하다.
　(D) 임대차 계약이 갱신되지 않았다.

14. What does the man suggest?

　(A) Providing outdoor dining
　(B) Relocating to a larger space
　(C) **Lowering prices**
　(D) Catering for business functions

어휘 relocate to ~로 이전하다, 이동하다 lower 내리다, 낮추다 cater 출장 뷔페를 제공하다 function 행사

해석 남자는 무엇을 갱신하는가?
　(A) 야외 식사 제공하기
　(B) 더 큰 공간으로 이전하기
　(C) 가격 낮추기
　(D) 비즈니스 행사에 출장 뷔페 제공하기

15. What does the woman ask the man to do?

　(A) Recruit an assistant
　(B) Organize a training session
　(C) Prepare for an inspection
　(D) **Create some food samples**

어휘 recruit 모집하다, 뽑다 assistant 조수, 보조원 training session 교육 (과정) inspection 시찰, 검열

■해석■ 여자는 남자에게 무엇을 하라고 요구하는가?
(A) 보조원을 뽑는다
(B) 교육을 준비한다
(C) 검열에 대비한다
(D) 음식 샘플을 만든다

■해설■ 여자가 대화를 시작하면서 문제가 있다고 말하고 있다(here's the problem). 작년 이맘때만큼의 고객 수를 확보하지 못했다는 것이므로(Over the last month, we haven't had as many customers as we had last year at this time.) 13번 문제는 이 부분을 패러프레이즈 한 선택지를 정답으로 골라야 한다. 해결책으로 남자가 제안한 것은 음식 가격을 낮추어 판매하는 할인 식사 주간인데, discount나 reduced price 같은 키워드만 알아들어도 14번의 정답을 알 수 있다. 여자는 남자의 아이디어에 찬성하면서 할인 제공할 요리를 준비해 보라고 지시하는데(Please go ahead and prepare those), 메뉴에 포함시키기 전에 시식을 먼저 하고 싶다고 했으므로(but I'd like to sample them first), 여기서 15번의 정답을 선택하면 된다. but으로 시작하는 문장에는 대부분 정답의 키워드가 들어 있다는 사실도 기억해 두자.

Questions 16 through 18 refer to the following conversation.

[M|Au] Linda! [16]You're still at your desk? I thought you were volunteering at our company's fund-raising event today.

[W|Am] Well, [I volunteered last year], [16]and now I'm addressing the delays in some of our translation projects this month.

[M|Au] Oh, I'm sorry to hear that. Can you tell me what happened?

[W|Am] [17]A group of clients are frustrated that they didn't receive their translations on time, and I'm feeling nervous about figuring out how to make up for the inconvenience.

[M|Au] I understand. Well, I have confidence in your ability to handle this. You've dealt with similar challenges in the past. I have to get to the fund-raiser now, [18]but I'll bring this problem up at our staff meeting tomorrow so that it doesn't happen again.

16–18번 문제는 다음 3인 대화에 관한 것입니다.

남: Linda! 아직도 자리에 있어요? 오늘 회사 기금 마련 행사에서 자원봉사 하는 줄 알았는데요.

여: 음, 자원봉사는 작년에 했고요, 지금은 이번 달 번역 프로젝트 중 일부가 지연된 걸 어떻게 할지 고심하고 있어요.

남: 아, 안 됐네요. 무슨 일인지 말해줄 수 있어요?

여: 몇몇 고객들이 제때 번역물을 받지 못해서 불만이 있는데요, 불편에 대해 보상할 방법을 생각해 내는 게 걱정이에요.

남: 알겠어요. 자, 나는 당신에게 이 문제를 해결할 능력이 있다고 믿어요. 전에도 비슷한 어려움을 다루어 봤잖아요. 지금은 내가 기금 마련 행사장에 가야 하는데, 이런 문제가 다시 생기지 않도록 내일 직원회의에서 얘기할게요.

■어휘■ fund-raising 기금 마련 address 고심하다, 다루다 translation 번역(물) frustrate 좌절감을 주다, 불만스럽게 만들다 on time 시간을 어기지 않고, 정각에 nervous 불안한, 초조한, 긴장한 figure out ~을 이해하다, 알아내다 make up for ~에 대해 보상하다 inconvenience 불편, 애로 confidence 신뢰, 확신 handle 처리하다 deal with (dealt-dealt) ~을 다루다, 처리하다 challenge 과제, 난제 fund-raiser 기금 마련 행사 bring up (화제를) 꺼내다

---

16. What does the woman imply when she says, "I volunteered last year"?

(A) She can aid in the training of other volunteers.

(B) She takes pride in her volunteer work.

(C) She did not have a good time at the event last year.

(D) She has no plans to be present at the event.

■어휘■ aid 돕다 take pride in ~에 대해 자부심이 있다 present 참석한, 출석한

■해석■ 여자는 "자원봉사는 작년에 했고요"라고 말할 때 무엇을 암시하는가?

(A) 다른 자원봉사자들의 교육을 도울 수 있다.

(B) 자원봉사 한 것에 대해 자부심이 있다.

(C) 작년 행사는 즐겁지 않았다.

(D) 행사에 참석하지 않을 계획이다.

17. What is the woman nervous about?

(A) Delivering a speech
(B) Responding to customer complaints
(C) Translating a complex document
(D) Assuming a new position

> **어휘** complex 복잡한 assume (직책, 임무 등을) 맡다

> **해석** 여자는 무엇에 대해 불안해하는가?
> (A) 연설하는 것
> (B) 고객의 불만에 응대하는 것
> (C) 복잡한 문서를 번역하는 것
> (D) 새 지위를 맡는 것

---

18. What does the man say he will do tomorrow?

(A) Reassign certain tasks
(B) Discuss an issue at a meeting
(C) Get ready to provide some feedback
(D) Conduct some preliminary research

> **어휘** reassign 재배치하다, 재배정하다 conduct (특정한 활동을) 하다 preliminary 예비의

> **해석** 남자는 내일 무엇을 하겠다고 말하는가?
> (A) 특정 업무를 재배정한다
> (B) 회의에서 사안을 논의한다
> (C) 피드백을 제공할 준비를 한다
> (D) 예비 조사를 수행한다

> **해설** 남자가 회사 기금 마련 행사에서 자원봉사를 하고 있을 줄 알았던 여자가 사무실에 있는 이유를 궁금해 하자(You're still at your desk? I thought you were volunteering at our company's fund-raising event today.) 자원봉사는 작년에도 했고(I volunteered last year), 지금은 다른 문제를 처리해야 한다고 대답하고 있으므로(and now I'm addressing the delays in some of our translation projects this month.), 여자는 올해 기금 마련 행사에 참석하지 않을 계획이다. 여기서 16번 문제의 정답을 선택하자. 여자가 불안해하는 이유는 번역물을 늦게 받은 고객들이 불만을 품자, 보상 방안을 마련하는 문제가 고민이기 때문이다(A group of clients are frustrated that they didn't receive their translations on time, and I'm feeling nervous about figuring out how to make up for the inconvenience). 여기서 17번의 정답을 골라야 한다. 18번은 but으로 시작하는 남자의 마지막 대사에서 정답을 알 수 있다. but I'll bring this problem up at our staff meeting tomorrow가 패러프레이즈 되어 있는 문장을 정답으로 선택해야 하는데, 문장을 알아들을 수 있게 따라 읽는 연습을 해두자. up at our 부분이 연음되므로 "어빼라ー r"이라고 읽어야 한다.

Questions 19 through 21 refer to the following conversation and packing slip.

M Cn I can help the next customer.

W Br Hi. ¹⁹I moved to a new house recently, and ended up breaking a few dishes in the process. I placed an order for replacements through your online store, and they were delivered yesterday. ²⁰The problem is, I received only three soup bowls instead of the seven I requested.

M Cn I apologize for the inconvenience. May I take a look at your packing slip?

W Br Yes, here it is.

M Cn Hmm... Unfortunately, this particular dish pattern's been discontinued. The three bowls you received are the last ones we had with that design. ²¹As a solution, I can offer you a refund for the entire purchase amount, and you can also keep the three bowls you received as a complimentary gift.

W Br Thanks a lot! I appreciate that.

19-21번 문제는 다음 대화와 운송 전표에 관한 것입니다.

> **남:** 다음 고객님 도와드리겠습니다.
> **여:** 안녕하세요. 최근에 새 집으로 이사했는데요. 과정 중에 접시 몇 개를 깨뜨려버렸어요. 온라인 스토어를 통해 교체품을 주문했고요. 어제 배달이 왔어요. 문제는 수프 그릇을 제가 요청한 일곱 개가 아니라 세 개만 받았다는 거예요.
> **남:** 불편을 끼쳐 드려 죄송합니다. 운송 전표를 볼 수 있을까요?
> **여:** 네, 여기 있어요.
> **남:** 음... 죄송하지만, 딱 이 접시 문양이 단종되어 버렸네요. 받으신 그릇 세 개가 저희가 그 디자인으로 가지고 있던 마지막 물건이었습니다. 해결책으로 구입하신 금액 전체를 환불해 드릴게요. 그리고 받으신 그릇 세 개도 무료 증정품으로 가지시면 됩니다.
> **여:** 그거 좋죠! 고맙습니다.

> **어휘** packing slip 운송 전표 end up V-ing 결국 ~하게 되다 place an order for ~을 주문하다 replacement 대체물, 교체물 pattern 무늬, 도안 discontinue 단종하다, 생산을 중단하다 complimentary 무료의

RALTON HOME FURNISHINGS

Order #45709

Quantity	Description	Total Price
5	Dinner Plate	$25
7	21 Soup Bowl	21 $42
4	Coffee Mug	$16
2	Teapot	$50

RALTON 가정용 가구

주문번호 45709

수량	품목	총 가격
5	정찬용 접시	25달러
7	수프 그릇	42달러
4	커피 머그	16달러
2	찻주전자	50달러

어휘 furnishings 가구 quantity 수량 description 종류, 품목 dinner plate 정찬용 접시, 식사의 메인 코스용 접시 teapot 찻주전자

---

19. What does the woman say happened when she moved?

(A) She was overcharged for a service.
(B) A carton was misplaced.
(C) A shipment was delivered to an incorrect location.
(D) Some items were damaged.

어휘 overcharge 과도하게 청구하다 carton 판지 상자 misplace 둔 곳을 잊다 shipment 수송품 incorrect 부정확한, 틀린

해석 여자는 이사할 때 무슨 일이 있었다고 말하는가?
(A) 서비스 요금이 과도하게 청구되었다.
(B) 상자를 잃어버렸다.
(C) 수송품이 잘못된 장소로 배달되었다.
(D) 일부 물품이 손상되었다.

---

20. Why does the woman need assistance?

(A) She is not pleased with her purchase.
(B) She is unable to access a Web site.
(C) She received an incomplete order.
(D) She lost a copy of an invoice.

어휘 access 접속하다 incomplete 불완전한, 불충분한 order 주문 invoice 명세서, 청구서

해석 여자는 왜 도움이 필요한가?
(A) 구입품에 대해 만족하지 못한다.
(B) 웹 사이트에 접속할 수 없다.

(C) 주문품을 다 받지 못했다.
(D) 청구서 사본을 잃어버렸다.

21. Look at the graphic. How much money will the woman be refunded?

(A) $25
(B) $42
(C) $16
(D) $50

해석 그래픽을 보라. 여자는 얼마나 되는 돈을 환불받을 것인가?
(A) 25달러
(B) 42달러
(C) 16달러
(D) 50달러

해설 여자가 최근에 새 집으로 이사하는 도중에 접시 몇 개가 깨졌다고 했으므로 breaking a few dishes가 패러프레이즈 되어 있는 문장을 19번 문제의 정답으로 선택해야 한다. 여자가 도움이 필요한 이유는 깨진 그릇을 대체하기 위해 새것을 주문했지만, 요청한 일곱 개가 아니라 세 개만 왔기 때문이므로(I received only three soup bowls instead of the seven I requested.) 이 부분을 패러프레이즈 한 문장을 20번의 정답으로 고르자. 남자는 해결책으로 일곱 개의 수프 그릇 전체에 대한 구입 금액을 환불해 주고, 여자가 이미 받은 세 개는 무료로 갖게 해주겠다고 했다(I can offer you a refund for the entire purchase amount, and you can also keep the three bowls you received as a complimentary gift). 운송 전표를 보고 수프 그릇의 총 구입 금액이 42달러임을 확인하면서 21번의 정답을 고르자.

Part 4

Questions 22 through 24 refer to the following excerpt from a meeting.

[M | Cn] As you know, a large number of employees make use of the coffee services provided in the company kitchens throughout the day. ²²We're thinking about changing coffee providers, ²³and so tomorrow, one of the vendors we're considering will be offering different coffee blends in the lobby. Feel free to grab a complimentary cup of any blend that suits your taste. We just ask that you provide us with your thoughts on the coffee by giving us some feedback. It should take only five minutes to fill out the feedback forms, ²⁴and you can leave your completed form with Marlene in Office B-14.

22-24번 문제는 다음 회의 발췌문에 관한 것입니다.

남: 아시다시피 많은 수의 직원들이 하루 종일 회사 식당에서 제공되는 커피 서비스를 이용합니다. 우리는 이 커피 제공 업체들을 바꾸려고 생각하고 있습니다. 그래서 내일 우리가 고려 중인 판매업체 중 하나가 로비에서 다양한 커피 블렌드를 제공할 예정입니다. 기호에 맞는 어느 블렌드든 자유롭게 무료로 한 잔씩 가져가시기 바랍니다. 우리가 요구하는 것은 약간의 피드백을 해주심으로써 커피에 대한 여러분의 생각을 우리에게 알려주는 것뿐입니다. 피드백 서식을 기입하는 데는 5분밖에 걸리지 않을 겁니다. 작성하신 서식은 B-14 사무실의 Marlene에게 가져다주시면 됩니다.

어휘 excerpt 발췌[인용] (부분) make use of ~을 이용하다, 활용하다 vendor 판매 회사 blend (차, 담배 등의) 블렌드, 혼합 (제품) grab ~을 손에 넣다 suit (기호, 요구 등에) 맞다 taste 입맛, 기호 fill out ~을 기입하다, 작성하다 leave 맡기다, 위탁하다 complete 작성하다

---

22. What does the speaker say the company is considering?

(A) **Contracting with a new vendor**
(B) Extending the lunch hour
(C) Establishing an intern program
(D) Refurbishing company kitchens

어휘 회사 establish 확립하다, 마련하다 refurbish 재단장하다

해석 화자는 회사가 무엇을 고려하고 있다고 말하는가?
(A) 새 업체와 계약하는 것
(B) 점심시간을 늘리는 것
(C) 인턴 프로그램을 마련하는 것
(D) 회사 식당을 재단장하는 것

---

23. What can listeners receive for free tomorrow?

(A) A coffee mug
(B) A clothing item
(C) A notebook
(D) **A beverage**

해석 청자들은 내일 무엇을 무료로 받을 수 있는가?
(A) 머그잔
(B) 의류 제품
(C) 공책
(D) 음료

---

24. Why should listeners visit Marlene's office?

(A) To acquire training materials
(B) To participate in a project
(C) To be awarded a prize
(D) **To submit a form**

어휘 materials 자료 award 수여하다

해석 청자들은 왜 Marlene의 사무실을 방문해야 하는가?
(A) 교육 자료를 얻기 위해
(B) 프로젝트에 참여하기 위해
(C) 상을 받기 위해
(D) 서식을 제출하기 위해

해석 22번 문제는 We're thinking about changing coffee providers가 패러프레이즈 되어 있는 선택지를 정답으로 고르면 된다. 이어지는 문장을 들어보면 내일 커피 제공 업체 중 하나가 로비에서 다양한 블렌드를 선보일 것이라고 알려주면서(tomorrow, one of the vendors we're considering will be offering different coffee blends in the lobby.) 한 잔씩 무료로 마셔볼 것을 직원들에게 권하고 있으므로(Feel free to grab a complimentary cup of any blend that suits your taste.), 23번의 정답은 coffee를 대신하는 단어 (D) A beverage이다. 직원들에게 커피를 맛본 후 피드백을 부탁하고 있으며 작성한 피드백 서식을 Marlene에게 제출하라고 했으므로(you can leave your completed form with Marlene in Office B-14.) 마지막 문장을 듣고 24번 문제의 정답을 선택하자.

Questions 25 through 27 refer to the following advertisement.

W Am Short on time for a meal? Need a burst of energy? Look no further! The Canadian consumer goods company that brought you Hercules Grains Cereal is now offering a new product. ²⁵Dr. Yummy is a wholesome treat that will help you feel full and satisfied. ²⁶With its high fiber content, low fat levels, and ample protein, this healthy snack is a perfect substitute for junk food. ²⁷[You won't be able to get enough!] Dr. Yummy is available in most grocery stores, so head to the nearest one today!

25-27번 문제는 다음 광고에 관한 것입니다.

여: 식사할 시간이 부족하세요? 폭발적인 에너지가 필요하세요? 더 이상 찾지 마세요! Hercules Grains Cereal을 선보인 캐나다 소비재 회사가 지금 신제품을 내놓습니다. Dr. Yummy는 건강에 좋은 간식이면서 포만감을 느끼도록 도와줍니다. 높은 섬유질 함유량과 낮은 지방 수치, 풍부한 단백질로, 이 건강에 좋은 간식은 정크 푸드의 완벽한 대용품입니다. 충분히 가질 수는 없을 겁니다(아무리 먹어도 더 먹고 싶을 거예요)! Dr. Yummy는 대부분의 식료품점에서 이용하실 수 있습니다. 오늘 가까운 곳에 가보세요!

➡️ **어휘** short on ~이 부족한 burst 폭발, 터뜨림 consumer goods 소비재 wholesome 건강에 좋은 treat 간식, 군것질거리 feel full and satisfied 포만감을 느끼다 fiber 섬유(질) content 함유량, 함량 ample 충분한, 풍부한 protein 단백질 substitute 대용품 head (특정 방향으로) 가다, 향하다

25. What product is being advertised?

(A) A seasoning
(B) A liquid refreshment
(C) A snack
(D) A vitamin supplement

➡️ **해석** 어떤 제품을 광고하고 있는가?
(A) 조미료
(B) 음료
(C) 간식
(D) 비타민 보충제

26. According to the speaker, what is the advantage of Dr. Yummy?

(A) It is highly nutritious.
(B) It is reasonably priced.
(C) It is sold in packs of six.
(D) It appeals to children.

➡️ **어휘** advantage 이점, 장점 nutritious 영양가가 높은 reasonably 적정하게 price 가격을 매기다 pack 묶음 appeal to ~의 관심을[흥미를] 끌다

➡️ **해석** 화자의 말에 따르면 Dr. Yummy의 장점은 무엇인가?
(A) 영양가가 매우 높다.
(B) 가격이 적정하다.
(C) 6개들이 묶음으로 판매한다.
(D) 어린이들의 관심을 끈다.

27. What does the speaker mean when she says, "You won't be able to get enough"?

(A) There are not enough items in stock.
(B) You will want plenty of these products.
(C) You cannot buy these goods in bulk.
(D) There is a diverse range of flavors to enjoy.

➡️ **어휘** stock 재고(품) in bulk 대량으로 diverse 다양한 range 범위, 범주

➡️ **해석** 화자는 "충분히 가질 수는 없을 겁니다."라고 말할 때 무엇을 의미하는가?
(A) 재고가 충분하지 않다.
(B) 이 제품을 많이 원할 것이다.
(C) 이 상품을 대량으로 살 수 없다.
(D) 다양한 맛을 즐길 수 있다.

➡️ **해설** 세 문제의 정답을 알려주는 문장들이 연속으로 나오기 때문에 순발력이 매우 중요하다. 선택지의 내용이 패러프레이즈 된 부분들을 알아들을 수 있게 단어도 많이 암기해 두자. 우선 Dr. Yummy is a wholesome treat를 들으면서 25번 문제의 정답을 선택하자. 바로 이어지는 문장에서 26번의 정답을 알아내야 하는데, With its high fiber content, low fat levels, and ample protein, this healthy snack is a perfect substitute for junk food.가 영양가 높은 식품을 묘사하고 있음을 이해해야 한다. 마지막 문장을 들으면서 27번의 정답을 골라야 한다. 대부분의 식료품점에서 살 수 있으니 지금 가까운 상점으로 가보라고 말하며 구입을 독려하고 있으므로(Dr. Yummy is available in most grocery stores, so head to the nearest one today!), 문맥이 자연스러우려면 앞 문장 You won't be able to get enough!의 의미는 "아무리 먹어도 더 먹고 싶을 거예요!" 즉, "이 제품을 많이 원하게 될 거예요."여야 한다.

Questions 28 through 30 refer to the following excerpt from a meeting and chart.

[W] [Am] 28As most of you know, I was certain that our new Web site would have all sorts of glitches, but to my surprise, I was mistaken. So far we haven't encountered any technical difficulties, and the majority of our customers are pleased with the new services we're providing. 29They particularly appreciate the feature of receiving e-mail alerts when out-of-stock products are restocked. I'm surprised, though, by how the Web site design is being perceived differently by various age groups. The outcomes depicted on this graph are, um, different from what I anticipated. 30Jeremy, could you please research why this specific age group shows the highest level of satisfaction with the site? Using that information, we can hopefully boost overall satisfaction.

28-30번 문제는 다음 회의 발췌문과 도표에 관한 것입니다.

여: 대부분 아시다시피 저는 우리의 새 웹 사이트에 온갖 종류의 결함이 다 있을 것이라고 확신했습니다. 하지만 놀랍게도 제가 잘못 생각하고 있었네요. 지금까지 우리는 어떠한 기술적인 어려움에도 맞닥뜨리지 않았으며, 대다수의 고객들은 우리가 제공하는 새 서비스에 만족하고 있습니다. 특별히 재고가 떨어졌던 상품이 다시 입고되었을 때 이메일 알림을 받는 기능의 진가를 인정하고 있어요. 하지만 웹 사이트 디자인이 다양한 연령대에 의해 어떻게 다르게 여겨지고 있는지는 놀랍습니다. 이 그래프에 나타난 결과는, 음, 제가 예상한 것과 다르네요. Jeremy, 왜 이 특정한 연령대가 웹 사이트에 대해 가장 높은 수준의 만족도를 보이는지 조사해 주겠어요? 그 정보를 이용해서 전체적인 만족도를 신장시킬 수 있기를 바랍니다.

어휘 excerpt 발췌[인용] (부분) sort 종류, 유형 glitch 작은 문제[결함] to one's surprise 놀랍게도 mistaken 잘못 알고 [판단하고] 있는 so far 지금까지 encounter 맞닥뜨리다 appreciate ~의 진가를 알아보다, 인정하다 feature (상품의 특징적) 기능 alert 알림 out-of-stock (일시적으로) 재고가 떨어진 restock 다시 채우다 though 그렇지만, 하지만 perceive ~을 (~로) 여기다 age group 연령대 outcome 결과 depict 묘사하다, 그리다 specific 특정한 hopefully 원하건대, (일이) 잘 되면 boost 신장시키다, 북돋우다

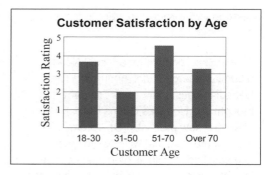

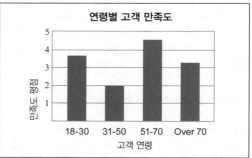

어휘 rating 평점

---

28. What does the speaker say she was wrong about?

(A) Increase in online sales
(B) A Web site malfunctioning
(C) The level of demand for a product
(D) The cost of enhancing a service

어휘 malfunction 제대로 작동하지 않다
해석 화자는 자신이 무엇에 대해 틀렸다고 말하는가?
(A) 온라인 판매량의 증가
(B) 제대로 작동하지 않는 웹 사이트
(C) 어떤 상품에 대한 수요의 정도
(D) 어떤 서비스를 향상시키는 비용

---

29. What does the speaker say is a popular Web site feature?

(A) Automated payment processing
(B) Reviews from customers
(C) Discounts on shipping
(D) E-mail notifications

해석 화자는 무엇이 인기 있는 웹 사이트 기능이라고 말하는가?
(A) 자동화된 결제 처리
(B) 고객들의 평가
(C) 배송비 할인

(D) 이메일 통보

30. Look at the graphic. What age group does the speaker ask Jeremy to investigate?

(A) 18-30
(B) 31-50
(C) 51-70
(D) Over 70

■ 해석 ■ 그래픽을 보라. 화자는 Jeremy에게 어느 연령대를 조사해 달라고 요구하는가?
(A) 18–30세
(B) 31–50세
(C) 51–70세
(D) 70세 이상

■ 해설 ■ 28번 문제의 정답은 첫 문장에서 알 수 있다. 새 웹 사이트에 많은 결함이 있을 것이라고 생각했는데, 그것이 틀린 생각이었다고 말하고 있다(I was certain that our new Web site would have all sorts of glitches, but to my surprise, I was mistaken.). 패러프레이즈 된 내용을 잘 파악하고 정답을 선택하자. 담화 중간에 나오는 They particularly appreciate the feature of receiving e-mail alerts를 들으면서 alerts가 notifications로 바뀌어 있다는 것을 간파하면 29번의 정답도 알 수 있다. 30번처럼 그래프가 사용될 때는 비교급이나 최상급 형용사/부사가 정답의 키워드인 경우가 많다. Jeremy에게 조사를 요구하는 문장인 could you please research why this specific age group shows the highest level of satisfaction with the site?에서 최상급 형용사 highest가 키워드다. 만족도가 가장 높은 연령대를 조사해달라고 지시했으므로 그래픽을 보면 51–70세임을 알 수 있다.

PART 1 Exercise

1 (B) **2** (C)

1. `M｜Au`

(A) A man is putting food items in a display case.
(B) A sales clerk is offering an item to a customer.
(C) A woman is hanging pictures on a wall.
(D) A customer is ready to pay the cashier.

어휘 cashier 출납원

해석 (A) 남자가 진열장에 식품을 넣고 있다.
(B) 점원이 고객에게 물건을 권하고 있다.
(C) 여자가 벽에 그림을 걸고 있다.
(D) 고객이 출납원에게 막 돈을 지불하려고 한다.

해설 putting, hanging, pay the cashier를 들으면서 (A), (C), (D)는 오답으로 잘 골라내자. 남자가 고객에게 물건을 권하는 장면이므로 offering an item이 정답 표현이다. 쇼핑하는 장면에서 사용되는 여러 가지 표현들을 잘 익혀 두자.

2. `M｜Cn`

(A) The man is removing his watch.
(B) The woman is staring into the distance.
(C) A game's being played on a table.
(D) The family is watching a performance.

어휘 remove (옷 등을) 벗다 stare into ~을 응시하다
distance 먼 곳

해석 (A) 남자가 손목시계를 벗고 있다.
(B) 여자가 먼 곳을 응시하고 있다.
(C) 테이블에서 게임을 하고 있다.
(D) 가족이 공연을 보고 있다.

해설 시계를 벗거나(removing his watch) 공연을 보는 (watching a performance) 장면은 아니므로 (A)와 (D) 는 오답이다. Day 01에서 공부한 staring into the distance를 기억하고 (B)도 오답으로 골라내자. 여가를 즐기는 여러 가지 장면에서 사용되는 표현들을 잘 익혀 두자.

PART 2 Exercise

1 (C)	**2** (A)	**3** (A)	**4** (B)	**5** (C)
6 (C)	**7** (A)	**8** (B)	**9** (C)	**10** (C)

1. `W｜Am` `M｜Cn`

Why do we have to reschedule the event?

(A) Maybe at the end of the month.
(B) I'll do it first thing tomorrow morning.
(C) I'm sorry, my doctor's appointment couldn't be moved.

어휘 first thing (아침에) 제일 먼저

→ 해석 행사 일정을 왜 다시 잡아야 하죠?

(A) 아마 월말이에요.
(B) 내일 아침에 제일 먼저 하겠습니다.
(C) 미안해요. 진료 예약을 옮길 수가 없어서요.

해설 (A)는 When 의문문의 정답으로 알맞은 대답이고, (B)는 어떤 제안이나 부탁을 받았을 때 할 수 있는 대답이다. 일정 변경의 이유를 묻는 질문은 반복적으로 출제되고 있으며 정답은 항상 누군가의 부재를 언급하는 대답이다.

---

2. [M|Au] [W|Am]

Why won't my computer turn on?

(A) There have been some issues with the battery in mine.
(B) Turn right at the stop sign.
(C) The computer cases are in the supply closet.

어휘 supply closet 비품 창고

→ 해석 제 컴퓨터가 왜 켜지지 않는 걸까요?
(A) 제 것에서는 배터리에 문제가 좀 있었어요.
(B) 정지 신호에서 우회전하세요.
(C) 컴퓨터 케이스는 비품 창고에 있습니다.

해설 Why에 대한 대답으로 기계적 결함을 언급하는 것은 항상 정답이다. (B)는 질문에 나온 turn을, (C)는 computer를 반복해서 들려줌으로써 오답을 유도하고 있다.

---

3. [W|Am] [M|Cn]

Why did the accounting department send that memo?

(A) You received a memo?
(B) I'm certain they can do that.
(C) Directly to Mr. Benjamin.

어휘 accounting 회계 (업무) memo 단체 메일, 회람

→ 해석 회계 팀이 왜 그 단체 메일을 보냈나요?
(A) 단체 메일을 받으셨다고요?
(B) 그들이 할 수 있다고 확신합니다.
(C) 직접 Mr. Benjamin에게요.

해설 (B)는 질문에 들어 있는 that을 반복하면서 오답을 유도하고 있고, (C)는 사람 이름으로 대답하고 있으므로 Who 의문문의 정답으로 알맞다. 내용을 도저히 알아들을 수 없을 때는 (A)처럼 반문하는 대답이 정답일 확률이 가장 높다는 사실을 기억하자.

---

4. [M|Cn] [W|Am]

Why are these guidelines so complicated?

(A) Thanks for coming in so early today.
(B) I've asked Chris to simplify them.
(C) There are enough copies available for everyone.

어휘 guidelines 지침 complicated 복잡한 simplify 간단하게[단순하게] 하다 copy (책, 신문 등의) 한 부

→ 해석 이 지침은 왜 이렇게 복잡한가요?
(A) 오늘 이렇게 일찍 와 주셔서 고맙습니다.
(B) Chris에게 간단하게 해 달라고 부탁해 놓았어요.
(C) 모든 사람이 이용할 만큼 충분한 부수가 있습니다.

해설 왜 이렇게 복잡하냐는 질문은 사실 불만을 말하는 것이며, 불만에 대한 해결책으로 동료에게 간소화를 부탁했다고 말하는 (B)가 자연스러운 대답이다. 따라 읽는 연습을 해 보자. 질문은 "와이 아r 디z 가이드라인 쏘우 캄플러케이릳?"이라고 읽는다. 대답의 동사 asked에서는 k와 d 발음이 탈락한다. 그래서 "아이배s 크리s 투 심플러파이 뎀."이라고 읽게 된다.

---

5. [W|Am] [W|Br]

Why was the advertising webinar canceled?

(A) A magazine advertisement.
(B) Mr. De Luca didn't like the color.
(C) I don't think it was.

어휘 webinar 웨비나(인터넷상의 세미나)

→ 해석 광고 웨비나는 왜 취소되었나요?
(A) 잡지 광고요.
(B) Mr. De Luca가 색상을 마음에 들어하지 않았어요.
(C) 취소되지 않았을 걸요.

해설 (A)는 질문의 advertising과 비슷한 발음을 들려주면서, (B)는 advertising, canceled에서 연상되는 대답으로 오답을 유도하고 있다. 행사가 취소된 이유를 묻는 질문에 대해 취소되지 않았다고 대답하는 (C)가 자연스러운 대화를 만들어 준다.

---

6. [W|Br] [M|Au]

Why is the vegetable soup missing from your lunch menu today?

(A) It suits you perfectly.
(B) Just the same amount of water.
(C) We're offering creamy tomato soup.

해석 오늘 점심 메뉴에는 왜 야채수프가 빠져 있나요?
  (A) 당신에게 완벽하게 어울립니다.
  (B) 꼭 같은 양의 물이요.
  (C) 저희가 크림 토마토 수프를 제공하고 있습니다.

해설 (A)는 질문에 나오는 soup와 발음이 비슷한 suits를 들려주면서, (B)는 the vegetable soup에서 연상되는 대답으로 오답을 유도하고 있다. 질문 앞부분 Why is the vegetable soup missing(왜 야채수프가 빠져 있나요?)에 집중하면 자연스러운 대답이 어느 것인지 알 수 있다.

---

7. ⟨W｜Br⟩⟨M｜Cn⟩

Why does Dr. Houston need another lab assistant?

(A) I didn't know she requested one.
(B) At least two years' experience.
(C) Yes, we toured the new lab.

어휘 lab(=laboratory) 실험실 assistant 조수, 비서 tour 둘러보다

해석 Houston 박사는 왜 실험실 조수가 필요하다는 거죠?
  (A) 그녀가 신청한 줄도 몰랐네요.
  (B) 최소 2년의 경력이요.
  (C) 네, 새 실험실을 둘러봤습니다.

해설 (B)는 질문의 need another lab assistant에서 연상되는 대답으로 오답을 유도하고 있으며, (C)는 Yes를 듣자마자 오답임을 알 수 있다. 오답을 잘 골라낼수록 고수가 된다!

---

8. ⟨W｜Br⟩⟨M｜Cn⟩

Why has there been such a delay in shipping these orders?

(A) Within the next forty-eight hours.
(B) Our stock of packing materials has been depleted.
(C) Mostly sporting goods.

어휘 ship 수송하다, 운송하다 stock 재고(품) packing 포장 deplete 고갈시키다 sporting goods 스포츠 용품

해석 이 주문품들을 보내는 게 왜 그렇게 지연된 거죠?
  (A) 앞으로 48시간 이내예요.
  (B) 포장 재료 재고가 다 떨어져서요.
  (B) 주로 스포츠 용품입니다.

해설 (A)는 When 의문문의, (C)는 What 의문문의 정답으로 알맞은 대답이다. Why 의문문의 정답이 명사 하나로만 이루어진 단답형 대답일 수는 없다. 오답을 잘 골라낼수록 고수가 된다!

---

9. ⟨M｜Au⟩⟨M｜Cn⟩

Why hasn't Ms. Lim been in the office all week?

(A) No, I haven't seen her.
(B) Typically until five o'clock or so.
(C) You'll have to ask her assistant.

어휘 typically 보통, 일반적으로 or so ~ 정도, ~쯤 assistant 조수, 비서

해석 Ms. Lim은 왜 일주일 내내 사무실에 없습니까?
  (A) 아니요, 저는 그녀를 못 봤습니다.
  (B) 보통은 5시 정도까지요.
  (C) 그녀의 비서에게 물어보셔야 할 거예요.

해설 (A)는 No를 듣는 순간 오답으로 골라낼 수 있고, (B)는 How late ~? 유형의 질문에서 정답으로 나올 만한 대답이다. "몰라" 유형의 대답들을 기억하고 있다가 들리면 정답으로 선택하자. Day 02에 정리된 목록을 보면 동사 ask가 들어가는 대답이 여러 가지 있는데, 보통 ask가 포함된 대답은 모른다는 뜻으로 하는 말이다.

---

10. ⟨M｜Au⟩⟨W｜Am⟩

Why didn't Steven come to the office?

(A) Take the stairs to your left.
(B) I think it was changed to two o'clock.
(C) All of the managers are at the staff meeting.

어휘 stairs 계단

해석 Steven은 왜 사무실로 오지 않았나요?
  (A) 왼쪽에 있는 계단으로 가세요.
  (B) 그건 두 시로 바뀌었을 거예요.
  (C) 매니저들은 모두 직원회의에 들어가 있습니다.

해설 (A)는 질문의 come to the office에서 연상되는 대답으로 오답을 유도하고 있으며, (B)는 it이 무엇을 가리키는지 알 수 없다. 질문 앞부분 Why didn't Steven come(Steven은 왜 오지 않았나요?)에 집중해서 자연스러운 대답을 알아내자.

PART 3 & 4 Exercise

1 (C) **2** (D) **3** (A) **4** (A) **5** (C) **6** (A)

Questions 1 through 3 refer to the following conversation.

[W] [Am] Hello. This is Mary Ying, customer service representative at Doylestown Bank. [1]I wanted to follow up on the message you left about your new account.

[M] [Au] Yes, thank you for getting back to me. I recently opened a checking account, [2]but the banker I talked to didn't show me how to access my account online.

[W] [Am] I'm happy to assist you with that. Just provide me with your e-mail, and I'll send you a detailed guide on how to conduct online transactions. [3]Alternatively, you can drop by tomorrow, and I can walk you through it personally.

[M] [Au] [3]That sounds good to me. I work in the neighborhood, so stopping by during my lunch break works well for me. I'll see you at one o'clock.

1-3번 문제는 다음 대화에 관한 것입니다.

여: 안녕하세요. Doylestown 은행 고객 서비스 담당자 Mary Ying입니다. 신규 계좌와 관련하여 남기신 메시지 때문에 연락드립니다.

남: 네, 연락 주셔서 고맙습니다. 최근에 당좌 예금을 개설했는데요, 상담해 주신 직원이 온라인으로 계좌에 접속하는 방법을 알려주지 않았어요.

여: 그거라면 제가 기꺼이 도와드리겠습니다. 이메일 주소만 알려 주시면 온라인으로 거래하는 법에 관한 자세한 안내서를 보내 드리겠습니다. 아니면, 내일 들러 주시면 제가 직접 보여 드릴 수도 있습니다.

남: 그게 좋겠네요. 인근에서 일하기 때문에 점심시간에 잠깐 들르는 게 저에게는 딱 좋아요. 1시에 뵐게요.

어휘 customer service representative 고객 서비스 직원 follow up on ~에 대응하여 조치하다 get back to ~에게 (나중에) 다시 연락하다 checking account 당좌 예금 access 접속하다 guide 안내서 conduct (특정한 활동을) 하다 transaction 거래 alternatively 그렇지 않으면, 그 대안으로 drop by(=stop by) 잠깐 들르다 walk A through B A에게 B를 하나하나 보여주다[가르쳐주다]

---

personally 직접, 몸소 neighborhood 근처, 인근 work for ~에게 문제없다, 좋다

---

1. Why does the woman call the man?

(A) To verify an e-mail address
(B) To reschedule an appointment
(C) To respond to a message
(D) To give directions to a place

어휘 verify 확인하다 directions (장소 찾기 위한) 길

해석 여자는 왜 남자에게 전화하는가?
(A) 이메일 주소를 확인하기 위해
(B) 약속을 다시 잡기 위해
(C) 메시지에 응답하기 위해
(D) 어떤 장소로 가는 길을 알려주기 위해

---

2. What problem does the man mention?

(A) He is unable to locate his keys.
(B) He cannot remember his password.
(C) He will not arrive on time for an appointment.
(D) He was not given some instructions.

어휘 locate ~의 위치를 찾아내다 on time 제시간에 instructions 설명

해석 남자는 어떤 문제를 언급하는가?
(A) 열쇠를 찾을 수 없다.
(B) 비밀번호가 기억나지 않는다.
(C) 약속 장소에 제시간에 도착하지 못할 것이다.
(D) 설명을 듣지 못했다.

---

3. What does the man say he will do tomorrow?

(A) Visit the bank
(B) Contact a client
(C) Work remotely
(D) Dine with a colleague

어휘 remotely 원격으로 dine 식사하다

해석 남자는 내일 무엇을 하겠다고 말하는가?
(A) 은행을 방문한다
(B) 고객에게 연락한다
(C) 원격으로 근무한다
(D) 동료와 함께 식사한다

대화의 목적을 묻는 질문은 거의 항상 첫 한두 문장에서 정답을 알 수 있다. I wanted to follow up on the message you left about your new account.가 패러프레이즈 된 표현이 1번 문제의 정답이다. but, no, actually, so가 들리면 더 집중하는 습관을 들이자. 남자의 대사 but the banker I talked to didn't show me how to access my account online.이 패러프레이즈 된 문장이 2번 문제의 정답이다. 남자의 문제를 알게 된 직원이 두 가지 해결책을 제시하는데, 이메일로 거래 방법을 알려주는 것과 그 대안인 내일 은행에 직접 들르는 것이다(you can drop by tomorrow, and I can walk you through it personally). 남자는 두 번째 해결책을 선호한다(That sounds good to me). 점심시간인 1시에 방문하겠다고 말하는 문장을 듣고 3번 문제의 정답을 선택하자(so stopping by during my lunch break works well for me. I'll see you at one o'clock).

Questions 4 through 6 refer to the following announcement.

M | Au ⁴I called this meeting to announce officially that our bank will be merging with Stratton Bank at the start of the upcoming year. The consolidation of our two banks will result in a positive impact on all of you as our employees. ⁵The most significant change is our transition to another building. This new building's conveniently located by the bus line, which will be advantageous for those of you who commute from the city. ⁶In addition, we will follow Stratton Bank's vacation policy, so all employees will be entitled to three extra days of vacation each year. Does anyone have any questions?

4-6번 문제는 다음 발표문에 관한 것입니다.

남: 우리 은행이 Stratton 은행과 내년 초에 합병하게 되었음을 공식적으로 발표하고자 이번 회의를 소집했습니다. 우리 두 은행의 통합은 모든 우리 직원 여러분에게 긍정적인 영향을 미칠 것입니다. 가장 중요한 변화는 다른 건물로 이동하는 것입니다. 이 새 건물은 편리하게도 버스 노선 옆에 위치해 있어서, 시내에서 통근하시는 분들에게 유리할 것입니다. 추가로 우리는 Stratton 은행의 휴가 정책을 따르기로 했습니다. 따라서 모든 직원들은 매년 추가 3일의 휴가를 받을 것입니다. 질문 있는 분 나요?

어휘 **merge** 합병하다 **upcoming** 다가오는, 곧 있을 **consolidation** 합병, 통합 **result in** ~을 낳다, 야기하다 **significant** 중요한, 커다란 **transition** 이동, 변화 **advantageous** 이로운, 유리한 **commute** 통근하다

be entitled to ~에 대한 자격을[권리를] 부여받다

---

4. What kind of business does the speaker work in?

(A) A financial institution
(B) A travel bureau
(C) A staffing firm
(D) An insurance provider

해석 화자는 어떤 회사에서 근무하는가?
(A) 금융 기관
(B) 여행사
(C) 인재 파견업체
(D) 보험 회사

---

5. According to the speaker, what advantage does the new location have?

(A) It has more spacious offices.
(B) It is close to a variety of cafés.
(C) It is easily accessible by public transit.
(D) It has exquisitely landscaped gardens.

어휘 **advantage** 이점, 장점 **spacious** 널찍한 **accessible** 접근 가능한 **public transit** 대중교통 **exquisitely** 아주 아름답게 **landscape** 조경을 하다

해석 화자의 말에 따르면 새 장소에는 어떤 장점이 있는가?
(A) 더 넓은 사무실이 있다.
(B) 다양한 카페와 가깝다.
(C) 대중교통으로 쉽게 접근할 수 있다.
(D) 매우 아름답게 조경이 된 정원이 있다.

---

6. What policy change does the speaker mention?

(A) Staff members will receive additional vacation time.
(B) The company will offer telecommuting as an option.
(C) Attendance at weekly meetings will be compulsory.
(D) The sharing of office spaces will be mandatory.

어휘 **telecommuting** 재택근무 **compulsory** 의무적인 **mandatory** 필수의

해석 화자는 어떤 정책 변경을 언급하는가?
(A) 직원들이 추가적인 휴가 기간을 받을 것이다.
(B) 회사가 재택근무를 선택 사항으로 제공할 것이다.

(C) 주간 회의 참석이 의무가 될 것이다.
(D) 사무실 공간의 공유가 필수적일 것이다.

> **해설** 첫 문장이 나오자마자 4번 문제의 정답을 선택하자. our bank라는 키워드만 알아들어도 알 수 있다. 두 은행의 합병으로 인해 생기는 가장 큰 변화는 새 건물로 옮겨 가는 것인데(The most significant change is our transition to another building.), 버스 노선에 인접해 있어서 시내에서 출근하는 직원들에게 장점이 된다고 말하고 있다(This new building's conveniently located by the bus line, which will be advantageous for those of you who commute from the city). 여기서 5번의 정답을 고르자. 이어지는 문장에서는 휴가 정책의 변화를 언급하고 있는데(we will follow Stratton Bank's vacation policy), 휴가를 추가로 3일씩 더 갈 수 있다고 말하고 있다(so all employees will be entitled to three extra days of vacation each year). 여기서 6번 문제의 정답을 선택해야 한다.

Actual Test

1 (D)	2 (D)	3 (A)	4 (C)	5 (C)
6 (B)	7 (C)	8 (A)	9 (B)	10 (A)
11 (B)	12 (B)	13 (D)	14 (B)	15 (D)
16 (A)	17 (B)	18 (C)	19 (D)	20 (A)
21 (C)	22 (B)	23 (A)	24 (D)	25 (B)
26 (B)	27 (A)	28 (A)	29 (D)	30 (C)

* 정답을 맞힌 문제도 해설을 읽어보세요.

Part 1

1. ⬚ W | Br ⬚

(A) A vehicle has been left in a garage.
(B) Pedestrians are crossing a street.
(C) Workers are replacing road signs.
(D) A sidewalk is being resurfaced.

> **어휘** pedestrian 보행자 sidewalk 인도, 보도 resurface (도로를) 다시 포장하다

> **해석** (A) 차량 한 대가 차고에 있다.
> (B) 보행자들이 길을 건너고 있다.
> (C) 인부들이 도로 표지판을 교체하고 있다.
> (D) 보도를 재포장하고 있다.

> **해설** 차량 한 대가 주차되어 있기는 하지만 차고에 있지는 않으므로 (A)는 오답이다. (B)는 crossing a street를 듣고 오답으로 골라낼 수 있다. (C)는 사진에 도로 표지판(road signs)이 없으므로 오답이다. 정답을 알아낼 수 있게 동사 resurface를 기억하자.

2. ⬚ W | Am ⬚

(A) Some safety cones are being removed from a work site.
(B) Some helmets have been placed on the ground.
(C) Some workers are directing traffic.
(D) A road is being dug up by some workers.

> **어휘** safety cone 안전 원뿔형 표지 direct traffic 교통정리를 하다 dig up 파내다, 파헤치다

> **해석** (A) 안전 원뿔형 표지들을 작업 현장에서 치우고 있다.
> (B) 헬멧들이 바닥에 놓여 있다.
> (C) 인부들이 교통정리를 하고 있다.
> (D) 인부들이 도로를 파헤치고 있다.

> **해설** (A)는 동작을 나타내는 진행 시제 수동태 문장이므로 정답이 되려면 치우는(remove) 동작을 하고 있어야 한다. (B)는 위치 표현 on the ground만 알아들으면 오답임을 알 수 있으며, (C)는 교통정리를 하고 있다고 (directing traffic) 했으므로 오답이다. '땅을 파헤치다'라는 뜻의 동사구 dig up을 기억하고 정답을 선택하자.

3. W|Am

(A) **A portion of the roof is unfinished.**
(B) Some roofing materials are being removed by a crane.
(C) A house is decorated with window boxes.
(D) A ladder is lying across a construction van.

어휘 portion 일부, 부분 unfinished 완성되지 않은 roofing 지붕 공사 crane 기중기, 크레인 window box (창가의) 화초 상자 lie 가로놓여 있다

해석 (A) 지붕 일부가 완성되지 않았다.
(B) 일부 지붕 재료를 기중기로 제거하고 있다.
(C) 집이 화초 상자들로 장식되어 있다.
(D) 사다리가 공사용 밴을 가로질러 놓여 있다.

해설 지붕 공사가 진행 중인 장면이므로 (A)가 정답이다. 사진에 보이지 않는 a crane과 window boxes, a construction van이 들리는 나머지 선택지는 모두 오답이다.

Part 2

4. W|Am M|Au

Why has the seminar been canceled?

(A) About thirty minutes ago.
(B) In Room Fifteen.
(C) **Because many people couldn't attend.**

해석 세미나가 왜 취소되었나요?
(A) 한 30분 전에요.
(B) 15호실에서요.
(C) 많은 사람이 참석할 수 없어서요.

해설 (A)는 질문이 When 의문문일 때, (B)는 Where 의문문일 때 정답으로 알맞은 대답이다. 일정 변경의 이유를 묻는 문제는 반복적으로 출제되며 누군가의 부재를 언급하는 대답은 항상 정답이다.

5. M|Cn W|Br

Why did Jeong-Won hire an assistant?

(A) She will submit an estimate in October.
(B) Anyhow, they thought I was late.
(C) **Aren't you aware of how hectic her schedule is?**

어휘 assistant 조수, 비서 estimate 견적서 anyhow 아무튼, 어쨌든 hectic 정신없이 바쁜, 빡빡한

해석 Jeong-Won이 왜 비서를 고용했죠?
(A) 10월에 견적서를 제출할 겁니다.
(B) 아무튼 그들은 제가 늦었다고 생각했어요.
(C) 그녀의 일정이 얼마나 바쁜지 모르세요?

해설 (A)는 질문이 How much ~?일 때 알맞은 대답이고, (B)는 they가 누구를 가리키는지 알 수 없다. 비서를 고용하는 이유를 묻는 질문이므로 일정이 얼마나 바쁜지 보면 알 수 있다고 대답하는 게 자연스럽다. 도저히 알 아들을 수 없는 문제가 출제되었을 때는 반문하는 대답이 정답일 확률이 가장 높다는 사실을 기억하자.

6. W|Br M|Au

Why did you put the food delivered this morning in the freezer?

(A) It's not working well at the moment.
(B) **I meant to put it in the refrigerator.**
(C) Shall we begin preparing dinner soon?

어휘 freezer 냉동고 at the moment 지금은, 현재 mean to-V ~하려고 하다

해석 오늘 아침에 배달 온 음식을 왜 냉동고에 넣었어요?
(A) 지금은 제대로 작동하고 있지 않아요.
(B) 냉장고에 넣으려고 했던 거예요.
(C) 저녁식사 준비를 곧 시작할까요?

해설 음식을 냉장고에 넣으려다가 실수로 냉동고에 넣었다는 뜻으로 하는 말이 자연스러운 대답이다.

7. W|Am W|Br

Why are we cleaning the laboratory?

(A) Just stack the books against that wall.
(B) I will be present if necessary.
(C) **Haven't you seen the inspection report?**

어휘 stack 쌓다 against ~에 붙여 present 참석한, 출석한 inspection 점검

[해석] 왜 실험실을 청소하고 있어요?
(A) 그 책들은 저 벽에 붙여 쌓아 두세요.
(B) 필요하다면 제가 참석하겠습니다.
(C) 점검 보고서 못 보셨어요?

[해설] 점검 보고서를 보면 실험실을 청소하는 이유를 알 수 있다는 뜻으로 하는 말이 자연스러운 대답이다. 도저히 알아들을 수 없는 문제가 출제되었을 때는 반문하는 대답이 정답일 확률이 가장 높다는 사실을 기억하자.

8. M Cn W Br

Why has our supplier decided to increase the delivery cost?

(A) I'll give them a call.
(B) Sure, last week.
(C) How many would you like?

[어휘] supplier 공급(업)자, 공급업체

[해석] 납품업체가 왜 배달료를 올리기로 했대요?
(A) 전화해 볼게요.
(B) 물론이죠, 지난주에요.
(C) 몇 개를 원하시나요?

[해설] "몰라" 유형의 대답은 정답이 될 수밖에 없다. 시험에서 자주 사용되어 온 Let me check ~.이나 I'll call[find out/ask] ~. 같은 표현을 기억해 두자. (B)는 Sure가 Yes를 대신하는 대답이므로 오답이며, (C)는 어떤 물건을 가리키는지 알 수 없다.

9. M Cn W Br

I'd like to know who's attending the exposition.

(A) Try turning the valve to the left.
(B) Registrations aren't due until next Friday.
(C) There are samples at Booth 306.

[어휘] exposition 박람회, 전시회 due (특정일까지 발생할) 예정인

[해석] 박람회에 누가 참석하는지 알고 싶습니다.
(A) 밸브를 왼쪽으로 돌려 보세요.
(B) 등록이 다음 주 금요일이 되어야 마감돼요.
(C) 306호 부스에 견본이 있어요.

[해설] 질문에 들어 있는 exposition을 position으로 잘못 알아들으면, 연상되는 단어 left를 듣고 (A)를 정답으로 잘못 선택할 수 있다. (C)도 the exposition에서 연상되는 대답으로 오답을 유도하고 있다. 박람회 등록 기간이 마감되려면 아직 멀었기 때문에 누가 참석할지 모른다는 뜻으로 말하는 (B)가 자연스러운 대답이다.

10. W Br M Au

Cynthia Stroman is the choreographer of this musical, isn't she?

(A) Yes, and it's beautifully done.
(B) No, I prefer classical music.
(C) There will be a dress rehearsal this evening.

[어휘] choreographer 안무가 beautifully 멋지게, 훌륭하게 dress rehearsal 총연습

[해석] Cynthia Stroman이 이 뮤지컬의 안무가죠?
(A) 네, 그리고 훌륭하게 짜졌어요.
(B) 아니요, 저는 클래식 음악을 선호합니다.
(C) 오늘 저녁에 총연습이 있을 거예요.

[해설] 일반 의문은 Yes, and[but] / (No), but으로 시작하는 대답이 들리면 정답이다. (B)는 질문에 들어 있는 musical과 발음이 비슷한 music을, (C)는 choreographer나 musical에서 연상되는 단어 dress rehearsal을 들려줌으로써 오답을 유도하고 있다.

11. M Cn W Br

Have the results of the new skincare line's testing come in yet?

(A) A focus group discussion moderator.
(B) They weren't what we expected.
(C) The launch date has been rescheduled.

[어휘] line 제품군 yet (의문문에서) 벌써, 이제 focus group 포커스 그룹 (테스트할 상품을 토의하는 소비자 그룹) moderator 사회자 launch 출시

[해석] 새 스킨케어 제품군 테스트 결과가 이제 나왔나요?
(A) 포커스 그룹 토론 사회자요.
(B) 우리가 기대했던 결과가 아니네요.
(C) 출시 날짜가 다시 정해졌어요.

[해설] (A)와 (C)는 모두 질문에서 연상될 수 있는 대답으로 오답을 유도하고 있다. 제품 테스트 결과가 나왔지만 예상했던 것과 다르다고 말하는 게 자연스러운 대답이다.

12. M Cn W Am

You can reschedule the charity event, can't you?

(A) Don't forget to sign up in advance.
(B) The invitations have already been sent out.
(C) Last year's was the biggest yet.

[어휘] charity 자선 sign up 등록하다 in advance 미리, 사전

에 **yet** (최상급과 함께) 이제[지금]까지

> **해석** 자선 행사 일정을 다시 잡을 수 있죠?
> (A) 미리 등록하는 거 잊지 마세요.
> (B) 초대장이 이미 발송되었는데요.
> (C) 작년 행사가 지금까지 했던 것 중 가장 컸어요.

> **해설** 질문 앞부분을 놓치면 event만 듣고 (A)와 (C)처럼 연상되는 대답을 정답으로 착각할 수 있다. 질문 앞부분 You can reschedule(일정을 다시 잡을 수 있죠?)에 집중하면 초대장이 이미 발송되었기 때문에 일정을 바꿀 수 없다고 말하는 게 자연스러운 대답이라는 것을 알 수 있다.

Part 3

Questions 13 through 15 refer to the following conversation with three speakers.

> **M Au** Thank you both for attending this meeting regarding the Dover building project. It was a productive session.
>
> **W Am** [13]Absolutely, Frank's done a terrific job with the project thus far, and I'm really looking forward to taking over from this point.
>
> **M Au** Frank, is there any other information that Mina should be aware of?
>
> **M Cn** One more detail to keep in mind - the client requires all communication in writing. [14]So make sure you send e-mails to confirm any discussions held over the phone or in person.
>
> **W Am** Got it. [15]So Frank, I've heard you'll be working overseas.
>
> **M Cn** Yeah, I've never been to Morocco before, so I'm really excited about my next building project in Marrakesh.

13-15번 문제는 다음 3인 대화에 관한 것입니다.

> **남1:** 두 사람 모두 Dover 건축 프로젝트와 관련하여 이번 회의에 참석해줘서 고마워요. 생산적인 시간이었어요.
> **여:** 정말 그래요. Frank가 지금까지 프로젝트를 맡아 일을 정말 잘 했어요. 이 시점부터 인계받는 게 정말 기대돼요.
> **남1:** Frank, Mina가 알아야 하는 다른 정보가 있나요?

> **남2:** 명심해야 할 세부 사항이 하나 더 있어요. 고객이 모든 커뮤니케이션을 서면으로 요구하거든요. 그래서 전화나 직접 만나서 하는 어떤 논의든지 반드시 이메일을 보내서 확인시켜 주세요.
> **여:** 알겠어요. 그런데 Frank, 당신은 해외에서 근무할 거라고 들었어요.
> **남2:** 네, 모로코에는 한 번도 가본 적이 없어서 Marrakesh에서 있을 다음번 건축 프로젝트 때문에 정말 신이 나 있어요.

> **어휘** regarding ~에 관하여 session (특정한 활동을 위한) 시간 terrific 아주 좋은, 훌륭한 thus far 지금까지 take over 인계받다 keep *sth* in mind ~을 명심하다, 유념하다 in writing 서면으로 make sure (that) 반드시 (~하도록) 하다 confirm 확인해 주다 in person 직접, 몸소 get it 이해하다

---

13. What are the speakers discussing?

(A) Securing financial backing
(B) Negotiating a company merger
(C) Making travel arrangements
(D) Handing over a project's leadership

> **어휘** secure 확보하다 backing 지원 negotiate 협상하다 arrangements 준비, 마련 hand over ~을 넘겨주다, 인계하다

> **해석** 화자들은 무엇을 논하고 있는가?
> (A) 재정적 지원 확보하기
> (B) 회사 합병 협상하기
> (C) 출장 준비하기
> (D) 프로젝트 지휘권 인계하기

---

14. What does Frank advise the woman to do?

(A) Conduct negotiations in person
(B) Forward confirmation e-mails
(C) Lower overhead costs
(D) Modify a budget

> **어휘** conduct (특정한 활동을) 하다 negotiation 협상 forward 보내다, 전달하다 confirmation 확인 lower 내리다, 낮추다 overhead costs 간접비 modify 수정하다, 변경하다

> **해석** Frank는 여자에게 무엇을 하라고 조언하는가?
> (A) 협상은 직접 진행한다
> (B) 확인 이메일을 보낸다
> (C) 간접비를 낮춘다
> (D) 예산안을 수정한다

15. What does Frank say he is excited about?

(A) Collaborating with new colleagues
(B) Receiving a pay raise
(C) Hiring an support staff member
(D) Working in foreign country

→ **어휘** collaborate 협력하다　pay raise 임금 인상

→ **해석** Frank는 무엇 때문에 신이 나 있다고 말하는가?
(A) 새 동료들과 협력하는 것
(B) 인상된 급여를 받는 것
(C) 지원 인력을 고용하는 것
(D) 외국에서 근무하는 것

해설 13번은 주제를 묻는 질문이므로 첫 문장부터 집중하도록 하자. 남자1이 회의에 참석해 주어서 고맙다고 말하는데(Thank you both for attending this meeting), 이어지는 여자의 대사를 들으면 회의 주제가 무엇이었는지 알 수 있다. 지금까지 Frank가 잘 해오던 일을 이제 여자가 인계받아 한다고 말하고 있으므로(Frank's done a terrific job with the project thus far, and I'm really looking forward to taking over from this point.) 프로젝트 지휘권 이양 문제를 놓고 의논했음을 알 수 있다. 14번 문제의 정답은 Frank의 대사 make sure you send e-mails to confirm any discussions에서 어렵지 않게 알아낼 수 있다. 대화 말미에 여자가 I've heard you'll be working overseas.라고 말하는데, 이에 대한 대답으로 Frank가 모로코 Marrakesh에는 가본 적이 없어서 그곳에서 진행하는 프로젝트가 기대된다고 말하고 있으므로(I've never been to Morocco before, so I'm really excited about my next building project in Marrakesh.), 그는 지금 외국에 나가서 일하게 된 것에 신이 나 있음을 알 수 있다. 여기서 15번의 정답을 선택하자.

Questions 16 through 18 refer to the following conversation.

M｜Cn Jennifer. ¹⁶So, about my presentation for the pharmacology conference...

W｜Br So sorry! I should've gotten back to you earlier.

M｜Cn That's fine. I know you've been concentrating on the trial for the new allergy medicine.

W｜Br Yeah, but the outcomes are promising. ¹⁷We're on track to launch the new medication within the year.

M｜Cn Excellent! So would you like to see some slides at the moment?

W｜Br Sure.

M｜Cn ¹⁸All right, I just wanted to double-check if I listed all the researchers' names on the credits slide.

W｜Br ¹⁸OK, let me see... hmm... yeah... Hold on. [Wasn't Akira involved in this project...] ?

M｜Cn Oh, you're right! I'm glad you caught that.

16-18번 문제는 다음 대화에 관한 것입니다.

남: Jennifer. 저기, 약리학 학회에서 할 내 프레젠테이션 말인데요...
여: 정말 미안해요! 더 일찍 당신에게 연락했어야 했어요.
남: 괜찮아요. 새 알레르기 치료제 임상 시험에 집중하고 있었다는 거 알고 있어요.
여: 맞아요, 그런데 결과가 조짐이 좋아요. 연내에 신약을 출시할 수 있도록 일이 착착 진행되고 있어요.
남: 잘 됐네요! 그럼 지금 바로 슬라이드를 좀 보시겠어요?
여: 물론이죠.
남: 좋아요, 내가 크레디트 슬라이드에 모든 연구원들의 이름을 포함했는지 다시 확인하기만 하면 돼요.
여: 알겠어요, 어디 봐요... 음... 맞고... 잠깐. Akira가 이 프로젝트에 관여하지 않았나요?
남: 아, 맞다! 발견해 줘서 다행이에요.

어휘 pharmacology 약리학　conference 회의, 학회　trial 임상 시험　outcome 결과　promising 조짐이 좋은　on track 제대로 진행되고 있는　launch 출시하다　medication 의약, 약물　at the moment 바로 지금　double-check 재확인하다　list 명단에 포함하다　credits 크레디트(제작진, 출연진 명단)　Hold on. 기다려, 멈춰.　be involved in ~에 관여하다

16. What industry do the speakers most likely work in?

(A) Pharmaceutical
(B) Banking
(C) Marketing
(D) Information technology

해석 화자들은 어느 업계에서 일하는가?
(A) 제약
(B) 은행업
(C) 마케팅
(D) 정보 기술

17. What does the woman say will happen this year?

(A) Some research will receive additional funding.

(B) A new product will be unveiled.

(C) There will be a merger of two companies.

(D) An award ceremony will take place.

18. What does the woman imply when she says, "Wasn't Akira involved in this project"?

(A) Certain findings are not ready yet.

(B) A project requires additional personnel.

(C) There is a lack of information on a slide.

(D) The man must meet with a researcher.

Questions 19 through 21 refer to the following conversation and chart.

M Cn Hi, I'm in search of an Internet provider, so I thought I'd stop by to learn about your service plans.

W Am Of course. We offer the most competitive rates in this area. As shown on this chart, the longer your contract period, the lower your monthly cost.

M Cn ¹⁹But what happens if I need to terminate the contract before its completion?

W Am ¹⁹Well... we do charge an extra fee for that.

M Cn ²⁰Umm... I'm getting transferred overseas in about a year, so I'm not interested in committing to the two-year plan. But I do want the lowest possible price.

W Am ²¹In that case, the one-year plan seems like the most suitable option. Shall we proceed with signing the contract?

M Cn ²¹Sure, let's get to it.

Contract Length	Cost per Month
3 months	$50.00
6 months	$40.00
[21]1 year	$30.00
2 years	$20.00

계약 기간	월 사용료
3개월	50.00달러
6개월	40.00달러
1년	30.00달러
2년	20.00달러

19. According to the woman, when is an extra fee charged?

(A) When a customer transfers to a new location

(B) When a payment is overdue

(C) When new application is installed

(D) When a contract is canceled early

🔹**어휘** transfer 전근 가다 overdue 기한이 지난 application 애플리케이션[응용 소프트웨어]

🔹**해석** 여자의 말에 따르면 언제 추가 요금이 부과되는가?
(A) 고객이 다른 곳으로 전근을 갈 때
(B) 대금 납입의 기한이 지났을 때
(C) 새 애플리케이션이 설치되었을 때
(D) 계약이 조기에 취소되었을 때

20. What does the man say he will do next year?

(A) Relocate abroad

(B) Complete an internship program

(C) Purchase another device

(D) Renew a contract

🔹**어휘** relocate 이전하다 renew 갱신하다, 연장하다

🔹**해석** 남자는 내년에 무엇을 할 것이라고 말하는가?
(A) 해외로 이전한다
(B) 인턴 프로그램을 이수한다
(C) 다른 장치를 구입한다
(D) 계약을 갱신한다

21. Look at the graphic. How much has the man agreed to pay per month?

(A) $50.00

(B) $40.00

(C) $30.00

(D) $20.00

🔹**해석** 그래픽을 보라. 남자는 매달 얼마를 내는 데 동의하는가?
(A) 50달러
(B) 40달러
(C) 30달러
(D) 20달러

🔹**해설** 19번 문제의 키워드 an extra fee charged가 여자의 대사 we do charge an extra fee for that.에 들어 있다. 바로 앞에 나오는 남자의 대사에서 추가 요금이 어떤 경우에 부과되는지 알 수 있다. 계약 기간이 다 되기 전에 종료하는 경우에 어떻게 되는지 묻고 있으므로(But what happens if I need to terminate the contract before its completion?) 이 내용을 기억하고 정답을 고르면 된다. 정답을 고를 때는 항상 순발력이 필요하다. 바로 이어지는 남자의 대사 I'm getting transferred overseas in about a year를 들으면서 20번의 정답을 알아내야 하기 때문이다. 대화 마지막 부분에 가면 여자가 남자에게 1년 계약을 추천하면서(the one-year plan seems like the most suitable option.) 계약서 작성을 종용하고 있는데(Shall we proceed with signing the contract?) 여기에 동의하는 남자의 대사 Sure, let's get to it.을 들으면서 21번의 정답을 고르자.

Part 4

Questions 22 through 24 refer to the following broadcast.

W | Br Good morning, RKZ Radio listeners! [22]Today on the Chester Business Show, we have professional career counselor Janet Lin as our guest. Over this next hour, Ms. Lin will outline strategies for discovering a profession that matches your skills, interests, and personality. Towards the end of the show, we would love to hear from our audience, [23]so don't hesitate to call in when the lines are open and let us know what you think. Well, let me start off by saying welcome, Ms. Lin. [24]It has come to my attention that you're bringing out a book on this topic, set to be published in print next month.

22-24번 문제는 다음 방송에 관한 것입니다.

여: RKZ 라디오 청취자 여러분, 안녕하세요! 오늘 Chester Business Show에서는 전문 직업 상담가 Janet Lin을 게스트로 모셨습니다. 앞으로 한 시간 동안 Ms. Lin이 여러분의 기술과 흥미, 성격에 맞는 직업을 발견하는 전략의 개요를 설명해 드립니다. 쇼가 끝날 무렵에는 우리 청취자 여러분의 목소리를 듣기 원합니다. 그러니까 회선이 열리면 주저 말고 전화 주셔서 의견을 말씀해 주세요. 자, Ms. Lin, 먼저 환영 인사를 전해 드리며 시작하겠습니다. 이 주제에 대해 책을 출간하신다는 사실을 알게 되었는데요. 다음 달에 출간될 예정이라고요.

> **어휘** outline ~의 개요를 서술하다 strategy 전략 profession 직업 towards ~ 무렵에 audience 청취자 hesitate 망설이다. 주저하다 call in 전화를 하다 line (전화) 회선 It has come to one's attention that ~을 알게 되다 bring out ~을 출간하다 set to-V ~할 준비가 된 in print 인쇄된

---

22. What is Ms. Lin's area of expertise?

(A) Management of nonprofit organizations

(B) Professional advice on career choices

(C) Event planning and coordination

(D) Individual financial planning

> **어휘** nonprofit 비영리의 coordination 조정, 조직화

> **해석** Ms. Lin의 전문 분야는 무엇인가?
> (A) 비영리 기관 운영
> (B) 직업 선택에 관한 전문적인 조언
> (C) 행사 기획과 진행
> (D) 개인 재무 설계

---

23. What are listeners encouraged to do?

(A) Share their opinions over the phone

(B) Update their résumés

(C) Participate in a workshop

(D) Keep track of household spending

> **어휘** update 갱신하다 keep track of ~을 기록하다

> **해석** 청취자들에게 무엇을 하도록 권장하는가?
> (A) 전화로 의견을 공유한다
> (B) 이력서를 갱신한다
> (C) 워크숍에 참가한다
> (D) 가계 지출을 기록한다

---

24. What does the speaker say will happen next month?

(A) An educational session will be conducted.

(B) A schedule will be altered.

(C) An interview is scheduled to take place.

(D) A book will become available.

> **어휘** session (특정한 활동을 위한) 시간 conduct (특정한 활동을) 하다 alter 바꾸다, 변경하다

> **해석** 화자는 다음 달에 무슨 일이 있을 것이라고 말하는가?
> (A) 교육이 실시된다.
> (B) 일정이 변경된다.
> (C) 면접이 있을 예정이다.
> (D) 책이 출간된다.

> **해설** 22번 문제는 professional career counselor Janet Lin이라는 소개만 알아들으면 쉽게 정답을 알 수 있다. 방송 중간에는 청취자들의 의견을 듣는 시간이 있음을 알리면서(Towards the end of the show, we would love to hear from our audience) 전화로 의견을 말해달라고 권장하고 있다(so don't hesitate to call in when the lines are open and let us know what you think.). 이 부분이 패러프레이즈 된 문장을 23번의 정답으로 선택하자. 24번 문제는 게스트가 다음 달에 책을 출간할 예정이라는 마지막 문장(you're bringing out a book on this topic, set to be published in print next month.)을 들으면서 정답을 알 수 있다.

Questions 25 through 27 refer to the following message.

[M | Au] Hi, Shawn. [25]I've just finished meeting with Tara Goldberg from product development. She approved our design for the company's upcoming line of raincoats, but she's requesting different colors than what we originally suggested. [26]I tried my best to convince her that a fresh and contemporary look was needed, but she was set on maintaining a traditional approach. There wasn't much more I could do. You know... [she's the head of the department]. [27]Anyway, I'm back at my desk now, so I'm going to schedule a time on our calendars tomorrow when we can get together and start working on these changes.

25-27번 문제는 다음 메시지에 관한 것입니다.

남: 안녕, Shawn. 지금 막 제품 개발팀의 Tara Goldberg와 회의를 하고 나왔어요. 곧 나올 우리 회사의 새 레인코트 제품군의 디자인은 승인했는데, 우리가 당초 제안한 것과는 다른 색상을 요청하고 있어요. 신선하고 현대적인 모습이 필요하다는 점을 납득시키려고 최선을 다해 봤지만, 전통적인 접근법을 유지하는 쪽으로 확고하더라고요. 더 이상 해 볼 수 있는 게 별로 없었어요. 당신도 알다시피... 그분이 부서장이잖아요. 어쨌든 저는 지금 자리로 돌아왔거든요. 그러니까 내일 우리 일정 중에 모여서 이 변경 작업을 시작할 수 있는 시간을 잡아 볼게요.

어휘 upcoming 다가오는, 곧 있을 line 제품군 convince 납득시키다, 확신시키다 contemporary 현대의, 당대의 be set on ~에 대해 (견해, 생각이) 확고한, 고정된 maintain 유지하다, 지속하다 approach 접근법

25. What did the speaker discuss with Tara Goldberg?

(A) A hiring policy
(B) A product design
(C) An order for supplies
(D) An itinerary for a trip

어휘 supplies 용품, 비품 itinerary 여행 일정
해석 화자는 Tara Goldberg와 무엇에 대해 의논했는가?
(A) 채용 정책
(B) 제품 디자인
(C) 비품 주문
(D) 출장 일정

26. What does the speaker imply when he says, "she's the head of the department"?

(A) He wants to introduce a new executive.
(B) He lacks the authority to make the final decision.
(C) A job title has been incorrectly printed.
(D) A colleague has achieved great success.

어휘 executive 경영 간부, 중역 authority 권한 incorrectly 틀리게
해석 화자는 "그분이 부서장이잖아요."라고 말할 때 무엇을 암시하는가?
(A) 자신이 새 중역을 소개하고 싶다.

(B) 자신은 최종 결정을 내릴 권한이 없다.
(C) 직함이 잘못 인쇄되었다.
(D) 동료가 큰 성공을 거두었다.

27. What will the speaker most likely do next?

(A) Set up a meeting
(B) Refer to a catalog
(C) Fill out a form
(D) Meet with a client

어휘 set up ~을 준비하다 refer to ~을 참조하다 fill out ~을 작성하다
해석 화자는 이후에 무엇을 하겠는가?
(A) 회의를 준비한다
(B) 카탈로그를 참조한다
(C) 서식을 작성한다
(D) 고객과 만난다

해설 첫 문장에서 제품 개발팀의 Tara Goldberg와 회의를 하고 나왔는데, 그녀가 새 제품군의 디자인을 승인했다고 말했으므로(I've just finished meeting with Tara Goldberg from product development. She approved our design for the company's upcoming line of raincoats), 회의 주제는 제품 디자인이었다. 여기서 25번 문제의 정답을 선택하자. 이어지는 내용을 들어 보면 Ms. Goldberg가 제품 색상을 바꾸라고 요청했고(but she's requesting different colors than what we originally suggested.), 화자는 신선하고 현대적인 색상을 사용하도록 그녀를 설득하려고 했지만(I tried my best to convince her that a fresh and contemporary look was needed), Ms. Goldberg는 전통적인 색상을 고집했다(but she was set on maintaining a traditional approach). 화자는 그녀를 설득하기 위해 할 수 있는 일이 별로 없었다(There wasn't much more I could do). 이 내용을 미루어 보았을 때 이어지는 문장 she's the head of the department는 자기는 부서장이 아니기 때문에 최종 결정의 권한이 있는 Ms. Goldberg의 의견에 따를 수밖에 없다는 뜻이다. 여기서 26번의 정답을 고르자. so로 시작하는 마지막 문장에서 27번 문제의 정답을 알려준다. 내일 모여서 색상 변경 작업을 시작할 만한 시간을 마련하겠다고 했으므로(I'm going to schedule a time on our calendars tomorrow when we can get together and start working on these changes.), 이 문장을 이해하고 정답을 알아내야 한다.

Questions 28 through 30 refer to the following experts from a meeting and survey.

> **W | Br** Let's start the staff meeting by going over the results of the member survey our fitness center recently completed. [28]It's crucial to ensure that our current members are content, which is why these results are significant. Here are the top four answers to the question, "What enhancements would you most like to see?" [29]While many expressed a desire for a larger pool, it is not feasible due to financial constraints. However, we can afford to hire a couple of new staff members so we can address the second most popular choice. [30]If you have any contacts who are qualified and might be interested in a position here, please pass on their details.

28-30번 문제는 다음 회의 발췌문과 설문 조사에 관한 것입니다.

> **여:** 최근 우리 헬스클럽이 완료한 회원 설문 조사의 결과를 검토하면서 직원회의를 시작합시다. 우리의 현 회원들의 만족을 보장하는 것은 매우 중요하며, 바로 이 점이 이 결과가 의미 있는 이유입니다. 여기 "무엇이 개선되기를 가장 원하십니까?"라는 질문에 대한 가장 많은 응답 네 개가 있습니다. 많은 회원들이 더 큰 수영장에 대한 바람을 피력했지만, 그것은 재정적인 제약으로 실현 가능하지 않습니다. 그러나 두 번째로 인기 있었던 선택 사항을 해결하기 위해 직원 두세 명 정도를 더 채용할 여력은 있습니다. 자격이 되면서 이곳의 자리에 관심이 있을 만한 아는 사람이 있다면 자세한 사항을 전달해주실 것을 부탁드립니다.

어휘 excerpt 발췌 부분, 인용구 go over ~을 점검하다, 검토하다 crucial 중대한 content 만족하는 significant 중요한, 의미 있는 feasible 실현 가능한 constraint 제약, 제한 can afford to-V (시간, 금전적으로) ~할 여유가 있다 so (that) + S + can[may/will] + V ~하기 위해서 address 다루다, 해결하려 하다 contact 연락을 주고받는 사람 pass on ~을 넘겨주다, 전달하다

Survey Results

Expanded swimming facility – 40%
Extended operating hours – 20%
Updated exercise equipment – 10%
Diverse classes – 30%

설문 조사 결과

수영 시설 확장 – 40%
운영 시간 연장 – 20%
운동 장비 교체 – 10%
다양한 수업 – 30%

어휘 extend 연장하다 diverse 다양한

---

28. According to the speaker, what is the center's main concern?

(A) Satisfying current members
(B) Complying with industry standards
(C) Minimizing operating expenses
(D) Developing successful marketing campaigns

어휘 concern 관심사 comply with ~에 따르다, ~을 준수하다 minimize 최소화하다

해석 헬스클럽의 주요 관심사는 무엇인가?
(A) 현 회원들을 만족시키는 것
(B) 업계 표준을 따르는 것
(C) 운영비를 최소화하는 것
(D) 성공적인 마케팅 캠페인을 만드는 것

---

29. Look at the graphic. What survey result does the speaker want to address?

(A) Expanded swimming facility
(B) Extended operating hours
(C) Updated exercise equipment
(D) Diverse classes

해석 그래픽을 보라. 화자는 설문 조사 결과의 어느 부분을 해결하고 싶은가?
(A) 수영 시설 확장
(B) 운영 시간 연장
(C) 운동 장비 교체
(D) 다양한 수업

---

30. What does the speaker ask the listeners to do?

(A) Perform safety assessments
(B) Enroll in a certification program
(C) Refer potential employees
(D) Tour a construction site

어휘 assessment 평가 enroll in ~에 등록하다 certification (기술, 자격의) 증명, 자격증 refer 소개하다 tour 둘러보다

(A) 안전 점검을 실시한다

(B) 자격증 프로그램에 등록한다

(C) 직원이 될 만한 사람을 소개한다

(D) 공사 현장을 둘러본다

해설 두 번째 문장 It's crucial to ensure that our current members are content가 28번 문제의 정답을 알려준다. 현 회원들의 만족을 보장하는 것이 매우 중요하다고 했으므로 이것이 이 헬스클럽의 주요 관심사다. 설문 조사 결과 가장 많은 회원들이 원하는 것으로 나타난 수영장 확장은 자금 부족 문제로 실현할 수 없다(While many expressed a desire for a larger pool, it is not feasible due to financial constraints). 그러나 두 번째로 많은 회원들이 바라는 수업을 더 다양하게 제공하는 것은 가능하다고 말한다(However, we can afford to hire a couple of new staff members so we can address the second most popular choice). 여기서 29번 문제의 정답을 선택하자. 순발력이 필요하다는 사실을 잊지 말자. 바로 이어지는 마지막 문장에서 30번 문제의 정답을 고를 수 있게 준비해야 한다. 자격이 있고 헬스클럽 취업에 관심이 있을 만한 지인을 소개해달라고 요청하고 있으므로(If you have any contacts who are qualified and might be interested in a position here, please pass on their details.), 여기서 정답을 알 수 있다.

PART 1 Exercise

1 (D)　**2** (C)

1. M Cn

(A) Some people are trying on aprons.
(B) Customers are waiting around a cash register.
(C) Artworks are being hung on the wall.
(D) Some artists are working on drawings.

어휘 try on (옷을) 입어 보다, (신발을) 신어 보다 apron 앞치마 cash register 금전 등록기 artwork 미술품 hang (hung-hung) 걸다, 매달다

해석 (A) 사람들이 앞치마를 입어보고 있다.
(B) 고객들이 금전 등록기 주변에서 기다리고 있다.
(C) 미술품들이 벽에 걸려 있다.
(D) 미술가들이 그림 작업을 하고 있다.

해설 trying on(입어보고 있다)과 a cash register(금전 등록기)를 듣고 (A)와 (B)는 오답으로 골라내자. 그림이 벽에 걸려 있지도(are being hung) 않으므로 (C)도 오답이다. working이 들어 있는 문장은 매우 자주 출제되므로 본책에 정리되어 있는 문장들을 여러 번 따라 읽으면서 잘 익혀두도록 하자.

2. W Am

(A) Some workers are polishing a corridor.
(B) Pieces of tile are being set into a floor.
(C) The people are concentrating on their tasks.
(D) One of the women is reaching for a paper cup.

어휘 polish (윤이 나도록) 닦다 corridor 복도 set (특정한 위치에) 놓다 reach (손, 팔을 ~쪽으로) 뻗다, 내밀다

해석 (A) 복도를 닦고 있다.
(B) 타일 조각들을 바닥에 놓고 있다.
(C) 업무에 집중하고 있다.
(D) 종이컵을 향해 손을 뻗고 있다.

해설 polishing, are being set, reaching 같은 동사들을 기억하면서 오답을 잘 골라내고, Part 1에서는 어떤 동작을 하고 있든 concentrating이 들리면 다 정답이라는 사실을 기억하자.

PART 2 Exercise

1 (C)	**2** (C)	**3** (A)	**4** (A)	**5** (B)
6 (A)	**7** (A)	**8** (A)	**9** (A)	**10** (A)

1. M Au　W Am

How soon can I expect to receive a response regarding my job application?

(A) No, it's later in the day.
(B) An exceptional résumé and cover letter.
(C) We'll call you in two weeks.

어휘 regarding ~에 관하여[대하여] exceptional 탁월한, 특출한 cover letter 자기소개서

해석 제 입사 지원에 대해 답변을 언제 받는 것으로 예상하면 될까요?
(A) 아니요, 그건 오후에 있습니다.
(B) 특출한 이력서와 자기소개서입니다.
(C) 2주 후에 전화 드리겠습니다.

해설 질문이 의문사 의문문이므로 (A)는 No를 듣자마자 오답인 것을 알 수 있으며, (B)는 질문에 들어 있는 expect와 발음이 비슷한 exceptional을 들려주면서 job application에서 연상되는 대답으로 오답을 유도하고

있다. How soon[quickly/late] ~?는 When 의문문과 같다고 생각하고 정답을 선택하자.

---

2. ⬚M|Cn⬚ ⬚W|Br⬚

How could I access my e-mail account on my tablet?

(A) The mail carrier will stop by soon.
(B) On the table next to the photocopier.
(C) Download the e-mail application.

🔹**어휘** mail carrier 우편집배원 stop by 잠시 들르다 photocopier 복사기 application 앱, 애플리케이션

🔹**해석** 태블릿에서는 어떻게 이메일 계정에 접속하나요?
(A) 우편집배원이 곧 들를 겁니다.
(B) 복사기 옆에 있는 테이블에요.
(C) 이메일 앱을 다운로드하세요.

🔹**해설** (A)는 질문에 들어 있는 mail을 반복시키면서, (B)는 tablet과 발음이 비슷한 table을 들려주면서 오답을 유도하고 있다. (B)는 Where 의문문의 정답으로 알맞은 대답이기도 하다. 질문이 How + 일반 동사 ~?일 때는 명령문이 들리면 정답이다.

---

3. ⬚W|Am⬚ ⬚M|Au⬚

How do you like your new job so far?

(A) I can work from home quite frequently.
(B) A career in mechanical engineering.
(C) My brother helped me apply.

🔹**어휘** so far 지금까지 frequently 자주, 흔히 mechanical engineering 기계 공학

🔹**해석** 새 일자리가 지금까지 어떤가요?
(A) 꽤 자주 재택근무를 할 수 있어요.
(B) 기계 공학 분야의 경력이요.
(C) 저희 형이 지원하도록 도와주었습니다.

🔹**해설** 의견을 묻는 질문인 How do you like ~?에서는 형용사나 부사를 사용하는 대답이 들리면 정답이다. 부사 frequently를 듣고 이 문장이 정답임을 알 수 있다. (B)와 (C)는 모두 질문의 new job에서 연상되는 대답으로 오답을 유도하고 있다.

---

4. ⬚W|Br⬚ ⬚M|Au⬚

How far away are you from the clinic?

(A) I'm near enough to walk.
(B) I'll make an appointment with the doctor.
(C) That clinic is pretty well known.

🔹**해석** 병원에서 어느 정도 거리에 사시나요?
(A) 걸어 다닐 만큼 충분히 가깝습니다.
(B) 제가 병원에 예약할게요.
(C) 저 병원은 상당히 유명해요.

🔹**해설** 질문 앞부분 How far away만 알아들어도 자연스러운 대답을 알 수 있다. (B)는 질문에 나오는 the clinic에서 연상되는 대답으로, (C)는 clinic을 반복시키면서 오답을 유도하고 있다.

---

5. ⬚W|Am⬚ ⬚M|Au⬚

How many more shipments are we expecting today?

(A) It was an impressive turnout.
(B) I can wait for them if you need to leave.
(C) No, it should be much less than that.

🔹**어휘** shipment 수송품 turnout 참가자 수

🔹**해석** 우리가 오늘 수송품을 몇 개 더 받아야 하나요?
(A) 인상적인 참가자 수였어요.
(B) 가셔야 하면 제가 기다릴게요.
(C) 아니요, 그것보다는 훨씬 더 적을 겁니다.

🔹**해설** 질문 앞부분이 How many more shipments(얼마나 더 많은 수송품)이므로 (A)는 자연스럽지 않은 대답이다. (C)는 No를 듣는 순간 오답임을 알 수 있다. 오답을 잘 골라낼수록 고수가 된다!

---

6. ⬚M|Au⬚ ⬚W|Am⬚

How can I reserve one of the meeting rooms at the library?

(A) Let me get the librarian to help you with that.
(B) They usually meet from ten to eleven A.M.
(C) That book's already been checked out.

🔹**어휘** librarian (도서관의) 사서 check out (도서관에서) 대출하다

🔹**해석** 도서관에서 회의실 중 하나를 예약하려면 어떻게 해야 하나요?
(A) 그건 사서에게 도와드리라고 할게요.
(B) 보통 오전 10시부터 11시까지 모입니다.
(C) 그 책은 이미 대출이 되었습니다.

🔹**해설** 질문 앞부분 How can I reserve(예약하려면 어떻게 해야 하나요)에 집중하면 자연스러운 대답을 선택할 수 있다. (B)는 When 의문문이나 What time ~?에 대한 대답으로 알맞은 문장이고, (C)는 How can I reserve? 에 대한 대답이 아니라, 이러한 질문을 하기 전에 들을 만한 말이다.

7. M|Cn W|Br

How often do you go back to Boston to visit?

(A) My parents don't live there anymore.
(B) We usually fly.
(C) Yes, it's one of my favorite destinations!

🔹어휘 fly 비행기로 가다 destination 여행지, 목적지

🔹해석 보스턴에는 얼마마다 한 번씩 돌아가 방문하시나요?
(A) 저희 부모님께서 더 이상 거기 살지 않으십니다.
(B) 보통은 비행기로 갑니다.
(C) 네, 제가 가장 좋아하는 여행지 중 하나예요!

🔹해설 How often ~?이라고 물었으므로 비행기를 탄다고 말하는 (B)는 오답이다. (C)는 Yes만 듣고 오답임을 알 수 있다. 오답을 잘 골라낼수록 고수가 된다!

8. W|Br M|Cn

How do you think we can meet the project deadline?

(A) It looks like we'll have to work extra hours.
(B) Can you turn off the projector?
(C) The meeting went longer than expected.

🔹어휘 projector 영사기

🔹해석 어떻게 하면 프로젝트 기한에 맞출 수 있을 거라고 생각하세요?
(A) 추가 근무를 해야 할 것 같은데요.
(B) 프로젝터 좀 꺼 주시겠어요?
(C) 회의가 예상보다 오래 지속되었어요.

🔹해설 (B)는 질문에 들어 있는 project와 발음이 비슷한 projector를, (C)는 meet이 포함된 meeting을 들려주면서 오답을 유도하고 있다. 오답을 잘 골라낼수록 고수가 된다!

9. W|Am M|Cn

How did you get the additional discount coupons?

(A) I signed up for them online.
(B) Usually twenty percent off.
(C) No, the package hasn't arrived.

🔹어휘 sign up (for) ~을 신청하다, 등록하다 off 할인하여

🔹해석 추가 할인 쿠폰은 어떻게 받으셨어요?

(A) 저는 온라인으로 신청했어요.
(B) 보통은 20퍼센트 할인이요.
(C) 아니요, 소포는 도착하지 않았어요.

🔹해설 질문 앞부분 How did you get(어떻게 받으셨어요?)에 집중하면 자연스러운 대답이 무엇인지 알 수 있다. (B)는 질문의 discount에서 연상되는 대답으로 오답을 유도하고 있고, (C)는 No라고 대답하고 있기 때문에 당연히 오답이다.

10. M|Cn W|Am

How do you want to showcase these new arrivals?

(A) Let's display them in the storefront.
(B) They're selling very quickly.
(C) You may be at the wrong gate.

🔹어휘 showcase 진열하다 new arrival 신착 상품 storefront 매장 앞쪽

🔹해석 새로 들어온 이 상품들을 어떻게 진열하고 싶으세요?
(A) 매장 앞쪽에 둡시다.
(B) 불티나게 팔리고 있어요.
(C) 게이트를 잘못 찾아오신 것 같은데요.

🔹해설 질문 앞부분 How do you want to showcase(어떻게 진열하고 싶으세요?)에 집중하면 자연스러운 대답을 선택할 수 있다. (B)와 (C)는 모두 질문에 들어 있는 new arrivals에서 연상되는 대답으로 오답을 유도하고 있다.

PART 3 Sample Questions

1-3번 문제는 다음 편지에 관한 것입니다.

여: 안녕하세요. 매장에서 첼로 레슨을 한다는 텔레비전 광고를 보고 등록하고 싶어서요.
남: 좋습니다. 첼로 경험이 있으신가요?
여: 음, 고등학교 오케스트라에서 조금 해 봤어요.
남: 알겠습니다. 중급반이 잘 맞을 것으로 보이네요. 수업은 다음 주에 시작될 예정입니다.
여: 좋아요.
남: 그 동안 저희 홈페이지에서 개별 지도 동영상을 보실 수 있는데, 주간 이메일을 구독하시면 됩니다. 회원이 되는 데 관심 있으신가요?
여: 아, 그거 좋겠네요. 제 이메일 주소는 elsa785@ mailexchange.com이에요.
남: 좋습니다. 준비는 다 되었고요, 첫 레슨은 다음 주 월요일 저녁 7시로 예정되어 있습니다. 거기서 뵙겠습니다.

어휘 intermediate 중급의 good fit 잘 맞는 것 in the meantime 그 동안[사이]에 tutorial 개별 지도 set 준비가 된

---

1. 여자는 고등학교에서 무엇을 했다고 말하는가?

(A) 동호회를 창설했다.
(B) 웹 사이트를 개발했다.
(C) 음악 단체에 참여했다.
(D) 온라인 수업을 들었다.

어휘 found 설립하다

---

2. 상점 웹 사이트에서 무엇을 이용할 수 있는가?

(A) 판촉 할인
(B) 교육용 동영상
(C) 음악가들과의 소통
(D) 매장 행사 일정

---

3. 여자가 "아, 그거 좋겠네요."라고 말할 때 무엇을 암시하는가?

(A) 이메일 주소가 기억하기 쉽다.
(B) 수업료가 적정하게 매겨져 있다.
(C) 악기가 조율되어 있다.
(D) 메일링 리스트에 가입할 수 있다.

어휘 reasonably 적정하게, 타당하게 price 가격을 매기다 [정하다] in tune 조율이 된

PART 3 & 4 Exercise

1 (D) **2** (A) **3** (C) **4** (B) **5** (D) **6** (A)

Questions 1 through 3 refer to the following conversation.

W Br ¹Evan, how did the marketing meeting go this morning? You were going to bring up our department's workload and ask for assistance, right?

M Au Yes! ¹ ²The company director has agreed to allocate an additional two hundred thousand dollars to our marketing department's budget.

W Br [That's a substantial rise from last year!] Do you have any details on how that money will be used?

M Au ³Well, the department managers have given their approval for most of the funds to go towards hiring two new staff members. Adding another artist and a digital advertising specialist to our team would be beneficial in dealing with our workload.

1-3번 문제는 다음 대화에 관한 것입니다.

여: Evan, 오전에 마케팅 회의 어떻게 됐어요? 우리 부서의 업무량 얘기를 꺼내서 지원을 요청하려고 했던 거 맞죠?

남: 네! 대표님이 추가로 20만 달러를 우리 마케팅부의 예산에 할당하는 데 동의하셨어요.

여: 그건 작년에 비해 상당한 증가잖아요! 그 돈이 어떻게 사용될 것인지 세부 사항을 알고 있나요?

남: 음. 부서장들이 대부분의 자금이 두 명의 새 직원을 채용하는 데 사용되는 것을 승인했어요. 우리 팀에 아티스트를 한 명 더 추가하고 디지털 광고 전문가까지 있으면 업무량을 감당하는 데 도움이 될 거예요.

어휘 bring up (화제를) 꺼내다 workload 업무량 company director 대표 이사 allocate 할당하다 substantial 상당한 give one's approval for ~을 승인하다 beneficial 유익한

---

1. What department do the speakers work in?

(A) Product development
(B) Human resources
(C) Accounting
(D) Marketing

해석 화자들은 어느 부서에서 근무하는가?
(A) 제품개발부
(B) 인사부
(C) 회계부
(D) 마케팅부

---

2. Why does the woman say, "That's a substantial rise from last year"?

(A) To suggest that some news is good
(B) To deny a proposed budget adjustment
(C) To indicate that a fee is appropriate
(D) To correct some inaccurate information

3. According to the man, what do the department managers plan to do?

(A) Purchase new equipment
(B) Organize a conference
(C) Recruit some more employees
(D) Diversify a product range

Questions 4 through 6 refer to the following talk.

M | Au To wrap up, I need to address some vacation requests. ⁴A number of drivers have asked me for time off towards the end of this month... but you know [it's the holiday season.] ⁴Shipping volumes will increase by forty percent over the next four weeks. ⁵And in fact, we're going to be so busy that we just hired some temporary help. ⁶So, for those of you who sent in requests, if you're considering taking time off after the holidays, I'll be sending back your request forms to you so you can update them with new dates.

4-6번 문제는 다음 담화에 관한 것입니다.

4. Why does the man say, "it's the holiday season"?

(A) To express his thrill
(B) To turn down a request
(C) To express dissatisfaction with a schedule
(D) To show appreciation to a colleague

5. What has the company recently done?

   (A) Adjusted a product price
   (B) Updated a policy
   (C) Established a new facility
   (D) Recruited temporary workers

▶어휘 adjust 조정하다 establish 설치하다, 개설하다 recruit 모집하다

▶해석 회사는 최근에 무엇을 했는가?
   (A) 제품 가격을 조정했다
   (B) 정책을 갱신했다
   (C) 새 시설을 개설했다
   (D) 임시 직원들을 모집했다

---

6. What will the man most likely do next?

   (A) Return some paperwork
   (B) Post some photographs
   (C) Revise a manual
   (D) Lead an orientation

▶어휘 post 게시하다, 게재하다 revise 수정하다

▶해석 남자는 이후에 무엇을 하겠는가?
   (A) 서류를 반환한다
   (B) 사진을 게재한다
   (C) 매뉴얼을 수정한다
   (D) 오리엔테이션을 진행한다

▶해설 4번 문제는 앞뒤 문장들의 내용을 고려하여 정답을 유추해야 하는데, 우선 앞문장에 들어 있는 have asked me의 호주식 발음을 익혀두자. asked를 '아스크트'라고 읽어야 하는데, 앞에 있는 have와 연음이 일어나고, 뒤에 me가 붙으면서 -ked 부분의 발음은 탈락한다. 그래서 '해바스미'라고 읽게 된다. 많은 기사들이 월말에 휴가를 신청했는데(A number of drivers have asked me for time off towards the end of this month), 지금을 휴가 기간이라서(but you know it's the holiday season.), 앞으로 4주간의 운송 물량이 크게 증가할 전망이다(Shipping volumes will increase by forty percent over the next four weeks). 담화의 맥락상 it's the holiday season.은 지금은 휴가를 가기에 알맞은 시기가 아니므로 신청을 반려하겠다는 뜻이다. 정답을 고를 때는 반드시 순발력을 발휘해야 하므로 선택지의 내용을 잘 기억하도록 노력하자. 재빨리 정답을 선택하고 바로 이어지는 문장에서 we just hired some temporary help.를 들으면서 5번 문제의 정답을 알아내야 한다. do next 문제의 정답은 언제나 마지막 문장에서 드러난다. I'll be sending back your request forms to you가 패러프레이즈 되어 있는 구문을 6번 문제의 정답으로 선택하자.

1 (C)	**2** (C)	**3** (D)	**4** (C)	**5** (B)
6 (C)	**7** (C)	**8** (A)	**9** (A)	**10** (C)
11 (B)	**12** (B)	**13** (C)	**14** (A)	**15** (B)
16 (D)	**17** (B)	**18** (A)	**19** (A)	**20** (C)
21 (B)	**22** (C)	**23** (D)	**24** (D)	**25** (D)
26 (B)	**27** (A)	**28** (A)	**29** (D)	**30** (D)

* 정답을 맞힌 문제도 해설을 읽어보세요.

Part 1

1. M | Au

   (A) One of the women is pointing at something on the board.
   (B) One of the men is entering the room.
   (C) One of the women has her back to a group of people.
   (D) One of the men is opening a folder.

▶어휘 point at ~을 가리키다 back 등; (등)허리

▶해석 (A) 여자 중 한 명이 칠판 위의 무언가를 가리키고 있다.
   (B) 남자 중 한 명이 방에 들어서고 있다.
   (C) 여자 중 한 명이 사람들을 등지고 있다.
   (D) 남자 중 한 명이 폴더를 열고 있다.

▶해설 pointing과 entering, opening은 모두 사진에 나타나지 않는 동작이다. have one's back to(~을 등지고 있다)를 기억하고 정답을 선택하자.

---

2. W | Br

(A) The man is riding a bicycle along the path.
(B) The man is taking off his helmet.
(C) The man is fastening his bike to the exterior of a vehicle.
(D) The man is moving a bicycle to the repair shop.

어휘 take off (옷 등을) 벗다 fasten 매다, 고정시키다 exterior 외부, 바깥면

해석 (A) 길을 따라 자전거를 타고 있다.
(B) 헬멧을 벗고 있다.
(C) 자전거를 차량 바깥에 고정시키고 있다.
(D) 자전거를 수리점으로 옮기고 있다.

해설 riding과 moving은 사진에 나타나지 않는 동작이므로 (A)와 (D)는 오답으로 골라내자. 복장을 묘사하기 위해 wearing을 사용하는 문장은 정답이 될 수 있지만, 입고 벗는 동작을 나타내는 putting on, removing, taking off가 들리는 문장은 오답이므로(Day 01 **주의 3 참조**) (B)도 골라내자. 동사 fastening을 기억하고 정답을 선택하자.

3. M | Cn

(A) The man is filling a bucket with water.
(B) The man is carrying a helmet.
(C) The man is leaning against a wall.
(D) The man is wearing safety gear.

어휘 carry 휴대하다, 들고 가다 lean ~에 기대다 safety gear 안전 장비

해석 (A) 양동이를 물로 채우고 있다.
(B) 헬멧을 들고 있다.
(C) 벽에 기대어 있다.
(D) 안전 장비를 착용하고 있다.

해설 채우고 있거나(filling) 기대어 있는(leaning) 장면이 아니므로 (A)와 (C)는 오답이다. 사진에 헬멧(a helmet)이 보이지 않으므로 (B)도 오답이다. 토익 시험에는 신체 보호용으로 착용하는 복장이나 장비의 통칭인 protective clothing, safety gear 같은 단어가 자주 나온다.

Part 2

4. M | Cn   W | Br

How much does this watch cost?

(A) Not so often these days.
(B) It's quarter to ten.
(C) Is the price tag missing?

어휘 quarter to ten 10시 15분 전 price tag 가격표 missing 없어진

해석 이 시계는 얼마인가요?
(A) 요즘에는 그리 자주 하지는 않습니다.
(B) 10시 15분 전입니다.
(C) 가격표가 없나요?

해설 (A)는 질문이 How often ~?일 때, (B)는 What time ~? 일 때 정답으로 알맞은 대답이다. 오답을 잘 골라낼수록 고수가 된다. 정답을 도저히 알 수 없을 때는 (C)처럼 반문하는 대답이 가장 확률이 높다는 사실을 기억하자.

5. W | Br   M | Au

How can I lower the projector screen?

(A) I owe him money for dinner.
(B) The control panel's next to the door.
(C) Which shelf is it on?

어휘 lower 내리다, 낮추다 projector 영사기 owe 빚지고 있다 control panel 제어판

해석 프로젝터 스크린은 어떻게 내리나요?
(A) 그에게 저녁 값을 갚아야 해요.
(B) 문 옆에 제어판이 있어요.
(C) 어느 선반에 있는데요?

해설 질문 앞부분 How can I lower(어떻게 내리나요?)에 집중하면 자연스러운 대답이 어느 것인지 알 수 있다.

6. W | Br   M | Au

How can we find summer interns for the marketing team?
(A) These are the summer rates.
(B) I'll check the storage room for them.

(C) Let's post some announcements on campus.

어휘 rate 요금 post 게시하다, 게재하다 announcement 알림, 공고

해석 마케팅팀의 여름 인턴사원들을 어떻게 찾을 수 있을까요?
(A) 이건 여름 요금입니다.
(B) 창고에서 찾아볼게요.
(C) 캠퍼스에 공고를 냅시다.

해설 (A)는 질문에 들어 있는 summer를 반복해서 들려주면서 오답을 유도하고 있다. 질문 앞부분 How can we find summer interns(여름 인턴사원들을 어떻게 찾을 수 있을까요?)에 집중해서 자연스러운 대답을 알아내자.

---

7. W Br M Au

How can we cut office expenses?

(A) It's on the fourth floor.
(B) I thought it was on sale.
(C) We use a significant amount of paper for printing.

어휘 on sale 할인[세일] 중인 significant 상당한

해석 사무실 운영 경비를 어떻게 절감할 수 있을까요?
(A) 4층에 있습니다.
(B) 할인 중인 줄 알았어요.
(C) 우리가 인쇄하는 데 상당량의 종이를 사용하잖아요.

해설 (A)는 Where 의문문의 정답으로 알맞은 대답이고, (B)는 질문의 cut과 expenses에서 연상되는 표현 on sale을 들려주면서 오답을 유도하고 있다. 오답을 잘 골라낼수록 고수가 된다!

---

8. M Cn W Am

How should I store these photographs?

(A) Rachel is responsible for that.
(B) From the company outing.
(C) Yes, the staff is very knowledgeable.

어휘 store 보관하다 outing 야유회 staff (모든) 직원 knowledgeable 아는 것이 많은

해석 이 사진들을 어떻게 보관할까요?
(A) 그 일은 Rachel 담당이에요.
(B) 회사 야유회에서요.
(C) 네, 직원들이 아는 것이 매우 많습니다.

해설 질문 앞부분 How should I store(어떻게 보관할까요?)에만 집중하면 자연스러운 대답을 선택할 수 있다. (B)는 질문에 들어 있는 photographs에서 연상되는 대답으로 오답을 유도하고 있으며, (C)는 Yes를 듣는 순간 오답임을 알 수 있다.

---

9. W Am W Br

Does this job candidate have good money-management skills?

(A) Here's a copy of her résumé.
(B) The bank closes at 5 P.M.
(C) A very long commute.

어휘 commute 통근 (거리)

해석 이 입사 지원자는 자산 관리 능력이 좋은가요?
(A) 그녀의 이력서 사본이 여기 있습니다.
(B) 은행은 오후 5시에 문 닫습니다.
(C) 매우 긴 통근 거리요.

해설 이력서를 주는 것은 입사 지원자의 자산 관리 능력이 좋은지 읽어 보고 확인하라는 말이므로 정답이 된다.

---

10. W Am M Au

Weren't the interns supposed to be working on this research project?

(A) She's with another patient.
(B) I'm going to start walking for exercise.
(C) Their training is not yet complete.

어휘 be supposed to-V ~하기로 되어 있다

해석 인턴사원들이 이 연구 프로젝트에 참여하기로 되어 있지 않았나요?
(A) 그녀는 다른 환자를 보고 있습니다.
(B) 운동으로 걷기를 시작하려고요.
(C) 교육이 아직 완료되지 않았어요.

해설 (A)는 질문에 나오는 interns에서 연상되는 단어 patient를, (B)는 working과 발음이 비슷한 walking을 들려주면서 오답을 유도하고 있다. 오답을 잘 골라낼수록 고수가 된다!

---

11. W Am M Cn

There has to be a faster way to drive to the headquarters.

(A) A commercial driver's license.
(B) Sorry, I'm not aware of any other routes.
(C) I'll be away for a quarter of an hour.

어휘 headquarters 본사 commercial 상업의, 이윤을 목적으로 한 away 자리에 없는

해설 본사까지 운전해서 가는 데는 틀림없이 더 빠른 길이 있을 텐데요.
(A) 영업용 운전면허요.
(B) 미안해요. 다른 경로는 모르겠어요.
(C) 15분 정도 자리를 비울 겁니다.

해설 (A)는 질문의 drive와 발음이 비슷한 driver를 들려주면서, (C)는 way와 발음이 비슷한 away를 들려주고, headquarters에 들어 있는 quarter를 반복시키면서 오답을 유도하고 있다. 질문 앞부분 There has to be a faster way(틀림없이 더 빠른 길이 있을 텐데요.)에 집중하면 자연스러운 대답이 어느 것인지 알 수 있다.

12. W Br W Am

Has the cleaning service confirmed for next Friday?

(A) The event was a tremendous success!

(B) I haven't checked my e-mail yet.

(C) Because it was too dirty.

어휘 confirm 확정하다 tremendous 엄청난, 대단한

해석 청소 업체가 서비스를 다음 주 금요일로 확정해 주었나요?
(A) 행사가 엄청난 성공이었어요!
(B) 아직 이메일을 확인하지 않았어요.
(C) 너무 더러웠거든요.

해설 "모른다"는 대답은 거의 항상 정답이다. I haven't checked. / Let me check ~. / Check with + 사람 / Check + 사물 같은 것들은 자주 출제되고 있으므로 기억해 두는 것이 좋다.

Part 3

Questions 13 through 15 refer to the following conversation.

M Cn Hi, Carly. [13]I tried to book seats for the play we planned to take our Taipei colleagues to, but there weren't any tickets left. Do you have any other ideas for activities we can do instead?

W Br Oh, that's unfortunate. Well, the weather is forecast to be lovely this weekend. [14]Have you considered treating them to a dinner at Port View Restaurant? It's located on a cruise ship on the riverfront, and I've brought guests there before.

M Cn I've been told about that ship, and the city landscape from the river is supposed to be spectacular. [15]Could you please look into the cost of the dinner cruise?

13-15번 문제는 다음 대화에 관한 것입니다.

남: 안녕, Carly. Taipei 동료들을 데리고 가려고 했던 연극 좌석을 예약하려고 했는데요, 남아 있는 표가 없었어요. 대신 할 만한 활동에 대한 다른 아이디어가 있나요?

여: 아, 안타깝게 됐네요. 음, 이번 주말에는 날씨가 화창할 것으로 예보되고 있잖아요. Port View 식당에서 저녁 식사를 대접하는 거 생각해 보셨어요? 강변 유람선에 있는데, 저도 전에 손님들을 데리고 거기 가 봤어요.

남: 그 배에 대해 들어봤어요. 강에서 보는 도시 전경도 장관이라고들 하더라고요. 유람선 타면서 하는 저녁 식사 비용을 좀 알아봐 주겠어요?

어휘 book 예약하다 treat A to B A에게 B를 대접하다 cruise ship 유람선 riverfront 강변 지대 city landscape 도시 전경 be supposed to-V (일반적으로) ~라고 한다 spectacular 장관인, 볼 만한 look into ~을 조사하다 cruise 유람선 여행

13. What problem does the man mention?

(A) A reservation is not accurate.

(B) A business trip has been deferred.

(C) An event is sold out.

(D) Credit card payments are not permitted.

어휘 defer 미루다, 연기하다 sold out 표가 매진된

해석 남자는 어떤 문제를 언급하는가?
(A) 예약이 정확하지 않다.
(B) 출장이 연기되었다.
(C) 행사 표가 매진되었다.
(D) 신용카드 납부가 허용되지 않는다.

14. What does the woman suggest offering their colleagues?

(A) A meal on a boat

(B) A room upgrade at a hotel

(C) Admission to a sporting event

(D) Gift certificates for a store

어휘 admission 들어감, 입장 gift certificate 상품권

해석 여자는 동료들에게 무엇을 제공하라고 제안하는가?
(A) 배에서 하는 식사
(B) 호텔 방 업그레이드
(C) 스포츠 행사 입장
(D) 상점 상품권

15. What does the man ask the woman to do?

(A) Contact a travel agent
(B) Research pricing information
(C) Make a payment beforehand
(D) Coordinate transportation

🔺어휘 travel agent 여행사 직원 beforehand 사전에, 미리
coordinate 편성하다 transportation 교통편

🔺해석 남자는 여자에게 무엇을 해 달라고 요구하는가?
(A) 여행사 직원에게 연락한다
(B) 가격 정보를 조사한다
(C) 미리 결제를 한다
(D) 교통편을 편성한다

🔺해설 대화를 시작하면서 남자가 문제를 언급한다. 연극
좌석을 예약하려고 했지만 남아 있는 표가 없다고 했으므
로(I tried to book seats for the play ~ but there weren't
any tickets left.) 여기서 13번 문제의 정답을 고르자. 연
극 공연 대신 동료들에게 제공하자고 여자가 제안하는 것
은 강변 유람선에서 운영하는 식당에서 하는 식사다(Have
you considered treating them to a dinner at Port View
Restaurant? It's located on a cruise ship on the
riverfront). 여기서 14번의 정답을 알 수 있다. 여자의 제
안을 들은 남자는 마지막 문장에서 유람선 식사 비용을
알아봐 달라고 부탁하고 있다(Could you please look
into the cost of the dinner cruise?). 여기서 15번 문제의
정답을 고르자.

Questions 16 through 18 refer to the following
conversation.

W Br I'm really impressed by how many
talented young scientists we've managed to
recruit recently, [16]but I'm also worried that our
research group lacks the kind of experience
we need for these upcoming projects.

M Au I've been giving that some thought as
well. We've identified some of the sharpest
up-and-coming chemists in the industry,
but they're in need of quality, hands-on
leadership. [17]We should really add a second
manager to the department, especially
one dedicated to training and professional
development.

W Br [Now that's an idea.] The greater the
support we give to the new employees, the
higher their productivity will be. [18]How about
we go over all the details so we can propose
this to the vice president?

16–18번 문제는 다음 대화에 관한 것입니다.

여: 최근에 우리가 재능 있는 젊은 과학자들을 이렇게 많
이 모집해 냈다는 게 정말 인상적이에요. 하지만 우리
연구팀이 이번에 다가오는 프로젝트를 위해 필요한
종류의 경험이 부족하다는 건 걱정이네요.
남: 나 역시 그 점을 조금 생각하고 있었어요. 우리가 업
계에서 가장 명석하고 전도유망한 화학자들 몇몇을
찾아내기는 했지만, 그들은 양질의 실무 지도가 필요
해요. 부서에 정말로 매니저를 한 명 더, 특히 교육과
전문성 개발을 전담해 줄 사람으로 뽑아야겠어요.
여: 어, 좋은 생각이에요. 신입 직원들에게 해주는 지원이
더 클수록 생산성도 더 높아질 거예요. 이걸 부사장님
께 제안할 수 있게 모든 세부 사항을 검토해 보는 게
어때요?

🔺어휘 impressed 인상 깊게 생각하는 talented 재능 있는
manage to–V (어려움에도) ~을 해내다 recruit 모집하다
upcoming 다가오는, 곧 있을 give sth thought 곰곰이
생각하다 identify 찾다, 발견하다 sharp 예리한, 명석한
up-and-coming 전도유망한 in need of ~이 필요한
quality 양질의 hands-on 실무형의, 직접 관여하는
dedicated to ~을 전담하는 professional
development 전문성 개발 productivity 생산성 go
over ~을 점검하다, 검토하다

---

16. What problem does the woman
mention?

(A) An error occurred during a research.
(B) Some project deadlines have
expired.
(C) A department lacks adequate
financial resources.
**(D) Some staff members are
inexperienced.**

🔺어휘 deadline 기한, 마감 일자 expire (기간이) 만료되다, 끝나다
adequate 충분한, 적절한 inexperienced 경험이 부족한,
미숙한

🔺해석 여자는 어떤 문제를 언급하는가?
(A) 연구 중 오류가 발생했다.
(B) 몇몇 프로젝트의 기한이 만료되었다.
(C) 부서에 충분한 재원이 부족하다.
(D) 일부 직원들이 경험이 부족하다.

---

17. What does the woman mean when she
says, "Now that's an idea"?

(A) She is seeking additional advice.
**(B) The man has come up with a
useful suggestion.**

(C) The existing plan is overly complicated.

(D) A change is occurring at the right time.

🔹**어휘** seek 청하다, 구하다 come up with (해답을) 찾아내다, 내놓다 existing 기존의 overly 지나치게, 너무

🔹**해석** 여자는 "어, 좋은 생각이에요."라고 말할 때 무엇을 의미하는가?
(A) 추가적인 조언을 구하고 있다.
(B) 남자가 유용한 제안을 내놓았다.
(C) 기존의 계획은 지나치게 복잡하다.
(D) 변화가 적시에 일어나고 있다.

---

18. What will the speakers most likely do next?

(A) Discuss a proposal
(B) Offer a promotion
(C) Arrange an interview
(D) Examine a report

🔹**어휘** arrange 마련하다, 주선하다

🔹**해석** 화자들은 이후에 무엇을 하겠는가?
(A) 제안에 대해 의논한다
(B) 승진을 제안한다
(C) 면접을 주선한다
(D) 보고서를 검토한다

🔹**해설** but으로 시작하는 문장은 정답을 알려줄 확률이 높다. 연구팀이 경험이 부족해서 걱정이라고 말하는 여자의 대사를 들으면서 16번 문제의 정답을 고르자(but I'm also worried that our research group lacks the kind of experience ~). Now that's an idea.는 부서에 매니저를 한 명 더 뽑자는 남자의 제안에 대한 응답이므로(We should really add a second manager to the department), 남자의 제안에 유용하다는 뜻으로 한 말이다. 대화의 맥락을 고려하여 17번 문제의 정답을 고르자. 18번은 do next? 문제로 거의 마지막 문장에서 정답을 알게 된다. 부사장에게 할 제안의 세부 사항을 검토하자는 제안이다(How about we go over all the details so we can propose this to the vice president?).

Questions 19 through 21 refer to the following conversation and spreadsheet.

[W | Br] [19]How's the new inventory-control software performing? It's been a month since I endorsed your purchase request for it.

[M | Au] [19] This software is really helpful. [20]It keeps track of our cleaning equipment, vacuum cleaners, floor polishers, and everything else. You may remember that I got it after some of our equipment got misplaced last year.

[W | Br] Indeed. So every piece of equipment is labeled with a bar code with this new software. And then it gets scanned into the system whenever it's removed and brought back?

[M | Au] That's correct. I can refer to a spreadsheet to monitor the current status of all the items in use. [21]Look, two items are scheduled to be checked in today.

19-21번 문제는 다음 대화와 스프레드시트에 관한 것입니다.

여: 새 재고 관리 소프트웨어 성능이 어때요? 내가 그 물건의 구매 요청을 승인한 지 한 달이 지났잖아요.
남: 이 소프트웨어 정말 도움이 됩니다. 청소 도구와 진공청소기, 바닥 광택기, 그 밖의 모든 것의 상태를 파악해 주거든요. 작년에 우리 장비 중 일부가 분실된 후에 제가 이걸 구입했다는 걸 기억하실 겁니다.
여: 물론이요. 그러니까 이 새 소프트웨어로 모든 장비에 바코드가 있는 라벨이 붙는 거군요. 그러고 나서 꺼내거나 도로 가져올 때마다 스캔되어 시스템에 입력되고요?
남: 맞습니다. 스프레드시트를 보면 사용 중인 모든 물품의 상태를 확인할 수 있습니다. 보세요, 오늘은 물건 두 개가 반납될 예정입니다.

🔹**어휘** inventory 재고(품) perform (기계가) 작동하다, 돌아가다 endorse 승인하다 keep track of ~에 대해 계속 알다[파악하다] vacuum cleaner 진공청소기 floor polisher 바닥 광택기 misplaced 잃어버린 refer to ~을 보다, 참조하다 monitor 감독하다, 주시하다 status 상태, 상황 check in 반납하다

Item #	Date Checked Out	Date Due
343	April 15	²¹April 17
228	April 16	²¹April 17
216	April 18	April 19
326	April 19	April 21

물품 #	대여 날짜	반납 기일
343	4월 15일	4월 17일
228	4월 16일	4월 17일
216	4월 18일	4월 19일
326	4월 19일	4월 21일

어휘 check out 빌리다 due 반납 기일이 되는

---

19. What did the business recently purchase?

(A) Some software
(B) Several trucks
(C) Office furniture
(D) Safety eyewear

해석 사업체는 최근에 무엇을 구입했는가?
(A) 소프트웨어
(B) 트럭 몇 대
(C) 사무실 가구
(D) 보호 안경

---

20. What type of business do the speakers most likely work for?

(A) A laundry service
(B) An electronics store
(C) A cleaning company
(D) A courier service

해석 화자들은 어떤 유형의 사업체에서 근무하겠는가?
(A) 세탁 서비스
(B) 전자 제품 매장
(C) 청소 회사
(D) 택배 서비스

---

21. Look at the graphic. When is the conversation taking place?

(A) On April 15
(B) On April 17
(C) On April 19
(D) On April 21

해석 그래픽을 보라. 대화를 언제 하고 있는가?
(A) 4월 15일에
(B) 4월 17일에
(C) 4월 19일에
(D) 4월 21일에

해설 여자가 한 달 전에 구입을 승인한 재고 관리 소프트웨어가 잘 작동하고 있는지 묻자(How's the new inventory-control software performing? It's been a month since I endorsed your purchase request for it.) 남자가 정말 도움이 많이 된다고 대답하고 있다(This software is really helpful). 여기서 19번 문제의 정답을 알 수 있다. 정답을 고를 때는 항상 순발력이 필요하다는 사실을 잊지 말자. 바로 이어지는 문장에서 our cleaning equipment, vacuum cleaners, floor polishers라는 키워드를 들으면서 화자들이 근무하는 곳은 청소 업체라는 사실을 알아내고 20번의 정답을 골라야 한다. 대화 말미에 남자가 여자에게 스프레드시트를 보여주면서 오늘 두 개의 물품이 반납될 예정이라고 말하는데(Look, two items are scheduled to be checked in today.), 그래픽을 보면 반납 기일이 4월 17일인 물품이 두 개 있다. 여기서 21번 문제의 정답을 알아내자.

Part 4

Questions 22 through 24 refer to the following talk.

W Am ²²The purpose of this meeting is to talk about an idea I have for the restaurant. ²⁴I believe it's time we increase the amount of vegetables we purchase from local farms. ²³Since we began using locally-grown lettuce and tomatoes in our salads, our customers have commented on the difference in taste. While I understand that these vegetables can be more costly compared to those bought from a major distributor, I believe they're well worth the higher price. ²³Because the vegetables are fresher, they have a lot more flavor, and our chefs have the opportunity to personally pick out the produce they require by visiting the farms. And besides, we'll probably make up any potential extra expenses by seeing a boost in customer numbers and enhanced restaurant reviews.

22-24번 문제는 다음 담화에 관한 것입니다.

여: 오늘 회의의 목적은 식당에 대해 제가 가지고 있는 아이디어에 대해 이야기하는 것입니다. 우리가 지역 농장들에서 사 오는 채소의 양을 늘릴 때가 되었다고 생각합니다. 샐러드에 이 지역에서 재배한 상추와 토마토를 사용하기 시작한 이후 고객들이 맛의 차이에 대해 언급하고 있습니다. 이 채소들이 대형 유통업체에서 구입하는 것들에 비해 비용이 더 많이 들 수 있다는 점은 저도 알고 있지만, 더 높은 가격을 들일 만한 가치는 충분히 있다고 믿습니다. 채소가 더 신선하기 때문에 풍미도 훨씬 더 많으며, 우리 셰프들은 농장을 방문함으로써 필요한 농산물을 직접 선택할 수 있는 기회를 갖게 됩니다. 이뿐만 아니라 고객 수가 증가하고 식당 평가가 좋아짐으로써 잠재적인 추가 경비를 보충할 수 있을 것입니다.

> **어휘** locally-grown 이 지역에서 재배한 lettuce 상추 comment on ~에 대해 의견을 말하다 costly 많은 비용이 드는 compared to ~와 비교하여 distributor 유통업체 well worth ~할 가치가 충분히 있는 flavor 풍미, 맛 personally 직접, 개인적으로 pick out ~을 고르다, 선택하다 produce 농산물, 농작물 make up ~을 보충하다 boost 증가 review 논평, 비평

- - - - -

22. Where does the speaker most likely work?

(A) On a vegetable farm
(B) In a grocery store
(C) At a dining establishment
(D) At a publishing company

> **어휘** dine 식사하다 establishment 기관, 시설
> **해석** 화자는 어디에서 근무하겠는가?
> (A) 채소 농장에서
> (B) 식료품 가게에서
> (C) 음식점에서
> (D) 출판사에서

- - - - -

23. What do customers like about fresh vegetables?

(A) The appearance
(B) The price
(C) The size
(D) The taste

> **해석** 신선한 채소와 관련하여 고객들은 무엇을 좋아하는가?
> (A) 겉모습
> (B) 가격
> (C) 크기
> (D) 맛

24. What does the speaker recommend?

(A) Increasing vegetable intake
(B) Cultivating one's own vegetables
(C) Requesting a discount from large wholesalers
(D) Sourcing more vegetables from local farms

> **어휘** intake 섭취 cultivate 재배하다 wholesaler 도매상 source 구입하다, 조달하다
> **해석** 화자는 무엇을 추천하는가?
> (A) 채소 섭취를 늘리는 것
> (B) 직접 채소를 재배하는 것
> (C) 대형 도매상에게 할인을 요청하는 것
> (D) 지역 농장들에서 더 많은 채소를 조달하는 것

> **해설** 22번과 같은 화자의 직업을 묻는 질문은 거의 대부분 첫 한두 문장으로 정답을 알 수 있다. 식당을 위한 아이디어를 논하는 회의를 열고 있으므로(The purpose of this meeting is to talk about an idea I have for the restaurant.) 화자의 직장은 식당인 것이 확실하다. 바로 이어지는 문장에서도 정답을 골라야 하므로 순발력이 매우 중요하다. 게다가 23번과 24번 문제는 순서를 바꿔서 정답을 선택해야 하므로 읽은 내용을 잘 기억하는 것도 중요하다. 우선 I believe it's time we increase the amount of vegetables we purchase from local farms.가 패러프레이즈 되어 있는 문장을 24번의 정답으로 골라야 한다. 여기서도 순발력 있게 정답을 고르고 바로 다음 문장을 들을 준비를 해야 한다. 지역에서 재배한 채소를 사용하기 시작한 이후(Since we began using locally-grown lettuce and tomatoes in our salads), 즉 더 신선한 채소를 사용하기 시작한 이후 고객들이 맛의 차이를 언급해 왔다고 말하고 있다(our customers have commented on the difference in taste). 여기서 23번의 정답을 골라야 한다. 이후에 나오는 Because the vegetables are fresher, they have a lot more flavor는 더 확신을 갖고 정답을 선택할 수 있게 도와준다.

Questions 25 through 27 refer to the following announcement.

[M | Au] I want to express my gratitude to the members of the media for being present at today's press conference. I'm Girolamo Vega, founder and CEO of Vega, Incorporated. ^{25 26}It's truly incredible to reflect on how our environmental consulting firm, which I co-founded with a small group of friends only five years back, has been growing. [Now, we have over four hundred people on staff.] And they are unparalleled in the industry. It's because of their contributions that our work on some of the largest wastewater projects in the world has been such a success. ²⁷In recognition of this, I'm announcing that employees will now have the option to acquire shares of stock in the company. I'm thrilled to offer this investment opportunity to our staff.

25-27번 문제는 다음 발표문에 관한 것입니다.

남: 오늘 기자 회견에 참석해 주신 것에 대해 언론인 여러분께 감사를 표하고 싶습니다. 저는 주식회사 Vega의 설립자이자 CEO인 Girolamo Vega입니다. 겨우 5년 전에 몇 명 안 되는 친구들과 함께 공동으로 창업한 우리 환경 컨설팅 회사가 성장해 온 과정을 되돌아보면 정말 놀랍습니다. 이제 우리에게는 400명 이상의 직원들이 있습니다. 게다가 이들은 업계에서 비길 데가 없는 사람들입니다. 세계 최대의 폐수 처리 프로젝트 중 몇몇을 맡아서 한 일이 그렇게 성공적이었던 것은 이들의 공헌 덕분입니다. 이를 인정하여 이제는 직원들이 회사 주식의 일정 지분을 취득할 수 있는 선택권을 갖게 될 것임을 발표하는 바입니다. 우리 직원들에게 이 투자 기회를 제공할 수 있게 되어 매우 기쁩니다.

🔸어휘 gratitude 고마움, 감사 press conference 기자 회견 founder 창립자, 설립자 Incorporated(Inc.) (회사명 뒤에) 주식회사 incredible 놀라운, 믿기 어려운 reflect on ~을 되돌아보다 firm 회사 co-found 공동 창업하다 unparalleled 비할[견줄] 데 없는 wastewater 폐수, 하수 in recognition of ~을 인정하여 acquire 취득하다 share 몫, 지분 stock (한 기업의) 주식 자본 thrilled 크게 기뻐하는, 흥분된

---

25. What type of company is Vega, Incorporated?

(A) Media and advertising
(B) Academic software
(C) Medical equipment
(D) Environmental consulting

🔸해석 주식회사 Vega는 어떤 유형의 회사인가?
(A) 미디어 및 광고
(B) 학술 소프트웨어
(C) 의료기기
(D) 환경 컨설팅

---

26. What does the speaker imply when he says, "Now, we have over four hundred people on staff"?

(A) A training program needs to be expanded.
(B) A company has experienced rapid growth.
(C) A department requires reorganization.
(D) An office building is overcrowded.

🔸어휘 rapid 빠른, 급속한 reorganization 재조직, 재편성 overcrowded 너무 붐비는, 초만원의

🔸해석 화자는 "이제 우리에게는 400명 이상의 직원들이 있습니다."라고 말할 때 무엇을 암시하는가?
(A) 교육 프로그램이 확대되어야 한다.
(B) 회사가 급속한 성장을 경험했다.
(C) 어떤 부서의 재편성이 필요하다.
(D) 사무실 건물이 초만원이다.

---

27. What is being announced?

(A) Employees will be able to invest in the company.
(B) Solar panels are scheduled for installation.
(C) A product is being discontinued.
(D) A board member will step down next year.

🔸어휘 solar panel 태양전지판 discontinue 생산을 중단하다 board 이사회 step down 사임하다, 퇴임하다

🔸해석 무엇을 발표하고 있는가?
(A) 직원들이 회사에 투자할 수 있게 될 것이다.
(B) 태양전지판이 설치될 예정이다.
(C) 어떤 제품이 단종될 것이다.
(D) 어떤 이사회 임원이 내년에 사임할 것이다.

Questions 28 through 30 refer to the following announcement and timetable.

W Am Attention, all passengers waiting for the five-thirty P.M. ferry to Ostar Island. ²⁸Please be advised that the ferry has been cancelled due to a storm along the coast. ²⁹Rest assured, though, the storm is moving swiftly and is expected to clear in time for the final departure of the day. In order to accommodate all the extra passengers on the final ferry trip, we will be using the upper deck of the boat. ³⁰It can get quite chilly up there, so you'd want to put on a sweater or jacket if you have one with you. We appreciate your patience and apologize for any inconvenience.

28-30번 문제는 다음 발표문과 시간표에 관한 것입니다.

여: 오후 5시 30분 Ostar 섬행(行) 카페리를 기다리는 모든 승객 여러분 주목해 주시기 바랍니다. 해안을 따라 일고 있는 폭풍우로 인해 해당 카페리는 운항이 취소되었음을 알려드립니다. 그러나 폭풍우가 빠르게 진행하고 있어서 오늘의 마지막 출발 시간에 맞춰 그칠 것으로 예상되오니 안심하시기 바랍니다. 마지막 카페리 운항에 추가 승객을 모두 수용하기 위하여 배의 상갑판을 사용할 예정입니다. 위로 올라가시면 상당히 추울 수 있어서 소지하고 계시다면 스웨터나 재킷을 입으시는 게 좋겠습니다. 양해에 감사드리며 불편에 대해 사과드립니다.

어휘 be advised that ~라는 것을 알리다 ferry (카)페리, 연락선 rest assured (that) ~라는 것에 대해 안심하다 though (문장 끝에서) 그렇지만, 하지만 swiftly 신속하게, 재빨리 clear (눈, 비 등이) 그치다 in time for ~하는 시간에 맞춰 accommodate 수용하다 chilly 쌀쌀한, 추운 inconvenience 불편

Ostar Island Ferry

Departures	Arrivals
10:00 A.M.	10:30 A.M.
12:00 P.M.	12:30 P.M.
5:30 P.M.	6:00 P.M.
7:30 P.M.	8:00 P.M.

Ostar 섬 카페리

출발	도착
오전 10:00	오전 10:30
오후 12:00	오후 12:30
오후 5:30	오후 6:00
오후 7:30	오후 8:00

28. What has caused a cancellation?

(A) Inclement weather
(B) Mechanical problems
(C) An unwell crew member
(D) Insufficient number of passengers

어휘 inclement (날씨가) 궂은, 사나운 mechanical 기계의 unwell 몸이 편치 않은, 아픈 crew 승무원 (전원) insufficient 불충분한

해석 취소의 원인은 무엇인가?
(A) 궂은 날씨
(B) 기계적 결함
(C) 몸 상태가 좋지 않은 승무원
(D) 불충분한 승객 수

29. Look at the graphic. What time will the ferry leave?

(A) 10:00 A.M.
(B) 12:00 P.M.
(C) 5:30 P.M.
(D) 7:30 P.M.

해석 그래픽을 보라. 카페리는 몇 시에 출발할 것인가?
(A) 오전 10:00
(B) 오후 12:00
(C) 오후 5:30
(D) 오후 7:30

30. What does the speaker say listeners may want to do?

(A) Travel the following day
(B) Retain a receipt
(C) Grab a bite to eat
(D) Dress in warm layers

어휘 retain 간직하다, 보관하다 grab a bite to eat 간단히 먹다
dress in (특정한 종류의) 옷을 입다

해석 화자는 청자들이 무엇을 하는 것이 좋겠다고 말하는가?
(A) 다음 날 이동한다
(B) 영수증을 보관한다
(C) 간단히 식사한다
(D) 따뜻한 옷을 여러 겹으로 입는다

해설 28번 문제는 a storm이 Inclement weather로 바뀌어 있다는 것만 알면 쉽게 정답을 고를 수 있다. 안내 방송에서 카페리 운항 취소를 알리면서 폭풍우가 마지막 출발 시간에 맞춰 그칠 것으로 예상된다는 소식을 전하고 있으므로(the storm is moving swiftly and is expected to clear in time for the final departure of the day.), 시간표를 보면서 마지막 출발 시간인 7시 30분에는 배가 정상적으로 출항할 것임을 알 수 있다. 여기서 29번의 정답을 선택하면 된다. 두 문장이 연속으로 정답의 키워드를 들려주고 있으므로 28번 문제의 정답을 고를 때 머뭇거리지 않도록 주의하자. 배의 상갑판을 개방할 예정인데, 올라가면 상당히 춥기 때문에 스웨터나 재킷을 입을 것을 권하고 있다(so you'd want to put on a sweater or jacket if you have one with you). 옷을 여러 겹으로 입으라는 권장이므로 여기서 30번의 정답을 알 수 있다.

PART 1 Exercise

1 (A)   **2** (B)

1. M | Au

(A) **Some skyscrapers are situated near the water's edge.**
(B) Some ferryboats are docked at a pier.
(C) The cityscape is reflected on the surface of the water.
(D) A line of vehicles are driving down the coastal road.

어휘 skyscraper 고층 건물 ferryboat 연락선, 페리보트 dock (배를) 부두에 대다 pier 부두 cityscape 도시 경관 coastal 해안의, 연안의

해석 (A) 고층 건물들이 물가에 위치해 있다.
(B) 페리보트들이 부두에 정박해 있다.
(C) 도시 경관이 물 표면에 비치고 있다.
(D) 차량들이 해안 도로를 따라 일렬로 달리고 있다.

해설 '~가 ~에 있다' 문장은 거의 매달 시험에 출제된다. 그중 '두다/놓다' 동사를 사용하여 '~가 ~에 놓여 있다'라고 말하는 문장이 가장 많이 사용되고 있으므로 철저한 공부가 필요하다. (B), (C), (D)는 각각 동사 are docked, is reflected, driving을 알아듣고 오답으로 골라내야 한다.

2. M | Cn

(A) Some equipment is being put in a rack.
(B) **Some cords are lying across the top of a counter.**
(C) A man is plugging a device into a power outlet.
(D) A man is aiming a flashlight ahead to find something.

어휘 rack 선반, 꽂이 cord 코드, 전깃줄 lie 가로놓여 있다 plug 플러그를 꽂다 plug A into B A를 B에 연결하다 power outlet 전기 콘센트 aim 겨누다 flashlight 손전등

해석 (A) 장비를 선반에 넣고 있다.
(B) 코드들이 카운터 위를 가로질러 놓여 있다.
(C) 기구를 전기 콘센트에 연결하고 있다.
(D) 손전등을 앞으로 비추며 무언가를 찾고 있다.

해설 (A)의 동사 is being put은 진행 시제 수동태이기 때문에 놓는 동작을 나타낸다. 장비가 이미 받침대에 놓여 있기 때문에 has been put이라고 해야 정답이 될 수 있다. (C)는 동사 plugging을 듣고, 혹은 a power outlet이 보이지 않기 때문에 오답으로 골라낼 수 있다. (D)는 to find something 부분이 추측을 나타내고 있기 때문에 정답이 될 수 없다.

PART 2 Exercise

1 (B)	**2** (B)	**3** (A)	**4** (B)	**5** (C)
6 (A)	**7** (A)	**8** (B)	**9** (A)	**10** (C)

1. M | Cn   W | Am

What will be discussed during the conference call?

(A) Only with customer service representatives.
(B) **Results from the customer satisfaction survey.**
(C) The discussion ended sooner than expected.

어휘 conference call 전화 회의 customer service representative 고객 서비스 상담원

해석 전화 회의에서는 무엇을 논의할 건가요?
(A) 고객 서비스 직원들만 함께 해요.

(B) 고객 만족도 설문조사의 결과요.
(C) 논의가 예상보다 일찍 끝났습니다.

해설 (A)처럼 사람 이름이나 직함을 이용한 대답은 Who 의문문의 정답으로 알맞다. (C)는 질문에 들어 있는 discussed와 발음이 비슷한 discussion을 들려주면서 오답을 유도하고 있다. 주제를 묻는 질문에는 대부분 명사(구)로만 이루어진 단답형 대답이 정답이다.

---

2. ⬚W Br⬚ ⬚M Au⬚

What type of chair would you prefer for your new office?

(A) That's a great choice.
(B) I'll just keep using the one I have.
(C) It won't arrive for another week.

어휘 keep V-ing ~을 계속하다, 반복하다

해설 새 사무실에는 어떤 유형의 의자를 선호하세요?
(A) 탁월한 선택입니다.
(B) 그냥 있는 걸 계속 사용할게요.
(C) 일주일은 더 있어야 도착할 겁니다.

해설 (A)는 What type of chair에서 연상되는 대답으로 오답을 유도하고 있으며, (C)는 When 의문문의 정답으로 알맞은 대답이다. What kind[type/form] of + 명사 ~? 유형의 질문이 나왔을 때 대답에 (the) one(s)이 들어 있으면 항상 정답이다.

---

3. ⬚W Br⬚ ⬚M Cn⬚

What was the highlight of your visit to the city last weekend?

(A) Definitely the Native Art Center!
(B) Thanks, but I already have other plans.
(C) Yes, the guidebook was quite useful.

어휘 highlight 가장 인상적인 것, 하이라이트 definitely 확실히 native art 민속 예술 guidebook 여행[관광] 안내서

해설 지난 주말 도시 방문에서 가장 인상적인 것은 뭐였어요?
(A) 당연히 민속 예술 센터죠!
(B) 고맙지만 이미 다른 계획이 있어요.
(C) 네, 여행 안내서가 상당히 유용했어요.

해설 질문 앞부분 What was the highlight of your visit(방문에서 가장 인상적인 것은 뭐였어요?)에 집중하면 자연스러운 대답을 찾을 수 있다. (B)는 Day 04에서 제안/부탁 의문문에 대해 거절하는 대답으로 공부했다. (C)는 Yes를 듣는 순간 오답임을 알 수 있다.

---

4. ⬚M Au⬚ ⬚W Br⬚

What should I do with the updated promotional brochures?

(A) She was promoted to manager.
(B) Send them to the subscribers on our mailing list.
(C) Put on the old shirt.

어휘 promotional 홍보의, 판촉의 brochure 안내 책자

해설 업데이트된 홍보 책자를 어떻게 할까요?
(A) 그녀는 매니저로 승진했어요.
(B) 우편 수신자 명단의 구독자들에게 보내세요.
(C) 오래된 셔츠를 입으세요.

해설 What should I[we] do ~?가 출제되면 명령문을 정답으로 선택하자. (A)는 질문의 promotional과 발음이 비슷한 promoted를 들려주면서 오답을 유도하고 있다. (C)는 명령문이지만 속지 말자. 질문의 brochures와 발음이 비슷한 old shirt('오우셔트'로 들린다)를 이용해서 오답을 유도하고 있다.

---

5. ⬚M Cn⬚ ⬚M Au⬚

What's the product code for this item?

(A) I saw a television advertisement about it.
(B) Batteries are included in the package.
(C) All the information is in the invoice.

어휘 invoice 송장(送狀), 청구서

해설 이 물건의 제품 코드가 뭐가요?
(A) 그것에 대한 텔레비전 광고를 봤어요.
(B) 배터리는 포장에 포함되어 있습니다.
(C) 모든 정보는 청구서에 있습니다.

해설 질문 앞부분 What's the product code(제품 코드가 뭐가요?)에 집중하자. 제품 코드를 비롯한 모든 정보가 청구서에 적혀 있다고 알려주는 문장이 자연스러운 대답이다.

---

6. ⬚M Cn⬚ ⬚W Am⬚

What time does your bus come?

(A) I'm going there on foot.
(B) A round-trip ticket.
(C) It's on Forty-Fifth Street.

어휘 on foot 걸어서, 도보로

해설 당신이 탈 버스는 몇 시에 오나요?
(A) 저는 거기 걸어서 갈 거예요.

(B) 왕복 티켓이요.
(C) 45번가에 있습니다.

> **해설** (B)는 질문에 들어 있는 bus에서 연상되는 대답으로 오답을 유도하고 있으며, (C)는 Where 의문문의 정답으로 알맞은 대답이다. 오답을 잘 골라낼수록 고수가 된다!

---

7. M Cn   M Au

What floor is Spellman Technologies on?

(A) There's a building directory right behind you.
(B) Mostly industrial machine parts.
(C) Yes, that's where they're located.

> **어휘** building directory 건물 안내판   part 부품

> **해석** Spellman Technologies는 몇 층에 있나요?
> (A) 당신 바로 뒤에 건물 안내판이 있습니다.
> (B) 주로 산업용 기계 부품이요.
> (C) 네, 거기가 그들이 있는 곳입니다.

> **해설** What 바로 뒤에 나오는 명사만 알아들으면 해결할 수 있다. What floor(몇 층?)라고 물었으므로 건물 안내판을 보라는 대답이 정답이다. (B)는 회사 이름에 들어 있는 Technologies에서 연상되는 대답으로 오답을 유도하고 있으며, (C)는 Yes를 듣고 오답으로 골라내야 한다.

---

8. M Cn   W Am

What did you do with the guest list that I sent you yesterday?

(A) Not until everyone received it.
(B) I passed it along to whoever needed it.
(C) We're expected to leave shortly.

> **어휘** pass along ~을 전달하다   shortly 곧, 얼마 안 있어

> **해석** 어제 보내 드린 초대 손님 명단으로 무엇을 하셨나요?
> (A) 모든 사람이 받을 때까지는 아닙니다.
> (B) 누구든 필요한 사람에게 전달했습니다.
> (C) 우리는 곧 떠날 것 같습니다.

> **해설** guest list의 발음을 연습해 보자. guest에서 t 발음이 탈락하고 "게스리스트"라고 읽게 된다. 질문 앞부분 What did you do with the guest list(초대 손님 명단으로 무엇을 하셨나요?)에 집중해서 자연스러운 대답을 선택하면 되는데, (B)가 발음하기도 알아듣기도 쉽지 않은 문장이다. "아이 패스티러롱 투 후에버 니디딧."이라고 읽어야 한다. 여러 번 연습해 보자.

---

9. M Au   W Am

What's the telephone number for Langford Restaurant?

(A) It's closed for remodeling.
(B) Steak or pasta?
(C) Our supervisor is expecting her call.

> **어휘** supervisor 감독관, 관리자

> **해석** Langford 식당 전화번호가 뭐죠?
> (A) 거기 리모델링 중이라서 문 닫았어요.
> (B) 스테이크요, 파스타요?
> (C) 저희 관리자가 그녀의 전화를 기다리고 있습니다.

> **해설** 식당 전화번호를 묻는 사람에게 지금 문을 닫아서 전화를 받지 않을 것이라고 말해주는 대답이 정답이다. (B)는 질문의 Restaurant에서 연상되는 대답으로, (C)는 telephone에서 연상되는 her call을 들려주면서 오답을 유도하고 있다. 오답을 잘 골라낼수록 고수가 된다!

---

10. W Br   M Au

What are your dinner specials tonight?

(A) At the corner of Jefferson Street and Elm Avenue.
(B) Those tables are reserved.
(C) Your server will be here momentarily.

> **어휘** momentarily 곧, 금방

> **해석** 오늘 저녁 특별 요리는 뭔가요?
> (A) Jefferson 가(街)와 Elm 가(街)가 만나는 모퉁이요.
> (B) 저 자리들은 예약이 되어 있습니다.
> (C) 담당 서빙 직원이 곧 올 겁니다.

> **해설** (A)는 Where 의문문의 정답으로 알맞은 대답이며, (B)는 질문에 들어 있는 dinner에서 연상되는 대답으로 오답을 유도하고 있다. 특별 요리가 무엇인지는 서빙하는 직원이 곧 와서 알려줄 것이라는 대답이 정답이다.

PART 3 & 4 Exercise

1 (A) **2** (C) **3** (D) **4** (B) **5** (A) **6** (D)

Questions 1 through 3 refer to the following conversation with three speakers.

[W Br] Hi, Oliver and Lydia. ¹You worked here in the sales division for several months before your first performance appraisal, right?

[M Cn] Yes, that sounds right.

[W Am] ¹It took four months for me to have my first evaluation. Why?

[W Br] ²I've already been with the company for four months, but no one has mentioned a performance appraisal to me yet. I'm wondering if I should bring it up.

[M Cn] Well, [the company doesn't have a policy in place for this.]

[W Am] ²That's true. It's a chance that your supervisor overlooked it. ³You know she's been away on business for the last week. She's having meetings with some potential clients in Tokyo.

[W Br] Well, once she returns, I'll ask her about it.

1-3번 문제는 다음 3인 대화에 관한 것입니다.

여1: Oliver, Lydia, 안녕하세요. 두 분 이곳 영업부에서 몇 달 근무하고 나서 첫 고과 평가가 있었던 거 맞죠?
남: 네, 그럴 거예요.
여2: 저는 첫 평가를 받는 데 4개월 걸렸어요. 왜요?
여1: 제가 회사를 다닌 지 벌써 4개월이 되었는데요, 아직까지 아무도 저에게 고과 평가에 대해 언급하지 않았어요. 제가 얘기를 꺼내야 하는 건지 궁금해서요.
남: 음, 이에 대해 회사에서 시행 중인 정책이 없어요.
여2: 맞아요. 당신의 관리자가 간과했을 가능성이 있어요. 지난주부터 출장 중이신 거 알죠? 도쿄에서 잠재 고객들과 만나고 있거든요.
여1: 음, 일단 그녀가 돌아오면 이 일에 대해 물어볼게요.

어휘 division (조직의) 부서 performance appraisal 인사 고과, 고과 평가 evaluation 평가 bring up (화제를) 꺼내다 in place 시행 중인 chance 가능성 supervisor 관리자 overlook 못 보고 넘어가다, 간과하다 be away on business 출장 중이다 potential client 잠재 고객

1. What are the speakers mainly discussing?

(A) An employee assessment
(B) A sales promotion
(C) A new patron
(D) An itinerary for a trip

어휘 assessment 평가 patron 고객 itinerary 여행 일정
해석 화자들은 주로 무엇을 논하고 있는가?
(A) 직원 평가
(B) 영업 보고서
(C) 신규 고객
(D) 여행 일정

2. Why does the man say, "the company doesn't have a policy in place for this"?

(A) To defer an announcement
(B) To grant approval to the woman
(C) To offer an explanation
(D) To propose a policy modification

어휘 defer 미루다, 연기하다 grant 승인하다, 허락하다 approval 승인, 허가 modification 수정, 변경
해석 남자는 왜 "이에 대해 회사에서 시행 중인 정책이 없어요."라고 말하는가?
(A) 발표를 연기하기 위해서
(B) 여자에게 승인을 내주기 위해서
(C) 설명을 해주기 위해서
(D) 정책 변경을 제안하기 위해서

3. Why is the manager unavailable?

(A) She is delivering a speech at a conference.
(B) She is training new hires.
(C) She is finishing a sales report.
(D) She is meeting some clients.

어휘 unavailable 만날 수 없는 deliver a speech 연설하다 conference 학회, 회의 (new) hire 신입 사원
해석 매니저는 왜 만날 수 없는가?
(A) 학회에서 연설하고 있다.
(B) 신입 사원들을 교육하고 있다.

(C) 영업 보고서를 마무리 짓고 있다.
(D) 고객들을 만나고 있다.

해설 주제를 묻는 질문은 첫 한두 문장에서 정답을 알 수 있다. 여자들의 대사에 들어 있는 performance appraisal 이나 my first evaluation 같은 키워드를 듣고 1번 문제의 정답을 고르자. 2번 문제는 대화의 맥락을 고려해서 풀자. 영국 여자가 회사에서 근무를 시작한 지 상당 기간이 지났는데도 고과 평가가 이루어지지 않는 이유를 궁금해 하고 있으므로(I've already been with the company for four months, but no one has mentioned a performance appraisal to me yet.) 이어지는 남자의 대사 the company doesn't have a policy in place for this(이 사안에 대해 시행되고 있는 방침은 없어요.)와 미국 여자의 대사 It's a chance that your supervisor overlooked it.(관리자가 잊고 있을 가능성이 있어요.)는 그 이유를 설명하는 대답이다. 3번에서 묻는 매니저를 만날 수 없는 이유는 마지막 문장을 보면, 출장 중인 매니저는 잠재 고객들과 만나고 있다고 알려주고 있다(You know she's been away on business for the last week. She's having meetings with some potential clients in Tokyo).

Questions 4 through 6 refer to the following announcement.

[W │ Br] Welcome to this month's all-staff meeting. To begin with, I have some exciting news. As the editor-in-chief of *Global Commerce* magazine, ⁴I am thrilled to announce the completion of our company's merger with Jenson Publishing. ⁵This means many great things for us, namely that we can take advantage of Jenson's exceptional technology department so we can elevate the quality of the online version of our magazine. [And why wouldn't we?] With Jenson's cutting-edge technology and our editorial expertise, we are poised to create an unparalleled digital experience for our readers. ⁶Now, Jenson has already granted all of us access to their publications. So, please use some time over the next few weeks to familiarize yourselves with their Web sites.

4-6번 문제는 다음 발표에 관한 것입니다.

여: 이번 달 전 직원 회의에 오신 것을 환영합니다. 우선 상당히 흥미진진한 소식이 있습니다. *Global Commerce* 잡지의 편집 주간으로서 저는 우리 회사와 Jenson 출판사의 합병이 완료되었음을 발표하게 되어 매우 기쁩니다. 이는 우리에게 많은 것을 의미하는데, 이를테면 Jenson 사(社)의 우수한 기술 부서를 활용하여 우리 잡지의 온라인 버전의 품질을 높일 수 있다는 점입니다. 그러면 우리가 왜 안 하겠어요? Jenson 사(社)의 최첨단 기술과 우리의 편집에 관한 전문 지식으로, 독자들에게 비할 데 없는 디지털 경험을 만들어 줄 준비를 갖추게 되었습니다. 자, Jenson 사(社)는 이미 우리 모두에게 자기들의 출판물들의 이용 권한을 주었습니다. 그러니까 앞으로 몇 주 동안은 시간을 내서 그들의 웹 사이트에 익숙해지기를 바랍니다.

어휘 to begin with 우선, 먼저 editor-in-chief 편집 주간 thrilled 크게 기뻐하는, 흥분된 merger 합병 namely 말하자면, 이를테면 take advantage of ~을 이용하다, 활용하다 exceptional 이례적일 정도로 우수한, 특출한 elevate 높이다 cutting-edge 최첨단의 editorial 편집의, 편집과 관련된 be poised to-V ~할 준비가 되어 있다 unparalleled 비할[견줄] 데 없는 grant (권리, 권한을) 부여하다 access 이용할 권리 publication 출판물, 간행물 familiarize oneself with ~에 익숙해지다

4. What is the purpose of the announcement?

(A) To scrutinize a budget proposal
(B) To discuss an upcoming merger
(C) To interpret some survey results
(D) To welcome new staff members

어휘 scrutinize 면밀히 조사하다, 검토하다 upcoming 다가오는, 곧 있을 interpret 해석하다, 이해하다

해석 발표의 목적은 무엇인가?
(A) 예산안을 면밀히 검토하는 것
(B) 다가오는 합병을 논하는 것
(C) 설문조사 결과를 해석하는 것
(D) 신입 직원들을 환영하는 것

5. What does the woman mean when she says, "And why wouldn't we"?

(A) She endorses a decision.
(B) She hopes to be transferred.
(C) She seeks input from the listeners.
(D) She is worried about a shipment.

어휘 endorse 지지하다 transfer 전근시키다 seek 청하다, 구하다 input (정보, 의견의) 제공, 투입 shipment 수송(품)

해석 여자는 "그렇다면 하지 않을 이유가 없겠죠?"라고 말할 때 무엇을 의미하는가?
(A) 어떤 결정을 지지한다.
(B) 전근하기를 바란다.
(C) 청자들의 의견을 구한다.
(D) 수송품에 대해 걱정한다.

---

6. What does the woman ask listeners to do?

(A) Participate in a training session
(B) Complete some documents
(C) Compile a set of questions
(D) Review some information online

어휘 complete (빠진 부분을 보충하여) 완성하다 compile (자료를 수집하여) 작성하다

해석 여자는 청자들에게 무엇을 하라고 요구하는가?
(A) 교육에 참가한다
(B) 문서를 완성한다
(C) 일련의 질문을 작성한다
(D) 온라인으로 정보를 검토한다

해설 주제나 질문은 거의 항상 첫 한두 문장을 잘 들으면 알 수 있다. 발표문 앞부분에 나오는 announce와 merger라는 키워드만 잘 듣고 4번 문제의 정답을 고르자. 바로 이어지는 문장을 잘 알아들어야 5번을 풀 수 있으므로 정답을 고를 때 순발력을 발휘하는 것도 잊지 말자. Jenson 사(社)와의 합병을 통해 그들의 기술 부서를 이용하여 잡지 온라인 버전의 품질을 높일 수 있다는 장점을 언급하고 있는데(we can take advantage of Jenson's exceptional technology department so we can elevate the quality of the online version of our magazine), 이것은 합병의 정당성을 설명하는 것이므로, 이어지는 And why wouldn't we?는 회사의 결정에 대한 지지를 나타내는 말이다. 마지막 두 문장은 각각 Now와 So로 시작하고 있는데, 이런 문장에는 정답의 키워드가 들어 있을 확률이 높다. Jenson 사(社)로부터 모든 출판물의 이용 권한을 부여받았으므로(Now, Jenson has already granted all of us access to their publications.) 그들의 웹 사이트에 익숙해질 것을 당부하고 있다(So, please use some time over the next few weeks to familiarize yourselves with their Web sites). 출판물들이 전자 자료이며 온라인으로 살펴보라는 말이므로 여기서 6번 문제의 정답을 알 수 있다.

Actual Test

1 (B)	**2** (C)	**3** (B)	**4** (A)	**5** (A)
6 (C)	**7** (B)	**8** (C)	**9** (A)	**10** (C)
11 (A)	**12** (C)	**13** (D)	**14** (C)	**15** (A)
16 (A)	**17** (A)	**18** (C)	**19** (C)	**20** (B)
21 (D)	**22** (D)	**23** (D)	**24** (C)	**25** (B)
26 (D)	**27** (A)	**28** (D)	**29** (A)	**30** (D)

* 정답을 맞힌 문제도 해설을 읽어보세요.

Part 1

1. M | Cn

(A) Some people are cleaning the plaza with brooms.
(B) A domed structure is visible in the distance.
(C) An open-air market is crowded despite the rain.
(D) A pedestrian is shaking the rain off her umbrella.

어휘 plaza 광장 broom 빗자루 domed 둥근 지붕의 structure 구조물, 건축물 in the distance 먼 곳에 open-air 야외의, 노천의 pedestrian 보행자

해석 (A) 사람들이 빗자루로 광장을 청소하고 있다.
(B) 먼 곳에 둥근 지붕의 건축물이 보인다.
(C) 비에도 불구하고 노천 시장이 붐빈다.
(D) 보행자가 우산을 흔들어 빗물을 털어 내고 있다.

해설 a domed structure나 visible 같은 것들은 자주 사용되는 키워드가 아니므로, 문장을 제대로 알아듣지 못해도 정답을 고를 수 있게 오답을 잘 골라내야 한다. cleaning, brooms, open-air market, crowded, shaking 같은 단어들을 잘 듣고 오답을 파악하자.

2. W | Br

(A) Some statues are being built on a bridge.
(B) Trees are lined up along the edge of a canal.
(C) A bridge with arches spans a waterway.
(D) A flight of stairs are fastened to a column.

🔵 어휘 **line up** ~을 일렬[한 줄]로 세우다[배열하다] **canal** 운하, 수로 **span** 가로지르다, ~에 걸쳐 있다 **waterway** 수로 **a flight of stairs** (두 층 사이에) 한 줄로 이어진 계단 **fasten** 단단히 고정시키다 **column** 기둥

🔵 해석 (A) 다리 위에 조각상을 만들고 있다.
(B) 나무들이 운하 가장자리를 따라 줄지어 배열되어 있다.
(C) 아치가 있는 다리가 수로 위를 가로지르고 있다.
(D) 계단 한 줄이 기둥에 고정되어 있다.

🔵 해설 진행 시제 수동태는 동작을 나타내므로 (A)가 정답이 되려면 조각상이 만들어진 상태가 아니라 만들어지는 중이어야 한다. 나무들이 줄지어 있지는 않으므로 (B)도 오답이고, 계단이 보이지 않으므로 (D)도 오답이다. 길, 계단, 난간, 다리 등이 뻗어 있다고 말할 때 extend, lead, run, span 같은 동사를 사용한다.

3. W | Am

(A) A woman's standing on a balcony.
(B) An awning extends over a shop entrance.
(C) A group of people is leaving a building.
(D) A brick patio is being swept.

🔵 어휘 **awning** 차양 **patio** 테라스

🔵 해석 (A) 어떤 여자가 발코니에 서 있다.
(B) 상점 입구 위에 차양이 뻗어 있다.
(C) 사람들이 건물에서 나가고 있다.
(D) 벽돌 테라스를 쓸고 있다.

🔵 해설 발코니에 서 있는 사람도(standing on a balcony), 건물에서 나가는 사람도(leaving a building), 테라스를 쓸고 있는 사람도(is being swept) 없으므로 (A)와 (C), (D)는 모두 오답이다. 길, 계단, 난간, 다리 등이 뻗어 있다고 말할 때 extend, lead, run, span 같은 동사를 사용한다.

Part 2

4. M | Cn   W | Am

What will be the cover story for this month's issue of our magazine?

(A) The editors are meeting later today to make a decision.
(B) July, August, and September.
(C) No, Shelley's having a computer issue.

🔵 어휘 **cover story** 표지 기사 **issue** (간행물의) 호; 문제, 걱정거리

🔵 해석 우리 잡지 이달 호 표지 기사는 무엇으로 할 건가요?
(A) 편집자들이 오늘 오후에 만나서 결정할 거예요.
(B) 7월과 8월, 9월이요.
(C) 아니요, Shelley는 컴퓨터에 문제가 있어요.

🔵 해설 질문 앞부분 What will be the cover story(표지 기사는 무엇으로 할 건가요?)에 집중하면 자연스러운 대답을 파악할 수 있다. (B)는 질문의 month에서 연상되는 대답으로 오답을 유도하고 있으며, (C)는 No만 들어도 오답임을 알 수 있다.

5. M | Au   W | Am

What's your opinion of the highlighted paragraphs in this document?

(A) I think they still need further revisions.
(B) You can find some storage space upstairs.
(C) The lighting in this room is very good.

🔵 어휘 **paragraph** 단락, 절 **further** 더 이상의, 추가의 **storage** 저장, 보관 **upstairs** 위층에서 **lighting** 조명

이 문서에서 하이라이트 표시된 단락에 대한 의견이 어떠신가요?
- (A) 아직 추가로 수정이 필요한 것 같은데요.
- (B) 위층에 수납 공간이 있습니다.
- (C) 이 방의 조명이 정말 좋습니다.

질문 앞부분 What's your opinion of에 집중하자. 의견을 묻는 질문이므로 의견을 말하는 대답이 정답이다. (B)는 질문에 들어 있는 this document에서 연상되는 대답으로, (C)는 highlighted와 발음이 비슷한 lighting을 들려주면서 오답을 유도하고 있다.

---

6. [W|Br] [M|Cn]

What was in that huge package?

(A) It arrived a few days ago, I think.
(B) I found it in the entrance hall.
(C) The floor lamps that I ordered.

entrance hall 현관홀, 입구 홀
저 엄청 큰 상자 안에는 뭐가 있었죠?
- (A) 아마 며칠 전에 도착했을 거예요.
- (B) 현관홀에서 발견했습니다.
- (C) 제가 주문한 플로어 스탠드요.

(A)는 When 의문문의, (B)는 Where 의문문의 정답으로 알맞은 대답이다. 오답을 잘 골라낼수록 고수가 된다!

---

7. [M|Au] [W|Am]

What should I prepare for the marketing workshop?

(A) A group of us attended.
(B) Didn't Miguel take care of everything?
(C) That should work.

work (계획, 방법 등이) 잘되다, 성공적이다
마케팅 워크숍을 위해 제가 무엇을 준비하면 될까요?
- (A) 우리 일행이 참석했어요.
- (B) Miguel이 모든 것을 처리하지 않았나요?
- (C) 그거면 될 겁니다.

질문 앞부분 What should I prepare(제가 무엇을 준비하면 될까요?)에 집중하자. Miguel이 모든 것을 준비했으므로 당신은 신경 쓸 것이 없다고 말하는 대답이 정답이다. (A)는 질문의 the marketing workshop에서 연상되는 대답으로, (C)는 workshop에 들어 있는 work를 반복시키면서 오답을 유도하고 있다. 저저히 정답을 모르겠다면 반문하는 대답이 정답일 확률이 가장 높다는 사실을 기억하자.

---

8. [W|Br] [M|Au]

Do you know if these towels are made of one hundred percent cotton?

(A) Please fold these T-shirts for display.
(B) Production increased by seventy percent.
(C) There should be a label stitched on the edge.

stitch 바느질하다, 꿰매다
이 수건들이 100% 면으로 만들어진 것인지 혹시 아세요?
- (A) 이 티셔츠들을 진열할 수 있게 개어 주세요.
- (B) 생산량이 70퍼센트 증가했습니다.
- (C) 가장자리에 라벨이 붙어 있을 거예요.

질문 앞부분을 놓치고 made of one hundred percent cotton만 알아들으면 연상되는 대답 (A)를 정답으로 잘못 고를 수 있다. (B)는 질문에 나왔던 percent를 반복시키면서 오답을 유도하고 있다. 오답을 잘 골라낼수록 고수가 된다!

---

9. [W|Br] [M|Cn]

Has the heating system been checked today?

(A) Elizabeth has the inspection report.
(B) Those tools on the shelf.
(C) I checked out of the hotel.

heating system 난방 장치 inspection 검사, 점검
오늘 난방 장치 점검했나요?
- (A) Elizabeth에게 점검 보고서가 있어요.
- (B) 선반 위에 있는 저 연장들이요.
- (C) 저는 호텔에서 체크아웃 했어요.

난방 장치 점검이 이루어졌는지는 보고서를 갖고 있는 Elizabeth가 알고 본인은 모르겠다고 말하는 대답이 정답이다. 모른다는 대답은 거의 항상 정답이다. (B)는 질문에서 연상될 수 있는 대답으로, (C)는 checked를 반복시키면서 오답을 유도하고 있다.

---

10. [M|Au] [W|Am]

Why don't we schedule the training session for when you get back?

(A) It stopped raining a while ago.
(B) I heard it'll be in front of the building.
(C) Mornings are best for me.

어휘 schedule *sth* for + 날짜/요일 ~로 ~의 일정을 잡다
a while ago 조금 전에

해석 교육 모임 일정을 당신이 돌아왔을 때에 맞춰 잡으면 어떨까요?
(A) 조금 전에 비가 그쳤습니다.
(B) 저는 그게 건물 앞에 있을 거라고 들었어요.
(C) 저는 오전이 가장 좋습니다.

해설 (A)는 질문에 나오는 training과 발음이 비슷한 stopped raining을 들려주면서, (B)는 back에서 연상되는 단어 front를 들려주면서 오답을 유도하고 있다. 오답을 잘 골라낼수록 고수가 된다!

⸺⸺⸺⸺⸺⸺⸺⸺⸺⸺⸺⸺⸺⸺

11. [M｜Cn] [W｜Br]

Don't I need manager approval to place this order?

(A) No, because it's less than thirty dollars.
(B) We can't turn left here.
(C) An additional dozen cases.

어휘 approval 승인　place an order 주문하다

해석 이 주문을 하려면 매니저의 승인이 필요하지 않나요?
(A) 아니에요, 30달러가 안 되니까요.
(B) 여기서는 좌회전을 할 수 없어요.
(C) 추가로 열두 상자요.

해설 질문 앞부분 Don't I need manager approval(매니저의 승인이 필요하지 않나요?)에 집중하면 (A)는 자연스러운 대답이고 (B)는 적절하지 않다는 것을 알 수 있다. (C)는 질문의 to place this order에서 연상되는 대답으로 오답을 유도하고 있다.

⸺⸺⸺⸺⸺⸺⸺⸺⸺⸺⸺⸺⸺⸺

12. [W｜Am] [M｜Au]

Why don't you assign some of the interns to support you on the project?

(A) A graph summarizing sales projections.
(B) I really enjoyed the internship.
(C) I haven't thought of that.

어휘 assign 배정하다　summarize 요약하다　projection 예상, 추정

해석 인턴 몇 명을 배정해서 프로젝트에서 당신을 지원하게 하지 그러세요?
(A) 매출 전망을 요약한 그래프입니다.
(B) 인턴 기간은 정말 즐거웠어요.
(C) 그 생각을 못 했네요.

해설 (A)는 질문에 나오는 project와 발음이 비슷한 projections를, (B)는 intern이 포함되는 internship을 들려주면서 오답을 유도하고 있다. 질문 앞부분 Why don't you에 집중하자. 제안하는 질문이므로 (C)와 같이 동의하는 대답이 정답이다.

Part 3

Questions 13 through 15 refer to the following conversation with three speakers.

[M｜Au] ¹³The last item on the agenda is the office renovations scheduled for next year, which are expected to be quite extensive. As a result, we won't be able to host client meetings here during that period. Does anyone have any suggestions to offer?

[W｜Am] Yaping and I were discussing this earlier and she referenced an advertisement she spotted in this morning's newspaper. What did it say again, Yaping?

[W｜Br] Well, there seems to be a place not too far from here called Get Space Solutions. ¹⁴They own the building and they have meeting rooms available for rent. I believe this would be suitable for our needs.

[M｜Au] OK. ¹⁵Could you head over there this afternoon and take a look around?

[W｜Br] ¹⁵Of course, I'll get that done.

13-15번 문제는 다음 3인 대화에 관한 것입니다.

남: 안건 중 마지막 항목은 내년으로 예정되어 있는 사무실 개조 공사인데, 상당히 대규모가 될 것으로 예상됩니다. 결과적으로 그 기간 동안은 여기서 고객들과의 회의를 진행할 수 없을 겁니다. 제안할 만한 사항 있는 분 계신가요?

여1: Yaping과 제가 아까 이 사안에 대해 이야기를 나누었는데요, 그녀가 오늘 조간신문에서 발견한 광고에 대해 언급했어요. 뭐라고 써 있다고 했지, Yaping?

여2: 음, 여기서 그리 멀지 않은 곳에 Get Space Solutions라는 장소가 있나 봐요. 건물이 그들 소유인데, 임차할 수 있는 회의실이 있습니다. 제 생각에는 이곳이 우리의 필요에 적합할 것 같아요.

남: 좋아요. 오늘 오후에 그곳에 가서 둘러봐 줄 수 있겠어요?

여2: 물론이죠, 그렇게 하겠습니다.

item 항목, 사항 agenda 의제, 안건 extensive 대규모의
as a result 결과적으로 host 주최하다 reference ~에
대해 언급하다 commercial 광고 (방송) own 소유하다
rent 임대, 임차 head (특정 방향으로) 가다, 향하다

13. According to the man, what will happen next year?

(A) A new product will be launched.
(B) Additional perks will be provided.
(C) Several employees will be hired.
(D) Some offices will be renovated.

→ 어휘 launch (상품을) 출시하다, 출간하다 perks (급료 이외의) 특전

→ 해석 남자의 말에 따르면 내년에 무슨 일이 있을 것인가?
(A) 신제품이 출시될 것이다.
(B) 추가 특전이 제공될 것이다.
(C) 여러 명의 직원이 채용될 것이다.
(D) 일부 사무실이 개조될 것이다.

14. What does Yaping suggest?

(A) Using online advertisements
(B) Supplementing details to a contract
(C) Hiring a venue for meetings
(D) Developing orientation materials

→ 어휘 supplement 보충하다, 추가하다 hire 빌리다, 세내다 venue 장소 materials 자료

→ 해석 Yaping은 무엇을 제안하는가?
(A) 온라인 광고 이용하기
(B) 계약서에 세부사항 추가하기
(C) 회의를 위한 장소 빌리기
(D) 오리엔테이션 자료 개발하기

15. What does Yaping agree to do?

(A) Investigate a location
(B) Interact with a client
(C) Complete a transaction
(D) Edit a document

→ 어휘 investigate 조사하다 interact 소통하다 transaction 거래, 매매

→ 해석 Yaping은 무엇을 하는 데 동의하는가?
(A) 장소를 조사한다
(B) 고객과 소통한다
(C) 거래를 완료한다
(D) 문서를 편집한다

해설 13번 문제의 정답은 첫 문장에 들어 있는 키워드 the office renovations scheduled for next year를 듣고 쉽게 알아낼 수 있다. 사무실 개조 공사 때문에 한동안 회사 건물 내에서는 고객과 회의를 할 수 없는데, 다행히 Yaping이 회의실을 대여하는 사업체를 찾아내어(they have meeting rooms available for rent.) 그곳을 이용할 것을 제안하고 있다(I believe this would be suitable for our needs). 여기서 순발력을 발휘하며 14번 문제의 정답을 고르고, 곧장 15번 문제로 연필을 옮기자. Yaping의 제안을 들은 남자가 오늘 그 건물을 찾아가 답사해 볼 것을 부탁하자(Could you head over there this afternoon and take a look around?), Yaping은 Of course, I'll get that done.이라는 말로 수락하고 있다.

Questions 16 through 18 refer to the following conversation.

M Au Hey, Yuko. I've been pondering - our outdoor dining area is available tonight. 16 17 Do you think we could have the Dully Manufacturing dinner outside?

W Am Well, I've just had a conversation with my contact at the company, 17 and they informed me about a video presentation that will be included along with the speeches. It's not possible to hold it outdoors.

M Au I guess that makes sense. [The recent weather has been quite pleasant, though!]

W Am Yeah. 18 You know, I think it'd be nice to serve the appetizers on the outdoor patio.

M Au That sounds like a good plan! We can easily arrange a few tables and chairs out there. It doesn't have to be a formal set-up.

16-18번 문제는 다음 대화에 관한 것입니다.

남: 저기, Yuko. 제가 생각해 봤는데요, 오늘 저녁에는 우리의 야외 식사 공간이 비잖아요. Dully Manufacturing의 만찬을 바깥에서 할 수 있을까요?

여: 음, 그 회사의 연락 담당자와 지금 막 얘기했는데요, 연설과 함께 포함될 동영상 프레젠테이션이 있다고 알려줬어요. 그걸 야외에서 하는 건 가능하지 않죠.

남: 그런 것 같네요. 하지만 최근에는 날씨가 참 쾌적하단 말이에요.

여: 그렇죠. 있잖아요, 제 생각에는 애피타이저는 야외 테라스에서 제공해도 좋을 것 같아요.

남: 좋은 계획인데요! 그곳이라면 테이블과 의자 몇 개는 쉽게 배치할 수 있죠. 격식을 갖춘 배열이어야 할 필요도 없고요.

어휘 ponder 숙고하다, 곰곰이 생각하다 contact 연락 담당자 make sense 타당하다 pleasant 쾌적한 though 하지만 patio 테라스 arrange 배열하다, 배치하다 set-up 구성, 배열

16. What event are the speakers discussing?

(A) **A company dinner**
(B) An inauguration ceremony
(C) A product launch
(D) An annual reunion

어휘 inauguration 개업; 취임 launch 출시 reunion (재회) 모임, 동창회

해석 화자들은 어떤 행사를 논하고 있는가?
(A) 기업 만찬
(B) 개업식
(C) 제품 출시 행사
(D) 연례 모임

17. What does the man imply when he says, "The recent weather has been quite pleasant, though"?

(A) **He feels disappointed at a decision.**
(B) He is reluctant to plan an outdoor function.
(C) He wishes for an increase in his vacation allowance.
(D) He anticipates a shift in the weather tonight.

어휘 reluctant 꺼리는, 마지못한 function 행사, 의식 vacation allowance 휴가 수당 shift 변화

해석 남자는 "하지만 최근에는 날씨가 참 쾌적하단 말이에요."라고 말할 때 무엇을 암시하는가?
(A) 결정으로 인해 실망감을 느끼고 있다.
(B) 야외 행사를 계획하는 것을 꺼려한다.
(C) 휴가 수당이 늘어나기를 바란다.
(D) 오늘 밤 날씨의 변화를 예상한다.

18. What does the woman suggest?

(A) Postponing a dinner appointment
(B) Setting up video equipment outdoors
(C) **Serving some food at an alternative place**
(D) Offering a markdown

어휘 set up ~을 설치하다 alternative 대안의, 대신의 markdown 가격 인하

해석 여자는 무엇을 제안하는가?
(A) 저녁 식사 약속을 연기하는 것
(B) 영상 장비를 야외에 설치하는 것
(C) 일부 음식을 대체 장소에서 제공하는 것
(D) 가격 할인을 제공하는 것

해설 16번과 같이 주제를 묻는 질문은 첫 한두 문장을 듣고 정답을 선택하자. 화자들은 Dully Manufacturing의 만찬 행사에 대해 논의하고 있다. 남자는 이 행사를 야외에서 치르고 싶어 하는데(Do you think we could have the Dully Manufacturing dinner outside?), 여자는 장비가 필요한 동영상 프레젠테이션이 포함되기 때문에 그렇게 할 수 없다고 대답하고 있다(they informed me about a video presentation that will be included along with the speeches. It's not possible to hold it outdoors). 이에 대한 남자의 응답 The recent weather has been quite pleasant, though!는 날씨가 좋음에도 불구하고 야외 공간을 이용할 수 없는 것에 대한 아쉬움을 나타내고 있으므로 여기서 17번 문제의 정답을 알 수 있다. 의견이 수용되지 않는 것에 실망하는 남자에게 여자는 전체 행사는 안 되겠지만, 애피타이저만큼은 야외 테라스에서 제공해 보자는 대안을 제시하고 있다(I think it'd be nice to serve the appetizers on the outdoor patio). 여기서 18번 문제의 정답을 고르자. 17번 문제의 정답 고르기를 머뭇거리면 바로 이어지는 문장을 놓쳐서 18번을 틀릴 수 있다. 토익 수험생에게는 언제나 순발력이 필요하다.

Questions 19 through 21 refer to the following conversation and chart.

M | Au Hi, Fatima. This is Larry, your editor at *Euro Directions* magazine. Is now a good time to chat?

W | Br Yes, I have a minute.

M | Au Great. [19] [20]Would you be able to increase the word count for your "Exploring Naples" article to two thousand words?

W | Br OK, there's plenty to cover on the topic. [20]But I have another article due that same day.

M | Au Ah, I see that on your assignment chart. [20]Let's extend the deadline for your other assignment by seven days. This will allow you to focus on Naples.

W | Br Thanks, I appreciate it. On another note, [21]I've been compiling some ideas for pieces to write this winter. I'll forward them to you later today for your feedback.

19–21번 문제는 다음 대화와 도표에 관한 것입니다.

남: 안녕하세요, Fatima. *Euro Directions* 지(誌)의 담당 편집자 Larry예요. 지금 이야기 나눌 시간 되세요?

여: 네, 시간 조금 있어요.

남: 잘 됐습니다. 당신이 쓰신 기사 '나폴리 탐방'의 단어 수를 2,000단어로 늘려주실 수 있을까요?

여: 알겠습니다. 그 주제에 대해서는 다룰 게 많죠. 하지만 제가 같은 날짜에 제출해야 하는 기사가 하나 더 있어요.

남: 아, 당신의 업무 차트를 보니 그게 있군요. 그 업무의 기한은 7일 더 연장합시다. 이렇게 하면 나폴리 기사에 집중할 수 있을 거예요.

여: 정말 고마워요. 그건 그렇고, 제가 올 겨울에 쓸 기사들의 아이디어를 정리하고 있거든요. 당신의 피드백을 받을 수 있게 오늘 오후에 보내드릴게요.

어휘 word count 총 단어 수 plenty 많은 양[수] cover 다루다, 포함시키다 due (특정일까지) 제출해야 하는 assignment 임무, 수행 업무 on another note 그건 그렇고 compile (자료를 수집하여) 작성하다, 정리하다 piece (신문, 잡지의) 기사 forward 보내다, 전달하다

Article	Deadline
[20]"Exploring Naples"	[20]September 14
[20]"Cheeses of Italy"	[20]September 14
"Affordable Tour Packages"	October 17
"Copenhagen by Bicycle"	November 12

기사	기한
'나폴리 탐방'	9월 14일
'이탈리아의 치즈'	9월 14일
'저렴한 패키지 여행'	10월 17일
'Copenhagen 자전거 여행'	11월 12일

어휘 affordable 살 만한 가격의, 저렴한

19. What does the man ask the woman to do?

(A) Extend an agreement
(B) Arrange a meeting for an interview
(C) Lengthen an article
(D) Proofread a document

어휘 agreement 협정, 계약 arrange 마련하다 lengthen 길게 하다, 늘이다 proofread 교정을 보다

해석 남자는 여자에게 무엇을 하라고 요청하는가?
(A) 계약을 연장한다
(B) 인터뷰를 위한 만남을 마련한다
(C) 기사 길이를 늘인다
(D) 문서를 교정 본다

20. Look at the graphic. Which article's deadline will be changed?

(A) "Exploring Naples"
(B) "Cheeses of Italy"
(C) "Affordable Tour Packages"
(D) "Copenhagen by Bicycle"

해석 그래픽을 보라. 어느 기사의 기한이 변경될 것인가?
(A) '나폴리 탐방'
(B) '이탈리아의 치즈'
(C) '저렴한 패키지 여행'
(D) 'Copenhagen 자전거 여행'

21. What does the woman say she will send the man?

(A) An itinerary for a tour
(B) An expense report
(C) Meeting minutes
(D) Ideas for upcoming articles

어휘 itinerary 여행 일정표 minutes 회의록

해석 여자는 남자에게 무엇을 보내겠다고 말하는가?
(A) 관광 일정표
(B) 지출 보고서
(C) 회의록
(D) 앞으로 쓸 기사의 아이디어

해설 19번 문제는 남자의 대사 중 Would you be able to increase the word count for your "Exploring Naples" article to two thousand words?가 패러프레이즈 되어 있는 표현을 정답으로 선택해야 한다. 여자는 기사를 더 길게 하는 것은 어렵지 않지만 같은 날 제출해야 하는 기사가 더 있다는 문제점을 알려주고 있다(But I have another article due that same day). 표를 보면 "Cheeses of Italy"라는 기사가 "Exploring Naples"와 기한이 같다는 것을 알 수 있다. 남자는 해결책으로 "Cheeses of Italy"의 기한을 일주일 연기하자고 제안하고 있으므로(Let's extend the deadline for your other assignment by seven days.) 여기서 20번의 정답을 고르자. 대화 끝에 여자가 올 겨울 기사에 활용하려고 수집, 정리하고 있는 아이디어를 남자에게 보내겠다고 말하고 있다(I've been compiling some ideas for pieces to write this winter. I'll forward them to you later today for your feedback). 여기서 21번 문제의 정답을 알 수 있다.

Part 4

Questions 22 through 24 refer to the following telephone message.

[W] [Am] Hello, this is Josephine Chen. ²²I wanted to inform you that the camera I bought from your online store had a scratched lens when it arrived. ²³I want to return it for an exchange at the post office this afternoon, but I'd like to have a conversation with a representative from your company before I send it. You see, I'm moving to a new house next week, so the replacement will need to be shipped to my new address. ²⁴Please call me back so I can be certain that the camera will be sent to the correct address by your shipping department.

22-24번 문제는 다음 전화 메세지에 관한 것입니다.

여: 안녕하세요, Josephine Chen입니다. 귀사의 온라인 상점에서 산 카메라가 도착했을 때 렌즈가 긁혀 있었다는 것을 알려드리고자 합니다. 교환을 위해 오늘 오후에 우체국에서 그 물건을 돌려보내려고 하는데요, 보내기 전에 귀사의 담당자와 대화를 나누고 싶어요. 음, 다음 주에 새 집으로 이사를 가거든요. 그래서 교체품은 저의 새 주소로 발송되어야 합니다. 배송 부서에서 카메라가 올바른 주소로 배송되는지 확인할 수 있도록 다시 전화해 주세요.

어휘 representative 대표(자), 대리인 you see 그러니까, 저, 있잖아 replacement 교체물, 대체물 ship 수송하다, 운송하다

22. What is wrong with the camera?
(A) It is missing a component.
(B) It is an outdated model.
(C) It weighs too much.
(D) It has been damaged.

어휘 miss 빠뜨리다, 빼놓다 component 부품 outdated 구식인 weigh 무게가 ~이다

해석 카메라에 무슨 문제가 있는가?
(A) 부품이 빠져 있다.
(B) 구식 모델이다.
(C) 무게가 너무 많이 나간다.
(D) 손상되었다.

23. Where does the speaker want to go this afternoon?
(A) To a warehouse
(B) To an electronics store
(C) To a real estate agency
(D) To a post office

해석 화자는 오늘 오후에 어디에 가고 싶은가?
(A) 창고에
(B) 전자 제품 매장에
(C) 부동산 중개업소에
(D) 우체국에

24. Why does the speaker request a return call?
(A) To cancel an order
(B) To inquire about a rental
(C) To verify a location
(D) To give driving directions

어휘 inquire 문의하다 rental 대여 verify 확인하다
directions 길 안내

해석 화자는 왜 회신 전화를 요청하는가?
(A) 주문을 취소하려고
(B) 대여에 대해 문의하려고
(C) 장소를 확인하려고
(D) 운전을 위한 길 안내를 해주려고

해설 22번 문제는 scratched라는 키워드만 들리면 쉽게 정답을 알 수 있다. 순발력을 발휘하는 것만 잊지 말자. 바로 이어지는 문장에서 23번의 정답을 고를 수 있게 준비해야 한다. 오후에 우체국에 가서 물건을 반품하겠다고 말하고 있다(I want to return it for an exchange at the post office this afternoon). 24번 문제의 정답은 마지막 문장에서 알 수 있는데, 자신이 이사 갈 주소를 판매사 측에서 확실히 알게 하기 위해 전화 통화를 원한다는 내용이다 (Please call me back so I can be certain that the camera will be sent to the correct address by your shipping department).

Questions 25 through 27 refer to the following broadcast.

M | Au Welcome to Business Tips and Tricks on WJNK Radio. ²⁵On today's show, I'll be talking with Tina Brownstein, who is a corporate trainer for customer service teams around the country. But that's not all she does. ²⁶She's also the creator of a software tool known as C3VR, which was released last month. Customer service representatives can enhance their communication skills through this interactive program that involves interacting with simulated, computer-generated customers. ²⁷However, Ms. Brownstein's most recent training software has faced criticism from some technology experts. [Only her employees had the opportunity to try out the product before its official release.] Therefore, there is much to talk about with her... right after this commercial break.

25–27번 문제는 다음 방송에 관한 것입니다.

남: 어서 오세요, WJNK 라디오 Business Tips and Tricks입니다. 오늘 방송에서는 Tina Brownstein과 이야기 나누려고 하는데요, 이분은 전국의 고객 서비스 팀들을 위한 기업 교육가이십니다. 하지만 그녀가 하는 일은 그뿐만이 아닙니다. C3VR이라고 알려진 소프트웨어 툴의 제작자이기도 하신데요, 이 제품은 지난달에 발매되었습니다. 고객 서비스 상담원은 컴퓨터가 만들어낸 가상 고객들과의 소통을 수반하는 이 쌍방향 프로그램을 통해 의사소통 능력을 향상시킬 수 있습니다. 그러나 Ms. Brownstein의 이 최신 훈련 소프트웨어는 일부 기술 전문가들의 비판에 직면했습니다. 공식 발매 전에는 오직 그녀의 직원들만 제품을 시험 사용해 볼 기회가 있었거든요. 그래서 그녀와 이야기 나눌 부분이 많습니다. 이 광고 하나만 듣고요.

어휘 corporate 기업의, 회사의 release 발매하다; 발매, 출시 customer service representative 고객 서비스 상담원 enhance 향상시키다 interactive 대화형의, 쌍방향의 involve 수반하다, 포함하다 interact 소통하다 simulated 모의의, 모조의 face ~에 직면하다 try out 시험해 보다 commercial break (TV, 라디오의) 중간광고 시간

25. What is Tina Brownstein's area of expertise?

(A) Online marketing
(B) Customer service
(C) Corporate accounting
(D) Business laws

어휘 accounting 회계 (업무)
해석 Tina Brownstein의 전문 영역은 무엇인가?
(A) 온라인 마케팅
(B) 고객 서비스
(C) 기업 회계
(D) 상법

26. What is C3VR?

(A) A digital camera brand
(B) An electronic reading device
(C) An automatic payment method
(D) A software program

해석 C3VR은 무엇인가?
(A) 디지털 카메라 브랜드
(B) 전자 독서 기기
(C) 자동 결제 방식
(D) 소프트웨어 프로그램

27. Why does the speaker say, "Only her employees had the opportunity to try out the product before its official release"?

(A) To explain why some experts are skeptical about a product
(B) To confirm whether testing on a product had to be terminated
(C) To inquire about the number of employees in a company
(D) To encourage the audience to test some merchandise

🔲 **어휘** release 발매, 출시 skeptical 의심이 많은, 회의적인
terminate 끝내다, 종료하다

🔲 **해석** 화자는 왜 "공식 발매 전에는 오직 그녀의 직원들만 제품을 시험 사용해 볼 기회가 있었거든요."라고 말하는가?
(A) 왜 일부 전문가들이 제품에 대해 회의적인지 설명하기 위해
(B) 제품에 대한 테스트가 종료되어야만 했음을 확인해주기 위해
(C) 회사의 직원 수에 대해 문의하기 위해
(D) 청취자들에게 상품을 테스트 해보라고 권하기 위해

🔲 **해설** 25번 문제의 정답은 화자가 Tina Brownstein을 고객 서비스 팀들을 위한 기업 교육가(a corporate trainer for customer service teams around the country)라고 소개하는 부분에서 알 수 있다. 26번은 a software tool known as C3VR이라는 키워드를 통해 쉽게 정답을 알 수 있다. 까다로운 문제는 27번이다. 화자는 이 제품이 일부 기술 전문가들의 비판을 받았다고 말하고 있는데(Ms. Brownstein's most recent training software has faced criticism from some technology experts.), 바로 이어지는 문장이 Only her employees had the opportunity to try out the product before its official release.이다. 공식 발매 전에는 오직 자사 직원들만 제품을 시험 사용해 보았다. 즉 소비자나 전문가 평가단의 피드백을 받는 등 별도의 절차가 없었던 것이 전문가들의 비판을 받는 원인이 되었음을 암시하고 있다. 따라서 주어진 문장은 전문가들이 제품에 대해 회의적인 이유를 설명하는 부분이라고 할 수 있다.

Questions 28 through 30 refer to the following talk and map.

W Am ²⁸Hello, welcome to the Visitors Center at Morrista National Park. I'm Sylvia, your guide for today's hike. ²⁹Normally we'd be taking the Zion Trail to the Picnic Area, but it's partially unavailable this week due to maintenance on its second section. So instead, we've decided to start off on the Zion Trail and make a switch to the La Quinta Trail halfway through our trek, as shown here on the map. Our lunch break will be at the end of the La Quinta Trail, and then we'll follow the Mary's Rock Trail back to the starting point. ³⁰It's supposed to be sunny today, so it's a good idea to protect yourself from the sun by applying sunscreen and wearing a hat.

28-30번 문제는 다음 담화와 지도에 관한 것입니다.

여: 안녕하세요, Morrista 국립공원 방문객 센터에 오신 것을 환영합니다. 저는 오늘 여러분의 하이킹 담당 가이드 Sylvia입니다. 평소라면 우리가 Zion 길을 타고 피크닉 구역까지 갈 텐데요, 후반 구간의 보수 공사 때문에 이번 주에는 부분적으로 이용하실 수 없습니다. 그래서 대신 여기 지도에서 보시는 바와 같이 Zion 길로 출발한 후 트레킹 중간쯤에 La Quinta 길로 옮겨 가기로 했습니다. 점심시간은 La Quinta 길이 끝나는 곳에서 있을 예정이고요, 그 후에는 Mary's Rock 길을 따라 출발점으로 돌아오려고 합니다. 오늘은 날씨가 화창할 것이기 때문에 자외선 차단제를 바르고 모자를 써서 햇빛으로부터 자신을 보호하는 것이 좋겠습니다.

🔲 **어휘** trail (산속의) 작은 길, 산길 partially 부분적으로
unavailable 이용할 수 없는 maintenance 유지 보수
halfway through 중간쯤에서 trek 트레킹 apply (화장품을) 바르다 sunscreen 자외선 차단제

Morrista 국립 공원 등산로 지도

---

28. Who most likely are the listeners?

(A) Park rangers
(B) Bus operators
(C) Maintenance workers
(D) Tourists

해석 청자들은 누구이겠는가?
(A) 공원 관리원들
(B) 버스 기사들
(C) 시설관리 직원들
(D) 관광객들

---

29. Look at the graphic. Where will the listeners be unable to go today?

(A) The North Pond
(B) The Picnic Area
(C) The Honeybee Garden
(D) The Visitor Center

해석 그래픽을 보라. 청자들은 오늘 어디에 갈 수 없는가?
(A) 북쪽 연못
(B) 피크닉 구역
(C) 꿀벌 정원
(D) 방문객 센터

---

30. What does the woman encourage the listeners to do?

(A) Study the park trail map
(B) Listen to the weather report
(C) Secure their belongings
(D) Use sun protection

어휘 study 살피다 secure 안전하게 지키다 belongings 소지품

해석 여자는 청자들에게 무엇을 하라고 권장하는가?
(A) 공원 등산로 지도를 살펴본다
(B) 일기예보를 듣는다
(C) 소지품을 잘 간수한다
(D) 햇빛 보호 조치를 취한다

해설 28번과 같이 청자들이 누구인지 묻는 문제는 대부분 첫 한두 문장에서 정답을 알 수 있다. 국립공원 방문객 센터에서 가이드의 환영 인사와 안내를 받는 사람들은 관광객들이다(Hello, welcome to the Visitors Center at Morrista National Park. I'm Sylvia, your guide for today's hike). 29번 문제는 가이드의 하이킹 경로 안내를 잘 들어야 풀 수 있다. 우선 평소에 이용하는 Zion 길은 보수 공사 때문에 후반 구간이 폐쇄되어 있다(Normally we'd be taking the Zion Trail to the Picnic Area, but it's partially unavailable this week due to maintenance on its second section). 그래서 관광객들은 Zion 길을 따라 가다가 중간에 La Quinta 길로 옮겨서 하이킹을 계속 할 것이다(So instead, we've decided to start off on the Zion Trail and make a switch to the La Quinta Trail halfway through our trek, as shown here on the map). 지도를 보면 평소대로 Zion 길을 따라 걸으면 북쪽 연못에 갈 수 있지만, 오늘은 그곳에 갈 수 없다는 것을 알 수 있다. 마지막에는 관광객들의 건강을 위한 당부가 나오는데, 날씨가 화창할 것이므로 자외선 차단제와 모자를 이용하라고 권장하고 있다(It's supposed to be sunny today, so it's a good idea to protect yourself from the sun by applying sunscreen and wearing a hat). 여기서 30번의 정답을 선택하자.

PART 1 Exercise

1 (C)   **2** (D)

1. [W|Am]

(A) One of the women is adjusting the angle of a mirror.
(B) An employee is putting laces into a pair of shoes.
(C) Many pairs of shoes are being displayed along a wall.
(D) One of the women has a shawl draped around her shoulders.

어휘 adjust 조정하다, 조절하다 angle 각, 각도 lace 끈, 줄 shawl 숄, 어깨걸이 drape 걸치다

해석 (A) 여자들 중 한 명이 거울의 각도를 조절하고 있다.
(B) 직원이 신발에 끈을 끼고 있다.
(C) 많은 신발이 벽을 따라 진열되어 있다.
(D) 여자들 중 한 명이 어깨에 숄을 걸치고 있다.

해설 adjusting, putting 같은 동사만 알아들으면 (A)와 (B)는 오답으로 골라낼 수 있다. (D)는 사진에 a shawl이 보이지 않으므로 오답이다. 신발이 진열되어 있으므로 키워드 display가 들리는 문장을 정답으로 고르면 된다. 동사 display는 진행 시제 수동태로 사용해도 예외적으로 '상태'를 나타낸다는 점도 기억하자.

2. [M|Cn]

(A) The shopkeeper is reaching inside a refrigerator.
(B) Some customers are standing side by side.
(C) Some bottles are arranged on a counter.
(D) Refreshments have been organized in refrigerated display cases.

어휘 shopkeeper 가게 주인 reach 손을 뻗다 refrigerated display case 냉장 진열장

해석 (A) 가게 주인이 냉장고 안으로 손을 뻗고 있다.
(B) 손님들이 나란히 서 있다.
(C) 병들이 카운터 위에 정리되어 있다.
(D) 음료가 냉장 진열장 안에 정리되어 있다.

해설 가게 주인으로 보이는 사람이 손을 뻗고 있는 듯한 자세이기는 하지만 냉장고 안으로(inside a refrigerator) 뻗지는 않았으므로 (A)는 오답이다. 사람이 한 명밖에 없는 사진인데 주어가 Some customers인 (B)도 오답이다. side by side에 속지 않도록 주의하자. (C)는 위치 표현 on a counter를 듣고 오답임을 알 수 있다. 물건이 진열되어 있는 장면은 매우 자주 출제되므로 진열된 상태를 나타내는 여러 동사들을 기억해 두자.

PART 2 Exercise

1 (A)	**2** (A)	**3** (B)	**4** (B)	**5** (C)
6 (A)	**7** (C)	**8** (C)	**9** (B)	**10** (A)

1. [W|Am] [W|Br]

Where can I get some tracking labels?

(A) They'll be attached at the loading dock.
(B) Yes, an overnight shipping.
(C) She doesn't live there.

어휘 track 추적하다 loading dock 하역장(건물에서 짐 싣고 내리는 곳) overnight shipping 익일 배송

해석 추적 라벨을 어디서 받을 수 있나요?
(A) 그건 하역장에서 붙일 거예요.
(B) 네, 익일 배송이요.
(C) 그녀는 거기 살지 않아요.

Where 의문문의 90%는 'in/at/on + 장소'의 패턴으로 정답이 출제된다. (B)는 Yes를 듣는 순간 오답임을 알 수 있고, (C)는 She가 누구를 가리키는지 알 수 없다는 사실만으로도 오답으로 골라낼 수 있다.

2. M|Au M|Cn

When will I find out if I won the contract?

(A) No later than Thursday.
(B) The public relations team.
(C) Haven't you found it?

어휘 find out ~을 알게 되다 win a contract 계약을 따내다 no later than 늦어도 ~까지는 public relations 홍보(활동)

해설 계약을 따내게 되면 언제 알게 되는 건가요?
(A) 늦어도 목요일까지요.
(B) 홍보팀이요.
(C) 못 찾았어요?

해설 When 의문문이므로 당연히 요일 이름이 들리는 선택지가 정답이다. (B)처럼 부서 이름으로 대답하는 경우는 Who 의문문의 정답으로 알맞고, (C)는 질문의 find와 발음이 비슷한 found를 들려주면서 오답을 유도하고 있다.

3. W|Am W|Br

Where will your new office be located?

(A) A couple of days from today.
(B) It'll be just round the corner.
(C) I don't think she's here today.

어휘 just round the corner 아주 가까운

해설 당신의 새 사무실은 어디가 될까요?
(A) 오늘로부터 2, 3일 후에요.
(B) 아주 가까울 거예요.
(C) 그녀는 오늘 여기에 없는 것 같아요.

해설 (A)는 When 의문문의 정답으로 알맞은 대답이고, (C)는 she가 누구를 가리키는지 알 수 없다는 사실만 파악해도 오답으로 골라낼 수 있다. Where 의문문의 정답에 자주 사용되는 장소 부사 (over) there, down the street, down the hall, (a)round the corner, online, downstairs, nearby 등을 기억하자.

4. M|Cn M|Au

When was the sculpture gallery added to the Port Franklin Museum?

(A) A significant amount of money.
(B) Three or four years ago.

(C) He's a local artist.

어휘 a significant amount of 상당량의, 상당한 금액의

해설 Port Franklin 미술관에 조각 전시관은 언제 추가된 거죠?
(A) 상당한 금액의 돈이요.
(B) 3, 4년 전에요.
(C) 그는 이 지역의 미술가입니다.

해설 (A)는 '상당한 금액의 돈'이라고 말하고 있으므로 의문사 When과는 무관하며, (C)는 Who 의문문의 정답으로 알맞은 대답이다. When 의문문이 과거 시제로 출제되면 대부분 정답에 last, ago, yesterday 같은 키워드가 들어간다.

5. W|Br W|Am

Where can I purchase fresh flowers this time of year?

(A) Nine thirty this morning.
(B) Yes, in March and April.
(C) Try the florist on South Avenue.

어휘 florist 꽃집

해설 연중 이맘때는 어디서 신선한 꽃을 살 수 있나요?
(A) 오늘 오전 9시 30분이요.
(B) 네, 3, 4월에요.
(C) South 가(街)에 있는 꽃집에 가 보세요.

해설 (A)는 시각으로 대답하고 있으므로 What time ~?의 정답으로 알맞은 대답이고, (B)는 Yes를 듣는 순간 오답임을 알 수 있다. Where 의문문의 정답으로 자주 사용되는 패턴으로 'try/check + 장소'도 기억해 두자.

6. M|Cn W|Am

When was your publishing house established?

(A) I've just started working here.
(B) The publicity officer.
(C) On Sullivan Street.

어휘 publishing house 출판사 publicity 홍보, 광고 officer 간부, 중역

해설 그쪽 출판사는 언제 설립되었나요?
(A) 저는 여기서 막 근무를 시작했어요.
(B) 홍보 담당 간부요.
(C) Sullivan 가(街)에요.

해설 (B)는 Who 의문문의, (C)는 Where 의문문의 정답으로 알맞은 대답이다. 오답을 잘 골라낼수록 고수가 된다!

7. [M|Cn] [W|Am]

Where are the copies of tomorrow's schedule?

(A) Just a small cup.
(B) Every Tuesday and Thursday.
(C) The printer's still out of order.

🔵 **어휘** out of order 고장 난

🔵 **해석** 내일 일정 복사본들 어디 있나요?
(A) 그냥 작은 컵이요.
(B) 매주 화요일과 목요일이요.
(C) 프린터가 아직 고장 나 있어요.

🔵 **해설** (A)는 질문의 copies와 발음이 비슷한 cup을 들려주면서 오답을 유도하고 있고, (B)는 When 의문문의 정답으로 알맞은 대답이다. 오답을 잘 골라낼수록 고수가 된다!

---

8. [W|Am] [M|Au]

When will we have the results of the customer survey?

(A) Around thirty questions.
(B) She's our best customer.
(C) We just sent it out this morning.

🔵 **어휘** send out (많은 사람에게) ~을 발송하다

🔵 **해석** 고객 설문조사 결과는 언제 나올까요?
(A) 약 30개의 질문이요.
(B) 그녀가 우리의 최고의 고객입니다.
(C) 겨우 오늘 오전에 발송했잖아요.

🔵 **해설** (A)는 질문에 나오는 the customer survey에서 연상되는 대답으로, (B)는 customer를 반복해서 들려주면서 오답을 유도하고 있다. 오답을 잘 골라낼수록 고수가 된다!

---

9. [W|Br] [M|Cn]

When are we going to launch the mobile phone application?

(A) Thanks, but I just ate.
(B) We're a bit behind schedule.
(C) Because I interviewed him previously.

🔵 **어휘** launch 출시하다 application (컴퓨터의) 애플리케이션, 앱 behind schedule 예정보다 늦게

🔵 **해설** 휴대폰 앱은 언제 출시할 건가요?
(A) 고맙지만 방금 먹었어요.
(B) 예정보다 약간 늦어졌어요.
(C) 전에 그를 인터뷰했기 때문이죠.

🔵 **해설** Thanks, but은 상대방의 제안을 거절할 때 쓰는 표현이므로 (A)는 오답이다. 또한 (A)는 질문의 launch를 lunch로 잘못 알아들었을 때 연상되는 대답이기도 하다. (C)처럼 Because로 시작하는 대답이 When 의문문의 정답이 될 수는 없다. 오답을 잘 골라낼수록 고수가 된다!

---

10. [W|Br] [M|Au]

Where should the new file cabinets be placed?

(A) Ms. Martin has the floor plan.
(B) Just the client files, please.
(C) I ordered more last month.

🔵 **어휘** floor plan 평면도

🔵 **해석** 새 파일 캐비닛들은 어디에 놓아야 할까요?
(A) Ms. Martin이 평면도를 갖고 있어요.
(B) 그냥 고객 파일만 주세요.
(C) 지난달에 더 주문했습니다.

🔵 **해설** (B)는 질문이 들어 있는 file을 반복시키면서 오답을 유도하고 있다. place an order(주문하다)라는 표현을 알고 있는 사람은 질문의 be placed에서 연상되는 단어 ordered를 들으면서 (C)를 정답으로 잘못 선택할 수 있다. (C)는 When 의문문의 정답으로 알맞은 대답이다. 오답을 잘 골라낼수록 고수가 된다!

PART 3 Sample Questions

1–3번 문제는 다음 대화에 관한 것입니다.

> **여:** Mike, 다음 달에 새 그래픽 디자이너가 합류할 거예요. 그래서 그에게 노트북과 추가 모니터를 제공해 주어야 해요. 그것들을 주문해 주실래요?
> **남:** 물론이죠. 판매업체가 가격을 올린 건 알고 있죠?
> **여:** 정말요?
> **남:** 네. 몇 분 전에 카탈로그를 봤는데, 최신 모델들이 이제 더 비싸졌어요.
> **여:** 그러네요. 음, 업무 공간마다 예산은 최대 1,200달러까지예요. 그러니까 그 가격 범주에 속하는 것 중 스크린이 가장 큰 걸로 주문하도록 해요.
> **남:** 알겠어요. 가격을 다시 한 번 살펴보고 나서 주문할게요.

🔵 **어휘** set A up with B A에게 B를 제공하다 place an order for ~을 주문하다 vendor 판매업체 fall within ~의 범위에 들어가다

Screen Size	System Price
11 inches	$999
13 inches	$1,099
[3]15 inches	[3]$1,199
17 inches	$1,299

스크린 크기	시스템 가격
11인치	999달러
13인치	1,099달러
15인치	1,199달러
17인치	1,299달러

1. 여자는 남자에게 무엇을 하라고 요구하는가?

(A) 장비를 주문한다
(B) 새 판매업체를 찾는다
(C) 노트북 컴퓨터를 수리한다
(D) 입사 지원자에게 연락한다

어휘 potential employee 입사 지원자, 잠재 직원

2. 남자는 어떤 문제를 언급하는가?

(A) 그래픽 디자이너가 회사를 그만두었다.
(B) 납품업체가 가격을 올렸다.
(C) 소프트웨어 프로그램이 단종되었다.
(D) 부서 예산이 낮아졌다.

어휘 supplier 납품업체 discontinue 단종하다 lower 내리다, 낮추다

3. 그래픽을 보라. 남자는 어느 크기의 스크린을 주문할 것인가?

(A) 11인치
(B) 13인치
(C) 15인치
(D) 17인치

PART 3 & 4 Exercise

1 (D)　**2** (D)　**3** (B)　**4** (B)　**5** (C)　**6** (C)

Questions 1 through 3 refer to the following conversation and list.

M | Au　Hi, I'm calling to gather some information about having an event catered at my company.

W | Am　Sure. Could you tell me the number of guests you anticipate and the budget you have in mind?

M | Au　[1]We're organizing a farewell event for one of our managers. We expect around thirty guests, [2]and we're working with a budget of no more than six hundred dollars.

W | Am　We do offer a package that meets your requirements. On our Web site, if you click on the Options tab, you can browse through the various menus there.

M | Au　[2]Oh, OK, you do have one that'll be suitable for us. I'd like to proceed with placing the order.

W | Am　[3]Sure, I'll just need a credit card number to hold the deposit.

1-3번 문제는 다음 대화와 목록에 관한 것입니다.

남: 안녕하세요, 회사에서 행사에 출장 뷔페를 제공받는 것에 대한 정보를 좀 얻으려고 전화했어요.
여: 잘 하셨어요. 예상하는 손님 수와 생각하는 예산을 말씀해 주시겠어요?
남: 매니저 중 한 분의 송별 행사를 준비 중입니다. 30명 정도의 손님을 예상하는데, 600달러밖에 안 되는 예산으로 진행하고 있어요.
여: 저희가 그 조건에 맞는 패키지 상품을 제공합니다. 저희 홈페이지에서 '옵션'을 클릭하면 거기서 다양한 메뉴를 둘러보실 수 있어요.
남: 아, 알겠습니다. 저희에게 알맞은 게 정말 있군요. 주문을 진행하고 싶어요.
여: 좋죠, 보증금을 받기 위해 신용카드 번호만 알려주시면 됩니다.

어휘 cater ~에 출장 뷔페를 제공하다 have *sth* in mind ~을 염두에 두다, 생각하다 organize 준비하다, 조직하다 farewell 작별 no more than 겨우 ~, 불과 ~ meet the requirements 조건에 맞다 browse through ~을 살펴보다, 열람하다 proceed with ~을 계속 진행하다 place an order 주문하다 deposit 보증금, 계약금

Options	
Seafood platter	$1,000
Steak platter	$850
Chicken platter	$700
[2]Vegetarian platter	[2]$550

옵션	
해산물 모듬	1,000달러
스테이크 모듬	850달러
치킨 모듬	700달러
채식 요리 모듬	550달러

어휘 platter 모듬 요리

---

1. What type of event is being organized?

   (A) A trade fair
   (B) A managers' meeting
   (C) A tour
   (D) A party

해석 어떤 유형의 행사를 준비하고 있는가?
   (A) 무역 박람회
   (B) 매니저 회의
   (C) 관광
   (D) 파티

---

2. Look at the graphic. What option will the man most likely select?

   (A) Seafood platter
   (B) Steak platter
   (C) Chicken platter
   (D) Vegetarian platter

해석 그래픽을 보라. 남자는 어느 옵션을 선택하겠는가?
   (A) 해산물 모듬
   (B) 스테이크 모듬
   (C) 치킨 모듬
   (D) 채식 요리 모듬

---

3. What information does the man still have to provide?

   (A) A purchase order number
   (B) Some payment information
   (C) The location of a business
   (D) A list of guests

해석 남자는 아직 어떤 정보를 제공해야 하는가?
   (A) 발주서 번호
   (B) 결제 정보
   (C) 사업체의 위치
   (D) 초대 손님 명단

해설 1번 문제의 정답은 남자가 회사 매니저 중 한 명의 송별 행사를 준비하고 있다고 말하는 문장에서 알 수 있다(We're organizing a farewell event for one of our managers). 그후 여자의 요청대로 예상 손님 수와 예산을 알려주고 있는데, 행사 예산이 600달러밖에 안 된다(we're working with a budget of no more than six hundred dollars). 목록을 보면 가격이 600달러 이하인 것은 Vegetarian platter밖에 없는데, 남자는 이것을 가리키면서 주문을 진행하겠다고 말한다(you do have one that'll be suitable for us. I'd like to proceed with placing the order). 여기서 2번 문제의 정답을 고르자. 곧바로 이어지는 문장에서 여자가 보증금을 위해 신용카드 번호를 요구하고 있다(I'll just need a credit card number to hold the deposit). 여기서 3번 문제의 정답을 선택하면 된다.

Questions 4 through 6 refer to the following excerpt from a meeting and sales graph.

[W][Am] There's one more topic I need to bring up during the staff meeting today. [4]I've just distributed a graph summarizing the yearly sales figures for our shoe store. And, well... I find this data quite intriguing, especially considering our move to a different neighborhood this year. As anticipated, the relocation led to a significant decrease in our sales at first. [5]We recorded the lowest shoe sales of the entire year during the quarter we moved. That was largely because the new community was unaware of our presence. [6]However, business picked up quickly towards the end of the year as a result of the newspaper ads and radio commercials we put out, leading to a record number of sales.

4-6번 문제는 다음 회의 발췌문과 판매량 그래프에 관한 것입니다.

> **여:** 오늘 직원회의에서 제기할 주제가 하나 더 있습니다. 방금 우리 신발 매장의 연간 매출액을 요약해 주는 그래프를 나눠 드렸죠. 그리고, 음... 저는 이 데이터가 상당히 흥미롭다고 생각하는데, 특별히 우리가 올해 다른 지역으로 이전했다는 사실을 고려하면 더 그렇습니다. 예상대로 처음에는 이 이전이 판매량의 상당한 감소로 이어졌어요. 이전을 한 분기 동안 우리는 한 해를 통틀어 가장 낮은 신발 판매를 기록했죠. 그것은 주로 새 지역 사회가 우리의 존재를 알지 못했기 때문입니다. 그러나 우리가 내보낸 신문 광고와 라디오 광고의 결과로 연말쯤에는 사업이 빠르게 회복되었고, 이것은 기록적인 판매량으로 이어졌습니다.

> **어휘** bring up (화제를) 꺼내다 summarize 요약하다 sales figures 매출액 find ~라고 여기다, 생각하다 intriguing 아주 흥미로운 considering ~을 고려하면, 감안하면 neighborhood (도시 내의) 지역, 동네 relocation 이전 lead to ~로 이어지다 significant 현저한, 상당한 record 기록하다; 기록적인 quarter 분기, 사분기 unaware of ~을 알지[눈치 채지] 못하는 presence 있음, 존재 pick up 회복되다, 개선되다 towards ~즈음에, 무렵에 commercial 광고 (방송) put out ~을 내보내다, 방송하다

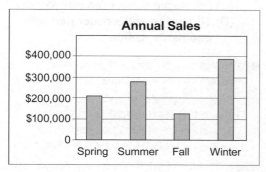

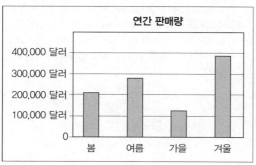

4. What type of product does the business sell?

(A) Apparel
(B) Footwear
(C) Electronic appliances
(D) Computer programs

> **해석** 사업체는 어떤 종류의 상품을 판매하는가?
> (A) 의류
> (B) 신발류
> (C) 전자 제품
> (D) 컴퓨터 프로그램

5. Look at the graphic. In what season did the business relocate?

(A) Spring
(B) Summer
(C) Fall
(D) Winter

> **어휘** relocate 이전하다, 이동하다
> **해석** 그래픽을 보라. 사업체가 어느 계절에 이전했는가?
> (A) 봄
> (B) 여름
> (C) 가을
> (D) 겨울

6. What did the business do after it relocated?

(A) It diversified its range of merchandise.
(B) It increased its workforce.
(C) It placed some advertisements.
(D) It organized an inauguration event.

> **어휘** diversify 다각화하다 workforce 총 근로자 수 place an advertisement 광고를 내다 inauguration 개시, 개업
> **해석** 사업체는 이전 후에 무엇을 했는가?
> (A) 상품의 범위를 다각화했다.
> (B) 직원 수를 늘렸다.
> (C) 광고를 냈다.
> (D) 개업식을 준비했다.

해설 4번 문제의 정답은 두 번째 문장 끝에 나오는 our shoe store라는 키워드만 알아들으면 쉽게 알 수 있다. 이 신발 매장은 올해 다른 지역으로 이전했는데, 이전한 분기에 연중 가장 낮은 판매량을 기록했다는 말이 나온다(We recorded the lowest shoe sales of the entire year during the quarter we moved). 그래프를 보면 이때가 가을이었음을 알 수 있다. 여기서 5번 문제의 정답을 고르자. 6번 문제의 정답은 However로 시작하는 문장에서 알 수 있다. 연말쯤에는 사업이 빠르게 회복되었는데, 이것은 신문과 라디오 광고 덕분이라고 설명하고 있다(business picked up quickly towards the end of the year as a result of the newspaper ads and radio commercials we put out). 여기서 이 사업체는 가을에 이전하자마자 광고 내는 일을 열심히 했음을 알 수 있다.

Actual Test

1 (C)	**2** (D)	**3** (C)	**4** (A)	**5** (C)
6 (B)	**7** (C)	**8** (C)	**9** (A)	**10** (A)
11 (A)	**12** (C)	**13** (D)	**14** (B)	**15** (C)
16 (C)	**17** (D)	**18** (A)	**19** (B)	**20** (D)
21 (A)	**22** (C)	**23** (A)	**24** (C)	**25** (C)
26 (B)	**27** (D)	**28** (B)	**29** (C)	**30** (D)

* 정답을 맞힌 문제도 해설을 읽어보세요.

Part 1

1. M | Au

(A) Some signs are posted on a column.
(B) People are attending a sporting event.
(C) Rows of lights are suspended above the display.
(D) People are working at an open-air market.

어휘 post 게시하다 column 기둥 suspend 매달다, 걸다
open-air 야외의, 노천의

해석 (A) 기둥에 표지판들이 게시되어 있다.
(B) 사람들이 스포츠 행사에 참석하고 있다.
(C) 여러 줄의 조명이 진열물 위에 매달려 있다.
(D) 사람들이 노천 시장에서 일하고 있다.

해설 사진에 기둥(a column)이 없으므로 (A)는 오답이며, 스포츠 행사(a sporting event)를 하는 장면도 아니므로 (B)도 오답이다. 지붕이 있는 장소라서 노천 시장(an open-air market)이라고 할 수도 없으므로 (D)도 오답이다. 물건이 진열되어 있는 장면에서 자주 키워드로 사용되는 display, 천장에 매달려 있는 장면의 키워드 hang(ing), hung, suspended, 줄지어 있는 장면의 키워드 line, row를 기억하자.

2. W | Br

(A) A park is crowded with pedestrians.
(B) A row of trees divides the plaza.
(C) People are sitting in an outdoor patio.
(D) The pavement is decorated with geometric design.

어휘 pedestrian 보행자 plaza 광장 patio 테라스
pavement 포장도로 geometric 기하학적인

해석 (A) 공원이 보행자들로 북적인다.
(B) 일렬로 된 나무들이 광장을 나누고 있다.
(C) 사람들이 야외 테라스에 앉아 있다.
(D) 포장도로가 기하학적인 디자인으로 장식되어 있다.

해설 사람이 없는 사진이므로 pedestrians와 People만 듣고도 (A)와 (C)는 오답으로 골라낼 수 있다. 나무가 일렬로 있지도 않고(A row of trees), 구역이 나누어져 있지도 않으므로(divides) (B)도 오답이다. 바닥이 무엇으로 장식되어 있는지 잘 듣고(geometric design) 정답을 선택하자.

3. W Am

(A) They're boarding up the windows of a building.
(B) Paint is being applied to a balcony.
(C) Ladders of different heights are propped up against the house.
(D) A paint can is being lowered from the roof.

어휘 board up (문, 창문 등을) 판자로 막다 apply (페인트, 크림 등을) 바르다 prop 기대어 세우다 lower 내리다, 낮추다

해석 (A) 건물 창문들에 판자를 대고 있다.
(B) 발코니에 페인트를 칠하고 있다.
(C) 서로 다른 높이의 사다리들이 집에 기대어 있다.
(D) 지붕에서 페인트 통을 내리고 있다.

해설 (A)는 동사 boarding up의 의미를 알고 오답으로 골라내야 한다. 페인트를 칠하는 위치가 발코니는 아니므로 (B)도 오답이다. 진행 시제 수동태는 '동작'을 나타내므로 (D)가 정답이 되려면 페인트 통을 내리고 있어야 한다(is being lowered). 사다리가 벽에 기대어 있으므로 키워드 propped를 듣고 정답을 선택하자.

Part 2

4. M Cn W Br

Where should I set up the equipment for the photo shoot?

(A) That's scheduled for next week.
(B) It was taken in Brussel.
(C) I bought it at the electronics store.

어휘 set up ~을 설치하다 photo shoot 사진 촬영

해석 사진 촬영 장비를 어디에 설치할까요?
(A) 그건 다음 주로 잡혀 있잖아요.
(B) Brussel에서 찍었어요.
(C) 전자 제품 매장에서 샀어요.

해설 (B)는 질문에 들어 있는 photo에서 연상되는 대답으로 오답을 유도하고 있고, (C)도 the equipment for the photo shoot에서 연상되는 대답이다. 또한 질문 앞부분 Where should I set up(어디에 설치할까요?)에 집중하면 (B)와 (C)는 모두 오답임을 알 수 있다.

5. M Au W Am

Where's the lecture being held?

(A) Next week is fine with me.
(B) A well-known psychologist.
(C) Oh, I didn't think you could make it.

어휘 psychologist 심리학자 make it (모임 등에) 가다, 참석하다

해석 강연회는 어디서 열리나요?
(A) 저는 다음 주 좋습니다.
(B) 유명한 심리학자요.
(C) 아, 참석 못 하시는 줄 알았어요.

해설 (A)는 When 의문의, (B)는 Who 의문문의 정답으로 알맞은 대답이다. 오답을 잘 골라낼수록 고수가 된다!

6. M Cn W Br

When's the new department director supposed to start?

(A) It's two hours long.
(B) Ms. Watson isn't retiring for several weeks.
(C) No, that department's downstairs.

어휘 director 책임자, 관리자 downstairs 아래층에

해석 새 부서 관리자는 언제 근무를 시작하기로 했나요?
(A) 두 시간 동안 합니다.
(B) Ms. Watson이 몇 주는 있어야 은퇴하잖아요.

(C) 아니요, 그 부서는 아래층에 있습니다.

해설 (A)는 How long ~?의 정답으로 알맞은 대답이고, (C)는 No가 들리는 순간 오답으로 골라낼 수 있다. 오답을 잘 골라낼수록 고수가 된다!

---

7. [M｜Au] [W｜Br]

Where can I donate some old office equipment?

(A) Because it starts at ten o'clock.
(B) No, you can't eat in here.
(C) What type of equipment is it?

어휘 donate 기증하다

해석 오래된 사무기기는 어디에 기증할 수 있을까요?
(A) 그건 10시에 시작하기 때문이죠.
(B) 아니요, 여기서는 드실 수 없습니다.
(C) 어떤 유형의 장비인데요?

해설 Where 의문문이므로 Because로 시작하는 (A)는 정답이 될 수 없고, (B)는 No만 듣고도 오답임을 알 수 있다. 도저히 정답을 알 수 없을 때는 반문하는 대답이 가장 확률이 높다는 사실을 기억하자.

---

8. [W｜Br] [M｜Cn]

When do you think we'll hear if we've won the Barclays account?

(A) I misplaced my accounting manual.
(B) One of our biggest clients.
(C) Ms. Pavlova might already know.

어휘 account 거래 (계약) misplace 어딘가에 두고 잊어버리다 accounting 회계 (업무)

해석 Barclays 사(社)와의 거래 계약을 따낸다면 언제 소식을 듣게 될 것 같으세요?
(A) 회계 매뉴얼을 잃어버렸어요.
(B) 우리의 가장 큰 고객 중 하나요.
(C) Ms. Pavlova가 이미 알고 있을 겁니다.

해설 (A)는 질문에 나오는 account와 발음이 비슷한 accounting을 들려주면서, (B)는 the Barclays account에서 연상되는 대답으로 오답을 유도하고 있다. "몰라" 유형의 대답은 거의 항상 정답인데, 그중 '사람 이름 + might[probably/should/would] know' 유형은 자주 출제되므로 반드시 기억해 두자.

---

9. [M｜Cn] [W｜Br]

Don't I need to make another appointment for a check-up?

(A) Most patients only come in once a year.
(B) I can't find my train ticket.
(C) They've appointed a new section head.

어휘 check-up (건강) 검진 section (조직의) 부서, 과

해석 건강 검진 예약을 한 번 더 해야 하지 않나요?
(A) 대부분의 환자들은 일 년에 한 번씩만 오세요.
(B) 제 기차표를 못 찾겠어요.
(C) 그들은 새 과장을 임명했어요.

해설 대부분은 일 년에 한 번씩만 건강 검진을 받고 있으니 지금 당장 추가 검진 예약을 할 필요는 없을 것 같다는 의견을 말하는 (A)가 정답이다. (C)는 질문의 appointment와 발음이 비슷한 appointed를 들려주면서 오답을 유도하고 있다.

---

10. [W｜Am] [M｜Cn]

Do I have to replace my car's tires?

(A) When did you buy your car?
(B) I know a nice place to eat.
(C) The elevator's on your right.

해석 제 차 타이어를 교체해야 할까요?
(A) 차를 언제 사셨는데요?
(B) 식사하기에 좋은 장소를 알고 있어요.
(C) 엘리베이터는 오른쪽에 있습니다.

해설 타이어를 교체해야 하는지는 자동차 구입 시기에 따라 결정해야 한다는 뜻으로 대답하고 있는 (A)가 정답이다. (B)는 질문에 나오는 replace와 발음이 비슷한 place를 들려주면서 오답을 유도하고 있다. 도저히 정답을 알 수 없을 때는 반문하는 대답이 확률이 높다는 사실을 기억하자.

---

11. [W｜Br] [M｜Au]

Isn't Juan moving into an apartment in the city?

(A) I haven't talked to him in a while.
(B) Those parts need to be counted.
(C) The ticket booth closes at nine P.M.

어휘 in a while 한동안 part 부품

해석 Juan은 시내에 있는 아파트로 이사 갈 예정 아닌가요?
(A) 한동안 그와 얘기를 안 해 봤어요.
(B) 저 부품들을 세어 보아야 해요.
(C) 매표소는 오후 9시에 닫습니다.

해설 질문 앞부분 Isn't Juan moving into(Juan은 이사 갈 예정 아닌가요?)에 집중하면 자연스러운 대답이 어느 것인지 알 수 있다. (B)는 질문에 나오는 apartment와 발

음이 비슷한 parts를 들려주면서, (C)는 moving과 발음이 비슷한 movie에서 연상되는 대답으로 오답을 유도하고 있다.

---

12. [M Au] [W Am]

Are there any openings on your company's graphic design team?

(A) The new design is very attractive.
(B) We're open until eight o'clock.
(C) You're welcome to submit an application.

어휘 opening 빈자리, 공석

해석 당신 회사 그래픽 디자인 팀에 공석이 있나요?
(A) 새 디자인이 매우 매력적이군요.
(B) 우리는 8시까지 영업합니다.
(C) 지원서를 제출하신다면 환영이에요.

해설 (A)는 질문에 들어 있는 design을, (B)는 open을 반복시키면서 오답을 유도하고 있다. 또한 질문 앞부분 Are there any openings(공석이 있나요?)에 집중하면 자연스러운 대답을 알아낼 수 있다.

Part 3

Questions 13 through 15 refer to the following conversation.

[M Cn] ^{13}Fatima, is everything ready for our interns' first day on Monday?

[W Br] Yes, their office set-up is complete, and I've just put together their information packets.

[M Cn] ^{14}And... don't forget to ask some staff if they can come in early on Monday to greet the interns as they arrive.

[W Br] ^{14}Oh, thanks for reminding me. I'm sure I'll be able to find some people willing to help with that. But how will the interns recognize the volunteers?

[M Cn] ^{15}How about providing volunteers with a T-shirt with the company logo? We have a few left over from the ones we ordered for our last trade fair. Let me go get them for you now.

13–15번 문제는 다음 대화에 관한 것입니다.

남: Fatima, 월요일 우리 인턴사원들의 근무 첫날을 위한 모든 준비는 끝났나요?
여: 네, 사무실 배치도 완료되었고요, 자료집도 지금 막 다 만들었어요.
남: 그리고... 몇몇 직원들에게 월요일에 일찍 출근해서 인턴들이 도착할 때 맞이해 줄 수 있는지 물어보는 거 잊지 마세요.
여: 아, 상기시켜 주셔서 고맙습니다. 분명히 그 일을 도와줄 의향이 있는 사람들을 몇 명 찾을 수 있을 거예요. 하지만 인턴들이 자원봉사자들을 어떻게 알아보죠?
남: 자원봉사자들에게 회사 로고가 새겨진 티셔츠를 제공하는 게 어떨까요? 지난 번 무역 박람회 때 주문한 것들 중 남은 게 몇 개 있어요. 내가 지금 가서 가져다줄게요.

어휘 set-up 배치 put together (이것저것을 모아) 만들다, 준비하다 information packet 자료집 greet 인사하다, 맞이하다 willing to-V ~할 의향이 있는 left over from (쓰고 난 뒤) 남은 trade fair 무역 박람회

13. What will happen on Monday?

(A) Some landscaping work will begin.
(B) A news conference will take place.
(C) Some clients will visit the company.
(D) An internship period will start.

어휘 landscaping 조경 news conference 기자 회견

해석 월요일에 무슨 일이 있을 것인가?
(A) 조경 작업이 시작될 것이다.
(B) 기자 회견이 있을 것이다.
(C) 고객들이 회사를 방문할 것이다.
(D) 인턴 근무 기간이 시작될 것이다.

14. What did the woman forget to do?

(A) Revise a schedule
(B) Seek out some volunteers
(C) Update a list of contacts
(D) Serve refreshments

어휘 revise 수정하다 seek out ~을 찾아내다 update 갱신하다 refreshments 다과

해석 여자는 무엇 하는 것을 잊었는가?
(A) 일정을 수정하는 것
(B) 자원봉사자들을 찾아내는 것
(C) 연락처 목록을 갱신하는 것
(D) 다과를 제공하는 것

15. What does the man say is available?

(A) Some notepads
(B) Cleaning products
(C) Customized clothing
(D) New flooring

어휘 notepad 노트패드(한 장씩 떼어 쓰게 된 메모장)
customize 맞춤 제작을 하다 flooring 바닥재

해석 남자는 무엇을 이용할 수 있다고 말하는가?
(A) 노트패드
(B) 청소용품
(C) 맞춤 제작 의상
(D) 새 바닥재

해설 남자의 첫 대사에 Monday라는 13번 문제의 키워드가 들어 있다. is everything ready for our interns' first day on Monday?에서 월요일에 인턴 근무 기간이 시작된다는 것을 알 수 있다. 남자의 두 번째 대사 don't forget to ask some staff if they can come in early on Monday to greet the interns as they arrive.를 들으면 월요일에 일찍 출근해서 인턴사원들을 맞이해 줄 자원봉사자들이 필요하다는 것을 알 수 있는데, thanks for reminding me.라는 여자의 대답을 통해 자원봉사자들을 찾는 일을 잊고 있었음을 짐작할 수 있다. 여기서 14번 문제의 정답을 고르자. 15번 문제의 정답은 남자의 세 번째 대사에서 알 수 있는데, 자원봉사자들에게 회사 로고가 새겨진 티셔츠를 지급하자고 제안하면서(How about providing volunteers with a T-shirt with the company logo?), 지난번 무역 박람회 때 사용하고 남은 것을 이번에 사용할 수 있다고 알려주고 있다(We have a few left over from the ones we ordered for our last trade fair).

Questions 16 through 18 refer to the following conversation.

[M | Au] ¹⁶Soo-mi, I'm ready to add the changes to the employee directory on our company Web site. Would you mind reviewing it before I upload them?

[W | Br] Hmm... it seems good so far, ¹⁷but, uh... hold on, there's an issue here. The vice president's name has been misspelled. Actually, her name should end with only one L.

[M | Au] ¹⁸Wow, I can't believe I overlooked that. Thank you for spotting it.

[W | Br] [It's easy to miss.] Once you make that change, it should be ready to upload. Let me know if you need any more help.

16–18번 문제는 다음 대화에 관한 것입니다.

남: Soo-mi, 직원 명부의 변경 사항을 회사 홈페이지에 추가할 준비가 다 되었어요. 업로드하기 전에 검토 좀 해주시겠어요?

여: 음... 여기까지는 좋아 보이는데요, 어... 잠깐만요. 여기 문제가 있네요. 부사장님 이름의 철자가 잘못 나와 있어요. 사실 그녀의 이름은 L자 하나로 끝나야 해요.

남: 와, 내가 그걸 못 보고 넘어가다니.... 발견해 줘서 고마워요.

여: 그런 건 놓치기 쉽죠. 일단 그걸 고치고 나면 업로드할 준비가 다 되겠네요. 도움이 더 필요하면 알려줘요.

어휘 directory 인명부 so far 지금까지 hold on (명령문으로) 기다려, 멈춰 issue 문제, 걱정거리 misspell ~의 철자를 잘못 쓰다 overlook 못 보고 넘어가다, 간과하다 spot 발견하다, 알아채다

16. What are the speakers mainly talking about?

(A) Creating a product catalog
(B) Ordering some visitor badges
(C) Updating a company's Web site
(D) Organizing a welcome reception

어휘 visitor badge 방문객 출입증 welcome reception 환영 연회

해석 화자들은 주로 무엇에 대해 이야기하고 있는가?
(A) 제품 카탈로그 만들기
(B) 방문객 출입증 주문하기
(C) 회사 홈페이지 갱신하기
(D) 환영 연회 준비하기

17. What problem does the woman notice?

(A) A report has not been filed.
(B) An identification badge is malfunctioning.
(C) A telephone number has been omitted.
(D) A name has been incorrectly spelled.

어휘 file 제출하다, 보내다 identification badge 신분증, 사원증 omit 빠뜨리다, 누락하다 incorrectly 부정확하게

해석 여자는 어떤 문제점을 알아차리는가?
(A) 보고서가 제출되지 않았다.
(B) 사원증이 오작동하고 있다.
(C) 전화번호가 누락되었다.
(D) 이름이 부정확하게 적혀 있다.

18. Why does the woman say, "It's easy to miss"?

(A) To express her understanding
(B) To clarify her responsibilities in a project
(C) To detail the steps involved in a process
(D) To inform the man of a detour

어휘 clarify 명확하게 하다 **detail** 상세히 설명하다 **involved in** ~에 관련된 **detour** 우회로

해석 여자는 왜 "그런 건 놓치지 쉽죠."라고 말하는가?
(A) 자신의 이해를 표현하려고
(B) 프로젝트에서 자신이 맡은 책임을 명확히 하려고
(C) 절차에 관련된 단계들을 상세히 설명하려고
(D) 남자에게 우회로를 알려주려고

해설 16번 문제는 주제를 묻고 있으므로 첫 문장에서 정답을 알 수 있을 것이라고 예상할 수 있다. 회사 홈페이지에 직원 명부의 변경 사항을 추가하는 것(I'm ready to add the changes to the employee directory on our company Web site.), 즉 홈페이지 갱신에 관한 대화다. 여자는 남자가 작성한 변경 사항을 검토하면서 부사장의 이름이 잘못 나와 있다는 문제를 알아챈다(there's an issue here. The vice president's name has been misspelled). 여기서 17번 문제의 정답을 고르자. 남자는 여자가 실수를 발견해준 것에 대해 감사를 표하면서 중요한 정보를 간과한 것에 대해 자책을 하자(I can't believe I overlooked that. Thank you for spotting it.), 여자가 It's easy to miss.라고 대답하는데, 이것은 실수에 대해 이해함을 나타내는 말로서 "그럴 수도 있지."라고 말하는 것과 같다. 이러한 점을 파악하고 18번의 정답을 선택하자.

Questions 19 through 21 refer to the following conversation and order form.

M Cn [19]Donna, we've started the preparations for our first play of the upcoming season. Could you please double-check the costume order before I send it off?

W Am Of course. Let's take a look... Alright... [20]Alright... um, we don't really need that many hats. Half that amount will do. We can reuse the ones from the spring production.

M Cn [20]OK, I'll lower that. Anything else?

W Am No issues with the rest. You go ahead and submit the order, [21]and I'll get started on installing the new ceiling lights. They're going to be suspended from the metal brackets we placed above the stage.

M Cn Oh, that'll look nice. Brighter is better.

19–21번 문제는 다음 대화와 주문서에 관한 것입니다.

남: Donna, 다가오는 시즌의 첫 연극을 위한 준비를 시작했어요. 의상 주문서를 발송하기 전에 재확인 좀 해주겠어요?
여: 물론이죠. 어디 봐요... 괜찮고... 괜찮고... 음, 모자는 사실 이렇게 많이 필요하지 않아요. 이 수량의 절반이면 충분할 거예요. 봄 작품에서 쓴 것들을 재사용하면 되거든요.
남: 알겠어요. 그건 낮출게요. 그밖에 다른 건요?
여: 나머지는 문제 없어요. 이대로 주문서 제출하시고 저는 새 천장 조명 설치하는 일을 시작할게요. 무대 위쪽에 놓은 금속 받침대에 매달리게 될 거예요.
남: 아, 그거 좋아 보이겠네요. 더 밝으면 더 좋죠.

어휘 upcoming 다가오는, 곧 있을 **double-check** 재확인하다 **costume** (연극, 영화의) 의상 **send off** ~을 발송하다 **do** 적절하다, 충분하다 **reuse** 재사용하다 **production** (연극, 영화, 방송의 제작된) 작품 **lower** 내리다, 낮추다 **issue** 문제, 걱정거리 **the rest** 나머지 **suspend** 매달다, 걸다 **bracket** 버팀대, 받침대

Item	Quantity	Total Price
Suit jackets	7	€175
Dresses	9	€270
Scarves	11	€33
[20]Hats	[20]17	€38
		Order Total = €516

품목	수량	총 가격
정장 재킷	7	175유로
드레스	9	270유로
스카프	11	33유로
모자	17	38유로
		주문 총액 = 516유로

19. Where do the speakers most likely work?

(A) At a travel bureau
(B) At a theater
(C) At a clothier
(D) At a tailor's shop

해석 화자들은 어디에서 근무하겠는가?

　(A) 여행사에서

　(B) 극장에서

　(C) 의류상에서

　(D) 양복점에서

20. Look at the graphic. Which quantity will be changed?

　(A) 7

　(B) 9

　(C) 11

　(D) 17

해석 그래픽을 보라. 어느 수량이 변경될 것인가?

　(A) 7

　(B) 9

　(C) 11

　(D) 17

21. What does the woman say she will do next?

　(A) Hang some light fixtures

　(B) Apply paint to the ceiling

　(C) Sanitize a piece of equipment

　(D) Take measurements of the actors

어휘 light fixture 조명 기구　apply (페인트, 크림 등을) 바르다　sanitize 위생 처리하다　take measurements 치수를 재다

해석 여자는 이후에 무엇을 할 것이라고 말하는가?

　(A) 조명 기구를 매단다

　(B) 천장에 페인트를 칠한다

　(C) 장비에 위생 처리를 한다

　(D) 배우들의 치수를 잰다

해설 19번에서 묻는 화자들이 근무하는 장소는 첫 문장에서 알 수 있다. 다가오는 시즌의 첫 연극 준비를 시작했다고 했으므로(we've started the preparations for our first play of the upcoming season.) 화자들이 일하는 곳은 극단임을 알 수 있다. 여자가 의상 주문서를 보면서 모자는 이 수량의 절반만 있어도 된다고 말하자(we don't really need that many hats. Half that amount will do.) 남자는 수량을 낮추겠다고 대답한다(OK, I'll lower that). 주문서에서 모자의 주문 수량이 17이므로 이 수치가 변경될 것임을 짐작할 수 있다. 여기서 20번의 정답을 고르자. 이어지는 대화는 여자가 남자에게 이대로 주문서를 보내라고 말하면서 자신은 천장 조명 설치를 시작하겠다고 한다 (You go ahead and submit the order, and I'll get started on installing the new ceiling lights). 여기서 21번 문제의 정답을 알 수 있다.

Part 4

Questions 22 through 24 refer to the following talk.

W Am Hello everyone, [22][23]and welcome to the architecture conference taking place at the East Wind Eco Inn. [23][24]This hotel was constructed last year using state-of-the-art energy-efficient and non-polluting materials. Additionally, the lodge provides convenient access to the surrounding forests and rivers that the region is well-known for. [23]We are pleased to be hosting your group of international architects. I'm sure you'll have plenty of questions about how efficient and cost-effective the materials we've utilized are, and why you should consider using them in your own architectural projects.

22–24번 문제는 다음 담화에 관한 것입니다.

여: 모두들 안녕하세요. East Wind Eco 호텔에서 열리는 건축학회에 오신 것을 환영합니다. 이 호텔은 작년에 지어졌는데요. 에너지 효율이 좋고 무공해인 최첨단 자재를 사용했습니다. 또한 이 산장 호텔은 이 지역이 유명하게 된 주변의 숲과 강에 대한 편리한 접근을 제공하기도 합니다. 여러 나라에서 오신 건축가 여러분을 모시게 되어 참 기쁩니다. 우리가 활용한 자재가 얼마나 효율적이며 비용 대비 효과가 좋은지, 또한 왜 그것을 여러분의 건축 프로젝트에 사용하기를 고려해야 하는지 분명 질문이 많으실 것이라고 생각합니다.

어휘 architecture 건축학　conference 학회　inn 소규모 호텔, 식당, 술집　state-of-the-art 최첨단의, 최신식의　energy-efficient 에너지 효율이 좋은　non-polluting 무공해의　lodge 산장　access 접근　surrounding 인근의, 주위의　host (주인으로서) 접대하다　architect 건축가　cost-effective 비용 효율[효과]이 높은　utilize 활용하다, 이용하다　architectural 건축의

22. Where is the talk taking place?

　(A) At an art museum

　(B) At a construction site

　(C) At a hotel

　(D) At a power plant

해석 담화는 어디에서 이루어지고 있는가?

　(A) 미술관에서

　(B) 공사 현장에서

(C) 호텔에서
(D) 발전소에서

---

23. Who most likely are the listeners?

(A) Architects
(B) Engineering students
(C) Hoteliers
(D) Event coordinators

▶해석 청자들은 누구이겠는가?
(A) 건축가들
(B) 공대생들
(C) 호텔 경영자들
(D) 행사 진행자들

---

24. What is mentioned about the materials used?

(A) They are manufactured locally.
(B) They are reasonably priced.
(C) They are environmentally friendly.
(D) They are hard to come by.

▶어휘 manufacture 제조하다, 생산하다 locally 그 지역에서 reasonably priced 적당한 가격인 environmentally friendly 환경 친화적인 come by 얻다, 구하다

▶해석 사용된 자재에 대해 무엇이 언급되는가?
(A) 이 지역에서 생산된다.
(B) 가격이 적당하다.
(C) 환경 친화적이다.
(D) 구하기 어렵다.

▶해설 22번 문제는 담화의 장소가 어디인지, 23번은 청자들이 누구인지 묻고 있으므로 두 문제 모두 대부분 첫 한두 문장에서 정답을 알 수 있는 유형이다. 그러므로 문제를 미리 읽으면서 두 문제의 정답을 동시에 골라야 할 수도 있다고 예상할 수 있다. 예상대로 첫 문장 welcome to the architecture conference taking place at the East Wind Eco Inn.을 들으면서 두 문제의 정답을 동시에 고르자. 업체 이름이 East Wind Eco Inn이므로 호텔임을 알 수 있고, 행사 이름이 architecture conference(건축학회)이므로 모여 있는 사람들은 건축가들임을 알 수 있다. 두 문제의 정답을 동시에 고르는 것도 쉽지 않은데, 순발력까지 필요한 고난도 문제다. 바로 이어지는 문장 This hotel was constructed last year using state-of-the-art energy-efficient and non-polluting materials.를 듣고 24번의 정답을 알아내야 한다. 에너지 효율성이 높은(energy-efficient) 무공해(non-polluting) 건축 자재라고 했으므로 친환경(environmentally friendly) 자재라는 말로 바꿔 부를 수 있다. 만약 첫 문장을 들으면서 22, 23번 문

제의 정답을 동시에 고르지 못했다면 이후에 등장하는 키워드 This hotel과 your group of international architects를 포착하고 다시 정답을 맞힐 수 있는 기회가 있다. 끝까지 포기하지 말고 집중해 보자.

Questions 25 through 27 refer to the following telephone message.

W Am Hey Stan, it's Min-hee. ²⁵I'm going through the design you created for the magazine advertisement for Clark Restaurant, and I wanted to share my thoughts with you. [It isn't what I was expecting.] ²⁶Clark Restaurant has always favored very traditional advertisements, and this one you made is quite contemporary. I apologize for not mentioning the client's preference earlier. I understand this is your first project with them. ²⁷You know, why don't you reach out to Shinji for assistance? He has experience working with Clark Restaurant before. Thanks, Stan. I'll speak to you later.

25-27번 문제는 다음 전화 메시지에 관한 것입니다.

여: Stan, 저 Min-hee예요. Clark 식당의 잡지 광고를 위해 당신이 한 디자인을 살펴보고 있는데요, 제 생각을 좀 공유하려고요. 이건 제가 기대했던 게 아니에요. Clark 식당은 언제나 매우 전통적인 광고를 선호해 왔는데, 당신이 만든 이건 상당히 현대적이네요. 고객이 선호하는 사항을 미리 알려주지 않은 점 사과할게요. 이번이 당신이 그들과 진행하는 첫 프로젝트라는 점도 이해해요. 있잖아요, Shinji에게 연락해서 도와달라고 하는 게 어떻겠어요? 그는 전에 Clark 식당과 협력해 본 경험이 있거든요. 고마워요, Stan. 나중에 다시 얘기해요.

▶어휘 go through ~을 살펴보다 favor 선호하다 contemporary 현대의 reach out 연락을 취하다

---

25. What industry does the speaker work in?

(A) Publishing
(B) Paper production
(C) Advertising
(D) Food service

▶해석 화자는 어느 업계에서 일하는가?
(A) 출판업
(B) 제지업

(C) 광고업
(D) 요식업

---

26. Why does the speaker say, "It isn't what I was expecting"?

(A) To explain the exceptional nature of a project

(B) To express disapproval for a design

(C) To suggest that a project's deadline be adjusted

(D) To indicate surprise at a surge in sales

어휘 exceptional 예외적인, 이례적인 nature 본질, 성격 disapproval 반감, 승인하지 않음 adjust 조정하다, 조절하다 surge 급증, 급등

해석 화자는 왜 "이건 제가 기대했던 게 아니에요."라고 말하는가?
(A) 프로젝트의 이례적인 성격을 설명하기 위해서
(B) 디자인을 승인하지 않음을 나타내기 위해서
(C) 프로젝트 기한을 조정할 것을 제안하기 위해서
(D) 판매량 급증에 놀랐음을 나타내기 위해서

---

27. What does the speaker suggest the listener do?

(A) Seek career advancement
(B) Organize a press conference
(C) Take some time off
(D) Consult with a colleague

어휘 seek 구하다, 추구하다 career advancement 경력 발전 press conference 기자 회견 time off 휴가, 휴식 기간 consult with ~와 상의하다

해석 화자는 청자에게 무엇을 하라고 제안하는가?
(A) 경력 발전을 모색한다
(B) 기자 회견을 준비한다
(C) 휴가를 간다
(D) 동료와 상의한다

해설 첫 문장을 들어보면 화자는 지금 청자가 만든 잡지 광고 디자인을 살펴보고 있고 그것에 대한 의견을 제시하려고 한다(I'm going through the design you created for the magazine advertisement for Clark Restaurant, and I wanted to share my thoughts with you). 여기서 화자가 광고업계에서 일하고 있음을 알아내고 25번 문제의 정답을 고르자. 화자는 It isn't what I was expecting(이건 제가 기대했던 게 아니에요).이라고 말하는데, 이어지는 문장에

서 고객이 원하는 광고의 성격(traditional)과 화자가 만든 것(contemporary)이 서로 상반된다고 설명하고 있다(Clark Restaurant has always favored very traditional advertisements, and this one you made is quite contemporary). 그러므로 화자는 청자의 디자인을 승인하지 않는다는 뜻으로 말한 것이다. 여기서 26번의 정답을 고르자. 해당 고객을 처음 상대해 보는 청자를 위해 전에 이 고객의 프로젝트를 맡아 본 적이 있는 Shinji에게 연락해서 도움을 구하라고 권하고 있다(why don't you reach out to Shinji for assistance? He has experience working with Clark Restaurant before). 여기서 27번의 정답을 알 수 있다.

Questions 28 through 30 refer to the following announcement and map.

[M | Au] Attention, all employees of Alfane Systems. ²⁸Please be reminded that the city's annual bicycle race will take place tomorrow, ²⁹causing the street that runs in front of the main entrance to be blocked off from six A.M. until ten A.M. So you'll need to plan accordingly. The other streets neighboring our building will remain accessible. No matter which route you choose to take to work, ³⁰please allow more commuting time as there will be a significant rise in traffic in the vicinity due to the race.

28-30번 문제는 다음 공지 사항과 지도에 관한 것입니다.

남: Alfane Systems의 모든 직원 여러분께 알립니다. 내일 시 주최 연례 자전거 경주가 개최됨으로 인해 정문 앞 도로가 오전 6시부터 10시까지 폐쇄됨을 다시 한 번 알려 드립니다. 그에 맞추어 계획을 잡으셔야 합니다. 우리 건물에 이웃한 다른 도로들은 계속 이용이 가능합니다. 어떤 경로로 출근하든 경주로 인해 주변 교통량이 크게 증가할 것이므로 통근 시간을 여유있게 잡기 바랍니다.

어휘 attention (안내 방송에서) 알립니다, 주목하세요 be reminded that ~라는 것을 알리다[상기시키다] run (길이) 뻗다, 이어지다 block off (도로나 출입구를) 차단하다, 봉쇄하다 accordingly 그에 맞춰 neighboring 이웃한, 인근의 accessible 접근[이용] 가능한 no matter which sth 어느 ~이든 상관없이 allow (시간, 돈 등을 어림하여) 잡다, 정하다, 할당하다 vicinity 부근, 인근

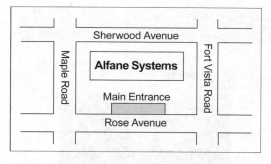

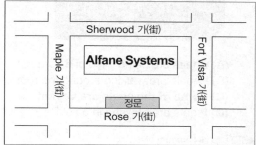

28. What will take place tomorrow morning?

(A) A road improvement project
(B) A competition
(C) A street performance
(D) An employee training session

🔹해석 내일 오전에 어떤 일이 있을 것인가?
(A) 도로 개선 프로젝트
(B) 대회
(C) 거리 공연
(D) 직원 교육

29. Look at the graphic. Which street will be closed?

(A) Sherwood Avenue
(B) Fort Vista Road
(C) Rose Avenue
(D) Maple Road

🔹해석 그래픽을 보라. 어느 도로가 폐쇄될 것인가?
(A) Sherwood 가(街)
(B) Fort Vista 가(街)
(C) Rose 가(街)
(D) Maple 가(街)

30. What does the speaker suggest?

(A) Arriving at the workplace in the afternoon
(B) Attending a corporate function
(C) Exploring certain study materials
(D) Allowing extra time for travel

🔹어휘 workplace 직장, 업무 현장 corporate 기업의, 회사의
function 행사, 의식 explore 탐구하다, 분석하다
travel 이동

🔹해석 화자는 무엇을 제안하는가?
(A) 직장에 오후에 출근하는 것
(B) 회사 행사에 참석하는 것
(C) 학습 자료를 분석하는 것
(D) 이동을 위한 추가 시간을 잡는 것

🔹해설 28번 문제는 키워드 tomorrow가 들어 있는 문장에서 또 다른 키워드 bicycle race만 알아들으면 쉽게 풀 수 있다. 중요한 것은 순발력이다. 바로 이어지는 분사구문에서 29번의 정답을 알아내야 한다. 자전거 대회 때문에 회사 정문 앞 도로가 폐쇄된다고 했다(causing the street that runs in front of the main entrance to be blocked off from six A.M. until ten A.M.). 지도를 보며 위치 표현을 잘 듣고 정답을 선택하자. 30번 문제는 please allow more commuting time이 패러프레이즈 되어 있는 구문을 정답으로 고르자.

PART 1 Exercise

1 (A)　　**2** (C)

1. W | Am

(A) Tabletop umbrellas have been closed.
(B) Some of the buildings face the lawn.
(C) A brick wall is being torn down.
(D) Most of the tables are occupied.

어휘 umbrella 우산, 파라솔　face ~에 면하다, ~을 향하다
lawn 잔디밭　tear down (tore-torn) (건물, 담 등을) 허물다,
헐다　occupied 사용 중인

해석 (A) 테라스 파라솔들이 접혀 있다.
(B) 건물들이 잔디에 면해 있다.
(C) 벽돌 담을 허물고 있다.
(D) 대부분의 테이블이 차 있다.

해설 두 단어 Tabletop umbrellas 사이에 일어나는 연음 현
상 때문에 알아듣기가 어려울 수 있다. '테이블타뻠브
렐러즈'라고 읽어야 한다. 읽는 연습을 충분히 해 두자.
사진에 잔디밭(the lawn)이 없으므로 (B)는 오답이다.
진행 시제 수동태는 '동작'을 나타내므로 (C)가 정답이
되려면 건물 철거 공사가 진행 중이어야 한다(is being
torn down). 대부분의 자리가 비어(unoccupied) 있으
므로 (D)는 사진의 장면을 반대로(occupied) 묘사하고
있다.

2. M | Au

(A) Chairs are being piled in a corner.
(B) People are walking around the room.
(C) Some of the seats are vacant.
(D) Plants are growing in a field.

어휘 pile 쌓다　vacant 비어 있는

해석 (A) 구석에 의자들을 쌓고 있다.
(B) 사람들이 방 안을 돌아다니고 있다.
(C) 몇몇 좌석이 비어 있다.
(D) 들판에서 식물들이 자라고 있다.

해설 진행 시제 수동태는 '동작'을 나타내므로 (A)가 정답이
되려면 쌓는 동작을 하고 있어야 한다(are being piled).
걸어 다니는(walking) 사람이 없으므로 (B)도 오답이다.
사진 배경이 들판(a field)이 아니므로 (D)도 오답이다.
자리가 비어 있음을 묘사하는 키워드 unoccupied,
empty, vacant, available을 기억하자.

PART 2 Exercise

1 (B)　　**2** (A)　　**3** (C)　　**4** (C)　　**5** (B)
6 (C)　　**7** (A)　　**8** (A)　　**9** (C)　　**10** (C)

1. W | Am　W | Br

Which office is Satoshi's?

(A) Sure, I can do that for you.
(B) It's the corner one.
(C) She's very organized.

어휘 organized 계획성 있는, 체계적인

해석 Satoshi의 사무실은 어느 것인가요?
(A) 물론이죠, 제가 해 드릴게요.
(B) 구석에 있는 거요.
(C) 그녀는 매우 체계적이에요.

Sure는 Yes라고 대답한 것과 같으므로 듣자마자 (A)가 오답인 것을 알 수 있다. (C)는 질문에 들어 있는 사람 이름 Satoshi에서 연상되는 대답으로 오답을 유도하고 있다. Which 의문문은 (The) one(s)이 들리면 무조건 정답이다.

---

2. M Cn W Am

Who informed the interns of the assignment changes?

(A) The coordinator of the program.
(B) Just a couple of minor changes.
(C) Along with the assigned interns.

어휘 assignment 임무, 업무 coordinator 진행자, 책임자 along with ~와 함께 assign 배정하다

해석 누가 인턴사원들에게 업무 변경에 대해 알려주었나요?
(A) 프로그램 진행자요.
(B) 단지 두세 개의 사소한 변경 사항이요.
(C) 배정된 인턴사원들과 함께요.

해설 Who 의문문의 90%는 사람 이름이나 직함이 들리는 대답이 정답이다. (B)는 질문에 나오는 changes를 반복시키면서, (C)는 assignment와 발음이 비슷한 assigned를 들려주고 interns를 반복시키면서 오답을 유도하고 있다.

---

3. M Au M Cn

Which committees are meeting tomorrow?

(A) She's very committed to the project.
(B) No, it was taken care of yesterday.
(C) Only the financial advisory committee.

어휘 committed 헌신적인, 열성적인 advisory committee 자문 위원회

해석 내일은 어떤 위원회가 회의하나요?
(A) 그녀는 그 프로젝트에 매우 열성적이에요.
(B) 아니요, 그건 어제 처리되었습니다.
(C) 재정 자문 위원회만 모여요.

해설 (A)는 질문의 committees와 발음이 비슷한 committed를 들려주면서 오답을 유도하고 있고, (B)는 No가 들리는 순간 오답임을 알 수 있다. Which 바로 뒤에 붙어 있는 committees만 알아들어도(어떤 위원회들) 자연스러운 대답이 어느 것인지 알 수 있다.

---

4. M Au W Am

Which part of the factory should I report to today?

(A) The times should be listed in the handbook.
(B) I wish I'd thought of that.
(C) Didn't your supervisor tell you about it?

어휘 report to ~에 도착을 보고하다 list 열거하다, 기재하다 handbook 편람, 안내서 supervisor 감독(자), 관리자

해석 제가 오늘은 공장 어느 구역에 가서 보고해야 하나요?
(A) 시간은 안내서에 기재되어 있을 거예요.
(B) 제가 그 생각을 못 했네요.
(C) 관리자가 그것에 대해 이야기해 주지 않았나요?

해설 Which 뒤에 붙어 있는 명사 part of the factory에만 집중하면(공장 어느 구역?) 자연스러운 대답을 파악할 수 있다. 도저히 정답을 알 수 없을 때는 (C)처럼 반문하는 대답이 확률이 가장 높다는 사실을 기억하자.

---

5. W Br M Au

Who's supposed to lead the orientation?

(A) She read it recently.
(B) The human resources team.
(C) Several copies of training manuals.

어휘 be supposed to-V ~하기로 되어 있다, ~해야 한다

해석 오리엔테이션은 누가 진행하기로 되어 있나요?
(A) 그녀는 최근에 그걸 읽었어요.
(B) 인사팀이요.
(C) 교육 매뉴얼 몇 부요.

해설 lead의 과거형이 led이므로 (A)는 발음이 비슷한 read를 들려주면서 오답을 유도하고 있다. 또한 She가 누구를 가리키는지도 알 수 없으므로 오답이다. (C)는 질문의 the orientation에서 연상되는 대답으로 오답을 유도하고 있다. Who 의문문은 대부분 사람을 들려주는 대답이 정답이지만, 회사나 부서 이름이 나올 때도 정답으로 선택해야 한다.

---

6. W Br M Cn

Who's involved in organizing the annual town festival?

(A) Parking, admission and activities are all free.
(B) It's next Saturday morning.
(C) Oh, are you interested in helping out?

해석 연례 마을 축제 준비에는 누가 관여하고 있나요?
(A) 주차와 입장, 활동이 모두 무료입니다.
(B) 다음 주 토요일 오전이에요.
(C) 아, 도와주실 생각이 있으신가요?

해설 (A)는 질문에 들어 있는 the annual town festival에서 연상되는 대답으로 오답을 유도하고 있지만, Who와는 관련이 없다. (B)는 When 의문문의 정답으로 알맞은 대답이다. 오답을 잘 골라낼수록 고수가 된다! 도저히 정답을 알 수 없을 때는 (C)처럼 반문하는 대답이 확률이 가장 높다는 사실을 기억하자.

7. W Am M Au

Don't you know how to use the new inventory management software?

(A) I was hoping you could train me.
(B) No, he doesn't use it.
(C) At the Fifth Street warehouse.

어휘 inventory 재고(품) warehouse 창고

해석 새 재고 관리 소프트웨어 사용법을 모르세요?
(A) 당신이 저를 교육해 주기를 바라고 있었는데요.
(B) 아니요, 그는 그것을 사용하지 않습니다.
(C) 5번가 창고에서요.

해설 간접 의문문은 중간에 나오는 의문사를 놓치지 않아야 한다. 질문 앞부분과 의문사 부분 Don't you know how to use(사용법을 모르세요?)에 집중하면 자연스러운 대답을 알아낼 수 있다. (B)는 질문에 나왔던 use를 반복시키고 Don't와 발음이 비슷한 doesn't를 들려주면서, (C)는 software와 발음이 비슷한 warehouse를 들려주면서 오답을 유도하고 있다. 게다가 (C)는 how to-V ~?가 아니라 Where 의문문의 정답으로 알맞은 대답이다.

8. M Au W Am

Who can open the office library?

(A) I have the key.
(B) I report to Mr. Park.
(C) Six new books.

어휘 report to ~의 밑에서 일하다

해석 누가 사무실 서고를 열 수 있어요?
(A) 저에게 열쇠가 있어요.
(B) 저는 Mr. Park 밑에서 일합니다.
(C) 새 책 여섯 권이요.

해설 질문 앞부분 Who can open(누가 열 수 있어요?)에 집중해서 자연스러운 대답이 어느 것인지 알아내야 한다. 사람 이름을 들려주면서 오답을 유도하고 있는 (B)에

속지 않도록 주의하자. (C)는 질문의 library에서 연상되는 대답으로 오답을 유도하고 있다.

9. W Br M Cn

Who's managing the bookstore this weekend?

(A) Mainly history and art books.
(B) At nine A.M.
(C) I just posted the staff schedule.

어휘 post 게시하다

해석 이번 주말에는 누가 서점을 관리할 건가요?
(A) 주로 역사와 미술 서적이요.
(B) 오전 9시에요.
(C) 제가 방금 직원 일정표를 게시했어요.

해설 (A)는 질문에 나왔던 bookstore와 발음이 비슷한 books를 들려주면서 오답을 유도하고 있고, (B)는 What time ~?의 정답으로 알맞은 대답이다. 오답을 잘 골라낼수록 고수가 된다!

10. W Am W Br

Who came up with our updated slogan?

(A) I heard it went pretty well.
(B) This elevator is going down.
(C) Someone in the marketing team.

어휘 come up with (아이디어, 계획 등을) 생각해내다, 내놓다 update 갱신하다 go well 잘 진행되다

해석 갱신된 슬로건은 누가 내놓은 건가요?
(A) 상당히 잘 진행되었다고 들었어요.
(B) 이 엘리베이터는 내려갑니다.
(C) 마케팅 부서 사람이요.

해설 (A)는 How ~ go(ing)?의 대답으로 알맞은 대답이며, (B)는 질문에 나오는 came up에서 연상되는 표현 going down을 들려주면서 오답을 유도하고 있다. Who 의문문은 Someone from[in]으로 시작하는 대답이 자주 정답으로 출제된다.

PART 3 & 4 Exercise

1 (C) **2** (C) **3** (A) **4** (A) **5** (A) **6** (C)

Questions 1 through 3 refer to the following conversation and sign.

[W][Am] Hi, Baolin. I'm just checking in. ²How's everything going up here? ¹ ²Have you finished cleaning the Batista Construction offices yet?

[M][Au] ¹ ²No, it's taking more time than I thought it would. I vacuumed the carpet, but there are a lot of stains. So I made the decision to shampoo it. But then I had to go downstairs to get the steam-cleaning machine and bring it back up here.

[W][Am] ³Well, before you start shampooing, could you come downstairs again? I could use a hand moving a large table in one of the conference rooms.

[M][Au] ³Sure, I'll head downstairs right away. This is a nice break for me from working on these carpets, anyway.

1–3번 문제는 다음 대화와 표지판에 관한 것입니다.

여: 안녕, Baolin. 그냥 확인차 들렀어요. 여기 일이 어떻게 되어가고 있어요? Batista 건설 사무실 청소는 이제 다 끝났나요?

남: 아니요. 생각했던 것보다 시간이 더 오래 걸리고 있어요. 카펫을 진공청소기로 청소했는데요. 얼룩이 많더라고요. 그래서 세제로 빨기로 했죠. 그런데 그러려면 아래층에 내려가서 스팀 청소기를 가지고 다시 여기로 올라와야 했죠.

여: 음, 빨기 시작하기 전에 아래층으로 다시 내려와 줄 수 있겠어요? 회의실 중 한 군데에서 큰 테이블을 옮기는 데 도움이 필요해요.

남: 물론이죠. 당장 아래층으로 갈게요. 이 카펫 작업을 쉴 수 있는 좋은 기회이기도 하겠네요.

어휘 check in (일의 진행을) 확인하다 vacuum 진공청소기로 청소하다 stain 얼룩 shampoo (카펫 등을 세제로) 빨다 downstairs 아래층으로 a hand 도움(의 손길) conference room 회의실 head ~로 향하다, 가다 right away 즉시, 곧바로

Office Directory
1st FL: OE Furniture Company
2nd FL: Gold Coast Imagination, Inc.
3rd FL: Batista Construction
4th FL: Brown & Sons

사무실 안내
1층: OE 가구 회사
2층: (주) Gold Coast Imagination
3층: Batista 건설
4층: Brown & Sons

어휘 directory (건물 내의) 안내판

1. Who most likely are the speakers?

(A) Carpet weavers
(B) Hair stylists
(C) Cleaning staff
(D) Construction workers

해석 화자들은 누구이겠는가?
(A) 카펫 직공들
(B) 헤어 디자이너들
(C) 청소 직원들
(D) 건설 근로자들

2. Look at the graphic. Where is the man currently working?

(A) On the first floor
(B) On the second floor
(C) On the third floor
(D) On the fourth floor

해석 그래픽을 보라. 남자는 현재 어디서 일하고 있는가?
(A) 1층에서
(B) 2층에서
(C) 3층에서
(D) 4층에서

3. What are the speakers probably going to do next?

(A) Rearrange a table
(B) Repair a machine
(C) Review some plans
(D) Conduct a conference call

어휘 rearrange 재배열하다, 재배치하다 review 검토하다
conduct 실시하다, 수행하다 conference call 전화 회의

해석 화자들은 이후에 무엇을 하겠는가?
(A) 테이블을 재배치한다
(B) 기계를 수리한다
(C) 계획을 검토한다
(D) 전화 회의를 한다

해설 화자들의 직업을 묻는 1번과 같은 문제는 대부분 첫 한두 문장에서 정답을 알려주므로 대화 시작과 동시에 정답 고를 준비를 하고 있어야 한다. 게다가 1번과 2번의 정답을 동시에 골라야 하는 경우이기 때문에 언제나 읽은 내용을 기억하려고 노력해야 한다는 사실도 중요하다. 여자가 남자의 작업 구역에 들러 일이 어떻게 되어가고 있는지(How's everything going up here?), Batista 건설 회사의 사무실 청소는 끝났는지 묻고 있다(Have you finished cleaning the Batista Construction offices yet?). 남자는 생각보다 오래 걸리고 있다고 대답하는데(No, it's taking more time than I thought it would.), 여기서 화자들의 직업이 건물 청소라는 것과 지금 남자가 있는 곳은 Batista 건설사가 있는 3층이라는 것을 알 수 있다. 3번과 같은 do next? 문제는 마지막 대사에서 정답을 알려준다. 여자가 테이블을 옮기기 위해 아래층에 내려와 줄 것을 부탁하고 있고(could you come downstairs again? I could use a hand moving a large table in one of the conference rooms.) 남자는 수락하고 있으므로(Sure, I'll head downstairs right away.) 대화가 끝난 후 화자들이 할 일은 테이블 재배치일 것이라고 짐작할 수 있다.

Questions 4 through 6 refer to the following instructions and flowchart.

[M][Au] Let's begin the meeting with some wonderful news - [4]thanks to the exceptional product designs created by this team, our line of kitchen appliances outsold all other competing brands on the market last quarter. Well done! Now I want to discuss the updates to our product development process. [5]As you can see from this flowchart, we've added an additional step between "Develop a Design"

and "Construct a Model." This new step means you'll have to be granted approval from the executive board before moving forward with your prototype. [6]Lately, some concern has arisen about the excessive time being wasted on prototypes that never actually become products. The introduction of this new process is intended to enhance our team's time efficiency and productivity.

4-6번 문제는 다음 지시 사항과 순서도에 관한 것입니다.

남: 신나는 소식으로 회의를 시작합시다. 이 팀이 만들어낸 탁월한 제품 디자인 덕분에 지난 분기에 우리 주방용품 제품군이 시장에 나와 있는 다른 모든 경쟁 브랜드들보다 더 많이 팔렸습니다. 잘 했습니다! 자, 이제 제품 개발 절차에 대한 갱신 사항을 논하고자 합니다. 이 순서도에서 보시다시피 '디자인 개발'과 '모형 제작' 사이에 추가 단계를 덧붙였습니다. 이 새로운 단계는 여러분이 시제품 제작을 진행하기 전에 이사회로부터 승인을 받아야 한다는 것을 의미합니다. 실제로는 전혀 상품이 되지 못하는 시제품에 낭비되고 있는 지나치게 많은 시간에 대해 최근에 약간의 우려가 생겼거든요. 이 새로운 절차의 도입은 우리 팀 시간 관리의 효율성과 생산성 향상을 목표로 하고 있습니다.

어휘 flowchart 플로 차트, 작업 순서도 exceptional 탁월한, 특출한 line 제품군 kitchen appliance 주방용품 outsell ～보다 더 많이 팔리다 Well done! 잘 했어!, 훌륭했어! update 갱신 construct 제작하다 grant (허가 등을) 하다, 주다, 부여하다 executive board 이사회 move forward with ～을 진행하다, 추진하다 prototype 시제품 lately 최근에 arise 생기다, 발생하다 excessive 지나친, 과도한 enhance 높이다, 향상시키다 efficiency 효율(성) productivity 생산성

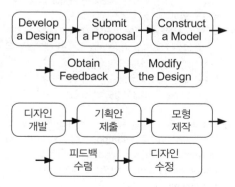

어휘 proposal 기획안 modify 변경하다, 수정하다

4. What does the speaker say about the company's kitchen appliances?

(A) They sold well in the previous quarter.
(B) They achieved success in a design contest.
(C) They are priced lower than competing products.
(D) They were featured in a trade magazine.

어휘 kitchen appliance 주방용품 sell 팔리다 price 가격을 매기다 feature 특집으로 다루다 trade magazine 업계지(誌)

해석 화자는 회사의 주방용품에 대해 무엇이라고 말하는가?
(A) 이전 분기에 잘 팔렸다.
(B) 디자인 대회에서 성공을 거두었다.
(C) 가격이 경쟁 상품들보다 낮게 매겨져 있다.
(D) 업계지에서 특집으로 다루어졌다.

5. Look at the graphic. According to the speaker, which step was recently added?

(A) Submit a proposal
(B) Construct a model
(C) Obtain feedback
(D) Modify the Design

해석 그래픽을 보라. 화자의 말에 따르면 어느 단계가 최근에 추가되었는가?
(A) 기획안 제출
(B) 모형 제작
(C) 피드백 수렴
(D) 디자인 수정

6. What concern does the speaker mention?

(A) Raw materials are in short supply.
(B) More appliances are being purchased online.
(C) Employees' time has been used inefficiently.
(D) A production deadline has been adjusted.

어휘 raw material 원자재 in short supply 공급이 딸리는 appliance (가정용) 기기 inefficiently 비효율[비능률]적으로 adjust 조정하다

해석 화자는 어떤 우려 사항을 언급하는가?
(A) 원자재의 공급이 부족하다.
(B) 더 많은 기기들이 온라인에서 구매되고 있다.
(C) 직원들의 시간이 비효율적으로 사용되어 왔다.
(D) 생산 기한이 조정되었다.

해설 4번 문제의 정답은 kitchen appliances라는 키워드가 들리는 문장에서 알아낼 수 있다. 지난 분기에 경쟁 브랜드들보다 더 많이 팔렸다고 알리고 있으므로 여기서 정답을 고르자(our line of kitchen appliances outsold all other competing brands on the market last quarter). 5번 문제는 순서도에 보이는 절차를 언급하는 문장에서 알 수 있다. '디자인 개발'과 '모형 제작' 사이에 단계를 추가했다고 말하고 있는데(we've added an additional step between "Develop a Design" and "Construct a Model."), 순서도를 보면 그 사이에 있는 단계는 '기획안 제출(Submit a proposal)'이다. 6번 문제의 정답은 concern이라는 키워드가 들어 있는 문장이 들릴 때 고르자. 상품화되지도 못할 시제품을 만드느라 너무 많은 시간이 낭비되고 있다는 우려 사항을 전달하고 있으므로 (some concern has arisen about the excessive time being wasted on prototypes that never actually become products.), 이 부분이 패러프레이즈 되어 있는 문장을 정답으로 선택하면 된다. 이어지는 문장에서 이 조치가 시간 관리의 효율성을 높이기 위한 것이라고 설명하고 있으므로(The introduction of this new process is intended to enhance our team's time efficiency and productivity.), 여기까지 들으면 더 확실하게 정답을 알 수 있다.

Actual Test

1 (B)	**2** (A)	**3** (D)	**4** (A)	**5** (C)
6 (C)	**7** (A)	**8** (A)	**9** (B)	**10** (B)
11 (C)	**12** (C)	**13** (D)	**14** (C)	**15** (B)
16 (A)	**17** (B)	**18** (D)	**19** (C)	**20** (D)
21 (B)	**22** (D)	**23** (A)	**24** (C)	**25** (C)
26 (C)	**27** (A)	**28** (D)	**29** (C)	**30** (D)

* 정답을 맞힌 문제도 해설을 읽어보세요.

Part 1

1. [M | Cn]

(A) A tank has been taken out of a building.
(B) Plastic sheets cover a building frame.
(C) Vertical beams have been erected on a construction site.
(D) A lawn is being mowed around the building.

어휘 plastic sheet 비닐 시트 frame (건물의) 뼈대 vertical 수직의 beam 기둥 erect (건물, 동상 등을) 세우다 lawn 잔디밭 mow (잔디를) 깎다

해석 (A) 탱크가 건물 밖으로 나와 있다.
(B) 비닐 시트가 건물 뼈대를 덮고 있다.
(C) 공사 현장에 수직 기둥들이 세워져 있다.
(D) 건물 주위에서 잔디를 깎고 있다.

해설 A tank, Vertical beams, a construction site 같은 단어들을 들으면 (A)와 (C)는 오답으로 골라낼 수 있다. 동작을 묘사하는 진행 시제 수동태는 사진에 사람이 있어야 정답이 될 수 있으므로 (D)도 오답이다. Plastic sheets(비닐 시트), a building frame(건물 뼈대) 같은 단어들을 잘 기억하고 정답을 선택하자.

2. [W | Br]

(A) A sitting area is illuminated by lamps.
(B) Refreshments have been left on a table.
(C) A couch is facing the fireplace.
(D) Some pictures are being framed for display.

어휘 illuminate (~에 불을) 비추다 refreshments 다과 couch 소파 face ~을 향하다, 향해 있다 fireplace 벽난로 frame 액자에 넣다

해석 (A) 램프가 휴식 공간을 비추고 있다.
(B) 테이블 위에 다과가 놓여 있다.
(C) 소파가 벽난로를 향해 있다.
(D) 그림을 전시하기 위해 액자에 넣고 있다.

해설 문제가 어렵게 출제될 때 동사 illuminate를 사용하는 문장이 나올 수 있음을 기억해 두자. 테이블 위에 다과 (Refreshments)가 없으므로 (B)는 오답이다. 소파가 향하는 방향은 벽난로 쪽이 아니므로 (C)도 오답이다. 동작을 묘사하는 진행 시제 수동태는 사진에 사람이 있어야 정답이 될 수 있으므로 (D)도 오답이다.

3. [W | Am]

(A) All of the balcony doors have been left open.
(B) There is a fence around the edge of the yard.
(C) Cartons of window glass are in a row on the ground.
(D) There are different styles of railings on the balconies.

어휘 carton 판지 상자 railing 난간

해석 (A) 모든 발코니 문이 열려 있다.

(B) 마당 가장자리를 둘러 울타리가 있다.

(C) 창유리 몇 상자가 바닥에 일렬로 있다.

(D) 발코니 난간들이 서로 다른 모양으로 생겼다.

해설 발코니 문은 모두 닫혀 있으므로 (A)는 오답이다. 사진에 보이지 않는 the edge of the yard(마당 가장자리)와 Cartons(판지 상자), the ground(땅바닥)를 들으면서 (B)와 (C)도 오답으로 골라내야 한다. 정답을 고를 수 있도록 크기나 모양을 비교하는 문장들을 잘 공부해두자.

Part 2

4. [W|Am] [M|Cn]

Who can pick up Mr. Hendrix from the airport?

(A) I don't have a car.
(B) It's a one-way ticket.
(C) No, it's not that heavy.

어휘 pick up ~을 차로 데리러 가다 one-way 편도의

해석 누가 공항에서 Mr. Hendrix를 데려올 수 있나요?

(A) 저는 차가 없어요.

(B) 편도 티켓입니다.

(C) 아니요, 그렇게 무겁지는 않아요.

해설 질문 앞부분 Who can pick up(누가 데려올 수 있나요?)에 집중하면 자연스러운 대답을 알 수 있다. (B)는 질문에 나오는 the airport에서 연상되는 단어로 오답을 유도하고 있고, (C)는 No만 듣고도 오답임을 알 수 있다.

5. [M|Cn] [M|Au]

Who's exhibiting in the Rattigan Art Gallery next month?

(A) Yes, it opens at six P.M.
(B) My friend Arshad is coming, too.
(C) It's a group of young Korean artists.

어휘 exhibit 작품을 전시하다, 전시회를 열다

해석 다음 달 Rattigan 미술관에서는 누가 전시회를 여나요?

(A) 네, 저녁 6시에 개관합니다.

(B) 제 친구 Arshad도 올 거예요.

(C) 젊은 한국 화가들 그룹입니다.

해설 일단 (A)는 Yes가 들리는 순간 오답으로 골라내야 한다. 사람 이름을 듣고 (B)를 정답으로 선택하지 않도록 주의하자. 질문 앞부분 Who's exhibiting(누가 전시회를 여나요?)에 집중해서 자연스러운 대답을 파악해야 한다.

6. [M|Au] [M|Cn]

Which supplier do you use for dairy products?

(A) Every now and then.
(B) In the supply room.
(C) The one on Lombard Street.

어휘 supplier 공급(업)자, 공급업체 dairy product 유제품 (every) now and then 때때로, 이따금씩 supply room 비품실

해석 유제품을 주문할 때 어느 공급업체를 이용하시나요?

(A) 이따금씩 합니다.

(B) 비품실에요.

(C) Lombard 가(街)에 있는 업체요.

해설 (A)는 How often ~?에서, (B)는 Where 의문문에서 정답으로 나올 만한 대답이다. Which 의문문은 The one이 들리면 무조건 정답이다.

7. [M|Cn] [W|Am]

Which parking facility is closest to the client's office?

(A) I usually take public transportation there.
(B) Around this time tomorrow, maybe.
(C) Wow, the view here is breathtaking!

어휘 breathtaking 숨이 멎을 정도로 멋진[놀라운]

해석 고객의 사무실에서 어느 주차 시설이 가장 가까운가요?

(A) 저는 보통 대중교통을 이용해서 거기에 가요.

(B) 아마 내일 이 시간쯤에요.

(C) 와, 여기 경치가 끝내주네요!

해설 항상 Which 바로 뒤에 붙는 명사만 알아들으면 문제를 해결할 수 있다. 질문이 Which parking facility(어느 주차 시설?)인 것만 생각하면 (B)와 (C)는 모두 오답인 것을 알 수 있다. 보통 대중교통을 타기 때문에 어느 주차 시설이 가장 가까운지 모른다고 대답하는 문장이 정답이다.

8. [W|Br] [W|Am]

I don't know how to get to the convention center from the train station.

(A) Wayne's printing out the directions.
(B) A complimentary lunch.
(C) Five hundred people attended.

어휘 directions 길 안내 complimentary 무료의

해설 기차역에서 컨벤션 센터까지 어떻게 가는지 모르겠
어요.
(A) Wayne이 길 안내를 인쇄하고 있어요.
(B) 무료 점심이요.
(C) 500명이 참석했습니다.

해설 질문 앞부분 I don't know how to get to(어떻게 가는지
모르겠어요)에만 집중하면 자연스러운 대답을 알 수 있
다. (B)와 (C)는 모두 질문에 들어 있는 convention에서
연상되는 대답으로 오답을 유도하고 있다.

---

9. [W | Am] [M | Au]

You know which floor the accounting
office is located on?

(A) The receipts are for November.
**(B) They've moved recently, so I'm
not sure.**
(C) The lights turn on and off
automatically.

어휘 accounting office 경리실
해설 경리실이 몇 층에 있는지 아세요?
(A) 그 영수증들은 11월분입니다.
(B) 최근에 옮겨가서, 저도 잘 모르겠어요.
(C) 조명은 자동으로 켜지고 꺼집니다.

해설 (A)는 질문의 accounting에서 연상되는 단어 receipts
를 들려주면서, (C)는 on을 반복시키면서 오답을 유도
하고 있다. 간접 의문문은 중간에 나오는 의문사를 놓
치지 않아야 한다. 질문 앞부분 Do you know which
floor(몇 층에 있는지 아세요?)에 집중하면 자연스러운
대답을 파악할 수 있다. "모른다"는 대답은 거의 항상
정답이다. 자주 출제되는 문장으로 I[We] don't know.
/ I have no idea. / I'm not sure. / I don't remember.
/ I can't recall. 같은 것들을 기억하고 있다가 들리면
정답으로 고르자.

---

10. [W | Br] [M | Cn]

This is the best Chinese restaurant in
town.

(A) Samantha is traveling in October.
(B) It's where I always take my clients.
(C) Fried rice and dumplings.

어휘 dumpling 만두
해설 여기가 시내에서 가장 좋은 중식당이에요.
(A) Samantha는 10월에 여행할 겁니다.
(B) 제가 항상 고객들을 데려오는 곳이죠.
(C) 볶음밥과 만두요.

해설 질문 앞부분을 놓치고 Chinese나 Chinese restaurant
만 듣고 문제를 풀려고 하면 (A)나 (C) 같은 연상되는
대답에 현혹될 수 있다. "이곳이 가장 좋은 중식당"이
라는 말에 "나도 항상 고객들을 여기에 데려온다"고 대
답하는 것이 의견 제시와 동의로 이루어진 자연스러운
대화가 된다.

---

11. [W | Am] [M | Cn]

You've been to the Bayside Center
before, right?

(A) Those shoes are tight.
(B) I'm actually left-handed.
(C) Mr. Mendez has.

어휘 left-handed 왼손잡이의
해설 전에 Bayside 센터에 가 보신 거 맞죠?
(A) 저 신발은 꽉 끼어요.
(B) 저는 사실 왼손잡이입니다.
(C) Mr. Mendez가 가 봤죠.

해설 (A)는 질문의 right과 발음이 비슷한 tight를, (B)는 right
에서 연상되는 단어 left를 들려주면서 오답을 유도하고
있다. 질문 앞부분 You've been to(가 보셨죠?)에 집중
해서 자연스러운 대답을 정답으로 선택하자.

---

12. [M | Au] [W | Br]

You said the financial report would be
completed this week, didn't you?

(A) No, she didn't pay for it.
(B) The keys were in the supply drawer.
(C) I did, but there's been a setback.

어휘 supply drawer 비품 서랍 setback 차질
해설 재무 보고서가 이번 주에 완료될 거라고 하지 않았던
가요?
(A) 아니요, 그녀는 그 값을 지불하지 않았습니다.
(B) 열쇠들은 비품 서랍에 있었어요.
(C) 그랬죠, 하지만 차질이 생겼어요.

해설 일반 의문문은 대답을 Yes, and[but] / (No), but으로
시작하면 다 정답이다. 매회 한 번 정도 등장할 수 있으
니 반드시 기억해 두자. I did, but이 들리는 순간 안심
하고 정답으로 선택하면 된다.

Part 3

Questions 13 through 15 refer to the following conversation with three speakers.

[M│Au] **13**I can't believe the Edmonton convention is just around the corner!

[W│Am] I know. It should be fantastic, especially with all those big-name speakers. **13**Are we good to go with transportation?

[M│Cn] **14**Uh, the plane tickets have already been sorted out, and you made arrangements for the rental car while we're there, right, Arvind?

[M│Au] **14**Oh, no! It completely slipped my mind to reserve the car! I've been preoccupied with organizing my workshop materials!

[M│Cn] All right... We're only forty-eight hours away from our departure. Getting a car now might be a challenge!

[W│Am] Let's not stress out about it. I read about a courtesy bus service to and from the hotel. **15**Let's speak with the hotel receptionist and find out.

13-15번 문제는 다음 3인 대화에 관한 것입니다.

남1: Edmonton 컨벤션 날짜가 얼마 남지 않았다니 믿기 지가 않네요!

여: 그래요. 정말 굉장할 거예요. 특히 그 모든 저명한 강 사들이 있으니까요. 우리 교통편은 다 준비되었나 요?

남2: 어, 비행기 표는 이미 다 준비되었고요, 거기 있 는 동안 쓸 렌터카 준비는 당신이 하기로 했죠, Arvind?

남1: 오, 이런! 차 예약하는 것을 완전히 잊어버리고 있었 어요! 워크숍 자료 정리하는 데 정신이 팔려 있었거 든요!

남2: 그래요... 출발할 시간이 48시간밖에 남지 않았네요. 지금 차를 구하는 건 어려울 것 같은데요!

여: 그걸로 스트레스 받지 말아요. 호텔까지 가고 오고 할 수 있는 무료 셔틀버스 서비스에 대해 읽었어요. 호텔 접수 직원과 통화해서 알아봐요.

어휘 around the corner (시간적으로) 아주 가까이, 임박하여 I know (동의, 공감의) 맞아, 그래 big-name 유명한, 저명한 good to go 준비가 다 된 transportation 교통수단, 차량

sort out ~을 처리하다 make arrangements for ~을 준비하다 slip one's mind 잊어버리다 preoccupied with ~에 정신이 팔린[사로잡힌] organize 정리하다, 구성하다 materials 자료 stress out 스트레스를 받다 courtesy bus (호텔, 전시장 등의) 무료 셔틀버스

---

13. What are the speakers mainly discussing?

(A) Strategies for minimizing a travel budget

(B) Attractions in Edmonton

(C) Potential venues for a conference

(D) Preparations for an upcoming business trip

어휘 strategy 전략 attraction 명소, 볼거리 potential 가능성 이 있는, 잠재적인 venue 장소

해석 화자들은 주로 무엇을 논하고 있는가?
(A) 출장 예산을 최소화하기 위한 전략
(B) Edmonton의 명소들
(C) 학회가 가능한 장소
(D) 다가오는 출장 준비

---

14. What problem do the speakers have?

(A) Their business cards are yet to be delivered.

(B) Their reservations are for the incorrect dates.

(C) Their transportation arrangements are incomplete.

(D) Their client in Edmonton is currently unavailable.

어휘 be yet to-V 아직 ~하지 않고 있다 incorrect 부정확한, 맞지 않는 transportation 교통수단, 차량 arrangements 준비, 마련 incomplete 불완전한, 미완성의 unavailable 만날 수 없는

해석 화자들은 어떤 문제를 갖고 있는가?
(A) 명함이 아직 배달되지 않았다.
(B) 예약 날짜가 잘못 되었다.
(C) 교통편 준비가 완료되지 않았다.
(D) 현재 Edmonton에 있는 고객을 만날 수 없다.

---

15. What does the woman suggest they do?

(A) Cancel an order

(B) Communicate with a hotel

(C) Arrange to deliver a speech

(D) Defer making a decision

어휘 arrange to-V ~하기 위한 준비를 하다 deliver a speech 연설하다 defer 미루다, 연기하다

해석 여자는 무엇을 하자고 제안하는가?
(A) 주문을 취소하자
(B) 호텔과 연락하자
(C) 연설할 준비를 하자
(D) 결정을 미루자

해설 13번 문제가 대화의 주제를 묻고 있으므로 첫 문장부터 집중해서 정답을 고를 준비를 하고 있어야 한다. 남자 1이 얼마 남지 않은 Edmonton 컨벤션에 대한 기대감을 표하자(I can't believe the Edmonton convention is just around the corner!) 여자가 Edmonton까지 갈 교통편이 준비되었는지 묻고 있다(Are we good to go with transportation?). 대화 주제는 타 지역에서 열리는 컨벤션 참석 준비, 즉 출장 준비이다. 정답을 고를 때는 언제나 순발력이 필요하다는 사실을 잊지 말자. 바로 이어지는 두 남자의 대화를 통해 14번의 정답을 알아내야 한다. 두 남자의 대사를 들어보면 비행편은 준비가 되었지만(Uh, the plane tickets have already been sorted out), Edmonton에서 이용할 렌터카는 예약이 되지 않았다(and you made arrangements for the rental car while we're there, right, Arvind? – Oh, no! It completely slipped my mind to reserve the car!). 교통편이 완비되지 않았다는 점이 화자들이 겪고 있는 문제다. 15번 문제의 정답은 여자의 마지막 대사 Let's speak with the hotel receptionist를 듣고 알 수 있다.

Questions 16 through 18 refer to the following conversation.

[M | Au] Eun-Jung, look at these scarves!

[W | Br] I know - aren't they fabulous! I got one for myself a while ago. ¹⁶They're handcrafted by local weavers, making each scarf one of a kind - a total original.

[M | Au] I'm impressed. ¹⁷I'd like to buy one for my office assistant. She has a birthday coming up. But... uhh... [I get paid only once a month.]

[W | Br] ¹⁷Oh, I'd be happy to lend you the money today. You can pay me back whenever you can.

[M | Au] Thank you very much! But... I can't recall ever seeing you wear a scarf like that at work before.

[W | Br] ¹⁸Actually, I let my sister borrow it one time, and she was so fond of it that I told her to keep it.

16-18번 문제는 다음 대화에 관한 것입니다.

남: Eun-Jung, 이 스카프들 좀 봐요!
여: 네, 기막히게 좋죠? 저도 얼마 전에 쓰려고 하나 샀어요. 이 지역 직공들이 수공예로 만들어서 각각의 스카프가 다른 곳에서는 찾아볼 수 없는 완전히 독창적인 것들이에요.
남: 인상적이네요. 사무실 비서에게 하나 사줬으면 좋겠어요. 생일이 다가오고 있거든요. 그런데... 어... 제가 급여를 한 달에 한 번만 받네요.
여: 아, 오늘은 제가 기꺼이 돈을 빌려줄게요. 언제든 갚을 수 있을 때 갚아요.
남: 정말 고마워요! 그런데... 전에 회사에서 당신이 그렇게 생긴 스카프를 하고 있는 걸 한 번도 본 기억이 없네요.
여: 실은 동생에게 한 번 빌려 쓰게 해줬더니 너무 좋아해서 그냥 가지라고 했어요.

어휘 I know (동의, 공감의) 맞아, 그래 fabulous 기막히게 좋은[멋진] a while ago 얼마 전에 handcrafted 수공예품인 weaver 직공, 방직공 one of a kind 독특한[유례를 찾기 힘든] 것 impressed 인상 깊게 생각하는 recall 기억해 내다 be fond of ~을 좋아하다

16. What does the woman say is special about the scarves?

(A) They are made by hand.
(B) They are exported overseas.
(C) They are made from velvet.
(D) They are sold only in designated stores.

어휘 designate 지정하다

해석 여자는 스카프들에 대해 무엇이 특별하다고 말하는가?
(A) 손으로 만들었다.
(B) 해외로 수출된다.
(C) 벨벳으로 만들었다.
(D) 지정된 매장에서만 판매된다.

17. What does the man imply when he says, "I get paid only once a month"?

(A) He used to be paid more frequently.
(B) He lacks the funds to make a purchase.
(C) He has to collect his paycheck today.
(D) He is planning to ask for a pay increase.

어휘 used to 전에는 ~였다 frequently 자주 collect 수령하다, 받다 paycheck 급여(로 받는 수표) pay increase 급여 인상

18. Why does the woman say she no longer wears her scarf?

(A) She misplaced it.
(B) She tore it.
(C) She returned it.
(D) She gave it away.

어휘 misplace ~을 어딘가에 두고 잊어버리다   tear (tore-torn) 찢다   give away ~을 선물로 주다

해석 여자는 왜 더 이상 스카프를 착용하지 않는다고 말하는가?
(A) 잃어버렸다.
(B) 찢어졌다.
(C) 반품했다.
(D) 선물로 주었다.

해설 16번 문제의 정답은 여자의 대사 중 handcrafted라는 키워드만 들으면 알 수 있다. 남자는 스카프들에 깊은 인상을 받으며 사무실 비서에게 선물하고 싶어 한다(I'd like to buy one for my office assistant). 하지만 급여를 한 달에 한 번만 받는다고 말하고 있는데(I get paid only once a month), 이어지는 여자의 대사 I'd be happy to lend you the money today(오늘은 내가 돈을 빌려줄게요).를 들으면, 한 달에 한 번만 급여를 받는다는 말은 현재 월급 때가 거의 다 되어서 선물을 살 돈이 없다는 뜻임을 추론할 수 있다. 여기서 17번의 정답을 고르자. 18번 문제의 정답은 여자의 마지막 대사를 듣고 선택해야 한다. she was so fond of it that I told her to keep it.을 알아들을 수 있게 여러 번 따라 읽는 연습을 해 보자. 패러프레이즈 된 문장을 정답으로 고르려면 give away의 뜻도 알고 있어야 한다.

Questions 19 through 21 refer to the following conversation and card.

[W|Br] I've been informed that there have been some dissatisfied customers lately.

[M|Cn] Yes, I'm afraid that's right. In fact, I've just had a conversation with one of them.

[W|Br] Oh. Well, uh, what was the feedback from the customer?

[M|Cn] She was far from satisfied. [19][20]Our driver picked her up on schedule, but encountered heavy traffic on the way to the airport, and she nearly missed her flight.

[W|Br] Hmm. We might want to examine the roadwork scheduled in the area. It could be impacting traffic more than we thought.

[M|Cn] Right. And we have some other concerns to address as well. [21]Take a look at the rest of these comments. We'll need to decide how to respond to them.

19-21번 문제는 다음 대화와 카드에 관한 것입니다.

여: 최근에 불만이 있는 고객들이 몇 명 있었다고 얘기를 들었어요.
남: 네, 유감스럽게도 그래요. 실은 지금 막 그중 한 명과 대화를 나누었어요.
여: 아, 그래요. 어, 그 고객으로부터의 피드백이 어떤 것이었나요?
남: 전혀 만족하지 못했죠. 우리 기사가 제때에 가서 그녀를 차에 태웠지만, 공항으로 가는 길에 교통체증을 만났대요. 그래서 거의 비행기를 놓칠 뻔했다는군요.
여: 음... 지역에서 예정되어 있는 도로 공사들을 살펴보는 게 좋겠어요. 우리가 생각했던 것보다 교통에 더 많은 영향을 미칠 수도 있어요.
남: 맞아요. 그리고 다루어야 할 다른 우려 사항들도 있어요. 나머지 의견들을 살펴보세요. 어떻게 대응해야 할지 결정해야 해요.

어휘 dissatisfied 불만스러워 하는   lately 최근에, 얼마 전에   far from 전혀[결코] ~이 아닌   pick up ~을 차로 데리러 가다   on schedule 예정대로   encounter 맞닥뜨리다   might want to-V ~ 하는 게 좋을 것 같다   impact 영향을 주다   concern 우려, 걱정   address 다루다, 대처하다   the rest 나머지

Name	Comment
Kevin Lee	Unclean seating
Jean Villiers	No price reduction
Anthony Choi	Web site inaccessible
[20]Robin Jarvela	[20]Running behind schedule

이름	평가
Kevin Lee	깨끗하지 않은 좌석
Jean Villiers	가격 할인 없음
Anthony Choi	홈페이지 접속 불가
Robin Jarvela	예정보다 늦게 운행

어휘 unclean 더러운, 깨끗하지 않은 seating 좌석, 자리 inaccessible 접근할 수 없는 run 운행하다 behind schedule 예정보다 늦게

19. Where do the speakers most likely work?

(A) At a cargo company
(B) At a car manufacturer
(C) At a taxi service company
(D) At an airport

해석 화자들은 어디에서 근무하겠는가?
(A) 화물 회사에서
(B) 자동차 제조업체에서
(C) 택시 서비스 회사에서
(D) 공항에서

20. Look at the graphic. Which customer are the speakers discussing?

(A) Kevin Lee
(B) Jean Villiers
(C) Anthony Choi
(D) Robin Jarvela

해석 그래픽을 보라. 화자들은 어느 고객을 논하고 있는가?
(A) Kevin Lee
(B) Jean Villiers
(C) Anthony Choi
(D) Robin Jarvela

21. What will the speakers do next?

(A) Examine fuel prices
(B) Scrutinize customer feedback
(C) Revise staffing schedules
(D) Organize training sessions

어휘 scrutinize 세심히 살피다 staffing 인력 배치 organize 준비하다, 조직하다

해석 화자들은 이후에 무엇을 할 것인가?
(A) 연료 가격을 살펴본다
(B) 고객들의 피드백을 자세히 살펴본다
(C) 직원 배치 일정을 수정한다
(D) 교육을 준비한다

해설 19번과 20번 문제의 정답을 동시에 골라야 한다. 이러한 유형의 문제를 원활하게 해결하려면 미리 읽은 문제의 내용을 기억하고 있어야 한다. 기사가 고객의 집을 제시간에 방문해서 그를 태우고 공항으로 갔는데, 교통체증을 만나 하마터면 비행기를 놓칠 뻔했다는 사연을 들으면(Our driver picked her up on schedule, but encountered heavy traffic on the way to the airport, and she nearly missed her flight.), 화자들이 근무하는 곳이 어디인지, 이 이야기가 카드에 나와 있는 고객 중 누가 겪은 일인지 알 수 있다. 21번과 같은 do next? 문제는 항상 마지막 대사에서 정답을 알 수 있다. 카드에 적혀 있는 나머지 피드백 읽어 보고 어떻게 대처하는 게 좋을지 결정하자는 제안이므로(Take a look at the rest of these comments. We'll need to decide how to respond to them.), 화자들이 이후에 할 일은 카드에 적힌 내용을 자세히 읽는 것임을 짐작할 수 있다.

Part 4

Questions 22 through 24 refer to the following excerpt from a meeting.

W Am Hello, **22**I've called this meeting with the software development team to communicate some good news. Our sales for the new software have exceeded our initial projections, **23**and I'd like to express my gratitude for the late nights and weekends you spent working to design such a great product. **24**So, the management has decided to reward you all with a bonus, which will be reflected in your upcoming paycheck. Thank you again for your outstanding performance!

22-24번 문제는 다음 회의 발췌문에 관한 것입니다.

여: 안녕하세요. 좋은 소식을 전하기 위해 소프트웨어 개발팀과 함께하는 이번 회의를 소집했습니다. 새 소프트웨어의 판매량이 처음의 예상치를 넘어섰습니다. 저는 여러분이 이렇게 훌륭한 제품을 디자인하느라 일하며 보낸 늦은 밤들과 주말들에 대해 감사를 표하고자 합니다. 그래서 우리 경영진은 여러분 모두에게 보너스로 보상해 드리기로 했으며, 이것은 여러분의 다음 급여에 반영될 것입니다. 탁월한 성과에 대해 다시 한번 감사드립니다!

어휘 excerpt 발췌 부분, 인용구 communicate (정보 등을) 전달하다 exceed 초과하다, 넘다 initial 최초의, 초기의 projection 예상, 추정 gratitude 감사, 고마움 management 경영진 reward 보상하다 reflect 반영

하다, 나타내다 **outstanding** 뛰어난, 걸출한
performance 실적, 성과

---

22. Who are the listeners?

    (A) Company stakeholders
    (B) Sales associates
    (C) Marketing experts
    (D) Software developers

어휘 stakeholder 투자자, 이해관계자 **sales associate**
영업 사원

해설 청자들은 누구인가?
    (A) 회사 투자자들
    (B) 영업 사원들
    (C) 마케팅 전문가들
    (D) 소프트웨어 개발자들

---

23. Why does the speaker thank the
listeners?

    (A) For working extended hours
    (B) For organizing a fundraiser
    (C) For decreasing expenditures
    (D) For assisting clients

어휘 fundraiser (기금) 모금 행사 **expenditure** 지출

해설 화자는 왜 청자들에게 고마워하는가?
    (A) 연장 근무를 해 주어서
    (B) 기금 마련 행사를 준비해 주어서
    (C) 지출을 줄여 주어서
    (D) 고객들을 도와주어서

---

24. What will the listeners receive?

    (A) An invitation to a banquet
    (B) Some extra time off work
    (C) Some additional money
    (D) A state-of-the-art device

어휘 banquet 연회, 만찬 **off work** 일을 쉬는
state-of-the-art 최첨단의, 최신식의

해설 청자들은 무엇을 받을 것인가?
    (A) 연회 초대
    (B) 추가 휴가
    (C) 추가 금액
    (D) 최첨단 기기

해설 청자들이 누구인지는 대부분 첫 한두 문장에서 알 수 있다. 이 회의가 소프트웨어 개발팀과 하는 것이라는 말을 듣고(this meeting with the software development team) 22번 문제의 정답을 선택하자. 화자는 청자들에게 감사를 표하고 있는데(I'd like to express my gratitude), 제품 디자인을 위해 야간과 주말에도 일한 것에 대한 감사다(for the late nights and weekends you spent working to design such a great product). 여기서 23번의 정답을 알 수 있다. 바로 이어지는 문장을 놓치지 않도록 반드시 순발력을 발휘하도록 하자. 또한 So로 시작하는 문장은 정답을 알려줄 확률이 높다는 점도 기억하자. 경영진이 직원들에게 감사를 표하기 위해 보너스를 지급하겠다고 했으므로(So, the management has decided to reward you all with a bonus) 여기서 24번의 정답을 알 수 있다.

Questions 25 through 27 refer to the following excerpt from a meeting.

[W] [Am] Thanks for joining us at this departmental head meeting. Our primary focus for today is budgeting. Our new video game is coming along, but the release date's been pushed back again. [25]This means a significant portion of our resources will be tied up until this project is finished, but [who knows when that will be.] For the time being, [26]we must reduce expenses elsewhere. So I request each of you to identify areas in your department where you can implement budget cuts. [27]I'm prepared to set aside time to work with you individually on reviewing your departmental budgets. Let me know your availability for this.

25-27번 문제는 다음 회의 발췌문에 관한 것입니다.

여: 이번 부서장 회의에 함께해 주셔서 고맙습니다. 오늘의 주요 논의 사항은 예산 편성입니다. 우리의 새 비디오 게임이 잘 되어 가고 있지만, 출시 날짜는 다시 미루어졌습니다. 이것은 이 프로젝트가 끝날 때까지 재원의 상당 부분이 묶이게 될 것을 의미합니다만, 그게 언제가 될지는 아무도 알 수 없습니다. 당분간은 다른 곳에서 지출을 줄여야 합니다. 그래서 여러분 각자에게 부서에서 예산 삭감을 시행할 수 있는 부분을 찾아보실 것을 요청하는 바입니다. 저는 여러분과 개별적으로 만나 여러분의 부서 예산을 검토하기 위해 따로 시간을 내려고 준비하고 있습니다. 이 일을 위해 언제 시간을 내실 수 있는지 알려주시기 바랍니다.

어휘 excerpt 발췌 부분, 인용구 **departmental** 부서의

head 책임자 primary 주된, 주요한 budget 예산을
세우다 come along (원하는 대로) 되어 가다 release
발매, 출시 push back ~을 미루다, 연기하다 resources
재원, 자금 tie up (돈을 쉽게 쓸 수 없도록) 묶어 두다
for the time being 당분간 elsewhere 다른 곳에서
identify 찾다, 발견하다 implement 시행하다 set aside
(돈, 시간을) 따로 떼어 두다 individually 개별적으로, 각각
따로 availability 시간을 낼 수 있음

---

25. What does the speaker imply when she
says, "Who knows when that will be"?

(A) She is unable to comprehend a
demand.
(B) She expects her staff to quicken their
pace.
**(C) She is uncertain when a project
will be completed.**
(D) She wants to receive feedback from
the audience.

어휘 comprehend 이해하다, 파악하다 quicken 빠르게 하다
pace 속도

해석 화자는 "그게 언제가 될지는 아무도 알 수 없습니다."
라고 말할 때 무엇을 암시하는가?
(A) 요구 사항을 이해할 수 없다.
(B) 직원들이 속도를 빨리 내주기를 기대한다.
(C) 프로젝트가 언제 완료될지 확실하지 않다.
(D) 청자들로부터 피드백을 받고 싶다.

---

26. What is the topic of the meeting?

(A) Hiring an accountant
(B) Promoting a product
(C) Lowering costs
(D) Planning a trade fair

어휘 accountant 회계사 lower 내리다, 낮추다 trade fair
무역 박람회

해석 회의의 주제는 무엇인가?
(A) 회계사 채용
(B) 제품 홍보
(C) 비용 절감
(D) 무역 박람회 기획

---

27. What does the speaker say she will
reserve time to do?

(A) Conduct one-on-one meetings
(B) Analyze data from a questionnaire
(C) Contact potential clients

(D) Draft a written contract

어휘 reserve 따로 남겨 두다 one-on-one 일대일의
questionnaire 설문지 potential client 잠재 고객
draft 초안을 작성하다

해석 화자는 무엇을 하기 위해 시간을 따로 남겨 두겠다고
말하는가?
(A) 일대일 회의를 하기 위해
(B) 설문지에서 나온 데이터를 분석하기 위해
(C) 잠재 고객들에게 연락하기 위해
(D) 서면 계약서 초안을 작성하기 위해

해설 논의 중인 프로젝트가 완료될 때까지 재원의 상당
부분이 묶여 있게 될 것이라고 말한 후에(a significant
portion of our resources will be tied up until this project
is finished.) Who knows when that will be(그게 언제가
될지는 아무도 알 수 없습니다.)라고 했으므로, 당연히 프
로젝트 완료가 언제일지 확실히 알 수 없다는 뜻으로 한
말이다. 여기서 25번 문제의 정답을 고르자. 순발력 있게
정답을 고른 후 바로 이어지는 문장들에 귀를 기울이자.
reduce expenses나 budget cuts 같은 키워드가 회의의
주제는 비용 절감임을 나타내고 있다. 여기서 26번의 정
답을 선택해야 한다. 빠른 속도로 정답을 고른 후, 이어지
는 문장에서 들리는 set aside time이라는 키워드가 27번
문제에 들어 있는 reserve time과 동의 표현임을 파악해
야 한다. 문장에 나오는 work with you individually on
reviewing your departmental budgets가 패러프레이즈
되어 있는 선택지가 정답이다.

Questions 28 through 30 refer to the following
excerpt from a meeting and chart.

[W] [Br] Alright everyone, let me present the
breakdown of this year's video game market
shares. [28]While we're still ranked among the
top four gaming companies, [29]we should
take note of GFQ's rapid growth - they just
surpassed us. Although we're not that far
behind with an eighteen percent share,
we need to keep up. [30]Our market experts
attribute GFQ's surge in popularity to its
innovative business model, where they offer
their games for free, with consumers making
extra purchases within the game. [30]We
believe implementing this business approach
may assist us in attracting new users, so
we're going to try it out with some of our
existing games in the upcoming quarter to
explore the possibility of growing beyond our
current eighteen-percent market share.

28-30번 문제는 다음 회의 발췌문과 도표에 관한 것입니다.

여: 자, 여러분, 올해의 비디오 게임 시장 점유율 분석 자료를 보여드리겠습니다. 우리가 여전히 최상위 4개 게임 회사들 중 하나에 올라 있기는 합니다만, GFQ의 급속한 성장에 주목해야 합니다. 그들이 지금 막 우리를 앞질렀습니다. 우리는 18퍼센트의 점유율로 그리 크게 뒤쳐지고 있지는 않지만, 따라잡아야 합니다. 우리 시장 전문가들은 GFQ의 인기가 갑자기 높아진 것은 획기적인 사업 모델 덕분이라고 보고 있는데, 그들은 게임을 무료로 제공하면서 소비자들이 게임 내에서 추가 구매를 하도록 하고 있습니다. 우리도 이 비즈니스 접근법을 시행한다면 신규 유저들을 끌어들이는 데 도움이 될 것이라고 믿고 있습니다. 그래서 다음 분기에는 기존의 게임 몇몇을 가지고 이것을 시험해 본 후 현재의 시장 점유율 18퍼센트를 넘어 성장해 나갈 수 있는 가능성을 타진할 것입니다.

어휘 excerpt 발췌 부분, 인용구 present 제시하다, 발표하다 breakdown (통계적) 분석, 분류 (market) share 시장 점유율 rank (등급, 순위를) 매기다 take note of ~에 주목하다 rapid 빠른 surpass 능가하다, 뛰어넘다 keep up 뒤쳐지지 않다, 따라가다 attribute A to B A를 B의 결과로 [덕분으로] 보다 surge 급증, 급등 innovative 획기적인 for free 무료로 implement 시행하다 approach 접근법, 처리 방법 try out ~을 시험해 보다 existing 기존의 upcoming 다가오는, 곧 있을 explore 탐구하다, 타진하다 current 현재의

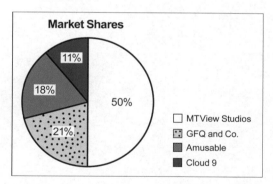

Market Shares

50% MTView Studios
21% GFQ and Co.
18% Amusable
11% Cloud 9

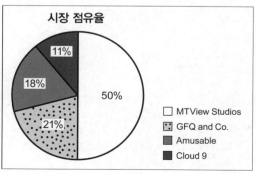

시장 점유율

50% MTView Studios
21% GFQ and Co.
18% Amusable
11% Cloud 9

---

28. What industry does the speaker work in?

(A) Interior design
(B) News reporting
(C) Film production
(D) Game development

해석 화자는 어느 업계에서 일하는가?
(A) 인테리어 디자인
(B) 뉴스 보도
(C) 영화 제작
(D) 게임 개발

---

29. Look at the graphic. What company does the speaker work for?

(A) MTView Studios
(B) GFQ and Co.
(C) Amusable
(D) Cloud 9

해석 그래픽을 보라. 화자는 어느 회사에서 근무하는가?
(A) MTView Studios
(B) GFQ and Co.
(C) Amusable
(D) Cloud 9

---

30. According to the speaker, what will the company do in the next quarter?

(A) Restructure a division
(B) Decrease production costs
(C) Negotiate a contract
(D) Adopt a new business strategy

어휘 restructure 구조를 조정하다 division 부서 negotiate (협상을 통해) 이끌어내다, 성사시키다 adopt 채택하다

해석 화자의 말에 따르면 회사는 다음 분기에 무엇을 할 것인가?
(A) 한 부서의 구조 조정을 한다
(B) 생산 원가를 낮춘다
(C) 계약을 성사시킨다
(D) 새 사업 전략을 채택한다

두 번째 문장에서 28번 문제의 정답을 알 수 있다. 화자의 회사는 현재 시장 점유율 최상위 4개의 게임 회사들 중 하나다(While we're still ranked among the top four gaming companies). 재빨리 정답을 고르고 이어지는 내용을 들으면서 29번의 정답도 고르자. GFQ가 자기들을 앞서기 시작했다고 알리고 있는데(we should take note of GFQ's rapid growth – they just surpassed us.), 도표를 보면 현재 시장 점유율에 있어 GFQ 다음 순위의 기업은 Amusable이다. 바로 이어지는 문장이 결정적으로 정답을 알려주고 있는데, 이 회사의 시장 점유율이 18퍼센트라고 말하고 있다(Although we're not that far behind with an eighteen percent share). 여기서 29번의 정답을 확신할 수 있다. 그 다음 문장을 들어보면 GFQ가 급성장할 수 있었던 것은 획기적인 사업 모델이 있었기 때문이다(Our market experts attribute GFQ's surge in popularity to its innovative business model). 화자는 마지막 문장에서 회사가 이러한 접근법을 긍정적으로 생각하고 있으며(We believe implementing this business approach may assist us in attracting new users), 다음 분기에는 자기들도 이것을 시험 삼아 도입해 볼 계획이라고 밝히고 있다(so we're going to try it out with some of our existing games in the upcoming quarter). 여기서 30번 문제의 정답을 알 수 있다.